0011 0aaa	DECI	Decimal input trap	d, n, s, sf, x, sx, sfx	NZV
0011 1aaa	DECO	Decimal output trap	i, d, n, s, sf, x, sx, sfx	
0100 0aaa	HEXO	Hexadecimal output trap	i, d, n, s, sf, x, sx, sfx	
0100 1aaa	STRO	String output trap	d, n, s, sf, x	
0101 0aaa	ADDSP	Add to stack pointer (SP)	i, d, n, s, sf, x, sx, sfx	NZVC
0101 1aaa	SUBSP	Subtract from stack pointer (SP)	i, d, n, s, sf, x, sx, sfx	NZVC
0110 raaa	ADDr	Add to r	i, d, n, s, sf, x, sx, sfx	NZVC
0111 raaa	SUBr	Subtract from r	i, d, n, s, sf, x, sx, sfx	NZVC
1000 raaa	ANDr	Bitwise AND to r	i, d, n, s, sf, x, sx, sfx	NZ
1001 raaa	ORr	Bitwise OR to r	i, d, n, s, sf, x, sx, sfx	NZ
1010 raaa	CPWr	Compare word to r	i, d, n, s, sf, x, sx, sfx	NZVC
1011 raaa	CPBr	Compare byte to r⟨8..15⟩	i, d, n, s, sf, x, sx, sfx	NZVC
1100 raaa	LDWr	Load word r from memory	i, d, n, s, sf, x, sx, sfx	NZ
1101 raaa	LDBr	Load byte r⟨8..15⟩ from memory	i, d, n, s, sf, x, sx, sfx	NZ
1110 raaa	STWr	Store word r to memory	d, n, s, sf, x, sx, sfx	
1111 raaa	STBr	Store byte r⟨8..15⟩ to memory	d, n, s, sf, x, sx, sfx	

Computer Systems

FIFTH EDITION

J. Stanley Warford
Pepperdine University

JONES & BARTLETT
LEARNING

World Headquarters
Jones & Bartlett Learning
5 Wall Street
Burlington, MA 01803
978-443-5000
info@jblearning.com
www.jblearning.com

Jones & Bartlett Learning books and products are available through most bookstores and online booksellers. To contact Jones & Bartlett Learning directly, call 800-832-0034, fax 978-443-8000, or visit our website, www.jblearning.com.

Substantial discounts on bulk quantities of Jones & Bartlett Learning publications are available to corporations, professional associations, and other qualified organizations. For details and specific discount information, contact the special sales department at Jones & Bartlett Learning via the above contact information or send an email to specialsales@jblearning.com.

Production Credits

VP, Executive Publisher: David D. Cella
Executive Editor: Matt Kane
Acquisitions Editor: Laura Pagluica
Editorial Assistant: Taylor Ferracane
Production Editor: Vanessa Richards
Director of Marketing: Andrea DeFronzo
VP, Manufacturing and Inventory Control: Therese Connell
Composition: S4Carlisle Publishing Services

Cover Design: Kristin E. Parker
Associate Director of Rights & Media: Joanna Lundeen
Rights & Media Specialist: Merideth Tumasz
Media Development Editor: Shannon Sheehan
Cover Image: © gkuna/Shutterstock
Printing and Binding: Edwards Brothers Malloy
Cover Printing: Edwards Brothers Malloy

Library of Congress Cataloging-in-Publication Data
Names: Warford, J. Stanley, 1944- author.
Title: Computer systems / J. Stanley Warford.
Description: Fifth edition. | Burlington, MA : Jones & Bartlett Learning,
    [2017] | Includes index.
Identifiers: LCCN 2015040618 | ISBN 9781284079630 (hardcover)
Subjects: LCSH: Computer systems.
Classification: LCC QA76 .W2372 2017 | DDC 004—dc23
LC record available at http://lccn.loc.gov/2015040618

6048

Printed in the United States of America
20 19 18 17 16   10 9 8 7 6 5 4 3 2 1

This book is dedicated to Lucy Ann, Douglas James, and Sara Sue.

Table of Contents

Level 3   Instruction Set Architecture   115

3. Information Representation   117

Preface

The fifth edition of *Computer Systems* offers a clear, detailed, step-by-step exposition of the central ideas in computer organization, assembly language, and computer architecture. The book is based in large part on a virtual computer, Pep/9, which is designed to teach the basic concepts of the classic von Neumann machine. The strength of this approach is that the central concepts of computer science are taught without getting entangled in the many irrelevant details that often accompany such courses. This approach also provides a foundation that encourages students to think about the underlying themes of computer science. Breadth is achieved by emphasizing computer science topics that are related to, but not usually included in, the treatment of hardware and its associated software.

Summary of Contents

Computers operate at several levels of abstraction; programming at a high level of abstraction is only part of the story. This book presents a unified concept of computer systems based on the level structure of **FIGURE P.1**.

The book is divided into seven parts, corresponding to the seven levels of Figure P.1:

Level App7	Applications
Level HOL6	High-order languages
Level ISA3	Instruction set architecture
Level Asmb5	Assembly
Level OS4	Operating system
Level LG1	Logic gate
Level Mc2	Microcode

The text generally presents the levels top-down, from the highest to the lowest. Level ISA3 is discussed before Level Asmb5, and Level LG1 is discussed before Level Mc2 for pedagogical reasons. In these two instances, it is more

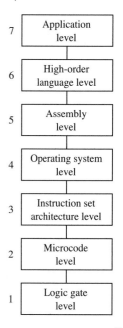

FIGURE P.1
The level structure of a typical computer system.

7	Application level
6	High-order language level
5	Assembly level
4	Operating system level
3	Instruction set architecture level
2	Microcode level
1	Logic gate level

natural to revert temporarily to a bottom-up approach so that the building blocks of the lower level will be in hand for construction of the higher level.

Level App7   Level App7 is a single chapter on application programs. It presents the idea of levels of abstraction and binary information and establishes the framework for the remainder of the book. A few concepts of relational databases are presented as an example of a typical computer application.

Level HOL6   Level HOL6 consists of one chapter, which reviews the C programming language. The chapter assumes that the student has experience in some imperative language, such as Java or Python—not necessarily C. The instructor can readily translate the C examples to other common Level HOL6 languages if necessary.

This chapter emphasizes the C memory model, including global versus local variables, functions with parameters, and dynamically allocated variables. The topic of recursion is treated because it depends on the mechanism of memory allocation on the run-time stack. A fairly detailed explanation is given on the details of the memory allocation process for function calls, as this mechanism is revisited at a lower level of abstraction later in the book.

Level ISA3   Level ISA3 is the instruction set architecture level. Its two chapters describe Pep/9, a virtual computer designed to illustrate computer concepts. Pep/9 is a small complex instruction set computer (CISC); a von Neumann machine. The central processing unit (CPU) contains an accumulator, an index register, a program counter, a stack pointer, and an instruction register. It has eight addressing modes: immediate, direct, indirect, stack-relative, stack-relative deferred, indexed, stack-indexed, and stack-deferred indexed. The Pep/9 operating system, in simulated read-only memory (ROM), can load and execute programs in hexadecimal format from students' text files. Students run short programs on the Pep/9 simulator and learn that executing a store instruction to ROM does not change the memory value.

Students learn the fundamentals of information representation and computer organization at the bit level. Because a central theme of this book is the relationship of the levels to one another, the Pep/9 chapters show the relationship between the ASCII representation (Level ISA3) and C variables of type `char` (Level HOL6). They also show the relationship between two's complement representation (Level ISA3) and C variables of type `int` (Level HOL6).

Level Asmb5   Level Asmb5 is the assembly level. The text presents the concept of the assembler as a translator between two levels—assembly and machine. It introduces Level Asmb5 symbols and the symbol table.

The unified approach really comes into play here. Chapters 5 and 6 present the compiler as a translator from a high-order language to assembly language. Previously, students learned a specific Level HOL6 language, C, and a specific von Neumann machine, Pep/9. These chapters continue the theme of relationships between the levels by showing the correspondence between (a) assignment statements at Level HOL6 and load/store instructions at Level Asmb5, (b) loops and `if` statements at Level HOL6 and branching instructions at Level Asmb5, (c) arrays at Level HOL6 and indexed addressing at Level Asmb5, (d) procedure calls at Level HOL6 and the run-time stack at Level Asmb5, (e) function and procedure parameters at Level HOL6 and stack-relative addressing at Level Asmb5, (f) `switch` statements at Level HOL6 and jump tables at Level Asmb5, and (g) pointers at Level HOL6 and addresses at Level Asmb5.

The beauty of the unified approach is that the text can implement the examples from the C chapter at this lower level. For example, the run-time stack illustrated in the recursive examples of Chapter 2 corresponds directly to the hardware stack in Pep/9 main memory. Students gain an understanding of the compilation process by translating manually between the two levels.

This approach provides a natural setting for the discussion of central issues in computer science. For example, the book presents structured programming at Level HOL6 versus the possibility of unstructured programming at Level Asmb5. It discusses the goto controversy and the structured programming/efficiency tradeoff, giving concrete examples from languages at the two levels.

Chapter 7, "Language Translation Principles," introduces students to computer science theory. Now that students know intuitively how to translate from a high-level language to assembly language, we pose the fundamental question underlying all of computing: What can be automated? The theory naturally fits in here because students now know what a compiler (an automated translator) must do. They learn about parsing and finite-state machines—deterministic and nondeterministic—in the context of recognizing C and Pep/9 assembly language tokens. This chapter includes an automatic translator between two small languages, which illustrates lexical analysis, parsing, and code generation. The lexical analyzer is an implementation of a finite-state machine. What could be a more natural setting for the theory?

Level OS4   Level OS4 consists of two chapters on operating systems. Chapter 8 is a description of process management. Two sections, one on loaders and another on trap handlers, illustrate the concepts with the Pep/9 operating system. Seven instructions have unimplemented opcodes that generate software traps. The operating system stores the process control block of the user's running process on the system stack, and the interrupt service routine interprets the instruction. The classic state transition diagram for running and waiting processes in an operating system is thus reinforced with a specific implementation of a suspended process. The chapter concludes with a description of concurrent processes and deadlocks. Chapter 9 describes storage management, both main memory and disk memory.

Level LG1   Level LG1 uses two chapters to present combinational and sequential circuits. Chapter 10 emphasizes the importance of the mathematical foundation of computer science by starting with the axioms of Boolean algebra. It shows the relationship between Boolean algebra and logic gates and then describes some common logic devices, including a complete logic design of the Pep/9 arithmetic logic unit (ALU). Chapter 11 illustrates the fundamental concept of a finite-state machine through the state transition diagrams of sequential circuits. It concludes with a description of common computer subsystems such as bidirectional buses, memory chips, and two-port memory banks.

Level Mc2   Chapter 12 describes the microprogrammed control section of the Pep/9 CPU. It gives the control sequences for a few sample instructions and addressing modes and provides a large set of exercises for the others. It also presents concepts of load/store architectures, contrasting the MIPS reduced instruction set computer (RISC) machine with the Pep/9 CISC machine. It concludes with performance issues by describing cache memories, pipelining, dynamic branch prediction, and superscalar machines.

Use in a Course

This book offers such broad coverage that instructors may wish to omit some of the material when designing a course. I use Chapters 1–7 in a computer systems course and Chapters 10–12 in a computer organization course.

In the book, Chapters 1–5 must be covered sequentially. Chapters 6 ("Compiling to the Assembly Level") and 7 ("Language Translation Principles") can be covered in either order. I often skip ahead to Chapter 7 to initiate a large software project, writing an assembler for a subset of Pep/9 assembly language, so students will have sufficient time to complete it during the semester. Chapter 11 ("Sequential Circuits") is obviously dependent on Chapter 10 ("Combinational Circuits"), but neither depends on Chapter 9 ("Storage Management"), which may be omitted. FIGURE P.2 , a chapter dependency graph, summarizes the possible chapter omissions.

Changes Made for the *Fifth Edition*

Improvements are in every chapter of this edition, and fall into one of two categories: a change in the virtual machine from Pep/8 to Pep/9 and other

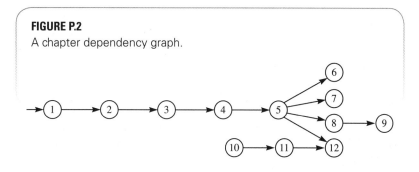

FIGURE P.2
A chapter dependency graph.

changes in content. The changes in content are too numerous to list, but major changes include the following:

> *HOL6 language*—This edition changes the HOL6 language from C++ to C. The C language is more common as a systems programming language and is more appropriate for a computer systems text. The previous edition refers to the memory model of C++ consisting of global variables allocated at a fixed location in memory, local variables and parameters allocated on the run-time stack, and dynamic variables allocated from the heap. But C++ is an OO language with a more complex memory model. The above model more accurately describes C than C++. The switch is visible in three places. Input/output (I/O) in the example programs use `scanf()` and `printf()` instead of `cin` and `cout`. The pass-by reference mechanism in C has the address operator `&` explicit in the actual parameter with a corresponding pointer type in the formal parameter. Memory allocation from the heap uses `malloc` instead of `new`.

> *Sidebars*—In this edition, the brief biographies formerly found in each chapter have been replaced with a different set of sidebars. Each sidebar is a real-world example of the concepts described in that chapter. As most of the chapters describe the Pep/9 virtual machine, the sidebars for those chapters show some corresponding implementations for the Intel x86 architecture. The new sidebars give a consistent running example of this architecture so students have a better idea of how the concepts of the virtual machine relate to real-world implementations.

> *New and expanded topics*—Chapter 1 now emphasizes how binary information is quantified in both space and time by presenting the performance equation and the concept of bandwidth. QR codes and color displays are detailed examples of these concepts. Chapter 3 describes Unicode as well as UTF-32 and UTF-8 encoding. Chapter 4 discusses

big-endian and little-endian order. Chapter 7 uses Java instead of C++ as the implementation language for the example translator. The microcode examples in Chapter 12 use the new UnitPre and UnitPost feature of the Pep/9 CPU simulator. The two-byte data bus now has simulator support, and that topic leads to an extended discussion of memory alignment issues and the new .ALIGN assembler directive.

Pep/8, the virtual machine for the two previous editions, has been superseded by Pep/9. As the instruction sets of the two machines are different, Pep/8 source and object programs are not compatible with those of Pep/9. Only a few instructions are affected, however, so much remains the same, including the set of eight addressing modes. The changes for Pep/9 include the following:

> *Replacement of* RETn *with* RET—In Pep/8, there are eight versions of the return statement, RET0, RET1, . . . , RET7. RETn deallocates *n* bytes from the run-time stack and then executes a return from a function call. The reasoning is that returns are always preceded by a deallocation of local variables, so programs are shorter if the assembly language programmer is not required to write an ADDSP instruction to explicitly deallocate the locals before the return.

> While this ISA design may be justified on architectural principles, it turned out to be deficient pedagogically. The problem is that students must learn two different concepts: the deallocation mechanism for data and the return mechanism for flow of control. Combining these two different concepts into one statement can be confusing during the learning process. Pep/9 now requires students to explicitly deallocate locals with the ADDSP statement. An added stylistic advantage is that the explicit ADDSP to deallocate locals at the end of a function corresponds directly to the SUBSP at the beginning of the function to allocate locals.

> *Memory-mapped I/O*—Of all the instructions in the Pep/8 instruction set, the most unrealistic are CHARI and CHARO for character input and output. Most real computer systems map input and output devices to main memory, which is now the design of Pep/9. In the new instruction set, there are no native input and output instructions. Instead, the Pep/8 instruction

```
CHARI alpha,ad
```

is replaced by the Pep/9 instructions

```
LDBA charIn,d ;Load byte to A from charIn
STBA alpha,ad ;Store byte from A to alpha
```

where `charIn` is the input device. The Pep/8 instruction

```
CHARO beta,ad
```

is replaced by the Pep/9 instructions

```
LDBA beta,ad ;Load byte to A from beta
STBA charOut,d ;Store byte to charOut
```

where `charOut` is the output device.

In the above code fragments, `ad` represents any valid addressing mode for the instruction. Symbols `charIn` and `charOut` are defined in the Pep/9 operating system and stored as machine vectors at the bottom of memory. Their values are included automatically in the symbol table of the assembler.

One disadvantage of memory-mapped I/O is that every `CHARI` and `CHARO` statement in a Pep/8 program must now be written as two statements, making programs longer. This disadvantage is mitigated by the fact that the trap instructions `DECI`, `DECO`, and `STRO` work as before, as the native I/O statements are hidden inside their trap routines.

The advantage is that students learn firsthand how memory-mapped I/O works by loading from the input device address and storing to the output device address. This requirement also illustrates the concept and the use of the memory map, a topic that students have a tendency to avoid with Pep/8. There is also a nice connection with the example in Chapter 11 on address decoding that shows how to wire an eight-port I/O chip into the memory map.

❯ *New native instruction* `CPBr`—In Pep/8, byte quantities must be compared with `CPr`, which compares two-byte quantities. Consequently, the high-order byte of the comparison must be considered, sometimes by clearing the high-order byte of the register before the comparison is made. The resulting assembler code for doing byte comparisons is convoluted.

`CPBr` is a new compare byte instruction that sets the status bits without regard to the high-order byte of the register. The resulting code is simpler to understand and to write.

❯ *Improved mnemonics*—Pep/9 renames the mnemonics for the compare, load, and store instructions, as FIGURE P.3 shows. The new scheme retains the letters `CP` for *compare*, `LD` for *load*, and `ST` for *store*; however, the scheme is now consistent in using the letters `W` for *word*, which is now required, and `B` for *byte* with this group of instructions. Not only is this naming convention more consistent, but there is a tendency for students to forget the meaning of a word (two

FIGURE P.3

New Pep/9 mnemonics.

Instruction	Pep/9	Pep/8
Compare word	CPWr	CPr
Compare byte	CPBr	Not available
Load word	LDWr	LDr
Load byte	LDBr	LDBYTEr
Store word	STWr	STr
Store byte	STBr	STBYTEr

bytes in the Pep computers). Including the letter W in the mnemonics for the two-byte instructions reinforces the meaning of "word."

> *New trap instruction* HEXO—Pep/9 eliminates the NOP2 and NOP3 trap instructions from the instruction set, which, together with the elimination of the RETn and character I/O instructions, allows the inclusion of another nonunary trap instruction. HEXO, which stands for *hexadecimal output*, was available in Pep/7 and is resurrected in Pep/9. It outputs a word as four hexadecimal characters.

> *Addressing mode nomenclature*—Pep/9 changes the name *stack-indexed deferred* addressing to *stack-deferred indexed* addressing and the corresponding assembler notation from sxf to sfx. This change more accurately reflects the semantics of the addressing mode, as the stack-deferred operation happens *before* the index operation.

> *Expanded MIPS coverage*—The MIPS architecture continues to be the RISC model contrasted with the Pep/9 CISC model. Its coverage is expanded with a more extensive and systematic description of all the MIPS addressing modes and instruction types and their implementation at the LG1 level. This edition also includes a more extensive exposition of RISC design principles, as illustrated by the MIPS architecture.

Unique Features

Computer Systems has several unique features that differentiate it from other texts on computer systems, assembly language, and computer organization.

> *Conceptual approach*—Many textbooks attempt to stay abreast of the field by including the latest technological developments, such as communication protocol specifications for the newest peripheral devices. They typically have how-this-device-works narrative explanations throughout. This text eschews such material in favor of selecting only those computing concepts that are fundamental, the mastery of which provides a basis for understanding both current and future technology. For instance, in mastering the concept of the space/time tradeoff, it is more important for students to experience the ideas with digital circuit design problems than to simply read about them in general. As another example, the concept of hardware parallelism is mastered best by learning how to combine cycles in a microcode implementation of an ISA instruction.

> *Problem-solving emphasis*—Students retain less when they only hear about or read about a subject. They retain more when they experience the subject. *Computer Systems* reflects this emphasis through the nearly 400 problem-solving exercises at the end of the chapters, many

with multiple parts. Rather than ask the student to repeat verbiage from the text, the exercises require quantitative answers, or the analysis or design of a program or digital circuit at one of the levels of abstraction of the system.

> *Consistent machine model*—The Pep/9 machine, a small CISC computer, is the vehicle for describing all the levels of the system. Students clearly see the relation between the levels of abstraction because they either program or design digital circuits for that machine at *all* the levels. For example, when they design an ALU component at the LG1 level, they know where the ALU fits in the implementation of the ISA3 level. They learn the difference between an optimizing and nonoptimizing compiler by translating C programs to assembly language as a compiler would. Using the same machine model for these learning activities at the different levels is a huge productivity advantage because the model is consistent from top to bottom. However, *Computer Systems* also presents the MIPS machine to contrast RISC design principles with microprogrammed CISC designs.

> *Complete program examples*—Many computer organization and assembly language texts suffer from the code fragment syndrome. The memory model, addressing modes, and I/O features of Pep/9 enable students to write complete programs that can be easily executed and tested without resorting just to code fragments. Real machines, and especially RISC machines, have complex function-calling protocols involving issues like register allocation, register spillover, and memory alignment constraints. Pep/9 is one of the few pedagogic machines—perhaps the only one—that permits students to write complete programs with input and output using the following: global and local variables, global and local arrays, call by value and by reference, array parameters, switch statements with jump tables, recursion, linked structures with pointers, and the heap. Assignments to write complete programs further the goal of learning by doing, as opposed to learning by reading code fragments.

> *Integration of theory and practice*—Some readers observe that Chapter 7 on language translation principles is unusual in a computer systems book. This observation is a sad commentary on the gulf between theory and practice in computer science curricula and perhaps in the field of computer science itself. Because the text presents the C language at Level HOL6, assembly language at Level Asmb5, and machine language at Level ISA3, and has as one goal understanding the relationship between the levels, a better question is: How could a chapter on language translation principles *not* be included? *Computer Systems* incorporates theory whenever possible to bolster practice.

For example, it presents Boolean algebra as an axiomatic system with exercises for proving theorems.

> *Breadth and depth*—The material in Chapters 1–6 is typical for books on computer systems or assembly language programming, and that in Chapters 8–12 for computer organization. Combining this breadth of material into one volume is unique and permits a consistent machine model to be used throughout the levels of abstraction of the complete system. Also unique is the depth of coverage at the digital circuit LG1 level, which takes the mystery out of the component parts of the CPU. For example, *Computer Systems* describes the implementations of the multiplexers, adders, ALUs, registers, memory subsystems, and bidirectional buses for the Pep/9 CPU. Students learn the implementation down to the logic gate level, with no conceptual holes in the grand narrative that would otherwise have to be taken on faith without complete understanding.

Computer Systems answers the question: What is the place of assembly language programming and computer organization in the computer science curriculum? It is to provide a depth of understanding about the architecture of the ubiquitous von Neumann machine. This text retains its unique goal to provide a balanced overview of all the main areas of the field, including the integration of software and hardware and the integration of theory and practice.

Computer Science Curricula 2013

The first edition of *Computer Systems* was published in 1999. From the beginning, its goal was to unify the presentation of computer systems using a single virtual machine, Pep/6 in the first edition, to illustrate the relationships between all seven levels of abstraction in a typical computer system. The text cut across many of the standard courses at the time (and even now), taking a breadth approach and, in so doing, sacrificing the depth of traditional details taught in standard assembly language, operating systems, computer architecture, computer organization, and digital circuit design courses.

The latest joint ACM/IEEE curriculum guidelines, Computer Science Curricula 2013[1] (CS2013), note the curriculum challenges arising from the rapid expansion of the field:

The growing diversity of topics potentially relevant to an education in Computer Science and the increasing integration of computing with other

---

[1] *Computer Science Curricula 2013, Curriculum Guidelines for Undergraduate Degree Programs in Computer Science*, The Joint Task Force on Computing Curricula, Association for Computing Machinery (ACM) IEEE Computer Society, December 20, 2013.

disciplines create particular challenges for this effort. Balancing topical growth with the need to keep recommendations realistic and implementable in the context of undergraduate education is particularly difficult.

One response to the challenge is the evolution of the guidelines in precisely the direction that *Computer Systems* has occupied since its first edition. CS2013 restructures previous "bodies of knowledge," deleting some old areas and creating some new ones. One of the new knowledge areas (KAs) of the guidelines is Systems Fundamentals:

> In previous curricular volumes, the interacting layers of a typical computing system, from hardware building blocks, to architectural organization, to operating system services, to application execution environments . . . were presented in independent knowledge areas. The new Systems Fundamentals KA presents a unified systems perspective and common conceptual foundation for other KAs . . . .

The goal of the new Systems Fundamentals KA in CS2013 is identical to the goal of *Computer Systems*, namely to present a "unified systems perspective" and a common conceptual foundation for other topics of computer science. *Computer Systems* is a mature text that uniquely satisfies this important new goal of the latest computer science curriculum guidelines.

Support Materials

The support material listed below is available from the publisher's website (go.jblearning.com/warford5e).

Pep/9 Assembler and Simulator   The Pep/9 machine is available for MS Windows, Mac OS X, and Unix/Linux systems. The assembler features the following:

> › An integrated text editor

> › Error messages that are inserted within the source code at the place where the error is detected

> › Student-friendly machine language object code in hexadecimal format

> › The ability to code directly in machine language, bypassing the assembler

> › The ability to redefine the mnemonics for the unimplemented opcodes that trigger synchronous traps

The simulator features the following:

> › Simulated ROM that is not altered by store instructions

> › A small operating system burned into simulated ROM that includes a loader and a trap handler system

> An integrated debugger that allows for break points, single-step execution, CPU tracing, and memory tracing

> The option to trace an application, the loader, or the operating system in any combination

> The ability to recover from endless loops

> The ability to modify the operating system by designing new trap handlers for the unimplemented opcodes

> Every example from the text built into the application, making it a useful tool for class demonstrations

Pep/9 CPU Simulator   A CPU simulator, also available for MS Windows, Mac OS X, and Unix/Linux systems, is available for use in the computer organization course. The CPU simulator features the following:

> Color-coded display paths that trace the data flow, depending on control signals to the multiplexers

> A single-cycle mode of operation with graphical user interface inputs for each control signal and instant visual display of the effects of the signal

> A multicycle mode of operation with an integrated text editor for the student to write Mc2 microcode sequences and execute them to implement ISA3 instructions

> New to this edition, a set of unit tests for every example and every microcode problem built into the application

Lecture Slides   A complete set of about 50 to 125 lecture slides per chapter is available in PDF format. The slides include every figure from the text as well as summary information, often in bullet-point format. They do not, however, include many examples, so they leave room for instructor presentation of examples and instructor-led discussions.

Exam Handouts   A set of exam handouts, including reference information such as the ASCII table, instruction set tables, etc., are provided for reference during exams and study sessions.

Digital Circuit Labs   A set of six digital circuit labs provides hands-on experience with physical breadboards. The labs illustrate the combinational and sequential devices from Chapters 10 and 11 with many circuits that are not in the book. Students learn practical digital design and implementation concepts that are beyond the scope of the text itself. They follow the sequence of topics from the text, beginning with combinational circuits and progressing through sequential circuits and ALUs.

Solutions Manual   Solutions to selected exercises are provided in an appendix. Solutions to all the exercises and problems are available to instructors who adopt the book.

For information on how qualified instructors can access these resources, please contact your Jones & Bartlett Learning representative.

Acknowledgments

Pep/1 had 16 instructions, one accumulator, and one addressing mode. Pep/2 added indexed addressing. John Vannoy wrote both simulators in Algol W. Pep/3 had 32 instructions and was written in Pascal as a student software project by Steve Dimse, Russ Hughes, Kazuo Ishikawa, Nancy Brunet, and Yvonne Smith. In an early review, Harold Stone suggested many improvements to the Pep/3 architecture that were incorporated into Pep/4 and carried into later machines. Pep/4 had special stack instructions, simulated ROM, and software traps. Pep/5 was a more orthogonal design, allowing any instruction to use any addressing mode. John Rooker wrote the Pep/4 system and an early version of Pep/5. Gerry St. Romain implemented a Mac OS version and an MS-DOS version. Pep/6 simplified indexed addressing and included the complete set of conditional branch instructions. John Webb wrote the trace facility using the BlackBox development system. Pep/7 increased the installed memory from 4 KiB to 32 KiB. Pep/8 increased the number of addressing modes from 4 to 8 and the installed memory to 64 KiB. The GUI version of the Pep/8 assembler and simulator was implemented in C++ and maintained by teams of students using the Qt development system. The teams included Deacon Bradley, Jeff Cook, Nathan Counts, Stuartt Fox, Dave Grue, Justin Haight, Paul Harvey, Hermi Heimgartner, Matt Highfield, Trent Kyono, Malcolm Lipscomb, Brady Lockhart, Adrian Lomas, Scott Mace, Ryan Okelberry, Thomas Rampelberg, Mike Spandrio, Jack Thomason, Daniel Walton, Di Wang, Peter Warford, and Matt Wells. Ryan Okelberry also wrote the Pep/8 CPU simulator. Luciano d'Ilori wrote the command line version of the assembler. The latest versions of Pep/8 and Pep/8 CPU, and the current version of Pep/9 and Pep/9 CPU, are complete rewrites in Qt by Emily Dimpfl and myself.

    More than any other book, Tanenbaum's *Structured Computer Organization* has influenced this text. This text extends the level structure of Tanenbaum's book by adding the high-order programming level and the applications level at the top.

The following reviewers of the manuscript, students, and users of the previous edition shaped the final product significantly: Kenneth Araujo, Ziya Arnavut, Wayne P. Bailey, Leo Benegas, Jim Bilitski, Noni Bohonak, Dan Brennan, Michael Yonshik Choi, Christopher Cischke, Collin Cowart, Lionel Craddock, William Decker, Fadi Deek, Peter Drexel, Gerald S. Eisman, Victoria Evans, Mark Fienup, Paula Ford, Brooke Fugate, Robert Gann, David Garnick, Ephraim P. Glinert, John Goulden, Dave Hanscom, Michael Hennessy, Paul Jackowitz, Mark Johnson, Michael Johnson, Amitava Karmaker, Michael Kirkpatrick, Peter MacPherson, Andrew Malton, Robert Martin, John Maxfield, John McCormick, Richard H. Mercer, Jonathan Mohr, Randy Molmen, Hadi Moradi, John Motil, Mohammad Muztaba Fuad, Peter Ng, Bernard Nudel, Carolyn Oberlink, Nelson Passos, Wolfgang Pelz, James F. Peters III, James C. Pleasant, Eleanor Quinlan, Glenn A. Richard, Gerry St. Romain, David Rosser, Sally Schaffner, Peter Smith, Harold S. Stone, Robert Tureman, J. Peter Weston, and Norman E. Wright. Joe Piasentin provided artistic consultation. Two people who influenced the design of Pep/8 significantly are Myers Foreman, who was a source of many ideas for the instruction set, and Douglas Harms, who suggested (among other improvements) the MOVSPA instruction that makes possible the passing of local variables by reference.

At Jones & Bartlett Learning, Acquisitions Editor Laura Pagluica, Director of Vendor Management Amy Rose, Production Editor Vanessa Richards, and Editorial Assistant Taylor Ferracane provided valuable support and with whom were a true joy to work. Kristin Parker captured the flavor of the book with her striking cover design.

I am fortunate to be at an institution that is committed to excellence in undergraduate education. Pepperdine University, in the person of Ken Perrin, provided the creative environment and the professional support in which the idea behind this project was able to evolve. My wife, Ann, provided endless personal support. To her I owe an apology for the time this project has taken, and my greatest thanks.

Stan Warford
Malibu, California

LEVEL

7

Application

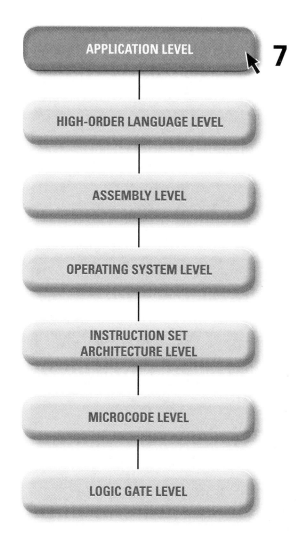

APPLICATION LEVEL — 7

HIGH-ORDER LANGUAGE LEVEL

ASSEMBLY LEVEL

OPERATING SYSTEM LEVEL

INSTRUCTION SET ARCHITECTURE LEVEL

MICROCODE LEVEL

LOGIC GATE LEVEL

CHAPTER 1

Computer Systems

The fundamental question of computer science

The fundamental question of computer science is: What can be automated? Just as the machines developed during the Industrial Revolution automated manual labor, computers automate the processing of information. When electronic computers were developed in the 1940s, their designers built them to automate the solution of mathematical problems. Since then, however, computers have applications as diverse as financial accounting, cinema production, and smartphones. The spread of computers is so relentless that new areas of computer automation appear almost daily.

The purpose of this text is to show how the computer automates the processing of information. Everything the computer does, you could do in principle. The major difference between computer and human execution of a job is that the computer can perform its tasks blindingly fast. However, to harness its speed, people must instruct, or program, the computer.

Programming languages

The nature of computers is best understood by learning how to program the machine. Programming requires that you learn a programming language. Before plunging into the details of studying a programming language, this chapter introduces the concept of *abstraction*, the theme on which this text is based. It then describes the hardware and software components of a computer system and concludes with a description of a database system as a typical application.

1.1 Levels of Abstraction

The concept of levels of abstraction is pervasive in the arts as well as in the natural and applied sciences. A complete definition of abstraction is multifaceted and, for our purposes, includes the following parts:

Definition of abstraction

> Suppression of detail to show the essence of the matter

> An outline structure

> Division of responsibility through a chain of command

> Subdivision of a system into smaller subsystems

The theme of this text is the application of abstraction to computer science. It begins, however, by considering levels of abstraction in areas other than computer science. The analogies drawn from these areas expand on the four parts of the preceding definition of abstraction and apply to computer systems as well.

Three common graphic representations of levels of abstraction are (1) level diagrams, (2) nesting diagrams, and (3) hierarchy, or tree, diagrams, as shown in FIGURE 1.1 . This section considers each of these representations of abstraction and shows how they relate to the analogies. The three diagrams also apply to levels of abstraction in computer systems throughout this text.

Figure 1.1(a) shows a *level diagram* as a set of boxes arranged vertically. The top box represents the highest level of abstraction, and the bottom box represents the lowest. The number of levels of abstraction depends on the system to be described. This figure would represent a system with three levels of abstraction.

Figure 1.1(b) shows a *nesting diagram*. Like the level diagram, a nesting diagram is a set of boxes. It always consists of one large outer box with the rest of the boxes nested inside it. In the figure, two boxes are nested immediately inside the one large outer box. The lower of these two boxes has one box nested, in turn, inside it. The outermost box of a nesting diagram corresponds to the top box of a level diagram. The nested boxes correspond to the lower boxes of a level diagram.

In a nesting diagram, none of the boxes overlap. That is, nesting diagrams never contain boxes whose boundaries intersect the boundaries of other boxes. A box is always completely enclosed within another box.

Figure 1.1(c) shows the third graphic representation of levels of abstraction, a *hierarchy*, or *tree*, *diagram*. In a tree, the big limbs branch off the trunk, the smaller limbs branch off the big limbs, and so on. The leaves are at the end of the chain, attached to the smallest branches. Tree diagrams such as Figure 1.1(c) have the trunk at the top instead of the bottom. Each box is called a *node*, with the single node at the top called the *root*. A node with no connections to a lower level is a *leaf*. This figure is a tree with one root node and three leaves. The top node in a hierarchy diagram corresponds to the top box of a level diagram.

Abstraction in Art

Henri Matisse was a major figure in the history of modern art. In 1909, he produced a bronze sculpture of a woman's back titled *The Back I*. Four years later, he created a work of the same subject but with a simpler rendering of the form, titled *The Back II*. After 4 more years, he created *The Back III*, followed by *The Back IV* 13 years later. shows the four sculptures.

A striking feature of the works is the elimination of detail as the artist progressed from one piece to the next. The contours of the back become less distinct in the second sculpture. The fingers of the right hand are hidden in the third. The hips are barely discernible in the fourth, which is the most abstract.

Matisse strove for expression. He deliberately suppressed visual detail in order to express the essence of the subject. In 1908, he wrote:

> In a picture, every part will be visible and will play the role conferred upon it, be it principal or secondary. All that is not useful in the picture is detrimental.

FIGURE 1.1
The three graphic representations of levels of abstraction.

(a) A level diagram.

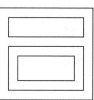

(b) A nesting diagram.

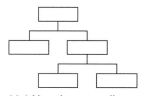

(c) A hierarchy, or tree, diagram.

FIGURE 1.2

Bronze sculptures by Henri Matisse. Each rendering is successively more abstract.
Matisse, Henri (1869–1954). *Nude from Behind*. Bas-relief in bronze. © 2015 Succession H. Matisse/Artists Rights Society (ARS), New York; Photo credit: © CNAC/MNAM/Dist. RMN-Grand Palais/Art Resource, NY.

The Back I   *The Back II*   *The Back III*   *The Back IV*
1909   1913   1917   1930

> A work of art must be harmonious in its entirety; for superfluous details would, in the mind of the beholder, encroach upon the essential elements.[1]

Suppression of detail is an integral part of the concept of levels of abstraction and carries over directly to computer science. In computer science terminology, *The Back IV* is at the highest level of abstraction and *The Back I* is at the lowest level. **FIGURE 1.3** is a level diagram that shows the relationship of these levels.

Like the artist, the computer scientist must appreciate the distinction between the essentials and the details. The chronological progression of creation in *The Back* series was from the most detailed to the most abstract. In computer science, however, the progression for problem solving should be from the most abstract to the most detailed. One goal of this text is to teach you how to think abstractly, that is, to suppress irrelevant detail when formulating a solution to a problem. Not that detail is unimportant in computer science! Detail is most important. However, in computing problems there is a natural tendency to be overly concerned with too much detail in the beginning stages of the progression. In solving problems in computer science, the essentials should come before the details.

FIGURE 1.3

The levels of abstraction in the Matisse sculptures. *The Back IV* is at the highest level of abstraction.

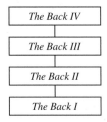

1. Alfred H. Barr, Jr., *Matisse: His Art and His Public* (New York: The Museum of Modern Art, 1951).

Abstraction in Documents

Levels of abstraction are also evident in the outline organization of written documents. An example is the United States Constitution, which consists of seven articles, each of which is subdivided into sections. The article and section headings shown in the following outline are not part of the Constitution itself.[2] They merely summarize the contents of the divisions.

Article I.	Legislative Department
Section 1.	Congress
Section 2.	House of Representatives
Section 3.	Senate
Section 4.	Elections of Senators and Representatives—Meetings of Congress
Section 5.	Powers and Duties of Each House of Congress
Section 6.	Compensation, Privileges, and Disabilities of Senators and Representatives
Section 7.	Mode of Passing Laws
Section 8.	Powers Granted to Congress
Section 9.	Limitations on Powers Granted to the United States
Section 10.	Powers Prohibited to the States
Article II.	Executive Department
Section 1.	The President
Section 2.	Powers of the President
Section 3.	Duties of the President
Section 4.	Removal of Executive and Civil Officers
Article III.	Judicial Department
Section 1.	Judicial Powers Vested in Federal Courts
Section 2.	Jurisdiction of United States Courts
Section 3.	Treason
Article IV.	The States and the Federal Government
Section 1.	Official Acts of the States
Section 2.	Citizens of the States
Section 3.	New States
Section 4.	Protection of States Guaranteed
Article V.	Amendments
Article VI.	General Provisions
Article VII.	Ratification of the Constitution

2. California State Senate, J. A. Beak, Secretary of the Senate, *Constitution of the State of California, the Constitution of the United States, and Related Documents* (Sacramento, 1967).

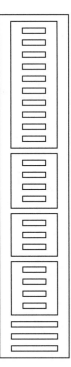

The Constitution as a whole is at the highest level of abstraction. A particular article, such as Article III, Judicial Department, deals with part of the whole. A section within that article, Section 2, Jurisdiction of United States Courts, deals with a specific topic and is at the lowest level of abstraction. The outline organizes the topics logically.

FIGURE 1.4 shows the outline structure of the Constitution in a nesting diagram. The big outer box is the entire Constitution. Nested inside it are seven smaller boxes, which represent the articles. Inside the articles are the section boxes.

This outline method of organizing a document is also important in computer science. The technique of organizing programs and information in outline form is called *structured programming*. In much the same way that English composition teachers instruct you to organize a report in outline form before writing the details, software designers organize their programs in outline form before filling in the programming details.

Abstraction in Organizations

Corporate organization is another area that uses the concept of levels of abstraction. For example, FIGURE 1.5 is a partial organization chart in the form of a hierarchy diagram for a hypothetical textbook publishing company. The president of the company is at the highest level and is responsible for the successful operation of the entire organization. The four vice presidents report to the president. Each vice president is responsible for just one major

FIGURE 1.5
A simplified organization chart for a hypothetical publishing company.

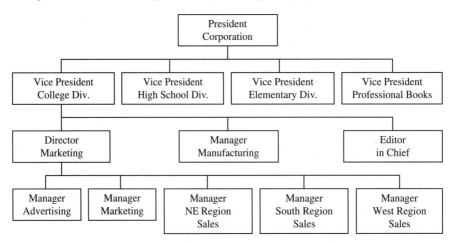

part of the operation. There are more levels, not shown in the figure, under each of the managers and vice presidents.

Levels in an organization chart correspond to responsibility and authority in the organization. The president acts in the best interest of the entire company. She delegates responsibility and authority to those who report to her. They in turn use their authority to manage their part of the organization and may delegate responsibilities to their employees. In businesses, the actual power held by individuals may not be directly reflected by their positions on the official chart. **FIGURE 1.6** is a level diagram that shows the line of authority in the organization. Each vice president reports to the president. Each director reports to a vice president, each manager reports to a director, and so on down the chain of command.

There is a direct relationship between the way an organization functions, as reflected by its organization chart, and the way a computer system functions. Like a large organization, a large computer system is typically organized as a hierarchy. Any given part of a computer system takes orders from the part immediately above it in the hierarchy diagram. In turn, it issues orders to be carried out by those parts immediately below it in the hierarchy.

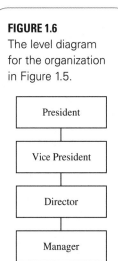

FIGURE 1.6
The level diagram for the organization in Figure 1.5.

Abstraction in Machines

Another example of levels of abstraction that is closely analogous to computer systems is the automobile. Like a computer system, the automobile is a man-made machine. It consists of an engine, a transmission, an electrical system, a cooling system, and a chassis. Each part of an automobile is subdivided. The electrical system has, among other things, a battery, headlights, and a voltage regulator.

People relate to automobiles at different levels of abstraction. Drivers are at the highest level of abstraction. They perform their tasks by knowing how to operate the car: for example, how to start it, how to use the accelerator, and how to apply the brakes.

At the next lower level of abstraction are the backyard mechanics. They understand more of the details under the hood than the casual drivers do. They know how to change the oil and the spark plugs. They do not need this detailed knowledge to drive the automobile.

At the next lower level of abstraction are the master mechanics. They can completely remove the engine, take it apart, fix it, and put it back together. They do not need this detailed knowledge to simply change the oil.

In a similar vein, people relate to computer systems at many different levels of abstraction. A complete understanding at every level is not necessary to use a computer. You do not need to be a mechanic to drive a car. Similarly, you do not need to be an experienced programmer to use a word processor.

FIGURE 1.7
The level structure of
a typical computer
system. Some systems
do not have Level 2.

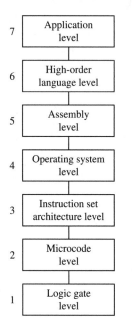

Abstraction in Computer Systems

FIGURE 1.7 shows the level structure of a typical computer system. Each of the seven levels shown in the diagram has its own language:

Level 7 (App7):	Language dependent on applications program
Level 6 (HOL6):	Machine-independent programming language
Level 5 (Asmb5):	Assembly language
Level 4 (OS4):	Operating system calls
Level 3 (ISA3):	Machine language
Level 2 (Mc2):	Microinstructions and register transfer
Level 1 (LG1):	Boolean algebra and truth tables

Programs written in these languages instruct the computer to perform certain operations. A program to perform a specific task can be written at any one of the levels of Figure 1.7. As with the automobile, a person writing a program in a language at one level does not need to know the language at any of the lower levels.

When computers were invented, only Levels LG1 and ISA3 were present. A human communicated with these machines by programming them in *machine language* at the instruction set architecture level. Machine language is great for machines but is tedious and inconvenient for a human programmer. *Assembly language*, at Level Asmb5, was invented to help the human programmer.

The first computers were large and expensive. Much time was wasted when one programmer monopolized the computer while the other users waited in line for their turns. Gradually, *operating systems* at Level OS4 were developed so many users could access the computer simultaneously. With today's personal computers, operating systems are still necessary to manage programs and data, even if the system services only one user.

In the early days, every time a company introduced a new computer model, the programmers had to learn the assembly language for that model. All their programs written for the old machine would not work on the new machine. *High-order languages* at Level HOL6 were invented so programs could be transferred from one computer to another with little modification and because programming in a high-order language is easier than programming at a lower level. The more popular Level HOL6 languages that you may be familiar with include the following:

> C   For programming operating systems

> C++   For general applications; C with added object-oriented features

> Python   A scripting language for web applications

> Java   For general-purpose and web applications

The widespread availability of computer systems spurred the development of many applications programs, also called *apps*, at Level App7. An *applications program* is one written to solve a specific type of problem, such as composing a document, statistically analyzing data, or routing a car to its destination. It allows you to use the computer as a tool without knowing the operational details at the lower levels.

Level LG1, the lowest level, consists of electrical components called *logic gates*. Along the way in the development toward higher levels, it was discovered that a level just above the logic gate level could be useful in helping designers build the Level ISA3 machine. *Microprogramming* at Level Mc2 is used on some computer systems today to implement the Level ISA3 machine. Level Mc2 was an important tool in the invention of the handheld calculator.

Your goal in studying this text is to communicate effectively with computers. To do so, you must learn the language. Languages at the higher levels are more human-oriented and easier to understand than languages at the lower levels. That is precisely why they were invented.

One goal of this text

As you study this text, you will gain some insight into the inner workings of a computer system by examining successively lower levels of abstraction. The lower you go in the hierarchy, the more details will come to light that were hidden at the higher levels. As you progress in your study, keep Figure 1.7 in mind. You must master a host of seemingly trivial details; it is the nature of the beast. Remember, however, that the beauty of computer science lies not in the diversity of its details but in the unity of its concepts.

1.2 **Hardware**

We build computers to solve problems. Early computers solved mathematical and engineering problems, and later computers emphasized information processing for business applications. Today, computers also control machines as diverse as automobile engines, robots, and microwave ovens. A computer system solves a problem from any of these domains by accepting input, processing it, and producing output. **FIGURE 1.8** illustrates the function of a computer system.

FIGURE 1.8
The three activities of a computer system.

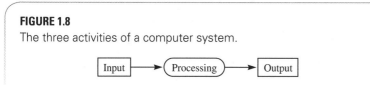

Computer systems consist of hardware and software. *Hardware* is the physical part of the system. Once designed, hardware is difficult and expensive to change. *Software* is the set of programs that instruct the hardware and is easier to modify than hardware. Computers are valuable because they are general-purpose machines that can solve many different kinds of problems, as opposed to special-purpose machines that can each solve only one kind of problem. Different problems can be solved with the same hardware by supplying the system with a different set of instructions—that is, with different software.

Every computer has three basic hardware components:

Components of hardware

> Central processing unit (CPU)

> Main memory

> Disk

FIGURE 1.9 shows these components in a block diagram. The lines between the blocks represent the flow of information. The information flows from one component to another on the *system bus*, which is simply a group of wires connecting the components. The preceding list of hardware components is in order of increasing storage capacity. The CPU has the smallest storage capacity, and the disk has the largest capacity. The list is also in order of decreasing speed. The CPU is the fastest device, and the disk is the slowest device.

Central Processing Unit

Registers are in the CPU.

Processing occurs in the CPU, which contains the circuitry to control all the other parts of the computer. It has a small set of memory, called *registers*, represented by the two blocks inside the CPU block in Figure 1.9. Although the figure shows only two registers, they typically number anywhere from

FIGURE 1.9
Block diagram of the three components of a computer system.

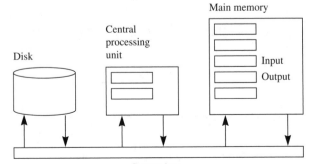

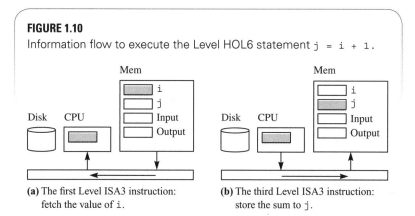

FIGURE 1.10
Information flow to execute the Level HOL6 statement j = i + 1.

(a) The first Level ISA3 instruction: fetch the value of i.

(b) The third Level ISA3 instruction: store the sum to j.

16 to 64. The CPU also has a set of instructions permanently wired into its circuitry. The instructions do such things as fetch information from main memory into a register; add, subtract, compare, and store information from a register back into main memory; and so on. What is not permanent is the order in which these instructions are executed. The order is determined by a program written in machine language at Level ISA3.

An example of how the CPU processes information is execution of the simple assignment j=i+1, which is a programming statement in Level HOL6 languages like C or Java. It adds 1 to integer variable i and assigns the sum to j. During execution of a program, the system stores the values of variables i and j in main memory. The single j=i+1 statement at Level HOL6 is translated to three statements at Level ISA3. Each of these three statements is one of the instructions wired into the CPU. The first instruction fetches the current value of i from memory into a CPU register, as FIGURE 1.10(a) shows. Information flows from the storage cell in memory onto the system bus and into a register in the CPU. The second instruction adds 1 to the value in the register. This instruction executes entirely within the CPU and involves no information flow along the system bus. The third instruction stores the incremented value back to the location of j in the main memory, as Figure 1.10(b) shows.

One statement at Level HOL6 can be three statements at Level ISA3.

Main Memory

Like the CPU, *main memory* has a set of memory cells to store information. It differs in two respects from the CPU. First, the number of storage cells is far greater than the number of cells in the CPU. Figure 1.9 shows only five cells in main memory, but a smartphone can have a few billion cells and a laptop more than 10 billion. These numbers compare with only dozens of registers in a typical CPU. Second, the CPU has a set of instructions wired into its circuitry to perform processing on the data in its registers. Although the capacity of main memory is huge compared to the capacity of the CPU, it cannot process the values that it stores. The only function it can perform is to remember the data values stored in its cells and produce them for the CPU or the disk on request.

Main memory stores four kinds of information:

> Data to be processed by the CPU

> Program instructions to be executed by the CPU

> Input connections to receive data from the external environment

> Output connections to send data to the external environment

An example of data storage are the integer values for i and j in Figure 1.10. Later during execution, if the program needs the value of j for another computation, main memory will deliver the value unchanged from the value previously stored.

When you purchase an application, say a word processor, you download it to the disk, which stores it until you want to use it. Then, when you execute the app, your computer system sends a copy of it from the disk to main memory. At any given time, main memory contains copies of all apps that are executing in the system. So, in addition to the values of variables i and j in Figure 1.10, main memory also stores the program instructions of the app. Because the CPU contains the circuitry to execute the app instructions, the computer system must fetch an instruction from main memory before it can execute the instruction. **FIGURE 1.11** shows the information flow to fetch an instruction. The information flow is similar to that in Figure 1.10(a) across the system bus, except that the information comes from the location where the instruction is stored instead of where i is stored. The instruction is copied to a special-purpose register in the CPU called the *instruction register*. The electronic circuitry in the CPU is designed to analyze the instruction in the instruction register and to execute it.

A few locations in main memory are reserved for input connections and output connections. This technique is called *memory-mapped input/output*, or *memory-mapped I/O*. A common example of an input device mapped to main memory is the keyboard. When you press a key on the keyboard, the circuitry inside the keyboard detects which key was pressed and sends information representing the character to the input connection in main memory. Then the keyboard sends a signal to the CPU informing it that a key was pressed. In response to the notification signal, the CPU fetches the character from the input connection so it can be processed. **FIGURE 1.12** shows the information flow to receive a character from the keyboard. In the same way that information flows when fetching data or an instruction from memory, the input information flows along the system bus to the CPU. The only difference is that the information comes from the input connection of the keyboard that is wired into the storage cell in main memory.

FIGURE 1.11
Information flow to fetch an instruction to be executed.

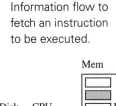

FIGURE 1.12
Information flow to receive a character from the keyboard.

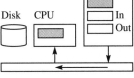

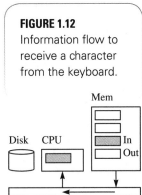

Memory-mapped I/O

Figure 1.12 might give the impression that the computer system has one large main memory device and that the keyboard is physically connected to one of the storage cells of that single device. Such a configuration is a convenient model for the programmer at Level ISA3. To get data from an input device, the ISA3 programmer writes an instruction to fetch the data from the input connection using the same coding techniques he would use to get the data value from a variable. The hardware designer at Level LG1, however, uses several separate devices to construct the main memory of the system. The designer does not connect the keyboard physically to a storage cell in a single central memory device. Instead, she connects the keyboard to the system bus to make it appear to the ISA3 programmer that there is a single memory device. This abstraction hides the connection details at Level LG1 from the programmer at Level ISA3.

The mouse, the trackpad, and the touch screen are three other common input devices. Inside a mouse is a small light-emitting diode that shines a beam of light down onto the surface of the desk. The light reflects back onto a sensor that samples the light 1500 times per second. A digital signal processor inside the mouse acts like a tiny computer programmed for only one task: to detect patterns in the images of the desktop and determine how far they have moved since the previous sample. The processor inside the mouse computes the direction and velocity of the mouse from the patterns and sends the data through the input connection to the computer, which in turn draws the cursor image on the screen.

The most visible output device is the screen of the computer system. Other devices include speakers for audio output and printers for hard copy output. In a small system like a handheld calculator, main memory contains one output connection for each number or letter that is visible on the calculator display. After the calculator computes the number to display, it sends each character of the number to the corresponding output connection. For example, if the number to display is 263, the computer sends the character 2 to the first output connection, the character 6 to the second output connection, and the character 3 to the third output connection. **FIGURE 1.13** shows the information flow over the system bus for one of the characters in the number.

Tablets and personal computers have pixel displays. A *pixel* is a picture element, which is a single dot on the display. The system forms an image on the display by setting the brightness and color of each individual pixel. Printers also form images by coloring each pixel on the paper with the proper mixture of ink. It is theoretically possible to have an output connection in main memory for each pixel in the output device. However, a typical screen can have around 10 million pixels. If the CPU had the task of keeping each pixel updated with the proper value, it would not have enough time to perform any other computations.

FIGURE 1.13
Information flow to send data to the output connection.

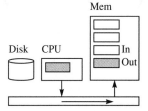

Pixels

Consequently, the main memory output connections for displays are not attached directly to each pixel of the display. Rather, they are attached to I/O modules containing separate special-purpose processors whose only function is to compute the color values for each pixel of the display. For example, to draw a line on the display, the CPU does not need to calculate the color values for all the pixels to render the line. Instead, it can send the endpoints of the line to the output connections, and then the I/O module can use that information to calculate and set the color values of the pixels in the display.

Disk

Like the CPU and main memory, the *disk* has a set of memory cells to store information. It differs from main memory in three respects. First, main memory is *volatile*. That is, when you turn the power off or when there is a power outage, the values in main memory are lost. In contrast, disk memory is nonvolatile. You can store information on a disk, turn the power off, and when you turn the power back on, the information is still there.

Disk memory is nonvolatile.

Second, the storage capacity of a disk is about a thousand times the capacity of main memory. The number of storage cells in main memory is typically in the billions, but the number of cells on a disk is typically in the trillions.

Disk memory capacity is greater than main memory capacity.

Third, although disk has high storage capacity, it has low speed compared to main memory. This speed difference is due to the different access methods of the two types of storage. The access method for main memory is *random*. In fact, the electronic components that make up main memory are often referred to as RAM (for *random access memory*) circuits. If you have just fetched some information from one end of main memory, you can immediately get information from the other end at random without passing over the information in between.

Random access

In contrast, the access method for a disk is *sequential*. A hard disk drive consists of a spinning platter with a thin magnetic coating on its surface that stores the information. A tiny sensor skims the surface of the disk and can move from the center to the edge of the disk to locate the position on the surface where the information is stored. If you have just fetched some information near the center of the disk, you cannot get information from the edge of the disk until you first move the sensor to the edge and then wait for the information to rotate to the sensor. The time to move the sensor to the proper location is called the *seek time*, and the time to wait for the information to rotate under the sensor is called the *latency*. These times are typically a few thousandths of a second. The time to access a value from RAM is typically a few billionths of a second. So, disk is about a million times slower than main memory.

Sequential access

Disk access is slower than main memory access.

Solid-state disks (SSDs) perform the same function as hard disk drives but are all electronic, with no moving parts. They do not have the high storage capacity of hard disk drives, but they are about a hundred times faster because they have no moving parts. The lack of moving parts makes them more reliable as well. Still, even an SSD is thousands of times slower than main memory.

FIGURE 1.14 shows the information flow between disk and main memory over the system bus. It differs from the previous information flows because the CPU is not an intermediary in the transaction. Information transfer between disk and main memory without going through the CPU registers is called *direct memory access,* or DMA. The disk has its own special-purpose processor, called a *DMA controller,* whose only function is to transfer information over the system bus between the disk and main memory. The CPU initiates the transfer request by sending a signal to the DMA controller. Then, while the CPU processes the information in its registers, the DMA controller simultaneously transfers the information over the bus. The disk controller signals the CPU when the transfer is complete.

Suppose you have a document you need to edit in a word processor. The word processor app is stored on disk. When you start up the app, the system sends a copy of the app from the disk to memory with a DMA transfer, as in Figure 1.14. Then, when you open your document, the system does the same kind of transfer, bringing your document into main memory. Figures 1.12 and 1.13 show the information flow when you type a key on the keyboard and view the results on the screen. When you save your document, the system does a DMA transfer similar to the one of Figure 1.14 but in the other direction, transferring your document from main memory to disk.

FIGURE 1.14
Direct memory access between a disk and main memory.

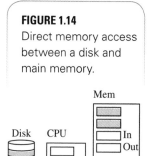

Direct memory access

1.3 Software

An *algorithm* is a set of instructions that, when carried out in the proper sequence, solves a problem in a finite amount of time. Algorithms do not require computers. FIGURE 1.15 is an algorithm in English that solves the problem of making six servings of stirred custard.

This recipe illustrates two important properties of algorithms—the finite number of instructions and execution in a finite amount of time. The algorithm has seven instructions—combine, stir, cook, remove, cool, add, and chill. Seven is a finite number. An algorithm cannot have an infinite number of instructions.

Even though the number of instructions in the custard algorithm is finite, there is a potential problem with its execution. The recipe instructs us to cook until the custard coats the metal spoon. What if it never coats the

Algorithms

FIGURE 1.15
An algorithm for making stirred custard.

Ingredients
   3 slightly beaten eggs
   ¼ cup sugar
   2 cups milk, scalded
   ½ teaspoon vanilla
Algorithm
   Combine eggs, sugar, and ¼ teaspoon salt.
   Slowly stir in slightly cooled milk.
   Cook in double boiler over hot, not boiling, water,
   stirring constantly.
   As soon as custard coats metal spoon, remove from heat.
   Cool at once—place pan in cold water and stir a minute
   or two.
   Add vanilla.
   Chill.

The finite requirement for an algorithm

spoon? Then, if we strictly followed the instructions, we would be cooking forever! A valid algorithm must never execute endlessly. It must provide a solution in a finite amount of time. Assuming that the custard will always coat the spoon, this recipe is indeed an algorithm.

Definition of a program

A *program* is an algorithm written for execution on a computer. Programs cannot be written in English. They must be written in a language for one of the seven levels of a computer system.

General-purpose computers can solve many different kinds of problems, from computing the company payroll to correcting a spelling mistake in a memorandum. The hardware gets its versatility from its ability to be programmed to do the different jobs. Programs that control the computer are called *software*.

Software

Software is classified into two broad groups:

› Systems software

› Applications software

Systems software versus applications software

Systems software makes the computer accessible to the applications designers. *Applications software*, in turn, makes the computer system accessible to the end user at Level App7. Generally speaking, a systems software engineer designs programs at Level HOL6 and below. These programs take care of the many details of the computer system with which the applications programmer does not want to bother.

Operating Systems

The most important software for a computer is the operating system. The *operating system* is the systems program that makes the hardware usable. Every general-purpose computer system includes both hardware and an operating system.

To study this text effectively, you must have access to a computer with an operating system. Some common commercial operating systems are Microsoft Windows, Mac OS X, Linux, Android, and iOS. Mac OS X and iOS are Unix operating systems, and Android is based on Linux, which is in turn a version of Unix.

An operating system has three general functions:

> File management

> Memory management

> Processor management

Functions of an operating system

Of these three functions, file management is the most visible to the user. The first thing a new computer user learns is how to manipulate the files of information on the operating system.

Disks, directories, and files in an operating system are analogous to filing cabinets, file folders, and documents in an office. In an office, the filing cabinet stores file folders, each of which contains a set of documents. In an operating system, disk drives store directories, each of which contains a set of files. The office worker assigns a name to a file folder that reflects the contents of the folder and makes it easy to pick out an individual file from the cabinet. Similarly, the computer user assigns a name to a directory that reflects the contents of the directory and makes it easy to pick out a file to open in an application.

Files can contain three types of information:

> Documents

> Programs

> Data

Three types of information contained in files

Documents may be company memoranda, music, photos, and the like. Files also store programs to be executed by the computer. To be executed, first they must be loaded from disk into main memory, as Figure 1.14 shows. Input data for an executing program can come from a file, and output data can also be sent to a file.

The files are physically scattered over the surface of the disk. To keep track of all these files of information, the operating system maintains a

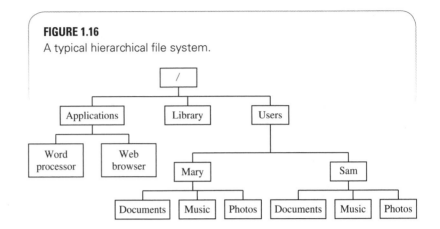

FIGURE 1.16
A typical hierarchical file system.

directory of them. The directory is a list of all the files on the disk. Each entry in the directory has the file's name, its size, its physical location on the disk, and any other information the operating system needs to manage the files. The directory itself is also stored on the disk.

FIGURE 1.16 shows a typical file system, which is hierarchical from the user's perspective. The box at the top is the root directory, labeled / in Unix systems. Below it are directories for storing applications, a library of software used by the applications, and each user's login account for the computer. Each user has a separate directory for files of documents, music, and photos.

The operating system provides the user with a way to manipulate the files on the disk. Common operating system commands include changing the name of a file or directory, deleting a file from the disk, and executing an application program. Experienced programmers can execute such commands on the command line with a terminal app. Most users initiate the commands with a point and click of the mouse. Your operating system is a program written for your computer by a team of systems programmers. When you issue the command to delete a file from the disk, a systems program executes that command. You, the user, are using a program that someone else, the systems programmer, wrote.

Software Analysis and Design

Software, whether systems or applications, has much in common with literature. Human authors write both. Other people read both, although computers can also read and execute programs. Both novelists and programmers are creative in that the solutions they propose are not unique. When a novelist has something to communicate, there is always more than one way to express it. The difference between a good novel and a bad one lies not only in the idea communicated, but also in the way the idea is expressed. Likewise, when a programmer has a problem to solve, there is always more than one way to program the solution. The difference between a good program and a bad one lies not only in the correctness of the solution to the problem, but also in other characteristics of the program, such as clarity, execution speed, and memory requirement.

As a student of literature, you participate in two distinct activities—reading and writing. Reading is analysis; you read what someone else has written and analyze its contents. Writing is design or synthesis; you have an idea to express, and your problem is how to communicate that idea effectively. Most people find writing more difficult than reading, because it requires more creativity. That is why there are more readers in the general population than authors.

Similarly, as a student of software, you will analyze and design programs. Remember that the three activities of a program are input, processing, and output. In analysis, you are given the input and the processing instructions. Your problem is to determine the output. In design, you are given the input and the desired output. Your problem is to write the processing instructions, that is, to design the software. **FIGURE 1.17** shows the difference between analysis and design.

As in reading and writing English literature, designing good software is more difficult than analyzing it. A familiar complaint of computer science students is "I understand the concepts, but I can't write the programs." This is a natural complaint because it reflects the difficulty of synthesis as opposed to analysis. Our ultimate goal is for you to be able to design software as well as analyze it. The following chapters will give you specific software design techniques.

Analysis versus design

But first you should become familiar with these general problem-solving guidelines, which also apply to software design:

> Understand the problem.

> Outline a solution.

> Solve each part of your outlined problem.

> Test your solution on the computer.

General problem-solving guidelines

FIGURE 1.17
The difference between analysis and design.

(a) Analysis—The input and processing are given. The output is to be determined.

(b) Design—The input and desired output are given. The processing is to be determined.

When faced with a software design problem, test your understanding of the problem by writing down some sample input and the corresponding output. You cannot solve a problem by computer if you do not know how to solve it by hand. To outline a solution, you must break down the problem into several subproblems. Because the subproblems are smaller than the original problem, they are easier to solve.

1.4 Digital Information

We live in a space–time universe. Every event in the universe occurs at a particular point in space and at a particular point in time. All computations in the universe, therefore, also occupy space and time. The space in a computer system consists of the electronic devices on the chip circuitry and the wires connecting them. The elapsed time of a computation consists of the time for the CPU to execute the instructions of the program plus the time to move the information between the components of the system.

Quantifying Space

Because computers are electronic, they store and process information in the form of electrical signals. The signals are voltage levels inside the electronic circuits. Each signal is either at a high voltage level, represented by the digit 1, or a low level, represented by the digit 0. Because there are only two possible values for the signal, it is called a *binary digit* or *bit*. A bit is the smallest unit of digital information. Each bit in a computer system occupies space in the circuit comprised of the electronic components that maintain its value.

Most data values represent either numbers or text. To process such data, a computer system represents numbers and text as a sequence of bits. The number of bits in a sequence is to a certain extent arbitrary. For integers, a long sequence of bits can store a wider range of numeric values than a small sequence can. For text, a long sequence of bits can store a wider range of characters. Different parts of a computer system have bit sequences with different lengths. For example, the registers in the CPU are usually sequences of 32 or 64 bits. The memory cells in main memory are always a sequence of 8 bits.

Because each bit can have two values, either 0 or 1, the number of values that can be stored in a sequence of n bits is fixed as follows:

> The number of values stored by a sequence of n bits is 2^n.

For example, FIGURE 1.18 shows all the possible values that can be stored by a sequence of three bits. Because $2^3 = 8$, there are eight possible

FIGURE 1.18

The eight values possible with three bits.

Decimal	Binary
0	000
1	001
2	010
3	011
4	100
5	101
6	110
7	111

Definition of bit

Information capacity of an n-bit cell

values that a sequence of three bits can store. If the three bits represent an integer, the eight integer values are 0, 1, 2, . . . , 7, as written in decimal.

How many bits does it take to store a single character in the English language? There are 26 letters in the alphabet. To include both uppercase letters and lowercase letters would require 2 × 26, which is 52 values. To include the 10 digit characters 0 through 9 brings the number of values up to 62. To include all the punctuation marks, like ? and !, add another dozen or so, which brings the total up to about 74. Now, six bits is not enough because 2^6 is 64 and we need to store at least 74 values. Seven bits works because 2^7 is 128, which exceeds our requirement of storing 74 values. The American Standard Code for Information Interchange (ASCII) specifies all possible 128 binary values and the English character that each bit pattern represents. It is common for storing textual information in computer systems. For example, a computer stores the lowercase letter q as the sequence of seven bits, 1110001, and the lowercase letter r as the sequence of seven bits, 1110010. See the back cover of this book for a table of ASCII characters.

A sequence of eight bits is called a *byte*, pronounced "bite." On all computer systems, each memory cell in main memory is one byte. To make a single seven-bit character fit into an eight-bit memory cell, the system prefixes an extra zero at the beginning of the seven-bit code for the character. So, q is stored as 0111 0001, and r is stored as 0111 0010. The rule of thumb to remember is:

Definition of byte

> It takes one byte, which is eight bits, to store one ASCII character.

Storage requirement for an ASCII character

FIGURE 1.19 shows the common metric prefixes for representing small quantities. An example of using a prefix for a small quantity would be to quote the seek time for a hard drive as 12 ms. The figure shows that the prefix letter *m* is an abbreviation for *milli-*, so the seek time is 12 milliseconds, or 12×10^{-3} seconds, or 0.012 seconds. Similarly, if the access time of a memory device is 430 ns, that time is 430×10^{-9} seconds, or 0.00000043 seconds.

FIGURE 1.19
Prefixes for small numbers in scientific notation.

Multiple	Prefix	Prefix Letter
10^{-3}	milli-	m
10^{-6}	micro-	μ
10^{-9}	nano-	n
10^{-12}	pico-	p

FIGURE 1.20
Prefixes for large numbers in scientific notation.

Decimal Multiples	Decimal Prefix	Decimal Prefix Letter	Binary Multiples	Binary Prefix	Binary Prefix Letters
$10^3 = 1000$	kilo-	K	$2^{10} = 1024$	kibi-	Ki
$10^6 = 1000^2$	mega-	M	$2^{20} = 1024^2$	mebi-	Mi
$10^9 = 1000^3$	giga-	G	$2^{30} = 1024^3$	gibi-	Gi
$10^{12} = 1000^4$	tera-	T	$2^{40} = 1024^4$	tebi-	Ti
$10^{15} = 1000^5$	peta-	P	$2^{50} = 1024^5$	pebi-	Pi

(a) The decimal and binary prefixes.

Decimal Multiples	Binary Multiples	Percent Difference
$10^3 = 1000$	$2^{10} = 1024$	2.4%
$10^6 = 1,000,000$	$2^{20} = 1,048,576$	4.9%
$10^9 = 1,000,000,000$	$2^{30} = 1,073,741,824$	7.4%
$10^{12} = 1,000,000,000,000$	$2^{40} = 1,099,511,627,776$	10.0%
$10^{15} = 1,000,000,000,000,000$	$2^{50} = 1,125,899,906,842,624$	12.6%

(b) The differences between the decimal and binary values.

The decimal prefixes in FIGURE 1.20(a) for the large values are common in science. For example, 45 MW is 45 megawatts, or 45×10^6 watts. These prefixes are also common for specifying hard disk drive capacities. However, they are not so common for specifying other memory capacities because the access methods for those devices are binary. Consequently, counting is frequently performed in base 2 instead of base 10. To distinguish between the two counting bases, the binary prefixes are modified by including the lowercase letter *i* after the corresponding decimal prefix letter. The binary prefixes in the figure show that a *binary kilo-* is designated as a *kibi-* and is 2^{10}, or 1024, and a *binary mega-* is 2^{20}, or 1024^2. Figure 1.20(b) shows the exact counting values for the decimal and corresponding binary multiples. For the first multiple, the difference between 1000 and 1024 is less than 3%, so you can think of a binary kilo-, or a kibi-, as being about 1000, even though it is a little more. The approximation for a mega- is a little worse but is still within 5%. The same applies to giga-, tera-, and peta-, but for peta- the difference is about 12.6%.

The abbreviation for a byte is the uppercase letter *B*. The abbreviation for a bit is the lowercase letter *b*. So, for example, a hard disk drive with a capacity of 780 GB can store 780×10^9 bytes using the standard meaning of giga-. On the other hand, a main memory of 8 GiB can store 8×2^{30} bytes, which is $8 \times 1{,}073{,}741{,}824$ bytes, or 8.59×10^9 bytes. As of this writing, the adoption of the binary prefixes is far from complete in the computing industry. Before the binary prefixes were standardized, the decimal prefixes were used to refer to both decimal values and binary values with no distinction between the two notations. Some manufacturers still quote main memory capacity, for example, as *8 GB* when they mean *8 GiB*. As another example, many computer engineers still refer to a *64-KB* storage unit when they mean *64 KiB*.

Abbreviations for byte and bit

Disk drive

Quantifying Time

All computations in a computer system occupy time as well as space. The two components of time in a computer system are the computation time, which is the time it takes the CPU to execute one of the instructions in its instruction set, and the transmission time, which is the time it takes to move information from one component of the system to another. The binary prefixes in Figure 1.20(a) are never used for specifying time.

A single machine instruction is fast by human standards. CPU speeds are commonly measured in GHz, which stands for *gigahertz*, a unit of frequency. A hertz is one cycle per second. So, a GHz is a billion cycles per second. For example, a CPU rated at 4.6 GHz executes at a rate of 4.6 billion cycles per second. Each computer instruction at Level Mc2 requires one cycle to execute. Each instruction at Level ISA3, however, is composed of several instructions at Level Mc2. When you purchase an app, you get a program of Level ISA3 instructions. So, when an ISA3 instruction in your app executes, it requires the execution of several Mc2 instructions, each of which requires one cycle.

Suppose you are running an app and you click on a button to perform a task. The following system performance equation computes the total execution time of the program task as the product of three terms:

$$\frac{\text{time}}{\text{program}} = \frac{\text{instructions}}{\text{program}} \times \frac{\text{cycles}}{\text{instruction}} \times \frac{\text{time}}{\text{cycle}}$$

The system performance equation

The first term is the number of Level ISA3 instructions that execute to perform the task. The second term is the average number of Mc2 instructions it takes to execute a single ISA3 instruction. The third term is the time it takes to complete one cycle and is related to the frequency as

$$T = \frac{1}{f}$$

where T, the period, is the number of seconds per cycle and f, the frequency rating of the CPU, is the number of cycles per second. As in all scientific calculations, the units in the three terms cancel to give the units of the product. *Instructions* in the numerator of the first term cancels with *instruction* in the denominator of the second term, and *cycles* in the numerator of the first term cancels with *cycle* in the denominator of the third term, to yield time per program for the result.

The number of cycles per ISA3 instruction varies greatly. Some ISA3 instructions are composed of only a single Mc2 cycle. Examples are instructions to add or subtract two integers and instructions to move a value from one register in the CPU to another. Some are composed of a few cycles. For example, to multiply two integers can take about four or five cycles. A complex computation like taking the cosine of a double value can take about 100 cycles. The average number of cycles per instruction in a given program task depends on the mix of ISA3 instructions that execute to perform the task.

Example 1.1 Suppose your CPU is rated at 2.5 GHz and you execute a program task on your app that requires the execution of 16 million ISA3 instructions. If each ISA3 instruction executes an average of 3.7 Mc2 instructions, what is the execution time of the program task?

    time/program
$=$ ⟨System performance equation⟩
    (instructions/program) × (cycles/instruction) × (time/cycle)
$=$ ⟨Substitute values with $T = 1/f$ for the third term⟩
    $(16 \times 10^6) \times (3.7) \times (1/(2.5 \times 10^9))$
$=$ ⟨Math⟩
    23.7 ms

So, the time is 23.7×10^{-3} seconds, or about 0.024 seconds. ∎

This example shows how to calculate the time it takes to execute a program task. The other aspect of time in a computer system is the time to move information from one component of the system to another. In general, the connection between the source and the destination over which information flows is called a *channel*. A channel could be the wires comprising the system bus in a computer system, or it could be the space between a cell phone tower and a cell phone. The *bandwidth* of the channel is the quantity of information that it can carry per unit of time. Channels with a high bandwidth can transfer more information per second than channels with a low bandwidth. It is common to quote channel bandwidths in units of bits per second, although occasionally it is quoted in bytes per second. Because a byte is eight bits, a channel with a bandwidth of 8.2 MB/s, for example, is equivalent to 8 × 8.2 or 65.6 Mb/s.

The bandwidth of a channel

The following bandwidth equation computes the total information transferred as the product of two terms:

$$\text{information} = \frac{\text{information}}{\text{time}} \times \text{time}$$

The bandwidth equation

The first term in the product is the bandwidth of the channel, and the second term is the transmission time.

Example 1.2   The bandwidth of a DMA channel between the hard drive and main memory in a computer system is quoted as 3 Gb/s. How long would it take to do a DMA transfer from the hard drive to main memory of the 400-MB thumbnail database from the photo library in your computer?

   time
= ⟨Solve bandwidth equation for time⟩
   information/(information/time)
= ⟨Substitute values with 8 bits per byte for information⟩
   $8 \times 500 \times 10^6/3 \times 10^9$
= ⟨Math⟩
   1.33 s ∎

Example 1.3   A typist is entering some text on a computer keyboard at the rate of 35 words per minute. How large must the bandwidth of the channel be to accommodate the information flow between the typist and the computer system? Assume that each word is followed by one space character, on average.

Including one space character after each word, the typist enters 36 characters per minute.

   bandwidth
= ⟨Definition of bandwidth⟩
   information/time
= ⟨Substitute values⟩
   (8(b/char) × 36 char)/(1(min) × 60(s/min))
= ⟨Math⟩
   4.8 b/s ∎

Quick Response Codes

The quick response code, or *QR code*, was invented in Japan to track items in the automotive industry. It is so versatile that it is now used for storing all kinds of textual information that can be conveniently scanned on mobile devices with built-in cameras. **FIGURE 1.21** shows two QR codes. Figure 1.21(a) shows the code for a web URL, and Figure 1.21(b) shows the code for the text of the first paragraph of this chapter.

FIGURE 1.21
Two QR codes.

(a) The QR code for a web URL.

(b) The QR code for the text of the first paragraph of this chapter.

A QR code is a square matrix of light and dark boxes of any color, each of which stores one bit of information. The QR terminology for a single box is a *module*. The following discussion refers to a module as a bit that stores 1 if it is black and 0 if it is white. There are 40 versions of QR codes, ranging in size from 21 × 21 bits for Version 1, 25 × 25 bits for Version 2, up to 177 × 177 bits for Version 40. Each version adds four bits per dimension to the previous version. Figure 1.21(a) is Version 3 with 29 × 29 bits, and Figure 1.21(b) is Version 11 with 81 × 81 bits. The larger the version, the more information can be stored. The code in part (b) stores all 564 characters of the first paragraph of this chapter.

Seven parts of the grid are reserved for alignment and format purposes as follows:

The QR code alignment and format regions

> Finder patterns

> Separators

> The dark module

> The format information area

> Timing patterns

> Alignment patterns (for Version 2 and higher only)

> The version information area (for Version 7 and higher only)

FIGURE 1.22(a) shows the first six of these regions for the Version 3 QR code of Figure 1.21(a). This version has no reserved version information area.

The finder patterns

The finder patterns located on three corners of the code are 7- × 7-square blocks that help the scanner determine the orientation of the code. Each consists of a black border seven bits wide surrounding a white border five bits wide, which in turn surrounds a 3×3 black matrix. The total number of bits occupied by the finder patterns is $7 \times 7 \times 3$, or 147 bits. The separators are the white borders around the inside boundaries of the finder patterns and occupy 15 bits each, for a total of 45 bits for the three. The dark module is a single black bit at the upper-right corner of the separator for the lower-left finder pattern. The format information area along the sides of the separators is shaded in the figure and totals 30 bits. These first four reserved regions always occupy the same area on the code and total $147 + 45 + 1 + 30$, which is 223 bits.

The separators

The dark module

The format information area

The timing patterns help the scanner identify the individual rows and columns in the grid. Each is a single track of alternating ones and zeros. The number of bits occupied by a timing pattern depends on the version of the code. The higher the version, the more bits in the timing pattern. For Version 3 with a 29- $\times$ 29-bit grid, the length is 29 minus the 8 bits on each end occupied by the finder pattern and separator. That is 13 bits for each timing pattern and 26 bits total for the two patterns.

The timing patterns

Each alignment pattern is a 5- $\times$ 5-square block and hence occupies 25 bits. However, the number of alignment patterns varies with the version, and the placement is such that an alignment pattern can intersect with a timing pattern. Version 3 in Figure 1.22(a) has one alignment pattern, which does not intersect a timing pattern. You should be able to spot the 13 alignment patterns in the QR code of Figure 1.21(b). Two of them intersect the top timing pattern, and two of them intersect the left timing pattern. To

The alignment patterns

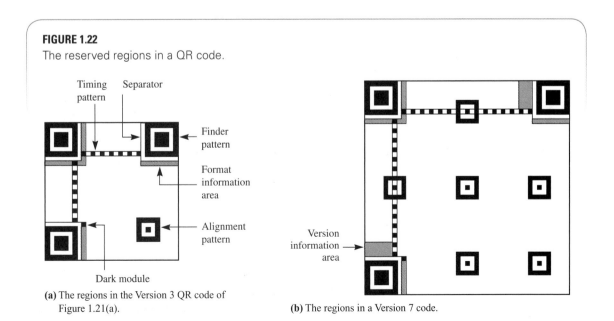

FIGURE 1.22
The reserved regions in a QR code.

(a) The regions in the Version 3 QR code of Figure 1.21(a).

(b) The regions in a Version 7 code.

*The version information
area*

calculate the total number of bits available for storing information, subtract the number of reserved bits from the total number in the grid. For Version 3 in Figure 1.22(a), that is 29×29 (or 841), minus 223 for the first group of regions, minus 26 for the timing patterns, minus 25 for the alignment pattern, which equals 567 bits.

The version information area is only present on Version 7 and higher. If it is present, it occupies two 3×6 blocks adjacent to the upper-right and lower-left finder patterns. Figure 1.22(b) for the 45×45 grid of Version 7 shows the placement of these two regions, each of which occupies 18 bits. This version also has six alignment patterns, two of which intersect the timing patterns. Each intersecting alignment pattern takes away only 20 bits from the total instead of 25, because the middle row or column is already accounted for by the bits in the timing pattern. Note that the alternating one–zero pattern of the timing track is not disturbed by the intersecting alignment pattern.

Example 1.4   How many bits are available for storing information in the Version 7 QR code of Figure 1.22(a)?

number of bits available for information
$=$ ⟨Subtract reserved areas from total⟩
$45 \times 45 - \mathit{fixed} - \mathit{timing} - \mathit{align} - \mathit{interalign} - \mathit{vinfo}$
$=$ ⟨Substitute values⟩
$45 \times 45 - 223 - 2(45 - 2 \times 8) - 4 \times 25 - 2 \times 20 - 2 \times 18$
$=$ ⟨Math⟩
$1496 \, \mathrm{b}$

where *fixed* is the number of bits in the first four reserved regions, *timing* is the number of bits in the two timing patterns, *align* is the number of bits in the four alignment patterns that do not intersect a timing pattern, *interalign* is the number of bits in the two alignment patterns that do intersect a timing pattern, and *vinfo* is the number of bits in the two version information areas. ∎

There are four kinds of information bits in a QR code.

*The QR code information
bits*

❭ The mode indicator

❭ The character count indicator

❭ The redundant bits for error correction

❭ The data bits

The mode indicator

The mode indicator is a four-bit string that specifies what kind of characters the code represents. The numeric mode is for codes that store only numbers. The alphanumeric mode stores only sequences of uppercase

English characters, the 10 decimal digits, and a few punctuation characters. The byte mode stores sequences of ASCII characters. There are two other modes, one of which stores Kanji characters for Asian languages.

The character count indicator contains anywhere from 8 to 16 bits, depending on the version and the mode. For example, in Version 10 using the numeric mode, the character count string is 12 bits long, but in Version 27 it is 14 bits long. Regardless of how many bits are in the character count indicator, it represents the number of characters stored in the code. The Version 3 QR code of Figure 1.21(a) uses the byte mode to store 43 ASCII characters of a URL address. Its character count indicator contains the 8 bits 0010 1011, because that is how to represent the integer 43 in binary.

The character count indicator

Whenever information is stored or transmitted, it is subject to errors. For example, a wireless signal might be distorted as you move your mobile device around the room. Or, on a QR code there might be a smudge of dirt that obscures the pattern of the code. The scanner might read the dirty smudge over a white bit as a 1 when the bit should be a 0. A common technique to handle such errors is to add extra bits to the data that allow the receiver to detect if an error has occurred and, if so, to correct it. Section 9.4 shows how error detection and correction codes work. The QR code uses the same error correction technique that is used to read Blu-ray discs when scratches on the surface of the disc can cause errors.

The redundant bits of error correction

FIGURE 1.23 shows the four possible correction levels in a QR code. The lowest correction level, L, can recover all the text in a QR code even if 7% of the code is damaged. The next higher correction level, M, can recover all the text even if 15% of the code is damaged. The higest level, H, can correct 30%. The higher the correction level, the more redundant bits are required, and so the fewer data bits can be stored in a given QR version. Levels L and M are most common in practice. The bits for the mode and character count indicators and the redundant bits for error correction represent overhead for the encoded message and must be subtracted from the information bits

FIGURE 1.23
The four possible correction levels in a QR code.

Correction at Level	Will Correct the Data With
L	7% damaged.
M	15% damaged.
Q	25% damaged.
H	30% damaged.

to determine how many data bits are available to store the message of the QR code. For the byte mode that stores a message of ASCII characters, the overhead is about 20% for Level L and 40% for Level M.

Example 1.5   How many ASCII characters can be stored in a 29 × 29 Version 3 QR code with one alignment pattern that does not intersect a timing pattern using Level L error correction with 25% overhead?

First, compute the number of information bits:

number of bits available for information
= ⟨Subtract reserved areas from total⟩
  $29 \times 29 - fixed - timing - align$
= ⟨Substitute values⟩
  $29 \times 29 - 223 - 2(29 - 2 \times 8) - 25$
= ⟨Math⟩
  567 b

If the mode and character count indicators and the redundant bits for error correction have a 25% overhead, then 100% − 25%, or 75% of the information bits are available for the data bits.

maximum number of characters
= ⟨Account for overhead⟩
  (fraction for data) × (number of characters)
= ⟨Substitute values⟩
  (1.00 − 0.25) × (567 b/8(b/char))
= ⟨Math⟩
  53.16
= ⟨Round down⟩
  53 characters

The URL in the QR code of Figure 1.21(a) is a Version 3 code with Level L error correction. It has 49 characters, which is just under the maximum limit of 53. ∎

Images

Images in a computer system include images on computer screens, scanned images of paper documents, and photographic images captured by cameras. Depending on the device, the image may be black and white, grayscale, or color. Regardless of the device, all images in a computer system are stored in binary.

FIGURE 1.24 shows four renderings of the letter *P* on four different display devices. In part (a), the image of the letter occupies a 5- × 8-pixel region of the display, and in (b) it occupies an 11- × 16-pixel region. You can

FIGURE 1.24
The letter *P* rendered in black and white and grayscale.

(a) Black and white, 5 × 8.

(b) Black and white, 11 × 16.

(c) Grayscale, 6 × 9.

(d) Grayscale, 11 × 17.

see from the two images that the more pixels that are available to store the image, the more accurate is the image. One way to increase the accuracy of the image is to increase the number of pixels per inch high enough that the human eye cannot perceive the individual pixels. Another way to increase the accuracy is to design the individual pixels with the ability to display shades of gray instead of just black and white. In part (c), the image of the letter has approximately the same number of pixels as in part (a), but some of the pixels have various shades of gray between pure black and pure white. Similarly, the image in part (d) has about the same number of pixels as the image in part (b) but is more accurate because of its grayscale, especially when viewed from a distance.

A black-and-white laser printer works on the same principle. It either does or does not deposit a dot of black toner on each pixel location on the paper. There is no gray toner, so product designers increase accuracy by increasing the number of dots per inch. A typical desktop laser printer can produce 600 or 1200 dots per inch. Commercial typesetting machines offer 2400 dots per inch or more. To print shades of gray, the printer deposits a pattern of black dots interspersed with white, which the human eye perceives as gray from a distance. Document scanners usually have the option to scan in black and white, grayscale, or color. When you view a scanned grayscale image on a screen, each screen pixel has the ability to display discrete shades of gray.

As with all information in a computer system, images are stored in binary. FIGURE 1.25(a) shows the binary storage for the black-and-white image in Figure 1.24(a). Each cell in the storage grid for the display contains a single bit that is 1 when the corresponding pixel is black and 0 when it is white. The total number of bits required to store the image is the total number of cells in the storage grid. The 5×8 grid requires 40 bits, which is 5 bytes, to store the image.

The *bit depth* of a stored image is the number of bits required to store *Bit depth* a single pixel. In Figure 1.25(a), the bit depth is one because there is one bit per pixel. Figure 1.25(b) shows the binary storage for the grayscale image in Figure 1.24(c). The bit depth for this image is three because it takes three bits to store each pixel. The table in Figure 1.18 lists the eight possible values with a memory cell of three bits. Each pixel in the image of Figure 1.25(b) is one of eight possible shades of gray. For example, the pixel in the lower-left corner is black, with a binary value of 111, and the pixel in the lower-right corner is white, with a value of 000. The pixel in the bottom row, second from the left, has a binary value of 010, which produces a light gray color, and the pixel just above that is darker, with a binary value of 101. The total number of bits required to display a grayscale image is the number of pixels times the bit depth.

FIGURE 1.25
Binary storage for black-and-white images and for grayscale images.

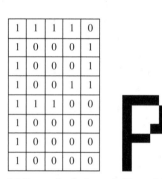

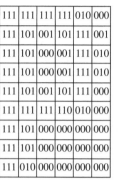

(a) Storage for the image in Figure 1.24(a).   (b) Storage for the image in Figure 1.24(c).

Example 1.6   An eReader has a 1072- × 1448-pixel grayscale display, with each pixel able to display 16 shades of gray. What is the KiB size of the display memory for the device?

First, determine the bit depth of the display. Because each pixel can display 16 shades of gray, and $2^4 = 16$, the bit depth is 4. Then compute the size of the display memory as follows:

size of display memory
= ⟨Product⟩
  (number of pixels) × (bit depth)
= ⟨Substitute values⟩
  (1072 × 1448 pixels) × 4(b/pixel)
= ⟨Math⟩
  6,209,024 b
= ⟨Convert to KiB⟩
  (6,209,024 b) × (1 B/8 b) × (1 KiB/1024 B)
= ⟨Math⟩
  758 KiB   ∎

In a color display, each pixel on the screen emits a color. The human eye captures the light rays from the field of pixels and focuses them on the retina. The retina contains two kinds of photoreceptor cells that are sensitive to light. It has about 6 million cone cells, which are sensitive to color, and 120 million rod cells, which are not sensitive to color and enable vision in low light conditions. The cells convert the light energy into electrical signals that are sent through the optic nerves to the brain. The brain combines all the signals from the photoreceptor cells to form an image in the mind. Strictly speaking, light rays do not have color. Color exists only in the human mind. When you view a photographic scene on a color display, the pixels emit points of light that are detected by the photoreceptor cells and processed by the brain so that the resulting image in the mind approximates the image that would be constructed by the brain were you to view the scene in nature.

Sunlight, which appears to be white in the human mind, is a mixture of a spectrum of colors. When the sun comes out on a rainy day, each droplet of water in the air is a tiny prism that separates the mixture of colors into the visible spectrum to make a rainbow. Each color in the spectrum is a pure color whose light rays have a single wavelength. **FIGURE 1.26** shows the wavelengths of light in the visible spectrum, which ranges from about 400 nm (nanometers) at the violet end of the spectrum to 700 nm at the red end. Colors outside the spectrum are mixtures of pure colors. For example, if a light ray is a mixture of the pure colors red and blue, the brain will interpret the signals from the cones to produce the color purple in the mind.

The retina has three types of cone cells that are sensitive to short, medium, and long wavelengths of light in the visible spectrum. **FIGURE 1.27** shows that each type of cone cell is sensitive to a range of wavelenths. The first type, known as an *S-cone* (for *short wavelength*), is sensitive to wavelengths of light between about 400 nm and 540 nm. It has peak sensitivity at about 430 nm, which corresponds to a blue-violet color. The peak sensitivity of the second, *M-cone* (for *medium wavelength*), is about 540 nm, corresponding roughly to green. The third, *L-cone* (for *long wavelength*), has the widest range of sensitivity and is more sensitive to red than the other cone types.

Figure 1.27 shows that if a source of light sends a pure 580-nm light ray to the human eye, both M-cones and L-cones will detect the ray and send their signals to the brain. The brain combines the signals from both types of cells to produce the color yellow in the mind. It is possible for two different light rays to produce the same color in the mind. For example, a light ray containing a mixture of pure red and pure green can also activate both M-cones and L-cones in such a way that their combined signals are identical to the signals sent by a pure 580-nm light ray. In that case, the mind will again perceive the color yellow.

Like grayscale displays, color displays are composed as a grid of pixels, with the difference that each pixel contains three subpixels: one that emits red light, one that emits green light, and one that emits blue light. **FIGURE 1.28(a)** shows the structure of a single-color pixel where R is the red subpixel, G is the green subpixel, and B is the blue subpixel. This layout of the subpixels, known as *RGB stripe*, is the most common, although some devices have a different arrangement of subpixels. A display is a two-dimensional grid of square pixels. Figure 1.28(b) is a 16 × 8 portion of a color display that shows the individual subpixels in each pixel. From a distance, the eye cannot

FIGURE 1.26
The colors of the visible spectrum.

Color	Wavelength
Violet	400–450 nm
Blue	450–495 nm
Green	495–570 nm
Yellow	570–590 nm
Orange	590–620 nm
Red	620–700 nm

FIGURE 1.27
Cone cell sensitivity as a function of wavelength.

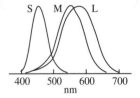

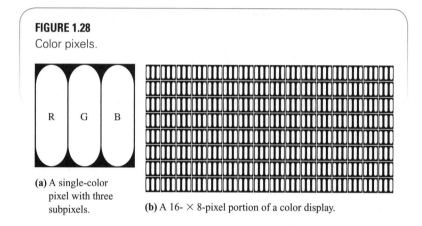

FIGURE 1.28
Color pixels.

(a) A single-color pixel with three subpixels.

(b) A 16- × 8-pixel portion of a color display.

distinguish between individual subpixels. The cone cells receive the light from a pixel as if it were a single source of light, with its color determined by the mixture of its red, green, and blue components.

When we look at our environment in nature, our eyes do not receive mixtures of only red, green, and blue. They receive mixtures of all the wavelengths from the visible spectrum. However, when we look at a scene on a computer display, our eyes receive mixtures of only the red, green, and blue from the subpixels. A scene on a display can appear realistic because the combination of red, green, and blue for each pixel produces the sensation of color in our minds that approximates the sensation produced by a different mixture of wavelengths in the real world. However, it is impossible with only three subpixels to produce all the colors the human eye can see in nature. The only colors a human can see on a display are those that are produced in our mind by mixtures of the colors from the red, green, and blue subpixels.

As with a grayscale image, the number of bits required to store a color image is equal to the total number of pixels in the display times the bit depth of each pixel. In Figure 1.25(b), the bit depth of the grayscale image is 3 because each bit can display eight shades of gray. Figure 1.28(a), however, shows that each color pixel consists of three subpixels. If each subpixel can display eight shades of its color, the total bit depth is 3 bits for each pixel times 3 pixels, which is 9. The total bit depth for a color pixel is sometimes referred to as the *color depth*. Color displays can typically produce 256 levels of brightness for each subpixel. Because 2^8 is 256, such displays require 8 bits each for the R, G, and B subpixels, for a total bit depth of 24. **FIGURE 1.29** shows some of the colors possible for such a pixel. The table shows the brightness levels in decimal, but as with all information in a computer system, they are physically stored as bits. A brightness of 255 is stored with 8 bits in binary as 1111 1111, a brightness of 192 is stored as 1100 0000, and a brightness of 128 is stored as 1000 0000. Chapter 3 describes these equivalences between decimal and binary.

FIGURE 1.29
Some colors produced by a color pixel with a bit depth of 24.

Color	Red	Green	Blue
White	255	255	255
Silver	192	192	192
Gray	128	128	128
Black	0	0	0
Red	255	0	0
Maroon	128	0	0
Yellow	255	255	0
Olive	128	128	0
Lime	0	255	0
Green	0	128	0
Aqua	0	255	255
Teal	0	128	128
Blue	0	0	255
Navy	0	0	128
Fuchsia	255	0	255
Purple	128	0	128

Example 1.7   A GPS system in an automobile has a 4.5- × 2.5-inch screen with 120 color pixels per inch. Each subpixel color can display 64 levels of brightness. What is the KiB size of the display memory?

First, determine the total number of pixels in the display.

number of pixels
= ⟨Product⟩
  (number in width) × (number in height)
= ⟨Substitute values⟩
  (4.5 in. × 120 pixels/in.) × (2.5 in. × 120 pixels/in.)
= ⟨Math⟩
  162,000 pixels

Because each subpixel can display 64 levels of brightness, and $2^6 = 64$, the number of bits for each subpixel is 6. Because there are 3 subpixels per pixel, the bit depth is 3×6, which is 18. Compute the size of the display memory as follows:

> size of display memory
> $=$ 〈Product〉
> (number of pixels) $\times$ (bit pixels)
> $=$ 〈Substitute values〉
> (162,000 pixels) $\times$ 18(b/pixel)
> $=$ 〈Math〉
> 2,916,000 b
> $=$ 〈Convert to KiB〉
> (2,916,000 b) $\times$ (1 B/8 b) $\times$ (1 KiB/1024 B)
> $=$ 〈Math〉
> 356 KiB   ∎

The fact that a color display cannot produce all the colors of nature but only an approximation of them is typical for all aspects of computer systems. Computers are useful because they perform tasks from the real world. In so doing, they *model* aspects of the real world. But computer models of the real world are always approximations.

For example, in a color display with a bit depth of 24, each pixel can produce 2^{24}, or 16,777,216, different colors. The human eye can distinguish about 10,000,000 colors, so it would seem that a color display can produce all the colors perceptible by the human eye. Yet it cannot, for two reasons. First, the human eye cannot distinguish between the color of one pixel and that of another with only a single level of brightness different in one subpixel. Consequently, the number of distinguishable colors from the set of 16,777,216 is less than the 10,000,000 distinguishable by the human eye. Second, the only way to produce all the colors perceptible by the human eye would be to have more than three subpixels per pixel and to have their wavelengths span the entire visible spectrum.

As another example, one mathematical property of integers is that there is no largest value. Consequently, there are an infinite number of integer values. However, all computers are finite. If there are n bits in a memory cell that stores an integer, then only 2^n values can be stored, not an infinite number of values. For a given storage cell, there is a largest integer value. So, the properties of integers stored in computers do not quite match the properties of mathematical integers.

The Intel Core i7 System

This text is an introduction to computer systems at all seven levels of abstraction. In practice, computer systems are complex and contain a massive amount of detail at each level—far too much detail to describe in an introductory text. Consequently, much of the detail at each level is hidden. The text presents a simplified model of each level that illustrates the fundamental principles that operate at that level. The principles govern all physical computer systems, but the model itself is only an approximation of systems in practice. This section is the first of a series of sidebars created to describe some of the omitted details and to show how the principles apply to systems in practice.

In the early history of computers, different manufacturers designed and sold many different computer systems. Over time, however, the number of different computer systems dwindled until the present,

when two computer systems dominate the commercial market—namely, the Intel/AMD systems and the ARM systems. Intel and Advanced Micro Devices (AMD) are the manufacturers of the x86 series of computer systems common in desktops and laptops. For mobile devices like smartphones and tablets, however, the Advanced RISC Machines (ARM) systems dominate the market. The *R* in the acronym *ARM* is itself an acronym and stands for *Reduced Instruction Set Computer (RISC)*. In contrast, the x86 series of computers use the Complex Instruction Set Computer (CISC) design. Chapter 12 describes the difference between CISC and RISC designs.

The Intel Core i7 system is a set of integrated circuits, also called *computer chips*, that form the basis of many Microsft Windows and Apple OS X desktops and laptops. FIGURE 1.30 shows some of the details of the Core i7 system that are not present in the corresponding

FIGURE 1.30
The Intel Core i7 system.

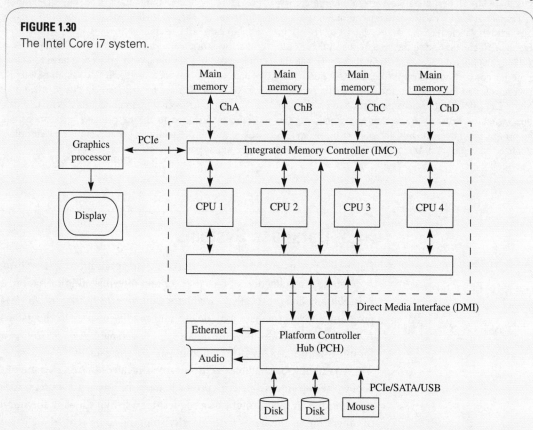

Figure 1.9. The dashed box represents a single physical package about 2 inches square that mounts on a circuit board. The integrated circuit inside the package has connections to a grid of pins on the bottom of the package that make electrical contact with the surface of the circuit board. The Platform Controller Hub (PCH) is another part mounted on the circuit board.

The most significant difference between the simplified model of Figure 1.9 and current systems is the existence of more than one CPU. A single chip typically contains several central processing units called *cores* that execute simultaneously. Having more than one CPU executing at the same time speeds up computations, much in the way that having several people working simultaneously on a single task shortens the time to complete the task. The Core i7 comprises a series of models, with the number of cores ranging from four, as in Figure 1.30, to eight, depending on the model.

Figure 1.9, which represents one primary system bus shared by all peripheral devices and main memory, is characteristic of early personal computer systems. The arrows labeled *Direct Media Interface (DMI)* in Figure 1.30 correspond to the system bus in Figure 1.9. All the peripheral devices, such as the disk drives and the Ethernet connection to the Internet, share the bus, which is connected to the CPUs on the neighboring package. The PCH controls the communication on the DMI bus, switching between the devices and scheduling the communication over the bus. In contrast to the system depicted in Figure 1.9, the main memory modules do not share the DMI system bus but are instead connected to the CPUs with separate paths called *channels*. The four memory channels are labeled *ChA*, *ChB*, *ChC*, and *ChD*. The integrated memory controller (IMC) inside the Core i7 package can connect any memory module to any CPU. Furthermore, each CPU cannot distinguish between individual main memory modules. The IMC makes all the memory modules appear like a single main memory to each CPU.

The connection between different subsystems on the circuit board is with one of several industry-standard buses: Peripheral Component Interconnect Express (PCIe), Serial Advanced Technology Attachment (SATA), or Universal Serial Bus (USB). PCIe usually connects two subsystems that are both permanently mounted on the circuit board. SATA is a common bus for connecting external disk drives to the circuit board. The USB bus is common for smaller peripherals like track pads and thumb drives. Two other common buses not shown in Figure 1.30 are Thunderbolt and High-Definition Multimedia Interface (HDMI). Thunderbolt is a combination of PCIe and another bus called *DisplayPort*, which was originally developed for video data. It is a high-speed bus common for transferring large amounts of data, as required, for example, in video-editing systems. HDMI is an interface for transferring digital video and audio signals between the components of a system. It was originally designed to be the primary interconnection link in home entertainment systems but is now common as an output port for computer systems as well.

1.5 Database Systems

Database systems are one of the most common applications at Level App7. A *database* is a collection of files that contain interrelated information, and a *database system* (also called a *database management system*, or *DBMS*) is a program that lets the user add, delete, and modify records in the database. A database system also permits queries of the database. A *query* is a request for information, usually from different parts of the database.

An example of a database is the information an online retailer maintains about the inventory, prices, product descriptions, and orders for its merchandise. A query might be a request for a listing showing the number of orders for all the items with priority shipping to be sent to a particular country at the end of the day. To produce the listing, the database system combines the information from different parts of the database, in this case from an order file and from a customer address file.

Relations

Relational database systems store information in files that appear to have a table structure. Each table has a fixed number of columns and a variable number of rows. FIGURE 1.31 is an example of the information in a relational database. Each table has a name. The table named Sor contains information about the members of a sorority, and the one named Frat contains information about the members of a fraternity. The user at Level App7 fixed the number of vertical columns in each table before entering the information in the body of the tables. The number of horizontal rows is variable so that individuals can be added to or deleted from the tables.

Relational database systems

Sor

S.Name	S.Class	S.Major	S.State
Beth	Soph	Hist	TX
Nancy	Jr	Math	NY
Robin	Sr	Hist	CA
Allison	Soph	Math	AZ
Lulwa	Sr	CompSci	CA

Frat

F.Name	F.Major	F.State
Emile	PolySci	CA
Sam	CompSci	WA
Ron	Math	OR
Mehdi	Math	CA
David	English	AZ
Jeff	Hist	TX
Craig	English	CA
Gary	CompSci	CA

FIGURE 1.31
An example of a relational database. This database contains two relations—Sor and Frat.

Relations, attributes, tuples, and domains

In relational database terminology, a table is called a *relation*. A column is an *attribute*, and a row is a *tuple* (rhymes with *couple*). In Figure 1.31, Sor and Frat are relations, (Nancy, Jr, Math, NY) is a 4-tuple of Sor because it has four elements, and F.Major is an attribute of Frat. The *domain* of an attribute is the set of all possible values of the attribute. The domain of S.Major and F.Major is the set {Hist, Math, CompSci, PolySci, English}.

Queries

Examples of queries from this database are requests for Ron's home state and for the names of all the sophomores in the sorority. Another query is a request for a list of those sorority and fraternity members who have the same major, and what that common major is.

In this small example, you can manually search through the database to determine the result of each of these queries. Ron's home state is OR, and Beth and Allison are the sophomores in the sorority. The third query is a little more difficult to tabulate. Beth and Jeff are both history majors. Nancy and Ron are both math majors, as are Nancy and Mehdi. Robin and Jeff are both history majors, and so on.

It is interesting that the result of each of these queries can be written in table form as in **FIGURE 1.32** . The result of the first query is a table with one column and one row, while the result of the second is a table with one column and two rows. The result of the third is a table with three columns and eight rows. So the result of a query of a relational database, which is a collection of relations, is itself a relation!

FIGURE 1.32
The result of three queries from the database of Figure 1.31. Each result is a relation.

Result1

F.State
OR

Result2

S.Name
Beth
Allison

Result3

S.Name	F.Name	Major
Beth	Jeff	Hist
Nancy	Ron	Math
Nancy	Mehdi	Math
Robin	Jeff	Hist
Allison	Ron	Math
Allison	Mehdi	Math
Lulwa	Sam	CompSci
Lulwa	Gary	CompSci

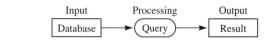

FIGURE 1.33
The relationship between the database, a query, and the result.

Query as a relation result

The fact that the result of a query is itself a relation is a powerful idea in relational database systems. The user at Level App7 views the database as a collection of relations. Her query is a request for another relation that the system derives from the existing relations in the database.

Remember that each level has a language. The language of a Level App7 relational DBMS is a set of commands that combines or modifies existing relations and produces new relations. The user at Level App7 issues the commands to produce the desired result. (FIGURE 1.33) shows the relationship between the database, a query, and the result. The database is the input. The query is a set of commands in the Level App7 language. As it does in every level in the computer system, the relationship takes this form: input, processing, output.

This chapter cannot describe every language of every relational database system on the market. Most of these lanugages are variations on a standard known as *Structured Query Language (SQL)*. Instead, it describes a simplified language typical of such systems. Most relational DBMS languages have many powerful commands. But three commands are fundamental— `select`, `project`, and `join`.

The `select` and `project` statements are similar because they both operate on a single relation to produce a modified relation. The `select` statement takes a set of rows from a given table that satisfies the condition specified in the statement. The `project` statement takes a set of columns from a given table according to the attributes specified in the statement. (FIGURE 1.34) illustrates the effect of the statements

```
select Frat where F.Major = English giving Temp1
```
and
```
project Sor over S.Name giving Temp2
```

The `project` statement can specify more than one column, in which case the attributes are enclosed in parentheses and separated by commas. For example,

```
project Sor over (S.Class, S.State) giving Temp3
```

selects two attributes from the `Sor` relation.

FIGURE 1.34

The `select` and `project` operators.

Temp1

F.Name	F.Major	F.State
David	English	AZ
Craig	English	CA

(a) `Select Frat where`
`  F.Major = English giving`
`  Temp1`

Temp2

S.Name
Beth
Nancy
Robin
Allison
Lulwa

(b) `Project`
`  Sor over`
`  S.Name`
`  giving`
`  Temp2`

Temp3

S.Class	S.State
Soph	TX
Jr	NY
Sr	CA
Soph	AZ

(c) `Project Sor over`
`  (S.Class, S.State)`
`  giving Temp3`

Note in Figure 1.34(c) that the pair (Sr, CA) is common from both 4-tuples (Robin, Sr, Hist, CA) and (Lulwa, Sr, CompSci, CA) in relation `Sor` (Figure 1.31). But the pair is not repeated in relation `Temp3`. A basic property of relations is that no row in any table may be duplicated. The `project` operator checks for duplicated rows and does not permit them. Mathematically, a relation is a set of tuples, and elements of a set cannot be duplicated.

`join` differs from `select` and `project` because its input is two tables, not one. A column from the first table and a column from the second table are specified as the `join` column. The `join` column from each table must have a common domain. The result of a `join` of two tables is one wide table whose columns are duplicates of the original columns, except that the `join` column appears only once. The rows of the resulting table are copies of those rows of the two original tables that have equal elements in the `join` column.

For example, in Figure 1.31 the columns `S.Major` and `F.Major` have a common domain. The statement

`join Sor and Frat over Major giving Temp4`

specifies that `Major` is the `join` column and that the relations `Sor` and `Frat` are to be joined over it. **FIGURE 1.35** shows that the only rows included in the `join` of the two tables are the ones with equal majors. The 4-tuple (Robin, Sr, Hist, CA) from `Sor` and the 3-tuple (Jeff, Hist, TX) from `Frat` are joined in `Temp4` because their majors, Hist, are equal.

Temp4

S.Name	S.Class	S.State	Major	F.Name	F.State
Beth	Soph	TX	Hist	Jeff	TX
Nancy	Jr	NY	Math	Ron	OR
Nancy	Jr	NY	Math	Mehdi	CA
Robin	Sr	CA	Hist	Jeff	TX
Allison	Soph	AZ	Math	Ron	OR
Allison	Soph	AZ	Math	Mehdi	CA
Lulwa	Sr	CA	CompSci	Sam	WA
Lulwa	Sr	CA	CompSci	Gary	CA

FIGURE 1.35
The `join` operator. The relation is from the statement `join Sor and Frat over Major` giving `Temp4`.

Structure of the Language

The statements in this Level App7 language have the following form:

```
select relation where condition giving relation
project relation over attributes giving relation
join relation and relation over attribute giving relation
```

The reserved words of the language are

```
select     project
join       and
where      over
giving
```

Reserved words

Each reserved word has a special meaning in the language, as the previous examples demonstrate. Words to identify objects in the language, such as Sor and Temp2 to identify relations and F.State to identify an attribute, are not reserved. They are created arbitrarily by the user at Level App7 and are called *identifiers*. The existence of reserved words and user-defined identifiers is common in languages at all the levels of a typical computer system.

Do you see how to use the `select`, `project`, and `join` statements to generate the results of the query in Figure 1.32? The statements for the first query, which asks for Ron's home state, are

```
select Frat where F.Name = Ron giving Temp5
project Temp5 over F.State giving Result1
```

The statements for the second query, which asks for the names of all the sophomores in the sorority, are

```
select Sor where S.Class = Soph giving Temp6
project Temp6 over S.Name giving Result2
```

The statements for the third query, which asks for a list of those sorority and fraternity members who have the same major and what that common major is, are

```
join Sor and Frat over Major giving Temp4
project Temp4 over (S.Name, F.Name, Major) giving
Result3
```

Chapter Summary

The fundamental question of computer science is: What can be automated? Computers automate the processing of information. The theme of this text is levels of abstraction in computer systems. Abstraction includes suppression of detail to show the essence of the matter, an outline structure, division of responsibility through a chain of command, and subdivision of a system into smaller systems. The seven levels of abstraction in a typical computer system are

Level 7 (App7):	Application
Level 6 (HOL6):	High-order language
Level 5 (Asmb5):	Assembly
Level 4 (OS4):	Operating system
Level 3 (ISA3):	Instruction set architecture
Level 2 (Mc2):	Microcode
Level 1 (LG1):	Logic gate

Each level has its own language, which serves to hide the details of the lower levels.

A computer system consists of hardware and software. Three components of hardware are the central processing unit, main memory, and disk storage. Of the three components, the disk has the highest storage capacity but is the slowest, and the CPU has the smallest capacity but is the fastest. Main memory is between the two in both capacity and speed.

Programs that control the hardware are called *software*. An algorithm is a set of instructions that, when carried out in the proper sequence, solves a problem in a finite amount of time. A program is an algorithm written for execution on a computer. A program inputs information, processes it, and outputs the results. Software analysis determines the output, given the input and the program. Software design determines the program, given the input and the desired output. The operating system is a large program that provides the human interface of the computer to the user. It manages files, memory, and processors.

The smallest unit of digital information is the binary digit, or bit. Each bit in a computer system occupies space. A computer system stores all information, such as numbers, text, and images, as collections of bits. A collection of eight bits is a byte. The number of values stored by a sequence of n bits is 2^n. It takes one byte, which is eight bits, to store one ASCII character.

All computations in a computer system occupy time as well as space. The two components of time in a computer system are the computation time, which is the time it takes the CPU to execute one of the instructions in its instruction set, and the transmission time, which is the time it takes to move information from one component of the system to another. The following system performance equation computes the total execution time of the program task as the product of three terms:

$$\frac{\text{time}}{\text{program}} = \frac{\text{instructions}}{\text{program}} \times \frac{\text{cycles}}{\text{instruction}} \times \frac{\text{time}}{\text{cycle}}$$

The following bandwidth equation computes the total information transferred as the product of two terms:

$$\text{information} = \frac{\text{information}}{\text{time}} \times \text{time}$$

The first term in the product is the bandwidth of the channel, and the second term is the transmission time.

A QR code stores a bit of information in a square on the QR grid. A dark square is the binary value 1, and a light square is the binary value 0. The more squares in the grid, the more information the QR code contains. An image in a computer system is a grid of pixels. A black-and-white image requires one bit per pixel. The bit depth of a grayscale image is the number of bits per pixel, which determines how many shades of gray each pixel can display. Color images require three subpixels—one red, one green, and one blue—for each color pixel.

Database systems are one of the most common applications at Level App7. Relational database systems store information in files that appear to have a table structure; this table is called a *relation*. The result of a query in a relational database system is itself a relation. The three fundamental operations in a relational database system are `select`, `project`, and `join`. A query is a combination of these three operations.

Exercises

At the end of each chapter in this text is a set of exercises and problems. Work the exercises on paper by hand. Answers to the starred exercises are in the back of the text. (For some multipart exercises, answers are supplied only for selected parts.) The problems are programs to be entered into the computer. This chapter contains only exercises.

Section 1.1

1. **(a)** Draw a hierarchy diagram that corresponds to the United States Constitution. **(b)** Based on Figure 1.5, draw a nesting diagram that corresponds to the organization of the hypothetical publishing company.

2. Genghis Khan organized his men into groups of 10 soldiers under a "leader of 10." Ten "leaders of 10" were under a "leader of 100." Ten "leaders of 100" were under a "leader of 1000." *(a) If Khan had an army of 10,000 soldiers at the lowest level, how many men in total were under him in his organization? **(b)** If Khan had an army of 5763 soldiers at the lowest level, how many men in total were under him in his organization? Assume that the groups of 10 should contain 10 if possible, but that one group at each level may need to contain fewer.

3. In the Bible, Exodus Chapter 18 describes how Moses was overwhelmed as the single judge of Israel because of the large number of trivial cases that were brought before him. His father-in-law, Jethro, recommended a hierarchical system of appellate courts where the lowest-level judge had responsibility for 10 citizens. Five judges of 10 sent the difficult cases that they could not resolve to a judge of 50 citizens. Two judges of 50 were under a judge of 100, and 10 judges of 100 were under a judge of 1000. The judges of 1000 citizens reported to Moses, who had to decide only the most difficult cases. *(a) If the population were exactly 2000 citizens (excluding judges), draw the three top levels of the hierarchy diagram. **(b)** In part (a), what would be the total population, including Moses, all the judges, and citizens? **(c)** If the population were exactly 10,000 citizens (excluding judges), what would be the total population, including Moses, all the judges, and citizens?

4. A full binary tree is a tree whose leaves are all at the same level, and every node that is not a leaf has exactly two nodes under it. FIGURE 1.36 is a full binary tree with three levels. *(a) Draw the full binary tree with four levels. *(b) How many nodes total are in a full binary tree with five levels? **(c)** With six levels? **(d)** With *n* levels in general?

FIGURE 1.36
Exercise 4: The full binary tree with three levels.

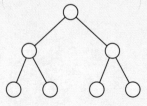

Section 1.2

5. True or false? (a) Main memory is volatile. (b) Main memory is accessed sequentially. (c) Disk memory is volatile. (d) Disk memory is accessed sequentially. (e) Main memory has greater storage capacity than disk memory. (f) Main memory has faster access time than disk memory.

Section 1.3

6. (a) What is an algorithm? (b) What is a program?

7. Answer the following questions about your operating system. (a) What is the name of your operating system? (b) Are certain characters disallowed or problematic in the names of the files? (c) Does your operating system distinguish between uppercase and lowercase characters in a file name?

8. Determine how to perform each of the following procedures with your operating system. (a) Set up a new user account. (b) Display the names of the files and subdirectories at the root directory. (c) Delete a file from the disk. (d) Change the name of a file. (e) Duplicate a file. (f) Display the size of a file. (g) Display the most recent modification time of a file.

Section 1.4

*9. If an app requires the execution of 20 million instructions to complete a task and your CPU is rated at 2.1 GHz, what is the execution time of the task? Assume that each ISA3 instruction executes an average of 4.5 Mc2 instructions.

10. If an app requires the execution of 30 million instructions to complete a task and your CPU is rated at 2.8 GHz, what is the execution time of the task? Assume that each ISA3 instruction executes an average of 7.3 Mc2 instructions.

11. How long would it take to transfer a 600-MB database from disk to memory over a DMA channel with a bandwidth of 2.5 GB/s?

*12. A typist is entering text on a keyboard at the rate of 40 words per minute. If each word is 5 characters long on average, what bandwidth in bits per second between the keyboard and main memory is required to transfer the information? A space is also a character. Assume that each word is followed by one space on average.

13. A typist is entering text on a keyboard at the rate of 30 words per minute. If each word is 6 characters long on average, what bandwidth in

bits per second between the keyboard and main memory is required to transmit the information? A space is also a character. Assume that each word is followed by one space on average.

14. How many total bits are stored in the grid of a Version 4 QR code?

15. **(a)** How many bits are available for storing information in a 49 × 49 Version 8 QR code? This version has four alignment patterns that do not intersect a timing pattern and two that do intersect a timing pattern. It also has two 18-bit version information areas. **(b)** If the overhead for the mode, character count, and Level M error correction is 37%, how many characters can be stored in the code?

16. **(a)** How many bits are available for storing information in a 57 × 57 Version 10 QR code? This version has four alignment patterns that do not intersect a timing pattern and two that do intersect a timing pattern. It also has two 18-bit version information areas. **(b)** If the overhead for the mode, character count, and Level L error correction is 22%, how many characters can be stored in the code?

17. **(a)** A desktop laser printer has a 300 dots-per-inch resolution. If each dot is stored in one bit of memory, how many MiB of memory are required to store the complete image of one 8.5- × 11-inch page of paper? **(b)** How many MiB of memory are required for a 1200 dots-per-inch printer?

18. An eReader has a 956- × 1290-pixel grayscale display with each pixel able to display 32 shades of gray. What is the KiB size of the display memory for the device?

19. A mobile phone has a 3.48- × 1.96-inch screen size with a resolution of 326 pixels per inch. **(a)** How many pixels does it have? **(b)** With 256 levels of brightness for each color of subpixel, what is the MiB size of the display memory?

20. A tablet has a 7.5- × 5.8-inch screen size with a resolution of 326 pixels per inch. **(a)** How many pixels does it have? **(b)** With 256 levels of brightness for each color subpixel, what is the MiB size of the display memory?

Section 1.5

21. Write the relations `Temp5` and `Temp6` from the discussion in Section 1.5 of the chapter.

22. Write the statements for the following queries of the database in Figure 1.31.
   *(a) Find Beth's home state. (b) List the fraternity members who are English majors. (c) List the sorority and fraternity members who have the same home state, and indicate what that home state is.

23. (a) Write the statements to produce Result2 in Figure 1.32, but with the project command before the select. (b) Write the statements to produce Result3 in Figure 1.22, but with join as the last statement.

LEVEL
6

High-Order Language

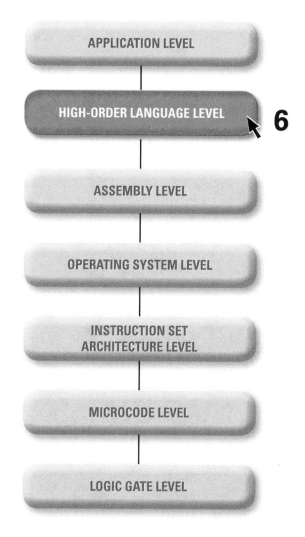

- APPLICATION LEVEL
- HIGH-ORDER LANGUAGE LEVEL 6
- ASSEMBLY LEVEL
- OPERATING SYSTEM LEVEL
- INSTRUCTION SET ARCHITECTURE LEVEL
- MICROCODE LEVEL
- LOGIC GATE LEVEL

CHAPTER 2

C

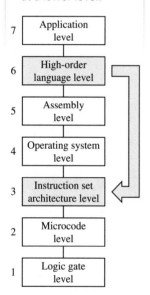

FIGURE 2.1

The function of a compiler, which translates a program in a Level 6 language to an equivalent program in a language at a lower level.

A program inputs information, processes it, and outputs the results. This chapter shows how a C program inputs, processes, and outputs values. It reviews programming at Level HOL6 and assumes that you have experience writing programs in some high-order language—not necessarily C—such as C++, Java, or Python. Because this text presents concepts that are common to all those languages, you should be able to follow the discussion despite any differences in the language with which you are familiar.

2.1 Variables

A computer can directly execute statements in machine language only at Level ISA3, the instruction set architecture level. So a Level HOL6 statement must first be translated to Level ISA3 before executing. FIGURE 2.1 shows the function of a compiler, which performs the translation from a Level HOL6 language to the Level ISA3 language. The figure shows translation to Level 3. Some compilers translate from Level 6 to Level 5, which then requires another translation from Level 5 to Level 3.

The C Compiler

To execute the programs in this text, you need access to a C compiler. Running a program is a three-step process:

> Write the program in C using a text editor. This version is called the *source program*.

> Invoke the compiler to translate, or compile, the source program from C to machine language. The machine language version is called the *object program*.

> Execute the object program.

Some systems allow you to specify the last two of these steps with a single command, usually called the *run* command. Whether or not you specify the compilation and execution separately, some translation is required before a Level HOL6 program can be executed.

When you write the source program, it will be saved in a file on disk just as any other text document would be. The compiler will produce another file, called a *code file*, for the object program. Depending on your compiler, the object program may or may not be visible on your file directory after the compilation.

If you want to execute a program that was previously compiled, you do not need to translate it again. You can simply execute the object program

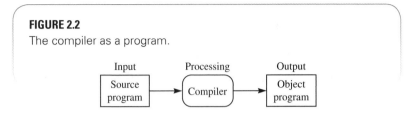

FIGURE 2.2
The compiler as a program.

directly. If you ever delete the object program from your disk, you can always get it back from the source program by compiling again. But the translation can go only from a high level to a low level. If you delete the source program, you cannot recover it from the object program.

Your C compiler is software, not hardware. It is a program that is stored in a file on your disk. Like all programs, the compiler has input, does processing, and produces output. **FIGURE 2.2** shows that the input to the compiler is the source program and the output is the object program.

Machine Independence

Level ISA3 languages are machine dependent. If you write a program in a Level ISA3 language for execution on a Brand X computer, it cannot run on a Brand Y computer. An important property of the languages at Level HOL6 is their machine independence. If you write a program in a Level HOL6 language for execution on a Brand X computer, it will run with only slight modification on a Brand Y computer.

FIGURE 2.3 shows how C achieves its machine independence. Suppose you write an applications program in C to do some statistical analysis. You want to sell it to people who own Brand X computers and to others who own Brand Y. The statistics program can be executed only if it is in machine language. Because machine language is machine dependent, you will need two machine-language versions, one for Brand X and one for Brand Y. Because C is a common high-order language, you will probably have access to a C compiler for the Brand X machine and a C compiler for the Brand Y machine. If so, you can simply invoke the Brand X C compiler on one machine to produce the Brand X machine-language version, and invoke the Brand Y C compiler on the other machine for the Brand Y version. You need to write only one C program.

The C Memory Model

The C programming language has three different kinds of variables—global variables, local variables, and dynamically allocated variables. The value of a variable is stored in the main memory of a computer, but where in memory

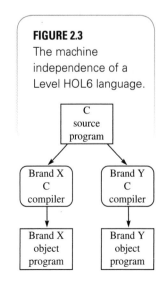

FIGURE 2.3
The machine independence of a Level HOL6 language.

it is stored depends on the kind of variable. There are three special sections of memory corresponding to the three kinds of variables:

The C memory model

> Global variables are stored at a fixed location in memory.
> Local variables and parameters are stored on the run-time stack.
> Dynamically allocated variables are stored on the heap.

Global variables are declared outside of any function and remain in place throughout the execution of the entire program. Local variables are declared within a function. They come into existence when the function is called and cease to exist when the function terminates. Dynamically allocated variables come into existence with the execution of the `malloc()` function and cease to exist with the execution of the `free()` function.

The push and pop operations

A stack is a container of values that stores values with the push operation and retrieves them with the pop operation. The policy for storage and retrieval is last in, first out. That is, when you pop a value from a stack, the value you get is the last one that was pushed. For this reason, a stack is sometimes called a *LIFO list*, where *LIFO* is an acronym for *last in, first out*.

Every C statement that executes is part of a function. A C function has a return type, a name, and a list of parameters. A program consists of a special function whose name is `main`, which is a function that is called by the operating system. A program executes by executing the statements in the main function. It is possible for a main statement to call another function. When a function executes, allocation on the run-time stack takes place in the following order:

Function call

> Push storage for the return value.
> Push the actual parameters.
> Push the return address.
> Push storage for the local variables.

Then, when the function terminates, deallocation from the run-time stack takes place in the opposite order:

Function return

> Pop the local variables.
> Pop the return address and use it to determine the next instruction to execute.
> Pop the parameters.
> Pop the return value and use it as specified in the calling statement.

These actions occur whether the function is the main function or is a function called by a statement in another function.

The programs in this chapter illustrate the memory model of the C programming language. Later chapters show the object code for the same programs after the compiler translates them to Level Asmb5.

Global Variables and Assignment Statements

Every C variable has three attributes:

> Name

> Type

> Value

The three attributes of a C variable

A variable's name is an identifier determined arbitrarily by the programmer. A variable's type specifies the kind of values it can have. FIGURE 2.4 shows a program that declares two global variables, inputs values for them, operates on the values, and outputs the result. This is a nonsense program whose sole purpose is to illustrate some features of the C language.

FIGURE 2.4

The assignment statement with global variables.

```c
// Stan Warford
// A nonsense program to illustrate global variables

#include <stdio.h>

char ch;
int j;

int main() {
    scanf("%c %d", &ch, &j);
    j += 5;
    ch++;
    printf("%c\n%d\n", ch, j);
    return 0;
}
```

Input
M 419

Output
N
424

The first two lines in Figure 2.4 are comments, which are ignored by the compiler. Comments in a C source program begin with two slash characters, //, and continue until the end of the line. The next line in the program is

```
#include <stdio.h>
```

which is a compiler directive to make a library of functions available to the program. In this case, the library file stdio.h, which stands for *standard input/ouput*, contains the input function scanf () and the output function printf (), used later in the program. This directive, or one similar to it, is necessary for all programs that use scanf () and printf ().

The next two lines in the program

```
char ch;
int j;
```

Global variables are declared outside of main().

declare two global variables. The name of the first variable is ch. Its type is character, as specified by the word char, which precedes its name. As with most variables, its value cannot be determined from the listing. Instead, it gets its value from an input statement. The name of the second variable is j with type integer, as specified by int. Every C program has a main function, which contains the executable statements of the program. In Figure 2.4, because the variables are declared outside the main program, they are global variables.

The next line in the program

```
int main() {
```

The returned value for main()

declares the main program to be a function that returns an integer. The C compiler must generate code that executes on a particular operating system. It is up to the operating system to interpret the value returned. The standard convention is that a return value of 0 indicates that no errors occurred during the program's execution. If an execution error does occur, the program is interrupted and returns some nonzero value without reaching the last executable statement of main(). What happens in such a case depends on the particular operating system and the nature of the error. All the C programs in this text use the common convention of returning 0 as the last executable statement in the main function.

The first executable statement in Figure 2.4 is

```
scanf("%c %d", &ch, &j);
```

The first parameter, "%c %d", is the format string, which contains two conversion specifiers, %c and %d. The second and third parameters are &ch and &j, which receive the values that are input. The standard input device can be either the keyboard or a disk file. In a Unix environment, the default input device is the keyboard. You can redirect the input to come from a disk file when you execute the program. This input statement gives the first value in the input stream to ch and the second value to j.

The conversion specifiers in the formatting string are placeholders and correspond in order to the remaining parameters in the parameter list. In Figure 2.4, placeholder %c corresponds to parameter &ch, and placeholder %d corresponds to parameter &j. Placeholder %c instructs the program to scan a character into variable ch, and specifier %d instructs the program to scan an optionally signed decimal integer into variable j. The ampersand *The address operator* character & is the C address operator and is required for variables in the scanf() function. Because the function changes the values of the variables, it requires the addresses of where the variables are stored in main memory instead of the values of the variables.

The space character between %c and %d tells the input scanner to ignore any white-space characters like spaces and tabs before the integer. You can put any number of spaces before the number 419 in the input and the output will remain unchanged. However, if you put a space before the input character M, the program will not work correctly, because ch will get the space character. If you want to allow any number of spaces before the input character, put a space before the %c placeholder in the format string.

The second executable statement is

```
j += 5;
```

The assignment operator in C is =, which is pronounced "gets." The *The C assignment operator* above statement is pronounced "j plus gets 5" and is equivalent to the assignment statement

```
j = j + 5;
```

which is pronounced "j gets j plus five."

Unlike some programming languages, C treats characters as if they were integers. You can perform arithmetic on them. The next executable statement

```
ch++;
```

adds 1 to ch with the increment operator. It is identical to the assignment statement

```
ch = ch + 1;
```

The next executable statement is

```
printf("%c\n%d\n", ch, j);
```

This output function uses the format string "%c\n%d\n" where %c and %d are again the placeholders for the remaining parameters ch and j.

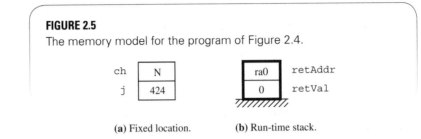

FIGURE 2.5
The memory model for the program of Figure 2.4.

(a) Fixed location.   **(b)** Run-time stack.

The standard output device can be either the screen or a disk file. In a Unix environment, the default output device is the screen. You can redirect the output to go to a disk file when you execute the program. \n is the newline character. This output statement sends the value of variable ch to the output device, moves the cursor to the start of the next line, sends the value of variable j to the output device, and then moves the cursor to the start of the next line. The printf() function does not use the & character in front of the variables because it does not change the values of the variables. Instead, it outputs the values they already have.

FIGURE 2.5 shows the memory model for the program of Figure 2.4 just before the program terminates. Storage for the global variables ch and j is allocated at a fixed location in memory, as Figure 2.5(a) shows.

Remember that when a function is called, four items are allocated on the run-time stack: return value, parameters, return address, and local variables. Because the main function in this program has no parameters and no local variables, the only items allocated on the stack are storage for the return value, labeled retVal, and the return address, labeled retAddr, in Figure 2.5(b). The figure shows the value for the return address as ra0, which is the address of the instruction in the operating system that will execute when the program terminates. The details of the operating system at Level OS4 are hidden from us at Level HOL6.

Local Variables

Local variables are declared within main().

Global variables are allocated at a fixed position in main memory. Local variables, however, are allocated on the run-time stack. In a C program, local variables are declared within the main program. The program in FIGURE 2.6 declares a constant and three local variables that represent two scores on exams for a course, and the total score computed as their average plus a bonus.

Before the first variable is the constant bonus. A constant is like a variable in that it has a name, a type, and a value. Unlike a variable, however,

---

FIGURE 2.6

A C program that processes three local integer values.

```c
#include <stdio.h>

int main() {
    const int bonus = 10;
    int exam1;
    int exam2;
    int score;
    scanf("%d %d", &exam1, &exam2);
    score = (exam1 + exam2) / 2 + bonus;
    printf("score = %d\n", score);
    return 0;
}
```

Input
68 84

Output
score = 86

---

the value of a constant cannot change. The value of this constant is 10, as specified by the initialization operator =.

The first executable statement in Figure 2.6 is

```c
scanf("%d %d", &exam1, &exam2);
```

which gives the first value in the input stream to exam1 and the second value to exam2. The second executable statement is

```c
score = (exam1 + exam2) / 2 + bonus;
```

which adds the values in exam1 and exam2, divides the sum by 2 to get their average, adds the bonus to the average, and then assigns the value to the variable score. Because exam1, exam2, and 2 are all integers, the division operator / represents integer division. If either exam1 or exam2 is declared to be a floating-point value, or if the divisor is written as 2.0 instead of 2, then the division operator represents floating-point division. Integer division truncates the remainder, whereas floating-point division maintains the fractional part. To output the value of a floating-point variable, use %f for the conversion specifier in the format string.

Integer versus floating-point division

Example 2.1   If the input of the program in Figure 2.6 is

```
68 85
```

then the output is still

```
score = 86
```

The sum of the exams is 153. If you divide 153 by 2.0, you get the floating-point value 76.5. But if you divide 153 by 2, the / operator represents integer division and the fractional part is truncated—in other words, chopped off—yielding 76.   ■

Example 2.2   If you declare score to have a double-precision, floating-point type as follows

```
double score;
```

and if you force the division to be floating point by changing 2 to 2.0 as follows

```
score = (exam1 + exam2) / 2.0 + bonus;
```

then the output is

```
score = 86.5
```

when the input is 68 and 85.   ■

Floating-point division of two numbers produces only one value, the quotient. However, integer division produces two values—the quotient and the remainder—both of which are integers. You can compute the remainder of an integer division with the C modulus operator %. FIGURE 2.7 shows some examples of integer division and the modulus operation.

FIGURE 2.7
Some examples of integer division and the modulus operation.

Expression	Value	Expression	Value
15 / 3	5	15 % 3	0
14 / 3	4	14 % 3	2
13 / 3	4	13 % 3	1
12 / 3	4	12 % 3	0
11 / 3	3	11 % 3	2

FIGURE 2.8

The memory model for the local variables in the program of Figure 2.6.

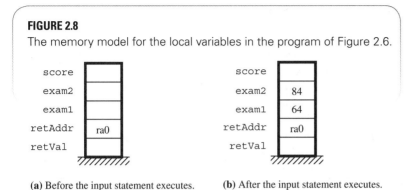

(a) Before the input statement executes.   (b) After the input statement executes.

FIGURE 2.8   shows the memory model for the local variables in the program of Figure 2.6. The computer allocates storage for all local variables on the run-time stack. When `main()` executes, storage for the return value, the return address, and local variables `exam1`, `exam2`, and `score` are pushed onto the stack. Because `bonus` is not a variable, it is not pushed onto the stack.

2.2 **Flow of Control**

A program operates by executing its statements sequentially—that is, one statement after the other. You can alter the sequence by changing the flow of control in two ways: selection and repetition. C has the `if` and `switch` statements for selection, and the `while`, `do`, and `for` statements for repetition. Each of these statements performs a test to possibly alter the sequential flow of control. The most common tests use one of the six relational operators shown in   FIGURE 2.9 .

FIGURE 2.9

The relational operators.

Operator	Meaning
==	Equal to
<	Less than
<=	Less than or equal to
>	Greater than
>=	Greater than or equal to
!=	Not equal to

The If/Else Statement

FIGURE 2.10 shows a simple use of the C if statement to perform a test with the greater-than-or-equal-to relational operator, >=. The program inputs a value for the integer variable num and compares it with the constant integer limit. If the value of num is greater than or equal to the value of limit, which is 100, the word high is output. Otherwise, the word low is output. It is legal to write an if statement without an else part.

You can combine several relational tests with the Boolean operators shown in FIGURE 2.11 . The double ampersand (&&) is the symbol for the AND operation, the double vertical bar (||) is for the OR operation, and the exclamation point (!) is for the NOT operation.

Example 2.3   If age, income, and tax are integer variables, the if statement

```
if ((age < 21) && (income <= 4000)) {
    tax = 0;
}
```

sets the value of tax to 0 if age is less than 21 and income is less than $4000. ∎

FIGURE 2.10
The C if statement.

```
#include <stdio.h>

int main() {
    const int limit = 100;
    int num;
    scanf("%d", &num);
    if (num >= limit) {
        printf("high\n");
    }
    else {
        printf("low\n");
    }
    return 0;
}
```

Input
75

Output
low

The if statement in Figure 2.10 has a single statement in each alternative. If you want more than one statement to execute in an alternative, you must enclose the statements in braces, { }. Otherwise, the braces are optional.

Example 2.4 The if statement in Figure 2.10 can be written

```
if (num >= limit)
    printf("high\n");
else
    printf("low\n");
```

without the braces around the output statements. ∎

FIGURE 2.11
The Boolean operators.

Symbol	Meaning
&&	AND
||	OR
!	NOT

The Switch Statement

The program in **FIGURE 2.12** uses the C switch statement to play a little guessing game with the user. It asks the user to pick a number. Then, depending on the number input, it outputs an appropriate message.

You can achieve the same effect yielded by the switch statement using the if statement. However, the equivalent if statement is not quite as efficient as switch.

FIGURE 2.12
The C switch statement.

```
#include <stdio.h>

int main() {
    int guess;
    printf("Pick a number 0..3: ");
    scanf("%d", &guess);
    switch (guess) {
        case 0: printf("Not close\n"); break;
        case 1: printf("Close\n"); break;
        case 2: printf("Right on\n"); break;
        case 3: printf("Too high\n");
    }
    return 0;
}
```

Interactive Input/Output
```
Pick a number 0..3: 1
Close
```

Example 2.5   The switch statement in Figure 2.12 can be written using the logically equivalent nested if statement:

```
if (guess == 0) {
    printf("Not close\n");
}
else if (guess == 1) {
    printf("Close\n");
}
else if (guess == 2) {
    printf("Right on\n");
}
else if (guess == 3) {
    printf("Too high\n");
}
```

However, this code is not as efficient as the switch. With this code, if the user guesses 3, all four tests will execute. With the switch statement, if the user guesses 3, the program jumps immediately to the "Too high" statement without having to compare guess with 0, 1, and 2.   ∎

The While Loop

The program in **FIGURE 2.13** takes as input a sequence of characters terminated with the asterisk, *. It outputs all the characters up to but not including the asterisk with each word on a separate line. An experienced C programmer would not use the asterisk as a sentinel character, so this example is unrealistic. Figure 2.13 and all the programs in this chapter are presented so that they can be analyzed at a lower level of abstraction in later chapters.

The program inputs the value of the first character into the global variable letter before entering the loop. The statement

```
while (letter != '*')
```

compares the value of letter with the asterisk character. If they are not equal, the body of the loop executes, which outputs either the character or a newline and then inputs the next character. Flow of control then returns to the test at the top of the loop.

This program would produce identical output if letter were local instead of global. Whether to declare a variable as local instead of global is a software design issue. The rule of thumb is to always declare variables to be local unless there is a good reason to do otherwise. Local variables enhance the modularity of software systems and make long programs easier to read and debug. The global variables in Figures 2.4 and 2.13 do not represent

FIGURE 2.13
The C while loop.

```
#include <stdio.h>

char letter;

int main() {
    scanf("%c", &letter);
    while (letter != '*') {
        if (letter == ' ') {
            printf("\n");
        }
        else {
            printf("%c", letter);
        }
        scanf("%c", &letter);
    }
    return 0;
}
```

Input
```
Hello, world!*
```

Output
```
Hello,
world!
```

good software design. They are presented because they illustrate the C memory model. Later chapters show how a C compiler would translate the programs presented in this chapter.

The Do Loop

The program in (FIGURE 2.14) illustrates the do statement. It is unusual because it has no input. The program produces the same output each time it executes. This is another nonsense program whose purpose is to illustrate flow of control.

A police officer is initially at a position of 0 units when he begins to pursue a driver who is initially at a position of 40 units. Each execution of the loop represents one time interval, during which the officer travels 25 units and the driver 20. The statement

```
cop += 25;
```

is C shorthand for

```
cop = cop + 25;
```

FIGURE 2.14
The C do loop.

```c
#include <stdio.h>

int cop;
int driver;

int main() {
    cop = 0;
    driver = 40;
    do {
        cop += 25;
        driver += 20;
    }
    while (cop < driver);
    printf("%d", cop);
    return 0;
}
```

Output
200

Unlike in the loop in Figure 2.13, the do statement has its test at the bottom of the loop. Consequently, the body of the loop is guaranteed to execute at least one time. When the statement

```c
while (cop < driver);
```

executes, it compares the value of cop with the value of driver. If cop is less than driver, flow of control transfers to do, and the body of the loop repeats.

Arrays and the For Loop

The program in **FIGURE 2.15** illustrates the for loop and the array. It allocates a local array of four integers, inputs values into the array, and then outputs the values in reverse order.

The statement

```c
int vector[4];
```

declares variable vector to be an array of four integers. In C, all arrays have their first index at 0. Hence, this declaration allocates storage for array elements

```c
vector[0] vector[1] vector[2] vector[3]
```

FIGURE 2.15

The C `for` loop with an array.

```c
#include <stdio.h>

int vector[4];
int j;

int main() {
    for (j = 0; j < 4; j++) {
        scanf("%d", &vector[j]);
    }
    for (j = 3; j >= 0; j--) {
        printf("%d %d\n", j, vector[j]);
    }
    return 0;
}
```

Input
2 26 -3 9

Output
3 9
2 -3
1 26
0 2

The number in the declaration that specifies how many elements will be allocated is always one more than the index of the last element. In this program, 4, which is the number of elements, is one more than 3, which is the index of the last element.

Every `for` statement has a pair of parentheses whose interior is divided into three compartments, each compartment separated from its neighbor by a semicolon. The first compartment initializes, the second compartment tests, and the third compartment increments. In this program, the `for` statement

```c
for (j = 0; j < 4; j++)
```

has `j = 0` for the initialization, `j < 4` for the test, and `j++` for the increment.

When the program enters the loop, `j` is set to 0. Because the test is at the top of the loop, the value of `j` is compared to 4. Because `j` is less than 4, the body of the loop

```c
scanf("%d", &vector[j]);
```

executes. The first integer value from the input stream is read into `vector[0]`. Control returns to the `for` statement, which increments `j` because of the expression `j++` in the third compartment. The value of `j` is then compared to 4, and the process repeats.

The values are printed in reverse order by the second loop because of the decrement expression

```
j--
```

which is C shorthand for

```
j = j - 1
```

The programming style with `for` loops in Figure 2.15 is not the preferred C style. The control variable `j` would rarely be declared as a global variable. Instead, it would be contained in the scope of the `for` statement, the first of which would be written as

```
for (int j = 0; j < 4; j++)
```

This text eschews this preferred coding style to more effectively teach the concepts of global versus local allocation on the run-time stack. A description of the allocation process for the preferred style would add an extra level of complication in the exposition.

2.3 Functions

In C, there are two kinds of functions: those that return void and those that return some other type. Function `main()` returns an integer, not void. The operating system uses the integer to determine if the program terminated normally. Functions that return void perform their processing without returning a value at all. Functions that return void are also called *procedures*. One common use of void functions is to input or output a collection of values.

Procedures are functions that return void.

Void Functions and Call-by-Value Parameters

The program in **FIGURE 2.16** uses a void function to print a bar chart of data values. The program reads the first value into the integer variable `numPts`. The global variable `j` controls the `for` loop in the main program, which executes `numPts` times. Each time the loop executes, it calls the void function `printBar()`. **FIGURE 2.17** shows a trace of the beginning of execution of the program in Figure 2.16.

FIGURE 2.16

A program that prints a bar chart. The void function prints a single bar.

```c
#include <stdio.h>

int numPts;
int value;
int j;

void printBar(int n) {
   int k;
   for (k = 1; k <= n; k++) {
      printf("*");
   }
   printf("\n");
}

int main() {
   scanf("%d", &numPts);
   for (j = 1; j <= numPts; j++) {
      scanf("%d", &value);
      printBar(value);
      //ra1
   }
   return 0;
}
```

Input
12 3 13 17 34 27 23 25 29 16 10 0 2

Output
```
***
*************
*****************
**********************************
**************************
*********************
*************************
***************************
****************
**********

**
```

FIGURE 2.17
The run-time stack for the program in Figure 2.16.

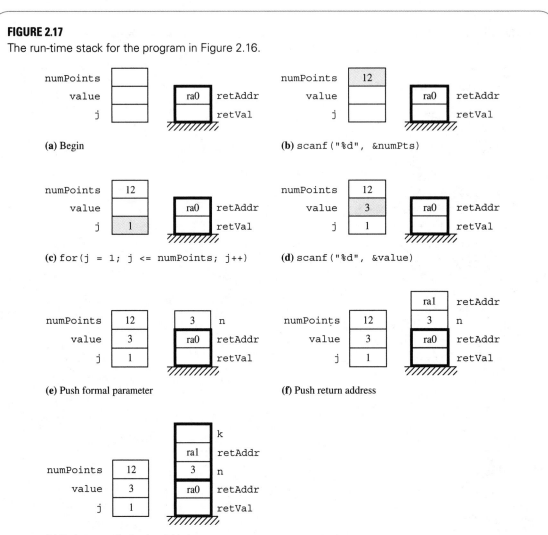

(a) Begin

(b) scanf ("%d", &numPts)

(c) for(j = 1; j <= numPoints; j++)

(d) scanf ("%d", &value)

(e) Push formal parameter

(f) Push return address

(g) Push storage for local variable k

Allocation takes place on the run-time stack in the following order when you call a void function:

The allocation process for a void function

> Push the actual parameters.

> Push the return address.

> Push storage for the local variables.

It is the same allocation as with a non-void function but without the initial push of storage for the return value. A *formal parameter* is the parameter in the function declaration. In Figure 2.16, n is the formal parameter. An *actual parameter* is the parameter in the function call. In Figure 2.16, value is the actual parameter.

Formal and actual parameters

Figure 2.17(e) is the start of the allocation process for Figure 2.16. The program pushes the value of actual parameter value for the formal parameter n. The effect is that formal parameter n gets the value of the actual parameter value. The program pushes the return address in Figure 2.17(f). In Figure 2.17(g), it pushes storage for the local variable, k. After the allocation process, the last local variable in the listing, k, is on top of the stack.

The collection of all the items pushed onto the run-time stack in a function call is known as a *stack frame* or *activation record*. In the program of Figure 2.16, the stack frame for the void function consists of three items—n, the return address, and k. The return address indicated by ra1 in the figure is the address of the end of the for statement of the main program. The stack frame for the main() function consists of two items—the return value and the return address.

Stack frames

After the procedure prints a single bar, control returns to the main program. The items on the run-time stack are deallocated in reverse order compared to their allocation. The process is:

The deallocation process for a void function

> Pop the local variables.

> Pop the return address and use it to determine the next instruction to execute.

> Pop the parameters.

The program uses the return address to know which statement to execute next in the main program after executing the last statement in the void function. Return address ra1 in the listing of the main program is the statement after the procedure call. It represents the point where j is incremented before the branch up to the test at the top of the loop.

Functions

The program in (**FIGURE 2.18**) uses a function to compute the value of the factorial of an integer. It prompts the user for a small integer and passes that integer as a parameter to function fact().

(**FIGURE 2.19**) shows the allocation process for the function in Figure 2.18, which returns the factorial of the actual parameter. Figure 2.19(c) shows storage for the return value pushed first. Figure 2.19(d) shows the value of actual parameter num, which is 3, pushed for the formal parameter n.

FIGURE 2.18

A program to compute the factorial of an integer with a function.

```c
#include <stdio.h>

int num;

int fact(int n) {
    int f, j;
    f = 1;
    for (j = 1; j <= n; j++) {
        f *= j;
    }
    return f;
}

int main() {
    printf("Enter a small integer: ");
    scanf("%d", &num);
    printf("Its factorial is: %d\n", fact(num)); // ra1
    return 0;
}
```

Interactive Input/Output

```
Enter a small integer: 3
Its factorial is: 6
```

The return address is pushed in Figure 2.19(e). Storage for local variables f and j is pushed in Figure 2.19(f) and (g).

The stack frame for this function has five items. The return address indicated by ra1 in the figure represents the address of the `printf()` function call in the main program. Control returns from the function to the calling statement. This is in contrast to a void function, in which control returns to the statement *following* the calling statement.

Returning control from void and nonvoid functions

Call-by-Reference Parameters

The procedures and functions in the previous programs all pass their parameters by value. In call by value, the formal parameter gets the value of the actual parameter. If the called procedure changes the value of its formal parameter, the corresponding actual parameter in the calling program does not change. Any changes made by the called procedure are made to the value

FIGURE 2.19

The run-time stack for the program in Figure 2.18.

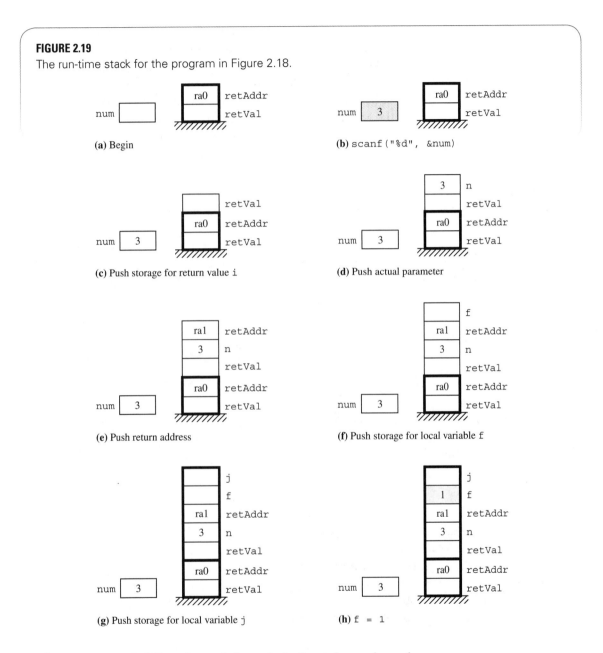

(a) Begin

(b) scanf ("%d", &num)

(c) Push storage for return value i

(d) Push actual parameter

(e) Push return address

(f) Push storage for local variable f

(g) Push storage for local variable j

(h) f = 1

on the run-time stack. When the stack frame is deallocated, any changed values are deallocated with it.

If the intent of the procedure is to change the value of the actual parameter in the calling program, then call by reference is used instead of call by value. In call by reference, the formal parameter gets a reference to the actual parameter. If the called procedure changes the value of its formal parameter, the

The & address operator

corresponding actual parameter in the calling program changes. To specify that a parameter is called by reference, you pass the address of the actual parameter with the & address operator. The corresponding formal parameter is a pointer and must be preceded by the asterisk, *, symbol. In C, a pointer is an address.

The program in FIGURE 2.20 uses call by reference to change the values of the actual parameters in main(). It prompts the user for two integer values and puts them in order. It has one void function, order(), that

FIGURE 2.20
A program to put two values in order. The void functions pass parameters by reference.

```c
#include <stdio.h>

int a, b;

void swap(int *r, int *s) {
    int temp;
    temp = *r;
    *r = *s;
    *s = temp;
}

void order(int *x, int *y) {
    if (*x > *y) {
        swap (x, y);
    }  // ra2
}

int main() {
    printf("Enter an integer: ");
    scanf("%d", &a);
    printf("Enter an integer: ");
    scanf("%d", &b);
    order(&a, &b);
    printf("Ordered they are: %d, %d\n", a, b); // ra1
    return 0;
}
```

Interactive Input/Output
```
Enter an integer: 6
Enter an integer: 2
Ordered they are: 2, 6
```

calls another void function, swap (). In main (), the call to order () has &a as the actual parameter and *x as the corresponding formal parameter. x is a pointer and, hence, is an address. Namely, x is the address of actual parameter a. When order () calls swap (), the actual parameter must again be an address. Because x is already an address, the & address operator is not prefixed to it in the actual parameter list in the call from order ().

Procedure order () shows how to access the value of the cell pointed to. The test for the if statement is

```
if (*x > *y)
```

Because x is a pointer, *x is the value in the memory cell to which x points. Variable x is a pointer to an int. The expression *x is an int. Similarly, *y is the value in the memory cell to which y points. The test

```
if (x > y)
```

would be an error because you would be testing whether the address of a is greater than the address of b instead of whether a is greater than b.

Procedure swap () also shows how the * operator is used to dereference a pointer. In the parameter list, the formal parameter

```
int *r
```

indicates that r is a pointer to an integer. That is, r is the address of an integer. In the assignment statement

```
temp = *r;
```

the asterisk * dereferences r. Because r is a pointer to an integer, *r is the integer to which it points. The assignment statement gives the integer value *r to the integer variable temp.

*The * pointer dereference operator*

FIGURE 2.21 shows the allocation and deallocation sequence for the entire program. The stack frame for order () in part (c) has three items. The formal parameters, x and y, are called by reference. The arrow pointing from x on the run-time stack to a in the main program indicates that x refers to a. Literally, x is the address of a. Similarly, the arrow from y to b indicates that y refers to b. The return address, indicated by ra1, is the address of the printf () statement that follows the call to order () in the main program.

The stack frame for swap () in Figure 2.21(d) has four items. r refers to x, which refers to a. Therefore, r refers to a. The arrow pointing from r on the run-time stack points to a, as does the arrow from x. Similarly, the arrow from s points to b, as does the arrow from y. The return address indicated by ra2 is the address after the last statement in order (). The statements in swap () exchange the values of r and s. Because r refers to a and s refers to b, they exchange the values of a and b in the main program.

FIGURE 2.21

The run-time stack for Figure 2.20.

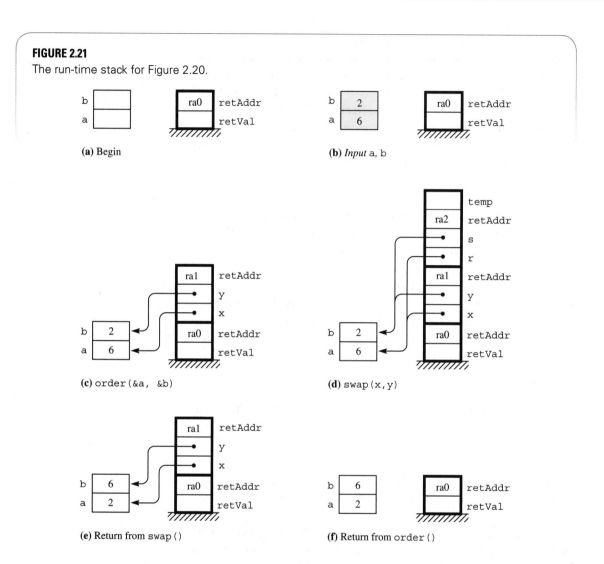

(a) Begin

(b) *Input* a, b

(c) order(&a, &b)

(d) swap(x,y)

(e) Return from swap()

(f) Return from order()

When a void function terminates and it is time to deallocate its stack frame, the return address in the frame tells the computer which instruction to execute next. Figure 2.21(e) shows the return from void function swap, deallocating its stack frame. The return address in the stack frame for swap tells the computer to execute the statement labeled ra2 in order() after deallocation. Although the listing shows no statement at ra2 in Figure 2.20, there is an implied return statement at the end of the void function that is invisible at Level HOL6.

In Figure 2.21(f), the stack frame for order() is deallocated. The return address in the stack frame for order() tells the computer to execute the printf() function in the main program after deallocation.

Because a stack is a LIFO structure, the last stack frame pushed onto the run-time stack will be the first one popped off at the completion of a function. The return address will, therefore, return control to the most recent calling function. This LIFO property of the run-time stack will be basic to your understanding of recursion in Section 2.4.

You may have noticed that `main ()` is always a function that returns an integer and that all the programs thus far have returned 0 to the operating system. Furthermore, all the main program functions thus far have no parameters. Although it is common for a main program to have parameters, none of the programs in this text do. To keep the figures simple, from now on they will omit the `retVal` and `retAddr` for the main program. A real C compiler must account for both of them.

A simplification for `main ()` *in this text*

2.4 Recursion

Did you ever look up the definition of some unknown word in the dictionary, only to discover that the dictionary defined it in terms of another unknown word? Then, when you looked up the second word, did you discover that it was defined in terms of the first word? That is an example of circular or indirect recursion. The problem with the dictionary is that you did not know the meaning of the first word to begin with. Had the second word been defined in terms of a third word that you knew, you would have been satisfied.

In mathematics, a *recursive definition* of a function is a definition that uses the function itself. For example, suppose a function, $f(n)$, is defined as follows:

Recursive definitions in mathematics

$$f(n) = nf(n-1)$$

You want to use this definition to determine $f(4)$, so you substitute 4 for n in the definition:

$$f(4) = 4 \times f(3)$$

But now you do not know what $f(3)$ is. So you substitute 3 for n in the definition and get

$$f(3) = 3 \times f(2)$$

Substituting this into the formula for $f(4)$ gives

$$f(4) = 4 \times 3 \times f(2)$$

But now you do not know what $f(2)$ is. The definition tells you it is 2 times $f(1)$. So the formula for $f(4)$ becomes

$$f(4) = 4 \times 3 \times 2 \times f(1)$$

You can see the problem with this definition. With nothing to stop the process, you will continue to compute $f(4)$ endlessly.

$$f(4) = 4 \times 3 \times 2 \times 1 \times 0 \times (-1) \times (-2) \times (-3) \cdots$$

It is as if the dictionary gave you an endless string of definitions, each based on another unknown word. To be complete, the definition must specify the value of $f(n)$ for a specific value of n. Then the preceding process will terminate, and you can compute $f(n)$ for any n.

Here is a complete recursive definition of $f(n)$:

$$f(n) = \begin{cases} 1 & \text{if } n \leq 1, \\ nf(n-1) & \text{if } n > 1. \end{cases}$$

This definition says you can stop the previous process at $f(1)$, which is called the *basis*. So $f(4)$ is

$$\begin{aligned} f(4) &= 4 \times f(4) \\ &= 4 \times 3 \times f(2) \\ &= 4 \times 3 \times 2 \times f(1) \\ &= 4 \times 3 \times 2 \times 1 \\ &= 24 \end{aligned}$$

You should recognize this definition as the factorial function.

A Factorial Function

Recursive functions in C

A *recursive function* in C is a function that calls itself. There is no special recursion statement with a new syntax to learn. The method of storage allocation on the run-time stack is the same as with nonrecursive functions. The only difference is that a recursive function contains a statement that calls itself.

The function in **FIGURE 2.22** computes the factorial of a number recursively. It is a direct application of the preceding recursive definition of $f(n)$.

FIGURE 2.23 is a trace that shows the run-time stack with the simplification of not showing the stack frame of the main program. The first function call is from the main program. Figure 2.23(c) shows the stack frame for the first call, assuming the user entered 4. The return address is ra1, which represents the address of the printf() function in the main program.

The first statement in the function tests n for 1. Because the value of n is 4, the else part executes. But the statement in the else part

```
return n * fact(n - 1) // ra2
```

contains a call to function fact() on the right side of the return statement.

FIGURE 2.22

A program to compute the factorial recursively.

```c
#include <stdio.h>

int num;

int fact(int n) {
    if (n <= 1) {
        return 1;
    }
    else {
        return n * fact(n - 1); // ra2
    }
}

int main() {
    printf("Enter a small integer: ");
    scanf("%d", &num);
    printf("Its factorial is: %d\n", fact(num)); // ra1
    return 0;
}
```

Interactive Input/Output

```
Enter a small integer: 4
Its factorial is: 24
```

This is a recursive call because it is a call to the function within the function itself. The same sequence of events happens as with any function call. A new stack frame is allocated, as Figure 2.23(d) shows. The return address in the second stack frame is the address of the calling statement in the function, represented by ra2.

The actual parameter is n - 1, whose value is 3 because the value of n in Figure 2.23(c) is 4. The formal parameter, n, is called by value. Therefore, the formal parameter n in the top frame of Figure 2.23(d) gets the value 3.

Figure 2.23(d) shows a curious situation that is typical of recursive calls. The program listing of Figure 2.22 shows only one declaration of n in the formal parameter list of fact. But Figure 2.23(d) shows two instances of n. The old instance of n has the value 4 from the main program. But the new instance of n has the value 3 from the recursive call.

Multiple instances of local variables and parameters

The computer suspends the old execution of the function and begins a new execution of the same function from its beginning. The first statement

FIGURE 2.23
The run-time stack for Figure 2.22.

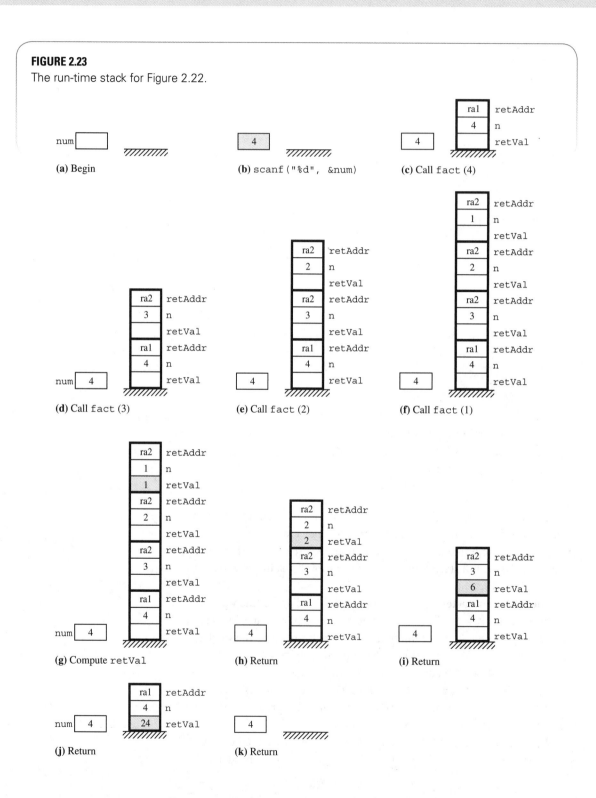

(a) Begin

(b) scanf("%d", &num)

(c) Call fact(4)

(d) Call fact(3)

(e) Call fact(2)

(f) Call fact(1)

(g) Compute retVal

(h) Return

(i) Return

(j) Return

(k) Return

in the function tests n for 1. But which n? Figure 2.23(d) shows two ns on the run-time stack. The rule is that any reference to a local variable or formal parameter is to the one on the top stack frame. Because the value of n is 3, the else part executes.

But now the function makes another recursive call. It allocates a third stack frame, as Figure 2.23(e) shows, and then a fourth, as Figure 2.23(f) shows. Each time, the newly allocated formal parameter gets a value one less than the old value of n because the function call is

```
fact(n - 1)
```

Finally, in Figure 2.23(g), n has the value 1. The function gives 1 to the cell on the stack labeled retVal. It skips the else part and terminates. That triggers a return to the calling statement.

The same events transpire with a recursive return as with a nonrecursive return. retVal contains the return value, and the return address tells which statement to execute next. In Figure 2.22(g), retVal is 1 and the return address is the calling statement in the function. The top frame is deallocated, and the calling statement

```
return n * fact(n - 1) // ra2
```

completes its execution. It multiplies its value of n, which is 2, by the value returned, which is 1, and assigns the result to retVal. So, retVal gets 2, as Figure 2.23(h) shows.

A similar sequence of events occurs on each return. Figure 2.23(i) and (j) show that the value returned from the second call is 6 and from the first call is 24. **FIGURE 2.24** shows the calling sequence for Figure 2.22. The main program calls fact. Then fact calls itself three times. In this example, fact is called a total of four times.

You see that the program computes the factorial of 4 the same way you would compute $f(4)$ from its recursive definition. You start by computing $f(4)$ as 4 times $f(3)$. Then you must suspend your computation of $f(4)$ to compute $f(3)$. After you get your result for $f(3)$, you can multiply it by 4 to get $f(4)$.

Similarly, the program must suspend its execution of the function to call the same function again. The run-time stack keeps track of the current values of the variables so they can be used when that instance of the function resumes.

Thinking Recursively

You can take two different viewpoints when dealing with recursion: microscopic and macroscopic. Figure 2.23 illustrates the microscopic viewpoint and shows precisely what happens inside the computer during execution. It is the viewpoint that considers the details of the run-time stack

FIGURE 2.24
The calling sequence for Figure 2.22. The solid arrows represent function calls. The dotted arrows represent returns. The value returned is next to each return arrow.

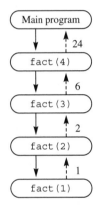

The microscopic and macroscopic viewpoints of recursion

during a trace of the program. The macroscopic viewpoint does not consider the individual trees. It considers the forest as a whole.

You need to know the microscopic viewpoint to understand how C implements recursion. The details of the run-time stack will be necessary when you study how recursion is implemented at Level Asmb5. But to write a recursive function, you should think macroscopically, not microscopically.

The most difficult aspect of writing a recursive function is the assumption that you can call the procedure that you are in the process of writing. To make that assumption, you must think macroscopically and forget about the run-time stack.

Proof by mathematical induction can help you think macroscopically. The two key elements of proof by induction are

> Establish the basis.

> Given the formula for n, prove it for $n + 1$.

The relation between proof by mathematical induction and recursion

Similarly, the two key elements of designing a recursive function are

> Compute the function for the basis.

> Assuming the function for $n - 1$, write it for n.

Imagine you are writing function fact (). You get to this point:

```
int fact(int n) {
    if (n <= 1) {
        return 1;
    }
    else {
```

and wonder how to continue. You have computed the function for the basis, n = 1. But now you must assume that you can call function fact (), even though you have not finished writing fact (). You must assume that fact (n - 1) will return the correct value for the factorial.

The importance of thinking macroscopically when you design a recursive function

Here is where you must think macroscopically. If you start wondering how fact (n - 1) will return the correct value, and if visions of stack frames begin dancing in your head, you are not thinking correctly. In proof by induction, you must assume the formula for n. Similarly, in writing fact (), you must assume that you can call fact (n - 1) with no questions asked.

The divide and conquer strategy

Recursive programs are based on a divide-and-conquer strategy, which is appropriate when you can solve a large problem in terms of a smaller one. Each recursive call makes the problem smaller and smaller, until the program reaches the smallest problem of all, the basis, which is simple to solve.

Recursive Addition

Here is another example of a recursive problem. Suppose `list` is an array of integers. You want to find the sum of all integers in the list recursively.

The first step is to formulate the solution of the large problem in terms of a smaller problem. If you knew how to find the sum of the integers between `list[0]` and `list[n - 1]`, you could simply add it to `list[n]`. You would then have the sum of all the integers.

The next step is to design a function with the appropriate parameters. The function will compute the sum of n integers by calling itself to compute the sum of n - 1 integers. So the parameter list must have a parameter that tells how many integers in the array to add. That should lead you to the following function head:

```
int sum(int a[], int n) {
// Returns the sum of the elements of a between a[0]
and a[n].
```

How do you establish the basis? That is simple. If n is 0, the function should add the sum of the elements between `a[0]` and `a[0]`. The sum of one element is just `a[0]`.

Now you can write

```
if (n == 0) {
    return a[0];
}
else {
```

Now think macroscopically. You can assume that `sum(a, n - 1)` will return the sum of the integers between `a[0]` and `a[n - 1]`. Have faith. All you need to do is add that sum to `a[n]`. **FIGURE 2.25** shows the function in a finished program.

Even though you write the function without considering the microscopic view, you can still trace the run-time stack. **FIGURE 2.26** shows the stack frames for the first two calls to sum. The stack frame consists of the value returned, the parameters a and n, and the return address. Because there are no local variables, no storage for them is allocated on the run-time stack.

In C, arrays are always called by reference without the & address operator in the actual parameter list. In Figure 2.25, the actual parameter `list` in the call

Arrays always called by reference

```
sum(list, 3)
```

is not prefixed with the & address operator, and yet it is called by reference. Hence, variable a in procedure sum refers to `list` in the main program. It literally contains the address of the first cell of the array. In this program, a contains the address of `list[0]`. The arrows in Figure 2.26(b) and (c) that

FIGURE 2.25
A recursive function that returns the sum of the first n numbers in an array.

```c
#include <stdio.h>

int list[4];

int sum(int a[], int n) {
// Returns the sum of the elements of a between a[0] and a[n].
    if (n == 0) {
        return a[0];
    }
    else {
        return a[n] + sum(a, n - 1); // ra2
    }
}

int main() {
    printf("Enter four integers: ");
    scanf("%d %d %d %d", &list[0], &list[1], &list[2], &list[3]);
    printf("Their sum is: %d\n", sum(list, 3));
    return 0;
}
```

Interactive Input/Output

```
Enter four integers: 3 2 6 4
Their sum is: 15
```

FIGURE 2.26
The run-time stack for the program in Figure 2.25.

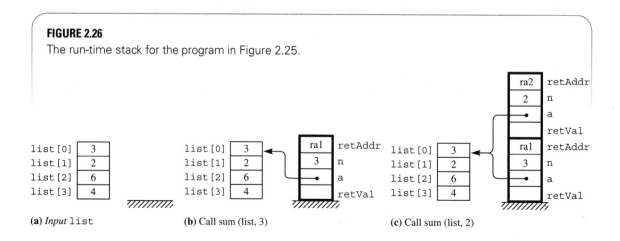

(a) *Input* list   (b) Call sum (list, 3)   (c) Call sum (list, 2)

point from the cells labeled a in the stack frame to the cell labeled list[0] indicate the reference of a to list.

In contrast to an array name without an index, an array name with an index is an individual element of an array and is treated like an individual variable. In Figure 2.25, the actual parameter list[1] in the call to scanf() is prefixed with the & address operator so it can be called by reference. To summarize, list[1] has type integer and requires the address operator to be called by reference. list has type array and is called by reference by default without the address operator.

A Binomial Coefficient Function

The next example of a recursive function has a more complex calling sequence. It is a function to compute the coefficient in the expansion of a binomial expression.

Consider the following expansions:

$$(x + y)^1 = x + y$$
$$(x + y)^2 = x^2 + 2xy + y^2$$
$$(x + y)^3 = x^3 + 3x^2y + 3xy^2 + y^3$$
$$(x + y)^4 = x^4 + 4x^3y + 6x^2y^2 + 4xy^3 + y^4$$

The coefficients of the terms are called *binomial coefficients*. If you write the coefficients without the terms, they form a triangle of values called *Pascal's triangle*. FIGURE 2.27 is Pascal's triangle for the coefficients up to the seventh power.

You can see from Figure 2.27 that each coefficient is the sum of the coefficient immediately above and the coefficient above and to the left. For example, the binomial coefficient in row 5, column 2, which is 10, equals 4 plus 6. Six is above 10, and 4 is above and to the left.

FIGURE 2.27

Pascal's triangle of binomial coefficients.

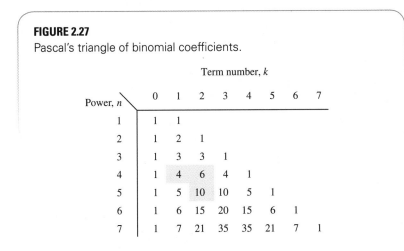

Power, n \ Term number, k	0	1	2	3	4	5	6	7
1	1	1						
2	1	2	1					
3	1	3	3	1				
4	1	4	6	4	1			
5	1	5	10	10	5	1		
6	1	6	15	20	15	6	1	
7	1	7	21	35	35	21	7	1

Mathematically, the binomial coefficient $b(n, k)$ for power n and term k is

$$b(n, k) = b(n - 1, k) + b(n - 1, k - 1)$$

That is a recursive definition because it defines the function $b(n, k)$ in terms of itself. You can also see that if k equals 0, or if n equals k, the value of the binomial coefficient is 1. The complete mathematical definition, including the two base cases, is

$$b(n, k) = \begin{cases} 1 & \text{if } k = 0, \\ 1 & \text{if } n = k, \\ b(n - 1, k) + b(n - 1, k - 1) & \text{if } 0 < k < n. \end{cases}$$

FIGURE 2.28 computes the value of a binomial coefficient recursively. It is based directly on the recursive definition of $b(n, k)$. FIGURE 2.29 shows a trace of the run-time stack. Parts (b), (c), and (d) show the allocation of the first three stack frames. They represent calls to binCoeff(3, 1),

FIGURE 2.28
A recursive computation of the binomial coefficient.

```c
#include <stdio.h>

int binCoeff(int n, int k) {
   int y1, y2;
   if ((k == 0) || (n == k)) {
      return 1;
   }
   else {
      y1 = binCoeff(n - 1, k); // ra2
      y2 = binCoeff(n - 1, k - 1); // ra3
      return y1 + y2;
   }
}

int main() {
   printf("binCoeff(3, 1) = %d\n", binCoeff(3, 1)); // ra1
   return 0;
}
```

Output
```
binCoeff(3, 1) = 3
```

FIGURE 2.29
The run-time stack for Figure 2.28.

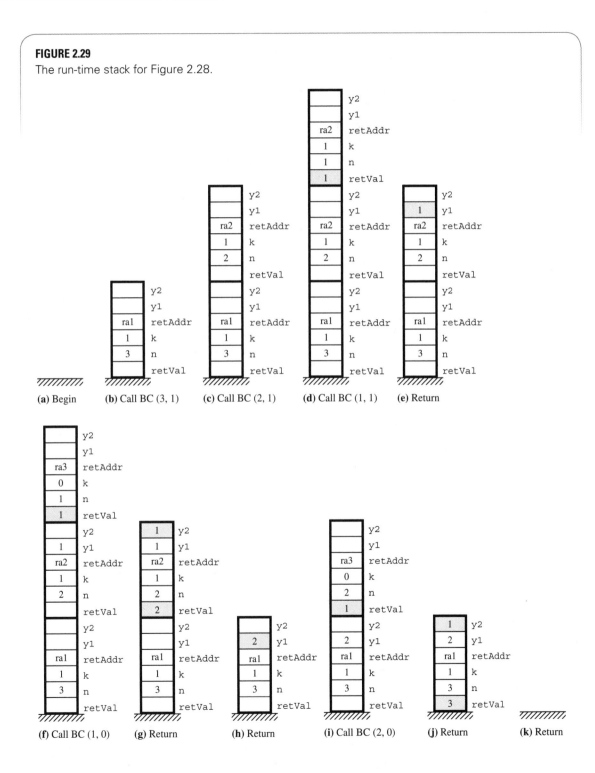

(a) Begin   (b) Call BC (3, 1)   (c) Call BC (2, 1)   (d) Call BC (1, 1)   (e) Return

(f) Call BC (1, 0)   (g) Return   (h) Return   (i) Call BC (2, 0)   (j) Return   (k) Return

binCoeff(2, 1), and binCoeff(1, 1). The first stack frame has the return address of the calling program in the main program. The next two stack frames have the return address of the y1 assignment statement. ra2 represents that statement.

Figure 2.29(e) shows the return from binCoeff(1, 1). y1 gets the value 1 returned by the function. Then the y2 assignment statement calls the function binCoeff(1, 0). Figure 2.29(f) shows the run-time stack during execution of binCoeff(1, 0). Each stack frame has a different return address.

The calling sequence for this program is different from those of the previous recursive programs. The other programs keep allocating stack frames until the run-time stack reaches its maximum height. Then they keep deallocating stack frames until the run-time stack is empty. This program allocates stack frames until the run-time stack reaches its maximum height. It does not deallocate stack frames until the run-time stack is empty, however. From Figure 2.29(d) to (e), it deallocates, but from 2.29(e) to (f), it allocates. From 2.29(f) to (g) to (h), it deallocates, but from 2.29(h) to (i), it allocates. Why? Because this function has two recursive calls instead of one. If the basis step is true, the function makes no recursive call. But if the basis step is false, the function makes two recursive calls, one for y1 and one for y2. **FIGURE 2.30** shows the calling sequence for the program. Notice that it is in the shape of a tree. Each node of the tree represents a function call. Except for the main program, a node has either two children or no children, corresponding to two recursive calls or no recursive calls.

Referring to Figure 2.30, the sequence of calls and returns is

The sequence of calls and returns for the program in Figure 2.30

```
Main program
    Call BC(3, 1)
        Call BC(2, 1)
            Call BC(1, 1)
        Return to BC(2, 1)
            Call BC(1, 0)
        Return to BC(2, 1)
    Return to BC(3, 1)
        Call BC(2, 0)
    Return to BC(3, 1)
Return to main program
```

With this indentation style, each indent from one line to the next represents a function call, and each outdent from one line to the next represents a function return. You can visualize the order of execution on the call tree by imagining that the tree is a coastline in an ocean. A boat starts from the left side of the main program and sails along the coast, always

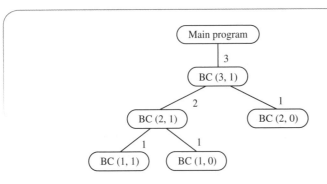

FIGURE 2.30
The call tree for the program in Figure 2.28.

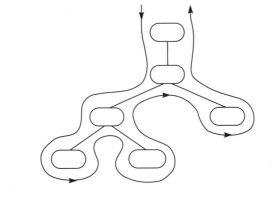

FIGURE 2.31
The order of execution of the program in Figure 2.28.

keeping the shore to its left. The boat visits the nodes in the same order from which they are called and returned. **FIGURE 2.31** shows the visitation path.

When analyzing a recursive program from a microscopic point of view, it is easier to construct the call tree before you construct the trace of the run-time stack. Once you have the tree, it is easy to see the behavior of the run-time stack. Every time the boat visits a lower node in the tree, the program allocates one stack frame. Every time the boat visits a higher node in the tree, the program deallocates one stack frame.

You can determine the maximum height of the run-time stack from the call tree. Just keep track of the net number of stack frames allocated when you get to the lowest node of the call tree. That will correspond to the maximum height of the run-time stack.

Drawing the call tree in the order of execution is not the easiest way. The previous execution sequence started

Main program
    Call BC(3, 1)
        Call BC(2, 1)
            Call BC(1, 1)

You should not draw the call tree in that order. It is easier to start with

Main program
    Call BC(3, 1)
    Return to BC(3, 1)
    Return to BC(3, 1)
  Return to main program

recognizing from the program listing that BC(3, 1) will call itself twice, BC(2, 1) once, and BC(2, 0) once. Then you can go back to BC(2, 1) and determine its children. In other words, determine all the children of a node before analyzing the deeper calls from any one of the children.

Constructing the call tree breadth first

This is a "breadth-first" construction of the tree, as opposed to the "depth-first" construction, which follows the execution sequence. The problem with the depth-first construction arises when you return up several levels in a complicated call tree to some higher node. You might forget the state of execution the node is in and not be able to determine its next child node. If you determine all the children of a node at once, you no longer need to remember the state of execution of the node.

Reversing the Elements of an Array

FIGURE 2.32 has a recursive procedure instead of a function. `reverse()` is a void function that reverses the elements in a local array of characters without returning a value. C allows the programmer to initialize an array of characters from a string constant enclosed in double quotes. In the main program, `word` is a local array of characters that is initialized from the string constant `"star"`. Because it is local, it is stored on the run-time stack in the stack frame for `main()`. The number of elements in the array is always one greater than the number of characters in the string constant because of an additional `\0` sentinel at the end of the string. In this program, `word` has five elements, four for the letters and one for the sentinel. In the `printf()` function calls, the placeholder `%s` causes the program to output the characters in array `word` from the first and up to, but not including, the sentinel.

The procedure reverses the characters in the array `str` between `str[j]` and `str[k]`. The main program wants to reverse the characters between `'s'` and `'r'`. So it calls `reverse()` with 0 for `j` and 3 for `k`.

The procedure solves this problem by breaking it down into a smaller problem. Because 0 is less than 3, the procedure knows that the characters between 0 and 3 need to be reversed. So it switches `str[0]` with `str[3]` and calls itself recursively to switch all the characters between `str[1]` and `str[2]`. If `j` is ever greater than or equal to `k`, no switching is necessary and the procedure does nothing. **FIGURE 2.33** shows the beginning of a trace of the run-time stack.

FIGURE 2.32
A recursive procedure to reverse the elements of a local array.

```c
#include <stdio.h>

void reverse(char *str, int j, int k) {
    char temp;
    if (j < k) {
        temp = str[j];
        str[j] = str[k];
        str[k] = temp;
        reverse(str, j + 1, k - 1);
    } // ra2
}

int main() {
    char word[5] = "star";
    printf("%s\n", word);
    reverse(word, 0, 3);
    printf("%s\n", word); // ra1
    return 0;
}
```

Output

```
star
rats
```

Towers of Hanoi

The Towers of Hanoi puzzle is a classic computer science problem that is conveniently solved by the recursive technique. The puzzle consists of three pegs and a set of disks with different diameters. The pegs are numbered 1, 2, and 3. Each disk has a hole at its center so that it can fit onto one of the pegs. The initial configuration of the puzzle consists of all the disks on one peg in a way that no disk rests directly on another disk with a smaller diameter. FIGURE 2.34 is the initial configuration for four disks.

The problem is to move all the disks from the starting peg to another peg under the following conditions:

> You may move only one disk at a time. It must be the top disk from one peg, which is moved to the top of another peg.

> You may not place one disk on another disk having a smaller diameter.

FIGURE 2.33
The run-time stack for the program in Figure 2.32.

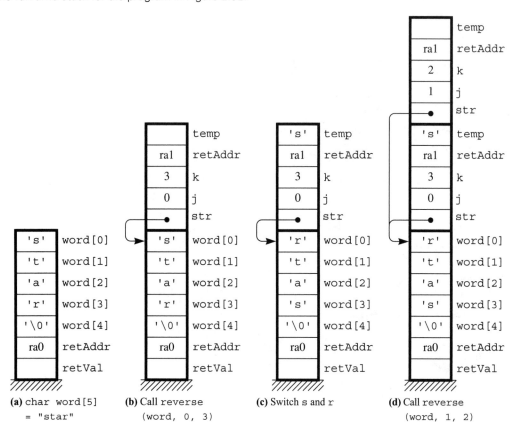

(a) char word[5]
   = "star"

(b) Call reverse
   (word, 0, 3)

(c) Switch s and r

(d) Call reverse
   (word, 1, 2)

The procedure for solving this problem has three parameters, n, j, and k, where

> n is the number of disks to move

> j is the starting peg

> k is the goal peg

j and k are integers that identify the pegs. Given the values of j and k, you can calculate the intermediate peg, which is the one that is neither the starting peg nor the goal peg, as 6 – j – k. For example, if the starting peg is 1 and the goal peg is 3, then the intermediate peg is 6 – 1 – 3 = 2.

To move the n disks from peg j to peg k, first check whether n = 1. If it does, then simply move the one disk from peg j to peg k. But if it does not, then decompose the problem into several smaller parts:

FIGURE 2.34
The Towers of Hanoi puzzle.

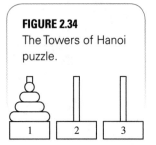

› Move n – 1 disks from peg j to the intermediate peg.

› Move one disk from peg j to peg k.

› Move n – 1 disks from the intermediate peg to peg k.

FIGURE 2.35 shows this decomposition for the problem of moving four disks from peg 1 to peg 3.

This procedure guarantees that a disk will not be placed on another disk with a smaller diameter, assuming that the original n disks are stacked correctly. Suppose, for example, that four disks are to be moved from peg 1 to peg 3, as in Figure 2.35. The procedure says that you should move the top three disks from peg 1 to peg 2, move the bottom disk from peg 1 to peg 3, and then move the three disks from peg 2 to peg 3.

In moving the top three disks from peg 1 to peg 2, you will leave the bottom disk on peg 1. Remember that it is the disk with the largest diameter, so any disk you place on it in the process of moving the other disks will be smaller. In order to move the bottom disk from peg 1 to peg 3, peg 3 must be empty. You will not place the bottom disk on a smaller disk in this step either. When you move the three disks from peg 2 to peg 3, you will place them on the largest disk, now on the bottom of peg 3. So the three disks will be placed on peg 3 correctly.

The procedure is recursive. In the first step, you must move three disks from peg 1 to peg 2. To do that, move two disks from peg 1 to peg 3, then one disk from peg 1 to peg 2, then two disks from peg 3 to peg 2. **FIGURE 2.36** shows this sequence. Using the previous reasoning, these steps will be carried out correctly. In the process of moving two disks from peg 1 to peg 3, you may place any of these two disks on the bottom two disks of peg 1 without fear of breaking the rules.

Eventually you will reduce the problem to the basis step, where you need to move only one disk. But the solution with one disk is easy. Programming

---

FIGURE 2.35

The solution for moving four disks from peg 1 to peg 3, assuming that you can move three disks from one peg to any other peg.

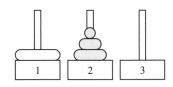 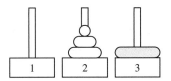 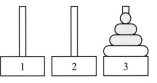

(**a**) Move three disks from peg 1 to peg 2.

(**b**) Move one disk from peg 1 to peg 3.

(**c**) Move three disks from peg 2 to peg 3.

FIGURE 2.36

The solution for moving three disks from peg 1 to peg 2, assuming that you can move two disks from one peg to any other peg.

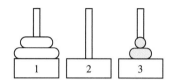
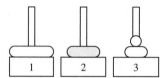
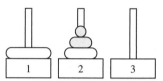

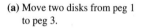

(a) Move two disks from peg 1 to peg 3.　　**(b)** Move one disk from peg 1 to peg 2.　　**(c)** Move two disks from peg 3 to peg 2.

the solution to the Towers of Hanoi puzzle is a problem at the end of the chapter.

Mutual Recursion

Some problems are best solved by procedures that do not call themselves directly but that are recursive nonetheless. Suppose a main program calls procedure a, and procedure a contains a call to procedure b. If procedure b contains a call to procedure a, then a and b are mutually recursive. Even though procedure a does not call itself directly, it does call itself indirectly through procedure b.

There is nothing different about the implementation of mutual recursion compared to plain recursion. Stack frames are allocated on the run-time stack the same way, with the return value allocated first, followed by parameters, followed by the return address, followed by local variables.

There is one slight problem in specifying mutually recursive procedures in a C program, however. It arises from the fact that procedures must be declared before they are used. If procedure a() calls procedure b(), the declaration of procedure b() must appear before the declaration of procedure a() in the listing. But if procedure b() calls procedure a(), the declaration of procedure a() must appear before the declaration of procedure b() in the listing. The problem is that if each calls the other, each must appear before the other in the listing, an obvious impossibility.

The function prototype

For this situation, C provides the *function prototype*, which allows the programmer to write the first procedure heading without the body. In a function prototype, you include the complete formal parameter list, but in place of the body, you put ;. After the function prototype comes the declaration of the second procedure, followed by the body of the first procedure.

Example 2.6   Here is an outline of the structure of the mutually recursive procedures a() and b() as just discussed:

Constants, types, variables of main program
```
void a(SomeType x);
void b(SomeOtherType y) {
    Body for b
}
void a(SomeType x) {
    Body for a
}
int main() {
    Executable statements of main program
}
```

If b() has a call to a(), the compiler will be able to verify that the number and types of the actual parameters match the formal parameters of a scanned earlier in the function prototype. If a() has a call to b(), the call will be in the body of a(). The compiler will have scanned the declaration of b() because it occurs before the block of a().   ∎

Although mutual recursion is not as common as recursion, some compilers are based on a technique called *recursive descent*, which uses mutual recursion heavily. You can get an idea of why this is so by considering the structure of C statements. It is possible to nest an if inside a while, which is nested in turn inside another if. A compiler that uses recursive descent has a procedure to translate if statements and another procedure to translate while statements. When the procedure that is translating the outer if statement encounters the while statement, it calls the procedure that translates while statements. But when that procedure encounters the nested if statement, it calls the procedure that translates if statements; hence the mutual recursion.

Mutual recursion in a recursive descent compiler

The Cost of Recursion

The selection of examples in this section was based on only one criterion: the ability of the example to illustrate recursion. You can see that recursive solutions require much storage for the run-time stack. It also takes time to allocate and deallocate the stack frames. Recursive solutions are expensive in both space and time.

If you can solve a problem easily without recursion, the nonrecursive solution will usually be better than the recursive solution. Figure 2.18, the nonrecursive function to calculate the factorial, is certainly better than the recursive factorial function of Figure 2.22. Both Figure 2.25, to find the sum of the numbers in an array, and Figure 2.32 can easily be programmed nonrecursively with a loop.

The binomial coefficient $b(n, k)$ has a nonrecursive definition that is based on factorials:

$$b(n, k) = \frac{n!}{k!(n - k)!}$$

If you compute the factorials nonrecursively, a program based on this definition may be more efficient than the corresponding recursive program. Here the choice is a little less clear because the nonrecursive solution requires multiplication and division, but the recursive solution requires only addition.

Some problems are recursive by nature and can be solved only nonrecursively with great difficulty. The problem of solving the Towers of Hanoi puzzle is recursive by nature. You can try to solve it without recursion to see how difficult it would be. Quick sort, one of the best-known sorting algorithms, falls into this category also. It is much more difficult to program quick sort nonrecursively than recursively.

Integrated Development Environments

The C programs in this chapter are short, with few, if any, additional functions other than main(). Furthermore, the additional functions are all contained in the same file as the main function. A typical commercial application consists of tens or hundreds of additional functions, which makes it impractical for the entire application to be contained in a single file.

A common convention for organizing a big software project is to collect small groups of related functions into separate files. In C, there are two types of files for these collections of functions—header files with file extension .h and source files with file extension .c. For example, the #include statement at the beginning of the program instructs the compiler to refer to the header file stdio.h for the input/output library. The header file contains the head of each function declaration—that is, the return type, the name of the function, and the formal parameter list. The corresponding source file contains not only the head of each function but also the C code that implements it.

An integrated development environment (IDE) is an application for software developers to write large programs containing many header files and source files. A typical IDE has an integrated text editor for writing source code and a point-and-click interface for managing all the header files and source files in the project. The text editor provides syntax highlighting for the source code and code completion for keywords and identifiers. The IDE provides a graphical user interface for the compiler and an integrated pane for program input and output.

Examples of some of the more popular IDEs are NetBeans, Eclipse, Qt Creator, Visual Studio, and Xcode. NetBeans is an open-source IDE that originated as a student project and was picked up by Sun Microsystems, the company that originated the Java programming language. When Oracle acquired Sun, they continued the NetBeans project and still maintain it. Eclipse is also an open-source IDE, originated by IBM. Both NetBeans and Eclipse are written in Java but provide developers with a choice of different programming languages to code in, including Java, C, and C++. Qt Creator is another open-source IDE and is maintained by The Qt Company, a subsidiary of Digia Plc. The Pep/9 software that accompanies this text is written in C++ with Qt Creator. In contrast to these open-source, cross-platform IDEs, Visual Studio and Xcode are proprietary

FIGURE 2.37
The NetBeans IDE with the program from Figure 2.32.

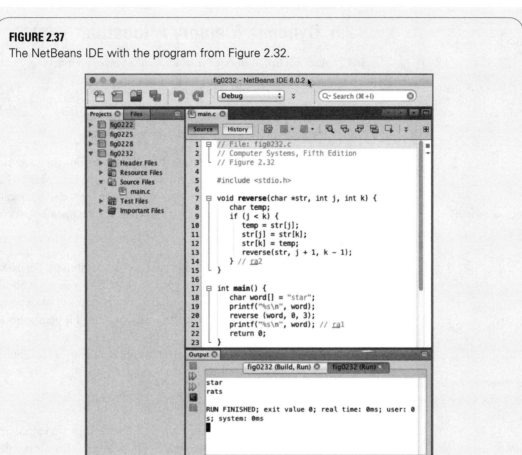

IDEs. Visual Studio is a Microsoft product for software development, primarily for the Windows operating system, and Xcode is an Apple product, primarily for the OS X and iOS operating systems.

FIGURE 2.37 shows the NetBeans IDE with the program from Figure 2.32. The left pane with the tab labeled Projects is for accessing all the files in a project. You can see that the IDE is managing four projects, with access to the project labeled fig0232. The IDE groups header files and source files separately. The programmer has opened the source file in the upper-right pane, which is the integrated text editor. She compiled and ran the program with a single click, producing the output in the bottom-right pane.

Another capability integrated into an IDE is version control. When many developers work on a single software project simultaneously, they need a way to manage potential conflicts when they modify the same source file. Version control systems manage the process by keeping track of all the changes made to the code and providing a systematic, documented process to resolve any conflicts. The two most popular version control systems are Subversion (SVN) and Git. Of the two, Git is the newer and more widespread. IDEs typically provide access to these version control systems through their graphical user interfaces. The Pep/9 software is maintained using Git and is available on GitHub, which is a software hosting service on the Internet.

2.5 Dynamic Memory Allocation

In C, values are stored in three distinct areas of main memory:

> Fixed locations in memory for global variables
> The run-time stack for local variables and parameters
> The heap for dynamically allocated variables

You do not control allocation and deallocation from the heap during procedure calls and returns. Instead, you allocate from the heap with the help of pointer variables. Allocation on the heap, which is not triggered automatically on the run-time stack by procedure calls, is known as *dynamic memory allocation*.

Dynamic memory allocation

Pointers

When you declare a global or local variable, you specify its type. For example, you can specify the type to be an integer, or a character, or an array. Similarly, when you declare a pointer, you must declare that it points to some type. The pointer itself can be global or local. The value to which it points, however, resides in the heap and is neither global nor local.

C provides two functions to control dynamic memory allocation:

Two operators that control dynamic memory allocation

> `malloc()`, to allocate from the heap
> `free()`, to deallocate from the heap

Omitting `free()` *is a simplification.*

Although memory deallocation with the `free()` function is important, this text does not describe how it operates. The programs that use pointers in this text are bad examples of software design because of this omission. The intent of the programs is to show the relationship between Levels HOL6 and Asmb5. This relationship will become evident in Chapter 6, which describes the translation of the programs.

The `malloc()` function expects the number of bytes of memory to allocate for its actual parameter. It does two things when it executes:

The two actions of the `malloc()` *function*

> It allocates a memory cell from the heap equal in size to the number of bytes as specified in its parameter.
> It returns a pointer to the newly allocated storage.

Two assignments are possible with pointers. You can assign a value to a pointer, or you can assign a value to the cell to which the pointer points. The first assignment is called a *pointer assignment*, which behaves according to the following rule:

The pointer assignment rule

> If p and q are pointers, the assignment p = q makes p point to the same cell to which q points.

FIGURE 2.38
A C nonsense program that illustrates the pointer type.

```c
#include <stdio.h>
#include <stdlib.h>
int *a, *b, *c;
int main() {
    a = (int *) malloc(sizeof(int));
    *a = 5;
    b = (int *) malloc(sizeof(int));
    *b = 3;
    c = a;
    a = b;
    *a = 2 + *c;
    printf("*a = %d\n", *a);
    printf("*b = %d\n", *b);
    printf("*c = %d\n", *c);
    return 0;
}
```

Output
```
*a = 7
*b = 7
*c = 5
```

FIGURE 2.38 is a nonsense program that illustrates the actions of the malloc() function and the pointer assignment rule. It uses global pointers, but the output would be the same if the pointers were local. If they were local, they would be allocated on the run-time stack instead of being at a fixed location in memory.

In the declaration of the global pointers

```c
int *a, *b, *c;
```

the asterisk before the variable name indicates that the variable, instead of being an integer, is a pointer to an integer. In FIGURE 2.39 , Figure 2.39(a) shows the pictorial representation of a pointer value to be a small black dot.

Figure 2.39(b) illustrates the action of the malloc() function. The sizeof() function takes a type and returns the number of bytes necessary to hold a value of that type. The expression (int *) in the first assignment is a type cast. Because malloc() returns a generic pointer, the type cast is necessary to convert the generic pointer to a pointer to an int. Consequently, the call to malloc() allocates a cell from the heap large enough to store an integer value, and it returns a pointer to the value. The assignment makes

FIGURE 2.39
A trace of the program in Figure 2.38.

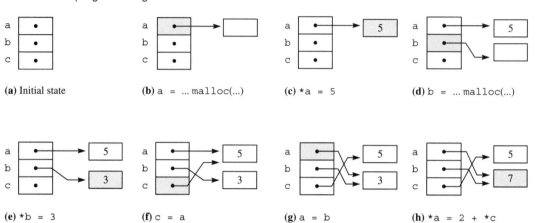

(a) Initial state   **(b)** a = ... malloc(...)   **(c)** *a = 5   **(d)** b = ... malloc(...)

(e) *b = 3   **(f)** c = a   **(g)** a = b   **(h)** *a = 2 + *c

a point to the newly allocated cell. Figure 2.39(c) shows how to access the cell to which a pointer points. Because a is a pointer, *a is the cell to which a points. Figure 2.39(f) illustrates the pointer assignment rule. The assignment c = a makes c point to the same cell to which a points. Similarly, the assignment a = b makes a point to the same cell to which b points. In Figure 2.39 (h), the assignment is not to pointer a but to the cell to which a points.

Structures

Structures are the key to data abstraction in C. They let the programmer consolidate variables with primitive types into a single abstract data type. Both arrays and structures are groups of values. However, all cells of an array must have the same type. Each cell is accessed by the numeric integer value of the index. With a structure, the cells can have different types. C provides the struct construct to group the values. The C programmer gives each cell, called a *field*, a field name.

FIGURE 2.40 shows a program that declares a struct named person that has four fields named first, last, age, and gender. The program declares a global variable named bill that has type person. Fields first, last, and gender have type char, and field age has type int.

To access the field of a structure, you place a period between the name of the variable and the name of the field you want to access. For example, the test of the if statement

```
if (bill.gender == 'm')
```

accesses the field named gender in the variable named bill.

FIGURE 2.40
The C structure.

```c
#include <stdio.h>

struct person {
    char first;
    char last;
    int age;
    char gender;
};
struct person bill;
int main() {
    scanf("%c%c%d %c", &bill.first, &bill.last, &bill.age, &bill.gender);
    printf("Initials: %c%c\n", bill.first, bill.last);
    printf("Age: %d\n", bill.age);
    printf("Gender: ");
    if (bill.gender == 'm') {
        printf("male\n");
    }
    else {
        printf("female\n");
    }
    return 0;
}
```

Input
bj 32 m

Output
Initials: bj
Age: 32
Gender: male

Linked Data Structures

Programmers frequently combine pointers and structures to implement linked data structures. The struct is usually called a *node*, a pointer points to a node, and the node has a field that is a pointer. The pointer field of the node serves as a link to another node in the data structure. FIGURE 2.41 is a program that implements a linked list data structure. The first loop inputs a sequence of integers terminated by the sentinel value –9999, placing the

FIGURE 2.41

A C program to input and output a linked list.

```c
#include <stdio.h>
#include <stdlib.h>

struct node {
    int data;
    struct node *next;
};
int main() {
    struct node *first, *p;
    int value;
    first = 0;
    scanf("%d", &value);
    while (value != -9999) {
        p = first;
        first = (struct node *) malloc(sizeof(struct node));
        first->data = value;
        first->next = p;
        scanf("%d", &value);
    }
    for (p = first; p != 0; p = p->next) {
        printf("%d ", p->data);
    }
    return 0;
}
```

Input
```
10 20 30 40 -9999
```

Output
```
40 30 20 10
```

first value in the input stream at the end of the linked list. The second loop outputs each element of the linked list. **FIGURE 2.42** is a trace of the first few statement executions of the program in Figure 2.41.

0 is a special pointer value.

The value 0 for a pointer is a special value that is guaranteed to point to no cell at all. It is commonly used in C programs as a sentinel value of linked structures. The statement

```c
first = 0;
```

assigns this special value to local pointer `first`. Figure 2.42(b) shows the value pictorially as a dashed triangle.

FIGURE 2.42
A trace of the first few statement executions of the program in Figure 2.41.

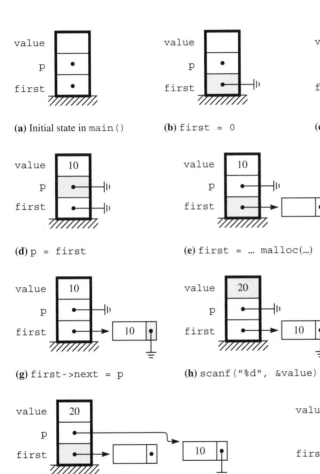

(a) Initial state in `main()`   **(b)** `first = 0`    **(c)** `scanf("%d", &value)`

(d) `p = first`   **(e)** `first = … malloc(…)`   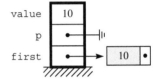 **(f)** `first->data = value`

(g) `first->next = p`   **(h)** `scanf("%d", &value)`   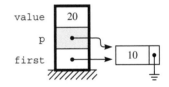 **(i)** `p = first`

(j) `first = … malloc(…)`   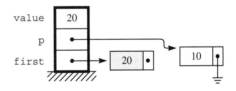 **(k)** `first->data = value`

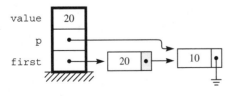

(l) `first->next = p`   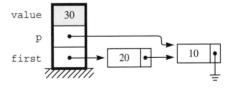 **(m)** `scanf("%d", &value)`

You use an asterisk to access the cell to which a pointer points, and a period to access the field of a structure. If a pointer points to a `struct`, you access a field of the `struct` using both the asterisk and the period.

Example 2.7　The following statement assigns the value of variable `value` to the data field of the structure to which it points.

```
(*first).data = value;
```
■

The -> operator

Because this combination of asterisk and period is so common, C provides the arrow operator `- >` formed by a hyphen followed immediately by a greater-than symbol. The statement in Example 2.7 can be written using this abbreviation as

```
first->data = value;
```

which Figure 2.42(f) and (k) shows. The program uses the same abbreviation to access the `next` field, which Figure 2.42(g) and (l) shows.

Chapter Summary

In C, values are stored in three distinct areas of main memory: fixed locations in memory for global variables, the run-time stack for local variables and parameters, and the heap for dynamically allocated variables. The two ways in which flow of control can be altered from the normal sequential flow are through selection and repetition. The C `if` and `switch` statements implement selection, and the `while`, `do`, and `for` statements implement repetition. All five statements use the relational operators to test the truth of a condition.

The LIFO nature of the run-time stack is required to implement function and procedure calls. The allocation process for a function is the following: Push storage for the return value, push the actual parameters, push the return address, and push storage for the local variables. The allocation process for a procedure is identical except that storage for the return value is not pushed. The stack frame consists of all the items pushed onto the run-time stack in one function or procedure call.

A recursive procedure is one that calls itself. To avoid calling itself endlessly, a recursive procedure must have an `if` statement that serves as an escape hatch to stop the recursive calls. Two different viewpoints in thinking about recursion are the microscopic and the macroscopic viewpoints. The microscopic viewpoint considers the details of the run-time stack during execution. The macroscopic viewpoint is based on a higher level of abstraction and is related to proof by mathematical induction. The microscopic viewpoint is useful for analysis; the macroscopic viewpoint is useful for design.

Allocation on the heap with the `malloc()` function is known as *dynamic memory allocation*. The `malloc()` function allocates a memory cell from the heap and returns a pointer to the newly allocated cell. A structure, indicated as `struct` in C, is a collection of values that need not all be the same type. Each value is stored in a field, and each field has a name. Linked data structures consist of nodes, which are structures that have pointers to other nodes. The node for a linked list has a field for a value and a field usually named `next` that points to the next node in the list.

Exercises

Section 2.4

1. The function `sum()` in Figure 2.25 is called for the first time by the main program. From the second time on, it is called by itself. *(a) How many times is it called altogether, including the call from `main()`? (b) Draw a picture of the main program variables and the run-time stack just after the function is called for the third time. Do not draw the stack frame for `main()`. You should have three stack frames. (c) Draw a picture of the main program variables and the run-time stack just before the return from the call of part (b). You should have three stack frames, but with different contents from part (b).

2. Each exercise below has five parts, as follows: (1) Draw the call tree in the style of Figure 2.30 for the function `binCoeff()` of Figure 2.28 assuming the given call statement from the main program. (2) Write down the sequence of calls and returns using the indentation notation on page 92. (3) How many times is the function called, including the call from the main program? (4) What is the maximum number of stack frames on the run-time stack during the execution, not counting the frame for the main program? (5) Draw the run-time stack in the style of Figure 2.29 at the given point during execution.

   *(a) Call statement `binCoeff(4, 1)` from the main program. For part (5), draw the run-time stack just before the return from `binCoeff(2, 1)`.

   (b) Call statement `binCoeff(5, 1)` from the main program. For part (5), draw the run-time stack just before the return from `binCoeff(3, 1)`.

   (c) Call statement `binCoeff(3, 2)` from the main program. For part (5), draw the run-time stack just before the return from `binCoeff(1, 0)`.

(d) Call statement binCoeff(4, 4) from the main program. For part (5), draw the run-time stack just before the return from binCoeff(4, 4).

(e) Call statement binCoeff(4, 2) from the main program. For part (5), binCoeff(2, 1) is called twice. Draw the run-time stack just before the return from the second call of the function.

3. Draw the call tree in the style of Figure 2.30 for the program in Figure 2.32 to reverse the letters of an array of characters, assuming the initial string is "Backward". How many times is function reverse() called, including the call from main()? What is the maximum number of stack frames allocated on the run-time stack, including the stack frame for main()? Draw the run-time stack just after the third call to function reverse(), including the stack frame for main().

4. The Fibonacci sequence is

0 1 1 2 3 5 8 13 21 . . .

Each Fibonacci number is the sum of the preceding two Fibonacci numbers. The sequence starts with the first two Fibonacci numbers and is defined recursively as

$$\text{fib}(n) = \begin{cases} 0 & \text{if } n = 0, \\ 1 & \text{if } n = 1, \\ \text{fib}(n-1) + \text{fib}(n-2) & \text{if } n < 1. \end{cases}$$

Draw the call tree in the style of Figure 2.30 for the following Fibonacci numbers:

(a) fib(3)   (b) fib(4)   (c) fib(5)

For each of these calls, how many times is fib() called, including the call from main()? What is the maximum number of stack frames allocated on the run-time stack, not including the stack frame for main()?

5. For your solution to the Towers of Hanoi in Problem 2.14, draw the call tree for the four-disk problem. How many times is your procedure called, including the call from main()? What is the maximum number of stack frames on the run-time stack, not including the stack frame for main()?

6. The mystery numbers are defined recursively as

$$\text{myst}(n) = \begin{cases} 2 & \text{if } n = 0, \\ 1 & \text{if } n = 1, \\ 2 \times \text{myst}(n-1) + \text{myst}(n-2) & \text{if } n > 1. \end{cases}$$

(a) Draw the call tree in the style of Figure 2.30 for myst(4).

(b) What is the value of myst(4)?

7. Examine the C program that follows: **(a)** Draw the run-time stack just after the procedure is called for the last time, including the stack frame for `main()`. **(b)** What is the output of the program?

```c
#include <stdio.h>
void what(char *word, int j) {
    if (j > 1) {
        word[j] = word[3 - j];
        what(word, j - 1);
    } // ra2
}
int main() {
    char str[5] = "abcd";
    what(str, 3);
    printf("%s\n", str); // ra1
    return 0;
}
```

Problems

Section 2.1

8. Write a C program that inputs two integers and outputs their quotient and remainder. To output the % character, you must write it as %% in the format string.

Sample Input

```
13   4
```

Sample Output

```
13/4 has value 3.
13%4 has value 1.
```

Section 2.2

9. Write a C program that inputs an integer and outputs whether the integer is even.

Sample Input

```
15
```

Sample Output

```
15 is not even.
```

10. Write a C program that inputs two integers and outputs the sum of the integers between them.

<u>Sample Input</u>

```
9   12
```

<u>Sample Output</u>

```
The sum of the numbers between 9 and 12 inclusive is 42.
```

Section 2.3

11. Write a C function

```
int rectArea (int len, int wid)
```

that returns the area of a rectangle with length `len` and width `wid`. Test it with a main program that inputs the length and width of a rectangle and outputs its area. Output the value in the main program, not in the function.

<u>Sample Input</u>

```
6   10
```

<u>Sample Output</u>

```
The area of a 6 by 10 rectangle is 60.
```

12. Write a C function

```
void rect(int *ar, int *per, int len, int wid)
```

that computes the area `ar` and perimeter `per` of a rectangle with length `len` and width `wid`. Test it with a main program that inputs the length and width of a rectangle and outputs its area and perimeter. Output the value in the main program, not in the procedure.

<u>Sample Input</u>

```
6   10
```

<u>Sample Output</u>

```
Length: 6
Width: 10
Area: 60
Perimeter: 32
```

Section 2.4

13. Write a C program that asks the user to input a small integer. Then use a recursive function that returns the value of that Fibonacci number as defined in Exercise 4. Do not use a loop. Output the value in the main program, not in the function.

Sample Input/Output

```
Which Fibonacci number? 8
The number is 21.
```

14. Write a C program that prints the solution to the Towers of Hanoi puzzle. It should ask the user to input the number of disks in the puzzle, the peg on which all the disks are placed initially, and the peg on which the disks are to be moved.

Sample Input/Output

```
How many disks do you want to move? 3
From which peg? 3
To which peg? 2

Move a disk from peg 3 to peg 2.
Move a disk from peg 3 to peg 1.
Move a disk from peg 2 to peg 1.
Move a disk from peg 3 to peg 2.
Move a disk from peg 1 to peg 3.
Move a disk from peg 1 to peg 2.
Move a disk from peg 3 to peg 2.
```

15. Write a recursive void function called `rotateLeft()` with two parameters, an array and an integer count n, that rotates the first n integers in the array to the left. To rotate n items left, rotate the first $n - 1$ items left recursively, and then exchange the last two items. For example, to rotate the five items

```
50    60    70    80    90
```

to the left, recursively rotate the first four items to the left:

```
60    70    80    50    90
```

and then exchange the last two items:

```
60    70    80    90    50
```

Test it with a main program that takes as input an integer count followed by the values to rotate. Output the original values and the rotated values. Do not use a loop in `rotateLeft()`. Output the value in the main program, not in the procedure.

Sample Input

```
5    50 60 70 80 90
```

Sample Output

```
Original list: 50   60   70   80   90
Rotated list: 60    70    80    90    50
```

16. Write a function

```
int maximum (int list[], int n)
```

that recursively finds the largest integer between `list[0]` and `list[n]`. Assume at least one element is in the list. Test it with a main program that takes as input an integer count followed by the values. Output the original values followed by the maximum. Do not use a loop in maximum. Output the value in the main program, not in the function.

Sample Input

```
5     50 30 90 20 80
```

Sample Output

```
Original list: 50   30   90   20   80
Largest value: 90
```

Section 2.5

17. The program in Figure 2.41 creates a linked list whose elements are in reverse order compared to their input order. Modify the first loop of the program to create the list in the same order as the input order. Do not modify the second loop.

Sample Input

```
10 20 30 40 -9999
```

Sample Output

```
10 20 30 40
```

18. Declare the following node for a binary search tree:

```
struct node {
   node *left;
   int data;
   node *right;
};
```

where `left` is a pointer to the left subtree and `right` is a pointer to the right subtree. Write a C program that inputs a sequence of integers with −9999 as a sentinel and inserts them into a binary search tree. Output them in ascending order with a recursive procedure that makes an inorder traversal of the search tree.

Sample Input

```
40 90 50 10 80 30 70 60 20 -9999
```

Sample Output

```
10 20 30 40 50 60 70 80 90
```

Instruction Set Architecture

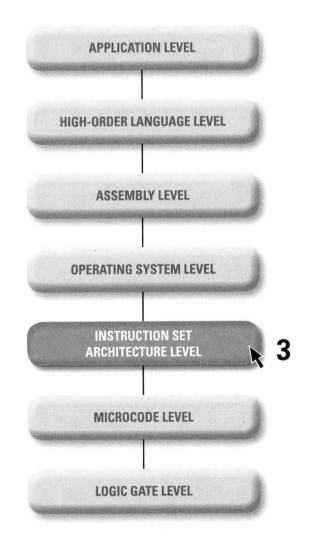

APPLICATION LEVEL

HIGH-ORDER LANGUAGE LEVEL

ASSEMBLY LEVEL

OPERATING SYSTEM LEVEL

INSTRUCTION SET
ARCHITECTURE LEVEL   3

MICROCODE LEVEL

LOGIC GATE LEVEL

CHAPTER 3

Information Representation

One of the most significant inventions of mankind is the printed word. The words on this page represent information stored on paper, which is conveyed to you as you read. Like the printed page, computers have memories for storing information. The central processing unit (CPU) has the ability to retrieve information from its memory much as you take information from words on a page.

Reading and writing, words and pages

Some computer terminology is based on this analogy. The CPU *reads* information from memory and *writes* information into memory. The information itself is divided into *words*. In some computer systems, large sets of words, usually anywhere from a few hundred to a few thousand, are grouped into *pages*.

Information representation at Level ISA3

In C, at Level HOL6, information takes the form of values that you store in a variable in main memory or in a file on disk. This chapter shows how the computer stores that information at Level ISA3. Information representation at the machine level differs significantly from that at the high-order languages level. At Level ISA3, information representation is less human-oriented. Later chapters discuss information representation at the intermediate levels, Levels Asmb5 and OS4, and show how they relate to Levels HOL6 and ISA3.

3.1 Unsigned Binary Representation

The Mark I computer

Early computers were electromechanical. That is, all their calculations were performed with moving switches called *relays*. The Mark I computer, built in 1944 by Howard H. Aiken of Harvard University, was such a machine. Aiken had procured financial backing for his project from Thomas J. Watson, president of International Business Machines (IBM). The relays in the Mark I computer could compute much faster than the mechanical gears that were used in adding machines at that time.

The ENIAC computer

Even before the completion of Mark I, John V. Atanasoff, working at Iowa State University, had finished the construction of an electronic computer to solve systems of linear equations. In 1941 John W. Mauchly visited Atanasoff's laboratory and in 1946, in collaboration with J. Presper Eckert at the University of Pennsylvania, built the famous Electronic Numerical Integrator and Calculator (ENIAC). ENIAC's 19,000 vacuum tubes could perform 5000 additions per second compared to 10 additions per second with the relays of the Mark I. Like the ENIAC, present-day computers are electronic, although their calculations are performed with integrated circuits (ICs) instead of with vacuum tubes.

Binary Storage

Electronic computer memories cannot store numbers and letters directly. They can store only electrical signals. When the CPU reads information from memory, it is detecting a signal whose voltage is about equal to that produced by two flashlight batteries.

Computer memories are designed with a most remarkable property. Each storage location contains either a high-voltage signal or a low-voltage signal—never anything in between. The storage location is like being pregnant. Either you are or you are not. There is no halfway.

The word *digital* means that the signal stored in memory can have only a fixed number of values. *Binary* means that only two values are possible. Practically all computers on the market today are binary. Hence, each storage location contains either a high voltage or a low voltage. The state of each location is also described as being either on or off, or, alternatively, as containing either a 1 or a 0.

Each individual storage unit is called a *binary digit* or *bit*. A bit can be only 1 or 0—never anything else, such as 2, 3, A, or Z. This is a fundamental concept. Every piece of information stored in the memory of a computer, whether it is the amount you owe on your credit card or your street address, is stored in binary as 1's and 0's.

In practice, the bits in a computer system are grouped together into *cells*. A seven-bit cell, for example, would store its information in groups of seven bits, as shows. You can think of a cell as a group of boxes, each box containing a 1 or a 0, and nothing else. Part (b) shows some possible binary values in a seven-bit cell. The values in part (c) are impossible because the digits in some boxes differ from 0 or 1.

Different parts of a computer system have different numbers of bits in each cell. Practically all computers today have eight bits per cell in their main memories and disks. An eight-bit cell is a *byte*. Other parts of the system have different sizes. This chapter shows examples with several different cell sizes to illustrate the general principle.

Information such as numbers and letters must be represented in binary form to be stored in memory. The representation scheme used to store information is called a *code*. This section examines a code for storing unsigned integers. The remainder of this chapter describes codes for storing other kinds of data. The next chapter examines codes for storing program commands in memory.

Integers

Numbers must be represented in binary form to be stored in a computer's memory. The particular code depends on whether the number has a fractional part or is an integer. If the number is an integer, the code depends on whether it is always nonnegative or whether it can be negative as well.

The *unsigned binary* representation is for integers that are always nonnegative. Before learning the binary system, we will review our own

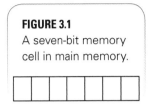

FIGURE 3.1
A seven-bit memory cell in main memory.

(a) A seven-bit cell.

0	1	1	0	1	0	1

1	1	0	1	1	0	0

0	0	0	0	0	0	0

(b) Some possible values in a seven-bit cell.

6	8	0	7	2	5	1

J	A	N	U	A	R	Y

(c) Some impossible values in a seven-bit cell.

Unsigned binary

base 10 (*decimal*, or *dec* for short) system, and then work our way down to the binary system.

Our decimal system was probably invented because we have 10 fingers with which we count and add. A book of arithmetic using this elegant system was written in India in the eighth century AD. It was translated into Arabic and was eventually carried by merchants to Europe, where it was translated from Arabic into Latin. The numbers came to be known as Arabic numerals because at the time it was thought that they originated in Arabia. But Hindu-Arabic numerals would be a more appropriate name because they actually originated in India.

Counting with Arabic numerals in base 10 looks like this (reading down, of course):

Counting in decimal

0	7	14	21	28	35
1	8	15	22	29	36
2	9	16	23	30	37
3	10	17	24	31	38
4	11	18	25	32	:
5	12	19	26	33	
6	13	20	27	34	

Starting from 0, the Indians simply invented a symbol for the next number, 1, then 2, and so on until they got to the symbol 9. At that point they looked at their hands and thought of a fantastic idea. On their last finger they did not invent a new symbol. Instead they used the first two symbols, 1 and 0, together to represent the next number, 10.

You know the rest of the story. When they got to 19 they saw that the 9 was as high as they could go with the symbols they had invented. So they dropped it down to 0 and increased the 1 to 2, creating 20. They did the same for 29 to 30 and, eventually, 99 to 100. On and on it went.

What if we only had 8 fingers instead of 10? What would have happened? At 7, the next number would be on our last finger, and we would not need to invent a new symbol. The next number would be represented as 10. Counting in base 8 (*octal*, or *oct* for short) looks like this:

Counting in octal

Base 8

0	7	16	25	34	43
1	10	17	26	35	44
2	11	20	27	36	45
3	12	21	30	37	46
4	13	22	31	40	:
5	14	23	32	41	
6	15	24	33	42	

The next number after 77 is 100 in octal.

Comparing the decimal and octal schemes, notice that 5 (oct) is the same number as 5 (dec), but that 21 (oct) is not the same number as 21 (dec). Instead, 21 (oct) is the same number as 17 (dec). Numbers have a tendency to look larger than they actually are when written in octal.

But what if we only had 3 fingers instead of 10 or 8? The pattern is the same. Counting in base 3 looks like this:

0	21	112	210	1001	1022	*Counting in base 3*
1	22	120	211	1002	1100	
2	100	121	212	1010	1101	
10	101	122	220	1011	1102	
11	102	200	221	1012	⋮	
12	110	201	222	1020		
20	111	202	1000	1021		

Finally, we have arrived at unsigned binary representation. Computers have only two fingers. Counting in base 2 (*binary*, or *bin* for short) follows the exact same method as counting in octal and base 3:

0	111	1110	10101	11100	100011	*Counting in binary*
1	1000	1111	10110	11101	100100	
10	1001	10000	10111	11110	100101	
11	1010	10001	11000	11111	100110	
100	1011	10010	11001	100000	⋮	
101	1100	10011	11010	100001		
110	1101	10100	11011	100010		

Binary numbers look a lot larger than they actually are. The number 10110 (bin) is only 22 (dec).

Base Conversions

Given a number written in binary, there are several ways to determine its decimal equivalent. One way is to simply count up to the number in binary and in decimal. That method works well for small numbers. Another method is to add up the place values of each 1 bit in the binary number.

Example 3.1   **FIGURE 3.2(a)** shows the place values for 10110 (bin). Starting with the 1's place on the right (called the *least significant bit*), each place has a value twice as great as the previous place value. Figure 3.2(b) shows the addition that produces the 22 (dec) value.   ∎

Example 3.2   The unsigned binary number system is analogous to our familiar decimal system. **FIGURE 3.3** shows the place values for 58,036 (dec). The figure 58,036 represents six 1's, three 10's, no 100's, eight 1000's, and

FIGURE 3.2
Converting from binary to decimal.

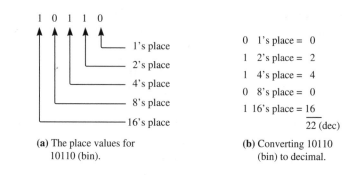

(a) The place values for 10110 (bin).

(b) Converting 10110 (bin) to decimal.

FIGURE 3.3
The place values for 58,036 (dec).

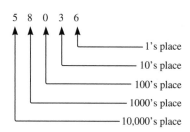

five 10,000's. Starting with the 1's place from the right, each place value is 10 times greater than the previous place value. In binary, each place value is 2 times greater than the previous place value. ∎

The value of an unsigned number can be conveniently represented as a polynomial in the base of the number system. (The base is also called the *radix* of the number system.) FIGURE 3.4 shows the polynomial representation of 10110 (bin) and 58,036 (dec). The value of the least significant place is

FIGURE 3.4
The polynomial representation of unsigned numbers.

$$1 \times 2^4 + 0 \times 2^3 + 1 \times 2^2 + 1 \times 2^1 + 0 \times 2^0$$

(a) The binary number 10110.

$$5 \times 10^4 + 8 \times 10^3 + 0 \times 10^2 + 3 \times 10^1 + 6 \times 10^0$$

(b) The decimal number 58,036.

always the base to the zeroth power, which is always 1. The next significant place is the base to the first power, which is the value of the base itself. You can see from the structure of the polynomial that the value of each place is the base times the value of the previous place.

In binary, the only place with an odd value is the 1's place. All the other places (2's, 4's, 8's, and so on) are even. If there is a 0 in the 1's place, the value of the binary number will come from adding several even numbers, and it therefore will be even. On the other hand, if there is a 1 in the 1's place of a binary number, its value will come from adding one to several even numbers, and it will be odd. As in the decimal system, you can tell whether a binary number is even or odd simply by inspecting the digit in the 1's place.

Determining the binary equivalent of a number written in decimal is a bit tricky. One method is to successively divide the original number by 2, keeping track of the remainders, which will form the binary number when listed in reverse order from how they were obtained.

Example 3.3 (FIGURE 3.5) converts 22 (dec) to binary. The number 22 divided by 2 is 11 with a remainder of 0, which is written in the right column. Then, 11 divided by 2 is 5, with a remainder of 1. Continuing until the number gets down to 0 produces a column of remainders, which, when read from the bottom up, form the binary number 10110. ∎

Notice that the least significant bit is the remainder when you divide the original value by 2. This fact is consistent with the observation that you can determine whether a binary number is even or odd by inspecting only the least significant bit. If the original value is even, the division will produce a remainder of 0, which will be the least significant bit. Conversely, if the original value is odd, the least significant bit will be 1.

Range for Unsigned Integers

All these counting schemes based on Arabic numerals let you represent arbitrarily large numbers. A real computer, however, has a finite number of bits in each cell. (FIGURE 3.6) shows how a seven-bit cell would store the number 22 (dec). Notice the two leading 0's, which do not affect the value of the number, but which are necessary for specifying the contents of the memory location. In dealing with a seven-bit cell, you should write the number without showing the boxes as

001 0110

The two leading 0's are still necessary. This text displays bit strings with a space (for legibility) between each group of four bits starting from the right.

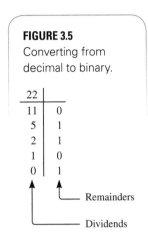

FIGURE 3.5
Converting from decimal to binary.

$$
\begin{array}{c|c}
22 & \\
11 & 0 \\
5 & 1 \\
2 & 1 \\
1 & 0 \\
0 & 1 \\
\end{array}
$$

Remainders

Dividends

FIGURE 3.6
The number 22 (dec) in a seven-bit cell.

0	0	1	0	1	1	0

The range of unsigned values depends on the number of bits in a cell. A sequence of all 0's represents the smallest unsigned value, and a sequence of all 1's represents the largest.

Example 3.4 The smallest unsigned integer a seven-bit cell can store is

    000 0000 (bin)

and the largest is

    111 1111 (bin)

The smallest is 0 (dec) and the largest is 127 (dec). A seven-bit cell cannot store an unsigned integer greater than 127.   ■

Unsigned Addition

Addition with unsigned binary numbers works like addition with unsigned decimal numbers. But it is easier because you only need to learn the addition rules for 2 bits instead of 10 digits. The rules for adding bits are

Binary addition rules

$$0 + 0 = \ \ 0$$
$$0 + 1 = \ \ 1$$
$$1 + 0 = \ \ 1$$
$$1 + 1 = 10$$

The carry technique in binary

The carry technique that you are familiar with in the decimal system also works in the binary system. If two numbers in a column add to a value greater than 1, you must carry 1 to the next column.

Example 3.5 Suppose you have a six-bit cell. To add the two numbers 01 1010 and 01 0001, simply write one number above the other and start at the least significant column:

```
          01 1010
   ADD    01 0001
          10 1011
```

Notice that when you get to the fifth column from the right, $1 + 1$ equals 10. You must write down the 0 and carry the 1 to the next column, where $1 + 0 + 0$ produces the leftmost 1 in the sum.

To verify that this carry technique works in binary, convert the two numbers and their sum to decimal:

    01 1010 (bin) = 26 (dec)
    01 0001 (bin) = 17 (dec)
    10 1011 (bin) = 43 (dec)

Sure enough, $26 + 17 = 43$ in decimal.   ■

Example 3.6   These examples show how the carry can propagate along several consecutive columns:

	00 0011			00 1111
ADD	01 0001		ADD	00 1001
	01 0100			01 1000

In the second example, when you get to the fourth column from the right, you have a carry from the previous column. Then $1 + 1 + 1$ equals 11. You must write down 1 and carry 1 to the next column. ∎

The Carry Bit

The range for the six-bit cell of the previous examples is 00 0000 to 11 1111 (bin), or 0 to 63 (dec). It is possible for two numbers to be in range but for their sum to be out of range. In that case, the sum is too large to fit into the six bits of the storage cell.

    To flag this condition, the CPU contains a special bit called the *carry bit*, denoted by the letter C. When two binary numbers are added, if the sum of the leftmost column (called the *most significant bit*) produces a carry, then C is set to 1. Otherwise C is cleared to 0. In other words, C always contains the carry from the leftmost column of the cell. In all the previous examples, the sum was in range. Hence the carry bit was cleared to 0.

The carry bit in addition

Example 3.7   Here are two examples showing the effect on the carry bit:

	01 0110			10 1010
ADD	10 0010		ADD	01 1010
C = 0	11 1000		C = 1	00 0100

In the second example, the CPU adds $42 + 26$. The correct result, which is 68, is too large to fit into the six-bit cell. Remember that the range is from 0 to 63. So the lowest order (that is, the rightmost) six bits are stored, giving an incorrect result of 4. The carry bit is also set to 1 to indicate that a carry occurred from the highest-order column. ∎

3.2 Two's Complement Binary Representation

The unsigned binary representation works for nonnegative integers only. If a computer is to process negative integers, it must use a different representation.

    Suppose you have a six-bit cell and you want to store the number −5 (dec). Because 5 (dec) is 101 (bin), you might try the pattern shown in **FIGURE 3.7** . But this is impossible because all bits, including the first, must

FIGURE 3.7
An attempt to store a negative number in binary.

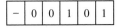

−	0	0	1	0	1

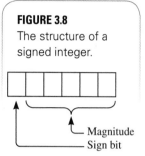

FIGURE 3.8
The structure of a
signed integer.

Magnitude
Sign bit

be 0 or 1. Remember that computers are binary. The above storage value
would require each box to be capable of storing a 0, or a 1, or a dash. Such a
computer would have to be ternary instead of binary.

The solution to this problem is to reserve the first box in the cell to
indicate the sign. Thus, the six-bit cell will have two parts—a one-bit sign
and a five-bit magnitude, as FIGURE 3.8 shows. Because the sign bit must
be 0 or 1, one possibility is to let a 0 sign bit indicate a positive number and
a 1 sign bit indicate a negative number. Then +5 could be represented as

> 00 0101

and −5 could be represented as

> 10 0101

In this code the magnitudes for +5 and −5 would be identical. Only the sign
bits would differ.

Few computers use the previous code, however. The problem is that if
you add +5 and −5 in decimal, you get 0, but if you add 00 0101 and 10 0101
in binary (sign bits and all), you get

$$
\begin{array}{r}
00\ 0101 \\
\underline{\text{ADD}\quad 10\ 0101} \\
\text{C} = 0\quad 10\ 1010
\end{array}
$$

A convenient property of
negative numbers

which is definitely not 0. It would be much more convenient if the hardware
of the CPU could add the numbers for +5 and −5, complete with sign bits
using the ordinary rules for unsigned binary addition, and get 0.

The *two's complement* binary representation has that property. The
positive numbers have a 0 sign bit and a magnitude as in the unsigned
binary representation. For example, the number +5 (dec) is still represented
as 00 0101.

But the representation of −5 (dec) is not 10 0101. Instead, it is 11 1011,
because adding +5 and −5 gives

$$
\begin{array}{r}
00\ 0101 \\
\underline{\text{ADD}\quad 11\ 1011} \\
\text{C} = 1\quad 00\ 0000
\end{array}
$$

Note that the six-bit sum is all 0's, as advertised.

The NEG operation

Under the rules of binary addition for a six-bit cell, the number 11 1011
is called the *additive inverse* of 00 0101. The operation of finding the additive
inverse is referred to as *negation*, abbreviated NEG. To negate a number is
also called *taking its two's complement*.

All we need now is the rule for taking the two's complement of a number.
A simple rule is based on the *ones' complement*, which is simply the binary

sequence with all the 1's changed to 0's and all the 0's changed to 1's. The ones' complement is also called the NOT operation.

The NOT operation

Example 3.8 The ones' complement of 00 0101 is

NOT 00 0101 = 11 1010

assuming a six-bit cell.

A clue to finding the rule for two's complement is to note the effect of adding a number to its ones' complement. Because 1 plus 0 is 1, and 0 plus 1 is 1, any number, when added to its ones' complement, will produce a sequence of all 1's. But then, adding a single 1 to a number of all 1's produces a number of all 0's.

Example 3.9 Adding 00 0101 to its ones' complement produces

$$
\begin{array}{rl}
 & 00\ 0101 \\
\text{ADD} & 11\ 1010 \\
\hline
C = 0 & 11\ 1111
\end{array}
$$

which is all 1's. Adding 1 to this produces

$$
\begin{array}{rl}
 & 11\ 1111 \\
\text{ADD} & 00\ 0001 \\
\hline
C = 1 & 00\ 0000
\end{array}
$$

which is all 0's.

In other words, adding a number to its ones' complement plus 1 gives all 0's. So the two's complement of a binary number must be found by adding 1 to its ones' complement.

Example 3.10 To find the two's complement of 00 0101, add 1 to its ones' complement.

NOT   00 0101 = 11 1010

$$
\begin{array}{rl}
 & 11\ 1010 \\
\text{ADD} & 00\ 0001 \\
\hline
 & 11\ 1011
\end{array}
$$

The two's complement of 00 0101 is therefore 11 1011. That is,

NEG 00 0101 = 11 1011

Recall that 11 1011 is indeed the negative of 00 0101 because they add to 0 as shown.

The general rule for negating a number regardless of how many bits the number contains is

The two's complement rule

> The two's complement of a number is 1 plus its ones' complement.

Or, in terms of the NEG and NOT operations,

> NEG x = 1 + NOT x

In our familiar decimal system, if you take the negative of a value that is already negative, you get a positive value. Algebraically,

$$-(-x) = x$$

where x is some positive value. If the rule for taking the two's complement is to be useful, the two's complement of a negative value should be the corresponding positive value.

Example 3.11   What happens if you take the two's complement of −5 (dec)?

$$\text{NOT}\quad 11\ 1011 = 00\ 0100$$

$$
\begin{array}{r}
00\ 0100 \\
\text{ADD}\quad 00\ 0001 \\
\hline
00\ 0101
\end{array}
$$

Voilà! You get +5 (dec) back again, as you would expect.   ∎

Two's Complement Range

Suppose you have a four-bit cell to store integers in two's complement representation. What is the range of integers for this cell?

The positive integer with the greatest magnitude is 0111 (bin), which is +7 (dec). It cannot be 1111 as in unsigned binary because the first bit is reserved for the sign and must be 0. In unsigned binary, you can store numbers as high as +15 (dec) with four bits. All four bits are used for the magnitude. In two's complement representation, you can store numbers only as high as +7 (dec), because only three bits are reserved for the magnitude.

What is the negative number with the greatest magnitude? The answer to this question might not be obvious. **FIGURE 3.9** shows the result of taking the two's complement of each positive number up to +7. What pattern do you see in the figure?

Notice that the two's complement operation automatically produces a 1 in the sign bit of the negative numbers, as it should. Even numbers still end in 0, and odd numbers end in 1.

Also, −5 is obtained from −6 by adding 1 to −6 in binary, as you would expect. Similarly, −6 is obtained from −7 by adding 1 to −7 in binary. We can squeeze one more negative integer out of our four bits by including −8.

FIGURE 3.9
The result of taking the two's complement in a four-bit cell.

Decimal	Binary
−7	1001
−6	1010
−5	1011
−4	1100
−3	1101
−2	1110
−1	1111

When you add 1 to −8 in binary, you get −7. The number −8 should therefore be represented as 1000. (**FIGURE 3.10**) shows the complete table for signed integers assuming a four-bit memory cell.

The number −8 (dec) has a peculiar property not shared by any of the other negative integers. If you take the two's complement of −7, you get +7, as follows:

NOT   1001 = 0110

        0110
ADD   0001
        0111

But if you take the two's complement of −8, you get −8 back again:

NOT   1000 = 0111

        0111
ADD   0001
        1000

This property exists because there is no way to represent +8 with only four bits.

We have determined the range of numbers for a four-bit cell with two's complement binary representation. It is

        1000 to 0111

as written in binary, or

        −8 to +7

as written in decimal.

The same patterns hold regardless of how many bits are contained in the cell. The largest positive integer is a single 0 followed by all 1's. The negative integer with the largest magnitude is a single 1 followed by all 0's. Its magnitude is 1 greater than the magnitude of the largest positive integer. The number −1 (dec) is represented as all 1's.

Example 3.12   The range for six-bit two's complement representation is

        10 0000 to 01 1111

as written in binary, or

        −32 to 31

as written in decimal. Unlike all the other negative integers, the two's complement of 10 0000 is itself, 10 0000. Also notice that −1 (dec) = 11 1111 (bin). ∎

FIGURE 3.10
The signed integers for a four-bit cell.

Decimal	Binary
−8	1000
−7	1001
−6	1010
−5	1011
−4	1100
−3	1101
−2	1110
−1	1111
0	0000
1	0001
2	0010
3	0011
4	0100
5	0101
6	0110
7	0111

Base Conversions

Converting from decimal to binary

To convert a negative number from decimal to binary is a two-step process. First, convert its magnitude from decimal to binary as in unsigned binary representation. Then negate it by taking the two's complement.

Example 3.13   How is −7 (dec) stored in a 10-bit cell? First, find the binary value of +7.

+7 (dec) = 00 0000 0111 (bin)

Then, take its two's complement.

NOT   00 0000 0111 = 11 1111 1000

$$
\begin{array}{r}
11\ 1111\ 1000 \\
\text{ADD}\quad 00\ 0000\ 0001 \\
\hline
11\ 1111\ 1001
\end{array}
$$

So −7 (dec) is 11 1111 1001 (bin).   ∎

Converting from binary to decimal

To convert a number from binary to decimal in a computer that uses two's complement representation, always check the sign bit first. If it is 0, the number is positive and you may convert, as in unsigned representation. If it is 1, the number is negative and you can choose one of two methods. One method is to make the number positive by negating it. Then convert to decimal as in unsigned representation.

Example 3.14   Say you have a 10-bit cell that contains 11 1101 1010. What decimal number does it represent? The sign bit is 1, so the number is negative. First negate the number:

NOT   11 1101 1010 = 00 0010 0101

$$
\begin{array}{r}
00\ 0010\ 0101 \\
\text{ADD}\quad 00\ 0000\ 0001 \\
\hline
00\ 0010\ 0110
\end{array}
$$

00 0010 0110 (bin) = 32 + 4 + 2 = 38 (dec)

So the original binary number must have been the negative of 38. That is,

11 1101 1010 (bin) = −38 (dec)   ∎

The other method is to convert directly without taking the two's complement. Simply add 1 to the sum of the place values of the 0's in the original binary number. This method works because the first step in taking

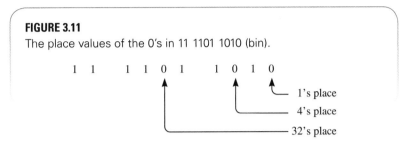

FIGURE 3.11
The place values of the 0's in 11 1101 1010 (bin).

the two's complement of a positive integer is to invert the bits. Those bits that were 1's, and thus contributed to the magnitude of the positive integer, become 0's. The 0's, not the 1's, of a negative integer contribute to its magnitude.

Example 3.15   FIGURE 3.11 shows the place values of the 0's in 11 1101 1010 (bin). Adding 1 to their sum gives

$$11\ 1101\ 1010\ (\text{bin}) = -(1 + 32 + 4 + 1) = -38\ (\text{dec})$$

which is the same result as with the previous method.   ∎

The Number Line

Another way of viewing binary representation is with the number line. FIGURE 3.12 shows the number line for a three-bit cell with unsigned binary representation. Eight numbers are represented.

You add by moving to the right on the number line. For example, to add 4 and 3, start with 4 and move three positions to the right to get 7. If you try to add 6 and 3 on the number line, you will fall off the right end. If you do it in binary, you will get an incorrect result because the answer is out of range:

```
          110
ADD       011
C = 1     001
```

The two's complement number line comes from the unsigned number line by breaking it between 3 and 4 and shifting the right part to the left side.

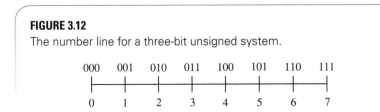

FIGURE 3.12
The number line for a three-bit unsigned system.

FIGURE 3.13

The number line for a three-bit two's complement system.

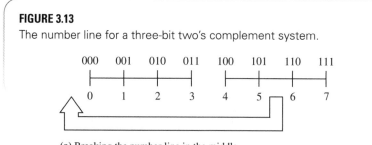

(a) Breaking the number line in the middle.

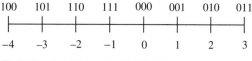

(b) Shifting the right part to the left side.

FIGURE 3.13 shows that the binary number 111 is now adjacent to 000, and what used to be +7 (dec) is now −1 (dec).

Addition is still performed by moving to the right on the number line, even if you pass through 0. To add −2 and 3, start with −2 and move three positions to the right to get 1. If you do it in binary, the answer is in range and correct:

$$
\begin{array}{r}
110 \\
\text{ADD}\quad 011 \\
\hline
\text{C}=1\quad 001
\end{array}
$$

These bits are identical to those for 6 + 3 in unsigned binary. Notice that the carry bit is 1, even though the answer is in range. With two's complement representation, the carry bit no longer indicates whether the result of the addition is in range.

Sometimes you can avoid the binary representation altogether by considering the shifted number line entirely in decimal. FIGURE 3.14 shows the two's complement number line with the binary number replaced by its

FIGURE 3.14

The two's complement number line with unsigned decimals.

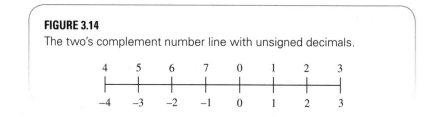

unsigned decimal equivalent. In this example, there are three bits in each memory location. Thus, there are 2^3, or 8, possible numbers.

Now the unsigned and signed numbers are the same from 0 up to 3. Furthermore, you can get the signed negative numbers from the unsigned numbers by subtracting 8:

$$7 - 8 = -1$$
$$6 - 8 = -2$$
$$5 - 8 = -3$$
$$4 - 8 = -4$$

Example 3.16 Suppose you have an eight-bit cell. There are 2^8, or 256, possible integer values. The nonnegative numbers go from 0 to 127. Assuming two's complement binary representation, what do you get if you add 97 and 45? In unsigned binary, the sum is

$$97 + 45 = 142 \text{ (dec, unsigned)}$$

But in two's complement binary, the sum is

$$142 - 256 = -114 \text{ (dec, signed)}$$

Notice that we get this result by avoiding the binary representation altogether. To verify the result, first convert 97 and 45 to binary and add:

$$97 \text{ (dec)} = 0110\ 0001 \text{ (bin)}$$
$$45 \text{ (dec)} = 0010\ 1101 \text{ (bin)}$$

```
        0110 0001
ADD     0010 1101
C = 0   1000 1110
```

This is a negative number because of the 1 in the sign bit. And now, to determine its magnitude:

$$\text{NEG } 1000\ 1110 = 0111\ 0010 \text{ (bin)}$$
$$= 114 \text{ (dec)}$$

This produces the expected result. ∎

The Overflow Bit

An important characteristic of binary storage at Level ISA3 is the absence of a type associated with a value. In the previous example, the sum 1000 1110, when interpreted as an unsigned number, is 142 (dec), but when interpreted in two's complement representation is −114 (dec). Although the value of the bit pattern depends on its type, whether unsigned or two's complement, the hardware makes no distinction between the two types. It stores only the bit pattern.

When the CPU adds the contents of two memory cells, it uses the rules for binary addition on the bit sequences, regardless of their types. In unsigned binary, if the sum is out of range, the hardware simply stores the (incorrect) result, sets the C bit accordingly, and goes on. It is up to the software to examine the C bit after the addition to see if a carry out occurred from the most significant column and to take appropriate action if necessary.

The C bit detects overflow for unsigned integers.

We noted above that in two's complement binary representation, the carry bit no longer indicates whether a sum is in range or out of range. An *overflow condition* occurs when the result of an operation is out of range. To flag this condition for signed numbers, the CPU contains another special bit called the *overflow bit*, denoted by the letter V. When the CPU adds two binary integers, if their sum is out of range when interpreted in the two's complement representation, then V is set to 1. Otherwise V is cleared to 0.

The V bit detects overflow for signed integers.

The CPU performs the same addition operation regardless of the interpretation of the bit pattern. As with the C bit, the CPU does not stop if a two's complement overflow occurs. It sets the V bit and continues with its next task. It is up to the software to examine the V bit after the addition.

Example 3.17   Here are some examples with a six-bit cell, showing the effects on the carry bit and on the overflow bit:

Adding two positives:		00 0011		01 0110
	ADD	01 0101	ADD	00 1100
	V = 0	01 1000	V = 1	10 0010
	C = 0		C = 0	

Adding a positive and a negative:		00 0101		00 1000
	ADD	11 0111	ADD	11 1010
	V = 0	11 1100	V = 0	00 0010
	C = 0		C = 1	

Adding two negatives:		11 1010		10 0110
	ADD	11 0111	ADD	10 0010
	V = 0	11 0001	V = 1	00 1000
	C = 1		C = 1	

Notice that all combinations of values are possible for V and C.   ∎

How can you tell if an overflow condition will occur? One way would be to convert the two numbers to decimal, add them, and see if their sum is outside the range as written in decimal. If so, an overflow has occurred.

The hardware detects an overflow by comparing the carry into the sign bit with the C bit. If they are different, an overflow has occurred, and V gets 1. If they are the same, V gets 0.

Instead of comparing the carry into the sign bit with C, you can tell directly by inspecting the signs of the numbers and the sum. If you add two positive numbers and get a negative sum, or if you add two negative numbers and get a positive sum, then an overflow occurred. It is not possible to get an overflow by adding a positive number and a negative number.

The Negative and Zero Bits

In addition to the C bit, which detects an overflow condition for unsigned integers, and the V bit, which detects an overflow condition for signed integers, the CPU maintains two other bits that the software can test after it performs an operation. They are the N bit, for detecting a negative result, and the Z bit, for detecting a zero result. In summary, the function of these four status bits is

> N = 1 if the result is negative.

  N = 0 otherwise.

> Z = 1 if the result is all zeros.

  Z = 0 otherwise.

> V = 1 if a signed integer overflow occurred.

  V = 0 otherwise.

> C = 1 if an unsigned integer overflow occurred.

  C = 0 otherwise.

The N bit is easy for the hardware to determine, as it is simply a copy of the sign bit. It takes a little more work for the hardware to determine the Z bit, because it must determine if every bit of the result is zero. Chapter 10 shows how the hardware computes the status bits from the result.

Example 3.18 Here are three examples of addition that show the effect of all four status bits on the result.

```
            01   0110              00   1000              00   1101
ADD    00   1100         ADD  11   1010        ADD   11   0011
N = 1  10   0010         N = 0 00   0010        N = 0 00   0000
Z = 0                    Z = 0                  Z = 1
V = 1                    V = 0                  V = 0
C = 0                    C = 1                  C = 1                  ∎
```

The default behavior for C and most other HOL6 languages is to ignore the V bit on integer overflow. (**FIGURE 3.15**) is a program that initializes n

FIGURE 3.15

An integer overflow in C.

```
#include <stdio.h>
#include <limits.h>

int main() {
    int n = INT_MAX - 2;
    for (int i = 0; i < 6; i++) {
        printf("n == %d\n", n);
        n++;
    }
    return 0;
}
```

Output
```
n == 2147483645
n == 2147483646
n == 2147483647
n == -2147483648
n == -2147483647
n == -2147483646
```

to two less than its maximum value, using INT_MAX from the limits.h library header file. It executes a loop six times, each time incrementing n by 1. The output is from execution on a computer that stores integers in 16-bit cells, making the two's complement range −2,147,483,648 to 2,147,483,647 as written in decimal or 1000 0000 0000 0000 to 0111 1111 1111 1111 as written in binary. When the program adds 1 to the maximum value, it sets C to 0 and V to 1. An overflow occurs, but the program keeps on executing, interpreting the incorrect sum of 1000 0000 0000 0000 as a negative number. Section 6.2 shows how to test the V bit at the Asmb5 level.

3.3 Operations in Binary

Because all information in a computer is stored in binary form, the CPU processes it with binary operations. The previous sections present the binary operations NOT, ADD, and NEG. NOT is a logical operator; ADD and NEG are arithmetic operators. This section describes some other logical and arithmetic operators that are available in the CPU of the computer.

FIGURE 3.16

The truth tables for the AND, OR, and XOR operators at Level ISA3.

p	q	p AND q
0	0	0
0	1	0
1	0	0
1	1	1

p	q	p OR q
0	0	0
0	1	1
1	0	1
1	1	1

p	q	p XOR q
0	0	0
0	1	1
1	0	1
1	1	0

(a) ISA3 table for AND.   **(b)** ISA3 table for OR.   **(c)** ISA3 table for XOR.

Logical Operators

You are familiar with the logical operations AND and OR. Another logical operator is the exclusive or, denoted XOR. The exclusive or of logical values p and q is true if p is true, or if q is true, but not both. That is, p must be true exclusive of q, or q must be true exclusive of p.

One interesting property of binary digits is that you can interpret them as logical quantities. At Level ISA3, a 1 bit can represent true, and a 0 bit can represent false. **FIGURE 3.16** shows the truth tables for the AND, OR, and XOR operators at Level ISA3.

At Level HOL6, AND and OR operate on Boolean expressions whose values are either true or false. They are used in if statements and loops to test conditions that control the execution of statements. An example of the AND operator is the C phrase

```
if ((ch >= 'a') && (ch <= 'z'))
```

FIGURE 3.17 shows the truth tables for AND, OR, and XOR at Level HOL6. They are identical to Figure 3.16, with 1 at Level ISA3 corresponding to true at Level HOL6, and 0 at Level ISA3 corresponding to false at Level HOL6.

Logical operations are easier to perform than addition because no carries are involved. The operation is applied bitwise to the corresponding bits in the sequence. Neither the carry bit nor the overflow bit is affected by logical operations.

Example 3.19 Some examples for a six-bit cell are

$$
\begin{array}{lll}
\quad\ 01\ 1010 & \quad\ 01\ 1010 & \quad\ 01\ 1010 \\
\text{AND}\ \ 01\ 0001 & \text{OR}\ \ \ 01\ 0001 & \text{XOR}\ \ 01\ 0001 \\
\hline
N = 0\ \ 01\ 0000 & N = 0\ \ 01\ 1011 & N = 0\ \ 00\ 1011 \\
Z = 0 & Z = 0 & Z = 0
\end{array}
$$

Note that when you take the AND of 1 and 1, the result is 1 with no carry. ∎

FIGURE 3.17
The truth tables for the AND, OR, and XOR operators at Level HOL6.

p	q	p AND q
true	true	true
true	false	false
false	true	false
false	false	false

(a) HOL6 table for AND.

p	q	p OR q
true	true	true
true	false	true
false	true	true
false	false	false

(b) HOL6 table for OR.

p	q	p XOR q
true	true	false
true	false	true
false	true	true
false	false	false

(c) HOL6 table for XOR.

Each of the operations AND, OR, and XOR combines two groups of bits to produce its result. But NOT and NEG operate on only a single group of bits. They are, therefore, called *unary operations*.

Register Transfer Language

The purpose of register transfer language (RTL) is to specify precisely the effect of a hardware operation. The RTL symbols might be familiar to you from your study of logic. FIGURE 3.18 shows the symbols.

The AND and OR operations are known as *conjunction* and *disjunction* in logic. The NOT operator is negation. The implies operator can be

FIGURE 3.18
The register transfer language operations and their symbols.

Operation	RTL Symbol
AND	∧
OR	∨
XOR	⊕
NOT	¬
Implies	⇒
Transfer	←
Bit index	⟨⟩
Informal description	{ }
Sequential separator	;
Concurrent separator	,

translated into English as "if/then." The transfer operator is the hardware equivalent of the assignment operator = in C. The memory cell on the left of the operator gets the quantity on the right of the operator. The bit index operator treats the memory cell as an array of bits starting with an index of 0 for the leftmost bit, the same way C indexes an array of elements. The braces enclose an informal English description when a more formal specification would not be helpful.

There are two separators. The sequential separator (semicolon) separates two actions that occur one after the other. The concurrent separator (comma) separates two actions that occur simultaneously.

Example 3.20 In the third computation of Example 3.19, suppose the first six-bit cell is denoted a, the second six-bit cell is denoted b, and the result is denoted c. An RTL specification of the exclusive OR operation is

$$c \leftarrow a \oplus b ; N \leftarrow c < 0 , Z \leftarrow c = 0$$

First, c gets the exclusive OR of a and b. After that action, two things happen simultaneously—N gets a Boolean value and Z gets a Boolean value. The Boolean expression $c < 0$ is 1 when c is less than zero and 0 when it is not. ∎

Arithmetic Operators

Two other unary operations are ASL, which stands for *arithmetic shift left*, and ASR, which stands for *arithmetic shift right*. As the name *ASL* implies, each bit in the cell shifts one place to the left. The bit that was on the leftmost end shifts into the carry bit. The rightmost bit gets 0. **FIGURE 3.19** shows the action of the ASL operation for a six-bit cell.

Example 3.21 Three examples of the arithmetic shift left operation are

    ASL 11 1100 = 11 1000,   N = 1, Z = 0, V = 0, C = 1
    ASL 00 0011 = 00 0110,   N = 0, Z = 0, V = 0, C = 0
    ASL 01 0110 = 10 1100,   N = 1, Z = 0, V = 1, C = 0   ∎

The operation is called an *arithmetic shift* because of the effect it has when the bits represent an integer. Assuming unsigned binary representation, the three integers in the previous example before the shift are

    60   3   22   (dec, unsigned)

After the shift, they are

    56   6   44   (dec, unsigned)

The effect of ASL is to double the number. ASL could not double the 60 because 120 is out of range for a six-bit unsigned integer. If the carry bit is 1

FIGURE 3.19
The action of the ASL operation for a six-bit cell.

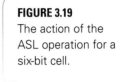

C

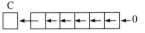

ASL doubles the number.

after the shift, an overflow has occurred when you interpret the binary sequence as an unsigned integer.

In the decimal system, a left shift produces the same effect, but the integer is multiplied by 10 instead of by 2. For example, a decimal ASL applied to 356 would give 3560, which is 10 times the original value.

What if you interpret the numbers in two's complement representation? Then the three integers before the shift are

$$-4 \quad 3 \quad 22 \qquad \text{(dec, signed)}$$

After the shift, they are

$$-8 \quad 6 \quad -20 \qquad \text{(dec, signed)}$$

Again, the effect of the ASL is to double the number, even if it is negative. This time ASL could not double the 22 because 44 is out of range when you assume two's complement representation. This overflow condition causes the V bit to be set to 1. The situation is similar to the ADD operation, where the C bit detects overflow of unsigned values, but the V bit is necessary to detect overflow of signed values.

The RTL specification for an arithmetic shift left on a six-bit cell r is

$$C \leftarrow r\langle 0 \rangle \,,\, r\langle 0..4 \rangle \leftarrow r\langle 1..5 \rangle \,,\, r\langle 5 \rangle \leftarrow 0\,;$$
$$N \leftarrow r < 0\,,\, Z \leftarrow r = 0\,,\, V \leftarrow \{\text{overflow}\}$$

Simultaneously, C gets the leftmost bit of r, the leftmost five bits of r get the values of the bits immediately to their right, and the last bit on the right gets 0. After the values are shifted, the N, Z, and V status bits are set according to the new values in r. It is important to distinguish between the semicolon, which separates two events (each of which has three parts), and the comma, which separates simultaneous events within the parts. The braces indicate less formally that the V bit is set according to whether the result overflowed when you interpret the value as a signed integer.

In the ASR operation, each bit in the group shifts one place to the right. The least significant bit shifts into the carry bit, and the most significant bit remains unchanged. **FIGURE 3.20** shows the action of the ASR operation for a six-bit cell. The ASR operation does not affect the V bit because an overflow is impossible when you divide a number by 2.

FIGURE 3.20

The action of the ASR operation for a six-bit cell.

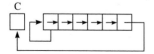

Example 3.22 Four examples of the arithmetic shift right operation are

$$\text{ASR } 01\ 0100 = 00\ 1010, \qquad N = 0, Z = 0, C = 0$$
$$\text{ASR } 01\ 0111 = 00\ 1011, \qquad N = 0, Z = 0, C = 1$$
$$\text{ASR } 11\ 0010 = 11\ 1001, \qquad N = 1, Z = 0, C = 0$$
$$\text{ASR } 11\ 0101 = 11\ 1010, \qquad N = 1, Z = 0, C = 1$$

The ASR operation is designed specifically for the two's complement representation. Because the sign bit does not change, negative numbers remain negative and positive numbers remain positive.

ASR halves the number.

Shifting to the left multiplies an integer by 2, whereas shifting to the right divides it by 2. Before the shift, the four integers in the previous example are

    20   23   −14   −11   (dec, signed)

After the shift, they are

    10   11   −7   −6   (dec, signed)

The even integers can be divided by 2 exactly, so there is no question about the effect of ASR on them. When odd integers are divided by 2, the result is always rounded down. For example, $23 \div 2 = 11.5$, and 11.5 rounded down is 11. Similarly, $-11 \div 2 = -5.5$, and −5.5 rounded down is −6. Note that −6 is less than −5.5 because it lies to the left of −5.5 on the number line.

Rotate Operators

In contrast to the arithmetic operators, the rotate operators do not interpret a binary sequence as an integer. Consequently, the rotate operations do not affect the N, Z, or V bits, but only the C bit. There are two rotate operators—rotate left, denoted ROL, and rotate right, denoted ROR. **FIGURE 3.21** shows the actions of the rotate operators for a six-bit cell. Rotate left is similar to arithmetic shift left, except that the C bit is rotated into the rightmost bit of the cell instead of 0 shifting into the rightmost bit. Rotate right does the same thing but in the opposite direction.

The RTL specification for a rotate left on a six-bit cell is

$$C \leftarrow r\langle 0 \rangle \,, r\langle 0 \,.\, .4 \rangle \leftarrow r\langle 1..5 \rangle \,, r\langle 5 \rangle \leftarrow C$$

Although the carry bit is the only status bit affected for the rotate left operation at Level ISA3, it affects the V bit at Level Mc2 (as discussed in Chapter 10).

FIGURE 3.21

The action of the rotate operators.

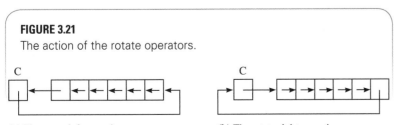

(a) The rotate left operation.   (b) The rotate right operation.

Example 3.23   Four examples of the rotate operation are

C = 1, ROL 01 1101 = 11 1011, C = 0
C = 0, ROL 01 1101 = 11 1010, C = 0
C = 1, ROR 01 1101 = 10 1110, C = 1
C = 0, ROR 01 1101 = 00 1110, C = 1

where the value of C before the rotate is on the left and the value of C after the rotate is on the right.   ∎

3.4 Hexadecimal and Character Representations

The binary representations in the previous sections are integer representations. This section deals with yet another number base, which will be used with the computer introduced in the next chapter. It also shows how that computer stores alphabetic information.

Hexadecimal

Suppose humans had 16 fingers instead of 10. What would have happened when Arabic numerals were invented? Remember the pattern. With 10 fingers, you start from 0 and keep inventing new symbols—1, 2, and so on until you get to your penultimate finger, 9. Then on your last finger you combine 1 and 0 to represent the next number, 10.

With 16 fingers, when you get to 9 you still have plenty of fingers left. You must go on inventing new symbols. These extra symbols are usually represented by the letters at the beginning of the English alphabet. So counting in base 16 (*hexadecimal*, or *hex* for short) looks like this:

Counting in hexadecimal

0	7	E	15	1C	23
1	8	F	16	1D	24
2	9	10	17	1E	25
3	A	11	18	1F	26
4	B	12	19	20	:
5	C	13	1A	21	
6	D	14	1B	22	

When the hexadecimal number contains many digits, counting can be a bit tricky. Consider counting the next five numbers in hexadecimal, starting with 8BE7, C9D, or 9FFE:

8BE7	C9D	9FFE
8BE8	C9E	9FFF
8BE9	C9F	A000
8BEA	CA0	A001
8BEB	CA1	A002
8BEC	CA2	A003

When written in octal, numbers have a tendency to look larger than they actually are. In hexadecimal, the effect is the opposite. Numbers have a tendency to look smaller than they actually are. Comparing the list of hexadecimal numbers with the list of decimal numbers shows that 18 (hex) is 24 (dec).

Base Conversions

In hexadecimal, each place value is 16 times greater than the previous place value. To convert from hexadecimal to decimal, simply multiply the place value by its digit and add.

Example 3.24 **FIGURE 3.22** shows how to convert 8BE7 from hexadecimal to decimal. The decimal value of B is 11, and the decimal value of E is 14. ▮

The procedure for converting from decimal to hexadecimal is analogous to the procedure for converting from decimal to binary. Instead of successively dividing the number by 2, you divide it by 16 and keep track of the remainders, which are the hexadecimal digits of the converted number.

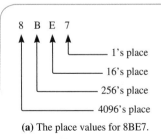

8 B E 7
- 1's place
- 16's place
- 256's place
- 4096's place

(a) The place values for 8BE7.

$$7 \times 1 = 7$$
$$14 \times 16 = 224$$
$$11 \times 256 = 2816$$
$$8 \times 4096 = 32{,}768$$
$$\overline{35{,}815}$$

(b) Converting 8BE7 to decimal.

FIGURE 3.22
Converting from hexadecimal to decimal.

FIGURE 3.23

The hexadecimal conversion chart.

	0	1	2	3	4	5	6	7	8	9	A	B	C	D	E	F
0_	0	1	2	3	4	5	6	7	8	9	10	11	12	13	14	15
1_	16	17	18	19	20	21	22	23	24	25	26	27	28	29	30	31
2_	32	33	34	35	36	37	38	39	40	41	42	43	44	45	46	47
3_	48	49	50	51	52	53	54	55	56	57	58	59	60	61	62	63
4_	64	65	66	67	68	69	70	71	72	73	74	75	76	77	78	79
5_	80	81	82	83	84	85	86	87	88	89	90	91	92	93	94	95
6_	96	97	98	99	100	101	102	103	104	105	106	107	108	109	110	111
7_	112	113	114	115	116	117	118	119	120	121	122	123	124	125	126	127
8_	128	129	130	131	132	133	134	135	136	137	138	139	140	141	142	143
9_	144	145	146	147	148	149	150	151	152	153	154	155	156	157	158	159
A_	160	161	162	163	164	165	166	167	168	169	170	171	172	173	174	175
B_	176	177	178	179	180	181	182	183	184	185	186	187	188	189	190	191
C_	192	193	194	195	196	197	198	199	200	201	202	203	204	205	206	207
D_	208	209	210	211	212	213	214	215	216	217	218	219	220	221	222	223
E_	224	225	226	227	228	229	230	231	232	233	234	235	236	237	238	239
F_	240	241	242	243	244	245	246	247	248	249	250	251	252	253	254	255

For numbers up to 255 (dec) or FF (hex), converting either way is easily done with the table in FIGURE 3.23. The body of the table contains decimal numbers. The left column and top row contain hexadecimal digits.

Example 3.25   To convert 9C (hex) to decimal, look up row 9 and column C to find 156 (dec). To convert 125 (dec), look it up in the body of the table and read off 7D (hex) from the left column and top row.   ■

If computers store information in binary format, why learn the hexadecimal system? The answer lies in the special relationship between hexadecimal and binary, as FIGURE 3.24 shows. There are 16 possible combinations of four bits, and there are exactly 16 hexadecimal digits. Each hexadecimal digit, therefore, represents four bits.

Hexadecimal as a shorthand for binary

Bit patterns are often written in hexadecimal notation to save space on the printed page. A computer manual for a 16-bit machine might state that a memory location contains 01D3. That is shorter than saying it contains 0000 0001 1101 0011.

To convert from unsigned binary to hexadecimal, partition the bits into groups of four starting from the rightmost end, and use the hexadecimal from Figure 3.23 for each group. To convert from hexadecimal to unsigned binary, simply reverse the procedure.

Example 3.26 To write the 10-bit unsigned binary number 10 1001 1100 in hexadecimal, start with the rightmost four bits, 1100:

10 1001 1100 (bin) = 29C (hex)

Because 10 bits cannot be partitioned into groups of four exactly, you must assume two additional leading 0's when looking up the leftmost digit in Figure 3.23. The leftmost hexadecimal digit comes from

10 (bin) = 0010 (bin) = 2 (hex)

in this example.   ∎

Example 3.27 For a 14-bit cell,

0D60 (hex) = 00 1101 0110 0000 (bin)

Note that the last hexadecimal 0 represents four binary 0's, but the first hexadecimal 0 represents only two binary 0's.   ∎

To convert from decimal to unsigned binary, you may prefer to use the hexadecimal table as an intermediate step. You can avoid any computation by looking up the hexadecimal value in Figure 3.22 and then converting each digit to binary according to Figure 3.23.

Example 3.28 For a six-bit cell,

29 (dec) = 1D (hex) = 01 1101 (bin)

where each step in the conversion is a simple table lookup.   ∎

In machine language program listings or program traces, numbers are rarely written in hexadecimal notation with negative signs. Instead, the sign bit is implicit in the bit pattern represented by the hexadecimal digits. You must remember that hexadecimal is only a convenient shorthand for a binary sequence. The hardware stores only binary values.

Example 3.29 If a 10-bit memory location contains 37A (hex), then the number in decimal is found by considering the following bit pattern:

37A (hex) = 11 0111 1010 (bin)

FIGURE 3.24
The relationship between hexadecimal and binary.

Hexadecimal	Binary
0	0000
1	0001
2	0010
3	0011
4	0100
5	0101
6	0110
7	0111
8	1000
9	1001
A	1010
B	1011
C	1100
D	1101
E	1110
F	1111

The sign bit is 1, so the number is negative. Converting to decimal gives

$$37A \text{ (hex)} = -134 \text{ (dec)}$$

Notice that the hexadecimal number is not written with a negative sign, even though it may be interpreted as a negative number. ∎

ASCII Characters

ASCII

Because computer memories are binary, alphabetic characters must be coded to be stored in memory. A widespread binary code for alphabetic characters is the *American Standard Code for Information Interchange*, also known as *ASCII* (pronounced *askey*).

ASCII contains all the uppercase and lowercase English letters, the 10 numeric digits, and special characters such as punctuation signs. Some of its symbols are nonprintable and are used mainly to transmit information between computers or to control peripheral devices.

ASCII is a seven-bit code. Because there are $2^7 = 128$ possible combinations of seven bits, there are 128 ASCII characters. **FIGURE 3.25** shows all these characters. The first column of the table shows the nonprintable characters, whose meanings are listed at the bottom. The rest of the table lists the printable characters.

Example 3.30 The sequence 000 0111, which stands for *bell*, causes a terminal to beep. Two other examples of nonprintable characters are *ACK* for *acknowledge* and *NAK* for *negative acknowledge*, which are used by some data transmission protocols. If the sender sends a packet of information over the channel that is detected error-free, the receiver sends an ACK back to the sender, which then sends the next packet. If the receiver detects an error, it sends a NAK back to the sender, which then resends the packet that was damaged in the initial transmission. ∎

Example 3.31 The name

　　Tom

would be stored in ASCII as

　　　101 0100
　　　110 1111
　　　110 1101

If that sequence of bits were sent to an output terminal, the word "Tom" would be displayed. ∎

FIGURE 3.25

The American Standard Code for Information Interchange (ASCII).

Char	Bin	Hex	Char	Bin	Hex	Char	Bin	Hex	Char	Bin	Hex
NUL	000 0000	00	SP	010 0000	20	@	100 0000	40	`	110 0000	60
SOH	000 0001	01	!	010 0001	21	A	100 0001	41	a	110 0001	61
STX	000 0010	02	"	010 0010	22	B	100 0010	42	b	110 0010	62
ETX	000 0011	03	#	010 0011	23	C	100 0011	43	c	110 0011	63
EOT	000 0100	04	$	010 0100	24	D	100 0100	44	d	110 0100	64
ENQ	000 0101	05	%	010 0101	25	E	100 0101	45	e	110 0101	65
ACK	000 0110	06	&	010 0110	26	F	100 0110	46	f	110 0110	66
BEL	000 0111	07	'	010 0111	27	G	100 0111	47	g	110 0111	67
BS	000 1000	08	(	010 1000	28	H	100 1000	48	h	110 1000	68
HT	000 1001	09	)	010 1001	29	I	100 1001	49	i	110 1001	69
LF	000 1010	0A	*	010 1010	2A	J	100 1010	4A	j	110 1010	6A
VT	000 1011	0B	+	010 1011	2B	K	100 1011	4B	k	110 1011	6B
FF	000 1100	0C	,	010 1100	2C	L	100 1100	4C	l	110 1100	6C
CR	000 1101	0D	–	010 1101	2D	M	100 1101	4D	m	110 1101	6D
SO	000 1110	0E	.	010 1110	2E	N	100 1110	4E	n	110 1110	6E
SI	000 1111	0F	/	010 1111	2F	O	100 1111	4F	o	110 1111	6F
DLE	001 0000	10	0	011 0000	30	P	101 0000	50	p	111 0000	70
DC1	001 0001	11	1	011 0001	31	Q	101 0001	51	q	111 0001	71
DC2	001 0010	12	2	011 0010	32	R	101 0010	52	r	111 0010	72
DC3	001 0011	13	3	011 0011	33	S	101 0011	53	s	111 0011	73
DC4	001 0100	14	4	011 0100	34	T	101 0100	54	t	111 0100	74
NAK	001 0101	15	5	011 0101	35	U	101 0101	55	u	111 0101	75
SYN	001 0110	16	6	011 0110	36	V	101 0110	56	v	111 0110	76
ETB	001 0111	17	7	011 0111	37	W	101 0111	57	w	111 0111	77
CAN	001 1000	18	8	011 1000	38	X	101 1000	58	x	111 1000	78
EM	001 1001	19	9	011 1001	39	Y	101 1001	59	y	111 1001	79
SUB	001 1010	1A	:	011 1010	3A	Z	101 1010	5A	z	111 1010	7A
ESC	001 1011	1B	;	011 1011	3B	[	101 1011	5B	{	111 1011	7B
FS	001 1100	1C	<	011 1100	3C	\	101 1100	5C	|	111 1100	7C
GS	001 1101	1D	=	011 1101	3D	]	101 1101	5D	}	111 1101	7D
RS	001 1110	1E	>	011 1110	3E	^	101 1110	5E	~	111 1110	7E
US	001 1111	1F	?	011 1111	3F	_	101 1111	5F	DEL	111 1111	7F

Abbreviations for Control Characters

NUL	null, or all zeros	**FF**	form feed	**CAN**	cancel
SOH	start of heading	**CR**	carriage return	**EM**	end of medium
STX	start of text	**SO**	shift out	**SUB**	substitute
ETX	end of text	**SI**	shift in	**ESC**	escape
EOT	end of transmission	**DLE**	data link escape	**FS**	file separator
ENQ	enquiry	**DC1**	device control 1	**GS**	group separator
ACK	acknowledge	**DC2**	device control 2	**RS**	record separator
BEL	bell	**DC3**	device control 3	**US**	unit separator
BS	backspace	**DC4**	device control 4	**SP**	space
HT	horizontal tabulation	**NAK**	negative acknowledge	**DEL**	delete
LF	line feed	**SYN**	synchronous idle		
VT	vertical tabulation	**ETB**	end of transmission block		

Example 3.32   The street address

```
52 Elm
```

would be stored in ASCII as

```
011 0101
011 0010
010 0000
100 0101
110 1100
110 1101
```

The blank space between 2 and E is a separate ASCII character.   ∎

The End of the Line

The ASCII standard was developed in the early 1960s and was intended for use on teleprinter machines of that era. A popular device that used the ASCII code was the Teletype Model 33, a mechanical printer with a continuous roll of paper that wrapped around a cylindrical carriage similar to a typewriter. The teleprinter received a stream of ASCII characters over a telephone line and printed the characters on paper.

The nonprintable characters are also known as *control characters* because they were originally used to control the mechanical aspects of a teleprinter. In particular, the ASCII LF control character stands for *line feed*. When the teleprinter received the LF character, it would rotate the carriage enough to advance the paper by one line. Another control character, CR, which stands for *carriage return*, would move the print head to the leftmost position of the page. Because these two mechanical operations were necessary to make the printer mechanism start at the beginning of a new line, the convention was to always use CR-LF to mark the beginning of a new line in a message that was to be sent to a teleprinter.

When early computer companies, notably Digital Equipment Corporation, adopted the ASCII code, they kept this CR-LF convention to denote the end of a line of text. It was convenient because many of those early machines used teleprinters as output devices. The convention was picked up by IBM and Microsoft when they developed the PC DOS and MS-DOS operating systems. MS-DOS eventually became Microsoft Windows, and the CR-LF convention has stuck to this day, despite the disappearance of the old teleprinter for which it was necessary.

Multics was an early operating system that was the forerunner of Unix. To simplify storage and processing of textual data, it adopted the convention of using only the LF character to denote the end of a line. This convention was picked up by Unix and continued by Linux, and is also the convention for OS X because it is Unix.

Figure 2.13 is a C program that reads a stream of characters from the input device and outputs the same stream of characters but substitutes the newline character, denoted \n in the string, for each space. The newline character corresponds to the ASCII LF control character. The program in Figure 2.13 works even if you run it in a Windows environment. The C standard specifies that if you output the \n character in a `printf()` string, the system will convert it to the convention for the operating system on which you are executing the program. In a Windows system, the \n character is converted to two characters, CR-LF, in the output stream. In a Unix system, it remains LF. If you ever need to process the CR character explicitly in a C program, you can write it as \r.

Unicode Characters

The first electronic computers were developed to perform mathematical calculations with numbers. Eventually, they processed textual data as well, and the ASCII code became a widespread standard for processing text with the Latin alphabet. As computer technology spread around the world, text processing in languages with different alphabets produced many incompatible systems. The Unicode Consortium was established to collect and catalog all the alphabets of all the spoken languages in the world, both current and ancient, as a first step toward a standard system for the worldwide interchange, processing, and display of texts in these natural languages.

Strictly speaking, the standard organizes characters into scripts, not languages. It is possible for one script to be used in multiple languages. For example, the extended Latin script can be used for many European and American languages. Version 7.0 of the Unicode standard has 123 scripts for natural language and 15 scripts for other symbols. Examples of natural language scripts are Balinese, Cherokee, Egyptian Hieroglyphs, Greek, Phoenician, and Thai. Examples of scripts for other symbols are Braille Patterns, Emoticons, Mathematical Symbols, and Musical Symbols.

Each character in every script has a unique identifying number, usually written in hexadecimal, and is called a *code point*. The hexadecimal number is preceded by "U+" to indicate that it is a Unicode code point. Corresponding to a code point is a *glyph*, which is the graphic representation of the symbol on the page or screen. For example, in the Hebrew script, the code point U+05D1 has the glyph ב.

FIGURE 3.26 shows some example code points and glyphs in the Unicode standard. The CJK Unified script is for the written languages of China, Japan,

Unicode Script	Code Point	Glyphs							
		0	1	2	3	4	5	6	7
Arabic	U+063_	ذ	ر	ز	س	ش	ص	ض	ط
Armenian	U+054_	Ձ	Ղ	Ճ	Մ	Յ	Ն	Շ	Ո
Braille Patterns	U+287_	⡀	⡁	⡂	⡃	⡄	⡅	⡆	⡇
CJK Unified	U+4EB_	京	佫	亲	亳	亵	裃	亶	廉
Cyrillic	U+041_	А	Б	В	Г	Д	Е	Ж	З
Egyptian Hieroglyphs	U+1300_	𓀀	𓀁	𓀂	𓀃	𓀄	𓀅	𓀆	𓀇
Emoticons	U+1F61_	😐	😑	😒	😓	😔	😕	😖	😗
Hebrew	U+05D_	א	ב	ג	ד	ה	ו	ז	ח
Basic Latin (ASCII)	U+004_	@	A	B	C	D	E	F	G
Latin-1 Supplement	U+00E_	à	á	â	ã	ä	å	æ	ç

FIGURE 3.26

A few code points and glyphs from the Unicode character set.

and Korea, which share a common character set with some variations. There are tens of thousands of characters in these Asian writing systems, all based on a common set of Han characters. To minimize unnecessary duplication, the Unicode Consortium merged the characters into a single set of unified characters. This Han unification is an ongoing process carried out by a group of experts from the Chinese-speaking countries, North and South Korea, Japan, Vietnam, and other countries.

Code points are backward compatible with ASCII. For example, from the ASCII table in Figure 3.25, the Latin letter S is stored with seven bits as 101 0011 (bin), which is 53 (hex). So, the Unicode code point for S is U+0053. The standard requires at least four hex digits following U+, padding the number with leading zeros if necessary.

A single code point can have more than one glyph. For example, an Arabic letter may be displayed with different glyphs depending on its position in a word. On the other hand, a single glyph might be used to represent two code points. The consecutive Latin code points U+0066 and U+0069 for f and i are frequently rendered with the ligature glyph fi.

The range of the Unicode code space is 0 to 10FFFF (hex), or 0 to 1 0000 1111 1111 1111 1111 (bin), or 0 to 1,114,111 (dec). About one-fourth of these million-plus code points have been assigned. Some values are reserved for private use, and each Unicode standard revision assigns a few more values to code points. It is theoretically possible to represent each code point with a single 21-bit number. Because computer memory is normally organized into eight-bit bytes, it would be possible to use three bytes to store each code point with the leading three bits unused.

However, most computers process information in chunks of either 32 bits (4 bytes) or 64 bits (8 bytes). It follows that the most effective method for processing textual information is to store each code point in a 32-bit cell, even though the leading 11 bits would be unused and always set to zeros. This method of encoding is called *UTF-32*, where *UTF* stands for *Unicode Transformation Format*. UTF-32 always requires eight hexadecimal characters to represent its four bytes.

Example 3.33 To determine how the letter z is stored in UTF-32, look up its value in the ASCII table as 7A (hex). Because Unicode code points are backward compatible with ASCII, the code point for the letter z is U+007A. The UTF-32 encoding in binary is obtained by prefixing zeros for a total of 32 bits as follows:

0000 0000 0000 0000 0000 0000 0111 1010

So, U+007A is encoded as 0000 007A (UTF-32).

Example 3.34 To determine the UTF-32 encoding of the emoticon ☺ with code point U+1F617, simply prefix the correct number of zeros. The encoding is 0001 F617 (UTF-32). ∎

Although UTF-32 is effective for processing textual information, it is inefficient for storing and transmitting textual information. If you have a file that stores mostly ASCII characters, three-fourths of the file space will be occupied by zeros. UTF-8 is a popular encoding standard that is able to represent every Unicode character. It uses one to four bytes to store a single character and therefore takes less storage space than UTF-32. The 64 Ki code points in the range U+0000 to U+FFFF, known as the *Basic Multilingual Plane*, contain characters for almost all modern languages. UTF-8 can represent each of these code points with one to three bytes and uses only a single byte for an ASCII character.

FIGURE 3.27 shows the UTF-8 encoding scheme. The first column, labeled *Bits*, represents the upper limit of the number of bits in the code point, excluding all leading zeros. The x's in the code represent the rightmost bits from the code point, which are spread out over one to four bytes.

The first row in the table corresponds to the ASCII characters, which have an upper limit of seven bits. An ASCII character is stored as a single byte whose first bit is 0 and whose last seven bits are identical to seven-bit ASCII. The first step in decoding a UTF-8 string is to inspect the first bit of the first byte. If it is zero, the first character is an ASCII character, which can be determined from the ASCII table, and the following byte is the first byte of the next character.

If the first bit of the first byte is 1, the first character is outside the range U+0000 to U+007F—that is, it is not an ASCII character, and it occupies more than one byte. In this case, the number of leading 1's in the first byte

FIGURE 3.27
The UTF-8 encoding scheme.

Bits	First Code Point	Last Code Point	Byte 1	Byte 2	Byte 3	Byte 4
7	U+0000	U+007F	0xxxxxxx			
11	U+0080	U+07FF	110xxxxx	10xxxxxx		
16	U+0800	U+FFFF	1110xxxx	10xxxxxx	10xxxxxx	
21	U+10000	U+1FFFFF	11110xxx	10xxxxxx	10xxxxxx	10xxxxxx

is equal to the total number of bytes occupied by the character. Some of the bits from the code point are stored in the first byte and some are stored in the remaining continuation bytes. Every continuation byte begins with the string 10 and stores six bits from the code point.

Example 3.35   To determine the UTF-8 encoding of the emoticon ☺ with code point U+1F617, first determine the upper limit of the number of bits in the code point. From Figure 3.27, it is in the range U+10000 to U+1FFFF; thus, the rightmost 21 bits from the code point are spread out over 4 bytes. The rightmost 21 bits from 1F617 (hex) are

   0 0001 1111 0110 0001 0111

where enough leading zeros are added to total 21 bits. The last row in Figure 3.27 shows the first three bits stored in Byte 1, the next six stored in Byte 2, the next six stored in Byte 3, and the last six stored in Byte 4. Regrouping the 21 bits accordingly yields

   000 011111 011000 010111

The format of Byte 1 from the table is 11110xxx, so insert the first three zeros in place of the x's to yield 11110000, and do the same for Bytes 3 and 4. The resulting bit pattern of the four bytes is

   11110000 10011111 10011000 10010111

So, U+1F617 is encoded as F09F 9897 (UTF-8), which is different from the four bytes of the UTF-32 encoding in Example 3.34.   ∎

Example 3.36   To determine the sequence of code points from the UTF-8 byte sequence 70 C3 A6 6F 6E, first write the byte sequence in binary as

   01110000 11000011 10100110 01101111 01101110

You can immediately determine that the first, fourth, and fifth bytes are ASCII characters because the leading bit is zero in those bytes. From the ASCII table, these bytes correspond to the letters p, o, and n, respectively. The leading 110 in the second byte indicates that 11 bits are spread out over 2 bytes per the second row in the body of the table in Figure 3.27. The leading 10 in the third byte is consistent, because that prefix denotes a continuation byte. Extracting the rightmost 5 bits from the second byte (first byte of the pair) and the rightmost 6 bytes from the third byte (second byte of the pair) yields the 11 bits:

   00011 100110

Prefixing this pattern with leading zeros and regrouping yields

   0000 0000 1110 0110

which is the code point U+00E6 corresponding to Unicode character æ. So, the original five-byte sequence is a UTF-8 encoding of the four code points U+0070, U+00E6, U+006F, U+006E and represents the string "pæon". ∎

Figure 3.27 shows that UTF-8 does not allow all possible bit patterns. For example, it is illegal to have the bit pattern

11100011 01000001

in a UTF-8–encoded file because the 1110 prefix of the first byte indicates that it is the first byte of a three-byte sequence, but the leading zero of the second byte indicates that it is a single ASCII character and not a continuation byte. If such a pattern is detected in a UTF-8–encoded file, the data is corrupted.

A major benefit of UTF-8 is its self-synchronization property. A decoder can uniquely identify the type of any byte in the sequence by inspection of the prefix bits. For example, if the first two bits are 10, it is a continuation byte. Or, if the first four bits are 1110, it is the first byte of a three-byte sequence. This self-synchronization property makes it possible for a UTF-8 decoder to recover most of the text when data corruption does occur.

UTF-8 is by far the most common encoding standard on the World Wide Web. It has become the default standard for multilingual applications. Operating systems are incorporating UTF-8 so that documents and files can be named in the user's native language. Modern programming languages such as Python and Swift have UTF-8 built in so a programmer can, for example, name a variable pæon or even ☺☺. Text editors that have traditionally processed only pure ASCII text, as opposed to word processors that have always been format friendly, are increasingly able to process UTF-8–encoded text files.

3.5 Floating-Point Representation

The numeric representations described in previous sections of this chapter are for integer values. C has three numeric types that have fractional parts:

- ❭ float — single-precision floating point
- ❭ double — double-precision floating point
- ❭ long double — extended-precision floating point

Values of these types cannot be stored at Level ISA3 with two's complement binary representation because provisions must be made for locating the decimal point within the number. Floating-point values are stored using a binary version of scientific notation.

Binary Fractions

Binary fractions have a binary point, which is the base 2 version of the base 10 decimal point.

Example 3.37 **FIGURE 3.28(a)** shows the place values for 101.011 (bin). The bits to the left of the binary point have the same place values as the corresponding bits in unsigned binary representation, as in Figure 3.2. Starting with the 1/2's place to the right of the binary point, each place has a value one-half as great as the previous place value. Figure 3.28(b) shows the addition that produces the 5.375 (dec) value. ∎

FIGURE 3.29 shows the polynomial representation of numbers with fractional parts. The value of the bit to the left of the radix point is always the base to the zeroth power, which is always 1. The next significant place to the left is the base to the first power, which is the value of the base itself. The value of the bit to the right of the radix point is the base to the power −1. The next significant place to the right is the base to the power −2. The value of each place to the right is 1/base times the value of the place on its left.

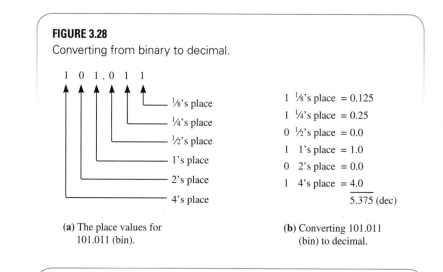

FIGURE 3.28
Converting from binary to decimal.

1 0 1 . 0 1 1

⅛'s place
¼'s place
½'s place
1's place
2's place
4's place

1 ⅛'s place = 0.125
1 ¼'s place = 0.25
0 ½'s place = 0.0
1 1's place = 1.0
0 2's place = 0.0
1 4's place = 4.0
                 5.375 (dec)

(a) The place values for 101.011 (bin).

(b) Converting 101.011 (bin) to decimal.

FIGURE 3.29
The polynomial representation of floating-point numbers.

$$1 \times 2^2 + 0 \times 2^1 + 1 \times 2^0 + 0 \times 2^{-1} + 1 \times 2^{-2} + 1 \times 2^{-3}$$

(a) The binary number 101.011.

$$5 \times 10^2 + 0 \times 10^1 + 6 \times 10^0 + 7 \times 10^{-1} + 2 \times 10^{-2} + 1 \times 10^{-3}$$

(b) The decimal number 506.721.

Determining the decimal value of a binary fraction requires two steps. First, convert the bits to the left of the binary point using the technique of Example 3.3 for converting unsigned binary values. Then, use the algorithm of successive doubling to convert the bits to the right of the binary point.

Example 3.38   **FIGURE 3.30** shows the conversion of 6.5859375 (dec) to binary. The conversion of the whole part gives 110 (bin) to the left of the binary point. To convert the fractional part, write the digits to the right of the decimal point in the heading of the right column of the table. Double the fractional part, writing the digit to the left of the decimal point in the column on the left and the fractional part in the column on the right. The next time you double, do not include the whole number part. For example, the value 0.34375 comes from doubling 0.171875, not from doubling 1.171875. The digits on the left from top to bottom are the bits of the binary fractional part from left to right. So, 6.5859375 (dec) = 110.1001011 (bin). ∎

The algorithm for converting the fractional part from decimal to binary is the mirror image of the algorithm for converting the whole part, from decimal to binary. Figure 3.5 shows that to convert the whole part, you use the algorithm of successive division by two. The bits you generate are the remainders of the division, and you generate them from right to left starting at the binary point. To convert the fractional part, you use the algorithm of successive multiplication by two. The bits you generate are the whole part of the multiplication, and you generate them from left to right starting at the binary point.

A number that can be represented with a finite number of digits in decimal may require an endless representation in binary.

Example 3.39   **FIGURE 3.31** shows the conversion of 0.2 (dec) to binary. The first doubling produces 0.4. A few more doublings produce 0.4 again. It is clear that the process will never terminate and that 0.2 (dec) = 0.001100110011 ... (bin) with the bit pattern 0011 endlessly repeating. ∎

Because all computer cells can store only a finite number of bits, the value 0.2 (dec) cannot be stored exactly and must be approximated. You should realize that if you add 0.2 + 0.2 in a Level HOL6 language like C, you will probably not get 0.4 exactly because of the roundoff error inherent in the binary representation of the values. For that reason, good numeric software rarely tests two floating point numbers for strict equality. Instead, the software maintains a small but nonzero tolerance that represents how close two floating point values must be to be considered equal. If the tolerance is, say, 0.0001, then the numbers 1.38264 and 1.38267 would be

FIGURE 3.30
Converting from decimal to binary.

6.5859375

↑

6 (dec) = 110 (bin)
(a) Convert the whole part.

	.5859375
1	.171875
0	.34375
0	.6875
1	.375
0	.75
1	.5
1	.0

(b) Convert the fractional part.

FIGURE 3.31
A decimal value with an unending binary representation.

	.2
0	.4
0	.8
1	.6
1	.2
0	.4
0	.8
1	.6
⋮	⋮

considered equal because their difference, which is 0.00003, is less than the tolerance.

Excess Representations

Floating-point numbers are represented with a binary version of the scientific notation common with decimal numbers. A nonzero number is *normalized* if it is written in scientific notation with the first nonzero digit immediately to the left of the radix point. The number zero cannot be normalized because it does not have a first nonzero digit.

Example 3.40   The decimal number -328.4 is written in normalized form in scientific notation as -3.284×10^2. The effect of the exponent 2 as the power of 10 is to shift the decimal point two places to the right. Similarly, the binary number -10101.101 is written in normalized form in scientific notation as -1.0101101×2^4. The effect of the exponent 4 as the power of 2 is to shift the binary point four places to the right. ▪

Example 3.41   The binary number 0.00101101 is written in normalized form in scientific notation as 1.01101×2^{-3}. The effect of the exponent -3 as the power of 2 is to shift the binary point three places to the left. ▪

In general, a floating point number can be positive or negative, and its exponent can be a positive or negative integer. FIGURE 3.32 shows a cell in memory that stores a floating point value. The cell is divided into three fields. The first field stores one bit for the sign of the number. The second field stores the bits representing the exponent of the normalized binary number. The third field, called the *significand*, stores bits that represent the magnitude of the value.

The more bits stored in the exponent, the wider the range of floating point values. The more bits stored in the significand, the higher the precision of the representation. A common representation is an 8-bit cell for the exponent and a 23-bit cell for the significand. To present the concepts of the floating point format, the examples in this section use a 3-bit cell for the exponent and a 4-bit cell for the significand. These are unrealistically tiny cell sizes, but they help to illustrate the format without an unwieldy number of bits.

Any signed representation for integers could be used to store the exponent. You might think that two's complement binary representation would be used, because that is the representation that most computers use to store signed integers. However, two's complement is not used. Instead, a biased representation is used for a reason that will be explained later.

FIGURE 3.32
Storage for a floating-point value.

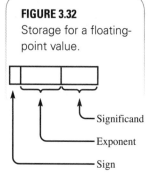

— Significand

— Exponent

— Sign

An example of a biased representation for a five-bit cell is excess 15. The range of numbers for the cell is −15 to 16 as written in decimal and 00000 to 11111 as written in binary. To convert from decimal to excess 15, you add 15 to the decimal value and then convert to binary as you would an unsigned number. To convert from excess 15 to decimal, you write the decimal value as if it were an unsigned number and subtract 15 from it. In excess 15, the first bit denotes whether a value is positive or negative. But unlike two's complement representation, 1 signifies a positive value, and 0 signifies a negative value.

Example 3.42   For a five-bit cell, to convert 5 from decimal to excess 15, add 5 + 15 = 20. Then convert 20 to binary as if it were unsigned, 20 (dec) = 10100 (bin). Therefore, 5 (dec) = 10100 (excess 15). The first bit is 1, indicating a positive value.   ∎

Example 3.43   To convert 00011 from excess 15 to decimal, convert 00011 as an unsigned value, 00011 (bin) = 3 (dec). Then subtract decimal values 3 − 15 = −12. So, 00011 (excess 15) = −12 (dec).   ∎

FIGURE 3.33 shows the bit patterns for a three-bit cell that stores integers with excess 3 representation compared to two's complement representation. Each representation stores eight values. The excess 3 representation has a range of −3 to 4 (dec), while the two's complement representation has a range of −4 to 3 (dec).

Decimal	Excess 3	Two's Complement
−4		100
−3	000	101
−2	001	110
−1	010	111
0	011	000
1	100	001
2	101	010
3	110	011
4	111	

FIGURE 3.33
The signed integers for a three-bit cell.

The Hidden Bit

Figure 3.32 shows one bit reserved for the sign of the number but no bit reserved for the binary point. A bit for the binary point is unnecessary because numbers are stored normalized, so the system can assume that the first 1 is to the left of the binary point. Furthermore, because there will always be a 1 to the left of the binary point, there is no need to store the leading 1 at all. To store a decimal value, first convert it to binary, write it in normalized scientific notation, store the exponent in excess representation, drop the leading 1, and store the remaining bits of the magnitude in the significand. The bit that is assumed to be to the left of the binary point but that is not stored explicitly is called the *hidden bit*.

Example 3.44   Assuming a three-bit exponent using excess 3 and a four-bit significand, how is the number 3.375 stored? Converting the whole number part gives 3 (dec) = 11 (bin). Converting the fractional part gives 0.375 (dec) = 0.011. The complete binary number is 3.375 (dec) = 11.011 (bin), which is 1.1011×2^1 in normalized binary scientific notation. The number is positive, so the sign bit is 0. The exponent is 1 (dec) = 100 (excess 3) from Figure 3.33. Dropping the leading 1, the four bits to the right of the binary point are .1011. So, 3.375 is stored as 0100 1011.   ∎

Of course, the hidden bit is assumed, not ignored. When you read a decimal floating point value from memory, the compiler assumes that the hidden bit is not stored. It generates code to insert the hidden bit before it performs any computation with the full number of bits. The floating point hardware even adds a few extra bits of precision called *guard digits* that it carries throughout the computation. After the computation, the system discards the guard digits and the assumed hidden bit and stores as many bits to the right of the binary point as the significand will hold.

Not storing the leading 1 allows for greater precision. In the previous example, the bits for the magnitude are 1.1011. Using a hidden bit, you drop the leading 1 and store .1011 in the four-bit significand. In a representation without a hidden bit, you would store the most significant bits, 1.011, in the four-bit significand and be forced to discard the least significant 0.0001 value. The result would be a value that only approximates the decimal value 3.375.

Because every memory cell has a finite number of bits, approximations are unavoidable even with a hidden bit. The system approximates by rounding off the least significant bits it must discard using a rule called "round to nearest, ties to even." **FIGURE 3.34** shows how the rule works for decimal and binary numbers. You round off 23.499 to 23 because 23.499 is closer to 23 than it is to 24. Similarly, 23.501 is closer to 24 than it is to 23. However, 23.5 is just as close to 23 as it is to 24, which is a tie. It rounds to 24 because 24

FIGURE 3.34
Round to nearest, ties to even.

Decimal	Decimal Rounded	Binary	Binary Rounded
23.499	23	1011.011	1011
23.5	24	1011.1	1100
23.501	24	1011.101	1100
24.499	24	1100.011	1100
24.5	24	1100.1	1100
24.501	25	1100.101	1101

is even. Similarly, the binary number 1011.1 is just as close to 1011 as it is to 1100, which is a tie. It rounds to 1100 because 1100 is even.

Example 3.45   Assuming a three-bit exponent using excess 3 and a four-bit significand, how is the number -13.75 stored? Converting the whole number part gives 13 (dec) = 1101 (bin). Converting the fractional part gives 0.75 (dec) = 0.11. The complete binary number is 13.75 (dec) = 1101.11 (bin), which is 1.10111×2^3 in normalized binary scientific notation. The number is negative, so the sign bit is 1. The exponent is 3 (dec) = 110 (excess 3). Dropping the leading 1, the five bits to the right of the binary point are .10111. However, only four bits can be stored in the significand. Furthermore, .10111 is just as close to .1011 as it is to .1100, and the tie rule is in effect. Because 1011 is odd and 1100 is even, round to .1100. So, -13.75 is stored as 1110 1100. ∎

Special Values

Some real values require special treatment. The most obvious is zero, which cannot be normalized because there is no 1 bit in its binary representation. You must set aside a special bit pattern for zero. Standard practice is to put all 0's in the exponent field and all 0's in the significand as well. What do you put for the sign? Most common is to have two representations for zero, one positive and one negative. For a three-bit exponent and four-bit significand, the bit patterns are

$$1\ 000\ 0000\ (\text{bin}) = -0.0\ (\text{dec})$$
$$0\ 000\ 0000\ (\text{bin}) = +0.0\ (\text{dec})$$

This solution for storing zero has ramifications for some other bit patterns. If the bit pattern for $+0.0$ were not special, then 0 000 0000 would be interpreted with the hidden bit as 1.0000×2^{-3} (bin) = 0.125, the smallest positive value that could be stored had the value not been reserved for zero. If this pattern is reserved for zero, then the smallest positive value that can be stored is

$$0\ 000\ 0001 = 1.0001 \times 2^{-3} \text{ (bin)} = 0.1328125$$

which is slightly larger. The negative number with the smallest possible magnitude is identical but with a 1 in the sign bit. The largest positive number that can be stored is the bit pattern with the largest exponent and the largest significand. The bit pattern for the largest value is

$$0\ 111\ 1111 \text{ (bin)} = +31.0 \text{ (dec)}$$

 FIGURE 3.35 shows the number line for the representation where zero is the only special value. As with integer representations, there is a limit to how large a value you can store. If you try to multiply 9.5 times 12.0, both of which are in range, the true value is 114.0, which is in the positive overflow region.

Unlike integer values, however, the real number line has an underflow region. If you try to multiply 0.145 times 0.145, which are both in range, the true value is 0.021025, which is in the positive underflow region. The smallest positive value that can be stored is 0.132815.

Numeric calculations with approximate floating point values need to have results that are consistent with what would be expected when calculations are done with exact precision. For example, suppose you multiply 9.5 and 12.0. What should be stored for the result? Suppose you store the largest possible value, 31.0, as an approximation. Suppose further that this is an intermediate value in a longer computation. If you later need to compute half of the result, you will get 15.5, which is far from what the correct value would have been.

FIGURE 3.35
The real number line with zero as the only special value.

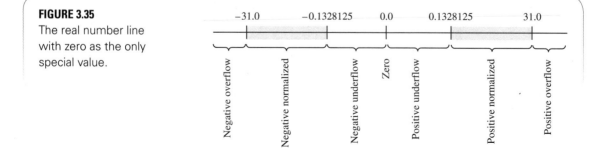

FIGURE 3.36
The special values
in floating-point
representation.

Special Value	Exponent	Significand
Zero	All zeros	All zeros
Denormalized	All zeros	Nonzero
Infinity	All ones	All zeros
Not a number	All ones	Nonzero

The same problem occurs in the underflow region. If you store 0.0 as an approximation of 0.021025, and you later want to multiply the value by 12.0, you will get 0.0. You risk being misled by what appears to be a reasonable value.

The problems encountered with overflow and underflow are alleviated somewhat by introducing more special values for the bit patterns. As is the case with zero, you must use some bit patterns that would otherwise be used to represent other values on the number line. In addition to zero, three special values are common—infinity, not a number (NaN), and denormalized numbers. **FIGURE 3.36** lists the four special values for floating-point representation and their bit patterns.

Infinity

Infinity is used for values that are in the overflow regions. If the result of an operation overflows, the bit pattern for infinity is stored. If further operations are done on this bit pattern, the result is what you would expect for an infinite value. For example, $3/\infty = 0$, $5 + \infty = \infty$, and the square root of infinity is infinity. You can produce infinity by dividing by 0. For example, $3/0 = \infty$, and $-4/0 = -\infty$. If you ever do a computation with real numbers and get infinity, you know that an overflow occurred somewhere in your intermediate results.

Not a number

A bit pattern for a value that is not a number is called a *NaN* (rhymes with *plan*). NaNs are used to indicate floating point operations that are illegal. For example, taking the square root of a negative number produces NaN, and so does dividing 0/0. Any floating point operation with at least one NaN operand produces NaN. For example, $7 + \text{NaN} = \text{NaN}$, and $7/\text{NaN} = \text{NaN}$.

Both infinity and NaN use the largest possible value of the exponent for their bit patterns. That is, the exponent field is all 1's. The significand is all 0's for infinity and can be any nonzero pattern for NaN. Reserving these bit patterns for infinity and NaN has the effect of reducing the range of values that can be stored. For a three-bit exponent and four-bit significand, the bit patterns for the largest magnitudes and their decimal values are

1 111 0000 (bin) $= -\infty$
1 110 1111 (bin) $= -15.5$ (dec)
0 110 1111 (bin) $= +15.5$ (dec)
0 111 0000 (bin) $= +\infty$

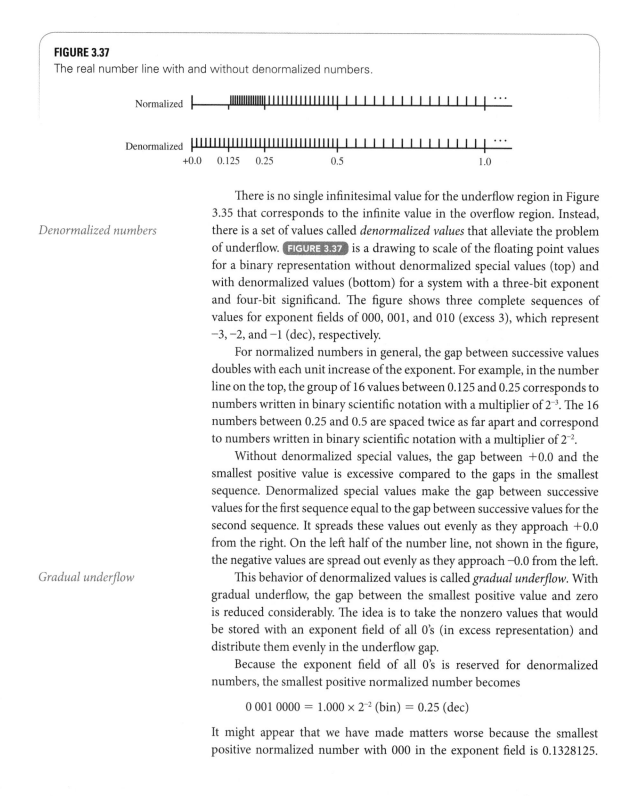

FIGURE 3.37

The real number line with and without denormalized numbers.

Denormalized numbers

There is no single infinitesimal value for the underflow region in Figure 3.35 that corresponds to the infinite value in the overflow region. Instead, there is a set of values called *denormalized values* that alleviate the problem of underflow. **FIGURE 3.37** is a drawing to scale of the floating point values for a binary representation without denormalized special values (top) and with denormalized values (bottom) for a system with a three-bit exponent and four-bit significand. The figure shows three complete sequences of values for exponent fields of 000, 001, and 010 (excess 3), which represent −3, −2, and −1 (dec), respectively.

For normalized numbers in general, the gap between successive values doubles with each unit increase of the exponent. For example, in the number line on the top, the group of 16 values between 0.125 and 0.25 corresponds to numbers written in binary scientific notation with a multiplier of 2^{-3}. The 16 numbers between 0.25 and 0.5 are spaced twice as far apart and correspond to numbers written in binary scientific notation with a multiplier of 2^{-2}.

Without denormalized special values, the gap between +0.0 and the smallest positive value is excessive compared to the gaps in the smallest sequence. Denormalized special values make the gap between successive values for the first sequence equal to the gap between successive values for the second sequence. It spreads these values out evenly as they approach +0.0 from the right. On the left half of the number line, not shown in the figure, the negative values are spread out evenly as they approach −0.0 from the left.

Gradual underflow

This behavior of denormalized values is called *gradual underflow*. With gradual underflow, the gap between the smallest positive value and zero is reduced considerably. The idea is to take the nonzero values that would be stored with an exponent field of all 0's (in excess representation) and distribute them evenly in the underflow gap.

Because the exponent field of all 0's is reserved for denormalized numbers, the smallest positive normalized number becomes

$$0\ 001\ 0000 = 1.000 \times 2^{-2} \text{ (bin)} = 0.25 \text{ (dec)}$$

It might appear that we have made matters worse because the smallest positive normalized number with 000 in the exponent field is 0.1328125.

But, the denormalized values are spread throughout the gap in such a way as to actually reduce it.

When the exponent field is all 0's and the significand contains at least one 1, special rules apply to the representation. Assuming a three-bit exponent and a four-bit significand,

> ❯ The hidden bit to the left of the binary point is assumed to be 0 instead of 1.

> ❯ The exponent is assumed to be stored in excess 2 instead of excess 3.

Representation rules for denormalized numbers

Example 3.46 For a representation with a three-bit exponent and four-bit significand, what decimal value is represented by 0 000 0110? Because the exponent is all 0's and the significand contains at least one 1, the number is denormalized. Its exponent is 000 (excess 2) = 0 − 2 = −2 (dec), and its hidden bit is 0, so its binary scientific notation is 0.0110×2^{-2}. The exponent is in excess 2 instead of excess 3 because this is the special case of a denormalized number. Converting to decimal yields 0.09375.   ∎

To see how much better the underflow gap is, compute the values having the smallest possible magnitudes, which are denormalized.

1 000 0001 (bin) = −0.015625 (dec)
1 000 0000 (bin) = −0.0
0 000 0000 (bin) = +0.0
0 000 0001 (bin) = +0.015625 (dec)

Without denormalized numbers, the smallest positive number is 0.1328125, so the gap has been reduced considerably.

FIGURE 3.38 shows some of the key values for a three-bit exponent and a four-bit significand using all four special values. The values are listed in numeric order from smallest to largest. The figure shows why an excess representation is common for floating point exponents. Consider all the positive numbers from +0.0 to +∞, ignoring the sign bit. You can see that if you treat the rightmost seven bits to be a simple unsigned integer, the successive values increase by one all the way from 000 0000 for 0 (dec) to 111 0000 for ∞. To do a comparison of two positive floating point values, say in a C statement like

```
if (x < y)
```

the computer does not need to extract the exponent field or insert the hidden bit. It can simply compare the rightmost seven bits as if they represented an integer to determine which floating point value has the larger magnitude. The circuitry for integer operations is considerably faster than that for

FIGURE 3.38
Floating-point values for a three-bit exponent and four-bit significand.

	Binary	Scientific Notation	Decimal
Not a number	1 111 nonzero		
Negative infinity	1 111 0000		$-\infty$
Negative normalized	1 110 1111	-1.1111×2^3	-15.5
	1 110 1110	-1.1110×2^3	-15.0
	. . .	. . .	. . .
	1 011 0001	-1.0001×2^0	-1.0625
	1 011 0000	-1.0000×2^0	-1.0
	1 010 1111	-1.1111×2^{-1}	-0.96875
	. . .	. . .	. . .
	1 001 0001	-1.0001×2^{-2}	-0.265625
	1 001 0000	-1.0000×2^{-2}	-0.25
Negative denormalized	1 000 1111	-0.1111×2^{-2}	-0.234375
	1 000 1110	-0.1110×2^{-2}	-0.21875
	. . .	. . .	. . .
	1 000 0010	-0.0010×2^{-2}	-0.03125
	1 000 0001	-0.0001×2^{-2}	-0.015625
Negative zero	1 000 0000		-0.0
Positive zero	0 000 0000		$+0.0$
Positive denormalized	0 000 0001	0.0001×2^{-2}	0.015625
	0 000 0010	0.0010×2^{-2}	0.03125
	. . .	. . .	. . .
	0 000 1110	0.1110×2^{-2}	0.21875
	0 000 1111	0.1111×2^{-2}	0.234375
Positive normalized	0 001 0000	1.0000×2^{-2}	0.25
	0 001 0001	1.0001×2^{-2}	0.265625
	. . .	. . .	. . .
	0 010 1111	1.1111×2^{-1}	0.96875
	0 011 0000	1.0000×2^0	1.0
	0 011 0001	1.0001×2^0	1.0625
	. . .	. . .	. . .
	0 110 1110	1.1110×2^3	15.0
	0 110 1111	1.1111×2^3	15.5
Positive infinity	0 111 0000		$+\infty$
Not a number	0 111 nonzero		

floating point operations, so using an excess representation for the exponent really improves performance.

The same pattern occurs for the negative numbers. The rightmost seven bits can be treated like an unsigned integer to compare magnitudes of the negative quantities. Floating-point quantities would not have this property if the exponents were stored using two's complement representation.

Figure 3.38 shows that -0.0 and $+0.0$ are distinct. At this low level of abstraction, negative zero is stored differently from positive zero. However, programmers at a higher level of abstraction expect the set of real number values to have only one zero, which is neither positive nor negative. For example, if the value of x has been computed as -0.0 vand y as $+0.0$, then the programmer should expect x to have the value 0 and y to have the value 0, and the expression $(x < y)$ to be false. Computers must be programmed to return false in this special case, even though the bit patterns indicate that x is negative and y is positive. The system hides the fact that there are two representations of zero at a low level of abstraction from the programmer at a higher level of abstraction.

With denormalization, to convert from decimal to binary you must first check if a decimal value is in the denormalized range to determine its representation. From Figure 3.38, for a three-bit exponent and a four-bit significand, the smallest positive normalized value is 0.25. Any value less than 0.25 is stored with the denormalized format.

Example 3.47   For a representation with a three-bit exponent and four-bit significand, how is the decimal value -0.078 stored? Because 0.078 is less than 0.25, the representation is denormalized, the exponent is all zeros, and the hidden bit is 0. Converting to binary, 0.078 (dec) $= 0.000100111\ldots$. Because the exponent is all zeros and the exponent is stored in excess 2 representation, the multiplier must be 2^{-2}. In binary scientific notation with a multiplier of 2^{-2}, $0.000100111\ldots = 0.0100111\ldots \times 2^{-2}$. As expected, the digit to the left of the binary point is 0, which is the hidden bit. The bits to be stored in the significand are the first four bits of $.0100111\ldots$, which rounds off to $.0101$. So the floating point representation for -0.078 is 1000 0101.   ∎

The IEEE 754 Floating-Point Standard

The Institute of Electrical and Electronic Engineers, Inc. (IEEE), is a professional society supported by its members that provides services in various engineering fields, one of which is computer engineering. The society has various groups that propose standards for the industry. Before the IEEE proposed its standard for floating point numbers, every computer manufacturer designed its own representation for floating point values, and they all differed from each other. In the early days before networks became prevalent and little data was shared between computers, this arrangement was tolerated.

Even without the widespread sharing of data, however, the lack of a standard hindered research and development in numerical computations. It was possible for two identical programs to run on two separate machines with the same input and produce different results because of the different approximations of the representations.

The IEEE set up a committee to propose a floating point standard, which it did in 1985. There are two standards: number 854, which is more applicable to handheld calculators than to other computing devices, and number 754, which was widely adopted for computers. The standard was revised with little change in 2008. Virtually every computer manufacturer now provides floating point numbers for their computers that conform to the IEEE 754 standard.

The floating point representation described earlier in this section is identical to the IEEE 754 standard except for the number of bits in the exponent field and in the significand. (**FIGURE 3.39**) shows the two formats for the standard. The single-precision format has an 8-bit cell for the exponent using excess 127 representation (except for denormalized numbers, which use excess 126) and 23 bits for the significand. It corresponds to C type `float`. The double-precision format has an 11-bit cell for the exponent using excess 1023 representation (except for denormalized numbers, which use excess 1022) and a 52-bit cell for the significand. It corresponds to C type double.

The single-precision format has the following bit values. Positive infinity is

> 0 1111 1111 000 0000 0000 0000 0000 0000

The hexadecimal abbreviation for the full 32-bit pattern arranges the bits into groups of four as

> 0111 1111 1000 0000 0000 0000 0000 0000

FIGURE 3.39

The IEEE 754 floating-point standard.

Bits 1   8   23

(a) Single precision.

Bits 1   11   52

(b) Double precision.

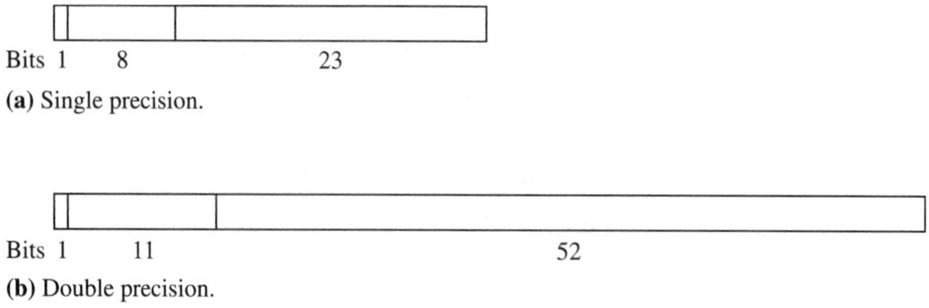

which is written 7F80 0000 (hex). The largest positive value is

    0 1111 1110 111 1111 1111 1111 1111 1111

or 7F7F FFFF (hex). It is exactly $2^{128} - 2^{104}$, which is approximately 2^{128} or 3.4×10^{38}. The smallest positive normalized number is

    0 0000 0001 000 0000 0000 0000 0000 0000

or 0080 0000 (hex). It is exactly 2^{-126}, which is approximately 1.2×10^{-38}. The smallest positive denormalized number is

    0 0000 0000 000 0000 0000 0000 0000 0001

or 0000 0001 (hex). It is exactly 2^{-149}, which is approximately 1.4×10^{-45}.

Example 3.48   What is the hexadecimal representation of −47.25 in single-precision floating point? The integer 47 (dec) = 101111 (bin), and the fraction 0.25 (dec) = 0.01 (bin). So, 47.25 (dec) = 101111.01 = 1.0111101×2^5. The number is negative, so the first bit is 1. The exponent 5 is converted to excess 127 by adding 5 + 127 = 132 (dec) = 1000 0100 (excess 127). The significand stores the bits to the right of the binary point, 0111101. So, the bit pattern is

    1 1000 0100 011 1101 0000 0000 0000 0000

which is C23D 0000 (hex).   ∎

Example 3.49   What is the number, as written in binary scientific notation, whose hexadecimal representation is 3CC8 0000? The bit pattern is

    0 0111 1001 100 1000 0000 0000 0000 0000

The sign bit is zero, so the number is positive. The exponent is 0111 1001 (excess 127) = 121 (unsigned) = 121 − 127 = −6 (dec). From the significand, the bits to the right of the binary point are 1001. The hidden bit is 1, so the number is 1.1001×2^{-6}.   ∎

Example 3.50   What is the number, as written in binary scientific notation, whose hexadecimal representation is 0050 0000? The bit pattern is

    0 0000 0000 101 0000 0000 0000 0000 0000

The sign bit is 0, so the number is positive. The exponent field is all 0's, so the number is denormalized. The exponent is 0000 0000 (excess 126) = 0 (unsigned) = 0 − 126 = −126 (dec). The hidden bit is 0 instead of 1, so the number is 0.101×2^{-126}.   ∎

The double-precision format has both wider range and greater precision because of the larger exponent and significand fields. The largest double value is approximately 2^{1023}, or 1.8×10^{308}. The smallest positive normalized number is approximately 2.2×10^{-308}, and the smallest denormalized number is approximately 4.9×10^{-324}.

Figure 3.37, which shows the denormalized special values, applies to IEEE 754 values with a few modifications. For single precision, the exponent field has eight bits. Thus, the three sequences in the top figure correspond to multipliers of 2^{-127}, 2^{-126}, and 2^{-125}. Because the significand has 23 bits, each of the three sequences has $2^{23} = 8,388,608$ values instead of 16 values. It is still the case that the spacing between successive values in each sequence is double the spacing between successive values in the preceding sequence.

For double precision, the exponent field has 11 bits. So, the three sequences in the top figure correspond to multipliers of 2^{-1023}, 2^{-1022}, and 2^{-1021}. Because the significand has 52 bits, each of the three sequences has $2^{52} = 4,503,599,627,370,496$ values instead of 16 values. With denormalization, each of the 4.5 quadrillion values in the left group are spread out evenly as they approach $+0.0$ from the right.

3.6 Models

A model is a simplified representation of some physical system. Workers in every scientific discipline, including computer science, construct models and investigate their properties. Consider some models of the solar system that astronomers have constructed and investigated.

Aristotle, who lived in Greece about 350 BC, proposed a model in which the earth was at the center of the universe. Surrounding the earth were 55 celestial spheres. The sun, moon, planets, and stars were each carried around the heavens on one of these spheres.

How well did this model match reality? It was successful in explaining the appearance of the sky, which looks like the top half of a sphere. It was also successful in explaining the approximate motion of the planets. Aristotle's model was accepted as accurate for hundreds of years.

Then in 1543 the Polish astronomer Copernicus published *De Revolutionibus*. In it he modeled the solar system with the sun at the center. The planets revolved around the sun in circles. This model was a better approximation to the physical system than the earth-centered model.

In the latter part of the 16th century, the Danish astronomer Tycho Brahe made a series of precise astronomical observations that showed a discrepancy in Copernicus's model. Then in 1609 Johannes Kepler proposed a model in which the earth and all the planets revolved around the sun not in circles, but in flattened circles called *ellipses*. This model was successful in explaining in detail the intricate motion of the planets as observed by Tycho Brahe.

Each of these models is a simplified representation of the solar system. None of the models is a completely accurate description of the real physical world. We know now, in light of Einstein's theories of relativity, that even Kepler's model is an approximation. No model is perfect. Every model is an approximation to the real world.

When information is represented in a computer's memory, that representation is only a model as well. Just as each model of the solar system describes some aspects of the underlying real system more accurately than other aspects, so does a representation scheme describe some property of the information more accurately than other properties.

Models as approximations of reality

For example, one property of positive integers is that there is an infinite number of them. No matter how large an integer you write down, someone else can always write down a larger integer. The unsigned binary representation in a computer does not describe that property very accurately. There is a limit to the size of the integer when stored in memory.

You may be aware that

$$\sqrt{2} = 1.4142135\ldots$$

The digits go on forever, never repeating. The representation scheme for storing real numbers is a model that only approximates numbers such as the square root of 2. It cannot represent the square root of 2 exactly. Any time a computer solves a problem, approximations are always involved because of limitations in the models.

All sorts of physical systems are commonly modeled with computers—inventories, molecules, accounting systems, and biological population systems, to name a few. In computer science, it is often the computer itself that is modeled.

Modeling the computer itself

The only physically real part of the computer is at Level LG1. Ultimately, a computer is just a complicated, organized mass of circuits and electrical signals. At Level ISA3, the high signals are modeled as 1's and the low signals as 0's. The programmer at Level ISA3 does not need to know anything about electrical circuits and signals to work with his model. Remember that at Level ISA3, the 1's and 0's represent the word Tom as

```
101 0100
110 1111
110 1101
```

The programmer at Level HOL6 does not need to know anything about bits to work with his model. In fact, programming the computer at any level requires only a knowledge of the model of the computer at that level.

A programmer at Level HOL6 can model the computer as a C machine. This model accepts C programs and uses them to process data. When the programmer instructs the machine to

```
printf("Tom");
```

he need not be concerned with how the computer is modeled as a binary machine at Level ISA3. Similarly, when a programmer at Level ISA3 writes a sequence of bits, he need not be concerned with how the computer is modeled as a combination of circuits at Level LG1.

This modeling of computer systems at successively higher levels is an idea that is not unique to computer science. Consider a large corporation with six divisions throughout the country. The president's model of the corporation is six divisions, with a vice president of each division reporting to him. He views the overall performance of the company in terms of the performance of each of the divisions. When he tells the vice president of the Widget Division to increase earnings, he does not need to be concerned with the vice president's model of the Widget Division. Likewise, when the vice president goes to each department manager within the Widget Division with an order, she does not need to be concerned with the department manager's model of his department. To have the president himself deal with the organization at the department level would be just about impossible. There are simply too many details at the department level of the entire corporation for one person to manage.

The computer user at Level App7 is like the president. He gives an instruction such as "compute the grade point average of all the sophomores" to a program originally written by a programmer at Level HOL6. He need not be concerned with the Level HOL6 model to issue the instruction. Eventually this command at Level App7 is transformed through successively lower levels to Level LG1. The end result is that the user at Level App7 can control the mass of electrical circuitry and signals with a very simplified model of the computer.

Chapter Summary

A binary quantity is restricted to one of two values. At the machine level, computers store information in binary. A bit is a binary digit whose value can be either 0 or 1. Nonnegative integers use unsigned binary representation. The rightmost bit is in the 1's place, the next bit to the left is in the 2's place, the next bit to the left is in the 4's place, and so on, with each place value double the preceding place value. Signed integers use two's complement binary representation in which the first bit is the sign bit and the remaining bits determine the magnitude. For positive numbers, the two's complement representation is identical to the unsigned representation. For negative numbers, however, the two's complement of a number is obtained by taking 1 plus the ones' complement of the corresponding positive number.

Every binary integer, signed or unsigned, has a range that is determined by the number of bits in the memory cell. The smaller the number of bits in the cell, the more limited the range. The carry bit, C, is used to flag an out-of-range condition for an unsigned integer, and the overflow bit, V, is used to flag an out-of-range condition for an integer in two's complement representation. Operations on binary integers include ADD, AND, OR, XOR, and NOT. ASL, which stands for *arithmetic shift left*, multiplies a binary value by 2, and ASR, which stands for *arithmetic shift right*, divides a binary value by 2.

The hexadecimal number system, which is a base 16 system, provides a compact notation for expressing bit patterns. The 16 hexadecimal digits are 0, 1, 2, 3, 4, 5, 6, 7, 8, 9, A, B, C, D, E, and F. One hexadecimal digit represents four bits. The American Standard Code for Information Interchange, abbreviated ASCII, is a common code for storing characters. It is a seven-bit code with 128 characters, including the uppercase and lowercase letters of the English alphabet, the decimal digits, punctuation marks, and nonprintable control characters. The Unicode character set extends ASCII to cover all the world's languages.

A floating point number is stored in a cell with three fields—a one-bit sign field, a field for the exponent, and a field for the significand. Except for special values, numbers are stored in binary scientific notation with a hidden bit to the left of the binary point that is assumed to be 1. The exponent is stored in an excess representation. Four special values are zero, infinity, NaN, and denormalized numbers. The IEEE 754 standard defines the number of bits in the exponent and significand fields to be 8 and 23 for single precision, and 11 and 52 for double precision.

A basic problem at all levels of abstraction is the mismatch between the form of the information to be processed and the language to represent it. A program in machine language processes bits. A program in a high-order language processes items such as arrays and records. Regardless of the level in which the program is written, the information must be cast into a format that the language can recognize. Matching the information to the language is a basic problem at all levels of abstraction and is a source of approximation in the modeling process of problem solving.

Exercises

Section 3.1

*1. Count the next 10 numbers (a) in octal starting from 267, (b) in base 3 starting from 2102, (c) in binary starting from 10101, and (d) in base 5 starting from 2433.

2. Count the next 10 numbers (a) in octal starting from 466, (b) in base 3 starting from 1201, (c) in binary starting from 11011, and (d) in base 5 starting from 3434.

*3. Convert the following numbers from binary to decimal, assuming unsigned binary representation:

   (a) 10010   (b) 110   (c) 1011
   (d) 1000   (e) 11111   (f) 1010101

4. Convert the following numbers from binary to decimal, assuming unsigned binary representation:

   (a) 10110   (b) 10   (c) 10101
   (d) 10000   (e) 1111   (f) 11110000

*5. Convert the following numbers from decimal to binary, assuming unsigned binary representation:

   (a) 25   (b) 16   (c) 1   (d) 14   (e) 5   (f) 41

6. Convert the following numbers from decimal to binary, assuming unsigned binary representation:

   (a) 12   (b) 35   (c) 3   (d) 0   (e) 27   (f) 16

7. With unsigned binary representation, what is the range of numbers as written in binary and in decimal for the following cells?

   *(a) a two-bit cell   *(b) a three-bit cell   (c) a four-bit cell
   (d) a five-bit cell   (e) an n-bit cell in general

*8. Perform the following additions on unsigned integers, assuming a seven-bit cell. Show the effect on the carry bit:

   (a)   010 1011   (b)   101 1001
         ADD   100 1001   ADD   011 0111
         C =   C =
   (c)   111 1111   (d)   111 1111
         ADD   111 1111   ADD   000 0001
         C =   C =

9. Perform the following additions on unsigned integers, assuming a nine-bit cell. Show the effect on the carry bit:

   (a)   0 0100 1011   (b)   1 0001 1101
         ADD   0 1101 0001   ADD   0 1110 1000
         C =   C =

(c)   1 1111 1111   (d)   1 1111 1111
    ADD   0 0000 0001   ADD   1 1111 1111
    C =   C =

10. Section 3.1 states that you can tell whether a binary number is even or odd only by inspecting the digit in the 1's place. Is that always possible for an arbitrary base? Explain.

11. Converting between octal and decimal is analogous to the technique of converting between binary and decimal. *(a) Write the polynomial representation of the octal number 70146 as in Figure 3.4. (b) Use the technique of Figure 3.5 to convert 7291 (dec) to octal.

12. Why do programmers at Level ISA3 confuse Halloween and Christmas? Hint: What does 31 (oct) equal?

Section 3.2

*13. Convert the following numbers from decimal to binary, assuming seven-bit two's complement binary representation:
    (a) 49   (b) −27   (c) 0
    (d) −64   (e) −1   (f) −2
    (g) What is the range for this computer as written in binary and in decimal?

14. Convert the following numbers from decimal to binary, assuming nine-bit two's complement binary representation:
    (a) 51   (b) −29   (c) −2
    (d) 0   (e) −256   (f) −1
    (g) What is the range for this cell as written in binary and in decimal?

*15. Convert the following numbers from binary to decimal, assuming seven-bit two's complement binary representation:
    (a) 001 1101   (b) 101 0101   (c) 111 1100
    (d) 000 0001   (e) 100 0000   (f) 100 0001

16. Convert the following numbers from binary to decimal, assuming nine-bit two's complement binary representation:
    (a) 0 0001 1010   (b) 1 0110 1010   (c) 1 1111 1100
    (d) 0 0000 0001   (e) 1 0000 0000   (f) 1 0000 0001

*17. Perform the following additions, assuming seven-bit two's complement binary representation. Show the effect on the status bits:
    (a)   010 1011   (b)   111 1001
        ADD   000 1110   ADD   000 1101
        N =   N =
        Z =   Z =
        V =   V =
        C =   C =

(c)   100 0110   (d)   110 0001
ADD   101 0101   ADD   111 0101
N =   N =
Z =   Z =
V =   V =
C =   C =

(e)   000 1101   (f)   100 1001
ADD   011 0100   ADD   010 1011
N =   N =
Z =   Z =
V =   V =
C =   C =

18. Perform the following additions, assuming nine-bit two's complement binary representation. Show the effect on the status bits:

(a)   0 1010 1100   (b)   1 1110 0101
ADD   0 0011 1010   ADD   0 0011 0101
N =   N =
Z =   Z =
V =   V =
C =   C =

(c)   1 0001 1011   (d)   1 1000 0101
ADD   1 0101 0100   ADD   1 1101 0110
N =   N =
Z =   Z =
V =   V =
C =   C =

(e)   0 0011 0100   (f)   1 0010 0111
ADD   0 1101 0010   ADD   0 1010 0111
N =   N =
Z =   Z =
V =   V =
C =   C =

19. With two's complement binary representation, what is the range of numbers as written in binary and in decimal notation for the following cells?

*(a) a two-bit cell   *(b)   a three-bit cell   (c)   a four-bit cell
(d) a five-bit cell   (e)   an n-bit cell in general

Section 3.3

*20. Perform the following logical operations, assuming a seven-bit cell:

<table>
<tr><td>(a)</td><td>010 1100</td><td>(b)</td><td>000 1111</td></tr>
<tr><td>AND</td><td>110 1010</td><td>AND</td><td>101 0101</td></tr>
<tr><td>N =</td><td></td><td>N =</td><td></td></tr>
<tr><td>Z =</td><td></td><td>Z =</td><td></td></tr>
<tr><td>(c)</td><td>010 1100</td><td>(d)</td><td>000 1111</td></tr>
<tr><td>OR</td><td>110 1010</td><td>OR</td><td>101 0101</td></tr>
<tr><td>N =</td><td></td><td>N =</td><td></td></tr>
<tr><td>Z =</td><td></td><td>Z =</td><td></td></tr>
<tr><td>(e)</td><td>010 1100</td><td>(f)</td><td>000 1111</td></tr>
<tr><td>XOR</td><td>110 1010</td><td>XOR</td><td>101 0101</td></tr>
<tr><td>N =</td><td></td><td>N =</td><td></td></tr>
<tr><td>Z =</td><td></td><td>Z =</td><td></td></tr>
</table>

(g) NEG   010 1100   (h) NOT   110 1010

21. Perform the following logical operations, assuming a nine-bit cell:

<table>
<tr><td>(a)</td><td>0 1001 0011</td><td>(b)</td><td>0 0000 1111</td></tr>
<tr><td>AND</td><td>1 0111 0101</td><td>AND</td><td>1 0111 0101</td></tr>
<tr><td>N =</td><td></td><td>N =</td><td></td></tr>
<tr><td>Z =</td><td></td><td>Z =</td><td></td></tr>
<tr><td>(c)</td><td>0 1001 0011</td><td>(d)</td><td>0 0000 1111</td></tr>
<tr><td>OR</td><td>1 0111 0101</td><td>OR</td><td>1 0111 0101</td></tr>
<tr><td>N =</td><td></td><td>N =</td><td></td></tr>
<tr><td>Z =</td><td></td><td>Z =</td><td></td></tr>
<tr><td>(e)</td><td>0 1001 0011</td><td>(f)</td><td>0 0000 1111</td></tr>
<tr><td>XOR</td><td>1 0111 0101</td><td>XOR</td><td>1 0111 0101</td></tr>
<tr><td>N =</td><td></td><td>N =</td><td></td></tr>
<tr><td>Z =</td><td></td><td>Z =</td><td></td></tr>
</table>

(g) NEG   1 1001 0011   (h) NOT   1 0111 0101

*22. Assuming seven-bit two's complement representation, convert each of the following decimal numbers to binary, show the effect of the ASL operation on it, and then convert the result back to decimal. Repeat with the ASR operation:

(a) 24   (b) 37   (c) −26
(d) 1   (e) 0   (f) −1

23. Assuming nine-bit two's complement representation, convert each of the following decimal numbers to binary, show the effect of the ASL

operation on it, and then convert the result back to decimal. Repeat with the ASR operation:

(a) 94	**(b)** 135	**(c)** −62
(d) 1	**(e)** 0	**(f)** −1

24. **(a)** Write the RTL specification for an arithmetic shift right on an eight-bit cell. **(b)** Write the RTL specification for an arithmetic shift left on an eight-bit cell.

*25. Assuming a seven-bit cell, show the effect of the rotate operation on each of the following values with the given initial value of C:

(a) C = 1, ROL 010 1101	**(b)** C = 0, ROL 010 1101
(c) C = 1, ROR 010 1101	**(d)** C = 0, ROR 010 1101

26. Assuming a nine-bit cell, show the effect of the rotate operation on each of the following values with the given initial value of C:

(a) C = 1, ROL 0 0110 1101	**(b)** C = 0, ROL 0 0110 1101
(c) C = 1, ROR 0 0110 1101	**(d)** C = 0, ROR 0 0110 1101

27. **(a)** Write the RTL specification for a rotate right on an eight-bit cell. **(b)** Write the RTL specification for a rotate left on an eight-bit cell.

Section 3.4

28. Count the next five numbers in hexadecimal, starting with the following:

*(**a**) 3AB7	**(b)** 6FD	**(c)** B9E

29. Convert the following numbers from hexadecimal to decimal:

*(**a**) 2D5E	**(b)** 2F	**(c)** 7

30. This chapter mentions the method of converting from decimal to hexadecimal but gives no examples. Use the method to convert the following decimal numbers to hexadecimal:

*(**a**) 26,831	**(b)** 4096	**(c)** 9

31. The technique for converting from decimal to any base will work, with some modification, for bases other than binary. **(a)** Explain the method to convert from decimal to octal. **(b)** Explain the method to convert from decimal to base n in general.

*32. Assuming seven-bit two's complement binary representation, convert the following numbers from hexadecimal to decimal. Remember to check the sign bit:

(a) 5D	**(b)** 2F	**(c)** 40

33. Assuming nine-bit two's complement binary representation, convert the following numbers from hexadecimal to decimal. Remember to check the sign bit:

(a) 1B4	**(b)** 0F5	**(c)** 100

*34. Assuming seven-bit two's complement binary representation, write the bit patterns for the following decimal numbers in hexadecimal:
   (a) −27   (b) 63   (c) −1

35. Assuming nine-bit two's complement binary representation, write the bit patterns for the following decimal numbers in hexadecimal:
   (a) −73   (b) −1   (c) 94

*36. Decode the following secret ASCII message (reading across):

```
100 1000     110 0001     111 0110     110 0101
010 0000     110 0001     010 0000     110 1110
110 1001     110 0011     110 0101     010 0000
110 0100     110 0001     111 1001     010 0001
```

37. Decode the following secret ASCII message (reading across):

```
100 1101     110 0101     110 0101     111 0100
010 0000     110 0001     111 0100     010 0000
110 1101     110 1001     110 0100     110 1110
110 1001     110 0111     110 1000     111 0100
010 1110
```

*38. How is the following string of nine characters stored in ASCII?
   Pay $0.92

39. How is the following string of 13 characters stored in ASCII?
   (321)497−0015

40. Convert the following Unicode code points to UTF-8:
   *(a) U+0542, Armenian ղ   (b) U+2873, Braille Pattern ⡳
   (c) U+4EB6, CJK Unified 亶 (d) U+13007, Egyptian Hieroglyphics 𓀇

41. Decode the following UTF-8 words:
   (a) 56 6F 69 C3 A0   (b) 4B C3 A4 73 65   (c) 70 C3 A2 74 65

42. You are the chief communications officer for the Lower Slobovian army at war with the Upper Slobovians. Your spies will infiltrate the enemy's command headquarters in an attempt to gain the "upper" hand. You know the Uppers are planning a major assault, and you also know the following: (1) It will be at either sunrise or sunset, (2) it will come by land, air, or sea, and (3) it will occur on March 28, 29, 30, or 31, or on April 1. Your spies must communicate with you in binary. Devise a suitable binary code for transmitting the information. Try to use the fewest number of bits possible.

43. Octal numbers are sometimes used instead of hexadecimal numbers to represent bit sequences.
   *(a) How many bits does one octal number represent?

How would you represent the decimal number −13 in octal with the following cells?

(b) A 15-bit cell   **(c)** A 16-bit cell   **(d)** An 8-bit cell

Section 3.5

*44. Convert the following numbers from binary to decimal:
   (a) 110.101001   **(b)** 0.000011   **(c)** 1.0

45. Convert the following numbers from binary to decimal:
   (a) 101.101001   **(b)** 0.000101   **(c)** 1.0

*46. Convert the following numbers from decimal to binary:
   (a) 13.15625   **(b)** 0.0390625   **(c)** 0.6

47. Convert the following numbers from decimal to binary:
   (a) 12.28125   **(b)** 0.0234375   **(c)** 0.7

48. Construct a table similar to Figure 3.33 that compares all the values with a four-bit cell for excess 7 and two's complement representation.

49. **(a)** With excess 7 representation, what is the range of numbers as written in binary and in decimal for a four-bit cell? **(b)** With excess 15 representation, what is the range of numbers as written in binary and in decimal for a five-bit cell? **(c)** With excess $2^{n-1} -1$ representation, what is the range of numbers as written in binary and in decimal for an n-bit cell in general?

50. Assuming a three-bit exponent field and a four-bit significand, write the bit pattern for the following decimal values:
   *(a) −12.5   **(b)** 13.0   **(c)** 0.43   **(d)** 0.1015625

51. Assuming a three-bit exponent field and a four-bit significand, what decimal values are represented by the following bit patterns?
   *(a) 0 010 1101   **(b)** 1 101 0110   **(c)** 1 111 1001
   (d) 0 001 0011   **(e)** 1 000 0100   **(f)** 0 111 0000

52. For IEEE 754 single-precision floating point, write the hexadecimal representation for the following decimal values:
   (a) 27.1015625   **(b)** −1.0   **(c)** −0.0
   (d) 0.5   **(e)** 0.6   **(f)** 256.015625

53. For IEEE 754 single-precision floating point, what is the number, as written in binary scientific notation, whose hexadecimal representation is the following?
   *(a) 4280 0000   **(b)** B350 0000   **(c)** 0061 0000
   (d) FF80 0000   **(e)** 7FE4 0000   **(f)** 8000 0000

54. For IEEE 754 single-precision floating point, write the hexadecimal representation for

  (a) positive zero

  (b) the smallest positive denormalized number

  (c) the largest positive denormalized number

  (d) the smallest positive normalized number

  (e) 1.0

  (f) the largest positive normalized number

  (g) positive infinity

55. For IEEE 754 double-precision floating point, write the hexadecimal representation for

  (a) positive zero

  (b) the smallest positive denormalized number

  (c) the largest positive denormalized number

  (d) the smallest positive normalized number

  (e) 1.0

  (f) the largest positive normalized number

  (g) positive infinity

Problems

Section 3.1

56. Write a program in C that takes as input a 4-digit octal number and prints the next 10 octal numbers. Define an octal number as

```
int octNum[4];
```

Use `octNum[0]` to store the most significant (i.e., leftmost) octal digit and `octNum[3]` to store the least significant octal digit. Test your program with interactive input.

57. Write a program in C that takes as input an 8-bit binary number and prints the next 10 binary numbers. Define a binary number as

```
int binNum[8];
```

Use `binNum[0]` to store the most significant (i.e., leftmost) bit and `binNum[7]` to store the least significant bit. Ask the user to input the first binary number with each bit separated by at least one space.

58. Defining a binary number as in Problem 57, write the function

```
int binToDec(const int bin[])
```

to convert an eight-bit unsigned binary number to a nonnegative decimal integer. Do not output the decimal integer in the function. Test your function with interactive input.

59. Defining a binary number as in Problem 57, write the function

```
void decToBin(int bin[], int dec)
```

to convert a nonnegative decimal integer to an eight-bit unsigned binary number. Do not output the binary number in the function. Test your function with interactive input.

60. Defining sum, bin1, and bin2 as binary numbers as in Problem 57, write the void function

```
void binaryAdd(int sum[], int *cBit,
               const int bin1[], const int bin2[])
```

to compute sum as the sum of the two binary numbers, bin1 and bin2. cBit should be the value of the carry bit after the addition. Do not output the carry bit or the sum in the function. Test your void function with interactive input.

Section 3.2

61. Defining a binary number as in Problem 57, write the function

```
int binToDec (const int bin[])
```

to convert an eight-bit two's complement binary number to a signed decimal integer. Do not output the decimal integer in the function. Test your function with interactive input.

62. Defining a binary number as in Problem 57, write the function

```
void decToBin(int bin[], int dec)
```

to convert a signed decimal integer to an eight-bit two's complement binary number. Do not output the binary number in the function. Test your function with interactive input.

Section 3.3

63. Defining bAnd, bin1, and bin2 as binary numbers as in Problem 57, write the void function

```
void binaryAnd(int bAnd[],
               const int bin1[], const int bin2[])
```

to compute bAnd as the AND of the two binary numbers bin1 and bin2. Do not output the binary number in the function. Test your function with interactive input.

64. Write the void function for Problem 63 renamed as binaryOr() using the OR operation.

65. Defining a binary number as in Problem 57, write the function

```
void shiftLeft(int binNum[], int *cBit)
```

to perform an arithmetic shift left on binNum. cBit should be the value of the carry bit after the shift. Do not output the shifted number or the carry bit in the function. Test your function with interactive input.

66. Write the function for Problem 65 renamed shiftRight(), using the arithmetic shift right operation.

Section 3.4

67. Write a program in C that takes as input a four-digit hexadecimal number and prints the next 10 hexadecimal numbers. Define a hexadecimal number as

```
int hexNum[4]
```

Allow upper- or lowercase letters for input and use uppercase letters for the hexadecimal output. For example, 3C6f should be valid input and should produce output 3C6F, 3C70, 3C71, ...

68. Defining a hexadecimal number as in Problem 67, write the function

```
int hexToDec(const int hexNum[])
```

to convert a four-digit hexadecimal number to a nonnegative decimal integer. Do not output the decimal integer in the function. Test your function with interactive input.

69. Defining a hexadecimal number as in Problem 67, write the function

```
void decToHex(int hexNum[], int decNum)
```

to convert a nonnegative decimal integer to a four-digit hexadecimal number. Do not output the hexadecimal number in the function. Test your function with interactive input.

70. Defining a hexadecimal number as in Problem 67, write the function

```
int hexToDec(const int hexNum[])
```

to convert a four-digit hexadecimal number to a signed decimal integer. Do not output the decimal integer in the function. Test your function with interactive input.

71. Defining a hexadecimal number as in Problem 67, write the function

```
void decToHex(int hex[], int dec)
```

to convert a signed decimal integer to a four-digit hexadecimal number. Do not output the hexadecimal number in the function. Test your function with interactive input.

72. Write a program in C to convert an unsigned number in an arbitrary base to a nonnegative decimal integer. For four-digit base 6 numbers, for example, declare

```
const int base = 6;
const int numDigits = 4;
int number[numDigits];
```

Write the function

```
void getNumber(int num[])
```

to input the unsigned number in the arbitrary base. Use the uppercase letters of the alphabet for input if required by the value of base. Write the function

```
int baseToDec(const int num[])
```

to convert the number in the arbitrary base to a nonnegative decimal value. You must be able to modify your program for operation with a different base by changing only the constant base. You must be able to modify the program for a different number of digits by changing only the constant numDigits.

73. Using the declarations as in Problem 72, write the function

```
void decToBase(int baseNum[], int decNum)
```

to convert the nonnegative decimal integer to the unsigned number in the arbitrary base. Write the function

```
void putNumber(const int baseNum[])
```

to output the unsigned number in the arbitrary base. Use the uppercase letters of the alphabet for output if required by the value of base. You must be able to modify your program for operation with a different base by changing only the constant base. You must be able to modify the program for a different number of digits by changing only the constant numDigits.

CHAPTER 4

Computer Architecture

An architect takes components such as walls, doors, and ceilings and arranges them together to form a building. Similarly, the computer architect takes components such as input devices, memories, and CPU registers and arranges them together to form a computer.

Buildings come in all shapes and sizes, and so do computers. This fact raises a problem. If we select one computer to study out of the dozens of popular models that are available, then our knowledge will be somewhat obsolete when that model is inevitably discontinued by its manufacturer. Also, this text would be less valuable to people who use the computers we choose not to study.

But there is another possibility. In the same way that a text on architecture could examine a hypothetical building, this text can explore a virtual computer that contains important features similar to those found on all real computers. This approach has its advantages and disadvantages.

One advantage is that the virtual computer can be designed to illustrate only the fundamental concepts that apply to most computer systems. We can then concentrate on the important points and not have to deal with the individual quirks that are present on all real machines. Concentrating on the fundamentals is also a hedge against obsolete knowledge. The fundamentals will continue to apply even as individual computers come and go in the marketplace.

The primary disadvantage of studying a virtual computer is that some of its details will be irrelevant to those who need to work with a specific real machine at the assembly language level or at the instruction set architecture level. If you understand the fundamental concepts, however, then you will easily be able to learn the details of any specific machine.

There is no 100% satisfactory solution to this dilemma. We have chosen the virtual computer approach mainly for its advantages in illustrating fundamental concepts. Our hypothetical machine is called the *Pep/9 computer*.

A virtual computer

Advantages and disadvantages of a virtual computer

The Pep/9 computer

4.1 Hardware

The Pep/9 hardware consists of three major components at the instruction set architecture level, ISA3:

> The central processing unit (CPU)

> The main memory with input/output devices

> The disk

The block diagram of FIGURE 4.1 shows each of these components as a block. The bus is a group of wires that connects the three major components. It carries the data signals and control signals sent between the blocks.

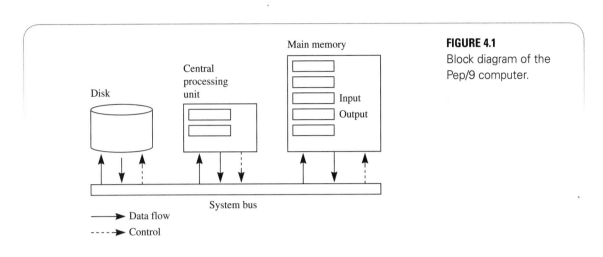

FIGURE 4.1
Block diagram of the Pep/9 computer.

Central Processing Unit (CPU)

The CPU contains six specialized memory locations called registers. As shown in FIGURE 4.2 , they are

> The 4-bit status register (NZVC)

> The 16-bit accumulator (A)

> The 16-bit index register (X)

> The 16-bit program counter (PC)

> The 16-bit stack pointer (SP)

> The 24-bit instruction register (IR)

Central processing unit (CPU)

Status bits (NZVC)

Accumulator (A)

Index register (X)

Program counter (PC)

Stack pointer (SP)

Instruction register (IR)

N Z V C

FIGURE 4.2
The CPU of the Pep/9 computer.

The N, Z, V, and C bits in the status register are the negative, zero, overflow, and carry bits (as discussed in Sections 3.1 and 3.2). The accumulator is the register that contains the result of an operation. The next three registers—X, PC, and SP—help the CPU access information in main memory. The index register is for accessing elements of an array. The program counter is for accessing instructions. The stack pointer is for accessing elements on the run-time stack. The instruction register holds an instruction after it has been accessed from memory.

In addition to these six registers, the CPU contains all the electronics (not shown in Figure 4.2) to execute the Pep/9 instructions.

Main Memory

FIGURE 4.3 shows the main memory of the Pep/9 computer. It contains 65,536 eight-bit storage locations. A group of eight bits is called a *byte* (pronounced *bite*). Each byte has an address similar to the number address on a mailbox. In decimal form, the addresses range from 0 to 65,535; in hexadecimal, they range from 0000 to FFFF. Main memory is sometimes called *core memory*.

Figure 4.3 shows the first three bytes of main memory on the first line, the next byte on the second line, the next three bytes on the next line, and, finally, the last two bytes on the last line. Whether you should visualize a line of memory as containing one, two, or three bytes depends on the context of the problem. Sometimes it is more convenient to visualize one byte on a line, sometimes two or three. Of course, in the physical computer a byte is a sequence of eight signals stored in an electrical circuit. The bytes would not be physically lined up as shown in the figure.

FIGURE 4.3
The main memory of the Pep/9 computer.

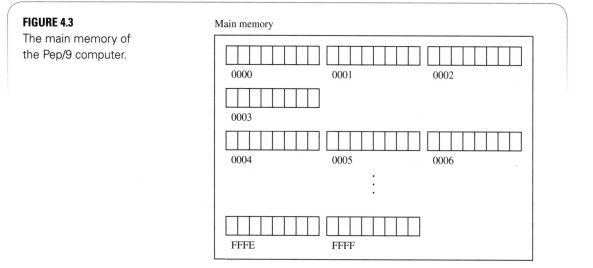

Main memory

Frequently it is convenient to draw main memory as in FIGURE 4.4 ,
with the addresses along the left side of the block. Even though the lines have
equal widths visually in the block, a single line may represent one or several
bytes. The address on the side of the block is the address of the leftmost byte
in the line.

You can tell how many bytes the line contains by the sequence of
addresses. In Figure 4.4, the first line must have three bytes because the
address of the second line is 0003. The second line must have one byte
because the address of the third line is 0004, which is one more than 0003.
Similarly, the third and fourth lines each have three bytes, the fifth has one,
and the sixth has two. From the figure, it is impossible to tell how many bytes
the seventh line has. The first three lines of Figure 4.4 correspond to the first
seven bytes in Figure 4.3.

Regardless of the way the bytes of main memory are laid out on paper,
the bytes with small addresses are referred to as the *top* of memory, and
those with large addresses are referred to as the *bottom*.

Most computer manufacturers specify a word to be a certain number of
bytes. In the Pep/9 computer, a word is two adjacent bytes. A word, therefore,
contains 16 bits. Most of the registers in the Pep/9 CPU are word registers.
In main memory, the address of a word is the address of the first byte of
the word. For example, FIGURE 4.5(a) shows two adjacent bytes at addresses
000B and 000C. The address of the 16-bit word is 000B.

It is important to distinguish between the content of a memory location
and its address. Memory addresses in the Pep/9 computer are 16 bits long.
Hence, the memory address of the word in Figure 4.5(a) could be written
in binary as 0000 0000 0000 1011. The content of the word at this address,
however, is 0000 0010 1101 0001. Do not confuse the content of the word
with its address. They are different.

To save space on the page, the content of a byte or word is usually
written in hexadecimal. Figure 4.5(b) shows the content in hexadecimal of
the same word at address 000B. In a machine language listing, the address of
the first byte of a group is printed, followed by the content in hexadecimal,
as in Figure 4.5(c). In this format, it is especially easy to confuse the address
of a byte with its content.

In the example in Figure 4.5, you can interpret the content of the
memory location several ways. If you consider the bit sequence 0000 0010
1101 0001 as an integer in two's complement representation, then the first
bit is the sign bit, and the binary sequence represents decimal 721. If you
consider the rightmost seven bits as an ASCII character, then the binary
sequence represents the character Q. The main memory cannot determine
which way the byte will be interpreted. It simply remembers the binary
sequence 0000 0010 1101 0001.

FIGURE 4.4
Another style for
depicting main
memory.

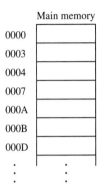

A Pep/9 word

FIGURE 4.5
The distinction between the content of a memory location and its address.

| 0 | 0 | 0 | 0 | 0 | 0 | 1 | 0 |

000B

| 1 | 1 | 0 | 1 | 0 | 0 | 0 | 1 |

000C

(a) The content in binary.

02	D1
000B	000C

(b) The content in hexadecimal.

000B   02D1

(c) The content in a machine
        language listing.

Input/Output Devices

You may be wondering where this Pep/9 hardware is located and whether you will ever be able to get your hands on it. The answer is, the hardware does not exist! At least it does not exist as a physical machine. Instead, it exists as a set of programs that you can execute on your computer system. *The Pep/9 virtual machine* The programs simulate the behavior of the Pep/9 virtual machine described in these chapters.

The Pep/9 system simulates two input/output (I/O) modes—interactive and batch. Before executing a program, you must specify the I/O mode. If you specify interactive, the input comes from the keyboard, and both input and output appear in a terminal window. If you specify batch, the input comes from an input pane and the output goes to an output pane. Batch mode simulates input from a file because the input pane must have data in it before the program executes, just as an input file contains data that a program processes.

Memory-mapped I/O Pep/9 simulates a common computer systems design called *memory-mapped I/O*. The input device is wired into main memory at one fixed address, and the output device is wired into main memory at another fixed address. In Pep/9, the input device is at address FC15 and the output device is at address FC16.

Data and Control

The solid lines connecting the blocks of Figure 4.1 are data flow lines. Data can flow from the input device at address FC15 on the bus to the CPU. It can also flow from the CPU on the bus to the output device at address FC16. Data cannot flow directly from the input device to another memory location without going first to the CPU. Nor can it flow directly from some other memory location to the output device without going first to the CPU. Most computer systems have a mechanism, called *direct memory access* (DMA), that allows data to flow between the disk and main memory directly without going through the CPU. Although this design is common, the Pep/9 simulator does not provide this feature.

The dashed lines are control lines. Control signals all originate from the CPU, which means that the CPU controls all the other parts of the computer. For example, to make data flow from the input device in main memory to the CPU along the solid data flow lines, the CPU must transmit a send signal along the dashed control line to the memory. The important point is that the processor really is central. It controls all the other parts of the computer.

Instruction Format

Each computer has its own set of instructions wired into its CPU. The instruction set varies from manufacturer to manufacturer. It often varies among computers made by the same company, although many manufacturers produce a family of models, each of which contains the same instruction set as the other models in that family.

The Pep/9 computer has 40 instructions in its instruction set, shown in **FIGURE 4.6**. Each instruction consists of either a single byte called the *instruction specifier,* or the instruction specifier followed immediately by a word called the *operand specifier.* Instructions that do not have an operand specifier are called *unary instructions.* **FIGURE 4.7** shows the structure of nonunary and unary instructions.

The instruction specifier and operand specifier

The eight-bit instruction specifier can have several parts. The first part is called the *operation code,* often referred to as the *opcode.* The opcode may consist of as many as eight bits and as few as four. For example, Figure 4.6 shows the instruction to move the stack pointer to the accumulator as having an eight-bit opcode of 0000 0011. The add to SP instruction, however, has the five-bit opcode 01010. Instructions with fewer than eight bits in the opcode subdivide their instruction specifier into several fields depending on the instruction. Figure 4.6 indicates these fields with the letters a, r, and n. Each one of these letters can be either 0 or 1.

The opcode

FIGURE 4.6
The Pep/9 instruction set at Level ISA3.

Instruction Specifier	Instruction
0000 0000	Stop execution
0000 0001	Return from CALL
0000 0010	Return from trap
0000 0011	Move SP to A
0000 0100	Move NZVC flags to A(12..15)
0000 0101	Move A(12..15) to NZVC flags
0000 011r	Bitwise invert r
0000 100r	Negate r
0000 101r	Arithmetic shift left r
0000 110r	Arithmetic shift right r
0000 111r	Rotate left r
0001 000r	Rotate right r
0001 001a	Branch unconditional
0001 010a	Branch if less than or equal to
0001 011a	Branch if less than
0001 100a	Branch if equal to
0001 101a	Branch if not equal to
0001 110a	Branch if greater than or equal to
0001 111a	Branch if greater than
0010 000a	Branch if V
0010 001a	Branch if C
0010 010a	Call subroutine
0010 011n	Unimplemented opcode, unary trap
0010 1aaa	Unimplemented opcode, nonunary trap
0011 0aaa	Unimplemented opcode, nonunary trap
0011 1aaa	Unimplemented opcode, nonunary trap
0100 0aaa	Unimplemented opcode, nonunary trap
0100 1aaa	Unimplemented opcode, nonunary trap
0101 0aaa	Add to stack pointer (SP)
0101 1aaa	Subtract from stack pointer (SP)
0110 raaa	Add to r
0111 raaa	Subtract from r
1000 raaa	Bitwise AND to r
1001 raaa	Bitwise OR to r
1010 raaa	Compare word to r
1011 raaa	Compare byte to r(8..15)
1100 raaa	Load word r from memory
1101 raaa	Load byte r(8..15) from memory
1110 raaa	Store word r to memory
1111 raaa	Store byte r(8..15) to memory

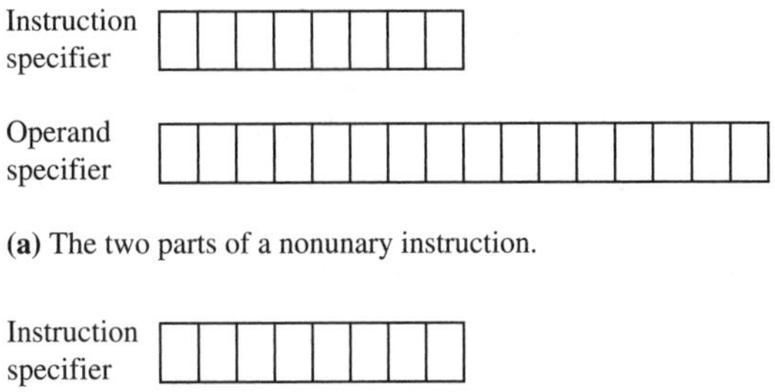

Instruction
specifier

Operand
specifier

(a) The two parts of a nonunary instruction.

Instruction
specifier

(b) A unary instruction.

FIGURE 4.7
The Pep/9 instruction
format.

Example 4.1 Figure 4.6 shows that the "branch if equal to" instruction has an instruction specifier of 0001 100a. Because the letter a can be zero or one, there are really two versions of the instruction—0001 1000 and 0001 1001. Similarly, there are eight versions of the decimal output trap instruction. Its instruction specifier is 0011 1aaa, where aaa can be any combination from 000 to 111. ∎

FIGURE 4.8 summarizes the meaning of the possible fields in the instruction specifier for the letters a and r. Generally, the letter a stands for addressing mode, and the letter r stands for register. When r is 0, the instruction operates on the accumulator. When r is 1, the instruction operates on the index register. Pep/9 executes each nonunary instruction in one of eight addressing modes—immediate, direct, indirect, stack-relative, stack-relative

FIGURE 4.8
The Pep/9 instruction specifier fields.

aaa	Addressing Mode
000	Immediate
001	Direct
010	Indirect
011	Stack-relative
100	Stack-relative deferred
101	Indexed
110	Stack-indexed
111	Stack-deferred indexed

(a) The addressing-aaa field.

a	Addressing Mode
0	Immediate
1	Indexed

(b) The addressing-a field.

r	Register
0	Accumulator, A
1	Index register, X

(c) The register-r field.

deferred, indexed, stack-indexed, or stack-deferred indexed. Later chapters describe the meaning of the addressing modes. For now, it is important only that you know how to use the tables of Figures 4.7 and 4.8 to determine which register and addressing mode a given instruction uses. The meaning of the letter n in the unary trap instruction is described in a later chapter.

Example 4.2   Determine the opcode, register, and addressing mode of the 1100 1011 instruction. Starting from the left, determine with the help of Figure 4.6 that the opcode is 1100. The next bit after the opcode is the r bit, which is 1, indicating the index register. The three bits after the r bit are the aaa bits, which are 011, indicating stack-relative addressing. Therefore, the instruction loads a word from memory into the index register using stack-relative addressing. ∎

The operand specifier, for those instructions that are not unary, indicates the operand to be processed by the instruction. The CPU can interpret the operand specifier several different ways, depending on the bits in the instruction specifier. For example, it may interpret the operand specifier as an ASCII character, as an integer in two's complement representation, or as an address in main memory where the operand is stored.

Instructions are stored in main memory. The address of an instruction in main memory is the address of the first byte of the instruction.

Example 4.3   **FIGURE 4.9** shows two adjacent instructions stored in main memory at locations 01A3 and 01A6. The instruction at 01A6 is unary; the instruction at 01A3 is not.

In this example, the instruction at 01A3 has

> Opcode: 0111
> Register-r field: 1
> Addressing-aaa field: 101
> Operand specifier: 0000 0011 0100 1110

FIGURE 4.9

Two instructions in main memory.

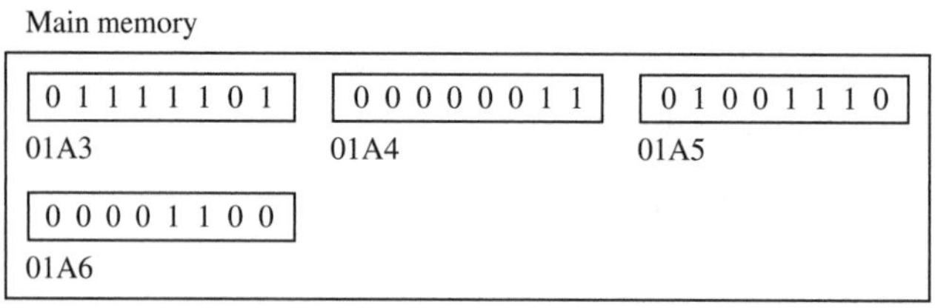

Main memory

0 1 1 1 1 1 0 1	0 0 0 0 0 0 1 1	0 1 0 0 1 1 1 0
01A3	01A4	01A5

0 0 0 0 1 1 0 0
01A6

where all the quantities are written in binary. According to the opcode chart of Figure 4.6, this is a subtract instruction. The register-r field indicates that the index register, as opposed to the accumulator, is affected. So this instruction subtracts the operand from the index register. The addressing-aaa field indicates indexed addressing, so the operand specifier is interpreted accordingly. In this chapter, we confine our study to the direct addressing mode. The other modes are taken up in later chapters.

The unary instruction at 01A6 has

Opcode: 0000 110
Register-r field: 0

The opcode indicates that the instruction will do an arithmetic shift right. The register-r field indicates that the accumulator is the register in which the shift will take place. Because this is a unary instruction, there is no operand specifier. ∎

In Example 4.3, the following form of the instructions is called *machine language*:

0111 1101 0000 0011 0100 1110
0000 1100

Machine language is a binary sequence—that is, a sequence of ones and zeros—that the CPU interprets according to the opcodes of its instruction set. A machine language listing would show these two instructions in hexadecimal, preceded by their memory addresses, as follows:

Machine language

01A3 FD034E
01A6 0C

If you have only the hexadecimal listing of an instruction, you must convert it to binary and examine the fields in the instruction specifier to determine what the instruction will do.

4.2 Direct Addressing

This section describes the operation of some of the Pep/9 instructions at Level ISA3. It describes how they operate in conjunction with the direct addressing mode. Later chapters describe the other addressing modes.

The addressing field determines how the CPU interprets the operand specifier. An addressing-aaa field of 001 indicates direct addressing. With direct addressing, the CPU interprets the operand specifier as the address in main memory of the cell that contains the operand. In mathematical notation,

Direct addressing

Oprnd = Mem[OprndSpec]

where *Oprnd* stands for *operand*, *OprndSpec* stands for *operand specifier*, and *Mem* stands for *main memory*.

The bracket notation indicates that you can think of main memory as an array and the operand specifier as the index of the array. In C, if v is an array and i is an integer, v[i] is the "cell" in the array that is determined by the value of the integer i. Similarly, the operand specifier in the instruction identifies the cell in main memory that contains the operand.

What follows is a description of some instructions from the Pep/9 instruction set. Each description lists the opcode and gives an example of the operation of the instruction when used with the direct addressing mode. Values of N, Z, V, and C are always given in binary. Values of other registers and of memory cells are given in hexadecimal. At the machine level, all values are ultimately binary. After describing the individual instructions, this chapter concludes by showing how you can put them together to construct a machine language program.

The Stop Instruction

The stop instruction has instruction specifier 0000 0000. When this instruction is executed, it simply makes the computer stop. Because Pep/9 is a simulated computer, you execute it by running the Pep/9 simulator on your computer. The simulator has a menu of command options for you to choose from. One of those options is to execute your Pep/9 program. When your Pep/9 program is executing, if it encounters this instruction it will stop and return the simulator to the menu of command options. The stop execution instruction is unary. It has no operand specifier.

The Load Word Instruction

The load word instruction has instruction specifier 1100 raaa. This instruction loads one word (two bytes) from a memory location into either the accumulator or the index register, depending on the value of r. It affects the N and Z bits. If the operand is negative, it sets the N bit to 1; otherwise it clears the N bit to 0. If the operand consists of 16 0's, it sets the Z bit to 1; otherwise it clears the Z bit to 0. The register transfer language (RTL) specification of the load instruction is

$$r \leftarrow Oprnd\,;\, N \leftarrow r < 0\,,\, Z \leftarrow r = 0$$

FIGURE 4.10

The load word instruction.

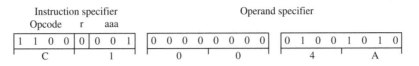

Example 4.4 Suppose the instruction to be executed is C1004A in hexadecimal, which (FIGURE 4.10) shows in binary. The register-r field in this example is 0, which indicates a load word to the accumulator instead of the index register. The addressing-aaa field is 001, which indicates direct addressing.

(FIGURE 4.11) shows the effect of executing the load word instruction, assuming Mem[004A] has an initial content of 92EF. The load word instruction does not change the content of the memory location. It sends a copy of the two memory cells (at addresses 004A and 004B) to the register. Whatever was in the register before the instruction was executed, in this case 036D, is destroyed. The N bit is set to 1 because the bit pattern loaded has 1 in the sign bit. The Z bit is set to 0 because the bit pattern is not all 0's. The V and C bits are unaffected by the load word instruction.

Figure 4.11 shows the data flow lines and control lines that the load word instruction activates. As indicated by the solid lines, data flows from the main memory on the bus to the CPU, and then into the register. For this data transfer to take place, the CPU must send a control signal (as indicated by the dashed lines) to main memory, telling it to put the data on the bus. The CPU also tells main memory the address from which to fetch the data. ∎

FIGURE 4.11

Execution of the load word instruction.

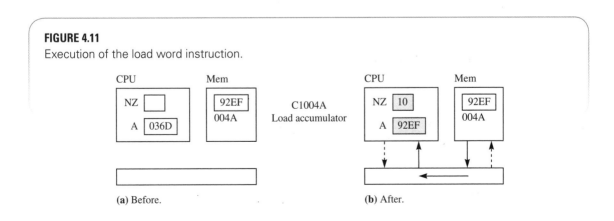

(a) Before.

(b) After.

The Store Word Instruction

The store word instruction has instruction specifier 1110 raaa. This instruction stores one word (two bytes) from either the accumulator or the index register to a memory location. With direct addressing, the operand specifies the memory location in which the information is stored. The RTL specification for the store instruction is

Oprnd ← r

Example 4.5 Suppose the instruction to be executed is E9004A in hexadecimal, which **FIGURE 4.12** shows in binary. This time, the register-r field indicates that the instruction will affect the index register. The addressing-aaa field, 001, indicates direct addressing.

FIGURE 4.13 shows the effect of executing the store instruction, assuming the index register has an initial content of 16BC. The store instruction does not change the content of the register. It sends a copy of the register to two memory cells (at addresses 004A and 004B). Whatever was in the memory cells before the instruction was executed, in this case F082, is destroyed. The store instruction affects none of the status bits. ∎

FIGURE 4.12

The store word instruction.

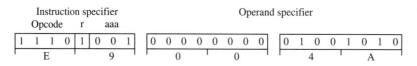

FIGURE 4.13

Execution of the store word instruction.

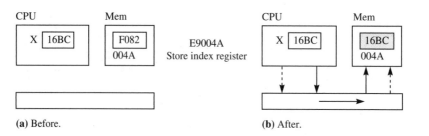

(a) Before.   (b) After.

The Add Instruction

The add instruction has instruction specifier 0110 raaa. It is similar to the load word instruction in that data is transferred from main memory to register r in the CPU. But with the add instruction, the original content of the register is not just written over by the content of the word from main memory. Instead, the content of the word from main memory is added to the content of the register. The sum is placed in the register, and all four status bits are set accordingly. As with the load word instruction, a copy of the memory word is sent to the CPU. The original content of the memory word is unchanged. The RTL specification of the add instruction is

$$r \leftarrow r + Oprnd ; N \leftarrow r < 0 , Z \leftarrow r = 0 , V \leftarrow \{overflow\} , C \leftarrow \{carry\}$$

Example 4.6 Suppose the instruction to be executed is 69004A in hexadecimal, which **FIGURE 4.14** shows in binary. The register-r field indicates that the instruction will affect the index register. The addressing-aaa field, 001, indicates direct addressing.

FIGURE 4.15 shows the effect of executing the add instruction, assuming the index register has an initial content of 0005 and Mem[004A]

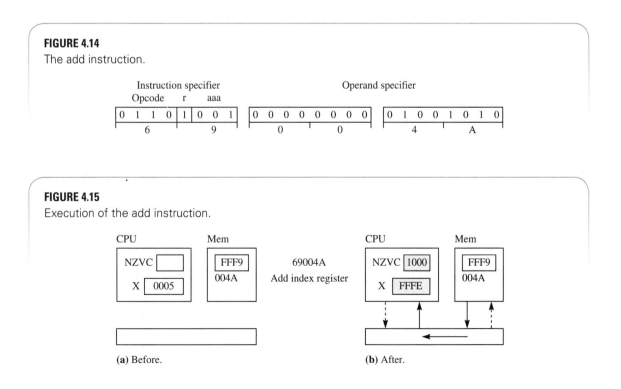

FIGURE 4.14
The add instruction.

FIGURE 4.15
Execution of the add instruction.

(a) Before.   (b) After.

has –7 (dec) = FFF9 (hex). In decimal, the sum 5 + (–7) is –2, which is shown as FFFE (hex) in Figure 4.15(b). The figure shows the NZVC bits in binary. The N bit is 1 because the sum is negative. The Z bit is 0 because the sum is not all 0's. The V bit is 0 because an overflow did not occur, and the C bit is 0 because a carry did not occur out of the most significant bit.　　▨

The Subtract Instruction

The subtract instruction has instruction specifier 0111 raaa. It is similar to the add instruction, except that the operand is subtracted from the register. The result is placed in the register, and the operand is unchanged. With subtraction, the C bit represents a carry from adding the negation of the operand. The RTL specification of the subtract instruction is

$$r \leftarrow r - \text{Oprnd} \; ; \; N \leftarrow r < 0 \, , \, Z \leftarrow r = 0 \, , \, V \leftarrow \{overflow\} \, , \, C \leftarrow \{carry\}$$

Example 4.7 Suppose the instruction to be executed is 71004A in hexadecimal, which FIGURE 4.16 shows in binary. The register-r field indicates that the instruction will affect the accumulator.

　　FIGURE 4.17 shows the effect of executing the subtract instruction, assuming the accumulator has an initial content of 0003 and Mem[004A] has 0009. In decimal, the difference 3 – 9 is –6, which is shown as FFFA (hex) in Figure 4.17(b). The figure shows the NZVC bits in binary. The N bit

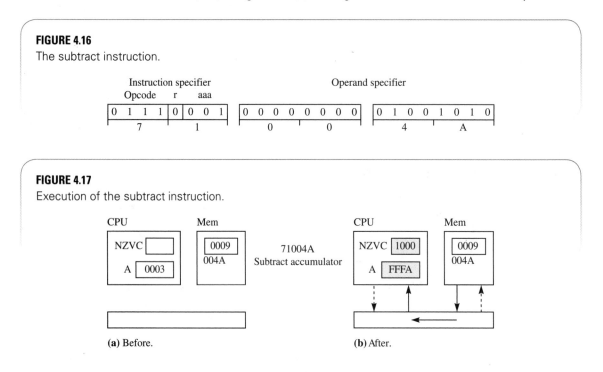

FIGURE 4.16
The subtract instruction.

FIGURE 4.17
Execution of the subtract instruction.

(a) Before.　　　　　　　　(b) After.

is 1 because the sum is negative. The Z bit is 0 because the sum is not all 0's. The V bit is 0 because an overflow did not occur, and the C bit is 0 because a carry did not occur when −9 was added to 3.   ∎

The And and Or Instructions

The and instruction has instruction specifier 1000 raaa, and the or instruction has instruction specifier 1001 raaa. Both instructions are similar to the add instruction. Rather than add the operand to the register, each instruction performs a logical operation on the register. The and operation is useful for masking out undesired 1 bits from a bit pattern. The or operation is useful for inserting 1 bits into a bit pattern. Both instructions affect the N and Z bits and leave the V and C bits unchanged. The RTL specifications for the and and or instructions are

$$r \leftarrow r \wedge Oprnd \,; N \leftarrow r < 0 \,, Z \leftarrow r = 0$$
$$r \leftarrow r \vee Oprnd \,; N \leftarrow r < 0 \,, Z \leftarrow r = 0$$

Example 4.8 Suppose the instruction to be executed is 89004A in hexadecimal, which **FIGURE 4.18** shows in binary. The opcode indicates that the and instruction will execute and the register-r field indicates that the instruction will affect the index register.

FIGURE 4.19 shows the effect of executing the and instruction, assuming the index register has an initial content of 5DC3 and Mem[004A] has 00FF. In binary, 00FF is 0000 0000 1111 1111. At every position where there is a 1 in Mem[004A], the corresponding bit in the index register is unchanged. At every position where there is a 0, the corresponding bit is cleared to 0. The figure shows the NZ bits in binary. The N bit is 0 because the quantity in the index register is not negative when interpreted as a signed integer. The Z bit is 0 because the index register is not all 0's.   ∎

Example 4.9 **FIGURE 4.20** shows the operation of the or instruction. The initial state is identical to that of Example 4.8, except that the opcode of the instruction specifier 99 is 1001, which indicates the or instruction. This time, at every position where there is a 0 in Mem[004A], the corresponding

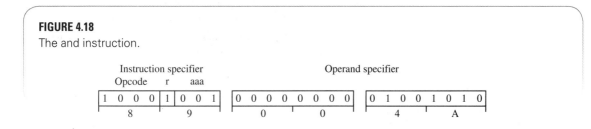

FIGURE 4.18

The and instruction.

FIGURE 4.19

Execution of the and instruction.

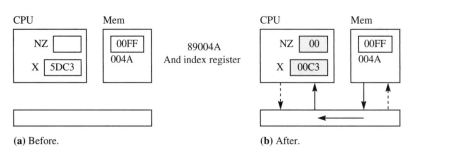

(a) Before.   (b) After.

FIGURE 4.20

Execution of the or instruction.

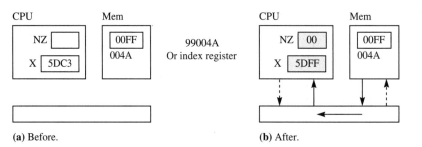

(a) Before.   (b) After.

bit in the index register is unchanged. At every position where there is a 1, the corresponding bit is set to 1. The N bit is 0 because the index register would not be negative if it were interpreted as a signed integer.

The Invert and Negate Instructions

The invert instruction has instruction specifier 0000 011r, and the negate instruction has instruction specifier 0000 100r. Both instructions are unary. They have no operand specifier. The invert instruction performs the NOT operation on the register. That is, each 1 is changed to 0, and each 0 is changed to 1. It affects the N and Z bits. The RTL specification of the invert instruction is

$$r \leftarrow \neg r ; N \leftarrow r < 0 , Z \leftarrow r = 0$$

The negate instruction interprets the register as a signed integer and negates it. The 16-bit register stores signed integers in the range −32768 to 32767. The negate instruction affects the N, Z, and V bits. The V bit is set only if the original value in the register is −32768, because there is no corresponding positive value of 32768. The RTL specification of the negate instruction is

$$r \leftarrow -r\,;\,N \leftarrow r < 0\,,\,Z \leftarrow r = 0\,,\,V \leftarrow \{overflow\}$$

Example 4.10 Suppose the instruction to be executed is 06 in hexadecimal, which **FIGURE 4.21** shows in binary. The opcode indicates that the invert instruction will execute, and the register-r field indicates that the instruction will affect the accumulator.

FIGURE 4.22 shows the effect of executing the invert instruction, assuming the accumulator has an initial content of 0003 (hex), which is 0000 0000 0000 0011 (bin). The not instruction changes the bit pattern to 1111 1111 1111 1100. The N bit is 1 because the quantity in the accumulator is negative when interpreted as a signed integer. The Z bit is 0 because the accumulator is not all 0's. ∎

Example 4.11 **FIGURE 4.23** shows the operation of the negate instruction. The initial state is identical to that of Example 4.10, except that the opcode of the instruction specifier 1A is 0000 100, which indicates the negate instruction. The negation of 3 is −3, which is 1111 1111 1111 1101 (bin) = FFFD (hex). ∎

FIGURE 4.21
The invert instruction.

Instruction specifier

Opcode							r
0	0	0	0	0	1	1	0

0   6

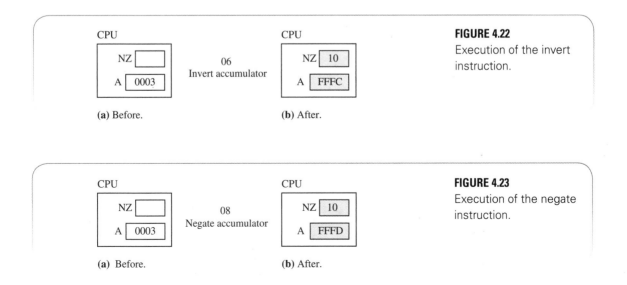

FIGURE 4.22
Execution of the invert instruction.

FIGURE 4.23
Execution of the negate instruction.

The Load Byte and Store Byte Instructions

These instructions, along with the two that follow, are byte instructions. Byte instructions operate on a single byte of information instead of a word. The load byte instruction has instruction specifier 1101 raaa, and the store byte instruction has instruction specifier 1111 raaa. The load byte instruction loads the operand into the right half of either the accumulator or the index register, and affects the N and Z bits. It leaves the left half of the register unchanged. The store byte instruction stores the right half of either the accumulator or the index register into a one-byte memory location and does not affect any status bits. The RTL specification of the load byte instruction is

$$r\langle 8..15\rangle \leftarrow \text{byte Oprnd} ; N \leftarrow 0 , Z \leftarrow r\langle 8..15\rangle = 0$$

and the RTL specification of the store byte instruction is

$$\text{byte Operand} \leftarrow r\langle 8..15\rangle$$

Example 4.12 Suppose the instruction to be executed is D1004A in hexadecimal, which FIGURE 4.24 shows in binary. The register-r field in this example is 0, which indicates a load to the accumulator instead of the index register. The addressing-aaa field is 001, which indicates direct addressing.

 FIGURE 4.25 shows the effect of executing the load byte instruction, assuming Mem[004A] has an initial content of 92. The N bit is always set to

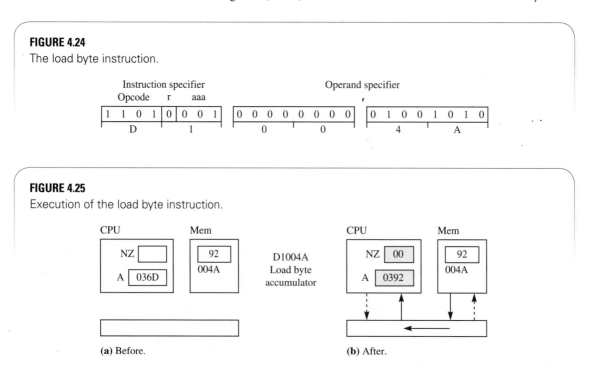

FIGURE 4.24

The load byte instruction.

FIGURE 4.25

Execution of the load byte instruction.

(a) Before.

(b) After.

FIGURE 4.26

Execution of the store byte instruction.

(a) Before.   (b) After.

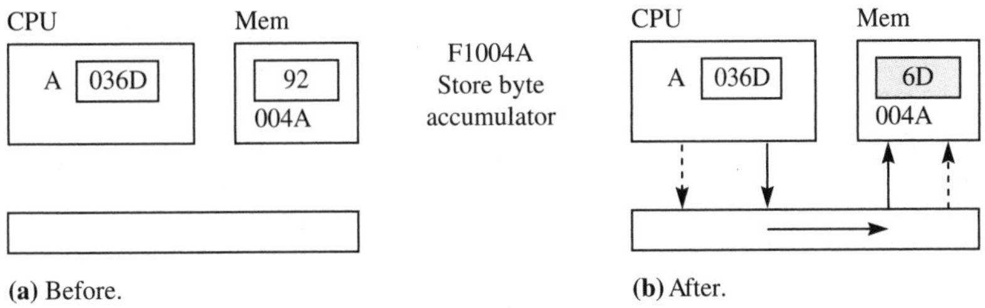

0 with this instruction. The Z bit is set to 0 because the eight bits loaded into the right half of the accumulator are not all 0's.   ▮

Example 4.13 `FIGURE 4.26` shows the effect of executing the store byte instruction. The initial state is the same as in Example 4.12, except that the instruction is store byte instead of load byte. The right half of the accumulator is 6D, which is sent to the memory cell at address 004A.   ▮

The Input and Output Devices

The input device is at address FC15, and is attached to an ASCII character input device like a keyboard. You get a character from the input device by executing the load byte instruction from address FC15. The output device is at address FC16 and is attached to an ASCII output device like a screen. You send a character to the output device by executing the store byte instruction to address FC16.

Example 4.14   Suppose the instruction to be executed is D1FC15 in hexadecimal, which is the load byte instruction from the input device with direct addressing. `FIGURE 4.27` shows the effect of executing the instruction, assuming that the next character in the input stream is W. The character from the input stream can come from the keyboard or from a file. The figure shows the keyboard wired into the memory location at address FC15. The user has pressed the W key. The ASCII value of the letter W is 57 (hex), which is sent to the accumulator.

The dashed lines from the CPU to main memory represent control signals that instruct the memory subsystem to put the byte from address FC15 onto the system bus. The memory subsystem has a special input circuit that detects when a memory load request is made from address FC15. It then performs all the necessary steps to put the next character from the input stream into Mem[FC15], which is then put on the system bus. This is an example of levels of abstraction in a computer system. The details of how the

FIGURE 4.27

The load byte instruction from the input device.

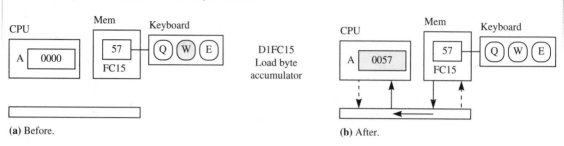

(a) Before.   **(b)** After.

character is transferred from the keyboard to Mem[FC15] are hidden from the Level ISA3 programmer, who only needs to know that to get the next ASCII character from the input stream you load a byte from that address. ∎

Example 4.15 Suppose the instruction to be executed is F1FC16 in hexadecimal, which is the store byte instruction to the output device with direct addressing. **FIGURE 4.28** shows the effect of executing the instruction, assuming that 69 (hex), which is the ASCII value for the letter i, is in the right half of the accumulator. The figure shows the screen wired into the memory location at address FC16. The ASCII value of the letter i is sent to Mem[FC16]. As with the input device, the memory subsystem has a special circuit that detects when a byte is stored to Mem[FC16] and routes it to the output stream to be displayed on the screen. ∎

Big Endian Versus Little Endian

There are two CPU design philosophies regarding the transfer of information between the registers of the CPU and the bytes in main memory. The problem arises because main memory is always byte-addressable and a

FIGURE 4.28

The store byte instruction to the output device.

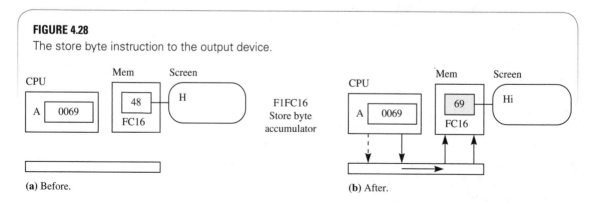

(a) Before.   **(b)** After.

register in a CPU typically contains more than one byte. The design question is, in what order should the sequence of bytes be stored in main memory? There are two choices. The CPU can store the most significant byte at the lowest address, called *big-endian order*, or it can store the least significant byte at the lowest address, called *little-endian order*. The choice of which order to use is arbitrary as long as the same order is used consistently for all instructions in the instruction set.

There is no dominant standard in the computing industry. Some processors use big-endian order, some use little-endian order, and some can use either order depending on a switch that is set by low-level software. Pep/9 is a big-endian CPU. Figure 4.13 shows the effect of the store instruction. The most significant byte in the register is 16, which is stored at the lowest address, 004A. The next byte in the register is BC and is stored at the next higher address, 004B. Figure 4.11 shows the load instruction, which is consistent. The most significant byte of the register gets 92, which is the byte from the lowest address at 004A. The next byte gets EF from the next higher address at 004B.

In contrast, FIGURE 4.29 shows what happens when a load instruction executes in a little-endian CPU. The byte at the lowest address, 004A, is 92 and is put in the least significant byte of the register. The byte from the next higher address, 004B, is put to the left of the low-order byte in the register. FIGURE 4.30 shows the effect of a load instruction in a CPU with 32-bit registers for both big-endian and little-endian ordering. A 32-bit register holds four bytes, which are loaded into the accumulator from most significant to least significant byte, or from least significant to most significant byte, depending on whether the CPU uses big-endian or little-endian ordering, respectively.

The word *endian* comes from Jonathan Swift's 1726 novel *Gulliver's Travels*, in which two competing kingdoms, Lilliput and Blefuscu, have different customs for breaking eggs. The inhabitants of Lilliput break their eggs at the little end, and hence are known as *little endians*, while the inhabitants of

FIGURE 4.29

The load instruction in a little-endian CPU.

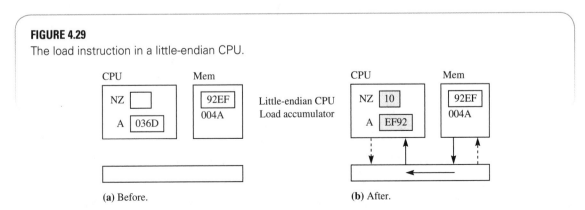

(a) Before. (b) After.

FIGURE 4.30
The load instruction with a 32-bit register.

	Initial State	Big Endian Final State	Little Endian Final State
Mem[019E]	89	89	89
Mem[019F]	AB	AB	AB
Mem[01A0]	CD	CD	CD
Mem[01A1]	EF	EF	EF
Accumulator		89 AB CD EF	EF CD AB 89

Blefuscu break their eggs at the big end, and hence are known as *big endians*. The novel is a parody reflecting the absurdity of war over meaningless issues. The terminology is fitting, as whether a CPU is big-endian or little-endian is of little fundamental importance.

4.3 von Neumann Machines

In the earliest electronic computers, each program was hand-wired. To change the program, the wires had to be manually reconnected, a tedious and time-consuming process. The Electronic Numerical Integrator and Calculator (ENIAC) computer described in Section 3.1 was an example of this kind of machine. Its memory was used only to store data.

In 1945, John von Neumann had proposed in a report published by the University of Pennsylvania that the United States Ordnance Department build a computer that would store in main memory not only the data, but the program as well. The stored-program concept was a radical idea at the time. Maurice V. Wilkes built the Electronic Delay Storage Automatic Calculator (EDSAC) at Cambridge University in England in 1949. It was the first computer to be built that used von Neumann's stored-program idea. Practically all commercial computers today are based on the stored-program concept, with programs and data sharing the same main memory. Such computers are called *von Neumann machines*, although some believe that J. Presper Eckert, Jr., originated the idea several years before von Neumann's paper.

The von Neumann Execution Cycle

The Pep/9 computer is a classic von Neumann machine. **FIGURE 4.31** is a pseudocode description of the steps required to execute a program:

> **FIGURE 4.31**
> A pseudocode description of the steps necessary to execute a
> program on the Pep/9 computer.
>
> *Load the machine language program*
> *Initialize* PC *and* SP
> do {
>   *Fetch the next instruction*
>   *Decode the instruction specifier*
>   *Increment* PC
>   *Execute the instruction fetched*
> }
> while (*the stop instruction does not execute*)

The do loop is called the *von Neumann execution cycle*. The cycle consists of
five operations:

> ❯ Fetch instruction at Mem[PC].
>
> ❯ Decode instruction fetched.
>
> ❯ Increment PC.
>
> ❯ Execute instruction fetched.
>
> ❯ Repeat the cycle.

The von Neumann execution cycle

The von Neumann cycle is wired into the CPU. The following is a more
detailed description of the steps in the execution process.

To load the machine language program into main memory, the first
instruction is placed at address 0000 (hex). The second instruction is placed
adjacent to the first. If the first instruction is unary, then the address of
the second instruction is 0001. Otherwise the operand specifier of the first
instruction will be contained in the bytes at 0001 and 0002. The address of
the second instruction would then be at 0003. The third instruction is placed
adjacent to the second similarly, and so on for the entire machine language
program.

Load the program

To initialize the program counter and stack pointer, PC is set to 0000
(hex), and SP is set to Mem[FFF4]. The purpose of the program counter is
to hold the address of the next instruction to be executed. Because the first
instruction was loaded into main memory at address 0000, the PC must be set
initially to 0000. The purpose of the stack pointer is to hold the address of the
top of the run-time stack. A later section explains why SP is set to Mem[FFF4].

Initialize PC and SP

Fetch instruction

The first operation in the von Neumann execution cycle is fetch. To fetch an instruction, the CPU examines the 16 bits in the PC and interprets them as an address. It then goes to that address in main memory to fetch the instruction specifier (one byte) of the next instruction. It brings the eight bits of the instruction specifier into the CPU and holds them in the first byte of the instruction register (IR).

Decode instruction specifier

The second operation in the von Neumann cycle is decode. The CPU extracts the opcode from the instruction specifier to determine which instruction to execute. Depending on the opcode, the CPU extracts the register specifier if there is one and the addressing field if there is one. Now the CPU knows from the opcode whether the instruction is unary. If it is not unary, the CPU fetches the operand specifier (one word) from memory and stores it in the last two bytes of the IR.

Increment PC

The third operation in the von Neumann execution cycle is increment. The CPU adds 0001 to the PC if the instruction was unary. Otherwise it adds 0003. Regardless of which number is added to the PC, its value after the addition will be the address of the following instruction because the instructions are loaded adjacent to one another in main memory.

Execute instruction fetched

The fourth operation in the von Neumann execution cycle is execute. The CPU executes the instruction that is stored in the IR. The opcode tells the CPU which of the 40 instructions to execute.

Repeat the cycle

The fifth operation in the von Neumann execution cycle is repeat. The CPU returns to the fetch operation unless the instruction just executed was the stop instruction. Pep/9 will also terminate at this point if the instruction attempts an illegal operation. Some instructions are not allowed to use certain addressing modes. The most common illegal operation that makes Pep/9 terminate is attempting execution of an instruction with a forbidden addressing mode.

FIGURE 4.32 is a more detailed pseudocode description of the steps to execute a program on the Pep/9 computer.

A Character Output Program

The Pep/9 system can take its input from the keyboard and send its output to the screen. These I/O devices are based on the ASCII character set. When you press a key, a byte of information representing a single ASCII character goes from the keyboard and is added to the input stream at the input device at Mem[FC15]. When the CPU sends a byte to the output device at Mem[FC16], the screen interprets the byte as an ASCII character, which it displays.

At Level ISA3, the machine level, computers usually have no input or output instructions for any type of data except bytes. The interpretation of the byte occurs in the input or output device, not in main memory. Pep/9's

FIGURE 4.32

A more detailed pseudocode description of the steps necessary to execute a program on the Pep/9 computer.

Load the machine language program into memory starting at address 0000.
PC ← 0000
SP ← Mem[FFF4]
do {
    Fetch the instruction specifier at address in PC
    PC ← PC + 1
    Decode the instruction specifier
    if (*the instruction is not unary*) {
        Fetch the operand specifier at address in PC
        PC ← PC + 2
    }
    Execute the instruction fetched
}
while ((*the stop instruction does not execute*) && (*the instruction is legal*))

only input instruction is load byte, which transfers a byte from the input device to a CPU register, and its only output instruction is store byte, which transfers a byte from a CPU register to the output device. Because these bytes are usually interpreted as ASCII characters, the I/O at Level ISA3 of the Pep/9 system is called *character I/O*.

FIGURE 4.33 shows a simple machine-language program that outputs the characters Hi on the output device. It uses three instructions: 1101 raaa, which is the load byte instruction from a memory location, 1111 raaa, which is the store byte instruction to the output device, and 0000 0000, which is the stop instruction. The first listing shows the machine language program in binary. Main memory stores this sequence of ones and zeros. The first column gives the address in hex of the first byte of the bit pattern on each line.

The second listing shows the same program abbreviated to hexadecimal. Even though this format is slightly easier to read, remember that memory stores bits, not literal hexadecimal characters as in the second listing. Each line in the listing has a comment that begins with a semicolon to separate it from the machine language. The comments are not loaded into memory with the program.

FIGURE 4.34 shows each step the computer takes to execute the first three instructions of the program. Figure 4.34(a) is the initial state of the Pep/9 computer. Neither the disk nor the input device is shown. Several of

FIGURE 4.33

A machine language program to output the characters `Hi`.

Address	Machine Language (bin)
0000	1101 0001 0000 0000 0000 1101
0003	1111 0001 1111 1100 0001 0110
0006	1101 0001 0000 0000 0000 1110
0009	1111 0001 1111 1100 0001 0110
000C	0000 0000
000D	0100 1000 0110 1001

Address	Machine Language (hex)
0000	D1000D ;Load byte accumulator 'H'
0003	F1FC16 ;Store byte accumulator output device
0006	D1000E ;Load byte accumulator 'i'
0009	F1FC16 ;Store byte accumulator output device
000C	00 ;Stop
000D	4869 ;ASCII "Hi" characters

Output

Hi

the CPU registers not used by this program are also omitted. Initially, the contents of the main memory cells and the CPU registers are unknown.

Figure 4.34(b) shows the first step of the process. The program is loaded into main memory, starting at address 0000. The details of where the program comes from and what puts it into memory are described in later chapters.

Figure 4.34(c) shows the second step of the process. The program counter is cleared to 0000 (hex). The figure does not show the initialization of SP because this program does not use the stack pointer.

Figure 4.34(d) shows the fetch part of the execution cycle. The CPU examines the bits in the PC and finds 0000 (hex). It signals the main memory to send the byte at that address to the CPU. When the CPU gets the byte, it stuffs it into the first part of the instruction register. Then it decodes the instruction specifier, determines from the opcode that the instruction is not unary, and brings the operand specifier into IR as well. The original bits at addresses 0000, 0001, and 0002 are not changed by the fetch. Main memory has sent a copy of the 24 bits to the CPU.

FIGURE 4.34

The von Neumann execution cycle for the program of Figure 4.33.

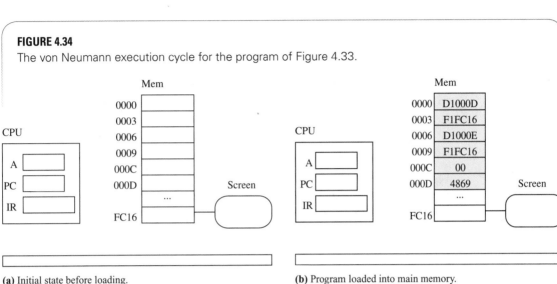

(a) Initial state before loading.

(b) Program loaded into main memory.

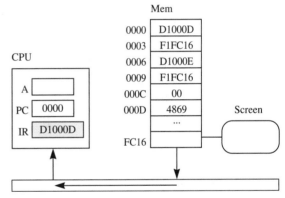

(c) PC ← 0000 (hex).

(d) Fetch instruction at Mem[PC].

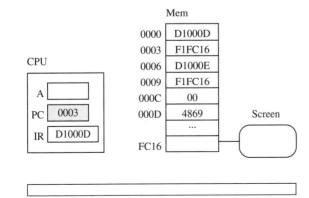

(e) Increment PC.

(f) Execute. Load byte for H to accumulator.

(*continues*)

FIGURE 4.34

The von Neumann execution cycle for the program of Figure 4.33. (*continued*)

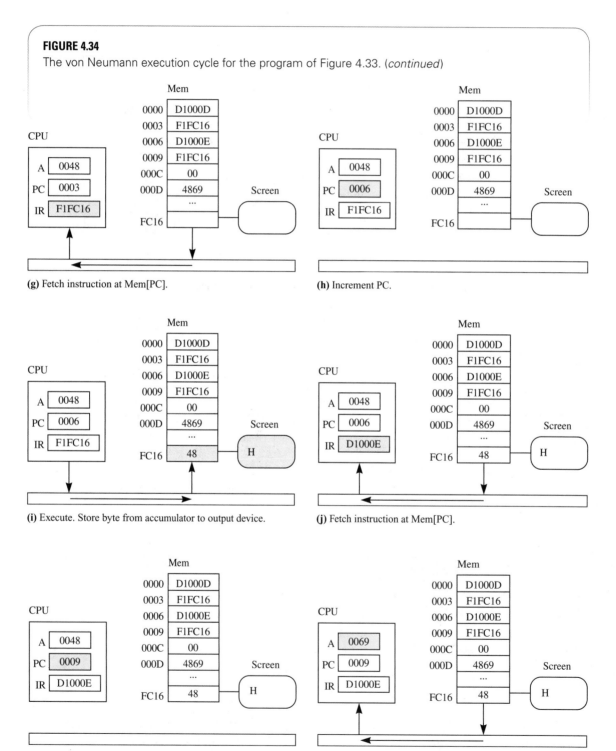

(g) Fetch instruction at Mem[PC].

(h) Increment PC.

(i) Execute. Store byte from accumulator to output device.

(j) Fetch instruction at Mem[PC].

(k) Increment PC.

(l) Execute. Load byte for i to accumulator.

Figure 4.34(e) shows the increment part of the execution cycle. The CPU adds 0003 to the PC.

Figure 4.34(f) shows the execute part of the execution cycle. The CPU examines the first four bits of IR and finds 1101. This opcode signals the circuitry to execute the load byte instruction. Consequently, the CPU examines the r-field and finds 0, which indicates the accumulator, and the addressing-aaa field and finds 001, which indicates direct addressing. It then examines the operand specifier and finds 000D (hex). It sends a control signal to main memory to go directly to address 000D and put the byte at that address on the system bus. The CPU then retrieves the value from the system bus and puts it into the right half of the accumulator.

Figure 4.34(g) shows the fetch part of the execution cycle. This time the CPU finds 0003 (hex) in the PC. It fetches a copy of the byte at address 0003, determines that the instruction is not unary, and then fetches the word at 0004. As a result, the original content of IR is destroyed.

Figure 4.34(h) shows the increment part of the execution cycle. The CPU adds 0003 to PC, making it 0006 (hex).

Figure 4.34(i) shows the execute part of the execution cycle. The CPU examines the first four bits of IR and finds 1111. This opcode signals the circuitry to execute the store byte instruction. Consequently, the CPU examines the r-field and finds 0, which indicates the accumulator, and the addressing-aaa field and finds 001, which indicates direct addressing. It then examines the operand specifier and finds FC16 (hex). It puts the byte from the right half of the accumulator on the bus and sends a control signal to main memory to store the data from the bus at address FC16, which is the output device. The output device interprets the byte as the ASCII character H and displays the character on the screen.

Figure 4.34(j) shows the fetch part of the execute cycle. Because PC contains 0006 (hex), the byte at that address comes to the CPU. When the CPU examines the opcode, it discovers that the instruction is not unary, so it fetches the word at address 0007.

Figure 4.34(k) shows the increment part of the execution cycle. The CPU adds 0003 to PC, making it 0009 (hex).

Figure 4.34(l) shows the execute part of the execution cycle. As with part (f), the CPU executes the load byte instruction—but this time loads from address 000E, which contains the ASCII code for the letter i. The figure does not show exection of the last two instructions. The following instruction sends the letter i to the output device, and the instruction after that causes the program to halt.

Just outputting two characters may seem a rather involved process, but it all happens quickly in human terms. The fetch part of the execution cycle takes less than about one nanosecond on many computers. Because the execution part of the execution cycle depends on the particular instruction, a complex instruction may take many nanoseconds to execute, whereas a simple instruction may take a few nanoseconds.

The computer does not attach any meaning to the electrical signals in its circuitry. Specifically, main memory does not know whether the bits at a particular address represent data or an instruction. It remembers only individual 1's and 0's.

von Neumann Bugs

In the program of Figure 4.33, the bits at addresses 0000 to 000C are used by the CPU as instructions, and the bits at 000D and 000E are used as data. The programmer placed the instruction bits at the beginning because she knew the PC would be initially cleared to 0000 and would be incremented by 0001 or 0003 on each iteration of the execution cycle. If the stop instruction (opcode 0000 0000) were omitted by mistake, the execution cycle would continue to fetch the next byte and interpret it as the instruction specifier of the next instruction, even though the programmer intended to have it interpreted as data.

Executing data as instructions

Because programs and data share the same memory, programmers at the machine level must be careful in allocating memory for each of them. Otherwise two types of problems can arise. The CPU may interpret a sequence of bits as an instruction when the programmer intended them to be data. Or the CPU may interpret a sequence of bits to be data when the programmer intended them to be an instruction. Both types of bugs occur at the machine level.

Interpreting instructions as data

Although the sharing of memory by both data and instructions can produce bugs if the programmer is not careful, it also presents an exciting possibility. A program is simply a set of instructions that is stored in memory. The programmer, therefore, can view the program as data for yet another program. It becomes possible to write programs that process other programs. Compilers, assemblers, and loaders are programs that adopt this viewpoint of treating other programs as data.

A Character Input Program

The program of **FIGURE 4.35** inputs two characters from the input device and outputs them in reverse order on the output device. It uses the character input instruction with direct addressing to get the characters from the input device.

The first instruction, D1FC15, has an opcode that specifies load byte from the input device at Mem[FC15], register-r field that specifies the accumulator, and addressing-aaa field that specifies direct addressing.

FIGURE 4.35
A machine language program to input two characters and output them in reverse order.

Address	Machine Language (bin)
0000	1101 0001 1111 1100 0001 0101
0003	1111 0001 0000 0000 0001 0011
0006	1101 0001 1111 1100 0001 0101
0009	1111 0001 1111 1100 0001 0110
000C	1101 0001 0000 0000 0001 0011
000F	1111 0001 1111 1100 0001 0110
0012	0000 0000

Address	Machine Language (hex)	
0000	D1FC15	;Input first character
0003	F10013	;Store first character
0006	D1FC15	;Input second character
0009	F1FC16	;Output second character
000C	D10013	;Load first character
000F	F1FC16	;Output first character
0012	00	;Stop

Input
up

Output
pu

It puts the first character from the input device into the right half of the accumulator. The second instruction, F10013, has an opcode that specifies store byte from the accumulator to Mem[0013]. Although this byte is not shown on the listing, it is surely available because memory goes all the way up to address FFFF.

The third instruction, D1FC15, is identical to the first and inputs the second character into the right half of the accumulator. The fourth instruction, F1FC16, has an opcode that specifies store byte, a register-r field that specifies the accumulator, and an addressing-aaa field that specifies direct addressing. It sends the byte from the accumulator to the output device at Mem[FC16]. The fifth instruction, D10013, loads the first character previously stored in Mem[0013] into the accumulator. The penultimate instruction, F1FC16, sends the second character from the accumulator to the output device at Mem[FC16]. The last instruction halts the program.

Converting Decimal to ASCII

FIGURE 4.36 shows a program that adds two single-digit numbers and outputs their single-digit sum. It illustrates the inconvenience of dealing with output at the machine level.

The two numbers to be added are 5 and 3. The program stores them at Mem[000D] and Mem[000F]. The first instruction loads the 5 into the accumulator, and then the second instruction adds the 3. At this point the sum is in the accumulator.

Now a problem arises. We want to output this result, but the only output instruction for this Level ISA3 machine is to store a byte in ASCII format to

FIGURE 4.36
A machine language program to add 5 and 3 and output the single-character result.

Address	Machine Language (bin)
0000	1100 0001 0000 0000 0000 1101
0003	0110 0001 0000 0000 0000 1111
0006	1001 0001 0000 0000 0001 0001
0009	1111 0001 1111 1100 0001 0110
000C	0000 0000
000D	0000 0000 0000 0101
000F	0000 0000 0000 0011
0011	0000 0000 0011 0000

Address	Machine Language (hex)	
0000	C1000D	;A<-first number
0003	61000F	;Add the two numbers
0006	910011	;Convert sum to character
0009	F1FC16	;Output the character
000C	00	;Stop
000D	0005	;Decimal 5
000F	0003	;Decimal 3
0011	0030	;Mask for ASCII char

Output

8

the output device at Mem[FC16]. The problem is that our result is 0000 1000 (bin). If the store byte instruction tries to output that, it will be interpreted as the backspace character, BS. (See the ASCII chart of Figure 3.25).

So, the program must convert the decimal number 8, 0000 1000 (bin), to the ASCII character 8, 0011 1000 (bin). The ASCII bits differ from the unsigned binary bits by the two extra 1's in the third and fourth bits. To do the conversion, the program inserts those two extra 1's into the result by ORing the accumulator with the mask 0000 0000 0011 0000, using the OR register instruction:

$$
\begin{array}{r}
0000\ 0000\ 0000\ 1000 \\
\mathrm{OR}\quad \underline{0000\ 0000\ 0011\ 0000} \\
0000\ 0000\ 0011\ 1000
\end{array}
$$

The accumulator now contains the correct sum in ASCII form. The store byte instruction sends it to the output device.

If you replace the word at Mem[0013] with 0009, what does this program output? Unfortunately, it does not output 14, even though the sum in the accumulator is

14 (dec) = 0000 0000 0000 1110 (bin)

after the add accumulator instruction executes. The OR instruction changes this bit pattern to 0000 0000 0011 1110 (bin), producing an output of >. Because the only output instruction at Level ISA3 is one that outputs a single byte, the program cannot output a result that should contain more than one character. Chapter 5 shows how to remedy this shortcoming.

A Self-Modifying Program

FIGURE 4.37 illustrates a curious possibility based on the von Neumann design principle. Notice that the program from 0006 to 0017 is identical to Figure 4.36 from 0000 to 0011. This program has two instructions at the beginning that are not in Figure 4.36, however. Because the instructions are shifted down six bytes, their operand specifiers are all greater by six than the operand specifiers of the previous program. Other than the adjustment by six bytes, however, the instructions beginning at 0006 would appear to duplicate the processing of Figure 4.36.

In particular, it appears that the load accumulator instruction would load the 5 into the accumulator, the add instruction would add the 3, the OR instruction would change the 8 (dec) to ASCII 8, and the store byte accumulator instruction would send the ASCII character for 8 to the output device at Mem[FC16]. Instead, the output is 2.

Because program and data share the same memory in a von Neumann machine, it is possible for a program to treat itself as data and modify

FIGURE 4.37

A machine language program that modifies itself. The add instruction changes to a subtract instruction.

Address	Machine Language (bin)
0000	1101 0001 0000 0000 0001 1001
0003	1111 0001 0000 0000 0000 1001
0006	1100 0001 0000 0000 0001 0011
0009	0110 0001 0000 0000 0001 0101
000C	1001 0001 0000 0000 0001 0111
000F	1111 0001 1111 1100 0001 0110
0012	0000 0000
0013	0000 0000 0000 0101
0015	0000 0000 0000 0011
0017	0000 0000 0011 0000
0019	0111 0001

Address	Machine Language (hex)	
0000	D10019	;Load byte accumulator
0003	F10009	;Store byte accumulator
0006	C10013	;A<-first number
0009	610015	;Add the two numbers
000C	910017	;Convert sum to character
000F	F1FC16	;Output the character
0012	00	;Stop
0013	0005	;Decimal 5
0015	0003	;Decimal 3
0017	0030	;Mask for ASCII char
0019	71	;Byte to modify instruction

Output

2

itself. The first instruction loads the byte 71 (hex) into the right half of the accumulator, and the second instruction puts it in Mem[0009]. What was at Mem[0009] before this change? The instruction specifier of the add accumulator instruction. Now the bits at Mem[0009] are 0111 0001. When the computer gets these bits in the fetch part of the von Neumann execution cycle, the CPU detects the opcode as 0111, the opcode for the subtract register instruction. The register specifier indicates the accumulator, and the addressing mode bits indicate direct addressing. The instruction subtracts 3 from 5 instead of adding it.

Of course, this is not a very practical program. If you wanted to subtract the two numbers, you would simply write the program of Figure 4.36 with the subtract instruction in place of the add instruction. But it does show that in a von Neumann machine, main memory places no significance on the bits it is storing. It simply remembers 1's and 0's and has no idea which are program bits, which are data bits, which are ASCII characters, and so on. Furthermore, the CPU cranks out the von Neumann execution cycle and interprets the bits accordingly, with no idea of their history. When it fetches the bits at Mem[0009], it does not know, or care, how they got there in the first place. It simply repeats the fetch, decode, increment, execute cycle over and over.

The x86 Architecture

The designation *x86* refers to a family of processors beginning with the 8086 introduced by Intel in 1978 and continuing with the 80186, 80286, 80386, 80486 series; the Pentium series; and the Core series. The CPU registers vary in size from 16 bits in the 8086, to 32 bits in the 80386, to 64 bits beginning with the Pentium 4. The processors are generally backward compatible. For example, the 64-bit processors have a 32-bit execution mode so that older software can run unchanged on the newer CPUs.

FIGURE 4.38 shows the registers in a typical 32-bit model. The x86 processors are little-endian and number the bits in a register starting from 0 for the least significant bit. The EFLAGS register has a number

FIGURE 4.38
The registers in a typical 32-bit x86 CPU.

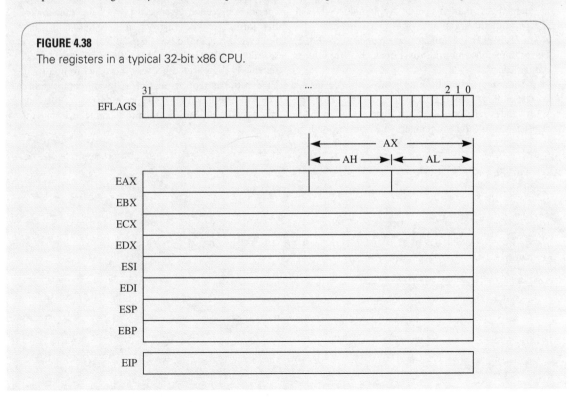

FIGURE 4.39

The x86 status bits corresponding to the Pep/9 status bits.

Status Bit	Intel Name	EFLAGS Position
N	SF	7
Z	ZF	6
V	OF	11
C	CF	0

of status bits besides the four NZVC bits in Pep/9. FIGURE 4.39 shows the location of the four bits that correspond to the Pep/9 status bits. *SF* stands for *sign flag*, and *OF* stands for *overflow flag*.

The x86 architecture has four general-purpose accumulators named *EAX*, *EBX*, *ECX*, and *EDX* that correspond to the single Pep/9 accumulator. Figure 4.38 shows that the rightmost two bytes of the EAX register are named *AX*, the left byte of AX is named *AH* for *A-high*, and the right byte of AX is named *AL* for *A-low*. The other accumulators are named accordingly. For example, the rightmost byte of the ECX register is named *CL*.

The x86 architecture has two index registers corresponding to the single X register of Pep/9. ESI is the source index register, and EDI is the destination index register. ESP is the stack pointer, which corresponds to the stack pointer SP of Pep/9. EBP is the base pointer, which points to the bottom of the current stack frame. Pep/9 has no corresponding register. EIP is called the *instruction pointer* in Intel terminology and corresponds to the program counter PC in Pep/9.

FIGURE 4.40 shows a machine language instruction that adds the content of the ECX register to the content of the EAX register and puts the sum in the ECX register. As with all von Neumann machines, a machine language instruction begins with an opcode field, 000000 in this example, which is the opcode for the add instruction. The following fields correspond to the register-r field and the addressing-aaa field of Pep/9 but with meaning specific to the x86 instruction set. The 1 in the s field indicates that the sum is on 32-bit quantities. If s were 0, only a single byte would be added. The 11 in the mod field indicates that the r/m field is a register. The 000 in the reg field, along with the 0 in the d field, indicates the EAX register, and the 001 in the r/m field, along with the 0 in the d field, indicates the ECX register. The hexadecimal abbreviation of the instruction is 01C1.

This is only one format from the x86 instruction set. There are multiple formats with some instruction specifiers preceded by special prefix bytes that change the format of the instruction specifier, and some followed by operand specifiers that might include a so-called scaled indexed byte. The instruction format scheme is complicated because it evolved from a small CPU with the requirement of backward compatibility. Pep/9 illustrates the concepts underlying machine languages in all von Neumann machines without the above complexities.

FIGURE 4.40

The x86 instruction format for the add register instruction.

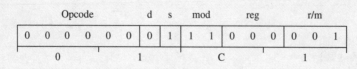

4.4 **Programming at Level ISA3**

To program at Level ISA3 is to write a set of instructions in binary. To execute the binary sequence, first you must load it into main memory. The operating system is responsible for loading the binary sequence into main memory.

An operating system is a program. Like any other program, a software engineer must design, write, test, and debug it. Most operating systems are so large and complex that teams of engineers must write them. The primary function of an operating system is to control the execution of application programs on the computer. Because the operating system is itself a program, it must reside in main memory in order to be executed. So main memory must store not only the application programs, but also the operating system.

In the Pep/9 computer, the bottom part of main memory—that is, the part with high memory addresses—is reserved for the operating system. The top part is reserved for the application program. **FIGURE 4.41** is a memory map of the Pep/9 computer system. It shows that the operating system starts at memory location FB8F and occupies the rest of main memory. That leaves memory locations 0000 to FB8E for the application program.

The loader is that part of the operating system that loads the application program into main memory so it can be executed. What loads the loader? The Pep/9 loader, along with several other parts of the operating system, is permanently stored in main memory.

Read-Only Memory

There are two types of electronic-circuit elements from which memory devices are manufactured—read/write circuit elements and read-only circuit elements.

In the program of Figure 4.35, when the store byte instruction, F10013, executed, the CPU transferred the content of the right half of the accumulator to Mem[0013]. The original content of Mem[0013] was destroyed, and the memory location then contained 0111 0101 (bin), the binary code for the letter u. When the load byte instruction, D10013, executed, the bits at location 0013 were sent back to the accumulator so they could be sent to the output device.

The circuit element at memory location 0013 is a read/write circuit. The store byte instruction did a write operation on it, which changed its content. The read byte instruction did a read operation on it, which sent a copy of its content to the accumulator. If the circuit element at location 0013 were a read-only circuit, the store byte instruction would not have changed its content.

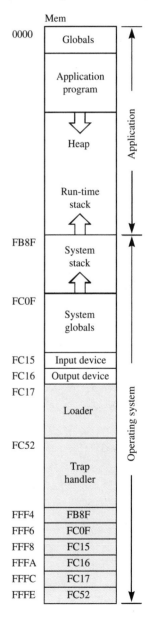

FIGURE 4.41
A memory map of the Pep/9 memory. The shaded part is read-only memory.

RAM should be called RWM.

Volatile memory

Both types of main-memory circuit elements—read/write and read-only—are random-access devices, as opposed to serial devices. When the load byte instruction does a read from memory location 0013, it does not need to start at location 0000 and sequentially go through 0001, 0002, 0003, and so on until it gets to 0013. Instead, it can go directly to location 0013. Because it can go to a random location in memory directly, the circuit element is called a *random-access* device.

Read-only memory devices are known as *ROM*. Read/write memory devices should be known as *RWM*. Unfortunately, they are known as *RAM*, which stands for *random-access memory*. That name is unfortunate because both read-only and read/write devices are random-access devices. The characteristic that distinguishes a read-only memory device from a read/write memory device is that the content of a read-only device cannot be changed by a store instruction. Because use of the term *RAM* is so pervasive in the computer industry, we also will use it to refer to read/write devices. But in our hearts we will know that ROMs are random also.

Main memory usually contains some ROM devices. Those parts of main memory that are ROM contain permanent binary sequences, which the store instruction cannot alter. Furthermore, when power to the computer is switched off at the end of the day and then switched on at the beginning of the next day, the ROM will retain those binary sequences in its circuitry. RAM will not retain its memory if the power is switched off. It is therefore called *volatile*.

There are two ways a computer manufacturer can buy ROM for a memory system. In the first approach, the computer manufacturer specifies to the circuit manufacturer the bit sequences desired in the memory devices. The circuit manufacturer then manufactures the devices accordingly. Alternatively, the computer manufacturer orders a programmable read-only memory (PROM), which is a ROM with all zeros. The computer manufacturer then permanently changes any desired location to a 1, in such a way that the device will contain the proper bit sequence. This process is called "burning in" the bit pattern.

The Pep/9 Operating System

Most of the Pep/9 operating system has been burned into ROM. In Figure 4.41, the ROM part of the operating system is shaded. It begins at location FC17 and continues down to FFFF. That part of main memory is permanent. A store instruction cannot change it. If the power is ever turned off, when it is turned on again, that part of the operating system will still be there. The region from FB8F to FC16 is the RAM part of the operating system for our computer.

The RAM part of the operating system is for the system variables and memory-mapped I/O devices. Variables will change while the operating system program is executing. The ROM part of the operating system contains the loader, which is a permanent fixture. Its job is to load the application program into RAM, starting at address 0000. On the Pep/9 virtual machine, you invoke the loader by choosing the loader option from the menu of the simulator program.

The bottom of the run-time stack for the application program, called the *user stack*, is at memory location FB8F, just above the operating system. The stack pointer register in the CPU contains the address of the top of the stack. When procedures are called, storage for the parameters, the return address, and the local variables are allocated on the stack at successively lower addresses. Hence the stack "grows upward" in memory toward the smaller addresses.

The run-time stack for the operating system begins at memory location FC0F, which is 128 bytes below the start of the user stack. When the operating system executes, the stack pointer in the CPU contains the address of the top of the system stack. Like the user stack, the system stack grows upward in memory. The operating system never needs more than 128 bytes on its stack, so there is no possibility that the system stack will try to store its data in the user stack region.

The Pep/9 operating system consists of two programs—the loader, which begins at address FC17, and the trap handler, which begins at address FC52. You will recall from Figure 4.6 that the instructions with opcodes 0010 011 through 0010 1 are unimplemented at Level ISA3. The trap handler implements these instructions for the assembly language programmer. Chapter 5 describes these instructions at Level Asmb5, the assembly level, and Chapter 8 shows how they are implemented at Level OS4, the operating system level.

Associated with the parts of the operating system are six words at the very bottom of ROM that are reserved for special use by the operating system. They are called *machine vectors* and are at addresses FFF4, FFF6, FFF8, FFFA, FFFC, and FFFE, as shown in Figure 4.41.

Machine vectors

When you choose the load option from the Pep/9 simulator menu, the following two events occur:

SP ← Mem[FFF6]
PC ← Mem[FFFC]

In other words, the content of memory location FFF6 is copied into the stack pointer, and the content of memory location FFFC is copied into the program counter. After these events occur, the execution cycle begins. FIGURE 4.42 illustrates these two events.

FIGURE 4.42

The Pep/9 load option.

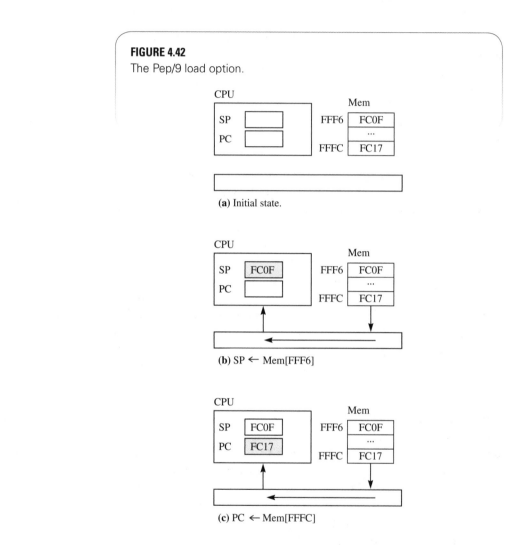

(a) Initial state.

(b) SP ← Mem[FFF6]

(c) PC ← Mem[FFFC]

Selecting the load option initializes the stack pointer and program counter to the predetermined values stored at FFF6 and FFFC. It just so happens that the value at address FFF6 is FC0F, the bottom of the system stack. FC0F is the value the stack pointer should have when the system stack is empty. It also happens that the value at address FFFC is FC17. In fact, FC17 is the address of the first instruction to be executed in the loader.

The system programmer who wrote the operating system decided where the system stack and the loader should be located. Realizing that the Pep/9 computer would fetch the vectors from locations FFFA and FFFC when the load option is selected, she placed the appropriate values in those locations. Because the first step in the execution cycle is fetch, the first instruction to be executed after selecting the load option is the first instruction of the loader program.

If you wish to revise the operating system, your loader might not begin at FC17. Suppose it begins at 7BD6 instead. When the user selects the load option, the computer will still go to location FFFC to fetch the vector. So you would need to place 7BD6 in the word at address FFFC.

This scheme of storing addresses at special reserved memory locations is flexible. It allows the system programmer to place the loader anywhere in memory that is convenient. A more direct but less flexible scheme would be to design the system to execute the following operations when the user selects the load option:

SP ← FC0F
PC ← FC17

The advantage of machine vectors

If selecting the load option produced these two events, the loader of the current operating system would still function correctly. However, it would be difficult to modify the operating system. The loader would always have to start at FC57, and the system stack would always have to start at FC4F. The system programmer would have no choice in the placement of the various parts of the system.

Using the Pep/9 System

To load a machine language program on the Pep/9 computer, fortunately you do not need to write it in binary. You may write it with ASCII hexadecimal characters in a text file. The loader will convert from ASCII to binary for you when it loads the program.

The listing in **FIGURE 4.43** shows how to prepare a machine language program for loading. It is the program of Figure 4.33, which outputs Hi. You simply write in a text file the binary sequence in hexadecimal without any addresses or comments. Terminate the list of bytes with lowercase zz, which the loader detects as a sentinel. The loader will put the bytes in memory one after the other, starting at address 0000 (hex).

The Pep/9 loader is extremely particular about the format of your machine-language program. To work correctly, the very first character in your text file must be a hexadecimal character. No leading blank lines or spaces are allowed. There must be exactly one space between bytes. If you wish to continue your byte stream on another line, you must not leave trailing spaces on the preceding line.

After you write your machine-language program and load it with the loader option, you must select the execute option to run it. The following two events occur when you select the execute option:

SP ← Mem[FFF4]
PC ← 0000

FIGURE 4.43

Preparing a program for the loader.

```
Address      Machine Language (hex)
0000         D1000D ;Load byte accumulator 'H'
0003         F1FC16 ;Store byte accumulator output device
0006         D1000E ;Load byte accumulator 'i'
0009         F1FC16 ;Store byte accumulator output device
000C         00     ;Stop
000D         4869   ;ASCII "Hi" characters


Hex Version for the Loader
D1 00 0D F1 FC 16 D1 00 0E F1 FC 16 00 48 69 zz


Output
Hi
```

Then the von Neumann execution cycle begins. Because PC has the value 0000, the CPU will fetch the first instruction from Mem[0000]. Fortunately, that is where the loader put the first instruction of the application program.

Figure 4.41 shows that Mem[FFF4] contains FB8F, the address of the bottom of the user stack. The application program in this example does not use the run-time stack. If it did, the application program could access the stack correctly because SP would be initialized to the address of the bottom of the user stack.

Enjoy!

Chapter Summary

Virtually all commercial computers are based on the von Neumann design principle, in which main memory stores both data and instructions. The three components of a von Neumann machine are the central processing unit (CPU), main memory with memory-mapped I/O devices, and disk. The CPU contains a set of registers, one of which is the program counter (PC), which stores the address of the instruction to be executed next.

The CPU has an instruction set wired into it. An instruction consists of an instruction specifier and an operand specifier. The instruction specifier, in turn, consists of an opcode and possibly a register field and an addressing mode field. The opcode determines which instruction in the instruction set is to be executed. The register field determines which register participates in the operation. The addressing mode field determines which addressing mode is used for the source or destination of the data.

Each addressing mode corresponds to a relationship between the operand specifier (OprndSpec) and the operand (Oprnd). In the direct addressing mode, the operand specifier is the address in main memory of the operand. In mathematical notation, Oprnd = Mem[OprndSpec].

To execute a program, a group of instructions and data are loaded into main memory, and then the von Neumann execution cycle begins. The von Neumann execution cycle consists of the following steps: (1) fetch the instruction specified by PC, (2) decode the instruction specifier, (3) increment PC, (4) execute the instruction fetched, and (5) repeat by going to Step 1.

Because main memory stores instructions as well as data, two types of errors at the machine level are possible. You may interpret data bits as instructions, or you may interpret instruction bits as data. Another possibility that is a direct result of storing instructions in main memory is that a program may be processed as if it were data. Loaders and compilers are important programs that take the viewpoint of treating instructions as data.

The operating system is a program that controls the execution of applications. It must reside in main memory along with the applications and data. On some computers, a portion of the operating system is burned into read-only memory (ROM). One characteristic of ROM is that a store instruction cannot change the content of a memory cell. The run-time stack for the operating system is located in random-access memory (RAM). A machine vector is an address of an operating system component, such as a stack or a program, used to access that component. Two important functions of an operating system are the loader and the trap handler.

Exercises

Section 4.1

*1. (a) How many bytes are in the main memory of the Pep/9 computer? (b) How many words are in it? (c) How many bits are in it? (d) How many total bits are in the Pep/9 CPU? (e) How many times bigger in terms of bits is the main memory than the CPU?

2. (a) Suppose the main memory of the Pep/9 were completely filled with unary instructions. How many instructions would it contain? **(b)** What is the maximum number of instructions that would fit in the main memory if none of the instructions is unary? **(c)** Suppose the main memory is completely filled with an equal number of unary and nonunary instructions. How many total instructions would it contain?

*3. Answer the following questions for the machine language instructions 6AF82C and D623D0. **(a)** What is the opcode in binary? **(b)** What does the instruction do? **(c)** What is the register-r field in binary? **(d)** Which register does it specify? **(e)** What is the addressing-aaa field in binary? **(f)** Which addressing mode does it specify? **(g)** What is the operand specifier in hexadecimal?

4. Answer the questions in Exercise 3 for the machine language instructions 7B00AC and F70BD3.

Section 4.2

*5. Suppose Pep/9 contains the following four hexadecimal values:

A: 19AC
X: FE20
Mem[0A3F]: FF00
Mem[0A41]: 103D

If it has these values before each of the following statements executes, what are the four hexadecimal values after each statement executes?

(a) C10A3F	**(b)** D10A3F	**(c)** D90A41
(d) F10A41	**(e)** E90A3F	**(f)** 790A41
(g) 710A3F	**(h)** 910A3F	**(i)** 07

6. Repeat Exercise 5 for the following statements:

(a) C90A3F	**(b)** D90A3F	**(c)** F10A41
(d) E10A41	**(e)** 690A3F	**(f)** 710A41
(g) 890A3F	**(h)** 990A3F	**(i)** 06

Section 4.3

7. Determine the output of the following Pep/9 machine language program. The left column is the memory address of the first byte on the line:

```
0000 D10013
0003 F1FC16
0006 D10014
```

```
0009 F1FC16
000C D10015
000F F1FC16
0012 00
0013 4A6F
0015 79
```

8. Determine the output of the following Pep/9 machine language program if the input is `tab`. The left column is the memory address of the first byte on the line:

```
0000 D1FC15
0003 F1001F
0006 D1FC15
0009 F10020
000C D1FC15
000F F10021
0012 D10020
0015 F1FC16
0018 D1001F
001B F1FC16
001E 00
```

9. Determine the output of the following Pep/9 machine language program. The left column in each part is the memory address of the first byte on the line:

*(a)	(b)
0000 C1000A	0000 C10008
0003 81000C	0003 06
0006 F1FC16	0004 F1FC16
0009 00	0007 00
000A A94F	0008 F0D4
000C FFFD	

Section 4.4

10. Suppose you need to process a list of 31,000 integers contained in Pep/9 memory at one integer per word. You estimate that 20% of the instructions in a typical program are unary instructions. What is the maximum number of instructions you can expect to be able to use in the program that processes the data? Keep in mind that your applications program must share memory with the operating system and with your data.

Problems

Section 4.4

11. Write a machine language program to output your name on the output device. The name you output must be longer than two characters. Write it in a format suitable for the loader and execute it on the Pep/9 simulator.

12. Write a machine language program to output the four characters Frog on the output device. Write it in a format suitable for the loader and execute it on the Pep/9 simulator.

13. Write a machine language program to output the three characters Cat on the output device. Write it in a format suitable for the loader and execute it on the Pep/9 simulator.

14. Write a machine language program to add the three numbers 2, –3, and 6 and output the sum on the output device. Store the –3 in hexadecimal. Do not use the subtract, negate, or invert instructions. Write the program in a format suitable for the loader and execute it on the Pep/9 simulator.

15. Write a machine language program to input two one-digit numbers, add them, and output the one-digit sum. There can be no space between the two one-digit numbers on input. Write the program in a format suitable for the loader and execute it on the Pep/9 simulator.

16. Write the program in Figure 4.35 in hexadecimal format for input to the loader. Verify that it works correctly by running it on the Pep/9 simulator with an input of up. Then modify the store byte instruction at 0003 so that the first character is stored at Mem[FCAA] and the load byte instruction at 000C is also from Mem[FCAA]. What is the output? Explain.

Assembly

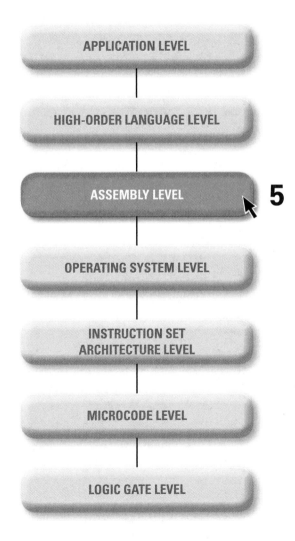

APPLICATION LEVEL

HIGH-ORDER LANGUAGE LEVEL

ASSEMBLY LEVEL   5

OPERATING SYSTEM LEVEL

INSTRUCTION SET
ARCHITECTURE LEVEL

MICROCODE LEVEL

LOGIC GATE LEVEL

CHAPTER 5

Assembly Language

TABLE OF CONTENTS

The Level-ISA3 language is machine language, sequences of 1's and 0's sometimes abbreviated to hexadecimal. Computer pioneers had to program in machine language, but they soon revolted against such an indignity. Memorizing the opcodes of the machine and having to continually refer to ASCII charts and hexadecimal tables to get their programs into binary was no fun. The assembly level was invented to relieve programmers of the tedium of programming in binary.

The assembly level uses the operating system below it.

Chapter 4 describes the Pep/9 computer at Level ISA3, the machine level. This chapter describes Level Asmb5, the assembly level. Between these two levels lies the operating system. Remember that the purpose of levels of abstraction is to hide the details of the system at the lower levels. This chapter illustrates that principle of information hiding. You will use the trap handler of the operating system without knowing the details of its operation. That is, you will learn what the trap handler does without learning how the handler does it. Chapter 8 reveals the inner workings of the trap handler.

5.1 Assemblers

The language at Level Asmb5 is called *assembly language*. It provides a more convenient way of writing machine language programs than binary does. The program of Figure 4.33, which outputs Hi, contains two types of bit patterns, one for instructions and one for data. These two types are a direct consequence of the von Neumann design, where program and data share the same memory with a binary representation for each.

The two types of bit patterns at Level ISA3

The two types of statements at Level Asmb5

Assembly language contains two types of statements that correspond to these two types of bit patterns. Mnemonic statements correspond to the instruction bit patterns, and pseudo-operations correspond to the data bit patterns.

Instruction Mnemonics

Suppose the machine language instruction

```
C0009A
```

is stored at some memory location. This is the load register r instruction. The register-r bit is 0, which indicates the accumulator and not the index register. The addressing-aaa field is 000, which specifies immediate addressing.

This instruction is written in the Pep/9 assembly language as

```
LDWA 0x009A,i
```

A mnemonic for the opcode

The mnemonic LDWA, which stands for *load word accumulator*, is written in place of the opcode, 1100, and the register-r field, 0. A mnemonic is a

FIGURE 5.1
The letters that specify the addressing mode in Pep/9 assembly language.

aaa	Addressing Mode	Letters
000	Immediate	i
001	Direct	d
010	Indirect	n
011	Stack-relative	s
100	Stack-relative deferred	sf
101	Indexed	x
110	Stack-indexed	sx
111	Stack-deferred indexed	sfx

memory aid. It is easier to remember that LDWA stands for the load word accumulator instruction than to remember that opcode 1100 and register-r 0 stand for the load word accumulator instruction. The operand specifier is written in hexadecimal, 009A, preceded by 0x, which stands for *hexadecimal constant*. In Pep/9 assembly language, you specify the addressing mode by placing one or more letters after the operand specifier with a comma between them. FIGURE 5.1 shows the letters that go with each of the eight addressing modes.

Letters for the addressing mode

Example 5.1   Here are some examples of the load word register r instruction written in binary machine language and in assembly language. LDWX corresponds to the same machine language statement as LDWA, except that the register-r bit for LDWX is 1 instead of 0.

```
1100 0011 0000 0000 1001 1010    LDWA 0x009A,s
1100 0110 0000 0000 1001 1010    LDWA 0x009A,sx
1100 1011 0000 0000 1001 1010    LDWX 0x009A,s
1100 1110 0000 0000 1001 1010    LDWX 0x009A,sx
```

FIGURE 5.2 summarizes the 40 instructions of the Pep/9 instruction set at Level Asmb5. It shows the mnemonic that goes with each opcode and the meaning of each instruction. The addressing modes column tells what addressing modes are allowed or whether the instruction is unary (U). The status bits column lists the status bits the instruction affects when it executes.

FIGURE 5.2

The Pep/9 instruction set at Level Asmb5.

Instruction Specifier	Mnemonic	Instruction	Addressing Mode	Status Bits
0000 0000	STOP	Stop execution	U	
0000 0001	RET	Return from CALL	U	
0000 0010	RETTR	Return from trap	U	
0000 0011	MOVSPA	Move SP to A	U	
0000 0100	MOVFLGA	Move NZVC flags to A⟨12..15⟩	U	
0000 0101	MOVAFLG	Move A⟨12..15⟩ to NZVC flags	U	
0000 011r	NOTr	Bitwise invert r	U	NZ
0000 100r	NEGr	Negate r	U	NZV
0000 101r	ASLr	Arithmetic shift left r	U	NZVC
0000 110r	ASRr	Arithmetic shift right r	U	NZC
0000 111r	ROLr	Rotate left r	U	C
0001 000r	RORr	Rotate right r	U	C
0001 001a	BR	Branch unconditional	i, x	
0001 010a	BRLE	Branch if less than or equal to	i, x	
0001 011a	BRLT	Branch if less than	i, x	
0001 100a	BREQ	Branch if equal to	i, x	
0001 101a	BRNE	Branch if not equal to	i, x	
0001 110a	BRGE	Branch if greater than or equal to	i, x	
0001 111a	BRGT	Branch if greater than	i, x	
0010 000a	BRV	Branch if V	i, x	
0010 001a	BRC	Branch if C	i, x	
0010 010a	CALL	Call subroutine	i, x	
0010 011n	NOPn	Unary no operation trap	U	
0010 1aaa	NOP	Nonunary no operation trap	i	

0011 0aaa	DECI	Decimal input trap	d, n, s, sf, x, sx, sfx	NZV
0011 1aaa	DECO	Decimal output trap	i, d, n, s, sf, x, sx, sfx	
0100 0aaa	HEXO	Hexadecimal output trap	i, d, n, s, sf, x, sx, sfx	
0100 1aaa	STRO	String output trap	d, n, s, sf, x	
0101 0aaa	ADDSP	Add to stack pointer (SP)	i, d, n, s, sf, x, sx, sfx	NZVC
0101 1aaa	SUBSP	Subtract from stack pointer (SP)	i, d, n, s, sf, x, sx, sfx	NZVC
0110 raaa	ADDr	Add to r	i, d, n, s, sf, x, sx, sfx	NZVC
0111 raaa	SUBr	Subtract from r	i, d, n, s, sf, x, sx, sfx	NZVC
1000 raaa	ANDr	Bitwise AND to r	i, d, n, s, sf, x, sx, sfx	NZ
1001 raaa	ORr	Bitwise OR to r	i, d, n, s, sf, x, sx, sfx	NZ
1010 raaa	CPWr	Compare word to r	i, d, n, s, sf, x, sx, sfx	NZVC
1011 raaa	CPBr	Compare byte to r⟨8..15⟩	i, d, n, s, sf, x, sx, sfx	NZVC
1100 raaa	LDWr	Load word r from memory	i, d, n, s, sf, x, sx, sfx	NZ
1101 raaa	LDBr	Load byte r⟨8..15⟩ from memory	i, d, n, s, sf, x, sx, sfx	NZ
1110 raaa	STWr	Store word r to memory	d, n, s, sf, x, sx, sfx	
1111 raaa	STBr	Store byte r⟨8..15⟩ to memory	d, n, s, sf, x, sx, sfx	

Figure 5.2 shows the unimplemented opcode instructions replaced by six new instructions:

NOPn	Unary no operation trap
NOP	Nonunary no operation trap
DECI	Decimal input trap
DECO	Decimal output trap
HEXO	Hexadecimal output trap
STRO	String output trap

The unimplemented opcode instructions at Level Asmb5

These new instructions are available to the assembly language programmer at Level Asmb5, but they are not part of the instruction set at Level ISA3. The operating system at Level OS4 provides them with its trap handler. At the assembly level, you may simply program with them as if they were part of the Level ISA3 instruction set, even though they are not. Chapter 8 shows in detail how the operating system provides these instructions. You do not need to know the details of how the instructions are implemented to program with them.

Pseudo-Operations

Pseudo-operations (pseudo-ops) are assembly language statements. Pseudo-ops do not have opcodes and do not correspond to any of the 40 instructions in the Pep/9 instruction set. Pep/9 assembly language has nine pseudo-ops:

The nine pseudo-ops of Pep/9 assembly language

.ADDRSS	The address of a symbol
.ALIGN	Padding to align at a memory boundary
.ASCII	A string of ASCII bytes
.BLOCK	A block of zero bytes
.BURN	Initiate ROM burn
.BYTE	A byte value
.END	The sentinel for the assembler
.EQUATE	Equate a symbol to a constant value
.WORD	A word value

All the pseudo-ops except .BURN, .END, and .EQUATE insert data bits into the machine language program. Pseudo means *false*. Pseudo-ops are so called because the bits that they generate do not correspond to opcodes, as do the bits generated by the 40 instruction mnemonics. They are not true instruction operations. Pseudo-ops are also called *assembler directives* or *dot commands* because each must be preceded by a . in assembly language.

The next three programs show how to use the .ASCII, .BLOCK, .BYTE, .END, and .WORD pseudo-ops. The other pseudo-ops are described later.

The .ASCII and .END Pseudo-ops

The line-oriented nature of assembly language

FIGURE 5.3 is Figure 4.33 written in assembly language instead of machine language. Pep/9 assembly language, unlike C, is line oriented. That is, each assembly language statement must be contained on only one line. You cannot continue a statement onto another line, nor can you place two statements on the same line.

Assembly language comments

Comments begin with a semicolon, ;, and continue until the end of the line. It is permissible to have a line with only a comment on it, but it must begin with a semicolon. The first four lines of this program are comment lines. The following lines also contain comments, but only after the assembly language statements. As in C, your assembly language programs should contain, at a minimum, your name, the date, and a description of the program. To conserve space in this text, however, the rest of the programs do not contain such a heading.

FIGURE 5.3

An assembly language program to output Hi. It is the assembly language version of Figure 4.33.

Assembler Input
```
;Stan Warford
;May 1, 2017
;A program to output "Hi"
;
LDBA        0x000D,d    ;Load byte accumulator 'H'
STBA        0xFC16,d    ;Store byte accumulator output device
LDBA        0x000E,d    ;Load byte accumulator 'i'
STBA        0xFC16,d    ;Store byte accumulator output device
STOP                    ;Stop
.ASCII      "Hi"        ;ASCII "Hi" characters
.END
```

Assembler Output
```
D1 00 0D F1 FC 16 D1 00 0E F1 FC 16 00 48 69 zz
```

Program Output
```
Hi
```

LDBA is the mnemonic for the load byte accumulator instruction, and STBA is the mnemonic for the store byte accumulator instruction. The statement

```
LDBA 0x000D,d
```

means "Load one byte from Mem[000D] using the direct addressing mode."

The .ASCII pseudo-op generates contiguous bytes of ASCII characters. In assembly language, you simply write .ASCII followed by a string of ASCII characters enclosed by double quotes. If you want to include a double quote in your string, you must prefix it with a backslash \. To include a backslash, prefix it with a backslash. You can put a newline character in your string by prefixing the letter n with a backslash and a tab character by prefixing the letter t with a backslash.

The .ASCII *pseudo-op*

The backslash prefix

Example 5.2   Here is a string that includes two double quotes:

```
"She said, \"Hello\"."
```

Here is one that includes a backslash character:

```
"My bash is \\."
```

And here is one with the newline character:

```
"\nThis sentence will output on a new line."
```
∎

Any arbitrary byte can be included in a string constant using the \x feature. When you include \x in a string constant, the assembler expects the next two characters to be hexadecimal digits, which specify the byte to be included in the string.

Example 5.3 The dot commands

```
.ASCII "Hello\nworld."
```

and

```
.ASCII "Hello\x0Aworld\x2E"
```

both generate the same sequence of bytes, namely

```
48 65 6C 6C 6F 0A 77 6F 72 6C 64 2E
```
∎

The .END *pseudo-op*

You must end your assembly language program with the .END command. It does not insert data bits into the program the way the .ASCII command does. It simply indicates the end of the assembly language program. The assembler uses .END as a sentinel to know when to stop translating.

Assemblers

Compare this program written in assembly language with the same program written in machine language. Assembly language is much easier to understand because of the mnemonics used in place of the opcodes. Also, the characters H and i written directly as ASCII characters are easier to read.

Unfortunately, you cannot simply write a program in assembly language and expect the computer to understand it. The computer can execute programs only by performing its von Neumann execution cycle (fetch, decode, increment, execute, repeat), which is wired into the CPU. The program must be stored in binary in main memory starting at address 0000 for the execution cycle to process it correctly (as shown in Chapter 4). The assembly language statements must somehow be translated into machine language before they are loaded and executed.

In the early days, programmers wrote in assembly language and then translated each statement into machine language by hand. The translation part was straightforward. It only involved looking up the binary opcodes for the instructions and the binary codes for the ASCII characters in the ASCII table. The hexadecimal operands could similarly be converted to binary with hexadecimal conversion tables. Only after the program was translated could it be loaded and executed.

The translation of a long program was a routine and tedious job. Soon programmers realized that a computer program could be written to do the translation. Such a program is called an *assembler*, and FIGURE 5.4 illustrates how it functions.

An assembler is a program whose input is an assembly language program and whose output is that same program translated into machine language in a format suitable for a loader. Input to the assembler is called the *source program*. Output from the assembler is called the *object program*. FIGURE 5.5 shows the effect of the Pep/9 assembler on the assembly language of Figure 5.3.

It is important to realize that an assembler merely translates a program into a format suitable for a loader. It does not execute the program. Translation and execution are separate processes, and translation always occurs first.

Because the assembler is itself a program, it must be written in some programming language. The computer pioneers who wrote the first assemblers had to write them in machine language. Or, if they wrote them in assembly language, they had to translate them into machine language by hand because no assemblers were available at the time. The point is that a machine can execute only programs that are written in machine language.

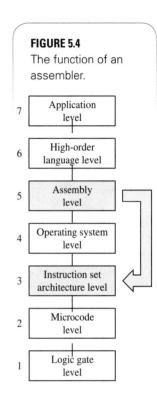

FIGURE 5.4
The function of an assembler.

The .BLOCK Pseudo-op

FIGURE 5.6 is the assembly language version of Figure 4.35. It inputs two characters and outputs them in reverse order.

FIGURE 5.5
The action of the Pep/9 assembler on the program of Figure 5.3.

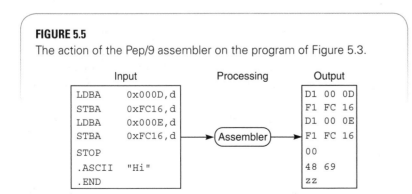

FIGURE 5.6

An assembly language program to input two characters and output them in reverse order. It is the assembly language version of Figure 4.35.

Assembler Input

```
LDBA    0xFC15,d    ;Input first character
STBA    0x0013,d    ;Store first character
LDBA    0xFC15,d    ;Input second character
STBA    0xFC16,d    ;Output second character
LDBA    0x0013,d    ;Load first character
STBA    0xFC16,d    ;Output first character
STOP                ;Stop
.BLOCK  1           ;Storage for first character
.END
```

Assembler Output

```
D1 FC 15 F1 00 13 D1 FC 15 F1 FC 16 D1 00 13 F1
FC 16 00 00 zz
```

Program Input

up

Program Output

pu

You can see from the assembler output that the first load statement, LDBA 0xFC15,d, translates to D1FC15, and the last store statement, STBA 0xFC16,d, translates to F1FC16. After that, the STOP statement translates to 00.

The .BLOCK pseudo-op generates the next byte of 0's. The dot command

```
.BLOCK 1
```

means "Generate a block of one byte of storage." The assembler interprets any number not prefixed with 0x as a decimal integer. The digit 1 is therefore interpreted as a decimal integer. The assembler expects a constant after the .BLOCK and will generate that number of bytes of storage, setting them to 0's.

The .WORD and .BYTE Pseudo-ops

FIGURE 5.7 is the same as Figure 4.36, computing 5 plus 3. It illustrates the .WORD pseudo-op.

Like the .BLOCK command, the .WORD command generates code for the loader, but with two differences. First, it always generates one

---

FIGURE 5.7

An assembly language program to add 5 and 3 and output the single-character result. It is the assembly language version of Figure 4.36.

Assembler Input

```
LDWA    0x000D,d    ;A <- first number
ADDA    0x000F,d    ;Add the two numbers
ORA     0x0011,d    ;Convert sum to character
STBA    0xFC16,d    ;Output the character
STOP                ;Stop
.WORD   5           ;Decimal 5
.WORD   3           ;Decimal 3
.WORD   0x0030      ;Mask for ASCII char
.END
```

Assembler Output

```
C1 00 0D 61 00 0F 91 00 11 F1 FC 16 00 00 05 00
03 00 30 zz
```

Program Output

```
8
```

---

word (two bytes) of code, not an arbitrary number of bytes. Second, the programmer can specify the content of the word. The dot command

```
.WORD 5
```

means "Generate one word with a value of 5 (dec)." The dot command

```
.WORD 0x0030
```

means "Generate one word with a value of 0030 (hex)."

The .BYTE command works like the .WORD command, except that it generates a byte value instead of a word value. In this program, you could replace

```
.WORD 0x0030
```

with

```
.BYTE 0x00
.BYTE 0x30
```

and generate the same machine language.

You can compare the assembler output of this assembly language program with the hexadecimal machine language of Figure 4.36 to see that they are identical. The assembler was designed to generate output that carefully follows the format expected by the loader. There are no leading blank lines or spaces. There is exactly one space between bytes, with no trailing spaces on a line. The byte sequence terminates with zz.

Using the Pep/9 Assembler

Execution of the program in Figure 5.6, the application program that outputs the two input characters in reverse order, requires the computer runs shown in FIGURE 5.8.

First the assembler is loaded into main memory and the application program is taken as the input file. The output from this run is the machine language version of the application program. It is then loaded into main memory for the second run. All the programs in the center boxes must be in machine language.

The Pep/9 system comes with an assembler as well as the simulator. When you execute the assembler, you must provide it with your assembly language program, previously created with the text editor. If you have made no errors in your program, the assembler will generate the object code in a format suitable for the loader. Otherwise, it will protest with one or more error messages and will generate no code. After you generate code from an error-free program, you can use it with the simulator (as described in Chapter 4).

When writing an assembly language program, you must place at least one space after the mnemonic or dot command. Other than that, there are no restrictions on spacing. Your source program may be in any combination of uppercase or lowercase letters. For example, you could write your source of Figure 5.6 as in FIGURE 5.9, and the assembler would accept it as valid and generate the correct code.

FIGURE 5.8

Two computer runs necessary for execution of the program in Figure 5.6.

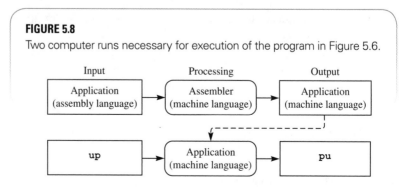

FIGURE 5.9
A valid source program and the resulting assembler listing.

Assembler Input

```
        ldwa 0x000D,d    ;A <- first number
  ADda   0x000F,d  ;Add the two numbers
        ORA     0x0011, d    ;Convert sum to character
  StBA    0Xfc16      ,    d    ;Output the character
        STop    ;Stop
   .WORD 5          ;Decimal 5
  .worD      3    ;Decimal 3
      .WORD  0x0030  ;Mask for ASCII char
    .end
```

Assembler Listing

```
- - - - - - - - - - - - - - - - - - - - - - - - - - - - - - - - - - - - - - - - - - - -
        Object
Addr    code      Mnemon  Operand     Comment
- - - - - - - - - - - - - - - - - - - - - - - - - - - - - - - - - - - - - - - - - - - -
0000    C1000D    LDWA    0x000D,d    ;A <- first number
0003    61000F    ADDA    0x000F,d    ;Add the two numbers
0006    910011    ORA     0x0011,d    ;Convert sum to character
0009    F1FC16    STBA    0xFC16,d    ;Output the character
000C    00        STOP                ;Stop
000D    0005      .WORD   5           ;Decimal 5
000F    0003      .WORD   3           ;Decimal 3
0011    0030      .WORD   0x0030      ;Mask for ASCII char
0013              .END
- - - - - - - - - - - - - - - - - - - - - - - - - - - - - - - - - - - - - - - - - - - -
```

In addition to generating object code for the loader, the assembler generates a program listing. The assembler listing converts the source program to a consistent format of uppercase and lowercase letters and spacing. Figure 5.9 shows the assembler listing from the unformatted source program.

The listing also shows the hexadecimal object code that each line generates and the address of the first byte where it will be loaded by the loader. Note that the .END command did not generate any object code.

This text presents the remaining assembly language programs as assembler listings, but without the column headings produced by the assembler, which are shown in the figure. The second column is the machine language object code, and the first column is the address where the loader will place that code in main memory. This layout is typical of most assemblers. It is a vivid presentation of the correspondence between machine language at Level ISA3 and assembly language at Level Asmb5.

Cross Assemblers

Machines built by one manufacturer generally have different instruction sets from those in machines built by another manufacturer. Hence, a program in machine language for one brand of computer will not run on another machine.

Resident assemblers

If you write an application in assembly language for a personal computer, you will probably assemble it on the same computer. An assembler written in the same language as the language to which it translates is called a *resident assembler*. The assembler resides on the same machine as the application program. The two runs of Figure 5.8 are on the same machine.

However, it is possible for the assembler to be written in Brand X machine language but to translate the application program into Brand Y machine language for a different machine. Then the application program cannot be executed on the same machine on which it was translated. It must first be moved from Brand X machine to Brand Y machine.

Cross assemblers

A *cross assembler* is an assembler that produces an object program for a machine different from the one that runs the assembler. Moving the machine language version of the application program from the output file of Brand X to the main memory of Brand Y is called *downloading*. Brand X is called the *host machine*, and Brand Y is called the *target machine*. In Figure 5.8, the first run would be on the host, and the second run would be on the target.

This situation often occurs when the target machine is a small special-purpose computer, such as a mobile device or the computer that controls the cooking cycles in a microwave oven. Assemblers are large programs that require significant main memory, as well as input and output peripheral devices. The processor that controls a microwave oven has a very small main memory. Its input is simply the buttons on the control panel and perhaps the input signal from the temperature probe. Its output includes the digital display and the signals to control the cooking element. Because it has no input/output (I/O) files, it cannot be used to run an assembler for itself. Its program must be downloaded from a larger host machine that has previously assembled the program into the target language.

5.2 Immediate Addressing and the Trap Instructions

With direct addressing, the operand specifier is the address in main memory of the operand. Mathematically,

Oprnd = Mem[OprndSpec]   *Direct addressing*

But with immediate addressing, the operand specifier *is* the operand:

Oprnd = OprndSpec   *Immediate addressing*

An instruction that uses direct addressing contains the address of the operand. But an instruction that uses immediate addressing contains the operand itself.

Immediate Addressing

Figure 5.10 shows how to write the program in Figure 5.3 with immediate addressing. It outputs the message Hi.

The assembler translates the load byte instruction

```
LDBA 'H',i
```

into object code D00048 (hex), which is

```
1101 0000 0000 0000 0100 1000
```

in binary. A check of Figure 5.2 verifies that 1101 0 is the correct opcode for the LDBA instruction. Also, the addressing-aaa field is 000 (bin), which indicates immediate addressing. As Figure 5.1 shows, the ,i specifies immediate addressing.

Character constants are enclosed in single quotes and always generate   *Character constants*
one byte of code. In the program of **FIGURE 5.10**, the character constant is placed in the operand specifier, which occupies two bytes. In this case, the character constant is positioned in the rightmost byte of the two-byte word.

That is how the assembler translates the statement to binary. But what happens when the loader loads the program and the first instruction executes? If the addressing mode were direct, the CPU would interpret 0048 as an address, and it would instruct main memory to put Mem[0048] on the bus to be loaded into the accumulator. Because the addressing mode is immediate, the CPU interprets 0048 as the operand itself (not the address of the operand) and puts 48 immediately in the accumulator without doing a memory fetch. The third instruction does likewise with 0069.

FIGURE 5.10

A program to output Hi using immediate addressing.

```
0000   D00048      LDBA      'H',i        ;Output 'H'
0003   F1FC16      STBA      0xFC16,d
0006   D00069      LDBA      'i',i        ;Output 'i'
0009   F1FC16      STBA      0xFC16,d
000C   00          STOP
000D               .END
```

Output

Hi

Two advantages of immediate addressing over direct addressing

Immediate addressing has two advantages over direct addressing. The program is shorter because the ASCII string does not need to be stored separately from the instruction. The program in Figure 5.3 has 15 bytes, and this program has 13 bytes. The instruction also executes faster because the operand is immediately available to the CPU in the instruction register. With direct addressing, the CPU must make an additional access to main memory to get the operand.

The DECI, DECO, and BR Instructions

Although the assembly language features we have learned so far are a big improvement over machine language, several irritating aspects remain. They are illustrated in the program of FIGURE 5.11, which inputs a decimal value, adds 1 to it, and outputs the sum.

The first instruction of Figure 5.7,

```
LDWA 0x000D,d ;A <- first number
```

The problem of address computation

puts the content of Mem[000D] into the accumulator. To write this instruction, the programmer had to know that the first number would be stored at address 000D (hex) after the instruction part of the program. The problem with placing the data at the end of the program is that you do not know exactly how long the instruction part of the program will be until you have finished it. Therefore, you do not know the address of the data while writing the instructions that require that address.

Another problem is program modification. Suppose you want to insert an extra statement in your program. That one modification will change the addresses of the data, and every instruction that refers to the data will need to be modified to reflect the new addresses. It would be easier to program at Level Asmb5 if you could place the data at the top of the program. Then you

FIGURE 5.11

A program to input a decimal value, add 1 to it, and output the sum.

```
0000   120005    BR       0x0005         ;Branch around data
0003   0000      .BLOCK   2              ;Storage for one integer
                 ;
0005   310003    DECI     0x0003,d       ;Get the number
0008   390003    DECO     0x0003,d       ;and output it
000B   D00020    LDBA     ' ',i          ;Output " + 1 = "
000E   F1FC16    STBA     0xFC16,d
0011   D0002B    LDBA     '+',i
0014   F1FC16    STBA     0xFC16,d
0017   D00020    LDBA     ' ',i
001A   F1FC16    STBA     0xFC16,d
001D   D00031    LDBA     '1',i
0020   F1FC16    STBA     0xFC16,d
0023   D00020    LDBA     ' ',i
0026   F1FC16    STBA     0xFC16,d
0029   D0003D    LDBA     '=',i
002C   F1FC16    STBA     0xFC16,d
002F   D00020    LDBA     ' ',i
0032   F1FC16    STBA     0xFC16,d
0035   C10003    LDWA     0x0003,d       ;A <- the number
0038   600001    ADDA     1,i            ;Add one to it
003B   E10003    STWA     0x0003,d       ;Store the sum
003E   390003    DECO     0x0003,d       ;Output the sum
0041   00        STOP
0042             .END
```

Input

-479

Output

-479 + 1 = -478

would know the address of the data when you write a statement that refers to that data.

Another irritating aspect of the program in Figure 5.7 is the restriction to single-character results because of the limitations of the output device at Mem[FC16]. Because the device can output only one byte as a single ASCII character, it is difficult to perform I/O on decimal values that require more than one digit for their ASCII representation.

The problem of restricting numeric operations to a single character

The unconditional branch,
BR

The program in Figure 5.11 alleviates both of these irritations. It is a program to input an integer, add 1 to it, and output the sum. It stores the data at the beginning of the program and permits large decimal values.

When you select the execute option in the Pep/9 simulator, the program counter (PC) gets the value 0000 (hex). The CPU will interpret the bytes at Mem[0000] as the first instruction to execute. To place data at the top of the program, we need an instruction that will cause the CPU to skip the data bytes when it fetches the next instruction. The unconditional branch, BR, is such an instruction. It simply places the operand of the instruction in the PC. In this program,

```
BR 0x0005  ;Branch around data
```

places 0005 (hex) in the PC. The RTL specification for the BR instruction is

$$PC \leftarrow Oprnd$$

During the fetch part of the next execution cycle, the CPU will get the instruction at 0005 instead of 0003, which would have happened if the PC had not been altered.

BR *defaults to immediate*
addressing

Because the branch instructions almost always use immediate addressing, the Pep/9 assembler does not require that the addressing mode be specified. If you do not specify the addressing mode for a branch instruction, the assembler will assume immediate addressing and generate 0 for the addressing-a field.

The correct operation of the BR instruction depends on the details of the von Neumann execution cycle. For example, you may have wondered why the cycle is fetch, decode, *increment, execute*, repeat instead of fetch, decode, *execute, increment*, repeat. Figure 4.34(f) shows the execution of instruction D1000D to load the byte for H while the value of PC is 0003, the address of instruction F1FC16. If the execute part of the von Neumann execution cycle had been before the increment part, then PC would have had the value 0000 when the instruction at address 0000, which was D1000D, executes. It seems to make more sense to have PC correspond to the *currently executing* instruction instead of the instruction *after* the currently executing one.

The reason increment must
come before execute in the
von Neumann execution
cycle

Why doesn't the von Neumann execution cycle have the execute part before the increment part? Because then BR would not work properly. In Figure 5.11, PC would get 0000; the CPU would fetch the BR instruction, 120005; and BR would execute, placing 0005 in PC. Then PC would increment to 0008. Instead of branching to 0005, your program would branch to 0008. Because the instruction set contains branching instructions, the increment part of the von Neumann execution cycle must be before the execute part.

DECI and DECO are two instructions the operating system provides at the assembly level that the Pep/9 hardware does not provide at the machine level. DECI, which stands for *decimal input*, converts a sequence of ASCII digit characters to a single word that corresponds to the two's complement representation of the value. DECO, decimal output, does the opposite conversion from the two's complement value in a word to a sequence of ASCII characters.

The DECI *instruction*

DECI permits any number of leading spaces or line feeds on input. The first printable character must be a decimal digit, a +, or a -. The following characters must be decimal digits. DECI sets Z to 1 if you input 0 and N to 1 if you input a negative value. It sets V to 1 if you enter a value that is out of range. Because a word is 16 bits and $2^{16} = 32768$, the range is –32768 to 32767 (dec). DECI does not affect the C bit.

The DECO *instruction*

DECO prints a - if the value is negative but does not print + if it is positive. It does not print leading 0's, and it outputs the minimum number of characters possible to properly represent the value. You cannot specify the field width. DECO does not affect the NZVC bits.

In Figure 5.11, the statement

```
DECI 0x0003,d ;Get the number
```

when confronted with input sequence -479, converts it to 1111 1110 0010 0001 (bin) and stores it in Mem[0003]. DECO converts the binary sequence to a string of ASCII characters and outputs them.

The STRO Instruction

You might have noticed that the program in Figure 5.11 requires seven pairs of LDBA and STBA instructions to output the string " + 1 = ", one pair for each ASCII character that is output. The program in (FIGURE 5.12) illustrates STRO, which means *string output*. It is another instruction that triggers a trap at the machine level but is a bona fide instruction at the assembly level. It lets you output the entire string of seven characters with only one instruction.

The STRO *instruction*

The operand for STRO is a contiguous sequence of bytes, each one of which is interpreted as an ASCII character. The last byte of the sequence must be a byte of all 0's, which the STRO instruction interprets as the sentinel. The instruction outputs the string of bytes from the beginning up to, but not including, the sentinel. In Figure 5.12, the pseudo-op

```
.ASCII " + 1 = \x00"
```

uses \x00 to generate the sentinel byte. The pseudo-op generates eight bytes including the sentinel, but only seven characters are output by the STRO instruction. Even though you could put the .ASCII pseudo-op at the beginning of the program and branch around it, our coding convention is to always put ASCII strings at the bottom of the program.

FIGURE 5.12

A program identical to that of Figure 5.11 but with the STRO instruction.

```
0000   120005     BR      0x0005        ;Branch around data
0003   0000       .BLOCK  2             ;Storage for one integer
                  ;
0005   310003     DECI    0x0003,d      ;Get the number
0008   390003     DECO    0x0003,d      ;and output it
000B   49001B     STRO    0x001B,d      ;Output " + 1 = "
000E   C10003     LDWA    0x0003,d      ;A <- the number
0011   600001     ADDA    1,i           ;Add one to it
0014   E10003     STWA    0x0003,d      ;Store the sum
0017   390003     DECO    0x0003,d      ;Output the sum
001A   00         STOP
001B   202B20     .ASCII  " + 1 = \x00"
       31203D
       2000
0023              .END
```

Input

-479

Output

-479 + 1 = -478

The assembler listing allocates room for only three bytes in the object code column. If the string in the .ASCII pseudo-op generates more than three bytes, the assembler listing continues the object code on subsequent lines.

Interpreting Bit Patterns: The HEXO Instruction

Chapters 4 and 5 progress from a low level of abstraction (ISA3) to a higher one (Asmb5). Even though assembly language at Level Asmb5 hides the machine language details, those details are there nonetheless. In particular, the machine is ultimately based on the von Neumann cycle of fetch, decode, increment, execute, repeat. Using pseudo-ops and mnemonics to generate the data bits and instruction bits does not change that property of the machine. When an instruction executes, it executes bits and has no knowledge of how those bits were generated by the assembler. FIGURE 5.13 shows a nonsense program whose sole purpose is to illustrate this fact. It generates data bits with one kind of pseudo-op that are interpreted by instructions in an unexpected way.

FIGURE 5.13

A nonsense program to illustrate the interpretation of bit patterns.

```
0000    120009    BR       0x0009       ;Branch around data
0003    FFFE      .WORD    0xFFFE       ;First
0005    00        .BYTE    0x00         ;Second
0006    55        .BYTE    'U'          ;Third
0007    0470      .WORD    1136         ;Fourth
                  ;
0009    390003    DECO     0x0003,d     ;Interpret First as dec
000C    D0000A    LDBA     '\n',i
000F    F1FC16    STBA     0xFC16,d
0012    390005    DECO     0x0005,d     ;Interpret Second and Third as dec
0015    F1FC16    STBA     0xFC16,d
0018    D0000A    LDBA     '\n',i
001B    410005    HEXO     0x0005,d     ;Interpret Second and Third as hex
001E    D0000A    LDBA     '\n',i
0021    F1FC16    STBA     0xFC16,d
0024    D10006    LDBA     0x0006,d     ;Interpret Third as char
0027    F1FC16    STBA     0xFC16,d
002A    D10008    LDBA     0x0008,d     ;Interpret Fourth as char
002D    F1FC16    STBA     0xFC16,d
0030    00        STOP
0031              .END
```

Output

```
-2
85
0055
Up
```

In the program, First is generated as a hexadecimal value with

```
.WORD 0xFFFE ;First
```

but is interpreted as a decimal number with

```
DECO 0x0003,d ;Interpret First as dec
```

which outputs -2. Of course, if the programmer meant for the bit pattern FFFE to be interpreted as a decimal number, he would have written the pseudo-op

```
.WORD -2 ;First
```

in the first place. This pseudo-op generates the same object code, and the object program would be identical to the original. When DECO executes, it does not know how the bits were generated during translation time. It only knows what they are during execution time.

The decimal output instruction

```
DECO 0x0005,d ;Interpret Second and Third as dec
```

interprets the bits at address 0005 as a decimal number and outputs 85. DECO always outputs the decimal value of two consecutive bytes. In this case, the bytes are 0055 (hex) = 85 (dec). The fact that the two bytes were generated from two different .BYTE dot commands and that one was generated from the hexadecimal constant 0x00 and the other from the character constant 'U' is irrelevant. During execution, the only thing that matters is what the bits are, not where they came from.

The hexadecimal output instruction

```
HEXO 0x0005,d ;Interpret Second and Third as hex
```

interprets the two bytes beginning at address 0005 as four hexadecimal digits and outputs them with no space between them. Again, it does not matter what pseudo-op created the bits. If the HEXO instruction were to output from address 0006, it would print 5504 instead of 0055.

The pair of instructions

```
LDBA 0x0006,d ;Interpret Third as char
STBA 0xFC16,d
```

interprets the bits at address 0006 as a character. There is no surprise here, because those bits were generated with the .BYTE command using a character constant. As expected, the letter U is output.

The last pair of instructions

```
LDBA 0x0008,d ;Interpret Fourth as char
STBA 0xFC16,d
```

outputs the letter p. Why? Because the bits at memory location 0008 are 70 (hex), which are the bits for the ASCII character p. Where did those bits come from? They are the second half of the bits that were generated by

```
.WORD 1136 ;Fourth
```

It just so happens that 1136 (dec) = 0470 (hex) and the second byte of that bit pattern is 70 (hex).

In all these examples, the instruction simply grinds through the von Neumann execution cycle. You must always remember that the translation process is different from the execution process and that translation happens before execution. After translation, when the instructions are executing, the origin of the bits is irrelevant. The only thing that matters is what the bits are, not where they came from during the translation phase.

Disassemblers

An assembler translates each assembly language statement into exactly one machine language statement. Such a transformation is called a *one-to-one mapping*. One assembly language statement maps to one machine language statement. This is in contrast to a compiler, which, as we shall see later, produces a *one-to-many mapping*.

The one-to-one mapping of an assembler

Given a single assembly language statement, you can always determine the corresponding machine language statement. But can you do the inverse? That is, given a bit sequence in a machine language program, can you determine the original assembly language statement from which the machine language came?

No, you cannot. Even though the transformation is one-to-one, the inverse transformation is not unique. Given the binary machine language sequence

The nonunique nature of the inverse mapping of an assembler

```
0101 0111
```

you cannot tell if the assembly language programmer originally used an ASCII assembler directive for the ASCII character W, or if she wrote the ADDSP mnemonic with stack-deferred indexed addressing. The assembler would have produced the exact same sequence of bits regardless of which of these two assembly language statements was in the original program.

Furthermore, during execution, main memory does not know what the original assembly language statements were. It remembers only the 1's and 0's that the CPU processes via its execution cycle.

FIGURE 5.14 shows two assembly language programs that produce the same machine language, and so produce identical output. Of course, a serious programmer would not write the second program because it is more difficult to understand than the first program.

Because of pseudo-ops, the inverse assembler mapping is not unique. If there were no pseudo-ops, there would be only one possible way to recover the original assembly language statements from binary object code. Pseudo-ops are for inserting data bits, as opposed to instruction bits, into memory. The fact that data and programs share the same memory is why the inverse assembler mapping is not unique.

The cause of the nonunique nature of the inverse mapping

The difficulty of recovering the source program from the object program can be a marketing benefit to the software developer. If you write

FIGURE 5.14

Two different source programs that produce the same object program and, therefore, the same output.

Assembly Language Program

```
0000   D10013     LDBA    0x0013,d
0003   F1FC16     STBA    0xFC16,d
0006   D10014     LDBA    0x0014,d
0009   F1FC16     STBA    0xFC16,d
000C   D10015     LDBA    0x0015,d
000F   F1FC16     STBA    0xFC16,d
0012   00         STOP
0013   50756E     .ASCII  "Pun"
0016              .END
```

Assembly Language Program

```
0000   D10013     LDBA    0x0013,d
0003   F1FC16     STBA    0xFC16,d
0006   D10014     LDBA    0x0014,d
0009   F1FC16     STBA    0xFC16,d
000C   D10015     LDBA    0x0015,d
000F   F1FC16     STBA    0xFC16,d
0012   00         STOP
0013   50756E     ADDSP   0x756E,i
0016              .END
```

Program Output

```
Pun
```

The advantage of object code for software distribution

an application in assembly language, there are two ways you can sell it. You can sell the source program and let your customer assemble it. Your customer would then have both the source program and the object program. Or you could assemble it yourself and sell only the object program.

In both cases, the customer has the object program necessary for executing the application program. But if he has the source program as well, he can easily modify it to suit his own purposes. He may even enhance it and then try to sell it as an improved version in direct competition with you, with little effort on his part. Modifying a machine language program would be much more difficult. Most commercial software products are sold only in object form to prevent the customer from tampering with the program.

The open-source software movement is an established development in the computer industry. The idea is that there is a benefit to the customer's having the source program because of support issues. If you own an object program and discover a bug that needs to be fixed or a feature that needs to be added, you must wait for the company who sold you the program to fix the bug or add the feature. But if you own the source, you can modify it yourself to suit your own needs. Some open-source companies give away the source code free of charge and derive their income by providing software support for the product. An example of this strategy is the Linux operating system, which is available for free from the Internet. Although such software is free, it requires a higher level of skill to use.

The advantage of source code for software distribution

A *disassembler* is a program that tries to recover the source program from the object program. It can never be 100% successful because of the nonunique nature of the inverse assembler mapping. The programs in this chapter place the data either before or after the instructions. In a large program, sections of data are typically placed throughout the program, making it difficult to distinguish data bits from instruction bits in the object code. A disassembler can read each byte and print it out several times— once interpreted as an instruction specifier, once interpreted as an ASCII character, once interpreted as an integer with two's complement binary representation, and so on. A person then can attempt to reconstruct the source program, but the process is tedious.

Disassemblers

5.3 **Symbols**

The previous section introduces BR as an instruction to branch around the data at the beginning of the program. Although this technique alleviates the problem of manually determining the address of the data cells, it does not eliminate the problem. You must still determine the addresses by counting in hexadecimal, and if the number of data cells is large, mistakes are likely. Also, if you want to modify the data section, say by removing a .WORD command, the addresses of all the data cells following the deletion will change. You must modify any instructions that refer to the modified addresses.

Assembly language symbols eliminate the problem of manually determining addresses. The assembler lets you associate a *symbol*, similar to a C identifier, with a *memory address*. Anywhere in the program you need to refer to the address, you can refer to the symbol instead. If you ever modify a program by adding or removing statements, when you reassemble the program the assembler will calculate the new address associated with the symbol. You do not need to rewrite the statements that refer to the changed addresses via the symbols.

The purpose of assembly language symbols

A Program with Symbols

The assembly language of FIGURE 5.15 produces object code identical to that of Figure 5.12. It uses three symbols, num, msg, and main.

The syntax rules for symbols are similar to the syntax rules for C identifiers. The first character must be a letter, and the following characters must be letters or digits. Symbols can be a maximum of only eight characters long. The characters are case sensitive. For example, Number would be a different symbol from number because of the uppercase N.

You can define a symbol on any assembly language line by placing it at the beginning of the line. When you define a symbol, you must terminate it with a colon :. No spaces are allowed between the last character of the symbol and the colon. In this program, the statement

```
num: .BLOCK 2 ;Storage for one integer #2d
```

defines the symbol num, in addition to allocating a block of two bytes. Although this line has spaces between the colon and the pseudo-op, the assembler does not require them.

The value of a symbol is an address.

When the assembler detects a symbol definition, it stores the symbol and its value in a symbol table. The value is the address in memory of where the first byte of the object code generated from that line will be loaded. If you define any symbols in your program, the assembler listing will include a printout of the symbol table with the values in hexadecimal. Figure 5.15 shows the symbol table printout from the listing of this program. You can see from the table that the value of the symbol num is 0003 (hex).

When you refer to the symbol, you cannot include the colon. The statement

```
LDWA num,d ;A <- the number
```

refers to the symbol num. Because num has the value 0003 (hex), this statement generates the same code that

```
LDWA 0x0003,d ;A <- the number
```

would generate. Similarly, the statement

```
BR main ;Branch around data
```

generates the same code that

```
BR 0x0005 ;Branch around data
```

would generate, because the value of main is 0005 (hex).

Note that the value of a symbol is an address, not the content of the cell at that address. When this program executes, Mem[0003] will contain

FIGURE 5.15

A program that adds 1 to a decimal value. It is identical to Figure 5.12 except that it uses symbols.

Assembler Listing

```
------------------------------------------------------------------
      Object
Addr  code   Symbol  Mnemon  Operand   Comment
------------------------------------------------------------------
0000  120005         BR      main      ;Branch around data
0003  0000   num:    .BLOCK  2         ;Storage for one integer #2d
                       ;
0005  310003 main:    DECI    num,d     ;Get the number
0008  390003         DECO    num,d     ;and output it
000B  49001B         STRO    msg,d     ;Output " + 1 = "
000E  C10003         LDWA    num,d     ;A <- the number
0011  600001         ADDA    1,i       ;Add one to it
0014  E10003         STWA    num,d     ;Store the sum
0017  390003         DECO    num,d     ;Output the sum
001A  00             STOP
001B  202B20 msg:    .ASCII  " + 1 = \x00"
      31203D
      2000
0023                 .END
------------------------------------------------------------------
```

Symbol table

```
------------------------------------------------
Symbol   Value      Symbol    Value
------------------------------------------------
main     0005       msg       001B
num      0003
------------------------------------------------
```

Input
```
-479
```

Output
```
-479 + 1 = -478
```

−479 (dec), which it gets from the input device. The value of num will still be 0003 (hex), not −479 (dec), which is different. It might help you to visualize the value of a symbol as coming from the address column on the assembler listing in the line that contains the symbol definition.

Symbols not only relieve you of the burden of calculating addresses manually, they also make your programs easier to read. num is easier on the eyes than 0x0003. Good programmers are careful to select meaningful symbols for their programs to enhance readability.

A von Neumann Illustration

When you program with symbols at Level Asmb5, it is easy to lose sight of the von Neumann nature of the computer. The two classic von Neumann bugs—manipulating instructions as if they were data and attempting to execute data as if they were instructions—are still possible.

For example, consider the following assembly language program:

```
this: DECO this,d
 STOP
 .END
```

You might think that the assembler would object to the first statement because it appears to be referring to itself as data in a nonsensical way. But the assembler does not look ahead to the ramifications of execution. Because the syntax is correct, it translates accordingly, as shown in the assembler listing in FIGURE 5.16 .

During execution, the CPU interprets 39 as the opcode for the decimal output instruction with direct addressing. It interprets the word at Mem[0000], which is 3900 (hex), as a decimal number and outputs its value, 14592.

FIGURE 5.16

A nonsense program that illustrates the underlying von Neumann nature of the machine.

```
Assembler Listing
0000   390000 this:   DECO    this,d
0003   00             STOP
0004                  .END

Output
14592
```

It is important to realize that computer hardware has no innate intelligence or reasoning power. The execution cycle and the instruction set are wired into the CPU. As this program illustrates, the CPU has no knowledge of the history of the bits it processes. It has no overall picture. It simply executes the von Neumann cycle over and over again. The same thing is true of main memory, which has no knowledge of the history of the bits it remembers. It simply stores 1's and 0's as commanded by the CPU. Any intelligence or reasoning power must come from software, which is written by humans.

x86 Assembly Language

Figure 5.8 shows two steps for the Pep/9 system—assemble, which translates from assembly language to machine language, followed by load, which puts the machine language in main memory for execution. **FIGURE 5.17** shows an additional step in typical systems called *linking*, which happens after assembly and before loading. Like the assembler and loader, the linker is a program that uses another program as data.

The linker is necessary if you want your assembly language program to use a previously written module stored in a static library. For example, it is possible for an assembly language program to call the `printf()` function to send values to the output stream. The code for `printf()` is stored in a static library, and the linker combines a copy of its code in the object file along with the object code from your assembly language program. In a Microsoft system, a static library file has extension `.lib` for library.

The only function of the Pep/9 loader is to load the object file into main memory. In an actual system, the loader has the additional function of setting up links to the dynamic library, also called the *shared library*. The idea behind a shared library is to decrease the size of the executable files in the system by not having the code for commonly used libraries duplicated in all the executable files. In a Microsoft system, a dynamic library file has extension `.dll` for *dynamic link library*.

Programming in assembly language for x86 is complicated by the fact that there are many different incompatible assembly languages for the same x86 instruction set. Also, there are many different incompatible object file formats, depending on the operating system. The following examples compare some Pep/9 assembly language features with those of the Microsoft assembler (MASM) in 32-bit mode available in the Visual Studio IDE.

Here is a code fragment from a Pep/9 assembler listing that allocates storage with some pseudo-ops:

```
0000    FFFE      first:    .WORD    0xFFFE
0002    00        second:   .BYTE    0x00
0003    55        third:    .BYTE    'U'
0004    0470      fourth:   .WORD    1136
0006    000000    fifth:    .BLOCK   4
        00
```

FIGURE 5.17
Preparation of an assembly language program for execution.

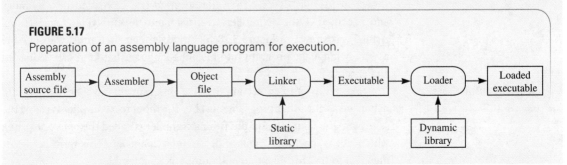

And here is the equivalent code fragment from the MASM listing:

```
00000000              .DATA
00000000 FFFE         first   WORD   0FFFEh
00000002 00           second  BYTE   00h
00000003 55           third   BYTE   'U'
00000004 0470         fourth  WORD   1136
00000006 00000000     fifth   DWORD  ?
```

The data section in a MASM program starts with .DATA. There is no dot before the BYTE and WORD pseudo-ops; nor is there a colon after the definition of a symbol. Hexadecimal constants terminate with the letter h. The leading 0 in 0FFFEh is necessary to prevent the assembler from interpreting FFFEh as a symbol. DWORD stands for *double word*, which is four bytes. QWORD stands for *quad word*, which is eight bytes. Instead of a separate .BLOCK pseudo-op to reserve storage without initialization, a ? denotes a value of all 0's in a BYTE, WORD, DWORD, or QWORD.

Here is a code fragment from the Pep/9 assembler listing for Figure 5.15:

```
000E C10003 LDWA num,d ;A <- the number
0011 600001 ADDA 1,i   ;Add one to it
0014 E10003 STWA num,d ;Store the sum
```

The equivalent code fragment from the MASM listing is at the bottom of this sidebar.

The mov mnemonic is used for both load and store. The first argument is always the destination, and the second argument is always the source. In the case of the add instruction, the first argument eax is the source and the destination. You can see from the listing that the mov instructions are five bytes long, and the add instruction is three bytes long. The mov instruction can transfer data only between two registers or between a memory cell and a register. It cannot transfer data between two memory cells. In the Pep/9 code, num is stored at Mem[0003], while in the MASM code, it is stored at Mem[0000000A].

```
00000000 A1 0000000A  mov eax, num ;EAX <- the number
00000005 83 C0 01      add eax, 1   ;Add one to it
00000008 A3 0000000A  mov num, eax ;Store the sum
```

5.4 Translating from Level HOL6

A compiler translates a program in a high-order language (Level HOL6) into a lower-level language, so eventually it can be executed by the machine. Some compilers translate directly into machine language (Level ISA3), as shown in **FIGURE 5.18(a)**. Then the program can be loaded into memory and executed. Other compilers translate into assembly language (Level Asmb5), as shown in Figure 5.18(b). An assembler then must translate the assembly language program into machine language before it can be loaded and executed.

Compilers and assemblers are programs

Like an assembler, a compiler is a program. It must be written and debugged as any other program must be. The input to a compiler is called the *source program*, and the output from a compiler is called the *object program*, whether it is machine language or assembly language. This terminology is identical to that for the input and output of an assembler.

FIGURE 5.18
The function of a compiler.

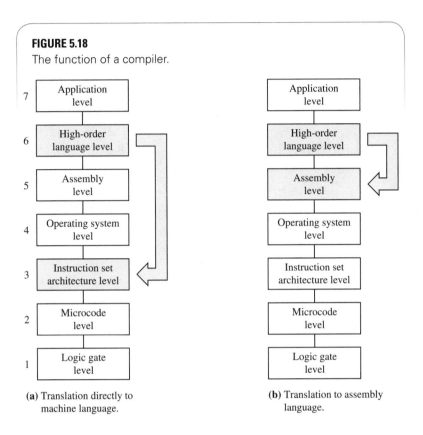

7 Application level

6 High-order language level

5 Assembly level

4 Operating system level

3 Instruction set architecture level

2 Microcode level

1 Logic gate level

Application level

High-order language level

Assembly level

Operating system level

Instruction set architecture level

Microcode level

Logic gate level

(a) Translation directly to machine language.

(b) Translation to assembly language.

This section describes the translation process from C to Pep/9 assembly language. It shows how a compiler translates scanf(), printf(), and assignment statements, and how it enforces the concept of type at the C level. Chapter 6 continues the discussion of the relationship between the high-order language level (Level HOL6) and the assembly level (Level Asmb5).

The Printf() Function

The program in FIGURE 5.19 shows how a compiler would translate a simple C program with one output statement into assembly language.

The compiler translates the single C statement

```
printf("Hello, world!\n");
```

Translating printf()

into one executable assembly language statement

```
STRO msg,d
```

and one dot command

FIGURE 5.19

The `printf()` function at Level HOL6 and Level Asmb5.

High-Order Language
```
#include <stdio.h>
int main() {
    printf("Hello, world!\n");
    return 0;
}
```

Assembly Language
```
0000   490004          STRO    msg,d
0003   00              STOP
0004   48656C msg:     .ASCII  "Hello, world!\n\x00"
       6C6F2C
       20776F
       726C64
       210A00
0013                   .END
```

Output
```
Hello, world!
```

```
msg: .ASCII "Hello, world!\n\x00"
```

This is a one-to-two mapping. In contrast to an assembler, the mapping for a compiler generally is not one-to-one, but one-to-many. This program and all the ones that follow place string constants at the bottom of the program. Data that corresponds to variable values is placed at the top of the program to correspond to its placement in the HOL6 program.

The compiler translates the C statement

Translating `return 0` *in* `main()`

```
return 0;
```

into the assembly language statement

```
STOP
```

`return` statements for C functions other than `main()` do not translate to `STOP`. This tranlation of `return` for `main()` is a simplification. A real C compiler must generate code that executes on a particular operating system. It is up to the operating system to interpret the value returned. A common convention is that a returned value of 0 indicates that no errors occurred during the program's execution. If an error did occur, the program returns some nonzero value, but what happens in such a case depends on the particular operating system. In the Pep/9 system, returning from `main()` corresponds to terminating the program. Hence, returning from `main()` will always translate to `STOP`. Chapter 6 shows how the compiler translates returns from functions other than `main()`.

Other elements of the C program are not even translated directly. For example,

```
#include <stdio.h>
```

does not appear in the assembly language program at all. A real compiler would use the `#include` statement to make the correct interface to the operating system and its library. The Pep/9 system ignores these kinds of details to keep things simple at the introductory level.

FIGURE 5.20 shows the input and output of a compiler with this program. Part (a) is a compiler that translates directly into machine language. The object program could be loaded and executed. Part (b) is a compiler that translates to assembly language at Level Asmb5. The object program would need to be assembled before it could be loaded and executed.

FIGURE 5.20
The action of a compiler on the program in Figure 5.19.

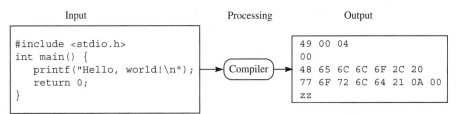

(a) A compiler that translates directly into machine language.

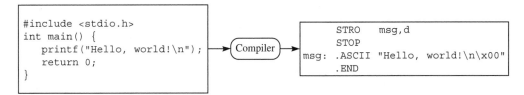

(b) A compiler that translates into assembly language.

Variables and Types

Every C variable has three attributes—name, type, and value. For each variable that is declared, the compiler reserves one or more memory cells in the machine language program. A variable in a high-order language is simply a memory location in a low-level language. Level-HOL6 programs refer to variables by names, which are C identifiers. Level-ISA3 programs refer to them by addresses. The value of the variable is the value in the memory cell at the address associated with the C identifier.

The symbol table for a compiler

The compiler must remember which address corresponds to which variable name in the Level-HOL6 program. It uses a symbol table to make the connection between variable names and addresses.

The symbol table for a compiler is similar to, but inherently more complicated than, the symbol table for an assembler. A variable name in C is not limited to eight characters, as is a symbol in Pep/9. In addition, the symbol table for a compiler must store the variable's type as well as its associated address.

A compiler that translates directly to machine language does not require a second translation with an assembler. **FIGURE 5.21(a)** shows the mapping produced by the symbol table for such a compiler. The programs in this text illustrate the translation process for a hypothetical compiler that translates to assembly language, however, because assembly language is easier to read than machine language. Variable names in C correspond to symbols in Pep/9 assembly language, as Figure 5.21(b) shows.

The correspondence in Figure 5.21(b) is unrealistic for compilers that translate to assembly language. Consider the problem of a C program that has two variables named discountRate1 and discountRate2. Because they are longer than eight characters, the compiler would have a difficult time mapping the identifiers to unique Pep/9 symbols. Our examples will limit the C identifiers to, at most, eight characters to make clear the correspondence between C and assembly language. Real compilers that translate to assembly language typically do not use assembly language symbols for the variable names.

FIGURE 5.21

The mapping a compiler makes between a Level-HOL6 variable and a Level-ISA3 storage location.

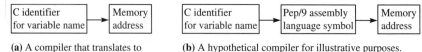

(a) A compiler that translates to machine language.

(b) A hypothetical compiler for illustrative purposes.

Global Variables and Assignment Statements

The C program in FIGURE 5.22 is from Figure 2.4. It shows assignment statements with global variables at Level HOL6 and the corresponding assembly language program, which the compiler produces. The object program contains comments. Real compilers do not generate comments because human programmers usually do not need to read the object program.

The assembly language listing shows two symbols that are used but apparently not defined—charIn, used with the LDBA instruction, and charOut, used with the STBA instruction. The assembler automatically includes these two symbols in its symbol table without the programmer needing to define them explicitly. The memory map of the Pep/9 computer in Figure 4.41 shows the input device at Mem[FC15] and the output device at Mem[FC16] within the operating system. Chapter 8 describes the Pep/9 operating system, and Figure 8.2 shows that charIn and charOut are defined in the operating system assembly language program.

If you modify the operating system, the input device may no longer be at Mem[FC15]. However, its location will still be in the machine vector at FFF8. Similarly, the location of the output device will always be in the machine vector at FFFA. The assembler takes the values of charIn and charOut from the symbol table of the operating system, which in turn sets up the machine vectors as follows:

Mem[FFF8] has the value of charIn
Mem[FFFA] has the value of charOut

During execution, the virtual machine uses these vectors to know where the input and output devices are in the memory map. From now on, you should use the symbols charIn and charOut when accessing the memory-mapped I/O devices, because they will always map to the correct locations in memory regardless of any modifications to the operating system.

Remember that a compiler is a program. It must be written and debugged just like any other program. A compiler to translate C programs can be written in any language—even C! The following program segment illustrates some details of this incestuous state of affairs. It is part of a simplified compiler that translates C source programs into assembly language object programs:

```
typedef int HexDigit;
enum KindType {sInt, sBool, sChar, sFloat};
struct SymbolTableEntry {
    char symbol[32];
    HexDigit value[4];
```

A symbol table definition for a hypothetical compiler

FIGURE 5.22

The assignment statement with global variables at Level HOL6 and Level Asmb5. The C program is from Figure 2.4.

High-Order Language

```c
#include <stdio.h>
char ch;
int j;
int main() {
    scanf("%c %d", &ch, &j);
    j += 5;
    ch++;
    printf("%c\n%d\n", ch, j);
    return 0;
}
```

Assembly Language

```
0000    120006          BR      main
0003    00      ch:     .BLOCK  1           ;global variable #1c
0004    0000    j:      .BLOCK  2           ;global variable #2d
                        ;
0006    D1FC15  main:   LDBA    charIn,d    ;scanf("%c %d", &ch, &j)
0009    F10003          STBA    ch,d
000C    310004          DECI    j,d
000F    C10004          LDWA    j,d         ;j += 5
0012    600005          ADDA    5,i
0015    E10004          STWA    j,d
0018    D10003          LDBA    ch,d        ;ch++
001B    600001          ADDA    1,i
001E    F10003          STBA    ch,d
0021    D10003          LDBA    ch,d        ;printf("%c\n%d\n", ch, j)
0024    F1FC16          STBA    charOut,d
0027    D0000A          LDBA    '\n',i
002A    F1FC16          STBA    charOut,d
002D    390004          DECO    j,d
0030    D0000A          LDBA    '\n',i
0033    F1FC16          STBA    charOut,d
0036    00              STOP
0037                    .END
```

Input

M 419

Output

N

424

```
    KindType kind;
};

SymbolTableEntry symbolTable[100];
```

An entry in a symbol table contains three parts—the symbol itself; its value, which is the address in Pep/9 memory where the value of the variable will be stored; and the kind of value that is stored, that is, the variable's type.

FIGURE 5.23 shows the entries in the symbol table for this program. The first variable has the symbolic name ch. The compiler allocates the byte at Mem[0003] by generating the .BLOCK command and stores its type as sChar in the symbol table, an indication that the variable is a C character. The second variable has the symbolic name j. The compiler allocates two bytes at Mem[0004] for its value and stores its type as sInt, indicating a C integer. It gets the types from the variable declaration of the C program.

During the code generation phase, the compiler translates

```
scanf("%c %d", &ch, &j);
```

into

```
LDBA 0xFC15,d
STBA 0x0003,d
DECI 0x0004,d
```

It consults the symbol table in Figure 5.23, which was filled at an earlier phase of compilation, to determine the addresses for the operands of the LDBA , STBA, and DECI instructions.

Note that the value stored in the symbol table is not the value of the variable during execution. It is the memory address of where that value will be stored. If the user enters 419 for j during execution, then the value stored at Mem[0004] will be 01A3 (hex), which is the binary representation of 419 (dec). The symbol table contains 0004, not 01A3, as the value of the symbol

FIGURE 5.23

The symbol table for a hypothetical compiler that translates the program in Figure 5.22.

	symbol	value	kind
[0]	ch	0003	sChar
[1]	j	0004	sInt
[2]	⋮	⋮	⋮

An assignment statement at
Level Asmb5

j at translation time. Values of C variables do not exist at translation time. They exist at execution time.

Assigning a value to a variable at Level HOL6 corresponds to storing a value in memory at Level Asmb5. The compiler translates the assignment statement

```
j += 5;
```

into

```
LDWA j,d
ADDA 5,i
STWA j,d
```

where the symbols are shown instead of the addresses. LDWA and ADDA perform the computation on the right-hand side of the assignment statement, leaving the result of the computation in the accumulator. STWA assigns the result back to j.

There is a distinction between the word "value" during translation versus during execution. During translation, the value of a symbol is an address. During execution, the value of a variable is the content of a memory cell. This assignment statement illustrates the general rules for accessing global variables:

The rules for accessing
global variables

> The value of a symbol for a variable is the address of the variable's value during execution.

> The value of a variable during execution is accessed with direct addressing.

In this case, the value of the symbol for the global variable j is the address 0004, and the LDWA and STWA statements access the value of the variable during execution with direct addressing.

Similarly, the compiler translates

The increment statement at
Level Asmb5

```
ch++
```

into

```
LDBA ch,d
ADDA 1,i
STBA ch,d
```

The same instruction that adds 5 to j, ADDA, performs the increment operation on ch. Again, because ch is a global variable, its value during translation is the address 0003, and the LDBA and STBA instructions use direct addressing to access the value of the variable during execution.

The compiler translates

The output operator at
Level Asmb5

```
printf("%c\n%d\n", ch, j);
```

into

```
LDBA ch,d
STBA charOut,d
LDBA '\n',i
STBA charOut,d
DECO j,d
LDBA '\n',i
STBA charOut,d
```

using direct addressing to output the values of the global variables ch and j.

The compiler must search its symbol table to make the connection between a symbol such as ch and its address, 0003. The symbol table is an array. If it is not maintained in alphabetic order by symbolic name, a sequential search would be necessary to locate ch in the table. If the symbolic names are in alphabetic order, a binary search is possible.

Type Compatibility

To see how type compatibility is enforced at Level HOL6, suppose you have two variables, integer j and floating-point y, in a C program. Also suppose that you have a computer unlike Pep/9 that is able to store and manipulate floating-point values. The compiler's symbol table for your program might look something like FIGURE 5.24 .

Now consider the operation j % 8 in C. % is the modulus operator, which is restricted to operate on integer values. In binary, to perform j % 8, you simply set all the bits except the rightmost three bits to 0. For example, if j has the value 61 (dec) = 0011 1101 (bin), then j % 8 has the value 5 (dec)

FIGURE 5.24
The compiler symbol table for a program with a floating-point variable.

	symbol	value	kind
[0]	j	0003	sInt
[1]	y	0005	sFloat
[2]	⋮	⋮	⋮

= 0000 0101 (bin), which is 0011 1101 with all bits except the rightmost three set to 0.

Suppose the following statement appears in your C program:

```
j = j % 8;
```

The compiler would consult the symbol table and determine that `kind` for the variable `j` is `sInt`. It would also recognize 8 as an integer constant and determine that the `%` operation is legal. It would then generate the object code

```
LDWA j,d
ANDA 0x0007,i
STWA j,d
```

Now suppose that the following statement appears in your C program:

Illegal at Level HOL6

```
y = y % 8;
```

The compiler would consult the symbol table and determine that `kind` for the variable `y` is `sFloat`. It would determine that the `%` operation is not legal because it can be applied only to integer types. It would then generate the error message

```
error: float operand for %
```

and would generate no object code. If, however, there were no type checking, the following code would be generated:

Legal at Level Asmb5

```
LDWA y,d
ANDA 0x0007,i
STWA y,d
```

Indeed, there is nothing to prevent an assembly language programmer from writing this code, even though its execution would produce meaningless results.

Type compatibility enforced by the compiler

Having the compiler check for type compatibility is a tremendous help. It keeps you from writing meaningless statements, such as performing a `%` operation on a float variable. When you program directly in assembly language at Level Asmb5, there are no type compatibility checks. All data consists of bits. When bugs occur due to incorrect data movements, they can be detected only at run time, not at translation time. That is, they are logical errors instead of syntax errors. Logical errors are notoriously more difficult to locate than syntax errors.

Pep/9 Symbol Tracer

Pep/9 has three symbolic trace features corresponding to the three parts of the C memory model—the global tracer for global variables, the stack tracer for parameters and local variables, and the heap tracer for dynamically allocated variables. To trace a variable, the programmer embeds trace tags in the comments associated with the variables and single steps through the program. The Pep/9 integrated development environment shows the run-time values of the variables.

There are two kinds of trace tags:

> Format trace tags

> Symbol trace tags

Trace tags

Trace tags are contained in assembly language comments and have no effect on generated object code. Each trace tag begins with the # character and supplies information to the symbol tracer on how to format and label the memory cell in the trace window. Trace tag errors show up as warnings when the code is assembled, allowing program execution without tracing turned on. However, they do prevent tracing until they are corrected.

The global tracer allows the user to specify which global symbol to trace by placing a format trace tag in the comment of the .BLOCK line where the global variable is declared. For example, these two lines from Figure 5.22,

```
ch: .BLOCK 1 ;global variable #1c
j:  .BLOCK 2 ;global variable #2d
```

have format trace tags #1c and #2d. You should read the first format trace tag as "one byte, character." This trace tag tells the symbol tracer to display the content of the one-byte memory cell at the address specified by the value of the symbol, along with the symbol ch itself. Similarly, the second trace tag tells the symbol tracer to display the two-byte cell at the address specified by j as a decimal integer.

The legal format trace tags are:

#1c	One-byte character
#1d	One-byte decimal
#2d	Two-byte decimal
#1h	One-byte hexadecimal
#2h	Two-byte hexadecimal

The format trace tags

Global variables do not require the use of symbol trace tags, because the Pep/9 symbol tracer takes the symbol from the .BLOCK line on which the trace tag is placed. Local variables, however, require symbol trace tags, which are described in Chapter 6.

The Shift and Rotate Instructions

Pep/9 has two arithmetic shift instructions and two rotate instructions. All four are unary, with the following instruction specifiers, mnemonics, and status bits that they affect:

The shift and rotate instructions

0000 101r	ASLr	Arithmetic shift left r	NZVC
0000 110r	ASRr	Arithmetic shift right r	NZC
0000 111r	ROLr	Rotate left r	C
0001 000r	RORr	Rotate right r	C

The shift and rotate instructions have no operand specifier. Each one operates on either the accumulator or the index register, depending on the value of r. A shift left multiplies a signed integer by 2, and a shift right divides a signed integer by 2 (as described in Chapter 3). Rotate left rotates each bit to the left by one bit, sending the most significant bit into C and C into the least significant bit. Rotate right rotates each bit to the right by one bit, sending the least significant bit into C and C into the most significant bit.

The register transfer language (RTL) specification for the ASLr instruction is

$$C \leftarrow r\langle 0\rangle , r\langle 0..14\rangle , \leftarrow r\langle 1..15\rangle , r\langle 15\rangle \leftarrow 0 ;$$
$$N \leftarrow r < 0 , Z \leftarrow r = 0 , V \leftarrow \{overflow\}$$

The RTL specification for the ASRr instruction is

$$C \leftarrow r\langle 15\rangle , r\langle 1..15\rangle \leftarrow r\langle 0..14\rangle ; N \leftarrow r < 0 , Z \leftarrow r = 0$$

The RTL specification for the ROLr instruction is

$$C \leftarrow r\langle 0\rangle , r\langle 0..14\rangle \leftarrow r\langle 1..15\rangle , r\langle 15\rangle \leftarrow C$$

The RTL specification for the RORr instruction is

$$C \leftarrow r\langle 15\rangle , r\langle 1..15\rangle \leftarrow r\langle 0..14\rangle , r\langle 0\rangle \leftarrow C$$

Example 5.4 Suppose the instruction to be executed is 0C in hexadecimal, which **FIGURE 5.25** shows in binary. The opcode indicates that the ASRr instruction will execute, and the register-r field indicates that the instruction will affect the accumulator.

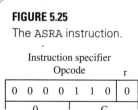

FIGURE 5.25
The ASRA instruction.

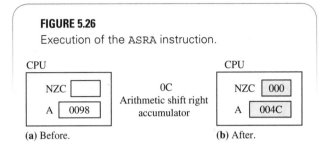

FIGURE 5.26

Execution of the ASRA instruction.

(a) Before. (b) After.

FIGURE 5.26 shows the effect of executing the ASRA instruction, assuming the accumulator has an initial content of 0098 (hex) = 152 (dec). The ASRA instruction changes the bit pattern to 004C (hex) = 76 (dec), which is half of 152. The N bit is 0 because the quantity in the accumulator is positive. The Z bit is 0 because the accumulator is not all 0's. The C bit is 0 because the least significant bit was 0 before the shift occurred. ∎

Constants and .EQUATE

.EQUATE is one of the few pseudo-ops to not generate any object code. Furthermore, the normal mechanism of taking the value of a symbol from the address of the object code does not apply. .EQUATE operates as follows:

> It must be on a line that defines a symbol.

> It equates the value of the symbol to the value that follows the .EQUATE.

> It does not generate any object code.

The operation of .EQUATE

The C compiler uses the .EQUATE dot command to translate C constants.

The C program in FIGURE 5.27 is identical to the one in Figure 2.6, except that the variables are global instead of local. It shows how to translate a C constant to machine language. It also illustrates the ASRA assembly language statement. The program calculates a value for score as the average of two exam grades plus a 10-point bonus.

The compiler translates

```
const int bonus = 10;
```

as

```
bonus:  .EQUATE 10
```

The assembly language listing in Figure 5.27 is notable on two counts. First, the line that contains the .EQUATE has no code in the machine language column. There is not even an address in the address column because there is no code to which the address would apply. This is consistent

FIGURE 5.27

A program for which the compiler translates a C constant to machine language.

High-Order Language

```
#include <stdio.h>
const int bonus = 10;
int exam1;
int exam2;
int score;

int main() {
   scanf("%d %d", &exam1, &exam2);
   score = (exam1 + exam2) / 2 + bonus;
   printf("score = %d\n", score);
   return 0;
}
```

Assembly Language

```
0000  120009         BR      main
              bonus:  .EQUATE 10          ;constant
0003  0000    exam1:  .BLOCK  2           ;global variable #2d
0005  0000    exam2:  .BLOCK  2           ;global variable #2d
0007  0000    score:  .BLOCK  2           ;global variable #2d
              ;
0009  310003 main:    DECI    exam1,d     ;scanf("%d %d", &exam1,
000C  310005          DECI    exam2,d     ; &exam2)
000F  C10003          LDWA    exam1,d     ;score = (exam1
0012  610005          ADDA    exam2,d     ; + exam2)
0015  0C              ASRA                ; / 2
0016  60000A          ADDA    bonus,i     ; + bonus
0019  E10007          STWA    score,d
001C  490029          STRO    msg,d       ;printf("score = %d\n",
001F  390007          DECO    score,d     ; score)
0022  D0000A          LDBA    '\n',i
0025  F1FC16          STBA    charOut,d
0028  00              STOP
0029  73636F msg:     .ASCII  "score = \x00"
      726520
      3D2000
0032                  .END
```

```
Symbol table
------------------------------------------
Symbol    Value         Symbol    Value
------------------------------------------
bonus     000A          exam1     0003
exam2     0005          main      0009
msg       0029          score     0007
------------------------------------------
```

Input
68 84

Output
score = 86

with the rule that .EQUATE does not generate code. Second, Figure 5.27 includes the symbol table from the assembler listing. You can see from the table that symbol bonus has the value 000A (hex), which is 10 (dec). In contrast, the symbol exam1 has the value 5 because the code generated for it by the .BLOCK dot command is at address 0005 (hex). But, there is no code for bonus, which is set to 000A by the .EQUATE dot command.

The I/O and assignment statements are similar to those in previous programs. scanf() translates to DECI, and printf() to DECO or STBA to charOut, all with direct addressing for the global variables. In general, assignment statements translate to

> load register,

> evaluate expression if necessary, and

> store register.

Translating assignment statements

To compute the expression

```
(exam1 + exam2) / 2 + bonus
```

the compiler generates code to load the value of exam1 into the accumulator, add the value of exam2 to it, and divide the sum by 2 with the ASRA instruction. The LDWA and ADDA instructions use direct addressing because exam1 and exam2 are global variables.

But how does the compiler generate code to add bonus? It cannot use direct addressing, because there is no object code corresponding to bonus, and hence no address. Instead, the statement

```
ADDA bonus,i
```

uses immediate addressing. In this case, the operand specifier is 000A (hex) = 10 (dec), which is the value to be added. The general rule for translating C constants to assembly language is

Translating C constants

> Declare the constant with .EQUATE.

> Access the constant with immediate addressing.

FIGURE 5.28

A translation of the C program in Figure 5.27 with a different placement of instructions and data.

```
0000   310020 main:    DECI     exam1,d        ;scanf("%d %d", &exam1,
0003   310022          DECI     exam2,d        ;  &exam2)
0006   C10020          LDWA     exam1,d        ;score = (exam1
0009   610022          ADDA     exam2,d        ;  + exam2)
000C   0C              ASRA                    ;  / 2
000D   60000A          ADDA     bonus,i        ;  + bonus
0010   E10024          STWA     score,d
0013   490026          STRO     msg,d          ;printf("score = %d\n",
0016   390024          DECO     score,d        ;  score)
0019   D0000A          LDBA     '\n',i
001C   F1FC16          STBA     charOut,d
001F   00              STOP
                ;
               bonus:   .EQUATE 10             ;constant
0020   0000    exam1:   .BLOCK  2              ;global variable #2d
0022   0000    exam2:   .BLOCK  2              ;global variable #2d
0024   0000    score:   .BLOCK  2              ;global variable #2d
0026   73636F msg:      .ASCII  "score = \x00"
       726520
       3D2000
002F                    .END

Symbol table
------------------------------------------------
Symbol     Value        Symbol     Value
------------------------------------------------
bonus      000A         exam1      0020
exam2      0022         main       0000
msg        0026         score      0024
------------------------------------------------
```

In a more realistic program, `score` would have type `float`, and you would compute the average with the real division operator. Pep/9 does not have hardware support for real numbers. Nor does its instruction set contain instructions for multiplying or dividing integers. These operations must be programmed with the shift left and shift right instructions.

Placement of Instructions and Data

The purpose this text is to show the correspondence between the levels of abstraction in a typical computer system. Consequently, the general program structure of an Asmb5 translation corresponds to the structure of the translated HOL6 program. Specifically, global variables appear before the main program in both the Asmb5 program and the HOL6 program. Real compilers do not have that constraint and often alter the placement of programs and data. **FIGURE 5.28** is a different translation of the C program in Figure 5.27. One benefit of this translation is the absence of the initial branch to the main program.

Chapter Summary

An assembler is a program that translates a program in assembly language into the equivalent program in machine language. The von Neumann design principle calls for instructions as well as data to be stored in main memory. Corresponding to each of these bit sequences are two types of assembly language statements. For program statements, assembly language uses mnemonics in place of opcodes and register-r fields, hexadecimal instead of binary for the operand specifiers, and mnemonic letters for the addressing modes. For data statements, assembly language uses pseudo-ops, also called *dot commands*.

With direct addressing, the operand specifier is the address in main memory of the operand. But with immediate addressing, the operand specifier is the operand. In mathematical notation, Oprnd = OprndSpec. Immediate addressing is preferable to direct addressing because the operand does not need to be stored separately from the instruction. Such instructions execute faster because the operand is immediately available to the CPU from the instruction register.

Assembly language symbols eliminate the problem of manually determining the addresses of data and instructions in a program. The value of a symbol is an address. When the assembler detects a symbol definition, it stores the symbol and its value in a symbol table. When the symbol is used, the assembler substitutes its value in place of the symbol.

A variable at the high-order language level (Level HOL6) corresponds to a memory location at the assembly level (Level Asmb5). An assignment statement at Level HOL6 that assigns an expression to a variable translates to a load, followed by an expression evaluation, followed by a store at Level Asmb5. Type compatibility at Level HOL6 is enforced by the compiler with the help of its symbol table, which is more complex than the symbol table of an assembler. At Level Asmb5, the only type is bit, and any operation can be performed on any bit pattern.

Exercises

Section 5.1

*1. Convert the following machine language instructions into assembly language, assuming that they were not generated by pseudo-ops:
   (a) 9AEF2A
   (b) 03
   (c) D7003D

2. Convert the following machine language instructions into assembly language, assuming that they were not generated by pseudo-ops:
   (a) 82B7DE
   (b) 04
   (c) DF63DF

*3. Convert the following assembly language instructions into hexadecimal machine language:
   (a) ASLA
   (b) DECI 0x000F,s
   (c) BRNE 0x01E6,i

4. Convert the following assembly language instructions into hexadecimal machine language:
   (a) ADDA 0x01FE,i
   (b) STRO 0x000D,sf
   (c) LDWX 0x01FF,s

*5. Convert the following assembly language pseudo-ops into hexadecimal machine language:
   (a) .ASCII "Bear\x00"
   (b) .BYTE 0xF8
   (c) .WORD 790

6. Convert the following assembly language pseudo-ops into hexadecimal machine language:

(a) `.BYTE 13`

(b) `.ASCII "Frog\x00"`

(c) `.WORD -6`

*7. Predict the output of the following assembly language program:

```
LDBA   0x0015,d
STBA   0xFC16,d
LDBA   0x0014,d
STBA   0xFC16,d
LDBA   0x0013,d
STBA   0xFC16,d
STOP
.ASCII  "gum"
.END
```

8. Predict the output of the following assembly language program:

```
LDBA   0x000E,d
STBA   0xFC16,d
LDBA   0x000D,d
STBA   0xFC16,d
STOP
.ASCII  "is"
.END
```

9. Predict the output of the following assembly language program if the input is g. Predict the output if the input is A. Explain the difference between the two results:

```
LDBA   0xFC15,d
ANDA   0x000A,d
STBA   0xFC16,d
STOP
.WORD   0x00DF
.END
```

Section 5.2

*10. Predict the output of the program in Figure 5.13 if the dot commands are changed to

```
.WORD 0xFFC7  ;First
.BYTE 0x00    ;Second
.BYTE 'H'     ;Third
.WORD 873     ;Fourth
```

11. Predict the output of the program in Figure 5.13 if the dot commands are changed to

```
.WORD 0xFE63  ;First
.BYTE 0x00    ;Second
.BYTE 'b'     ;Third
.WORD 1401    ;Fourth
```

12. Determine the object code and predict the output of the following assembly language programs:

*(a)

```
DECO  'm',i
LDBA  '\n',i
STBA  0xFC16,d
DECO  "mm",i
LDBA  '\n',i
STBA  0xFC16,d
LDBA  0x0026,i
STBA  0xFC16,d
STOP
.END
```

(b)

```
DECO  'Q',i
LDBA  '\n',i
STBA  0xFC16,d
DECO  0xFFC3,i
LDBA  '\n',i
STBA  0xFC16,d
LDBA  0x007D,i
STBA  0xFC16,d
STOP
.END
```

Section 5.3

*13. In the following code, determine the values of the symbols here and there. Write the object code in hexadecimal. (Do not predict the output.)

```
        BR     there
here:   .WORD  9
there:  DECO   here,d
        STOP
        .END
```

14. In the following code, determine the values of the symbols this, that, and theOther. Write the object code in hexadecimal. (Do not predict the output.)

```
          BR     theOther
this:     .WORD  17
that:     .WORD  19
theOther: DECO   this,d
          DECO   that,d
          STOP
          .END
```

*15. In the following code, determine the value of the symbol `this`. Predict and explain the output of the assembly language program:

```
this:    HEXO     this,d
         STOP
         .END
```

16. In the following code, determine the value of the symbol `this`. Predict and explain the output of the assembly language program:

```
this:    DECO     this,d
         STOP
         .END
```

Section 5.4

17. How are the symbol table of an assembler and a compiler similar? How do they differ?

*18. How does a C compiler enforce type compatibility?

19. Assume you have a Pep/9-type computer and the following disk files:

> File A: A Pep/9 assembly language assembler written in machine language

> File B: A C-to-assembly-language compiler written in assembly language

> File C: A C program that will read numbers from a data file and print their median

> File D: A data file for the median program of file C

To compute the median, you must make the four computer runs described schematically in FIGURE 5.29 . Each run involves an input file that will be operated on by a program to produce an output file. The output file produced by one run may be used either as the input file or as the program of a subsequent run. Describe the content of files E, F, G, and H, and label the empty blocks in Figure 5.29 with the appropriate file letter.

FIGURE 5.29

The computer runs for Exercise 19.

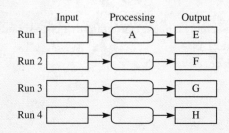

Problems

Section 5.1

20. Write an assembly language program that prints your first name on the screen. Use the `.ASCII` pseudo-op to store the characters at the bottom of your program. Use the `LDBA` instruction with direct addressing to output the characters from the string. The name you print must contain more than two letters.

Section 5.2

21. Write an assembly language program that prints your first name on the screen. Use immediate addressing with a character constant to designate the operand of `LDBA` for each letter of your name.

22. Write an assembly language program that prints your first name on the screen. Use immediate addressing with a decimal constant to designate the operand of `LDBA` for each letter of your name.

23. Write an assembly language program that prints your first name on the screen. Use immediate addressing with a hexadecimal constant to designate the operand of `LDBA` for each letter of your name.

Section 5.4

The following C programs do not show the include statement for `<studio.h>`, which would be required for the programs to compile.

24. Write an assembly language program that corresponds to the following C program:

```
int num1;
int num2;

int main () {
    scanf("%d %d", &num1, &num2);
    printf("%d\n%d\n", num2, num1);
    return 0;
}
```

25. Write an assembly language program that corresponds to the following C program:

```
const char chConst = 'a';
char ch1;
char ch2;
```

```
int main () {
    scanf("%c%c", &ch1, &ch2);
    printf("%c%c%c\n", ch1, chConst, ch2);
    return 0;
}
```

26. Write an assembly language program that corresponds to the following
    C program:

```
const int amount = 20000;
int num;
int sum;

int main () {
    scanf("%d", &num);
    sum = num + amount;
    printf("sum = %d\n", sum);
    return 0;
}
```

Test your program twice. The first time, enter a value for num to make the sum within the allowed range for the Pep/9 computer. The second time, enter a value that is in range but that makes sum outside the range. Note that the out-of-range condition does not cause an error message but just gives an incorrect value. Explain the value.

27. Write an assembly language program that corresponds to the following
    C program:

```
int width;
int length;
int perim;

int main () {
    scanf("%d %d", &width, &length);
    perim = (width + length) * 2;
    printf("width = %d\n", width);
    printf("length = %d\n\n", length);
    printf("perim = %d\n", perim);
    return 0;
}
```

28. Write an assembly language program that corresponds to the following C program:

```c
char ch;

int main () {
    scanf("%c", &ch);
    ch--;
    printf("%c\n", ch);
    return 0;
}
```

29. Write an assembly language program that corresponds to the following C program:

```c
int num1;
int num2;

int main () {
    scanf("%d", &num1);
    num2 = -num1;
    printf("num1 = %d\n", num1);
    printf("num2 = %d\n", num2);
    return 0;
}
```

30. Write an assembly language program that corresponds to the following C program:

```c
int num;

int main () {
    scanf("%d", &num);
    num = num / 16;
    printf("num = %d\n", num);
    return 0;
}
```

31. Write an assembly language program that corresponds to the following C program:

```c
int num;

int main () {
    scanf("%d", &num);
    num = num % 16;
    printf("num = %d\n", num);
    return 0;
}
```

CHAPTER 6

Compiling to the Assembly Level

The theme of this text is the application of the concept of levels of abstraction to computer systems. This chapter continues the theme by showing the relationship between the high-order languages level and the assembly level. It examines features of the C language at Level HOL6 and shows how a compiler might translate programs that use those features to the equivalent program at Level Asmb5.

One major difference between Level-HOL6 languages and Level-Asmb5 languages is the absence of extensive data types at Level Asmb5. In C, you can define integers, reals, arrays, Booleans, and structures in almost any combination. But assembly language has only bits and bytes. If you want to define an array of structures in assembly language, you must partition the bits and bytes accordingly. The compiler does that job automatically when you program at Level HOL6.

Another difference between the levels concerns the flow of control. C has if, while, do, for, switch, and function statements to alter the normal sequential flow of control. You will see that assembly language is limited by the basic von Neumann design to more primitive control statements. This chapter shows how the compiler must combine several primitive Level-Asmb5 control statements to execute a single, more powerful Level-HOL6 control statement.

6.1 Stack Addressing and Local Variables

When a program calls a function, the program allocates storage on the run-time stack for the returned value, the parameters, and the return address. Then the function allocates storage for its local variables. Stack-relative addressing allows the function to access the information that was pushed onto the stack.

You can consider main() of a C program to be a function that the operating system calls. You might be familiar with the fact that the main program can have parameters named argc and argv as follows:

```
int main(int argc, char* argv[])
```

With main declared this way, argc and argv are pushed onto the run-time stack, along with the return address and any local variables.

A simplification with
main()

To keep things simple, this text always declares main() without the parameters, and it ignores the fact that storage is allocated for the integer returned value and the return address. Hence, the only storage allocated for main() on the run-time stack is for local variables. Figure 2.19(a) shows the memory model with the returned value and the return address on the run-time stack. Figure 2.23(a) shows the memory model with this simplification.

Stack-Relative Addressing

With stack-relative addressing, the relation between the operand and the operand specifier is

Oprnd = Mem[SP + OprndSpec]   *Stack-relative addressing*

The stack pointer acts as a memory address to which the operand specifier is added. Figure 4.41 shows that the user stack grows upward in main memory starting at address FB8F. When an item is pushed onto the run-time stack, its address is smaller than the address of the item that was on the top of the stack.

The stack grows upward in main memory.

You can think of the operand specifier as the offset from the top of the stack. If the operand specifier is 0, the instruction accesses Mem[SP], the value on top of the stack. If the operand specifier is 2, it accesses Mem[SP + 2], the value two bytes below the top of the stack.

The Pep/9 instruction set has two instructions for manipulating the stack pointer directly, ADDSP and SUBSP. (CALL, RET, and RETTR manipulate the stack pointer indirectly.) ADDSP simply adds a value to the stack pointer, and SUBSP subtracts a value. The register transfer language (RTL) specification of ADDSP is

SP ← SP + Oprnd   *The ADDSP instruction*

and the RTL specification of SUBSP is

SP ← SP – Oprnd   *The SUBSP instruction*

Neither instruction changes the status bits.

Even though you can add to and subtract from the stack pointer, you cannot set the stack pointer with a load instruction. There is no LDSP instruction. Then how is the stack pointer ever set? When you select the execute option in the Pep/9 simulator, the following two actions occur:

SP ← Mem[FFF4]
PC ← 0000

The first action sets the stack pointer to the content of memory location FFF4. That location is part of the operating system ROM, and it contains the address of the top of the application's run-time stack. Therefore, when you select the execute option, the stack pointer is initialized correctly. The default Pep/9 operating system initializes the stack pointer to FB8F. The application never needs to set it to anything else. In general, the application only needs to subtract from the stack pointer to push items onto the run-time stack, and add to the stack pointer to pop items off of the run-time stack.

FIGURE 6.1
Stack-relative addressing.

```
0000   D00042   LDBA   'B',i        ;move B to stack
0003   F3FFFF   STBA   -1,s
0006   D0004D   LDBA   'M',i        ;move M to stack
0009   F3FFFE   STBA   -2,s
000C   D00057   LDBA   'W',i        ;move W to stack
000F   F3FFFD   STBA   -3,s
0012   C0014F   LDWA   335,i        ;move 335 to stack
0015   E3FFFB   STWA   -5,s
0018   D00069   LDBA   'i',i        ;move i to stack
001B   F3FFFA   STBA   -6,s
001E   580006   SUBSP  6,i          ;push 6 bytes onto stack
0021   D30005   LDBA   5,s          ;output B
0024   F1FC16   STBA   charOut,d
0027   D30004   LDBA   4,s          ;output M
002A   F1FC16   STBA   charOut,d
002D   D30003   LDBA   3,s          ;output W
0030   F1FC16   STBA   charOut,d
0033   3B0001   DECO   1,s          ;output 335
0036   D30000   LDBA   0,s          ;output i
0039   F1FC16   STBA   charOut,d
003C   500006   ADDSP  6,i          ;pop 6 bytes off stack
003F   00       STOP
0040            .END
```

Output
BMW335i

Accessing the Run-Time Stack

FIGURE 6.1 shows how to push data onto the stack, access it with stack-relative addressing, and pop it off the stack. The program pushes the string BMW onto the stack, followed by the decimal integer 335, followed by the character 'i'. Then it outputs the items and pops them off the stack.

FIGURE 6.2(a) shows the values in the stack pointer (SP) and main memory before the program executes. The machine initializes SP to FB8F from the vector at Mem[FFF4].

The first two instructions

```
0000 D00042 LDBA 'B',i ;move B to stack
0003 F3FFFF STBA -1,s
```

put an ASCII 'B' character in the byte just above the top of the stack. LDBA puts the 'B' byte in the right half of the accumulator, and STBA puts it above the stack. The store instruction uses stack-relative addressing with an operand specifier of –1 (dec) = FFFF (hex). Because the stack pointer has the value FB8F, the 'B' is stored at Mem[FB8F + FFFF] = Mem[FB8E]. The next two instructions put 'M' and 'W' at Mem[FB8D] and Mem[FB8C], respectively.

The decimal integer 335, however, occupies two bytes. The program must store it at an address that differs from the address of the 'W' by two. That is why the instruction to store the 335 is

```
0015 E3FFFB STWA -5,s
```

and not STWA -4,s. In general, when you push items onto the run-time stack, you must take into account how many bytes each item occupies and set the operand specifier accordingly.

The subtract stack pointer instruction

```
001E 580006 SUBSP 6,i ;push 6 bytes onto stack
```

subtracts 6 from the stack pointer, as Figure 6.2(b) shows. That completes the push operation.

Tracing a program that uses stack-relative addressing does not require you to know the absolute value in the stack pointer. The push operation would work the same if the stack pointer were initialized to some other value, say FA18. In that case, 'B', 'M', 'W', 335, and 'i' would be at Mem[FA17], Mem[FA16], Mem[FA15], Mem[FA13], and Mem[FA12], respectively, and the stack pointer would wind up with a value of FA12. The values would be at the same locations relative to the top of the stack, even though they would be at different absolute memory locations.

FIGURE 6.3 is a more convenient way of tracing the operation and makes use of the fact that the value in the stack pointer is irrelevant. Rather than show the value in the stack pointer, it shows an arrow pointing to the memory cell whose address is contained in the stack pointer. Rather than show the address of the cells in memory, it shows their offsets from the stack pointer. Figures depicting the state of the run-time stack will use this drawing convention from now on.

The instruction

```
0021 D30005 LDBA 5,s ;output B
```

loads the ASCII 'B' character from the stack. Note that the stack-relative address of the 'B' before SUBSP executes is –1, but its address after SUBSP executes is 5. Its stack-relative address is different because the stack pointer has changed. Both

```
0003 F3FFFF STBA -1,s
```

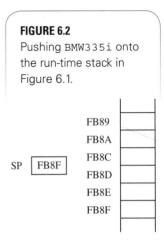

FIGURE 6.2

Pushing BMW335i onto the run-time stack in Figure 6.1.

(a) Before the program executes.

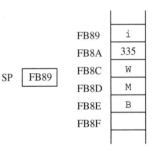

(b) After SUBSP executes.

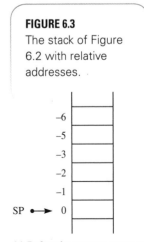

FIGURE 6.3

The stack of Figure 6.2 with relative addresses.

(a) Before the program executes.

(*continues*)

FIGURE 6.3
The stack of
Figure 6.2 with
relative addresses.
(*continued*)

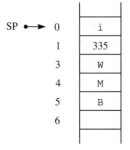

SP ● ➤	0	i
	1	335
	3	W
	4	M
	5	B
	6	

(b) After SUBSP executes.

and

```
0021 D30005 LDBA 5,s ;output B
```

access the same memory cell because SP has a different value when each of them executes. The other items are output similarly using their stack offsets, as shown in Figure 6.3(b).

The instruction

```
003C 500006 ADDSP 6,i ;pop 6 bytes off stack
```

deallocates six bytes of storage from the run-time stack by adding 6 to SP. Because the stack grows upward toward smaller addresses, you push storage by subtracting from the stack pointer, and you pop storage by adding to the stack pointer.

Local Variables

The previous chapter shows how the compiler translates programs with global variables. It allocates storage for a global variable with a .BLOCK dot command and accesses the global variable with direct addressing. Local variables, however, are allocated on the run-time stack. To translate a program with local variables, the compiler

The rules for accessing local variables

> pushes local variables onto the stack with SUBSP,

> accesses local variables with stack-relative addressing, and

> pops local variables off the stack with ADDSP.

The memory model for global versus local variables

An important difference between global and local variables is the time at which the allocation takes place. The .BLOCK dot command is not an executable statement. Storage for global variables is reserved at a fixed location before the program executes. In contrast, the SUBSP statement is executable. Storage for local variables is created on the run-time stack during program execution.

The C program in **FIGURE 6.4** is from Figure 2.6. It is identical to the program of Figure 5.27 except that the variables are declared local to main(). Although this difference is not perceptible to the user of the program, the translation performed by the compiler is significantly different. **FIGURE 6.5** shows the run-time stack for the program. bonus is a constant and is defined with the .EQUATE command (as in Figure 5.27). However, local variables are also defined with .EQUATE. With a constant, .EQUATE specifies the value of the constant, but with a local variable, .EQUATE specifies the stack offset on the run-time stack. For example, Figure 6.5 shows that the stack offset for local variable exam1 is 4. Therefore, the assembly language program equates the symbol exam1 to 4. Note from the assembly language listing that .EQUATE does not generate any code for the local variables.

.EQUATE specifies the stack offset for a local variable

FIGURE 6.4

A program with local variables. The C program is from Figure 2.6.

High-Order Language

```
#include <stdio.h>

int main() {
   const int bonus = 10;
   int exam1;
   int exam2;
   int score;
   scanf("%d %d", &exam1, &exam2);
   score = (exam1 + exam2) / 2 + bonus;
   printf("score = %d\n", score);
   return 0;
}
```

Assembly Language

```
0000   120003           BR      main
                bonus:  .EQUATE 10          ;constant
                exam1:  .EQUATE 4           ;local variable #2d
                exam2:  .EQUATE 2           ;local variable #2d
                score:  .EQUATE 0           ;local variable #2d
                      ;
0003   580006 main:     SUBSP   6,i         ;push #exam1 #exam2 #score
0006   330004           DECI    exam1,s     ;scanf("%d %d", &exam1, &exam2)
0009   330002           DECI    exam2,s
000C   C30004           LDWA    exam1,s     ;score = (exam1 + exam2) / 2 + bonus
000F   630002           ADDA    exam2,s
0012   0C               ASRA
0013   60000A           ADDA    bonus,i
0016   E30000           STWA    score,s
0019   490029           STRO    msg,d       ;printf("score = %d\n", score)
001C   3B0000           DECO    score,s
001F   D0000A           LDBA    '\n',i
0022   F1FC16           STBA    charOut,d
0025   500006           ADDSP   6,i         ;pop #score #exam2 #exam1
0028   00               STOP
0029   73636F msg:      .ASCII  "score = \x00"
       726520
       3D2000
0032                    .END
```

Format trace tags

Symbol trace tags

FIGURE 6.5

The run-time stack for the program of Figure 6.4.

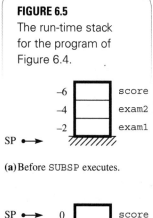

(a) Before SUBSP executes.

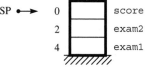

(b) After SUBSP executes.

Translation of the executable statements in main() differs in two respects from the version with global variables. First, SUBSP and ADDSP push and pop storage on the run-time stack for the locals. Second, all accesses to the variables use stack-relative addressing instead of direct addressing. Other than these differences, the translation of the assignment and output statements is the same.

Figure 6.4 shows how to write trace tags for debugging with local variables. The assembly language program uses the format trace tag #2d with the .EQUATE pseudo-op to tell the debugger that the values of exam1, exam2, and score should be displayed as two-byte decimal values.

These local variables are pushed onto the run-time stack with the SUBSP instruction. Consequently, to debug your program you specify the three symbol trace tags #exam1, #exam2, and #score in the comment for SUBSP. When you single-step through the program, the Pep/9 system displays a figure on the screen like that of Figure 6.5(b), with the symbolic labels of the cells on the right of the run-time stack. For the debugger to function accurately, you must list the symbol trace tags in the comment field in the exact order they are pushed onto the run-time stack. In this program, exam1 is pushed first, followed by exam2 and then score. Furthermore, this order must be consistent with the offset values in the .EQUATE pseudo-op.

The variables are popped off the stack with the ADDSP instruction. So you must list the variables that are popped off the run-time stack in the proper order. Because the variables are popped off in the opposite order they are pushed on, you list them in the opposite order from the order in the SUBSP instruction. In this program, score is popped off, followed by exam2 and then exam1.

Although trace tags are not necessary for the program to execute, they serve to document the program. The information provided by the symbol trace tags is valuable for the reader of the program, because it describes the purpose of the SUBSP and ADDSP instructions. The assembly language programs in this chapter all include trace tags for documentation purposes, and your programs should as well.

6.2 Branching Instructions and Flow of Control

The Pep/9 instruction set has eight conditional branches:

BRLE	Branch on less than or equal to
BRLT	Branch on less than
BREQ	Branch on equal to

```
BRNE      Branch on not equal to
BRGE      Branch on greater than or equal to
BRGT      Branch on greater than
BRV       Branch on V
BRC       Branch on C
```

Each of these conditional branches tests one or two of the four status bits, N, Z, V, and C. If the condition is true, the operand is placed in the program counter (PC), causing the branch. If the condition is not true, the operand is not placed in PC, and the instruction following the conditional branch executes normally. You can think of them as comparing a 16-bit result to 0000 (hex). For example, BRLT checks whether a result is less than zero, which happens if N is 1. BRLE checks whether a result is less than or equal to zero, which happens if N is 1 or Z is 1. Here is the RTL specification of each conditional branch instruction.

BRLE	$N = 1 \vee Z = 1 \Rightarrow PC \leftarrow Oprnd$	*The conditional branch*
BRLT	$N = 1 \Rightarrow PC \leftarrow Oprnd$	*instructions*
BREQ	$Z = 1 \Rightarrow PC \leftarrow Oprnd$	
BRNE	$Z = 0 \Rightarrow PC \leftarrow Oprnd$	
BRGE	$N = 0 \Rightarrow PC \leftarrow Oprnd$	
BRGT	$N = 0 \wedge Z = 0 \Rightarrow PC \leftarrow Oprnd$	
BRV	$V = 1 \Rightarrow PC \leftarrow Oprnd$	
BRC	$C = 1 \Rightarrow PC \leftarrow Oprnd$	

Whether a branch occurs depends on the value of the status bits. The status bits are in turn affected by the execution of other instructions. For example,

```
LDWA num,s
BRLT place
```

causes the content of num to be loaded into the accumulator. If the word represents a negative number—that is, if its sign bit is 1—then the N bit is set to 1. BRLT tests the N bit and causes a branch to the instruction at place. On the other hand, if the word loaded into the accumulator is not negative, then the N bit is cleared to 0. When BRLT tests the N bit, the branch does not occur and the instruction after BRLT executes next.

Translating the If Statement

FIGURE 6.6 shows how a compiler would translate an if statement from C to assembly language. The program computes the absolute value of an integer.

The assembly language comments show the statements that correspond to the high-level program. The scanf() function call translates to DECI,

FIGURE 6.6

The `if` statement at Level HOL6 and Level Asmb5.

High-Order Language

```
#include <stdio.h>

int main() {
    int number;
    scanf("%d", &number);
    if (number < 0) {
        number = -number;
    }
    printf("%d", number);
    return 0;
}
```

Assembly Language

```
0000   120003          BR       main
               number:  .EQUATE 0            ;local variable #2d
                   ;
0003   580002 main:    SUBSP    2,i          ;push #number
0006   330000          DECI     number,s     ;scanf("%d", &number)
0009   C30000 if:      LDWA     number,s     ;if (number < 0)
000C   1C0016          BRGE     endIf
000F   C30000          LDWA     number,s     ;number = -number
0012   08              NEGA
0013   E30000          STWA     number,s
0016   3B0000 endIf:   DECO     number,s     ;printf("%d", number)
0019   500002          ADDSP    2,i          ;pop #number
001C   00              STOP
001D                   .END
```

and the `printf()` function call translates to `DECO`. The assignment statement translates to the sequence `LDWA`, `NEGA`, `STWA`.

The compiler translates the `if` statement into the sequence `LDWA`, `BRGE`. The RTL specification of `LDWr` is

The `LDWr` instruction

$$r \leftarrow \text{Oprnd}; N \leftarrow r < 0, Z \leftarrow r = 0$$

When `LDWA` executes, if the value loaded into the accumulator is positive or zero, the N bit is cleared to 0. That condition calls for skipping the body of the `if` statement. (**FIGURE 6.7(a)**) shows the structure of the `if` statement at Level HOL6. *S1* represents the `scanf()` function call, *C1* represents the condition `number < 0`, *S2* represents the statement `number = -number`, and *S3* represents the statement `printf()` function call. Figure 6.7(b) shows the structure with the more primitive branching instructions at Level Asmb5. The dot following *C1* represents the conditional branch, `BRGE`.

The braces { and } for delimiting a compound statement have no counterpart in assembly language. The sequence

> *Statement 1*
> ```
> if (number >= 0) {
> ```
> > *Statement 2*
> > *Statement 3*
>
> ```
> }
> ```
> *Statement 4*

translates to

> > *Statement 1*
> ```
> if:    LDWA number,d
>        BRLT endIf
> ```
> > *Statement 2*
> > *Statement 3*
> ```
> endIf:
> ```
> *Statement 4*

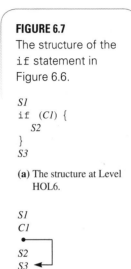

FIGURE 6.7

The structure of the `if` statement in Figure 6.6.

```
S1
if (C1) {
    S2
}
S3
```

(a) The structure at Level HOL6.

```
S1
C1
•
S2
S3
```

(b) The same structure at Level Asmb5.

Optimizing Compilers

You may have noticed an extra load statement that was not strictly required in Figure 6.6. You can eliminate the `LDWA` at 000F because the value of `number` will still be in the accumulator from the previous load at 0009.

The question is, what would a compiler do? The answer depends on the compiler. A compiler is a program that must be written and debugged. Imagine that you must design a compiler to translate from C to assembly language. When the compiler detects an assignment statement, you program it to generate the following sequence: (a) load accumulator, (b) evaluate expression if necessary, (c) store result to variable. Such a compiler would generate the code of Figure 6.6, with the `LDWA` at 000F.

Imagine how difficult your compiler program would be if you wanted it to eliminate the unnecessary load. When your compiler detected an assignment statement, it would not always generate the initial load. Instead, it would analyze the previous instructions generated and remember the content of the accumulator. If it determined that the value in the accumulator was the same as the value that the initial load put there, it would not generate the initial load.

In Figure 6.6, the compiler would need to remember that the value of `number` was still in the accumulator from the code generated for the `if` statement.

The purpose of an optimizing compiler

A compiler that expends extra effort to make the object program shorter and faster is called an *optimizing compiler*. You can imagine how much more difficult an optimizing compiler is to design than a nonoptimizing one. Not only are optimizing compilers more difficult to write, they also take longer to compile because they must analyze the source program in much greater detail.

The advantages and disadvantages of an optimizing compiler

Which is better, an optimizing or a nonoptimizing compiler? That depends on the use to which you put the compiler. If you are developing software, a process that requires many compiles for testing and debugging, then you would want a compiler that translates quickly—that is, a nonoptimizing compiler. If you have a large fixed program that will be executed repeatedly by many users, you would want fast execution of the object program—hence, an optimizing compiler. Most compilers offer a wide range of options that allow the developer to specify the level of optimization desired. Software is normally developed and debugged with little optimization and then translated one last time with a high level of optimization for the end users.

The examples in this chapter occasionally present object code that is partially optimized. Most assignment statements, such as the one in Figure 6.6, are presented in nonoptimized form.

Translating the If/Else Statement

FIGURE 6.8 illustrates the translation of the `if/else` statement. The C program is identical to the one in Figure 2.10. The `if` body requires an extra unconditional branch around the `else` body. If the compiler omitted the BR at 0015 and the input were 127, the output would be `highlow`.

Unlike Figure 6.6, the `if` statement in Figure 6.8 does not compare a variable's value with zero. It compares the variable's value with another nonzero value using CPWA, which stands for *compare word accumulator*. CPWA subtracts the operand from the accumulator and sets the NZVC status bits accordingly. CPWr is identical to SUBr except that SUBr stores the result of the subtraction in register r (accumulator or index register), whereas CPWr ignores the result of the subtraction. The RTL specification of CPWr is

The CPWr instruction

$$T \leftarrow r - Oprnd; N \leftarrow T < 0, Z \leftarrow T = 0, V \leftarrow \{overflow\}, C \leftarrow \{carry\};$$
$$N \leftarrow N \oplus V$$

where T represents a temporary value.

(There is an adjustment to the N bit, $N \leftarrow N \oplus V$, that is not present in the subtract instruction. N is replaced by the exclusive OR of N and V. If the result of the subtraction yields an overflow and the N bit were set as usual, the subsequent conditional branch instruction might execute an erroneous branch. Consequently, if the CPWr subtraction operation overflows and sets the V bit,

FIGURE 6.8
The `if`/`else` statement at Level HOL6 and Level Asmb5. The C program is from Figure 2.10.

High-Order Language

```c
#include <stdio.h>

int main() {
   const int limit = 100;
   int num;
   scanf("%d", &num);
   if (num >= limit) {
      printf("high\n");
   }
   else {
      printf("low\n");
   }
   return 0;
}
```

Assembly Language

```
0000  120003            BR       main
                limit:  .EQUATE  100          ;constant
                num:    .EQUATE  0            ;local variable #2d
                        ;
0003  580002 main:      SUBSP    2,i          ;push #num
0006  330000            DECI     num,s        ;scanf("%d", &num)
0009  C30000 if:        LDWA     num,s        ;if (num >= limit)
000C  A00064            CPWA     limit,i
000F  160018            BRLT     else
0012  49001F            STRO     msg1,d       ;printf("high\n")
0015  12001B            BR       endIf
0018  490025 else:      STRO     msg2,d       ;printf("low\n")
001B  500002 endIf:     ADDSP    2,i          ;pop #num
001E  00                STOP
001F  686967 msg1:      .ASCII   "high\n\x00"
      680A00
0025  6C6F77 msg2:      .ASCII   "low\n\x00"
      0A00
002A                    .END
```

FIGURE 6.9

The structure of the if/else statement in Figure 6.8.

```
S1
if (C1) {
    S2
}
else {
    S3
}
S4
```

(a) The structure at Level HOL6.

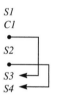

```
S1
C1

S2

S3
S4
```

(b) The same structure at Level Asmb5.

then the N bit is inverted from its normal value and does not duplicate the sign bit. With this adjustment, the compare operation extends the range of valid comparisons. Even though there is an overflow, the N bit is set as if there were no overflow so that a subsequent conditional branch will operate as expected.)

This program computes num - limit and sets the NZVC bits. BRLT tests the N bit, which is set if

$$num - limit < 0$$

that is, if

$$num < limit$$

That is the condition under which the else part must execute.

FIGURE 6.9 shows the structure of the control statements at the two levels. Part (a) shows the Level-HOL6 control statement, and part (b) shows the Level-Asmb5 translation for this program.

Translating the While Loop

Translating a loop requires branches to previous instructions. FIGURE 6.10 shows the translation of a while statement. The C program is identical to the one in Figure 2.13. It echoes ASCII input characters to the output, replacing a space character with a newline character, using the sentinel

FIGURE 6.10

The while statement at Level HOL6 and Level Asmb5. The C program is from Figure 2.13.

High-Order Language

```c
#include <stdio.h>

char letter;

int main() {
    scanf("%c", &letter);
    while (letter != '*') {
        if (letter == ' ') {
            printf("\n");
        }
        else {
            printf("%c", letter);
        }
        scanf("%c", &letter);
    }
    return 0;
}
```

Assembly Language

```
0000   120004              BR      main
0003   00      letter:     .BLOCK  1           ;global variable #1c
       ;
0004   D1FC15  main:       LDBA    charIn,d    ;scanf("%c", &letter)
0007   F10003              STBA    letter,d
000A   D10003  while:      LDBA    letter,d    ;while (letter != '*')
000D   B0002A              CPBA    '*',i
0010   18002E              BREQ    endWh
0013   B00020  if:         CPBA    ' ',i       ;if (letter == ' ')
0016   1A0022              BRNE    else
0019   D0000A              LDBA    '\n',i      ;printf("\n")
001C   F1FC16              STBA    charOut,d
001F   120025              BR      endIf
0022   F1FC16  else:       STBA    charOut,d   ;printf("%c", letter)
0025   D1FC15  endIf:      LDBA    charIn,d    ;scanf("%c", &letter)
0028   F10003              STBA    letter,d
002B   12000A              BR      while
002E   00      endWh:      STOP
002F                       .END
```

technique with * as the sentinel. If the input is `Hello, world!*` on a single line, the output is `Hello,` on one line and `world!` on the next.

The test for a `while` statement is made with a conditional branch at the top of the loop. This program tests a character value, which is a byte quantity. Every `while` loop ends with an unconditional branch to the test at the top of the loop. The unconditional branch at 002B brings control back to the initial test. **FIGURE 6.11** shows the structure of the `while` statement at the two levels.

The RTL specification of CPBr is

$$T \leftarrow r\langle 8..15 \rangle - \text{byte Oprnd}; N \leftarrow T < 0, Z \leftarrow T = 0, V \leftarrow 0, C \leftarrow 0$$

where T represents an eight-bit temporary value. The instruction sets the status bits according to the eight-bit value without regard to the high-order byte of register r. The CPBA instruction in Figure 6.10(b) would still function correctly even if the accumulator had some 1's in its high-order byte.

The RTL specification of LDBr is

$$r\langle 8..15 \rangle \leftarrow \text{byte Oprnd}; N \leftarrow 0, Z \leftarrow r\langle 8..15 \rangle = 0$$

As with CPBr, the instruction sets the status bits according to the eight-bit value without regard to the high-order byte of register r. If you ever need to

FIGURE 6.11

The structure of the `while` statement in Figure 6.10.

```
S1
while (C1) {
  S2
}
S3
```

(a) The structure at Level HOL6.

```
S1
C1
S2
S3
```

(b) The same structure at Level Asmb5.

check for the ASCII NUL byte, you can load the byte into the accumulator and execute BREQ straightaway without using the compare byte instruction.

Translating the Do Loop

A highway patrol officer parks behind a sign. A driver passes by, traveling 20 meters per second, which is faster than the speed limit. When the driver is 40 meters down the road, the officer gets his car up to 25 meters per second to pursue the offender. How far from the sign is the officer when he catches up to the speeder?

The program in FIGURE 6.12 solves the problem by simulation. It is identical to the one in Figure 2.14. The values of cop and driver are the positions of the two motorists, initialized to 0 and 40, respectively. Each

FIGURE 6.12

The do statement at Level HOL6 and Level Asmb5. The C program is from Figure 2.14.

High-Order Language

```c
#include <stdio.h>

int cop;
int driver;

int main() {
    cop = 0;
    driver = 40;
    do {
        cop += 25;
        driver += 20;
    }
    while (cop < driver);
    printf("%d", cop);
    return 0;
}
```

Assembly Language

```
0000  120007          BR      main
0003  0000    cop:    .BLOCK  2          ;global variable #2d
0005  0000    driver: .BLOCK  2          ;global variable #2d
                      ;
0007  C00000  main:   LDWA    0,i        ;cop = 0
000A  E10003          STWA    cop,d
```

```
000D  C00028          LDWA    40,i        ;driver = 40
0010  E10005          STWA    driver,d
0013  C10003 do:      LDWA    cop,d       ;cop += 25
0016  600019          ADDA    25,i
0019  E10003          STWA    cop,d
001C  C10005          LDWA    driver,d    ;driver += 20
001F  600014          ADDA    20,i
0022  E10005          STWA    driver,d
0025  C10003 while:   LDWA    cop,d       ;while (cop < driver)
0028  A10005          CPWA    driver,d
002B  160013          BRLT    do
002E  390003          DECO    cop,d       ;printf("%d", cop)
0031  00              STOP
0032                  .END
```

execution of the do loop represents one second of elapsed time, during which the officer travels 25 meters and the driver 20, until the officer catches the driver.

A do statement has its test at the bottom of the loop. In this program, the compiler translates the while test to the sequence LDWA, CPWA, BRLT. BRLT executes the branch if N is set to 1. Because CPWA computes the difference, cop - driver, N will be 1 if

```
cop - driver < 0
```

that is, if

```
cop < driver
```

That is the condition under which the loop should repeat. **FIGURE 6.13** shows the structure of the do statement at Levels 6 and 5.

Translating the For Loop

for statements are similar to while statements because the test for both is at the top of the loop. The compiler must generate code to initialize and to increment the control variable. The program in **FIGURE 6.14** shows how a compiler generates code for the for statement. It translates the for statement into the following sequence at Level Asmb5:

> ❯ Initialize the control variable.

> ❯ Test the control variable.

> ❯ Execute the loop body.

> ❯ Increment the control variable.

> ❯ Branch to the test.

FIGURE 6.13
The structure of the do statement in Figure 6.12.

S1
do {
    S2
}
while (*C1*)
S3

(a) The structure at Level HOL6.

S1
S2
C1
S3

(b) The same structure at Level Asmb5.

FIGURE 6.14

The `for` statement at Level HOL6 and Level Asmb5.

High-Order Language

```
#include <stdio.h>

int main() {
    int j;
    for (j = 0; j < 3; j++) {
        printf("j = %d\n", j);
    }
    return 0;
}
```

Assembly Language

```
0000   120003            BR      main
               j:         .EQUATE 0              ;local variable #2d
               ;
0003   580002 main:      SUBSP   2,i            ;push #j
0006   C00000            LDWA    0,i            ;for (j = 0
0009   E30000            STWA    j,s
000C   A00003 for:       CPWA    3,i            ;j < 3
000F   1C002A            BRGE    endFor
0012   49002E            STRO    msg,d          ;printf("j = %d\n", j)
0015   3B0000            DECO    j,s
0018   D0000A            LDBA    '\n',i
001B   F1FC16            STBA    charOut,d
001E   C30000            LDWA    j,s            ;j++)
0021   600001            ADDA    1,i
0024   E30000            STWA    j,s
0027   12000C            BR      for
002A   500002 endFor:    ADDSP   2,i            ;pop #j
002D   00                STOP
002E   6A203D msg:       .ASCII  "j = \x00"
       2000
0033                     .END
```

In this program, CPWA computes the difference, j - 3. BRGE branches out of the loop if N is 0—that is, if

$$j - 3 \geq 0$$

or, equivalently,

```
j >= 3
```

The body executes three times for j having the values 0, 1, and 2. After the last execution, j increments to 3, the loop terminates, and the value of 3 is not written by the output statement.

Spaghetti Code

At the assembly level, a programmer can write control structures that do not correspond to the control structures in C. **FIGURE 6.15** shows one possible flow of control that is not directly possible in many Level-HOL6 languages. Condition *C1* is tested, and if it is true, a branch is taken to the middle of a loop whose test is *C2*.

Assembly language programs generated by a compiler are usually longer than programs written by humans directly in assembly language. Not only that, but they often execute more slowly. If human programmers can write shorter, faster assembly language programs than compilers, why does anyone program in a high-order language? One reason is the ability of the compiler to perform type checking (as mentioned in Chapter 5). Another is the additional burden of responsibility that is placed on the programmer when given the freedom of using primitive branching instructions. If you are not careful when you write programs at Level Asmb5, the branching instructions can get out of hand.

The program in **FIGURE 6.16** is an extreme example of the problem that can occur with unbridled use of primitive branching instructions. It

FIGURE 6.15
A flow of control not possible directly in many HOL6 languages.

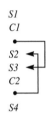

FIGURE 6.16
A mystery program.

```
0000   120009           BR       main
0003   0000    n1:       .BLOCK   2           ;#2d
0005   0000    n2:       .BLOCK   2           ;#2d
0007   0000    n3:       .BLOCK   2           ;#2d
                         ;
0009   310005  main:     DECI     n2,d
000C   310007           DECI     n3,d
000F   C10005           LDWA     n2,d
0012   A10007           CPWA     n3,d
0015   16002A           BRLT     L1
0018   310003           DECI     n1,d
```
(continues)

FIGURE 6.16

A mystery program. (*continued*)

```
001B  C10003          LDWA    n1,d
001E  A10007          CPWA    n3,d
0021  160074          BRLT    L7
0024  120065          BR      L6
0027  E10007          STWA    n3,d
002A  310003 L1:      DECI    n1,d
002D  C10005          LDWA    n2,d
0030  A10003          CPWA    n1,d
0033  160053          BRLT    L5
0036  390003          DECO    n1,d
0039  390005          DECO    n2,d
003C  390007 L2:      DECO    n3,d
003F  00              STOP
0040  390005 L3:      DECO    n2,d
0043  390007          DECO    n3,d
0046  120081          BR      L9
0049  390003 L4:      DECO    n1,d
004C  390005          DECO    n2,d
004F  00              STOP
0050  E10003          STWA    n1,d
0053  C10007 L5:      LDWA    n3,d
0056  A10003          CPWA    n1,d
0059  160040          BRLT    L3
005C  390005          DECO    n2,d
005F  390003          DECO    n1,d
0062  12003C          BR      L2
0065  390007 L6:      DECO    n3,d
0068  C10003          LDWA    n1,d
006B  A10005          CPWA    n2,d
006E  160049          BRLT    L4
0071  12007E          BR      L8
0074  390003 L7:      DECO    n1,d
0077  390007          DECO    n3,d
007A  390005          DECO    n2,d
007D  00              STOP
007E  390005 L8:      DECO    n2,d
0081  390003 L9:      DECO    n1,d
0084  00              STOP
0085                  .END
```

is difficult to understand because of its lack of comments and indentation and its inconsistent branching style. Actually, the program performs a very simple task. Can you discover what it does?

The body of an `if` statement or a loop in C is a block of statements, sometimes contained in a compound statement delimited by braces, `{ }`. Additional `if` statements and loops can be nested entirely within these blocks. (**FIGURE 6.17(a)**) pictures this situation schematically. A flow of control that is limited to nestings of the `if/else`, `switch`, `while`, `do`, and `for` statements is called *structured flow of control*.

Structured flow of control

The branches in the mystery program do not correspond to the structured control constructs of C. Although the program's logic is correct for performing its intended task, it is difficult to decipher because the branching statements branch all over the place. This kind of program is called *spaghetti code*. If you draw an arrow from each branch statement to the statement to which it branches, the picture looks rather like a bowl of spaghetti, as Figure 6.17(b) shows.

Spaghetti code

It is often possible to write efficient programs with unstructured branches. Such programs execute faster and require less memory for storage than if they were written in a high-order language with structured flow of control. Some specialized applications require this extra measure of efficiency and are therefore written directly in assembly language.

Balanced against this savings in execution time and memory space is difficulty in comprehension. When programs are hard to understand, they are hard to write, debug, and modify. The problem is economic. Writing, debugging, and modifying are all human activities that are labor intensive and, therefore, expensive. The question you must ask is whether the extra efficiency justifies the additional expense.

FIGURE 6.17
Two different styles of flow of control.

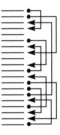

(a) Structured flow.

Flow of Control in Early Languages

Computers had been around for many years before structured flow of control was discovered. In the early days, there were no high-order languages. Everyone programmed in assembly language. Computer memories were expensive, and CPUs were slow by today's standards. Efficiency was all-important. Because a large body of software had not yet been generated, the problem of program maintenance was not appreciated.

The first widespread high-order language was Fortran, developed in the 1950s. Because people were used to dealing with branch instructions, they included them in the language. An unconditional branch in Fortran is

(b) Spaghetti code.

```
GOTO 260
```

A goto statement at Level HOL6

where 260 is the statement number of another statement. It is called a *goto statement*. A conditional branch is

```
IF (NUMBER .GE. 100) GOTO 500
```

where `.GE.` means "is greater than or equal to." This statement compares the value of variable `NUMBER` with 100. If it is greater than or equal to 100, the next statement executed is the one with a statement number of 500. Otherwise, the statement after the `IF` is executed.

Fortran's conditional `IF` is a big improvement over Level-Asmb5 branch instructions. It does not require a separate compare instruction to set the status bits. But notice how the flow of control is similar to Level-Asmb5 branching: If the test is true, do the `GOTO`. Otherwise, continue to the next statement.

As people developed more software, they noticed that it would be convenient to group statements into blocks for use in `if` statements and loops. The most notable language to make this advance was Algol 60, developed in 1960. It was the first widespread block-structured language, although its popularity was limited mainly to Europe.

The Structured Programming Theorem

The preceding sections show how high-level structured control statements translate into primitive branch statements at a lower level. They also show how you can write branches at the lower level that do not correspond to the structured constructs. This raises an interesting and practical question: Is it possible to write an algorithm with goto statements that will perform some processing that is impossible to perform with structured constructs? That is, if you limit yourself to structured flow of control, are there some problems you will not be able to solve that you could solve if unstructured gotos were allowed?

The structured programming theorem

Corrado Bohm and Giuseppe Jacopini answered this important question in a computer science journal article in 1966.[1] They proved mathematically that any algorithm containing gotos, no matter how complicated or unstructured, can be written with only nested `if` statements and `while` loops. Their result is called the *structured programming theorem*.

Bohm and Jacopini's paper was highly theoretical. It did not attract much attention at first because programmers generally had no desire to limit the freedom they had with goto statements. Bohm and Jacopini showed what could be done with nested `if` statements and `while` loops, but left unanswered why programmers would want to limit themselves that way.

---

1. Corrado Bohm and Giuseppe Jacopini, "Flow-Diagrams, Turing Machines and Languages with Only Two Formation Rules," *Communications of the ACM 9* (May 1966): 366–371.

People experimented with the concept anyway. They would take an algorithm in spaghetti code and try to rewrite it using structured flow of control without goto statements. Usually the new program was much clearer than the original. Occasionally it was even more efficient.

The Goto Controversy

Two years after Bohm and Jacopini's paper appeared, Edsger W. Dijkstra of the Technological University at Eindhoven, the Netherlands, wrote a letter to the editor of the same journal in which he stated his personal observation that good programmers used fewer gotos than poor programmers.[2]

In his opinion, a high density of gotos in a program indicated poor quality. He stated in part:

> More recently I discovered why the use of the goto statement has such disastrous effects, and I became convinced that the goto statement should be abolished from all "higher level" programming languages (i.e., everything except, perhaps, plain machine code). ... The goto statement as it stands is just too primitive; it is too much an invitation to make a mess of one's program.

To justify these statements, Dijkstra developed the idea of a set of coordinates that are necessary to describe the progress of the program. When a human tries to understand a program, he must maintain this set of coordinates mentally, perhaps unconsciously. Dijkstra showed that the coordinates to be maintained with structured flow of control were vastly simpler than those with unstructured gotos. Thus he was able to pinpoint the reason that structured flow of control is easier to understand.

Dijkstra acknowledged that the idea of eliminating gotos was not new. He mentioned several people who influenced him on the subject, one of whom was Niklaus Wirth, who had worked on the Algol 60 language.

Dijkstra's letter set off a storm of protest, now known as the famous *goto controversy*. To theoretically be able to program without goto was one thing. But to advocate that goto be abolished from high-order languages such as Fortran was altogether something else.

Old ideas die hard. However, the controversy has died down, and it is now generally recognized that Dijkstra was, in fact, correct. The reason is cost. When software managers began to apply the structured flow of control discipline, along with other structured design concepts, they found that the

---

2. Edsger W. Dijkstra, "Goto Statement Considered Harmful," *Communications of the ACM 11* (March 1968): 147–648.

resulting software was much less expensive to develop, debug, and maintain. It was usually well worth the additional memory requirements and extra execution time.

Fortran 77 was a more recent version of Fortran standardized in 1977. The goto controversy influenced its design. It contains a block style IF statement with an ELSE part similar to C. For example,

```
IF (NUMBER .GE. 100) THEN
    Statement 1
ELSE
    Statement 2
ENDIF
```

You can write the IF statement in Fortran 77 without goto.

One point to bear in mind is that the absence of gotos in a program does not guarantee that the program is well structured. It is possible to write a program with three or four nested if statements and while loops when only one or two are necessary. Also, if a language at any level contains only goto statements to alter the flow of control, they can always be used in a structured way to implement if statements and while loops. That is precisely what a C compiler does when it translates a program from Level HOL6 to Level Asmb5.

6.3 Function Calls and Parameters

A C function call changes the flow of control to the first executable statement in the function. At the end of the function, control returns to the statement following the function call. The compiler implements function calls with the CALL instruction, which has a mechanism for storing the return address on the run-time stack. It implements the return to the calling statement with RET, which uses the saved return address on the run-time stack to determine which instruction to execute next.

Translating a Function Call

FIGURE 6.18 shows how a compiler translates a function call without parameters. The program outputs three triangles of asterisks.

The CALL instruction pushes the content of the program counter onto the run-time stack and then loads the operand into the program counter. Here is the RTL specification of the CALL instruction:

The CALL instruction

$$SP \leftarrow SP - 2; Mem[SP] \leftarrow PC; PC \leftarrow Oprnd$$

The return address for the procedure call is pushed onto the stack and a branch to the procedure is executed.

FIGURE 6.18
A procedure call at Level HOL6 and Level Asmb5.

High-Order Language
```
#include <stdio.h>

void printTri() {
   printf("*\n");
   printf("**\n");
   printf("***\n");
   printf("****\n");
}

int main() {
   printTri();
   printTri();
   printTri();
   return 0;
}
```

Assembly Language
```
0000   120019            BR       main
                ;
                ;******* void printTri()
0003   49000D printTri:STRO      msg1,d      ;printf("*\n")
0006   490010           STRO     msg2,d      ;printf("**\n")
0009   490014           STRO     msg3,d      ;printf("***\n")
000C   01               RET
000D   2A0A00 msg1:     .ASCII   "*\n\x00"
0010   2A2A0A msg2:     .ASCII   "**\n\x00"
       00
0014   2A2A2A msg3:     .ASCII   "***\n\x00"
       0A00
                ;
                ;******* int main()
0019   240003 main:     CALL     printTri    ;printTri()
001C   240003           CALL     printTri    ;printTri()
001F   240003           CALL     printTri    ;printTri()
0022   00               STOP
0023                    .END
```

The default addressing mode for CALL is immediate.

As with the branch instructions, CALL usually executes in the immediate addressing mode, in which case the operand is the operand specifier. If you do not specify the addressing mode, the Pep/9 assembler will assume immediate addressing.

Here is the RTL specification of RET:

The RET instruction

$$PC \leftarrow Mem[SP]; SP \leftarrow SP + 2$$

The instruction moves the return address from the top of the stack into the program counter. Then it adds 2 to the stack pointer, which completes the pop operation.

In Figure 6.18,

```
0000 120019 BR main
```

puts 0019 into the program counter. The next statement to execute is, therefore, the one at 0019, which is the first CALL instruction. The discussion of the program in Figure 6.1 explains how the stack pointer is initialized to FB8F. FIGURE 6.19 shows the run-time stack before and after execution of the first CALL statement. As usual, the initial value of the stack pointer is FB8F.

The operations of CALL and RET crucially depend on the von Neumann execution cycle: fetch, decode, increment, execute, repeat. In particular, the increment step happens before the execute step. As a consequence, the statement that is executing is not the statement whose address is in the program counter. It is the statement that was fetched before the program counter was incremented and that is now contained in the instruction register. Why is that so important in the execution of CALL and RET?

Figure 6.19(a) shows the content of the program counter as 001C before execution of the first CALL instruction. It is not the address of the first CALL instruction, which is 0019. Why not? Because the program counter was incremented to 001C before execution of the CALL. Therefore, during execution of the first CALL instruction, the program counter contains the address of the instruction in main memory located just after the first CALL instruction.

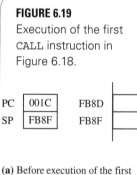

FIGURE 6.19

Execution of the first CALL instruction in Figure 6.18.

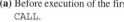

(a) Before execution of the first CALL.

(b) After execution of the first CALL.

What happens when the first CALL executes? First, SP ← SP – 2 subtracts two from SP, giving it the value FB8D. Then, Mem[SP] ← PC puts the value of the program counter, 001C, into main memory at address FB8D—that is, on top of the run-time stack. Finally, PC ← Oprnd puts 0003 into the program counter, because the operand specifier is 0003 and the addressing mode is immediate. The result is Figure 6.19(b).

The von Neumann cycle continues with the next fetch. But now the program counter contains 0003. So, the next instruction to be fetched is the one at address 0003, which is the first instruction of the printTri procedure. The output instructions of the procedure execute, producing the pattern of a triangle of asterisks.

Eventually the RET instruction at 000C executes. (**FIGURE 6.20(a)**) shows the content of the program counter as 000D just before execution of RET. This might seem strange, because 000D is not even the address of an instruction. It is the address of the string "*\x00". Why? Because RET is a unary instruction and the CPU incremented the program counter by one. The first step in the execution of RET is PC ← Mem[SP], which puts 001C into the program counter. Then SP ← SP + 2 changes the stack pointer back to FB8F.

The von Neumann cycle continues with the next fetch. But now the program counter contains the address of the second CALL instruction. The same sequence of events happens as with the first call, producing another triangle of asterisks in the output stream. The third call does the same thing, after which the STOP instruction executes. Note that the value of the program counter after the STOP instruction executes is 0023 and not 0022, which is the address of the STOP instruction.

Now you should see why increment comes before execute in the von Neumann execution cycle. To store the return address on the run-time stack, the CALL instruction needs to store the address of the instruction following the CALL. It can do that only if the program counter has been incremented before the CALL statement executes.

The reason increment must come before execute in the von Neumann execution cycle

Translating Call-by-Value Parameters with Global Variables

The allocation process when you call a void function in C is

> Push the actual parameters.

> Push the return address.

> Push storage for the local variables.

At Level HOL6, the instructions that perform these operations on the stack are hidden. The programmer simply writes the function call, and during execution the stack pushes occur automatically.

At the assembly level, however, the translated program must contain explicit instructions for the pushes. The program in (**FIGURE 6.21**), which is identical to the program in Figure 2.16, is a Level-HOL6 program that prints a bar chart and the program's corresponding Level-Asmb5 translation. It shows the Level-Asmb5 statements, not explicit at Level HOL6, that are required to push the parameters.

The caller in main() is responsible for pushing the actual parameters and executing CALL, which pushes the return address onto the stack. The callee in printBar() is responsible for pushing storage on the stack for its local variables. After the callee executes, it must pop the storage for the

FIGURE 6.20
The first execution of the RET instruction in Figure 6.18.

PC | 000D   FB8D | 001C
SP | FB8D   FB8F |

(a) Before the first execution of RET.

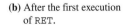

PC | 001C   FB8D | 001C
SP | FB8F   FB8F |

(b) After the first execution of RET.

FIGURE 6.21
Call-by-value parameters with global variables. The C program is from Figure 2.16.

High-Order Language

```c
#include <stdio.h>

int numPts;
int value;
int j;

void printBar(int n) {
   int k;
   for (k = 1; k <= n; k++) {
      printf("*");
   }
   printf("\n");
}

int main() {
   scanf("%d", &numPts);
   for (j = 1; j <= numPts; j++) {
      scanf("%d", &value);
      printBar(value);
   }
   return 0;
}
```

Assembly Language

```
0000   120034            BR      main
0003   0000    numPts:   .BLOCK  2           ;global variable #2d
0005   0000    value:    .BLOCK  2           ;global variable #2d
0007   0000    j:        .BLOCK  2           ;global variable #2d
                         ;
                         ;******* void printBar(int n)
               n:        .EQUATE 4           ;formal parameter #2d
               k:        .EQUATE 0           ;local variable #2d
0009   580002 printBar:SUBSP     2,i         ;push #k
000C   C00001            LDWA    1,i         ;for (k = 1
000F   E30000            STWA    k,s
0012   A30004 for1:      CPWA    n,s         ;k <= n
0015   1E002A            BRGT    endFor1
0018   D0002A            LDBA    '*',i       ;printf("*")
```

```
001B  F1FC16          STBA    charOut,d
001E  C30000          LDWA    k,s         ;k++)
0021  600001          ADDA    1,i
0024  E30000          STWA    k,s
0027  120012          BR      for1
002A  D0000A endFor1: LDBA    '\n',i      ;printf("\n")
002D  F1FC16          STBA    charOut,d
0030  500002          ADDSP   2,i         ;pop #k
0033  01              RET
              ;
              ;****** main()
0034  310003 main:    DECI    numPts,d    ;scanf("%d", &numPts)
0037  C00001          LDWA    1,i         ;for (j = 1
003A  E10007          STWA    j,d
003D  A10003 for2:    CPWA    numPts,d    ;j <= numPts
0040  1E0061          BRGT    endFor2
0043  310005          DECI    value,d     ;scanf("%d", &value)
0046  C10005          LDWA    value,d     ;move value
0049  E3FFFE          STWA    -2,s
004C  580002          SUBSP   2,i         ;push #n
004F  240009          CALL    printBar    ;printBar(value)
0052  500002          ADDSP   2,i         ;pop #n
0055  C10007          LDWA    j,d         ;j++)
0058  600001          ADDA    1,i
005B  E10007          STWA    j,d
005E  12003D          BR      for2
0061  00     endFor2: STOP
0062                  .END
```

local variables and then pop the return address by executing RET. Before the caller can continue, it must pop the actual parameters.

In summary, the caller and callee procedures do the following:

> Caller pushes actual parameters (executes SUBSP).
> Caller pushes return address (executes CALL).
> Callee pushes storage for local variables (executes SUBSP).
> Callee executes its body.
> Callee pops local variables (executes ADDSP).
> Callee pops return address (executes RET).
> Caller pops actual parameters (executes ADDSP).

FIGURE 6.22

Call-by-value parameters with global variables.

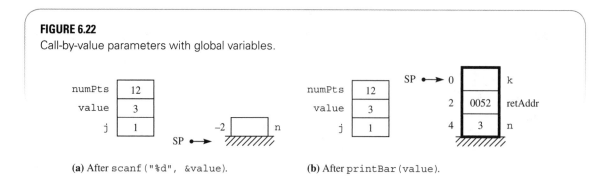

(a) After scanf ("%d", &value).   (b) After printBar (value).

Note the symmetry of the operations. The last three operations undo the first three operations in reverse order. That order is a consequence of the last-in, first-out property of the stack.

The global variables in the Level-HOL6 main program—numPts, value, and j—correspond to the identical Level-Asmb5 symbols, whose symbol values are 0003, 0005, and 0007, respectively. These are the addresses of the memory cells that will hold the run-time values of the global variables. FIGURE 6.22(a) shows the global variables on the left with their symbols in place of their addresses. The values for the global variables are the ones after

```
scanf ("%d", &value);
```

executes for the first time.

What do the formal parameter, n, and the local variable, k, correspond to at Level Asmb5? Not absolute addresses, but stack-relative addresses. Procedure printBar defines them with

```
n: .EQUATE 4 ;formal parameter #2d
k: .EQUATE 0 ;local variable #2d
```

Remember that .EQUATE does not generate object code. The assembler does not reserve storage for them at translation time. Instead, storage for n and k is allocated on the stack at run time. The decimal numbers 4 and 0 are the stack offsets appropriate for n and k during execution of the procedure, as Figure 6.22(b) shows. The procedure refers to them with stack-relative addressing.

The statements that correspond to the procedure call in the caller are

```
0046  C10005  LDWA   value,d
0049  E3FFFE  STWA   -2,s
004C  580002  SUBSP  2,i        ;push #n
004F  240009  CALL   printBar   ;printBar (value)
0052  500002  ADDSP  2,i        ;pop #n
```

Because the parameter is a global variable that is called by value, LDWA uses direct addressing. That puts the run-time value of variable value in the accumulator, which STWA then moves onto the stack. The offset is –2 because value is a two-byte integer quantity, as Figure 6.22(a) shows.

The statements that correspond to the procedure call in the callee are

```
0009  580002 printBar:SUBSP  2,i   ;push #k
...
0030  500002          ADDSP   2,i   ;pop #k
0033  01              RET
```

SUBSP subtracts 2 because the local variable, k, is a two-byte integer quantity. Figure 6.22(a) shows the run-time stack just after the first input of global variable value and just before the first procedure call. It corresponds directly to Figure 2.17(d). Figure 6.22(b) shows the stack just after the procedure call and corresponds directly to Figure 2.17(g). Note that the return address, which is labeled ra1 in Figure 2.17, is here shown to be 0052, which is the machine language address of the instruction following the CALL instruction.

The stack address of n is 4 because both k and the return address occupy two bytes on the stack. If there were more local variables, the stack address of n would be correspondingly greater. The compiler must compute the stack addresses from the number and size of the quantities on the stack.

In summary, to translate call-by-value parameters with global variables, the compiler generates code as follows:

> To get the actual parameter in the caller, it generates a load instruction with direct addressing.

> To get the formal parameter in the callee, it generates a load instruction with stack-relative addressing.

The translation rules for call-by-value parameters with global variables

Translating Call-by-Value Parameters with Local Variables

The program in **FIGURE 6.23** is identical to the one in Figure 6.21 except that the variables in main() are local instead of global. Although the program behaves like the one in Figure 6.21, the memory model and the translation to Level Asmb5 are different.

You can see that the versions of void function printBar() at Level HOL6 are identical in Figure 6.21 and Figure 6.23. Hence, it should not be surprising that the compiler generates identical object code for the two versions of printBar() at Level Asmb5. The only difference between the

FIGURE 6.23
Call-by-value parameters with local variables.

High-Order Language
```
#include <stdio.h>

void printBar(int n) {
   int k;
   for (k = 1; k <= n; k++) {
      printf("*");
   }
   printf("\n");
}

int main() {
   int numPts;
   int value;
   int j;
   scanf("%d", &numPts);
   for (j = 1; j <= numPts; j++) {
      scanf("%d", &value);
      printBar(value);
   }
   return 0;
}
```

Assembly Language
```
0000  12002E           BR       main
                 ;
                 ;******* void printBar(int n)
                 n:       .EQUATE 4           ;formal parameter #2d
                 k:       .EQUATE 0           ;local variable #2d
0003  580002 printBar:SUBSP   2,i            ;push #k
0006  C00001           LDWA    1,i            ;for (k = 1
0009  E30000           STWA    k,s
000C  A30004 for1:    CPWA    n,s            ;k <= n
000F  1E0024           BRGT    endFor1
0012  D0002A           LDBA    '*',i          ;printf("*")
0015  F1FC16           STBA    charOut,d
0018  C30000           LDWA    k,s            ;k++)
```

```
001B  600001          ADDA    1,i
001E  E30000          STWA    k,s
0021  12000C          BR      for1
0024  D0000A endFor1: LDBA    '\n',i      ;printf("\n")
0027  F1FC16          STBA    charOut,d
002A  500002          ADDSP   2,i         ;pop #k
002D  01              RET
                  ;
                  ;******* main()
              numPts:  .EQUATE 4           ;local variable #2d
              value:   .EQUATE 2           ;local variable #2d
              j:       .EQUATE 0           ;local variable #2d
002E  580006 main:    SUBSP   6,i         ;push #numPts #value #j
0031  330004          DECI    numPts,s    ;scanf("%d", &numPts)
0034  C00001          LDWA    1,i         ;for (j = 1
0037  E30000          STWA    j,s
003A  A30004 for2:    CPWA    numPts,s    ;j <= numPts
003D  1E005E          BRGT    endFor2
0040  330002          DECI    value,s     ;scanf("%d", &value)
0043  C30002          LDWA    value,s     ;move value
0046  E3FFFE          STWA    -2,s
0049  580002          SUBSP   2,i         ;push #n
004C  240003          CALL    printBar    ;printBar(value)
004F  500002          ADDSP   2,i         ;pop #n
0052  C30000          LDWA    j,s         ;j++)
0055  600001          ADDA    1,i
0058  E30000          STWA    j,s
005B  12003A          BR      for2
005E  500006 endFor2: ADDSP   6,i         ;pop #j #value #numPts
0061  00              STOP
0062                  .END
```

two programs is in `main()`. (FIGURE 6.24(a)) shows the allocation of `numPts`, `value`, and `j` on the run-time stack in the main program. Figure 6.24(b) shows the stack after `printTri` is called for the first time. Because `value` is a local variable, the compiler generates `LDWA value,s` with stack-relative addressing to get the actual value of `value`, which it then puts in the stack cell for formal parameter `n`.

In summary, to translate call-by-value parameters with local variables, the compiler generates code as follows:

> ❯ To get the actual parameter in the caller, it generates a load instruction with stack-relative addressing.

> ❯ To get the formal parameter in the callee, it generates a load instruction with stack-relative addressing.

Translating Non-void Function Calls

The allocation process when you call a function is

> ❯ Push storage for the return value.

> ❯ Push the actual parameters.

> ❯ Push the return address.

> ❯ Push storage for the local variables.

Allocation for a non-void function call differs from that for a procedure (void function) call by the extra value that you must allocate for the returned function value.

FIGURE 6.25 shows a program that computes a binomial coefficient recursively and is identical to the one in Figure 2.28. It is based on Pascal's triangle of coefficients (shown in Figure 2.27). The recursive definition of the binomial coefficient is

$$b(n, k) = \begin{cases} 1 & \text{if } k = 0, \\ 1 & \text{if } n = k, \\ b(n-1, k) + b(n-1, k-1) & \text{if } 0 < k < n. \end{cases}$$

The translation rules for call-by-value parameters with local variables

FIGURE 6.24
The first execution of the function call in Figure 6.23.

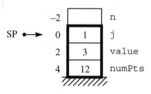

(a) After scanf ("%d", &value).

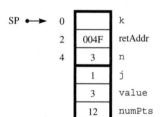

(b) After printBar (value).

FIGURE 6.25
A recursive nonvoid function at Level HOL6 and Level Asmb5. The C program is from Figure 2.28.

High-Order Language
```
#include <stdio.h>

int binCoeff(int n, int k) {
    int .y1, y2;
    if ((k == 0) || (n == k)) {
        return 1;
    }
```

```
   else {
      y1 = binCoeff(n - 1, k); // ra2
      y2 = binCoeff(n - 1, k - 1); // ra3
      return y1 + y2;
   }
}
int main() {
   printf("binCoeff(3, 1) = %d\n", binCoeff(3, 1)); // ra1
   return 0;
}
```

Assembly Language

```
0000  12006B            BR        main
               ;
               ;******* int binomCoeff(int n, int k)
               retVal:  .EQUATE 10          ;return value #2d
               n:       .EQUATE 8           ;formal parameter #2d
               k:       .EQUATE 6           ;formal parameter #2d
               y1:      .EQUATE 2           ;local variable #2d
               y2:      .EQUATE 0           ;local variable #2d
0003  580004 binCoeff:SUBSP    4,i          ;push #y1 #y2
0006  C30006 if:       LDWA     k,s          ;if ((k == 0)
0009  180015           BREQ     then
000C  C30008           LDWA     n,s          ;|| (n == k))
000F  A30006           CPWA     k,s
0012  1A001F           BRNE     else
0015  C00001 then:     LDWA     1,i          ;return 1
0018  E3000A           STWA     retVal,s
001B  500004           ADDSP    4,i          ;pop #y2 #y1
001E  01               RET
001F  C30008 else:     LDWA     n,s          ;move n - 1
0022  700001           SUBA     1,i
0025  E3FFFC           STWA     -4,s
0028  C30006           LDWA     k,s          ;move k
002B  E3FFFA           STWA     -6,s
002E  580006           SUBSP    6,i          ;push #retVal #n #k
0031  240003           CALL     binCoeff     ;binCoeff(n - 1, k)
0034  500006 ra2:      ADDSP    6,i          ;pop #k #n #retVal
0037  C3FFFE           LDWA     -2,s         ;y1 = binomCoeff(n - 1, k)
003A  E30002           STWA     y1,s
```

(continues)

FIGURE 6.25

A recursive nonvoid function at Level HOL6 and Level Asmb5. The C program is from Figure 2.28. (*continued*)

```
003D  C30008          LDWA    n,s            ;move n - 1
0040  700001          SUBA    1,i
0043  E3FFFC          STWA    -4,s
0046  C30006          LDWA    k,s            ;move k - 1
0049  700001          SUBA    1,i
004C  E3FFFA          STWA    -6,s
004F  580006          SUBSP   6,i            ;push #retVal #n #k
0052  240003          CALL    binCoeff       ;binomCoeff(n - 1, k - 1)
0055  500006 ra3:     ADDSP   6,i            ;pop #k #n #retVal
0058  C3FFFE          LDWA    -2,s           ;y2 = binomCoeff(n - 1, k - 1)
005B  E30000          STWA    y2,s
005E  C30002          LDWA    y1,s           ;return y1 + y2
0061  630000          ADDA    y2,s
0064  E3000A          STWA    retVal,s
0067  500004 endIf:   ADDSP   4,i            ;pop #y2 #y1
006A  01              RET
              ;
              ;******* main()
006B  49008D main:    STRO    msg,d          ;printf("binCoeff(3, 1) = %d\n",
006E  C00003          LDWA    3,i            ;move 3
0071  E3FFFC          STWA    -4,s
0074  C00001          LDWA    1,i            ;move 1
0077  E3FFFA          STWA    -6,s
007A  580006          SUBSP   6,i            ;push #retVal #n #k
007D  240003          CALL    binCoeff       ;binCoeff(3, 1)
0080  500006 ra1:     ADDSP   6,i            ;pop #k #n #retVal
0083  3BFFFE          DECO    -2,s
0086  D0000A          LDBA    '\n',i
0089  F1FC16          STBA    charOut,d
008C  00              STOP
008D  62696E msg:     .ASCII  "binCoeff(3, 1) = \x00"
      ...
009F                  .END
```

The function tests for the base cases with an `if` statement, using the OR Boolean operator. If neither base case is satisfied, it calls itself recursively twice—once to compute $b(n - 1, k)$ and once to compute $b(n - 1, k - 1)$. Figure 2.29 shows the run-time stack produced by a call from the main program with actual parameters $(3, 1)$. The function is called twice more with parameters $(2, 1)$ and $(1, 1)$, followed by a return. Then a call with parameters $(1, 0)$ is executed, followed by a second return, and so on. **FIGURE 6.26** shows the run-time stack at the assembly level immediately after the second return. It corresponds directly to the Level-HOL6 diagram of Figure 2.29(g). The return address labeled ra2 in Figure 2.29(g) is 0034 in Figure 6.26, the address of the instruction after the first CALL in the function. Similarly, the address labeled ra1 in Figure 2.29(g) is 0080 in Figure 6.26.

At the start of the main program when the stack pointer has its initial value, the first actual parameter has a stack offset of –4, and the second has a stack offset of –6. In a procedure call (a void function), these offsets would be –2 and –4, respectively. Their magnitudes are greater by 2 because of the two-byte value returned on the stack by the function. The SUBSP instruction at 007A allocates six bytes, two for the return value and two each for the actual parameters.

When the function returns control to ADDSP at 0080, the value it returns will be on the stack below the two actual parameters. ADDSP pops the parameters and return value by adding 6 to the stack pointer, after which it points to the cell directly below the returned value. So DECO outputs the value with stack-relative addressing and an offset of –2.

The function calls itself by allocating actual parameters according to the standard technique. For the first recursive call, it computes $n - 1$ and k and pushes those values onto the stack along with storage for the returned value. After the return, the sequence

```
0034   500006 ra2:   ADDSP   6,i    ;pop #k #n #retVal
0037   C3FFFE          LDWA    -2,s   ;y1 = binomCoeff(n - 1, k)
003A   E30002          STWA    y1,s
```

pops the two actual parameters and return value and assigns the return value to `y1`. For the second call, it pushes $n - 1$ and $k - 1$ and assigns the return value to `y2` similarly.

Translating Call-by-Reference Parameters with Global Variables

C provides call-by-reference parameters so that the called procedure can change the value of the actual parameter in the calling procedure. Figure 2.20 shows a program at Level HOL6 that uses call by reference to put two global

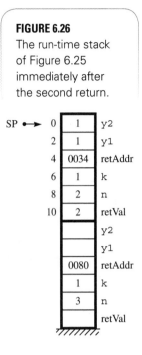

FIGURE 6.26
The run-time stack of Figure 6.25 immediately after the second return.

variables, a and b, in order. (FIGURE 6.27) shows the same program together with the object program that a compiler would produce.

Parameters called by reference differ from parameters called by value in C because the actual parameter provides a reference to a variable in the caller instead of the value of the variable. At the assembly level, the code that pushes the actual parameter onto the stack pushes the address of the actual parameter, which corresponds to the & address operator in the parameter list. When the actual parameter is a global variable, its address is available as the value of its symbol. So, the code to get the address of a global variable

FIGURE 6.27
Call-by-reference parameters with global variables. The C program is from Figure 2.20.

High-Order Language

```c
#include <stdio.h>

int a, b;

void swap(int *r, int *s) {
    int temp;
    temp = *r;
    *r = *s;
    *s = temp;
}

void order(int *x, int *y) {
    if (*x > *y) {
        swap(x, y);
    } // ra2
}

int main() {
    printf("Enter an integer: ");
    scanf("%d", &a);
    printf("Enter an integer: ");
    scanf("%d", &b);
    order(&a, &b);
    printf("Ordered they are: %d, %d\n", a, b); // ra1
    return 0;
}
```

Assembly Language

```
0000  12003F        BR      main
0003  0000   a:      .BLOCK  2           ;global variable #2d
0005  0000   b:      .BLOCK  2           ;global variable #2d
             ;
             ;****** void swap(int *r, int *s)
             r:      .EQUATE 6           ;formal parameter #2h
             s:      .EQUATE 4           ;formal parameter #2h
             temp:   .EQUATE 0           ;local variable #2d
0007  580002 swap:   SUBSP   2,i         ;push #temp
000A  C40006         LDWA    r,sf        ;temp = *r
000D  E30000         STWA    temp,s
0010  C40004         LDWA    s,sf        ;*r = *s
0013  E40006         STWA    r,sf
0016  C30000         LDWA    temp,s      ;*s = temp
0019  E40004         STWA    s,sf
001C  500002         ADDSP   2,i         ;pop #temp
001F  01            RET
             ;
             ;****** void order(int *x, int *y)
             x:      .EQUATE 4           ;formal parameter #2h
             y:      .EQUATE 2           ;formal parameter #2h
0020  C40004 order:  LDWA    x,sf        ;if (*x > *y)
0023  A40002         CPWA    y,sf
0026  14003E         BRLE    endIf
0029  C30004         LDWA    x,s         ;move x
002C  E3FFFE         STWA    -2,s
002F  C30002         LDWA    y,s         ;move y
0032  E3FFFC         STWA    -4,s
0035  580004         SUBSP   4,i         ;push #r #s
0038  240007         CALL    swap        ;swap(x, y)
003B  500004         ADDSP   4,i         ;pop #s #r
003E  01     endIf:  RET
             ;
             ;****** main()
003F  490073 main:   STRO    msg1,d      ;printf("Enter an integer: ")
0042  310003         DECI    a,d         ;scanf("%d", &a)
0045  490073         STRO    msg1,d      ;printf("Enter an integer: ")
0048  310005         DECI    b,d         ;scanf("%d", &b)
004B  C00003         LDWA    a,i         ;move &a
```

(continues)

FIGURE 6.27

Call-by-reference parameters with global variables. The C program is from Figure 2.20. (*continued*)

```
004E   E3FFFE          STWA     -2,s
0051   C00005          LDWA     b,i            ;move &b
0054   E3FFFC          STWA     -4,s
0057   580004          SUBSP    4,i            ;push #x #y
005A   240020          CALL     order          ;order(&a, &b)
005D   500004 ra1:     ADDSP    4,i            ;pop #y #x
0060   490086          STRO     msg2,d         ;printf("Ordered they are: %d, %d\n"
0063   390003          DECO     a,d            ;, a
0066   490099          STRO     msg3,d
0069   390005          DECO     b,d            ;, b)
006C   D0000A          LDBA     '\n',i
006F   F1FC16          STBA     charOut,d
0072   00              STOP
0073   456E74 msg1:    .ASCII   "Enter an integer: \x00"
       . . .
0086   4F7264 msg2:    .ASCII   "Ordered they are: \x00"
       . . .
0099   2C2000 msg3:    .ASCII   ", \x00"
009C                   .END
```

is a load instruction with immediate addressing. In Figure 6.27, the code to get the address of a is

```
004B C00003 LDWA a,i ;move &a
```

The value of the symbol a is 0003, the address of where the a is stored. The machine code for this instruction is C00003. C0 is the instruction specifier for the load accumulator instruction with addressing-aaa field of 000 to indicate immediate addressing. With immediate addressing, the operand specifier is the operand. Consequently, this instruction loads 0003 into the accumulator. The store instruction

```
004E E3FFFE STWA -2,s
```

then puts the address of a on the run-time stack.

Similarly, the code to push the address of b is

```
0051 C00005 LDWA b,i ;move &b
```

The machine code for this instruction is C00005, where 0005 is the address of b. This instruction loads 0005 into the accumulator with immediate addressing, after which the store instruction puts it on the run-time stack.

In procedure order(), the compiler translates the if statement

```
if (*x > *y)
```

at Level HOL6 into the three statements

```
0020   C40004 order:   LDWA   x,sf    ;if (*x > *y)
0023   A40002          CPWA   y,sf
0026   14003E          BRLE   endIf
```

at Level Asmb5. The addressing mode letters for the load and compare instructions are sf, which stands for *stack-relative deferred addressing*.

Remember that the relation between the operand and the operand specifier with stack-relative addressing is

Oprnd = Mem[SP + OprndSpec]   *Stack-relative addressing*

The relation between the operand and the operand specifier with stack-relative deferred addressing is

Oprnd = Mem[Mem[SP + OprndSpec]]   *Stack-relative deferred*
                                               addressing

In other words, Mem[SP + OprndSpec] is the address of the operand, rather than the operand itself.

In the preceding LDWA instruction, x is the operand specifier. It is the formal parameter stored on the run-time stack. It is the address of a, which was put on the stack by the caller. In procedure order(), the two expressions x and *x at Level HOL6 correspond to Level Asmb5 as follows:

> › Pointer x at Level HOL6 is at Mem[SP + x] at Level Asmb5. You access it with stack-relative addressing, s.

> › Integer *x at Level HOL6 is at Mem[Mem[SP + x]] at Level Asmb5. You access it with stack-relative deferred addressing, sf.

Procedure order() calls swap(x, y). Because the actual parameter is x and not *x, procedure order() simply transfers the address for swap() to use. The statement

```
0029 C30004 LDWA x,s ;move x
```

uses stack-relative addressing to get the address into the accumulator. The next instruction puts it on the run-time stack.

In procedure order(), the compiler must translate

```
temp = *r;
```

It must load the value of *r into the accumulator and then store it in temp. Because it is loading *r instead of r, it uses stack-relative deferred addressing instead of stack-relative addressing. The compiler generates the following object code to translate the assignment statement:

```
000A  C40006   LDWA   r,sf    ;temp = *r
000D  E30000   STWA   temp,s
```

The next assignment statement in procedure swap()

```
*r = *s;
```

has the * dereference operator on both variables. Consequently, the compiler generates LDWA and STWA both with stack-relative deferred addressing.

```
0010  C40004   LDWA   s,sf   ;*r = *s
0013  E40006   STWA   r,sf
```

FIGURE 6.28 shows the run-time stack at Level HOL6 and Level Asmb5. The address of a is 0003, which main() pushes onto the run-time stack for formal parameter x when it calls order(). Procedure order() pushes the same address onto the run-time stack when it calls procedure swap().

In summary, to translate call-by-reference parameters with global variables, the compiler generates code as follows:

The translation rules for call-by-reference parameters with global variables

> To get the actual parameter in the caller, it generates a load instruction with immediate addressing.

> To get the formal parameter x in the callee, it generates a load instruction with stack-relative addressing.

> To get the dereferenced formal parameter *x in the callee, it generates a load instruction with stack-relative deferred addressing.

FIGURE 6.28

The run-time stack for Figure 6.27 at Level HOL6 and Level Asmb5.

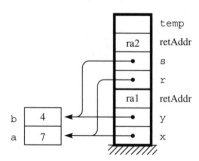

(a) The run-time stack at Level HOL6.

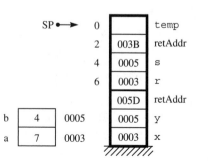

(b) The run-time stack at Level Asmb5.

Translating Call-by-Reference Parameters with Local Variables

FIGURE 6.29 shows a program that computes the perimeter of a rectangle given its width and height. The main program prompts the user for the width and the height, which it inputs into two local variables named `width` and `height`. A third local variable is named `perim`. The main program calls

FIGURE 6.29
Call-by-reference parameters with local variables.

High-Order Language
```
#include <stdio.h>

void rect(int *p, int w, int h) {
   *p = (w + h) * 2;
}

int main() {
   int perim, width, height;
   printf("Enter width: ");
   scanf("%d", &width);
   printf("Enter height: ");
   scanf("%d", &height);
   rect(&perim, width, height);
   // ra1
   printf("Perimeter = %d\n", perim);
   return 0;
}
```

Assembly Language
```
0000   12000E            BR      main
                     ;
                     ;******* void rect(int *p, int w, int h)
                     p:        .EQUATE 6          ;formal parameter #2h
                     w:        .EQUATE 4          ;formal parameter #2d
                     h:        .EQUATE 2          ;formal parameter #2d
0003   C30004 rect:   LDWA    w,s                ;*p = (w + h) * 2
0006   630002         ADDA    h,s
0009   0A             ASLA
000A   E40006         STWA    p,sf
000D   01             RET
```

(continues)

FIGURE 6.29

Call-by-reference parameters with local variables. (*continued*)

```
                ;
                ;******* main()
                perim:   .EQUATE 4        ;local variable #2d
                width:   .EQUATE 2        ;local variable #2d
                height:  .EQUATE 0        ;local variable #2d
000E  580006 main:      SUBSP   6,i       ;push #perim #width #height
0011  490049            STRO    msg1,d    ;printf("Enter width: ")
0014  330002            DECI    width,s   ;scanf("%d", &width)
0017  490057            STRO    msg2,d    ;printf("Enter height: ")
001A  330000            DECI    height,s  ;scanf("%d", &height)
001D  03                MOVSPA            ;move &perim
001E  600004            ADDA    perim,i
0021  E3FFFE            STWA    -2,s
0024  C30002            LDWA    width,s   ;move width
0027  E3FFFC            STWA    -4,s
002A  C30000            LDWA    height,s  ;move height
002D  E3FFFA            STWA    -6,s
0030  580006            SUBSP   6,i       ;push #p #w #h
0033  240003            CALL    rect      ;rect(&perim, width, height)
0036  500006 ra1:       ADDSP   6,i       ;pop #h #w #p
0039  490066            STRO    msg3,d    ;printf("Perimeter = %d\n", perim);
003C  3B0004            DECO    perim,s
003F  D0000A            LDBA    '\n',i
0042  F1FC16            STBA    charOut,d
0045  500006            ADDSP   6,i       ;pop #height #width #perim
0048  00                STOP
0049  456E74 msg1:      .ASCII  "Enter width: \x00"
      ...
0057  456E74 msg2:      .ASCII  "Enter height: \x00"
      ...
0066  506572 msg3:      .ASCII  "Perimeter = \x00"
      ...
0073                    .END
```

Input/Output

```
Enter width: 8
Enter height: 5
Perimeter = 26
```

a procedure (a void function) named `rect()`, passing `width` and `height` by value and `perim` by reference. The figure shows the input and output when the user enters 8 for the width and 5 for the height.

FIGURE 6.30 shows the run-time stack at Level HOL6 for the program. Compare it to Figure 6.28(a) for a program with global variables that are called by reference. In that program, formal parameters x, y, r, and s refer to global variables a and b. At Level Asmb5, a and b are allocated at translation time with the `.EQUATE` dot command. Their symbols are their addresses. However, Figure 6.30 shows `perim` to be allocated on the run-time stack. The statement

```
000E 580006 main: SUBSP 6,i
```

allocates storage for `perim`, whose symbol is defined by

```
perim: .EQUATE 4 ;local variable #2d
```

Its symbol is not its absolute address. Its symbol is its address relative to the top of the run-time stack, as FIGURE 6.31(a) shows. Its absolute address is FB8D. Why? Because that is the location of the bottom of the application run-time stack, as the memory map in Figure 4.41 shows.

So, the compiler cannot generate code to push parameter `perim` with

```
LDWA perim,i
STWA -2,s
```

as it does for global variables. If it generated those instructions, procedure `rect()` would modify the content of Mem[0004], and 0004 is not where `perim` is located.

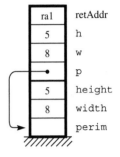

FIGURE 6.30
The run-time stack for Figure 6.29 at Level HOL6.

FIGURE 6.31
The run-time stack for Figure 6.29 at Level Asmb5.

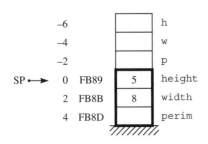

(a) Before the procedure call.

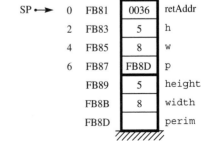

(b) After the procedure call.

The absolute address of perim is FB8D. Figure 6.31(a) shows that you could calculate it by adding the value of perim, 4, to the value of the stack pointer. Fortunately, there is a unary instruction MOVSPA that moves the content of the stack pointer to the accumulator. The RTL specification of MOVSPA is

$$A \leftarrow SP$$

To push the address of perim, the compiler generates the following instructions at 001D in Figure 6.29:

```
001D  03      MOVSPA             ;move &perim
001E  600004  ADDA     perim,i
0021  E3FFFE  STWA     -2,s
```

The first instruction moves the content of the stack pointer to the accumulator. The accumulator then contains FB89. The second instruction adds the value of perim, which is 4, to the accumulator, making it FB8D. The third instruction puts the address of perim in the cell for p, which procedure rect() uses to store the perimeter. Figure 6.31(b) shows the result.

The compiler translates *p in rect() as it would any dereferenced call-by-reference parameter. Namely, at 000A it stores the value using stack-relative deferred addressing:

```
000A E40006 STWA p,sf
```

With stack-relative deferred addressing, the address of the operand is on the stack. The operand is

Stack-relative deferred addressing

$$Oprnd = Mem[Mem[SP + OprndSpec]]$$

This instruction adds the stack pointer FB81 to the operand specifier 6, yielding FB87. Because Mem[FB87] is FB8D, it stores the accumulator at Mem[FB8D] in the stack.

In summary, to translate call-by-reference parameters with local variables, the compiler generates code as follows:

The translation rules for call-by-reference parameters with local variables

> To get the actual parameter in the caller, the compiler generates the unary MOVSPA instruction followed by the ADDA instruction with immediate addressing.

> To get the formal parameter x in the callee, the compiler generates a load instruction with stack-relative addressing.

> To get the dereferenced formal parameter *x in the callee, the compiler generates a load instruction with stack-relative deferred addressing.

Translating Boolean Types

Several schemes exist for storing Boolean values at the assembly level. The one most appropriate for C is to treat the values true and false as integer constants. The values are

```
const int true = 1;
const int false = 0;
```

FIGURE 6.32 is a program that declares a Boolean function named inRange(). The library stdbool.h defines the bool type as if true and false were declared as above.

FIGURE 6.32
Translation of a Boolean type.

High-Order Language

```c
#include <stdio.h>
#include <stdbool.h>

const int LOWER = 21;
const int UPPER = 65;

bool inRange(int a) {
   if ((LOWER <= a) && (a <= UPPER)) {
      return true;
   }
   else {
      return false;
   }
}

int main() {
   int age;
   scanf("%d", &age);
   if (inRange(age)) {
      printf("Qualified\n");
   }
   else {
      printf("Unqualified\n");
   }
   return 0;
}
```

(continues)

FIGURE 6.32

Translation of a Boolean type. (*continued*)

Assembly Language

```
0000   120023          BR      main
                true:  .EQUATE 1
                false: .EQUATE 0
                ;
                LOWER: .EQUATE 21              ;const int
                UPPER: .EQUATE 65              ;const int
                ;
                ;******* bool inRange(int a)
                retVal: .EQUATE 4             ;returned value #2d
                a:      .EQUATE 2             ;formal parameter #2d
0003   C00015 inRange: LDWA   LOWER,i         ;if ((LOWER <= a)
0006   A30002 if:      CPWA   a,s
0009   1E001C          BRGT   else
000C   C30002          LDWA   a,s             ;&& (a <= UPPER))
000F   A00041          CPWA   UPPER,i
0012   1E001C          BRGT   else
0015   C00001 then:    LDWA   true,i          ;return true
0018   E30004          STWA   retVal,s
001B   01              RET
001C   C00000 else:    LDWA   false,i         ;return false
001F   E30004          STWA   retVal,s
0022   01              RET
                ;
                ;******* main()
                age:    .EQUATE 0             ;local variable #2d
0023   580002 main:    SUBSP  2,i             ;push #age
0026   330000          DECI   age,s           ;scanf("%d", &age)
0029   C30000          LDWA   age,s           ;move age
002C   E3FFFC          STWA   -4,s
002F   580004          SUBSP  4,i             ;push #retVal #a
0032   240003          CALL   inRange         ;inRange(age)
0035   500004          ADDSP  4,i             ;pop #a #retVal
0038   C3FFFE          LDWA   -2,s            ;if (inRange(age))
003B   180044          BREQ   else2
003E   49004B then2:   STRO   msg1,d          ;printf("Qualified\n")
0041   120047          BR     endif2
```

```
0044   490056 else2:   STRO    msg2,d      ;printf("Unqualified\n");
0047   500002 endif2: .ADDSP   2,i         ;pop #age
004A   00              STOP
004B   517561 msg1:    .ASCII  "Qualified\n\x00"
       . . .
0056   556E71 msg2:    .ASCII  "Unqualified\n\x00"
       . . .
0063                   .END
```

Representing false and true at the bit level as 0000 and 0001 (hex) has advantages and disadvantages. Consider the logical operations on Boolean quantities and the corresponding assembly instructions ANDr, ORr, and NOTr. If p and q are global Boolean variables, then

```
p && q
```

translates to

```
LDWA p,d
ANDA q,d
```

If you AND 0000 and 0001 with this object code, you get 0000 as desired. The OR operation, ||, also works as desired. The NOT operation is a problem, however, because if you apply NOT to 0000, you get FFFF instead of 0001. Also, applying NOT to 0001 gives FFFE instead of 0000. Consequently, the compiler does not generate the NOT instruction when it translates the C assignment statement

```
p = !q
```

Instead, it uses the exclusive-or operation XOR, which has the mathematical symbol $\oplus$. It has the useful property that if you take the XOR of any bit value b with 0, you get b. And if you take the XOR of any bit value b with 1, you get the logical negation of b. Mathematically,

$$b \oplus 0 = b$$
$$b \oplus 1 = \neg\, b$$

Unfortunately, the Pep/9 computer does not have an XORr instruction in its instruction set. If it did have such an instruction, the compiler would generate the following code for the above assignment:

```
LDWA q,d
XORA 0x0001,i
STWA p,d
```

If q is false, it has the representation 0000 (hex), and 0000 XOR 0001 equals 0001, as desired. Also, if q is true, it has the representation 0001 (hex), and 0001 XOR 0001 equals 0000.

The type bool was not included in the C-language standard library until 1999. Older compilers use the convention that the Boolean operators operate on integers. They interpret the integer value 0 as false and any nonzero integer value as true. To preserve backward compatibility, current C compilers maintain this convention.

6.4 Indexed Addressing and Arrays

A variable at Level HOL6 is a memory cell at Level ISA3. A variable at Level HOL6 is referred to by its name; at Level ISA3, by its address. A variable at Level Asmb5 can be referred to by its symbolic name, but the value of that symbol is the address of the cell in memory.

What about an array of values? An array contains many elements, and so consists of many memory cells. The memory cells of the elements are contiguous; that is, they are adjacent to one another. An array at Level HOL6 has a name. At Level Asmb5, the corresponding symbol is the address of the first cell of the array. This section shows how the compiler translates source programs that allocate and access elements of one-dimensional arrays. It does so with several forms of indexed addressing.

At Level Asmb5, the value of the symbol of an array is the address of the first cell of the array.

FIGURE 6.33 summarizes all the Pep/9 addressing modes. Previous programs illustrate immediate, direct, stack-relative, and stack-relative

FIGURE 6.33
The Pep/9 addressing modes.

Addressing Mode	aaa	Letters	Operand
Immediate	000	i	OprndSpec
Direct	001	d	Mem[OprndSpec]
Indirect	010	n	Mem[Mem[OprndSpec]]
Stack-relative	011	s	Mem[SP + OprndSpec]
Stack-relative deferred	100	sf	Mem[Mem[SP + OprndSpec]]
Indexed	101	x	Mem[OprndSpec + X]
Stack-indexed	110	sx	Mem[SP + OprndSpec + X]
Stack-deferred indexed	111	sfx	Mem[Mem[SP + OprndSpec] + X]

deferred addressing. Programs with arrays use indexed, stack-indexed, or stack-deferred indexed addressing. The column labeled *aaa* shows the address-aaa field at Level ISA3. The column labeled *Letters* shows the assembly language designation for the addressing mode at Level Asmb5. The column labeled *Operand* shows how the CPU determines the operand from the operand specifier (OprndSpec).

Translating Global Arrays

The C program in FIGURE 6.34 is the same as the one in Figure 2.15, except that the variables are global instead of local. It shows a program at Level HOL6 that declares a global array of four integers named vector and a global integer named j. The main program inputs four integers into the array with a for loop and outputs them in reverse order together with their indexes.

FIGURE 6.34
A global array.

High-Order Language

```
#include <stdio.h>

int vector[4];
int j;

int main() {
   for (j = 0; j < 4; j++) {
      scanf("%d", &vector[j]);
   }
   for (j = 3; j >= 0; j--) {
      printf("%d %d\n", j, vector[j]);
   }
   return 0;
}
```

Assembly Language

```
0000  12000D          BR      main
0003  000000 vector:  .BLOCK  8           ;global variable #2d4a
      000000
      0000
000B  0000   j:       .BLOCK  2           ;global variable #2d
               ;
               ;******* main()
```

(continues)

FIGURE 6.34

A global array. (*continued*)

```
000D  C80000 main:    LDWX    0,i          ;for (j = 0
0010  E9000B          STWX    j,d
0013  A80004 for1:    CPWX    4,i          ;j < 4
0016  1C0029          BRGE    endFor1
0019  0B              ASLX                 ;two bytes per integer
001A  350003          DECI    vector,x     ;scanf("%d", &vector[j])
001D  C9000B          LDWX    j,d          ;j++)
0020  680001          ADDX    1,i
0023  E9000B          STWX    j,d
0026  120013          BR      for1
0029  C80003 endFor1: LDWX    3,i          ;for (j = 3
002C  E9000B          STWX    j,d
002F  A80000 for2:    CPWX    0,i          ;j >= 0
0032  160054          BRLT    endFor2
0035  39000B          DECO    j,d          ;printf("%d %d\n", j, vector[j])
0038  D00020          LDBA    ' ',i
003B  F1FC16          STBA    charOut,d
003E  0B              ASLX                 ;two bytes per integer
003F  3D0003          DECO    vector,x
0042  D0000A          LDBA    '\n',i
0045  F1FC16          STBA    charOut,d
0048  C9000B          LDWX    j,d          ;j--)
004B  780001          SUBX    1,i
004E  E9000B          STWX    j,d
0051  12002F          BR      for2
0054  00     endFor2: STOP
0055                  .END
```

Input

60 70 80 90

Output

3 90
2 80
1 70
0 60

FIGURE 6.35 shows the memory allocation for integer `j` and array `vector`. As with all global integers, the compiler translates

```
int j;
```

at Level HOL6 as the following statement at Level Asmb5:

```
000B 0000 j:      .BLOCK 2 ;global variable #2d
```

The compiler translates

```
int vector[4];
```

at Level HOL6 as the following statement at Level Asmb5:

```
0003  000000  vector:   .BLOCK  8  ;global variable #2d4a
      000000
      0000
```

It allocates eight bytes because the array contains four integers, each of which is two bytes. Figure 6.35 shows that 0003 is the address of the first element of the array. The second element is at 0005, and each element is at an address two bytes greater than the previous element.

Format trace tags for arrays specify how many cells are in the array as well as the number of bytes. You should read the format trace tag `#2d4a` as "two byte decimal, four cell array." With this specification, the Pep/9 debugger will produce a figure similar to that of Figure 6.35 with each array cell individually labeled.

The compiler translates the first `for` statement

```
for (j = 0; j < 4; j++)
```

as usual. It accesses `j` with direct addressing because `j` is a global variable. But how does it access `vector[j]`? It cannot simply use direct addressing, because the value of symbol `vector` is the address of the first element of the array. If the value of `j` is 2, it should access the third element of the array, not the first.

The answer is that it uses indexed addressing. With indexed addressing, the CPU computes the operand as

$$\text{Oprnd} = \text{Mem}[\text{OprndSpec} + X]$$

It adds the operand specifier and the index register and uses the sum as the address in main memory from which it fetches the operand.

In Figure 6.34, the compiler translates

```
scanf("%d", &vector[j]);
```

Format trace tags for arrays

Indexed addressing

FIGURE 6.35
Memory allocation for the global array of Figure 6.34.

0003		vector[0]
0005		vector[1]
0007		vector[2]
0009		vector[3]
000B		j

at Level HOL6 as

```
0019  0B      ASLX             ;two bytes per integer
001A  350003  DECI  vector,x   ;scanf("%d", &vector[j])
```

at Level Asmb5. This is an optimized translation. The compiler analyzed the previous code generated and determined that the index register already contained the current value of j. A nonoptimizing compiler would generate the following code:

```
LDWX j,d
ASLX
DECI vector,x
```

Suppose the value of j is 2. LDX puts the value of j in the index register. (Or, an optimizing compiler determines that the current value of j is already in the index register.) ASLX multiplies the 2 times 2, leaving 4 in the index register. DECI uses indexed addressing. So, the operand is computed as

Mem[OprndSpec + X]
Mem[0003 + 4]
Mem[0007]

which Figure 6.35 shows is vector[2]. Had the array been an array of characters, the ASLX operation would be unnecessary because each character occupies only one byte. In general, if each cell in the array occupies *n* bytes, the value of j is loaded into the index register, multiplied by *n*, and the array element is accessed with indexed addressing.

Similarly, the compiler translates the output of vector[j] as

```
003E  0B      ASLX             ;two bytes per integer
003F  3D0003  DECO  vector,x
```

with indexed addressing.

In summary, to translate global arrays, the compiler generates code as follows:

The translation rules for global arrays

› To allocate storage for the array, it generates .BLOCK *tot*, where *tot* is the total number of bytes occupied by the array.

› To get an element of the array, it generates LDWX to put the index into the index register, generates code to multiply the index by the number of bytes per cell (ASLX in the case of an array of integers with two bytes per integer), and uses indexed addressing.

Translating Local Arrays

Like all local variables, local arrays are allocated on the run-time stack during program execution. The SUBSP instruction allocates the array and the ADDSP instruction deallocates it. FIGURE 6.36 is a program identical to the one of Figure 6.34 except that the index j and the array vector are local to main().

FIGURE 6.36
A local array. The C program is from Figure 6.34 but with local variables.

High-Order Language
```
#include <stdio.h>

int main() {
    int vector[4];
    int j;
    for (j = 0; j < 4; j++) {
        scanf("%d", &vector[j]);
    }
    for (j = 3; j >= 0; j--) {
        printf("%d %d\n", j, vector[j]);
    }
    return 0;
}
```

Assembly Language
```
0000   120003              BR      main
                       ;
                       ;******* main ()
                       vector:  .EQUATE 2       ;local variable #2d4a
                       j:       .EQUATE 0       ;local variable #2d
0003   58000A main:       SUBSP   10,i          ;push #vector #j
0006   C80000             LDWX    0,i           ;for (j = 0
0009   EB0000             STWX    j,s
000C   A80004 for1:       CPWX    4,i           ;j < 4
000F   1C0022             BRGE    endFor1
0012   0B                 ASLX                  ;two bytes per integer
0013   360002             DECI    vector,sx     ;scanf("%d", &vector[j])
0016   CB0000             LDWX    j,s           ;j++)
```

(continues)

FIGURE 6.36
A local array. The C program is from Figure 6.34 but with local variables. (*continued*)

```
0019  680001          ADDX    1,i
001C  EB0000          STWX    j,s
001F  12000C          BR      for1
0022  C80003 endFor1: LDWX    3,i            ;for (j = 3
0025  EB0000          STWX    j,s
0028  A80000 for2:    CPWX    0,i            ;j >= 0
002B  16004D          BRLT    endFor2
002E  3B0000          DECO    j,s            ;printf("%d %d\n", j, vector[j])
0031  D00020          LDBA    ' ',i
0034  F1FC16          STBA    charOut,d
0037  0B              ASLX                   ;two bytes per integer
0038  3E0002          DECO    vector,sx
003B  D0000A          LDBA    '\n',i
003E  F1FC16          STBA    charOut,d
0041  CB0000          LDWX    j,s            ;j--)
0044  780001          SUBX    1,i
0047  EB0000          STWX    j,s
004A  120028          BR      for2
004D  50000A endFor2: ADDSP   10,i           ;pop #j #vector
0050  00              STOP
0051                  .END
```

FIGURE 6.37 shows the memory allocation on the run-time stack for the program of Figure 6.36. The compiler translates

```
int vector[4];
int j;
```

at Level HOL6 as

```
0003 58000A main: SUBSP 10,i ;push #vector #j
```

at Level Asmb5. It allocates eight bytes for vector and two bytes for j, for a total of 10 bytes. It sets the values of the symbols with

```
vector:   .EQUATE 2  ;local variable #2d4a
j:        .EQUATE 0  ;local variable #2d
```

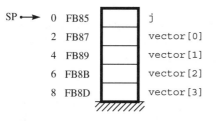

FIGURE 6.37
Memory allocation for the local array of Figure 6.36.

where 2 is the stack-relative address of the first cell of vector and 0 is the stack-relative address of j as Figure 6.37 shows.

How does the compiler access vector[j]? It cannot use indexed addressing, because the value of symbol vector is not the address of the first element of the array. It uses stack-indexed addressing. With stack-indexed addressing, the CPU computes the operand as

Oprnd = Mem[SP + OprndSpec + X]

Stack-indexed addressing

It adds the stack pointer plus the operand specifier plus the index register and uses the sum as the address in main memory from which it fetches the operand.

In Figure 6.36, the compiler translates

```
scanf("%d", &vector[j]);
```

at Level HOL6 as

```
0012  0B      ASLX                 ;two bytes per integer
0013  360002  DECI   vector,sx     ;scanf("%d", &vector[j])
```

at Level Asmb5. As in the previous program, this is an optimized translation. A nonoptimizing compiler would generate the following code:

```
LDWX j,d
ASLX
DECI vector,sx
```

Suppose the value of j is 2. LDWX puts the value of j in the index register. ASLX multiplies the 2 times 2, leaving 4 in the index register. DECI uses stack-indexed addressing. So, the operand is computed as

Mem[SP + OprndSpec + X]
Mem[FB85 + 2 + 4]
Mem[FB8B]

which Figure 6.37 shows is `vector[2]`. You can see how stack-indexed addressing is made for arrays on the run-time stack. SP is the address of the top of the stack. OprndSpec is the stack-relative address of the first cell of the array, so SP + OprndSpec is the absolute address of the first cell of the array. With j in the index register (multiplied by the number of bytes per cell of the array), the sum SP + OprndSpec + X is the address of cell j of the array.

In summary, to translate local arrays, the compiler generates code as follows:

The translation rules for
local arrays

> To allocate storage for the array, it generates `SUBSP` *tot* with immediate addressing where *tot* is the total number of bytes occupied by the array.

> To get an element of the array, it generates `LDWX` to put the index into the index register, generates code to multiply the index by the number of bytes per cell (`ASLX` in the case of an array of integers with two bytes per integer), and uses stack-indexed addressing.

Translating Arrays Passed as Parameters

In C, the name of an array without the square brackets, `[]`, is the address of the first element of the array. When you pass an array, even if you do not use the & designation in the actual parameter list, you are passing the address of the first element of the array. The effect is as if you called the array by reference. The designers of the C language reasoned that programmers almost never want to pass an array by value because such calls are so inefficient. They require large amounts of storage on the run-time stack because the stack must contain the entire array. And they require a large amount of time because the value of every cell must be copied onto the stack. Consequently, the default behavior in C is for arrays to be called as if by reference.

FIGURE 6.38 shows how a compiler translates a program that passes a local array as a parameter. The main program passes an array of integers `vector` and an integer `numItms` to procedures `getVect()` and `putVect()`. `getVect()` inputs values into the array and sets `numItms` to the number of items input. `putVect()` outputs the values of the array.

Figure 6.38 shows that the compiler translates the local variables

```
int vector[8];
int numItms;
```

as

```
              vector:  .EQUATE 2      ;local variable #2d8a
              numItms: .EQUATE 0      ;local variable #2d
0057  580012  main:    SUBSP   18,i ;push #vector #numItms
```

FIGURE 6.38
Passing a local array as a parameter.

High-Order Language
```c
#include <stdio.h>

void getVect(int v[], int *n) {
   int j;
   scanf("%d", n);
   for (j = 0; j < *n; j++) {
      scanf("%d", &v[j]);
   }
}

void putVect(int v[], int n) {
   int j;
   for (j = 0; j < n; j++) {
      printf("%d ", v[j]);
   }
   printf("\n");
}
int main() {
   int vector[8];
   int numItms;
   getVect(vector, &numItms);
   putVect(vector, numItms);
   return 0;
}
```

Assembly Language
```
0000  120058            BR      main
                  ;
                  ;******* getVect(int v[], int *n)
                  v:       .EQUATE 6           ;formal parameter #2h
                  n:       .EQUATE 4           ;formal parameter #2h
                  j:       .EQUATE 0           ;local variable #2d
0003  580002 getVect: SUBSP  2,i              ;push #j
0006  340004            DECI   n,sf            ;scanf("%d", n)
0009  C80000            LDWX   0,i             ;for (j = 0
000C  EB0000            STWX   j,s
000F  AC0004 for1:      CPWX   n,sf            ;j < *n
```

(continues)

FIGURE 6.38
Passing a local array as a parameter. (*continued*)

```
0012  1C0025           BRGE    endFor1
0015  0B               ASLX                    ;two bytes per integer
0016  370006           DECI    v,sfx           ;scanf("%d", &v[j])
0019  CB0000           LDWX    j,s             ;j++)
001C  680001           ADDX    1,i
001F  EB0000           STWX    j,s
0022  12000F           BR      for1
0025  500002  endFor1: ADDSP   2,i             ;pop #j
0028  01               RET
               ;
               ;******* putVect(int v[], int n)
               v2:      .EQUATE 6               ;formal parameter #2h
               n2:      .EQUATE 4               ;formal parameter #2d
               j2:      .EQUATE 0               ;local variable #2d
0029  580002  putVect: SUBSP   2,i             ;push #j2
002C  C80000           LDWX    0,i             ;for (j = 0
002F  EB0000           STWX    j2,s
0032  AB0004  for2:    CPWX    n2,s            ;j < n
0035  1C004E           BRGE    endFor2
0038  0B               ASLX                    ;two bytes per integer
0039  3F0006           DECO    v2,sfx          ;printf("%d ", v[j])
003C  D00020           LDBA    ' ',i
003F  F1FC16           STBA    charOut,d
0042  CB0000           LDWX    j2,s            ;j++)
0045  680001           ADDX    1,i
0048  EB0000           STWX    j2,s
004B  120032           BR      for2
004E  D0000A  endFor2: LDBA    '\n',i          ;printf("\n")
0051  F1FC16           STBA    charOut,d
0054  500002           ADDSP   2,i             ;pop #j2
0057  01               RET
               ;
               ;******* main()
               vector:  .EQUATE 2               ;local variable #2d8a
               numItms: .EQUATE 0               ;local variable #2d
0058  580012  main:    SUBSP   18,i            ;push storage for #vector #numItms
005B  03               MOVSPA                  ;move (&)vector
005C  600002           ADDA    vector,i
```

```
005F   E3FFFE           STWA      -2,s
0062   03               MOVSPA                 ;move &numItms
0063   600000           ADDA      numItms,i
0066   E3FFFC           STWA      -4,s
0069   580004           SUBSP     4,i          ;push #v #n
006C   240003           CALL      getVect      ;getVect(vector, &numItms)
006F   500004           ADDSP     4,i          ;pop #n #v
0072   03               MOVSPA                 ;move (&)vector
0073   600002           ADDA      vector,i
0076   E3FFFE           STWA      -2,s
0079   C30000           LDWA      numItms,s    ;move numItms
007C   E3FFFC           STWA      -4,s
007F   580004           SUBSP     4,i          ;push #v2 #n2
0082   240029           CALL      putVect      ;putVect(vector, numItms)
0085   500004           ADDSP     4,i          ;pop #n2 #v2
0088   500012           ADDSP     18,i         ;pop #numItms #vector
008B   00               STOP
008C                    .END
```

Input

5 40 50 60 70 80

Output

40 50 60 70 80

The SUBSP instruction pushes 18 bytes on the run-time stack, 16 bytes for the eight integers of the array, and 2 bytes for the integer. The .EQUATE dot commands set the symbols to their stack offsets, as FIGURE 6.39(a) shows.

The compiler translates

```
getVect(vector, &numItms);
```

by first generating code to move the address of the first cell of vector to the stack

```
005B   03       MOVSPA               ;move (&)vector
005C   600002   ADDA    vector,i
005F   E3FFFE   STWA    -2,s
```

and then by generating code to move the address of numItms to the stack.

```
0062   03       MOVSPA               ;move &numItms
0063   600000   ADDA    numItms,i
0066   E3FFFC   STWA    -4,s
```

FIGURE 6.39

The run-time stack for the program of Figure 6.38.

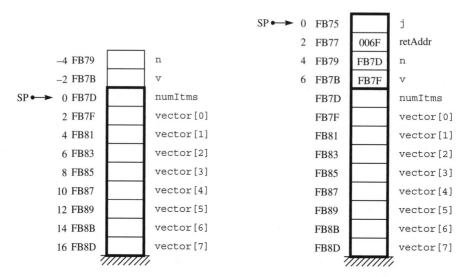

(a) Before calling getVect ( ).   (b) After calling getVect ( ).

Even though the first actual parameter in C is vector and not &vector, the compiler nevertheless writes code to push the address of v with the MOVSPA and ADDA instructions. As usual, the second actual parameter &numItms has the address operator & prefixed so the compiler will push its address the same way. Remember that arrays in C are a special case and are called by reference by default without using the & addressing operator in the actual parameter list. Figure 6.39(b) shows v with FB7F, the address of vector[0], as well as n with FB79, the address of numItms.

Figure 6.39(b) also shows the stack offsets for the parameters and local variables in getVect (). The compiler defines the symbols

```
v: .EQUATE 6 ;formal parameter #2h
n: .EQUATE 4 ;formal parameter #2h
j: .EQUATE 0 ;local variable #2d
```

accordingly. It translates the input statement as

```
0006 340004 DECI n,sf ;scanf("%d", n)
```

where stack-relative deferred addressing is used because n is called by reference and the address of n is on the stack.

But how does the compiler translate

```
scanf("%d", &v[j]);
```

It cannot use stack-indexed addressing, because the array of values is not in the stack frame for getVect(). The value of v is 6, which means that the address of the first cell of the array is six bytes below the top of the stack. The array of values is in the stack frame for main(). Stack-deferred indexed addressing is designed to access the elements of an array whose address is in the top stack frame but whose actual collection of values is not. With stack-deferred indexed addressing, the CPU computes the operand as

Oprnd = Mem[Mem[SP + OprndSpec] + X]

Stack-deferred indexed addressing

It adds the stack pointer plus the operand specifier and uses the sum as the address of the first element of the array, to which it adds the index register. The compiler translates the input statement as

```
0015   0B       ASLX            ;two bytes per integer
0016   370006   DECI   v,sfx    ;scanf("%d", &v[j])
```

where the letters sfx indicate stack-deferred indexed addressing, and the compiler has determined that the index register will contain the current value of j.

For example, suppose the value of j is 2. The ASLX instruction doubles it to 4. The computation of the operand is

Mem[Mem[SP + OprndSpec] + X]
Mem[Mem[FB75 + 6] + 4]
Mem[Mem[FB7B] + 4]
Mem[FB7F + 4]
Mem[FB83]

which is vector[2], as expected from Figure 6.39(b).

The formal parameters in procedures getVect() and putVect() in Figure 6.39 have the same names. At Level HOL6, the scope of the parameter names is confined to the body of the function. The programmer knows that a statement containing n in the body of getVect() refers to the n in the parameter list for getVect() and not to the n in the parameter list of putVect(). The scope of a symbol name at Level Asmb5, however, is the entire assembly language program. The compiler cannot use the same symbol for the n in putVect() that it uses for the n in getVect(), as duplicate symbol definitions would be ambiguous. All compilers must have some mechanism for managing the scope of name declarations in Level-HOL6 programs when they transform them to symbols at Level Asmb5. The compiler in Figure 6.38 makes the identifiers unambiguous by appending the digit 2 to the symbol name. Hence, the compiler translates variable name n in putVect() at Level HOL6 to symbol n2 at Level Asmb5. It does the same with v and j.

With procedure putVect (), the array is passed as a parameter but n is called by value. In preparation for the procedure call, the address of vector is pushed onto the stack as before, but this time the value of numItms is pushed, not its address. In procedure putVect (), n2 is accessed with stack-relative addressing

```
0032   AB0004   for2:   CPWX   n2,s   ;j < n
```

because it is called by value. v2 is accessed with stack-deferred indexed addressing

```
0038   0B         ASLX              ;two bytes per integer
0039   3F0006   DECO   v2,sfx   ;printf("%d ", v[j])
```

as it is in getVect ().

In Figure 6.38, vector is a local array. If it were a global array, the translations of getVect () and putVect () would be unchanged. v[j] would still be accessed with stack-deferred indexed addressing, which expects the address of the first element of the array to be in the top stack frame. The only difference would be in the code to push the address of the first element of the array in preparation of the call. As in the program of Figure 6.34, the value of the symbol of a global array is the address of the first cell of the array. Consequently, to push the address of the first cell of the array, the compiler would generate an LDWA instruction with immediate addressing followed by an STWA instruction with stack-relative addressing to do the push.

In summary, to pass an array as a parameter, the compiler generates code as follows:

The translation rules for passing an array as a parameter

> To get the actual parameter in the caller, which is the address of the first element of the array, it generates either (a) MOVSPA followed by ADDA with immediate addressing for a local array, or (b) LDWA with immediate addressing for a global array.

> To get an element of the array in the callee, it generates LDWX to put the index into the index register, generates code to multiply the index by the number of bytes per cell (ASLX in the case of an array of integers with two bytes per integer), and uses stack-deferred indexed addressing.

Translating the Switch Statement

The program in (**FIGURE 6.40**), which is also in Figure 2.12, shows how a compiler translates the C switch statement. It uses an interesting combination of indexed addressing with the unconditional branch, BR. The switch statement is not the same as a nested if statement. If a user

FIGURE 6.40
Translation of a `switch` statement. The C program is from Figure 2.12.

High-Order Language
```c
#include <stdio.h>

int main() {
    int guess;
    printf("Pick a number 0..3: ");
    scanf("%d", &guess);
    switch (guess) {
        case 0: printf("Not close\n"); break;
        case 1: printf("Close\n"); break;
        case 2: printf("Right on\n"); break;
        case 3: printf("Too high\n");
    }
    return 0;
}
```

Assembly Language
```
0000   120003              BR       main
                   ;
                   ;******* main()
                   guess:   .EQUATE 0          ;local variable #2d
0003   580002 main:        SUBSP    2,i        ;push #guess
0006   490034              STRO     msgIn,d    ;printf("Pick a number 0..3: ")
0009   330000              DECI     guess,s    ;scanf("%d", &guess)
000C   CB0000              LDWX     guess,s    ;switch (guess)
000F   0B                  ASLX                ;two bytes per address
0010   130013              BR       guessJT,x
0013   001B   guessJT: .ADDRSS case0
0015   0021            .ADDRSS case1
0017   0027            .ADDRSS case2
0019   002D            .ADDRSS case3
001B   490049 case0:       STRO     msg0,d     ;printf("Not close\n")
001E   120030              BR       endCase    ;break
0021   490054 case1:       STRO     msg1,d     ;printf("Close\n")
0024   120030              BR       endCase    ;break
0027   49005B case2:       STRO     msg2,d     ;printf("Right on\n")
002A   120030              BR       endCase    ;break
```

(continues)

FIGURE 6.40

Translation of a `switch` statement. The C program is from Figure 2.12. (*continued*)

```
002D   490065 case3:   STRO    msg3,d      ;printf("Too high\n")
0030   500002 endCase: ADDSP   2,i         ;pop #guess
0033   00             STOP
0034   506963 msgIn:   .ASCII  "Pick a number 0..3: \x00"
       . . .
0049   4E6F74 msg0:    .ASCII  "Not close\n\x00"
       . . .
0054   436C6F msg1:    .ASCII  "Close\n\x00"
       . . .
005B   526967 msg2:    .ASCII  "Right on\n\n\x00"
       . . .
0065   546F6F msg3:    .ASCII  "Too high\n\x00"
       . . .
006F                   .END
```

Symbol table

Symbol	Value	Symbol	Value
case0	001B	case1	0021
case2	0027	case3	002D
endCase	0030	guess	0000
guessJT	0013	main	0003
msg0	0049	msg1	0054
msg2	005B	msg3	0065
msgIn	0034		

----

enters 2 for guess, the switch statement branches directly to the third alternative without comparing guess to 0 or 1. An array is a random access data structure because the indexing mechanism allows the programmer to access any element at random without traversing all the previous elements. For example, to access the third element of a vector of integers, you can write vector[2] directly without having to traverse vector[0] and vector[1] first. Main memory is, in effect, an array of bytes whose addresses correspond to the indexes of the array. To translate the switch statement, the compiler allocates an array of addresses called a *jump table*. Each entry in the jump table is the address of the first statement of a section of code that corresponds to one of the cases of the switch statement. With indexed addressing, the program can branch directly to case 2.

Jump tables

Figure 6.40 shows the jump table at 0013 in the assembly language program. The code generated at 0013 is 001B, which is the address of the first statement of case 0. The code generated at 0015 is 0021, which is the address of the first statement of case 1, and so on. The compiler generates the jump table with .ADDRSS pseudo-ops. Every .ADDRSS command must be followed by a symbol. The code generated by .ADDRSS is the value of the symbol. For example, case2 is a symbol whose value is 0027, the address of the code to be executed if guess has a value of 2. Therefore, the object code generated by

The .ADDRSS *pseudo-op*

```
.ADDRSS case2
```

at 0017 is 0027.

Suppose the user enters 2 for the value of guess. The statement

```
000C CB0000 LDWX guess,s ;switch (guess)
```

puts 2 in the index register. The statement

```
000F 0B ASLX ;two bytes per address
```

doubles the 2, leaving 4 in the index register. The statement

```
0010 130013 BR guessJT,x
```

is an unconditional branch with indexed addressing. The value of the operand specifier guessJT is 0013, the address of the first word of the jump table. For indexed addressing, the CPU computes the operand as

Oprnd = Mem[OprndSpec + X]

Indexed addressing

Therefore, the CPU computes

Mem[OprndSpec + X]
Mem[0013 + 4]
Mem[0017]
0027

as the operand. The RTL specification for the BR instruction is

PC ← Oprnd

and so the CPU puts 0027 in the program counter. Because of the von Neumann cycle, the next instruction to be executed is the one at address 0027, which is precisely the first instruction for case 2.

The break statement in C is translated as a BR instruction to branch to the end of the switch statement. If you omit the break in your C program, the compiler will omit the BR and control will fall through to the next case.

If the user enters a number not in the range 0..3, a run-time error will occur. For example, if the user enters 4 for guess, the ASLX instruction will multiply it by 2, leaving 8 in the index register, and the CPU will compute the operand as

Mem[OprndSpec + X]
Mem[0013 + 8]
Mem[001B]
4100

so the branch will be to memory location 4100 (hex). The problem is that the bits 001B were generated by the assembler for the STRO instruction and were never meant to be interpreted as a branch address. To prevent such indignities from happening to the user, C specifies that nothing should happen if the value of guess is not one of the cases. It also provides a default case for the switch statement to handle any case not encountered by the previous cases. The compiler must generate an initial conditional branch on guess to handle the values not covered by the other cases. The problems at the end of the chapter explore this characteristic of the switch statement.

Compiling to x86 Assembly Language

The C compiler in Microsoft's Visual Studio IDE normally compiles direct to machine code. However, it has the capability to output to an assembly language called *Microsoft Macro Assembler (MASM)* as an intermediate step, which you can then inspect and compare with your C source code. Following are some code fragments from the assembly language translation of the C program in Figure 6.10.

The program has a single global variable declared as

```
char letter;
```

in C. The compiler translates this declaration to

```
_DATA SEGMENT
COMM _letter:BYTE
_DATA ENDS
```

in MASM. It creates the assembly language symbol _letter to represent the global variable letter in C.

Global variables are stored in a data segment, which is a fixed location in memory.

The compiler translates the loop test

```
while (letter != '*')
```

as shown in FIGURE 6.41(a).

As with the Pep/9 listing, the first column is the address in memory, the second column is the machine code in hexadecimal, the third column is the assembly language mnemonic, and the remaining columns specify one or more operands.

The movsx instruction is move with sign extend, which puts the value of letter in the EAX register. Rather than having different versions of mov for different sizes of operands, the language uses PTR to denote the number of bytes in the operand. The cmp instruction is the compare instruction, which compares

FIGURE 6.41

MASM translations from C.

```
0003a  0f be 05 00 00
       00 00 00         movsx eax, BYTE PTR _letter
00041  83 f8 2a         cmp   eax, 42 ; 0000002aH
00044  74 62            je    SHORT $LN3@main
```

(a) Translation of the while loop test.

```
0007c  a1 00 00 00 00 mov   eax, DWORD PTR _value
00081  50             push  eax
00082  e8 00 00 00 00 call  _printBar
00087  83 c4 04       add   esp, 4
```

(b) Translation of the printBar() function call.

```
0001e  c7 45 f8 01 00 ; k = 1
       00 00          mov   DWORD PTR _k$[ebp], 1
00025  eb 09          jmp   SHORT $LN3@printBar
$LN2@printBar:        ; k++
00027  8b 45 f8       mov   eax, DWORD PTR _k$[ebp]
0002a  83 c0 01       add   eax, 1
0002d  89 45 f8       mov   DWORD PTR _k$[ebp], eax
$LN3@printBar:        ; k <= n
00030  8b 45 f8       mov   eax, DWORD PTR _k$[ebp]
00033  3b 45 08       cmp   eax, DWORD PTR _n$[ebp]
00036  7f 19          jg    SHORT $LN1@printBar
```

(c) Translation of the for loop.

```
0004f  eb d6          jmp SHORT $LN2@printBar
$LN1@printBar:
```

(d) The branch to the top of the loop.

the content of the EAX register with 42 (dec), which is 2A (hex), which is the ASCII character *. As with Pep/9, a semicolon is the beginning of a comment, which the compiler produced for the listing. Hexadecimal constants terminate with the letter H. The je instruction is *jump if equal*, which is equivalent to the Pep/9 BREQ instruction. The compiler generates the symbol $LN3@ main as the target of the branch, which it defines later in the program.

The code fragment in Figure 6.41(b) is an example of MASM assembly code generated by the function call

```
printBar(value)
```

in the C program of Figure 6.21.

The push instruction automatically subtracts 4 from the stack pointer ESP when it pushes _value onto the run-time stack. The add instruction pops the bytes off the stack.

Although the preceding code fragment is close to the equivalent Pep/9 translation, the code fragment for the setup code at the beginning of printBar() is more complex. In addition to the stack pointer, there is a base pointer for the stack frame that must be managed. The compiler sets up values for formal parameter n and local variable k in the text segment at the beginning of the printBar() function:

```
; COMDAT _printBar
_TEXT SEGMENT
_k$ = -8   ; size = 4
_n$ = 8    ; size = 4
_printBar PROC ; COMDAT
```

Unlike Pep/9, the offsets are relative to the base pointer, not the stack pointer, and can be negative. The setup code at the beginning of the function takes nine instructions and is not shown here.

The code fragment in Figure 6.41(c) is the compiler's translation of

```
for (k = 1; k <= n; k++)
```

inside the function.

The first statement initializes k to 1. DWORD designates double word, which is four bytes. MASM treats the brackets, [], like the addition operator. Thus, the expression _k$[ebp] denotes an addressing mode where the operand is Mem[EBP + OprndSpec], with the value of _k$ one of the operand specifiers. This addressing mode is equivalent to stack relative in Pep/9 but with the base pointer EBP instead of the stack pointer.

You can see the operand specifiers in the object code. The value of symbol _k$ is –8 (dec), which is 1111 1000 (bin) or f8 in the object code. Similarly, you can see that _n$ is 08 in the object code.

jmp is the unconditional jump, equivalent to BR in Pep/9. jg is the jump if greater than, equivalent to BRGT in Pep/9. The two statements in Figure 6.41(d) are at the bottom of the loop. The first branches back to the test, and the second is the symbol that terminates the loop.

The x86 jump instructions use PC-relative addressing, which is common but not used in Pep/9 to keep the translations simple. With PC-relative addressing, the operand specifier is not the address of the target, but rather the offset from the current value of the PC necessary to reach the target. In other words, the operand is PC + OprndSpec.

Example 6.1   Consider the jmp instruction at 00025 in Figure 6.41(c). The instruction specifier is eb and the operand specifier is 09. The branch is not to Mem[09], but rather to Mem[PC + 09]. After the instruction has been fetched and the program counter incremented, the value of the program counter, EIP in the x86 architecture, is 00027. Thus, the branch is to Mem[00027 + 09], which is Mem[00030], where the addition is in hexadecimal. Sure enough, the target of the branch is $LN3@printBar: at 00030.   ∎

Example 6.2   Consider the jmp instruction at 0004f in Figure 6.41(d). After the instruction has been fetched and the program counter incremented, the value of the program counter is 00051. From the object code listing, the operand specifier is d6. It is considered an eight-bit signed integer 1101 0110, and there is a 1 in the sign bit making it negative—namely –42 (dec). Adding –42 (dec) to 00051 (hex) with the proper base conversions yields the hexadecimal address 00027. As expected, the target of the branch is $LN2@printBar: at 00027 in Figure 6.41(c).

The x86 architecture, like Pep/9, describes a complex instruction set (CISC) machine. You can see from the preceding object code that x86 instructions come in many different sizes. Chapter 12 describes the MIPS machine, which is a reduced instruction set (RISC) machine. The primary design goal for RISC machines is for all instructions to have the same size. Chapter 12 shows how the MIPS machine also uses PC-relative addressing for its branch instructions.   ∎

6.5 Dynamic Memory Allocation

Abstraction of control

The purpose of a compiler is to create a high level of abstraction for the programmer. For example, it lets the programmer think in terms of a single while loop instead of the detailed conditional branches at the assembly level that are necessary to implement the loop on the machine. Hiding the details of a lower level is the essence of abstraction.

But abstraction of program control is only one side of the coin. The other side is abstraction of data. At the assembly and machine levels, the only data types are bits and bytes. Previous programs show how the compiler translates character, integer, and array types. Each of these types can be global, allocated with .BLOCK, or local, allocated with SUBSP on the run-time stack. But C programs can also contain structures and pointers, the basic building blocks of many data structures. At Level HOL6, pointers access structures allocated from the heap with the malloc() function. This section shows the operation of a simple heap at Level Asmb5 and how the compiler translates programs that contain pointers and structures.

Abstraction of data

Translating Global Pointers

FIGURE 6.42 shows a C program with global pointers and its translation to Pep/9 assembly language. The C program is identical to the one in Figure 2.38. Figure 2.39 shows the allocation from the heap as the program executes at Level HOL6. The heap is a region of memory different from the stack. The

---

FIGURE 6.42
Translation of global pointers. The C program is from Figure 2.38.

High-Order Language
```
#include <stdio.h>
#include <stdlib.h>

int *a, *b, *c;

int main() {
    a = (int *) malloc(sizeof(int));
    *a = 5;
    b = (int *) malloc(sizeof(int));
    *b = 3;
    c = a;
    a = b;
    *a = 2 + *c;
    printf("*a = %d\n", *a);
    printf("*b = %d\n", *b);
    printf("*c = %d\n", *c);
    return 0;
}
```

(continues)

FIGURE 6.42

Translation of global pointers. The C program is from Figure 2.38. (*continued*)

Assembly Language

```
0000   120009            BR       main
0003   0000    a:        .BLOCK   2         ;global variable #2h
0005   0000    b:        .BLOCK   2         ;global variable #2h
0007   0000    c:        .BLOCK   2         ;global variable #2h
               ;
               ;******* main ()
0009   C00002  main:     LDWA     2,i       ;a = (int *) malloc(sizeof(int))
000C   240073            CALL     malloc    ;allocate #2d
000F   E90003            STWX     a,d
0012   C00005            LDWA     5,i       ;*a = 5
0015   E20003            STWA     a,n
0018   C00002            LDWA     2,i       ;b = (int *) malloc(sizeof(int))
001B   240073            CALL     malloc    ;allocate #2d
001E   E90005            STWX     b,d
0021   C00003            LDWA     3,i       ;*b = 3
0024   E20005            STWA     b,n
0027   C10003            LDWA     a,d       ;c = a
002A   E10007            STWA     c,d
002D   C10005            LDWA     b,d       ;a = b
0030   E10003            STWA     a,d
0033   C00002            LDWA     2,i       ;*a = 2 + *c
0036   620007            ADDA     c,n
0039   E20003            STWA     a,n
003C   490061            STRO     msg0,d    ;printf("*a = %d\n", *a)
003F   3A0003            DECO     a,n
0042   D0000A            LDBA     '\n',i
0045   F1FC16            STBA     charOut,d
0048   490067            STRO     msg1,d    ;printf("*b = %d\n", *b)
004B   3A0005            DECO     b,n
004E   D0000A            LDBA     '\n',i
0051   F1FC16            STBA     charOut,d
0054   49006D            STRO     msg2,d    ;printf("*c = %d\n", *c)
0057   3A0007            DECO     c,n
005A   D0000A            LDBA     '\n',i
005D   F1FC16            STBA     charOut,d
0060   00                STOP
```

```
0061   2A6120 msg0:    .ASCII    "*a = \x00"
       3D2000
0067   2A6220 msg1:    .ASCII    "*b = \x00"
       3D2000
006D   2A6320 msg2:    .ASCII    "*c = \x00"
       3D2000
                   ;
                   ;******* malloc()
                   ;          Precondition: A contains number of bytes
                   ;          Postcondition: X contains pointer to bytes
0073   C9007D malloc:  LDWX     hpPtr,d      ;returned pointer
0076   61007D          ADDA     hpPtr,d      ;allocate from heap
0079   E1007D          STWA     hpPtr,d      ;update hpPtr
007C   01              RET
007D   007F   hpPtr:   .ADDRSS  heap         ;address of next free byte
007F   00     heap:    .BLOCK   1            ;first byte in the heap
0080                   .END
```

Output

```
*a = 7
*b = 7
*c = 5
```

compiler, in cooperation with the operating system under which it runs, must generate code to perform the allocation and deallocation from the heap.

When you program with pointers in C, you allocate storage from the heap with the malloc() function. When your program no longer needs the storage that was allocated, you deallocate it with the free() function. It is possible to allocate several cells of memory from the heap and then deallocate one cell from the middle. The memory management algorithms must be able to handle that scenario. To keep things simple at this introductory level, the programs that illustrate the heap do not show the deallocation process. The heap is located in main memory at the end of the application program. Function malloc() works by allocating storage from the heap, so that the heap grows downward. Once memory is allocated, it can never be deallocated. This feature of the Pep/9 heap is unrealistic but easier to understand than if it were presented more realistically.

Simplification in the Pep/9 heap

The assembly language program in Figure 6.42 shows the heap starting at address 007F, which is the value of the symbol heap. The allocation algorithm maintains a global pointer called `hpPtr`, which stands for *heap pointer*. The statement

```
007D 007F hpPtr: .ADDRSS heap ;address of next free byte
```

initializes `hpPtr` to the address of the first byte in the heap. The application supplies `malloc()` with the number of bytes needed. The `malloc()` function returns the current value of `hpPtr` and then increments it by the number of bytes requested. Hence, the invariant maintained by `malloc()` is that `hpPtr` points to the address of the next byte to be allocated from the heap.

The calling protocol for function `malloc()`

The calling protocol for `malloc()` is different from the calling protocol for other functions. With other functions, information is passed via parameters on the run-time stack. With `malloc()`, the application puts the number of bytes to be allocated in the accumulator and executes the CALL statement to invoke the function. The function puts the current value of `hpPtr` in the index register for the application. So, the precondition for the successful operation of `malloc()` is that the accumulator contains the number of bytes to be allocated from the heap. The postcondition is that the index register contains the address in the heap of the first byte allocated by `malloc()`.

The calling protocol for function `malloc()` is more efficient than the calling protocol for other functions. The implementation of `malloc()` requires only four lines of assembly language code, including the RET statement. The statement

```
0073 C9007D malloc: LDWX hpPtr,d ;returned pointer
```

puts the current value of the heap pointer in the index register. The statement

```
0076 61007D ADDA hpPtr,d ;allocate from heap
```

adds the number of bytes to be allocated to the heap pointer, and the statement

```
0079 E1007D STWA hpPtr,d ;update hpPtr
```

updates `hpPtr` to the address of the first unallocated byte in the heap.

This efficient calling protocol is possible for two reasons. First, there is no long parameter list as is possible with other functions. The application only needs to supply óne value to `malloc()`. The calling protocol for other functions must be designed to handle arbitrary numbers of parameters. If a parameter list had, say, four parameters, there would not be enough registers in the Pep/9 CPU to hold them all. But the run-time stack can store an arbitrary number of parameters. Second, `malloc()` does not call any other function. Specifically, it makes no recursive calls. The calling protocol for functions must be designed in general to allow for functions to call other functions or to call themselves recursively. The run-time stack is essential for such calls but unnecessary for `malloc()`.

[FIGURE 6.43(a)] shows the memory allocation for the C program at Level HOL6 just before the first `printf()` statement. It corresponds to Figure 2.39(h). Figure 6.43(b) shows the same memory allocation at Level Asmb5. Global pointers a, b, and c are stored at 0003, 0005, and 0007. As with all global variables, they are allocated with .BLOCK by the statements

```
0003 0000 a:  .BLOCK 2 ;global variable #2h
0005 0000 b:  .BLOCK 2 ;global variable #2h
0007 0000 c:  .BLOCK 2 ;global variable #2h
```

A pointer at Level HOL6 is an address at Level Asmb5. Addresses occupy two bytes. Hence, each global pointer is allocated two bytes. Pointers have format trace tags #2h because pointers are addresses, typically displayed in hexadecimal.

Pointers are addresses.

The compiler translates the statement

```
a = (int *) malloc(sizeof(int));
```

as

```
0009  C00002  main:  LDWA  2,i      ;a = (int *) malloc …
000C  240073          CALL  malloc  ;allocate #2d
000F  E90003          STWX  a,d
```

The LDWA instruction puts 2 in the accumulator. The CALL instruction calls the `malloc()` function, which allocates two bytes of storage from the heap and puts the pointer to the allocated storage in the index register. The comment has format trace tag #2d because the cell pointed to by a contains a two-byte decimal value. The STWX instruction stores the returned pointer in the global variable a. Because a is a global variable, STWX uses direct addressing. After this sequence of statements executes, a has the value 007F, and `hpPtr` has the value 0081 because it has been incremented by two.

How does the compiler translate

```
*a = 5;
```

At this point in the execution of the program, the global variable a has the address of where the 5 should be stored. (This point does *not* correspond to Figure 6.43, which is later in the execution.) The store word instruction cannot use direct addressing to put 5 in a, as that would replace the address

FIGURE 6.43

Memory allocation for Figure 6.42 just before the first `printf()` statement.

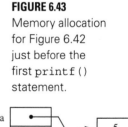

(a) Global pointers at Level HOL6.

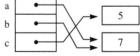

0003	0081	a
0005	0081	b
0007	007F	c

| 007F | 5 |
| 0081 | 7 |

(b) The same global pointers at Level Asmb5.

with 5, which is not the address of the allocated cell in the heap. Pep/9 provides the indirect addressing mode, in which the operand is computed as

Indirect addressing

Oprnd = Mem[Mem[OprndSpec]]

With indirect addressing, the operand specifier is the address in memory of the address of the operand. The compiler translates the assignment statement as

```
0012   C00005   LDWA   5,i   ;*a = 5
0015   E20003   STWA   a,n
```

where n in the store word instruction indicates indirect addressing. At this point in the execution, the operand is computed as

Mem[Mem[OprndSpec]]
Mem[Mem[0003]]
Mem[007F]

which is the first cell in the heap. The store word instruction stores 5 in main memory at address 007F.

The compiler translates the assignment of global pointers the same as it would translate the assignment of any other type of global variable. It translates

```
c = a;
```

as

```
0027   C10003   LDWA   a,d   ;c = a
002A   E10007   STWA   c,d
```

using direct addressing. At this point in the program, a contains 007F, the address of the first cell in the heap. The assignment gives c the same value, the address of the first cell in the heap, so that c points to the same cell to which a points.

Contrast the access of a global pointer to the access of the cell to which it points. The compiler translates

```
*a = 2 + *c;
```

as

```
0033   C00002   LDWA   2,i   ;*a = 2 + *c
0036   620007   ADDA   c,n
0039   E20003   STWA   a,n
```

where the add and store word instructions use indirect addressing. Whereas access to a global pointer uses direct addressing, access to the cell to which it points uses indirect addressing. You can see that the same principle applies to the translation of the printf() statement. Because printf() outputs

*a—that is, the cell to which a points—the DECO instruction at 003F uses indirect addressing.

In summary, to translate a global pointer, the compiler generates code as follows:

> › To allocate storage for the pointer, it generates .BLOCK 2 because an address occupies two bytes.

> › To get the pointer, it generates LDWA with direct addressing.

> › To get the content of the cell pointed to by the pointer, it generates LDWA or LDBA, depending on the type in the cell with indirect addressing.

The translation rules for global pointers

Translating Local Pointers

The program in FIGURE 6.44 is the same as the program in Figure 6.42 except that the pointers a, b, and c are declared to be local instead of global. There is no difference in the output of the program compared to the program where the pointers are declared to be global. However, the memory model is quite different because the pointers are allocated on the run-time stack.

FIGURE 6.44
Translation of local pointers.

High-Order Language
```
#include <stdio.h>
#include <stdlib.h>

int main() {
    int *a, *b, *c;
    a = (int *) malloc(sizeof(int));
    *a = 5;
    b = (int *) malloc(sizeof(int));
    *b = 3;
    c = a;
    a = b;
    *a = 2 + *c;
    printf("*a = %d\n", *a);
    printf("*b = %d\n", *b);
    printf("*c = %d\n", *c);
    return 0;
}
```

(continues)

FIGURE 6.44

Translation of local pointers. (*continued*)

Assembly Language

```
0000   120003           BR       main
                 ;
                 ;******* main()
                 a:       .EQUATE 4          ;local variable #2h
                 b:       .EQUATE 2          ;local variable #2h
                 c:       .EQUATE 0          ;local variable #2h
0003   580006 main:      SUBSP    6,i        ;push #a #b #c
0006   C00002           LDWA     2,i        ;a = (int *) malloc(sizeof(int))
0009   240073           CALL     malloc     ;allocate #2d
000C   EB0004           STWX     a,s
000F   C00005           LDWA     5,i        ;*a = 5
0012   E40004           STWA     a,sf
0015   C00002           LDWA     2,i        ;b = (int *) malloc(sizeof(int))
0018   240073           CALL     malloc     ;allocate #2d
001B   EB0002           STWX     b,s
001E   C00003           LDWA     3,i        ;*b = 3
0021   E40002           STWA     b,sf
0024   C30004           LDWA     a,s        ;c = a
0027   E30000           STWA     c,s
002A   C30002           LDWA     b,s        ;a = b
002D   E30004           STWA     a,s
0030   C00002           LDWA     2,i        ;*a = 2 + *c
0033   640000           ADDA     c,sf
0036   E40004           STWA     a,sf
0039   490061           STRO     msg0,d     ;printf("*a = %d\n", *a)
003C   3C0004           DECO     a,sf
003F   D0000A           LDBA     '\n',i
0042   F1FC16           STBA     charOut,d
0045   490067           STRO     msg1,d     ;printf("*b = %d\n", *b)
0048   3C0002           DECO     b,sf
004B   D0000A           LDBA     '\n',i
004E   F1FC16           STBA     charOut,d
0051   49006D           STRO     msg2,d     ;printf("*c = %d\n", *c)
0054   3C0000           DECO     c,sf
0057   D0000A           LDBA     '\n',i
005A   F1FC16           STBA     charOut,d
005D   500006           ADDSP    6,i        ;pop #c #b #a
```

```
0060   00                  STOP
0061   2A6120 msg0:        .ASCII   "*a = \x00"
       3D2000
0067   2A6220 msg1:        .ASCII   "*b = \x00"
       3D2000
006D   2A6320 msg2:        .ASCII   "*c = \x00"
       3D2000
                        ;
                        ;******* malloc()
                        ;         Precondition: A contains number of bytes
                        ;         Postcondition: X contains pointer to bytes
0073   C9007D malloc:    LDWX     hpPtr,d      ;returned pointer
0076   61007D            ADDA     hpPtr,d      ;allocate from heap
0079   E1007D            STWA     hpPtr,d      ;update hpPtr
007C   01                RET
007D   007F   hpPtr:     .ADDRSS heap          ;address of next free byte
007F   00     heap:      .BLOCK  1             ;first byte in the heap
0080                     .END
```

FIGURE 6.45 shows the memory allocation for the program in Figure 6.44 just before execution of the first `printf()` statement. As with all local variables, a, b, and c are allocated on the run-time stack. Figure 6.44(b) shows their offsets from the top of the stack as 4, 2, and 0. Consequently, the compiler translates

```
int *a, *b, *c;
```

as

```
a: .EQUATE 4   ;local variable #2h
b: .EQUATE 2   ;local variable #2h
c: .EQUATE 0   ;local variable #2h
```

Because a, b, and c are local variables, the compiler generates code to allocate storage for them with SUBSP and deallocates storage with ADDSP.

The compiler translates

```
a = (int *) malloc(sizeof(int));
```

as

```
0006  C00002 LDWA  2,i     ;a = (int *) malloc(sizeof(int))
0009  240073 CALL  malloc  ;allocate #2d
000C  EB0004 STWX  a,s
```

FIGURE 6.45
Memory allocation for Figure 6.44 just before the first `printf()` statement.

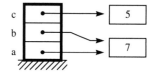

(a) Local pointers at Level HOL6.

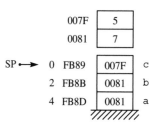

(b) The same local pointers at Level Asmb5.

The LDWA instruction puts 2 in the accumulator in preparation for calling the malloc() function, because an integer occupies two bytes. The CALL instruction invokes malloc(), which allocates the two bytes from the heap and puts their address in the index register. In general, assignments to local variables use stack-relative addressing. Therefore, the STWX instruction uses stack-relative addressing to assign the address to a.

How does the compiler translate the assignment

```
*a = 5;
```

a is a pointer, and the assignment gives 5 to the cell to which a points. a is also a local variable. This situation is identical to the one where a parameter is called by reference in the programs of Figures 6.27 and 6.29. Namely, the address of the operand is on the run-time stack. The compiler translates the assignment statement as

```
000F   C00005   LDWA   5,i     ;*a = 5
0012   E40004   STWA   a,sf
```

where the store instruction uses stack-relative deferred addressing.

The compiler translates the assignment of local pointers the same as it would translate the assignment of any other type of local variable. It translates

```
c = a;
```

as

```
0024   C30004   LDWA   a,s    ;c = a
0027   E30000   STWA   c,s
```

using stack-relative addressing. At this point in the program, a contains 007F, the address of the first cell in the heap. The assignment gives c the same value, the address of the first cell in the heap, so that c points to the same cell to which a points.

The compiler translates

```
*a = 2 + *c;
```

as

```
0030   C00002   LDWA   2,i     ;*a = 2 + *c
0033   640000   ADDA   c,sf
0036   E40004   STWA   a,sf
```

where the add instruction uses stack-relative deferred addressing to access the cell to which c points and the store instruction uses stack-relative deferred addressing to access the cell to which a points. The same principle applies to the translation of printf() statements where the DECO instructions also use stack-relative deferred addressing.

In summary, to access a local pointer, the compiler generates code as follows:

The translation rules for local pointers

> ❯ To allocate storage for the pointer, it generates SUBSP with two bytes for each pointer because an address occupies two bytes.

> ❯ To get the pointer, it generates LDWA with stack-relative addressing.

> ❯ To get the content of the cell pointed to by the pointer, it generates LDWA with stack-relative deferred addressing.

Translating Structures

Structures are the key to data abstraction at Level HOL6, the high-order languages level. They let the programmer consolidate variables with primitive types into a single abstract data type. The compiler provides the struct construct at Level HOL6. At Level Asmb5, the assembly level, a structure is a contiguous group of bytes, much like the bytes of an array. However, all cells of an array must have the same type and, therefore, the same size. Each cell is accessed by the numeric integer value of the index.

With a structure, the cells can have different types and, therefore, different sizes. The C programmer gives each cell, called a *field*, a field name. At Level Asmb5, the field name corresponds to the offset of the field from the first byte of the structure. The field name of a structure corresponds to the index of an array. It should not be surprising that the fields of a structure are accessed much like the elements of an array. Instead of putting the index of the array in the index register, the compiler generates code to put the field offset from the first byte of the structure in the index register. Apart from this difference, the remaining code for accessing a field of a structure is identical to the code for accessing an element of an array.

Fields in a structure

FIGURE 6.46 shows a program that declares a struct named person that has four fields named first, last, age, and gender. It is identical to the program in Figure 2.40. The program declares a global variable name bill that has type person. **FIGURE 6.47** shows the storage allocation for the structure at Levels HOL6 and Asmb5. Fields first, last, and gender have type char and occupy one byte each. Field age has type int and occupies two bytes. Figure 6.47(b) shows the address of each field of the structure. To the left of the address is the offset from the first byte of the structure. The offset of a structure is similar to the offset of an element on the stack except that there is no pointer to the top of the structure that corresponds to SP.

FIGURE 6.46

Translation of a structure. The C program is from Figure 2.40.

High-Order Language

```
#include <stdio.h>

struct person {
   char first;
   char last;
   int age;
   char gender;
};
struct person bill;

int main() {
   scanf("%c%c%d %c", &bill.first, &bill.last, &bill.age, &bill.gender);
   printf("Initials: %c%c\n", bill.first, bill.last);
   printf("Age: %d\n", bill.age);
   printf("Gender: ");
   if (bill.gender == 'm') {
      printf("male\n");
   }
   else {
      printf("female\n");
   }
   return 0;
}
```

Assembly Language

```
0000  120008           BR      main
              first:   .EQUATE 0   ;struct field #1c
              last:    .EQUATE 1   ;struct field #1c
              age:     .EQUATE 2   ;struct field #2d
              gender:  .EQUATE 4   ;struct field #1c
0003  000000 bill:     .BLOCK  5   ;globals #first #last #age #gender
      0000
              ;
              ;******* main()
0008  C80000 main:     LDWX    first,i     ;scanf("%c%c%d %c",
000B  D1FC15           LDBA    charIn,d    ;&bill.first,
000E  F50003           STBA    bill,x
0011  C80001           LDWX    last,i      ;&bill.last,
```

```
0014   D1FC15          LDBA    charIn,d
0017   F50003          STBA    bill,x
001A   C80002          LDWX    age,i        ;&bill.age,
001D   350003          DECI    bill,x
0020   C80004          LDWX    gender,i     ;&bill.gender)
0023   D1FC15          LDBA    charIn,d
0026   F50003          STBA    bill,x
0029   49006C          STRO    msg0,d       ;printf("Initials: %c%c\n",
002C   C80000          LDWX    first,i      ;bill.first,
002F   D50003          LDBA    bill,x
0032   F1FC16          STBA    charOut,d
0035   C80001          LDWX    last,i       ;bill.last)
0038   D50003          LDBA    bill,x
003B   F1FC16          STBA    charOut,d
003E   D0000A          LDBA    '\n',i
0041   F1FC16          STBA    charOut,d
0044   490077          STRO    msg1,d       ;printf("Age:   %d\n",
0047   C80002          LDWX    age,i        ;bill.age)
004A   3D0003          DECO    bill,x
004D   D0000A          LDBA    '\n',i
0050   F1FC16          STBA    charOut,d
0053   49007D          STRO    msg2,d       ;printf("Gender: ")
0056   C80004          LDWX    gender,i     ;if (bill.gender == 'm')
0059   D50003          LDBA    bill,x
005C   B0006D          CPBA    'm',i
005F   1A0068          BRNE    else
0062   490086          STRO    msg3,d       ;printf("male\n")
0065   12006B          BR      endIf
0068   49008C else:    STRO    msg4,d       ;printf("female\n")
006B   00     endIf:   STOP
006C   496E69 msg0:    .ASCII  "Initials: \x00"
       . . .
0077   416765 msg1:    .ASCII  "Age: \x00"
       . . .
007D   47656E msg2:    .ASCII  "Gender: \x00"
       . . .
0086   6D616C msg3:    .ASCII  "male\n\x00"
       . . .
008C   66656D msg4:    .ASCII  "female\n\x00"
       . . .
0094                   .END
```

(continues)

FIGURE 6.46

Translation of a structure. The C program is from Figure 2.40. (*continued*)

Input
```
bj 32 m
```

Output
```
Initials: bj
Age: 32
Gender: male
```

FIGURE 6.47

Memory allocation for Figure 6.46 just after the `scanf()` statement.

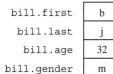

bill.first	b
bill.last	j
bill.age	32
bill.gender	m

(a) A global structure at Level HOL6.

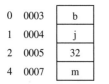

0	0003	b
1	0004	j
2	0005	32
4	0007	m

(b) The same global structure at Asmb5.

The compiler translates

```
struct person {
    char first;
    char last;
    int age;
    char gender;
};
```

with equate dot commands as

```
first:    .EQUATE 0   ;struct field #1c
last:     .EQUATE 1   ;struct field #1c
age:      .EQUATE 2   ;struct field #2d
gender:   .EQUATE 4   ;struct field #1c
```

The name of a field equates to the offset of that field from the `first` byte of the structure. `first` equates to 0 because it is the first byte of the structure. `last` equates to 1 because `first` occupies one byte. `age` equates to 2 because `first` and `last` occupy a total of two bytes. And `gender` equates to 4 because `first`, `last`, and `age` occupy a total of four bytes. The compiler translates the global variable

```
person bill;
```

as

```
0003 000000 bill: .BLOCK 5 ;globals #first #last…
     0000
```

To access a field of a global structure, the compiler generates code to load the index register with the offset of the field from the first byte of the structure. It accesses the field as it would the cell of a global array using indexed addressing. For example, the compiler translates the `scanf()` of `&bill.age` as

```
001A  C80002  LDWX  age,i    ;&bill.age,
001D  350003  DECI  bill,x
```

The load instruction uses immediate addressing to load the offset of field `age` into the index register. The decimal input instruction uses indexed addressing to access the field.

The compiler translates

```
if (bill.gender == 'm')
```

similarly as

```
0056  C80004  LDWX  gender,i ;if (bill.gender == 'm')
0059  D50003  LDBA  bill,x
005C  B0006D  CPBA  'm',i
```

The load word instruction puts the offset of the `gender` field into the index register. The load byte instruction accesses the field of the structure with indexed addressing and puts it into the rightmost byte of the accumulator. Finally, the compare instruction compares `bill.gender` with the letter `m`.

In summary, to access a global structure, the compiler generates code as follows:

> ❭ It equates each field of the structure to its offset from the first byte of the structure.

> ❭ To allocate storage for the structure, it generates `.BLOCK` *tot* where *tot* is the total number of bytes occupied by the structure.

> ❭ To get a field of the structure, it generates `LDWX` to load the offset of the field into the index register with immediate addressing, followed by an `LDBA` or `LDWA` instruction with indexed addressing.

The translation rules for global structures

In the same way that accessing the field of a global structure is similar to accessing the element of a global array, accessing the field of a local structure is similar to accessing the element of a local array. Local structures are allocated on the run-time stack. The name of each field equates to its offset from the first byte of the structure. The name of the local structure equates to its offset from the top of the stack. The compiler generates `SUBSP` to allocate storage for the structure and any other local variables, and `ADDSP` to deallocate storage. It accesses a field of the structure by loading the offset of the field into the index register

The translation rules for local structures

with immediate addressing followed by an instruction with stack-indexed addressing. Translating a program with a local structure is a problem for the student at the end of this chapter.

Translating Linked Data Structures

Programmers frequently combine pointers and structures to implement linked data structures. The `struct` is usually called a *node*, a pointer points to a node, and the node has a field that is a pointer. The pointer field of the node serves as a link to another node in the data structure. FIGURE 6.48 is

FIGURE 6.48
Translation of a linked list. The C program is from Figure 2.42.

High-Order Language

```
#include <stdio.h>
#include <stdlib.h>

struct node {
    int data;
    struct node *next;
};

int main() {
    struct node *first, *p;
    int value;
    first = 0;
    scanf("%d", &value);
    while (value != -9999) {
        p = first;
        first = (struct node *) malloc(sizeof(struct node));
        first->data = value;
        first->next = p;
        scanf("%d", &value);
    }
    for (p = first; p != 0; p = p->next) {
        printf("%d ", p->data);
    }
    return 0;
}
```

Assembly Language

```
0000   120003             BR      main
               data:     .EQUATE 0              ;struct field #2d
               next:     .EQUATE 2              ;struct field #2h
               ;
               ;******* main ()
               first:    .EQUATE 4              ;local variable #2h
               p:        .EQUATE 2              ;local variable #2h
               value:    .EQUATE 0              ;local variable #2d
0003   580006 main:      SUBSP   6,i            ;push #first #p #value
0006   C00000            LDWA    0,i            ;first = 0
0009   E30004            STWA    first,s
000C   330000            DECI    value,s        ;scanf("%d", &value);
000F   C30000 while:     LDWA    value,s        ;while (value != -9999)
0012   A0D8F1            CPWA    -9999,i
0015   18003F            BREQ    endWh
0018   C30004            LDWA    first,s        ;p = first
001B   E30002            STWA    p,s
001E   C00004            LDWA    4,i            ;first = (...) malloc(...)
0021   24006A            CALL    malloc         ;allocate #data #next
0024   EB0004            STWX    first,s
0027   C30000            LDWA    value,s        ;first->data = value
002A   C80000            LDWX    data,i
002D   E70004            STWA    first,sfx
0030   C30002            LDWA    p,s            ;first->next = p
0033   C80002            LDWX    next,i
0036   E70004            STWA    first,sfx
0039   330000            DECI    value,s        ;scanf("%d", &value)
003C   12000F            BR      while
003F   C30004 endWh:     LDWA    first,s        ;for (p = first
0042   E30002            STWA    p,s
0045   C30002 for:       LDWA    p,s            ;p != 0
0048   A00000            CPWA    0,i
004B   180066            BREQ    endFor
004E   C80000            LDWX    data,i         ;printf("%d ", p->data)
0051   3F0002            DECO    p,sfx
0054   D00020            LDBA    ' ',i
0057   F1FC16            STBA    charOut,d
005A   C80002            LDWX    next,i         ;p = p->next)
005D   C70002            LDWA    p,sfx
```

(continues)

FIGURE 6.48
Translation of a linked list. The C program is from Figure 2.42. (*continued*)

```
0060   E30002            STWA      p,s
0063   120045            BR        for
0066   500006 endFor:    ADDSP     6,i          ;pop #value #p #first
0069   00                STOP
               ;
               ;******* malloc()
               ;         Precondition: A contains number of bytes
               ;         Postcondition: X contains pointer to bytes
006A   C90074 malloc:    LDWX      hpPtr,d      ;returned pointer
006D   610074            ADDA      hpPtr,d      ;allocate from heap
0070   E10074            STWA      hpPtr,d      ;update hpPtr
0073   01                RET
0074   0076   hpPtr:     .ADDRSS   heap         ;address of next free byte
0076   00     heap:      .BLOCK    1            ;first byte in the heap
0077                     .END
```

Input
10 20 30 40 -9999

Output
40 30 20 10

a program that implements a linked list data structure. It is identical to the program in Figure 2.42.

The compiler equates the fields of the struct

```
struct node {
    int data;
    node* next;
};
```

to their offsets from the first byte of the struct. data is the first field, with an offset of 0. next is the second field, with an offset of 2 because data occupies two bytes. The translation is

```
data:   .EQUATE 0   ;struct field #2d
next:   .EQUATE 2   ;struct field #2h
```

The compiler translates the local variables

```
node *first, *p;
int value;
```

as it does all local variables. It equates the variable names with their offsets from the top of the run-time stack. The translation is

```
first:   .EQUATE 4   ;local variable #2h
p:       .EQUATE 2   ;local variable #2h
value:   .EQUATE 0   ;local variable #2d
```

FIGURE 6.49(b) shows the offsets for the local variables. The compiler generates SUBSP at 0003 to allocate storage for the locals and ADDSP at 0066 to deallocate storage.

When you use malloc() in C, the computer must allocate enough memory from the heap to store the item to which the pointer points. In this program, a node occupies four bytes. Therefore, the compiler translates

```
first = (struct node *) malloc(sizeof(struct node));
```

by allocating four bytes in the code it generates to call malloc(). The translation is

```
001E  C00004  LDWA  4,i       ;first = (struct node *) …
0021  24006A  CALL  malloc    ;allocate #data #next
0024  EB0004  STWX  first,s
```

FIGURE 6.49
Memory allocation for Figure 6.48 just before scanning 40 from the input stream.

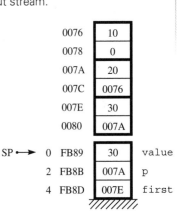

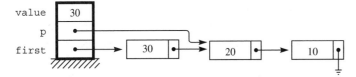

(a) The linked list at Level HOL6.

(b) The same linked list at Level Asmb5.

The load word instruction puts 4 in the accumulator in preparation for the call to `malloc()`. The call instruction calls `malloc()`, which puts the address of the first byte of the allocated node in the index register. When you allocate a structure, you supply symbol trace tags for the fields, #data and #next in this case, to be used by the symbolic debugger. The store word instruction completes the assignment to local variable `first` using stack-relative addressing.

How does the compiler generate code to access the field of a node to which a local pointer points? Remember that a pointer is an address. A local pointer implies that the address of the node is on the run-time stack. Furthermore, the field of a `struct` corresponds to the index of an array. If the address of the first cell of an array is on the run-time stack, you access an element of the array with stack-deferred indexed addressing. That is precisely how you access the field of a node. Instead of putting the value of the index in the index register, you put the offset of the field in the index register. The compiler translates

```
first->data = value;
```

as

```
0027   C30000   LDWA   value,s      ;first->data = value
002A   C80000   LDWX   data,i
002D   E70004   STWA   first,sfx
```

Similarly, it translates

```
first->next = p;
```

as

```
0030   C30002   LDWA   p,s          ;first->next = p
0033   C80002   LDWX   next,i
0036   E70004   STWA   first,sfx
```

To see how stack-deferred indexed addressing works for a local pointer to a node, remember that the CPU computes the operand as

Stack-deferred indexed addressing

$$Oprnd = Mem[Mem[SP + OprndSpec] + X]$$

It adds the stack pointer plus the operand specifier and uses the sum as the address of the first field, to which it adds the index register. Figure 6.49(b) shows the computation state just after STWA at 0036 executes with stack-deferred indexed addressing. The call to `malloc()` has returned the address of the newly allocated node, 007E, and stored it in `first`. The LDWA instruction at 0030 has put the value of p, 007A at this point in the program, in the accumulator. The LDWX instruction at 0033 has put the value of next, offset 2, in the index register. The STWA instruction at 0036 executes with stack-deferred indexed addressing. The operand specifier is 4, the value of first. The computation of the operand is

Mem[Mem[SP + OprndSpec] + X]
Mem[Mem[FB89 + 4] + 2]
Mem[Mem[FB8D] + 2]
Mem[007E + 2]
Mem[0080]

which is the next field of the node to which first points.

In summary, to access a field of a node pointed to by a local pointer, the compiler generates code as follows:

> To specify a field of a node, it generates .EQUATE to equate the offset of the field from the first byte of the node.

> To allocate storage for the node, it generates SUBSP *tot* with immediate addressing, where *tot* is the total number of bytes occupied by the structure.

> To get the field pointed to by p, it generates LDWX with stack-relative addressing to move the value of p into the index register, followed by LDWA or LDBA, depending on the type in the cell with stack-deferred indexed addressing.

The translation rules for accessing the field of a node to which a local pointer points

You should be able to determine how the compiler translates programs with global pointers to nodes. Formulation of the translation rules is an exercise for the student at the end of this chapter. Translation of a C program that has global pointers to nodes is also a problem for the student.

Chapter Summary

A compiler uses conditional branch instructions at the machine level to translate if statements and loops at the high-order languages level. An if/else statement requires a conditional branch instruction to test the if condition and an unconditional branch instruction to branch around the else part. The translation of a while or do loop requires a branch to a previous instruction. The for loop requires, in addition, instructions to initialize and increment the control variable.

The structured programming theorem, proved by Bohm and Jacopini, states that any algorithm containing gotos, no matter how complicated or unstructured, can be written with only nested if statements and while loops. The goto controversy was sparked by Dijkstra's famous letter, which stated that programs without gotos were not only possible but desirable.

The compiler allocates global variables at a fixed location in main memory. Procedures and functions allocate parameters and local variables on the run-time stack. Values are pushed onto the stack by incrementing the stack pointer (SP) and popped off the stack by decrementing SP. The subroutine call instruction pushes the contents of the program counter (PC), which acts as the return address, onto the stack. The subroutine return instruction pops the return address off the stack into the PC. Instructions access global values with direct addressing and values on the run-time stack with stack-relative addressing. A parameter that is called by reference has its address pushed onto the run-time stack. It is accessed with stack-relative deferred addressing. Boolean variables are stored with a value of 0 for false and a value of 1 for true.

Array values are stored in consecutive main memory cells. You access an element of a global array with indexed addressing, and an element of a local array with stack-indexed addressing. In both cases, the index register contains the index value of the array element, which must be multiplied by the number of bytes per cell. An array passed as a parameter always has the address of the first cell of the array pushed onto the run-time stack. You access an element of the array with stack-deferred indexed addressing. The compiler translates the switch statement with an array of addresses, each of which is the address of the first statement of a case. The array of addresses is called a *jump table*.

Pointer and struct types are common building blocks of data structures. A pointer is an address of a memory location in the heap. The malaloc() function allocates memory from the heap. You access a cell to which a global pointer points with indirect addressing. You access a cell to which a local pointer points with stack-relative deferred addressing. A struct has several named fields and is stored as a contiguous group of bytes. You access a field of a global struct with indexed addressing, with the index register containing the offset of the field from the first byte of the struct. Linked data structures commonly have a pointer to a struct called a *node*, which in turn contains a pointer to yet another node. If a local pointer points to a node, you access a field of the node with stack-deferred indexed addressing.

Exercises

Section 6.1

1. Explain the difference in the C memory model between global and local variables. How is each allocated and accessed?

Section 6.2

2. What is an optimizing compiler? When would you want to use one? When would you not want to use one? Explain.

*3. The object code for Figure 6.14 has a CPWA at 000C to test the value of j. Because the program branches to that instruction from the bottom of the loop, why doesn't the compiler generate an LDWA j,d at that point before CPA?

4. Discover the function of the mystery program of Figure 6.16, and state in one short sentence what it does.

5. Read the papers by Bohm and Jacopini and by Dijkstra that are referred to in this chapter and write a summary of them.

Section 6.3

*6. Draw the values just before and just after the second CALL at 001C of Figure 6.18 executes, as they are drawn in Figure 6.19.

7. Figure 6.26 is the run-time stack just after the second return. Draw the run-time stack, as in that figure, that corresponds to the time just before the second return.

Section 6.4

*8. In the Pep/9 program of Figure 6.40, if you enter 4 for Guess, what statement executes after the branch at 0010? Why?

9. Section 6.4 does not show how to access an element from a two-dimensional array. Describe how a two-dimensional array might be stored and the assembly language object code that would be necessary to access an element from it.

Section 6.5

10. What are the translation rules for accessing the field of a node pointed to by a global pointer?

Problems

Section 6.2

11. Translate the following C program to Pep/9 assembly language.

```c
#include <stdio.h>

int main() {
   int number;
   scanf("%d", &number);
   if (number % 2 == 0) {
      printf("Even\n");
   }
   else {
      printf("Odd\n");
   }
   return 0;
}
```

12. Translate the following C program to Pep/9 assembly language.

```c
#include <stdio.h>

const int limit = 5;

int main() {
   int number;
   scanf("%d", &number);
   while (number < limit) {
      number++;
      printf("%d ", number);
   }
   return 0;
}
```

13. Translate the following C program to Pep/9 assembly language.

```c
#include <stdio.h>

int main() {
   char ch;
   scanf("%c", &ch);
   if ((ch >= 'A') && (ch <= 'Z')) {
      printf("A");
   }
```

```
    else if ((ch >= 'a') && (ch <= 'z')) {
        printf("a");
    }
    else {
        printf("$");
    }
    printf("\n");
    return 0;
}
```

14. Translate the C program in Figure 6.12 to Pep/9 assembly language but with the do loop test changed to

```
    while (cop <= driver);
```

15. Translate the following C program to Pep/9 assembly language.

```
#include <stdio.h>

int main() {
    int numItms, j, data, sum;
    scanf("%d", &numItms);
    sum = 0;
    for (j = 1; j <= numItms; j++) {
        scanf("%d", &data);
        sum += data;
    }
    printf("Sum: %d\n", sum);
    return 0;
}
```

Sample Input
```
4 8 -3 7 6
```

Sample Output
```
Sum: 18
```

Section 6.3

16. Translate the following C program to Pep/9 assembly language.

```
#include <stdio.h>

int myAge;

void putNext(int age) {
    int nextYr;
    nextYr = age + 1;
```

```
        printf("Age: %d\n", age);
        printf("Age next year: %d\n", nextYr);
    }

    int main () {
        scanf("%d", &myAge);
        putNext(myAge);
        putNext(64);
        return 0;
    }
```

17. Translate the C program in Problem 16 to Pep/9 assembly language, but declare myAge to be a local variable in main().

18. Translate the following C program to Pep/9 assembly language. It multiplies two integers using a recursive shift-and-add algorithm. mpr stands for *multiplier* and mcand stands for *multiplicand*.

A recursive integer multiplication algorithm

```
#include <stdio.h>

int times(int mpr, int mcand) {
    if (mpr == 0) {
        return 0;
    }
    else if (mpr % 2 == 1) {
        return times(mpr / 2, mcand * 2) + mcand;
    }
    else {
        return times(mpr / 2, mcand * 2);
    }
}

int main() {
    int n, m;
    scanf("%d %d", &n, &m);
    printf("Product: %d\n", times(n, m));
    return 0;
}
```

19. Write a C program that converts an uppercase character to a lowercase character. Declare function

```
char toLower(char ch);
```

to do the conversion. If ch is not an uppercase character, the function should return ch unchanged. If it is an uppercase character, add the difference of 'a' and 'A' to ch as the return value. **(a)** Write your program with a global variable for the actual parameter. Translate your C program to Pep/9 assembly language. **(b)** Write your program with a local variable for the actual parameter. Translate your C program to Pep/9 assembly language.

20. Write a C program that defines

```
int minimum(int j1, int j2)
```

which returns the smaller of `j1` and `j2`. **(a)** Write your program with a global variable for the actual parameter. Translate your C program to Pep/9 assembly language. **(b)** Write your program with a local variable for the actual parameter. Translate your C program to Pep/9 assembly language.

21. Translate to Pep/9 assembly language your C solution from Problem 2.13 that computes a Fibonacci term using a recursive function.

22. Translate to Pep/9 assembly language your C solution from Problem 2.14 that outputs the instructions for the Towers of Hanoi puzzle.

23. The recursive binomial coefficient function in Figure 6.25 can be simplified by omitting `y1` and `y2` as follows:

```
int binCoeff(int n, int k) {
   if ((k == 0) || (n == k)) {
      return 1;
   }
   else {
      return binCoeff(n - 1, k) + binCoeff(n - 1, k - 1);
   }
}
```

Write a Pep/9 assembly language program that calls this function. Keep the value returned from the `binCoeff(n - 1, k)` call on the stack, and push the actual parameters for the call to `binCoeff(n - 1, k - 1)` on top of it. **FIGURE 6.50** shows a trace of the run-time stack where the stack frame contains four words (for retVal, n, k, and retAddr) and the shaded word is the value returned by a function call. The trace is for a call of `binCoeff(3,1)` from the main program.

24. Translate the following C program to Pep/9 assembly language. It multiplies two integers using an iterative shift-and-add algorithm.

```
#include <stdio.h>

int product, n, m;

void times(int *prod, int mpr, int mcand) {
```

An iterative integer multiplication algorithm

FIGURE 6.50
Trace of the run-time stack for Figure 6.25.

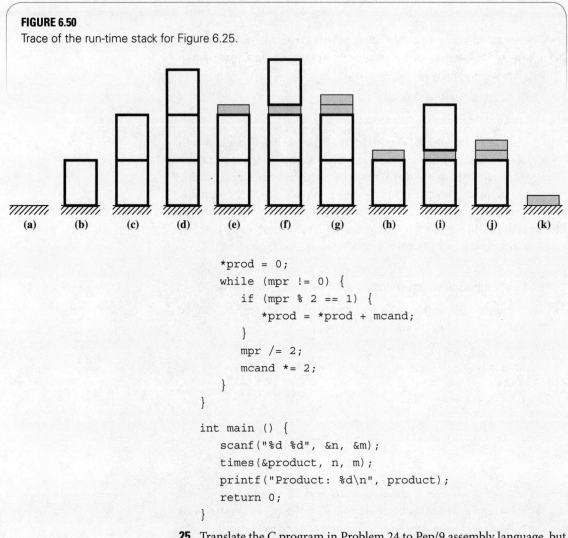

(a)   (b)   (c)   (d)   (e)   (f)   (g)   (h)   (i)   (j)   (k)

```
*prod = 0;
while (mpr != 0) {
    if (mpr % 2 == 1) {
        *prod = *prod + mcand;
    }
    mpr /= 2;
    mcand *= 2;
}
}

int main () {
    scanf("%d %d", &n, &m);
    times(&product, n, m);
    printf("Product: %d\n", product);
    return 0;
}
```

25. Translate the C program in Problem 24 to Pep/9 assembly language, but declare product, n, and m to be local variables in main().

26. **(a)** Rewrite the C program of Figure 2.22 to compute the factorial recursively, but use procedure times() in Problem 24 to do the multiplication. Use one extra local variable in fact() to store the product. **(b)** Translate your C program to Pep/9 assembly language.

Section 6.4

27. Translate the following C program to Pep/9 assembly language:

```
#include <stdio.h>

int list[16];
```

```
int j, numItems;
int temp;

int main() {
    scanf("%d", &numItems);
    for (j = 0; j < numItems; j++) {
        scanf("%d", &list[j]);
    }
    temp = list[0];
    for (j = 0; j < numItems - 1; j++) {
        list[j] = list[j + 1];
    }
    list[numItems - 1] = temp;
    for (j = 0; j < numItems; j++) {
        printf("%d ", list[j]);
    }
    printf("\n");
    return 0;
}
```

Sample Input
```
5
11 22 33 44 55
```

Sample Output
```
22 33 44 55 11
```

The test in the second `for` loop is awkward to translate because of the arithmetic expression on the right side of the < operator. You can simplify the translation by transforming the test to the following mathematically equivalent test:

```
j + 1 < numItems;
```

28. Translate the C program in Problem 27 to Pep/9 assembly language, but declare `list`, `j`, `numItems`, and `temp` to be local variables in `main()`.

29. Translate the following C program to Pep/9 assembly language:

```
#include <stdio.h>

void getList(int ls[], int *n) {
    int j;
    scanf("%d", n);
    for (j = 0; j < *n; j++) {
```

```
            scanf("%d", &ls[j]);
        }
    }

    void putList(int ls[], int n) {
        int j;
        for (j = 0; j < n; j++) {
            printf("%d ", ls[j]);
        }
        printf("\n");
    }

    void rotate(int ls[], int n) {
        int j;
        int temp;
        temp = ls[0];
        for (j = 0; j < n - 1; j++) {
            ls[j] = ls[j + 1];
        }
        ls[n - 1] = temp;
    }

    int main() {
        int list[16];
        int numItems;
        getList(list, &numItems);
        putList(list, numItems);
        rotate(list, numItems);
        putList(list, numItems);
        return 0;
    }
```

Sample Input

```
5
11 22 33 44 55
```

Sample Output

```
11 22 33 44 55
22 33 44 55 11
```

30. Translate the C program in Problem 29 to Pep/9 assembly language, but declare list and numItems to be global variables.

31. Translate to Pep/9 assembly language the C program from Figure 2.25 that adds four values in an array using a recursive function.

32. Translate to Pep/9 assembly language the C program from Figure 2.32 that reverses the elements of a local array using a recursive procedure. Initialize word to "star" with five pairs of load byte, store byte instructions (including the zero sentinel), and translate the printf() statement with STRO using stack-relative addressing.

33. Translate the following C program to Pep/9 assembly language:

```
#include <stdio.h>

int main () {
    int guess;
    printf("Pick a number 0..3: ");
    scanf("%d", &guess);
    switch (guess) {
        case 0: case 1: printf("Too low"); break;
        case 2: printf("Right on"); break;
        case 3: printf("Too high");
    }
    printf("\n");
    return 0;
}
```

The program is identical to Figure 6.40 except that two of the cases execute the same code. Your jump table must have exactly four entries, but your program must have only three case symbols and three cases.

34. Translate the following C program to Pep/9 assembly language.

```
#include <stdio.h>

int main () {
    int guess;
    printf("Pick a number 0..3: ");
    scanf("%d", &guess);
    switch (guess) {
        case 0: printf("Not close"); break;
        case 1: printf("Too low"); break;
        case 2: printf("Right on"); break;
        case 3: printf("Too high"); break;
        default: printf("Illegal input");
    }
```

```
        printf("\n");
        return 0;
}
```

Section 6.5

35. Translate to Pep/9 assembly language the C program from Figure 6.46 that accesses the fields of a structure, but declare `bill` as a local variable in `main()`.

36. Translate to Pep/9 assembly language the C program from Figure 6.48 that manipulates a linked list, but declare `first`, `p`, and `value` as global variables.

37. Insert the following C code fragment in `main()` of Figure 6.48 just before the `return` statement:

```
sum = 0; p = first;
while (p != 0) {
    sum += p->data;
    p = p->next;
}
printf("Sum: %d\n", sum);
```

and translate the complete program to Pep/9 assembly language. Declare `sum` to be a local variable along with the other locals as follows:

```
struct node *first, *p;
int value, sum;
```

38. Insert the following C code fragment between the declaration of `node` and `main()` in Figure 6.48:

```
void reverse(struct node *list) {
    if (list != 0) {
        reverse(list->next);
        printf("%d ", list->data);
    }
}
```

and the following code fragment in `main()` just before the `return` statement:

```
printf("\n");
reverse(first);
printf("\n");
```

Translate the complete C program to Pep/9 assembly language. The added code outputs the linked list in reverse order.

39. Insert the following C code fragment in `main()` of Figure 6.48 just before the `return` statement:

```
first2 = 0; p2 = 0;
for (p = first; p != 0; p = p->next) {
   p2 = first2;
   first2 = (struct node *) malloc(sizeof (struct node));
   first2->data = p->data;
   first2->next = p2;
}
for (p2 = first2; p2 != 0; p2 = p2->next) {
   printf("%d ", p2->data);
}
printf("\n");
```

Declare `first2` and `p2` to be local variables along with the other locals as follows:

```
struct node *first, *p, *first2, *p2;
int value;
```

Translate the complete program to Pep/9 assembly language. The added code creates a copy of the first list in reverse order and outputs it.

40. Translate to Pep/9 assembly language your C solution from Problem 2.18 that inputs an unordered list of integers with –9999 as a sentinel into a binary search tree, then outputs them with an inorder traversal of the tree.

41. This problem is a project to write a simulator in C for the Pep/9 computer.

(a) Write a loader that takes a Pep/9 object file in standard format and loads it into the main memory of a simulated Pep/9 computer. Declare main memory as an array of integers as follows:

```
int Mem[65536]; // Pep/9 main memory
```

Take your input as a string of characters from the standard input. Write a memory dump function that outputs the content of main memory as a sequence of decimal integers that represents the program. For example, if the input is

```
D1 00 0D F1 FC 16 D1 00 0E F1 FC 16 00 48 69 zz
```

as in Figure 4.42, then the program should convert the hexadecimal numbers to integers and store them in the first 15 cells of Mem. The output should be the corresponding integer values as follows:

```
209 0 13 241 252 22 209 0 14 241 252 22 0 72 105
```

(b) Implement instructions LDBr, STBr, and STOP and addressing modes immediate and direct. Use Figure 4.32 as a guide for implementing the von Neumann execution cycle. If an instruction stores a byte to Mem[FC16], output the corresponding character to the standard output stream. If an instruction loads a byte from Mem[FC15], input the corresponding character from the standard input stream. For example, with the input as in part (a), the output should be Hi.

(c) Implement DECO as if it were a native instruction. That is, you should not implement the trap mechanism described in Section 8.2.

(d) Implement instructions BR, LDWr, STWr, SUBSP, and ADDSP and addressing mode stack relative. Test your implementation by assembling the program of Figure 6.1 with the Pep/9 assembler, then inputting the hexadecimal program into your simulator. The output should be BMW335i.

(e) Implement instructions ADDr, SUBr, ASLr, and ASRr. Implement instructions DECI and STRO as if they were native instructions. Take the input from the standard input stream and send your output to the standard output stream of C. Test your implementation by executing the program of Figure 6.4.

(f) Implement the conditional branch instructions BRLE, BRLT, BREQ, BRNE, BRGE, BRGT, BRV; the unary instructions NOTr and NEGr; and the compare instructions CPWr and CPBr. Test your implementation by executing the programs of Figures 6.6, 6.8, 6.10, 6.12, and 6.14.

(g) Implement instructions CALL and RET. Test your implementation by executing the programs of Figures 6.18, 6.21, 6.23, and 6.25.

(h) Implement instruction MOVSPA and addressing mode stack relative deferred. Test your implementation by executing the programs of Figures 6.27 and 6.29.

(i) Implement addressing modes indexed, stack-indexed, and stack-deferred indexed. Test your implementation by executing the programs of Figures 6.34, 6.36, 6.38, 6.40, and 6.48.

(j) Implement the indirect addressing mode. Test your implementation by executing the program of Figure 6.42.

CHAPTER 7

Language Translation Principles

The fundamental question of computer science

You are now multilingual because you understand at least four languages—English, C, Pep/9 assembly language, and machine language. The first is a natural language, and the other three are artificial languages.

Keeping that in mind, let's turn to the fundamental question of computer science, which is: What can be automated? We use computers to automate everything from writing payroll checks to correcting spelling errors in manuscripts. Although computer science has been moderately successful in automating the translation of natural languages, say from German to English, it has been quite successful in translating artificial languages. You have already learned how to translate between the three artificial languages of C, Pep/9 assembly language, and machine language. Compilers and assemblers automate this translation process for artificial languages.

Automatic translation

Because each level of a computer system has its own artificial language, the automatic translation between these languages is at the very heart of computer science. Computer scientists have developed a rich body of theory about artificial languages and the automation of the translation process. This chapter introduces the theory and shows how it applies to the translation of C and Pep/9 assembly language.

Syntax and semantics

Two attributes of an artificial language are its syntax and semantics. A computer language's *syntax* is the set of rules that a program listing must obey to be declared a valid program of the language. Its *semantics* is the meaning or logic behind the valid program. Operationally, a syntactically correct program will be successfully translated by a translator program. The semantics of the language determine the result produced by the translated program when the object program is executed.

The part of an automatic translator that compares the source program with the language's syntax is called the *parser*. The part that assigns meaning to the source program is called the *code generator*. Most computer science theory applies to the syntactic rather than the semantic part of the translation process.

Three common techniques to describe a language's syntax are

Techniques to specify syntax

> Grammars

> Finite-state machines

> Regular expressions

This chapter introduces grammars and finite-state machines. It shows how to construct a software finite-state machine to aid in the parsing process. The last section shows a complete program, including code generation, that automatically translates between two languages. Space limitations preclude a presentation of regular expressions.

7.1 Languages, Grammars, and Parsing

Every language has an alphabet. Formally, an *alphabet* is a finite, nonempty set of characters. For example, the C alphabet is the nonempty set

```
{  a,  b,  c,  d,  e,  f,  g,  h,  i,  j,  k,  l,  m,  n,
   o,  p,  q,  r,  s,  t,  u,  v,  w,  x,  y,  z,  A,  B,
   C,  D,  E,  F,  G,  H,  I,  J,  K,  L,  M,  N,  O,  P,
   Q,  R,  S,  T,  U,  V,  W,  X,  Y,  Z,  0,  1,  2,  3,
   4,  5,  6,  7,  8,  9,  +,  -,  *,  /,  =,  <,  >,  [,
   ],  (,  ),  {,  },  .,  ,,  :,  ;,  &,  !,  %,  ',  ",
   _,  \,  #,  ?,  ^,  |,  ~}
```

The C alphabet

The alphabet for Pep/9 assembly language is similar except for the punctuation characters, as shown in the following set:

```
{  a,  b,  c,  d,  e,  f,  g,  h,  i,  j,  k,  l,  m,  n,
   o,  p,  q,  r,  s,  t,  u,  v,  w,  x,  y,  z,  A,  B,
   C,  D,  E,  F,  G,  H,  I,  J,  K,  L,  M,  N,  O,  P,
   Q,  R,  S,  T,  U,  V,  W,  X,  Y,  Z,  0,  1,  2,  3,
   4,  5,  6,  7,  8,  9,  \,  .,  ,,  :,  ;,  ',  "}
```

The Pep/9 assembly language alphabet

Another example of an alphabet is the alphabet for the language of real numbers, not in scientific notation. It is the set

```
{  0,  1,  2,  3,  4,  5,  6,  7,  8,  9,  +,  -,  .  }
```

The alphabet for real numbers

Concatenation

An abstract data type is a set of possible values together with a set of operations on the values. Notice that an alphabet is a set of values. The pertinent operation on this set of values is *concatenation*, which is simply the joining of two or more characters to form a string. An example from the C alphabet is the concatenation of ! and = to form the string !=. In the Pep/9 assembly alphabet, you can concatenate 0 and x to make 0x, the prefix of a hexadecimal constant. And in the language of real numbers, you can concatenate -, 2, 3, ., and 7 to make -23.7.

Concatenation

Concatenation applies not only to individual characters in an alphabet to construct a string, but also to strings concatenated to construct longer strings. From the C alphabet, you can concatenate void, printBar, and (int n) to produce the procedure heading

```
void printBar(int n)
```

The length of a string is the number of characters in the string. The string void has a length of four. The string of length zero, called the *empty string*, is denoted by the Greek letter ε to distinguish it from the English characters in an alphabet. Its concatenation properties are

The empty string

$$\varepsilon x = x\varepsilon = x$$

where x is a string. The empty string is useful for describing syntax rules.

In mathematics terminology, ε is the identity element for the concatenation operation. In general, an *identity element*, i, for an operation is one that does not change a value, x, when x is operated on by i.

Identity elements

Example 7.1   One is the identity element for multiplication because

$$1 \cdot x = x \cdot 1 = x$$

and true is the identity element for the AND operation because

$$\text{true AND } q = q \text{ AND true} = q. \qquad \blacksquare$$

Languages

The closure of an alphabet

If T is an alphabet, the closure of T, denoted T^*, is the set of all possible strings formed by concatenating elements from T. T^* is extremely large. For example, if T is the set of characters and punctuation marks of the English alphabet, T^* includes all the sentences in the collected works of Shakespeare, in the English Bible, and in all the English encyclopedias ever published. It includes all strings of those characters ever printed in all the libraries in all the world throughout history, and then some.

Not only does it include all those meaningful strings, it includes meaningless ones as well. Here are some elements of T^* for the English alphabet:

```
To be or not to be, that is the question.
Go fly a kite.
Here over highly toward?
alkeu jfoj ,9nm20mfq23jk l?x!jeo
```

Some elements of T^* where T is the alphabet of the language for real numbers are

```
-2894.01
24
+78.3.80
--234---
6
```

You can easily construct many other elements of T^* with the two alphabets just mentioned. Because strings can be infinitely long, the closure of any alphabet has an infinite number of elements.

What is a language? In the examples of T^* that were just presented, some of the strings are in the language and some are not. In the English example, the first two strings are valid English sentences; that is, they are in the language. The last two strings are not in the language. A *language* is a subset of the closure of its alphabet. Of the infinite number of strings you can construct from concatenating strings of characters from its alphabet, only some will be in the language.

The definition of a language

Example 7.2   Consider the following two elements of T^*, where T is the alphabet for the C language:

```
#include <stdio.h>
int main() {
    printf("Valid");
    return 0;
}

#include <stdio.h>
int main(); {
    printf("Valid");
    return 0;
}
```

The first element of T^* is in the C language, but the second is not because it has a syntax error. ∎

Grammars

To define a language, you need a way to specify which of the many elements of T^* are in the language and which are not. A *grammar* is a system that specifies how you can concatenate the characters of alphabet T to form a legal string in a language. Formally, a grammar contains four parts:

> N, a nonterminal alphabet

> T, a terminal alphabet

> P, a set of rules of production

> S, the start symbol, which is an element of N

The four parts of a grammar

An element from the nonterminal alphabet, N, represents a string of characters from the terminal alphabet, T. A nonterminal symbol is frequently enclosed in angle brackets, <>. You see the terminal symbols when you read the language. You do not see the nonterminal symbols. The rules of production use the nonterminals to describe the structure of the language, which may not be readily apparent when you read the language.

Example 7.3   In the C grammar, the nonterminal <compound-statement> might represent the following group of terminals:

```
{
  int i;
  scanf ("%d", &i);
  i++;
  printf ("%d", i);
}
```

The listing of a C program always contains terminals, never nonterminals. You would never see a C listing like this:

```
#include <stdio.h>
main ()
<compound-statement>
```

The nonterminal symbol, <compound-statement>, is useful for describing the structure of a C program.   ∎

Every grammar has a special nonterminal called the *start symbol*, *S*. Notice that *N* is a set, but *S* is not. *S* is one of the elements of set *N*. The start symbol, along with the rules of production, *P*, enables you to decide whether a string of terminals is a valid sentence in the language. If, starting from *S*, you can generate the string of terminals using the rules of production, then the string is a valid sentence.

A Grammar for C Identifiers

The grammar in (FIGURE 7.1) specifies a C identifier. Even though a C identifier can use any uppercase or lowercase letter or digit, to keep the example small, this grammar permits only the letters a, b, and c and the digits 1, 2, and 3. You know the rules for constructing an identifier. The first character must be a letter, and the remaining characters, if any, can be letters or digits in any combination.

This grammar has three nonterminals, namely, <identifier>, <letter>, and <digit>. The start symbol is <identifier>, one of the elements from the set of nonterminals.

FIGURE 7.1
A grammar for C identifiers.

$N = \{$ <identifier> , <letter> , <digit> $\}$
$T = \{$ a , b , c , 1 , 2 , 3 $\}$
$P = $ the productions
    1. <identifier> $\rightarrow$ <letter>
    2. <identifier> $\rightarrow$ <identifier> <letter>
    3. <identifier> $\rightarrow$ <identifier> <digit>
    4. <letter> $\rightarrow$ a
    5. <letter> $\rightarrow$ b
    6. <letter> $\rightarrow$ c
    7. <digit> $\rightarrow$ 1
    8. <digit> $\rightarrow$ 2
    9. <digit> $\rightarrow$ 3
$S = $ <identifier>

The rules of production are of the form

Productions

$$A \rightarrow w$$

where A is a nonterminal and w is a string of terminals and nonterminals. The symbol $\rightarrow$ means "produces." You should read production rule number 3 in Figure 7.1 as, "An identifier produces an identifier followed by a digit."

The grammar specifies the language by a process called a *derivation*. To derive a valid sentence in the language, you begin with the start symbol and substitute for nonterminals from the rules of production until you get a string of terminals. The following is a derivation of the identifier cab3 from this grammar. The symbol $\Rightarrow$ means "derives in one step."

Derivations

<identifier>	$\Rightarrow$ <identifier> <digit>	Rule 3
	$\Rightarrow$ <identifier> 3	Rule 9
	$\Rightarrow$ <identifier> <letter> 3	Rule 2
	$\Rightarrow$ <identifier> b 3	Rule 5
	$\Rightarrow$ <identifier> <letter> b 3	Rule 2
	$\Rightarrow$ <identifier> a b 3	Rule 4
	$\Rightarrow$ <letter> a b 3	Rule 1
	$\Rightarrow$ c a b 3	Rule 6

Next to each derivation step is the production rule on which the substitution is based. For example, Rule 2,

<identifier> → <letter>

was used to substitute for <identifier> in the derivation step

<identifier> 3 ⇒ <identifier> <letter> 3

You should read this derivation step as "Identifier followed by 3 derives in one step identifier followed by letter followed by 3."

Analogous to the closure operation on an alphabet is the closure of the derivation operation. The symbol ⇒* means "derives in zero or more steps." You can summarize the previous eight derivation steps as

<identifier> ⇒* c a b 3

This derivation proves that cab3 is a valid identifier because it can be derived from the start symbol, <identifier>. A language specified by a grammar consists of all the strings derivable from the start symbol using the rules of production. The grammar provides an operational test for membership in the language. If it is impossible to derive a string, the string is not in the language.

A Grammar for Signed Integers

The grammar in **FIGURE 7.2** defines the language of signed integers, where d represents a decimal digit. The start symbol is I, which stands for *integer*. F is the first character, which is an optional sign, and M is the magnitude.

Sometimes the rules of production are not numbered and are combined on one line to conserve space on the printed page. You can write the rules of production for this grammar as

```
I  →  FM
F  →  +  |  -  |  ε
M  →  d  |  dM
```

where the vertical bar, |, is the alternation operator and is read as "or." Read the last line as "M produces d, or d followed by M."

Here are some derivations of valid signed integers in this grammar:

I ⇒ FM	I ⇒ FM	I ⇒ FM
⇒ FdM	⇒ FdM	⇒ FdM
⇒ FddM	⇒ Fdd	⇒ FddM
⇒ Fddd	⇒ dd	⇒ FdddM
⇒ -ddd		⇒ Fdddd
		⇒ +dddd

Note how the last step of the second derivation uses the empty string to derive dd from Fdd. It uses the production F → ε and the fact that εd = d.

FIGURE 7.2

A grammar for signed integers.

$N = \{I, F, M\}$
$T = \{+, -, d\}$
P = the productions
   1. I → FM
   2. F → +
   3. F → -
   4. F → ε
   5. M → dM
   6. M → d
$S = I$

This production rule with the empty string is a convenient way to express the fact that a positive or negative sign in front of the magnitude is optional.

Some illegal strings from this grammar are `ddd+`, `+-ddd`, and `ddd+dd`. Try to derive these strings from the grammar to convince yourself that they are not in the language. Can you informally prove from the rules of production that each of these strings is not in the language?

The productions in both of the sample grammars have recursive rules in which a nonterminal is defined in terms of itself. Rule 3 of Figure 7.1 defines an <identifier> in terms of an <identifier> as

Recursive productions

<identifier> → <identifier> <digit>

and Rule 5 of Figure 7.2 defines M in terms of M as

M → dM

Recursive rules produce languages with an infinite number of legal sentences. To derive an identifier, you can keep substituting <identifier> <digit> for <identifier> as long as you like to produce an arbitrarily long identifier.

As in all recursive definitions, there must be an escape hatch to provide the basis for the definition. Otherwise, the sequence of substitutions for the nonterminal could never stop. The rule M → d provides the basis for M in Figure 7.2.

A Context-Sensitive Grammar

The production rules for the previous grammars always contain a single nonterminal on the left side. The grammar in **FIGURE 7.3** has some production rules with both a terminal and nonterminal on the left side.

Here is a derivation of a string of terminals with this grammar:

A ⇒ aABC	Rule 1
⇒ aaABCBC	Rule 1
⇒ aaabCBCBC	Rule 2
⇒ aaabBCCBC	Rule 3
⇒ aaabBCBCC	Rule 3
⇒ aaabBBCCC	Rule 3
⇒ aaabbBCCC	Rule 4
⇒ aaabbbCCC	Rule 4
⇒ aaabbbcCC	Rule 5
⇒ aaabbbccC	Rule 6
⇒ aaabbbccc	Rule 6

An example of a substitution in this derivation is using Rule 5 in the step

aaabbbCCC ⇒ aaabbbcCC

FIGURE 7.3
A context-sensitive grammar.

$N = \{A, B, C\}$
$T = \{a, b, c\}$
P = the productions
    1. A → aABC
    2. A → abC
    3. CB → BC
    4. bB → bb
    5. bC → bc
    6. cC → cc
$S = A$

Rule 5 says that you can substitute c for C, but only if the C has a b to its left.

In the English language, to quote a phrase out of context means to quote it without regard to the other phrases that surround it. Rule 5 is an example of a context-sensitive rule. It does not permit the substitution of C by c unless C is in the proper context—namely, immediately to the right of a b.

Context-sensitive grammars

Loosely speaking, a *context-sensitive grammar* is one in which the production rules may contain more than just a single nonterminal on the left side. In contrast, grammars that are restricted to a single nonterminal on the left side of every production rule are called *context-free*. (The precise theoretical definitions of *context-sensitive* and *context-free grammars* are more restrictive than these definitions. For the sake of simplicity, this chapter uses the previous definitions, although you should be aware that a more rigorous description of the theory would not define them as we have here.)

Some other examples of valid strings in the language specified by this grammar are abc, aabbcc, and aaaabbbbcccc. Two examples of invalid strings are aabc and cba. You should derive these valid strings and also try to derive the invalid strings to prove their invalidity to yourself. Some experimentation with the rules should convince you that the language is the set of strings that begins with one or more a's, followed by an equal number of b's, followed by the same number of c's. Mathematically, this language, *L*, can be written

$$L = \{a^n b^n c^n \mid n > 0\}$$

which you should read as "The language *L* is the set of strings $a^n b^n c^n$ such that *n* is greater than 0." The notation a^n means the concatenation of *n* a's.

The Parsing Problem

Deriving valid strings from a grammar is fairly straightforward. You can arbitrarily pick some nonterminal on the right side of the current intermediate string and select rules for the substitution repeatedly until you get a string of terminals. Such random derivations can give you many sample strings from the language.

An automatic translator, however, has a more difficult task. You give a translator a string of terminals that is supposed to be a valid sentence in an artificial language. Before the translator can produce the object code, it must determine whether the string of terminals is indeed valid. The only way to determine whether a string is valid is to derive it from the start symbol of the grammar. The translator must attempt such a derivation. If it succeeds, it knows the string is a valid sentence. The problem of determining whether a given string of terminal characters is valid for a specific grammar is called *parsing* and is illustrated schematically in **FIGURE 7.4** .

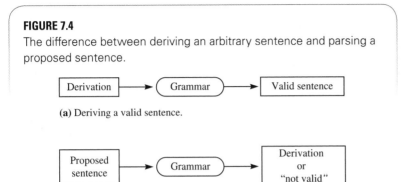

FIGURE 7.4
The difference between deriving an arbitrary sentence and parsing a proposed sentence.

(a) Deriving a valid sentence.

(b) The parsing problem.

Parsing a given string is more difficult than deriving an arbitrary valid string. The parsing problem is a form of searching. The parsing algorithm must search for just the right sequence of substitutions to derive the proposed string. Not only must it find the derivation if the proposed string is valid, but it must also admit the possibility that the proposed string may not be valid. If you look for a lost diamond ring in your room and do not find it, that does not mean the ring is not in your room. It may simply mean that you did not look in the right place. Similarly, if you try to find a derivation for a proposed string and do not find it, how do you know that such a derivation does not exist? A translator must be able to prove that no derivation exists if the proposed string is not valid.

A Grammar for Expressions

To see some of the difficulty a parser may encounter, consider ⟨ **FIGURE 7.5** ⟩, which shows a grammar that describes an arithmetic infix expression. Suppose you are given the string of terminals

```
( a * a ) + a
```

and the production rules of this grammar, and are asked to parse the proposed string. The correct parse is

$E \Rightarrow E + T$	Rule 1
$\Rightarrow T + T$	Rule 2
$\Rightarrow F + T$	Rule 4
$\Rightarrow (E) + T$	Rule 5
$\Rightarrow (T) + T$	Rule 2
$\Rightarrow (T * F) + T$	Rule 3
$\Rightarrow (F * F) + T$	Rule 4

FIGURE 7.5
A grammar for expressions. Nonterminal E represents the expression. T represents a term and F a factor in the expression.

$N = \{ E, T, F \}$
$T = \{ +, *, (,), a \}$
$P =$ the productions
    1. $E \rightarrow E + T$
    2. $E \rightarrow T$
    3. $T \rightarrow T * F$
    4. $T \rightarrow F$
    5. $F \rightarrow (E)$
    6. $F \rightarrow a$
$S = E$

$\Rightarrow$ (a * F) + T	Rule 6
$\Rightarrow$ (a * a) + T	Rule 6
$\Rightarrow$ (a * a) + F	Rule 4
$\Rightarrow$ (a * a) + a	Rule 6

The reason this could be difficult is that you might make a bad decision early in the parse that looks plausible at the time but that leads to a dead end. For example, you might spot the "(" in the string that you were given and choose Rule 5 immediately. Your attempted parse might be

$E \Rightarrow T$	Rule 2
$\Rightarrow F$	Rule 4
$\Rightarrow$ (E)	Rule 5
$\Rightarrow$ (T)	Rule 2
$\Rightarrow$ (T * F)	Rule 3
$\Rightarrow$ (F * F)	Rule 4
$\Rightarrow$ (a * F)	Rule 6
$\Rightarrow$ (a * a)	Rule 6

Until now, you have seemingly made progress toward your goal of parsing the original expression because the intermediate string looks more like the original string at each successive step of the derivation. Unfortunately, now you are stuck because there is no way to get the + a part of the original string.

After reaching this dead end, you may be tempted to conclude that the proposed string is invalid, but that would be a mistake. Just because you cannot find a derivation does not mean that such a derivation does not exist.

One interesting aspect of a parse is that it can be represented as a tree. The start symbol is the root of the tree. Each interior node of the tree is a nonterminal, and each leaf is a terminal. The children of an interior node are the symbols from the right side of the production rule substituted for the parent node in the derivation. The tree is called a *syntax tree*, for obvious reasons. **FIGURE 7.6** shows the syntax tree for (a * a) + a with the grammar in Figure 7.5, and **FIGURE 7.7** shows it for dd with the grammar in Figure 7.2.

A C Subset Grammar

The rules of production for the grammar in **FIGURE 7.8** specify a small subset of the C language. The only primitive types in this language are integer and character. The language has no provision for constant or type declarations and does not permit reference parameters. It also omits switch and for statements. Despite these limitations, it gives an idea of how the syntax for a real language is formally defined.

FIGURE 7.6
The syntax tree for the parse of (a * a) + a in Figure 7.5.

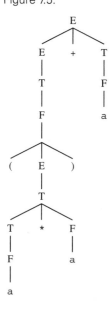

FIGURE 7.7
The syntax tree for the parse of dd in Figure 7.2.

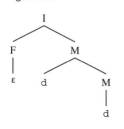

FIGURE 7.8
A grammar for a subset of the C language.

```
<translation-unit> →
    <external-declaration>
    | <translation-unit> <external-declaration>
<external-declaration> →
    <function-definition>
    | <declaration>
<function-definition> →
    <type-specifier> <identifier> ( <parameter-list> ) <compound-statement>
    | <identifier> ( <parameter-list> ) <compound-statement>
<declaration> → <type-specifier> <declarator-list> ;
<type-specifier> → void | char | int
<declarator-list> →
    <identifier>
    | <declarator-list> , <identifier>
<parameter-list> →
    ε
    | <parameter-declaration>
    | <parameter-list> , <parameter-declaration>
<parameter-declaration> → <type-specifier> <identifier>
<compound-statement> → { <declaration-list> <statement-list> }
<declaration-list> →
    ε
    | <declaration>
    | <declaration-list> <declaration>
<statement-list> →
    ε
    | <statement>
    | <statement-list> <statement>
<statement> →
    <compound-statement>
    | <expression-statement>
    | <selection-statement>
    | <iteration-statement>
<expression-statement> → <expression> ;
<selection-statement> →
    if ( <expression> ) <statement>
```

(continues)

FIGURE 7.8

A grammar for a subset of the C language. (*continued*)

```
            | if ( <expression> ) <statement> else <statement>
    <iteration-statement> →
            while ( <expression> ) <statement>
            | do <statement> while ( <expression> ) ;
    <expression> →
            <relational-expression>
            | <identifier> = <expression>
    <relational-expression> →
            <additive-expression>
            | <relational-expression> < <additive-expression>
            | <relational-expression> > <additive-expression>
            | <relational-expression> <= <additive-expression>
            | <relational-expression> >= <additive-expression>
    <additive-expression> →
            <multiplicative-expression>
            | <additive-expression> + <multiplicative-expression>
            | <additive-expression> – <multiplicative-expression>
    <multiplicative-expression> →
            <unary-expression>
            | <multiplicative-expression> * <unary-expression>
            | <multiplicative-expression> / <unary-expression>
    <unary-expression> →
            <primary-expression>
            | <identifier> ( <argument-expression-list> )
    <primary-expression> →
            <identifier>
            | <constant>
            | ( <expression> )
    <argument-expression-list> →
            <expression>
            | <argument-expression-list> , <expression>
    <constant> →
            <integer-constant>
            | <character-constant>
    <integer-constant> →
            <digit>
            | <integer-constant> <digit>
```

```
<character-constant> → ' <letter> '
<identifier> →
      <letter>
    | <identifier> <letter>
    | <identifier> <digit>
<letter> →
      a | b | c | d | e | f | g | h | i | j | k | l | m |
      n | o | p | q | r | s | t | u | v | w | x | y | z |
      A | B | C | D | E | F | G | H | I | J | K | L | M |
      N | O | P | Q | R | S | T | U | V | W | X | Y | Z
<digit> →
      0 | 1 | 2 | 3 | 4 | 5 | 6 | 7 | 8 | 9
```

The nonterminals for this grammar are enclosed in angle brackets, <>. Any symbol not in brackets is in the terminal alphabet and may literally appear in a C program listing. The start symbol for this grammar is the nonterminal <translation-unit>.

The specification of a programming language by the rules of production of its grammar is called *Backus Naur Form*, abbreviated *BNF*. In BNF, the production symbol → is sometimes written ::=. The Algol 60 language, designed in 1960, popularized BNF.

Backus Naur Form (BNF)

The following example of a parse with this grammar shows that

```
while ( a <= 9 )
     S1;
```

is a valid <statement>, assuming that *S1* is a valid <expression>. The parse consists of the derivation in **FIGURE 7.9**.

FIGURE 7.10 shows the corresponding syntax tree for this parse. The nonterminal <statement> is the root of the tree because the purpose of the parse is to show that the string is a valid <statement>.

With this example in mind, consider the task of a C compiler. The compiler has programmed into it a set of production rules similar to the rules of Figure 7.8. A programmer submits a text file containing the source program, a long string of terminals, to the compiler. First, the compiler must determine whether the string of terminal characters represents a valid C translation unit. If the string is a valid <translation-unit>, then the compiler must generate the corresponding object code in a lower-level language. If it is not, the compiler must issue an appropriate syntax error.

FIGURE 7.9

The derivation of nonterminal <statement> `while ( a <= 9 )` *S1*; for the grammar in Figure 7.8.

```
<statement>
    ⇒  <iteration-statement>
    ⇒  while ( <expression> ) <statement>
    ⇒  while ( <relational-expression> ) <statement>
    ⇒  while ( <relational-expression> <= <additive-expression> ) <statement>
    ⇒  while ( <additive-expression> <= <additive-expression> ) <statement>
    ⇒  while ( <multiplicative-expression> <= <additive-expression> ) <statement>
    ⇒  while ( <unary-expression> <= <additive-expression> ) <statement>
    ⇒  while ( <primary-expression> <= <additive-expression> ) <statement>
    ⇒  while ( <identifier> <= <additive-expression> ) <statement>
    ⇒  while ( <letter> <= <additive-expression> ) <statement>
    ⇒  while ( a <= <additive-expression> ) <statement>
    ⇒  while ( a <= <multiplicative-expression> ) <statement>
    ⇒  while ( a <= <unary-expression> ) <statement>
    ⇒  while ( a <= <primary-expression> ) <statement>
    ⇒  while ( a <= <constant> ) <statement>
    ⇒  while ( a <= <integer-constant> ) <statement>
    ⇒  while ( a <= <digit> ) <statement>
    ⇒  while ( a <= 9 ) <statement>
    ⇒  while ( a <= 9 ) <expression-statement>
    ⇒  while ( a <= 9 ) <expression> ;
    ⇒* while ( a <= 9 ) S1;
```

There are literally hundreds of rules of production in the standard C grammar. Imagine what a job the C compiler has, sorting through those rules every time you submit a program to it! Fortunately, computer science theory has developed to the point where parsing is not difficult for a compiler. When designed using the theory, C compilers can parse a program in a way that guarantees they will correctly decide which production to use for the substitution at every step of the derivation. If their parsing algorithm does not find the derivation of <translation-unit> to match the source, they can prove that such a derivation does not exist and that the proposed source program must have a syntax error.

Code generation is more difficult than parsing for compilers. The reason is that the object code must run on a specific machine produced by a specific manufacturer. Because every manufacturer's machine has a different architecture with different instruction sets, code-generation techniques

FIGURE 7.10

The syntax tree for a parse of nonterminal <statement> while (a <= 9) *S1;* for the grammar in Figure 7.9.

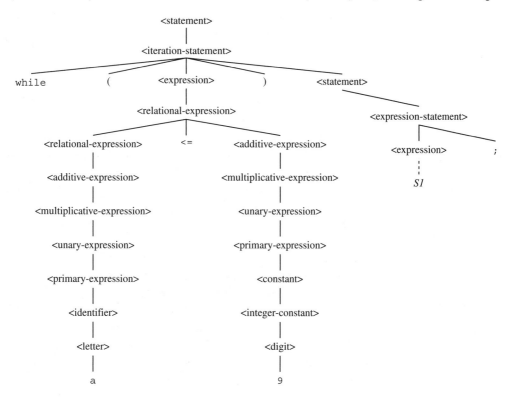

for one machine may not be appropriate for another. A single, standard von Neumann architecture based on theoretical concepts does not exist. Consequently, not as much theory for code generation has been developed to guide compiler designers in their compiler construction efforts.

Context Sensitivity of C

It appears from Figure 7.8 that the C language is context-free. Every production rule has only a single nonterminal on the left side. This is in contrast to a context-sensitive grammar, which can have more than a single nonterminal on the left, as in Figure 7.3. Appearances are deceiving. Even though the grammar for this subset of C, as well as the full standard C language, is context-free, the language itself has some context-sensitive aspects.

C has a context-free grammar.

Consider the grammar in Figure 7.3. How do its rules of production guarantee that the number of c's at the end of a string must equal the number of a's at the beginning of the string? Rules 1 and 2 guarantee that for each a generated, exactly one C will be generated. Rule 3 lets the C commute to the right of B. Finally, Rule 5 lets you substitute c for C in the context of having a b to the left of C. The language could not be specified by a context-free grammar because it needs Rules 3 and 5 to get the C's to the end of the string.

C is not a context-free language.

There are context-sensitive aspects of the C language that Figure 7.8 does not specify. For example, the definition of <parameter-list> allows any number of formal parameters, and the definition of <argument-expression-list> allows any number of actual parameters. You could write a C program containing a procedure with three formal parameters and a procedure call with two actual parameters that is derivable from <translation-unit> with the grammar in Figure 7.8. If you try to compile the program, however, the compiler will declare a syntax error.

The fact that the number of formal parameters must equal the number of actual parameters in C is similar to the fact that the number of a's at the beginning of the string must equal the number of c's at the end of the string in the language defined by the grammar in Figure 7.3. The only way to put that restriction in C's grammar would be to include many complicated, context-sensitive rules. It is easier for the compiler to parse the program with a context-free grammar and check for any violations after the parse—usually with the help of its symbol table—that the grammar cannot specify.

7.2 Finite-State Machines

Finite-state machines (FSMs) are another way to specify the syntax of a sentence in a language. In diagram form, an FSM is a finite set of states represented by circles called *nodes* and transitions between the states represented by *arcs* between the circles. Each arc begins at one state, ends at another, and contains an arrowhead at the ending state. Each arc is also labeled with a character from the terminal alphabet of the language.

One state of the FSM is designated as the start state and at least one, possibly more, is designated a final state. On a diagram, the start state has an incoming arrow and a final state is indicated by a double circle.

Mathematically, such a collection of nodes connected by arcs is called a *graph*. When the arcs are directed, as they are in an FSM, the structure is called a *directed graph* or *digraph*.

FIGURE 7.11
An FSM to parse an identifier.

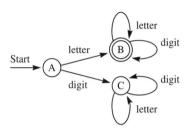

An FSM to Parse an Identifier

FIGURE 7.11 shows an FSM that parses an identifier as defined by the grammar in Figure 7.1. The set of states is {A, B, C}. A is the start state, and B is the final state. There is a transition from A to B on a letter, from A to C on a digit, from B to B on a letter or a digit, and from C to C on a letter or a digit.

To use the FSM, imagine that the input string is written on a piece of paper tape. Start in the start state, and scan the characters on the input tape from left to right. Each time you scan the next character on the tape, make a transition to another state of the FSM. Use only the transition that is allowed by the arc corresponding to the character you have just scanned. After scanning all the input characters, if you are in a final state, the characters are a valid identifier. Otherwise they are not.

Example 7.4   To parse the string cab3, you would make the following transitions:

Current state: A	Input: cab3	Scan c and go to B.
Current state: B	Input: ab3	Scan a and go to B.
Current state: B	Input: b3	Scan b and go to B.
Current state: B	Input: 3	Scan 3 and go to B.
Current state: B	Input:	Check for final state.

Because there is no more input and the last state is B, a final state, cab3 is a valid identifier. ∎

You can also represent an FSM by its state transition table. FIGURE 7.12 is the state transition table for the FSM of Figure 7.11. The table lists the next state reached by the transition from a given current state on a given input symbol.

FIGURE 7.12
The state transition table for the FSM of Figure 7.11.

Current State	Next State	
	Letter	Digit
→ A	B	C
Ⓑ	B	B
C	C	C

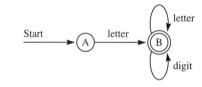

FIGURE 7.13
The FSM of Figure 7.11 without the failure state.

Simplified FSMs

It is often convenient to simplify the diagram for an FSM by eliminating the state whose sole purpose is to provide transitions for illegal input characters. State C in this machine is such a state. If the first character is a digit, the string will not be a valid identifier, regardless of the following characters. State C acts like a failure state. Once you make a transition to C, you can never make a transition to another state, and you know the input string eventually will be declared invalid. (FIGURE 7.13) shows the simplified FSM of Figure 7.11 without the failure state.

When you parse a string with this simplified machine, you will not be able to make a transition when you encounter an illegal character in the input string. There are two ways to detect an illegal sentence in a simplified FSM:

> You may run out of input and not be in a final state.

> You may be in some state, and the next input character does not correspond to any of the transitions from that state.

(FIGURE 7.14) is the corresponding state transition table for Figure 7.13. The state transition table for a simplified machine has no entry for a missing transition. Note that this table has no entry under the digit column for the current state of A. The remaining machines in this chapter are written in simplified form.

Nondeterministic FSMs

When you parse a sentence using a grammar, frequently you must choose between several production rules for substitution in a derivation step. Similarly, nondeterministic FSMs require you to decide between more than one transition when parsing the input string. (FIGURE 7.15) is a nondeterministic FSM to parse a signed integer. It is nondeterministic because there is at least one state that has more than one transition from it on the same character. For example, state A has a transition to both B and C on a digit. There is also some nondeterminism at state B because,

FIGURE 7.14
The state transition table for the FSM of Figure 7.13.

Current State	Next State	
	Letter	**Digit**
→A	B	
Ⓑ	B	B

FIGURE 7.15
A nondeterministic FSM to parse a signed integer.

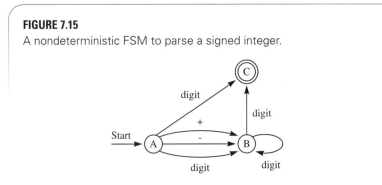

given that the next input character is a digit, a transition both to B and to C is possible.

Example 7.5   You must make the following decisions to parse +203 with this nondeterministic FSM:

Current state: A	Input: +203	Scan + and go to B.
Current state: B	Input: 203	Scan 2 and go to B.
Current state: B	Input: 03	Scan 0 and go to B.
Current state: B	Input: 3	Scan 3 and go to C.
Current state: C	Input:	Check for final state.

Because there is no more input and you are in the final state C, you have proven that the input string +203 is a valid signed integer. ∎

When parsing with rules of production, you run the risk of making an incorrect choice early in the parse. You may reach a dead end where no substitution will get your intermediate string of terminals and nonterminals closer to the given string. Just because you reach such a dead end does not necessarily mean that the string is invalid. All invalid strings will produce dead ends in an attempted parse. But even valid strings have the potential for producing dead ends if you make a wrong decision early in the derivation.

The same principle applies with nondeterministic FSMs. With the machine of Figure 7.15, if you are in the start state, A, and the next input character is 7, you must choose between the transitions to B and to C. Suppose you choose the transition to C and then find that there is another input character to scan. Because there are no transitions from C, you have reached a dead end in your attempted parse. You must conclude, therefore, that either the input string was invalid—or it was valid and you made an incorrect choice at an earlier point.

FIGURE 7.16
The state transition table for the FSM of Figure 7.15.

Current State	Next State +	−	Digit
→ A	B	B	B, C
B			B, C
Ⓒ			

FIGURE 7.16 is the state transition table for the machine of Figure 7.15. The nondeterminism is evident from the multiple entries (B, C) in the digit column. They represent a choice that must be made when attempting a parse.

Machines with Empty Transitions

In the same way that it is convenient to incorporate the empty string into production rules, it is sometimes convenient to construct FSMs with transitions on the empty string. Such transitions are called *empty transitions*. FIGURE 7.17 is an FSM that corresponds closely to the grammar in Figure 7.2 to parse a signed integer, and FIGURE 7.18 is its state transition table.

In Figure 7.17, F is the state after the first character, and M is the magnitude state analogous to the F and M nonterminals of the grammar. In the same way that a sign can be +, -, or neither, the transition from I to F can be on +, -, or ε.

FIGURE 7.17
An FSM with an empty transition to parse a signed integer.

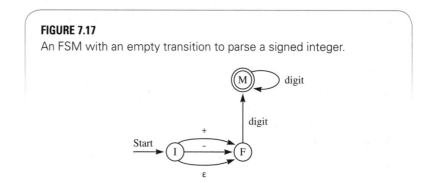

FIGURE 7.18
The state transition table for the FSM of Figure 7.17.

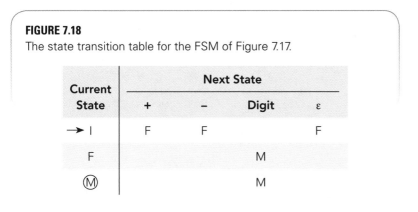

Current State	Next State			
	+	−	Digit	ε
→ I	F	F		F
F			M	
Ⓜ			M	

Example 7.6 To parse `32` requires the following decisions:

Current state: I	Input: `32`	Scan ε and go to F.
Current state: F	Input: `32`	Scan `3` and go to M.
Current state: M	Input: `2`	Scan `2` and go to M.
Current state: M	Input:	Check for final state.

The transition from I to F on ε does not consume an input character. When you are in state I, you can do one of three things: (a) scan + and go to F, (b) scan - and go to F, or (c) scan nothing (that is, the empty string) and go to F. ∎

Machines with empty transitions are always considered nondeterministic. In Example 7.6, the nondeterminism comes from the decision you must make when you are in state I and the next character is +. You must decide whether to go from I to F on + or from I to F on ε. These are different transitions because they leave you with different input strings, even though they are transitions to the same state.

Machines with empty transitions are considered nondeterministic.

Given an FSM with empty transitions, it is always possible to transform it to an equivalent machine without the empty transitions. There are two steps in the algorithm to eliminate an empty transition.

> Given a transition from p to q on ε, for every transition from q to r on a, add a transition from p to r on a.

> If q is a final state, make p a final state.

The algorithm to remove an empty transition

This algorithm follows from the concatenation property of ε:

εa = a

Example 7.7 FIGURE 7.19 shows how to remove an empty transition from the machine in part (a), resulting in the equivalent machine in part (b). Because there is a transition from state X to state Y on ε, and from state Y

FIGURE 7.19
Removing an empty transition.

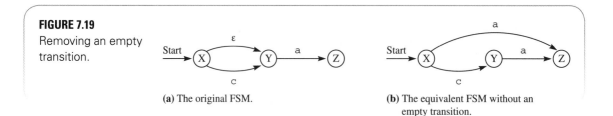

(a) The original FSM.

(b) The equivalent FSM without an empty transition.

to state Z on a, you can eliminate the empty transition if you construct a transition from state X to state Z on a. If you are in X, you might just as well go to Z directly on a. The state and remaining input will be the same as if you went from X to Z via Y on ε.   ∎

Example 7.8   (FIGURE 7.20) shows this transformation on the FSM of Figure 7.17. The empty transition from I to F is replaced by the transition from I to M on digit, because there is a transition from F to M on digit.   ∎

In Example 7.8, there is only one transition from F to M, so the empty transition from I to F is replaced by only one transition from I to M. If an FSM has more than one transition from the destination state of the empty transition, you must add more than one transition when you eliminate the empty transition.

Example 7.9   To eliminate the empty transition from W to X in (FIGURE 7.21(a)), you need to replace it with two transitions, one from W to Y on a and one from W to Z on b. In this example, because X is a final state in Figure 7.21(a), W becomes a final state in the equivalent machine of Figure 7.21(b) in accordance with the second step of the algorithm.   ∎

Removing the empty transition from Figure 7.17 produced a deterministic machine. In general, however, removing all the empty transitions does not guarantee that the FSM is deterministic. Even though

FIGURE 7.20
Removing the empty transition from the FSM of Figure 7.17.

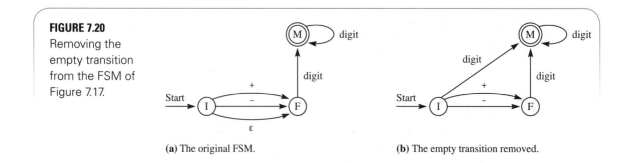

(a) The original FSM.

(b) The empty transition removed.

all machines with empty transitions are nondeterministic, an FSM with no empty transitions may still be nondeterministic. Figure 7.15 is such a machine, for example.

Given the choice, you are always better off parsing with a deterministic rather than a nondeterministic FSM. With a deterministic machine, there is no possibility of making a wrong choice with a valid input string and terminating in a dead end. If you ever terminate at a dead end, you can conclude with certainty that the input string is invalid.

The advantage of a deterministic FSM

Computer scientists have been able to prove that for every nondeterministic FSM there is an equivalent deterministic FSM. That is, there is a deterministic machine that recognizes exactly the same language. Unfortunately, the proof of this useful result is beyond the scope of this text. The proof consists of a recipe that tells how to construct an equivalent deterministic machine from the nondeterministic one.

Multiple Token Recognizers

A *token* is a string of terminal characters that has meaning as a group. The characters usually correspond to some nonterminal in a language's grammar. For example, consider the Pep/9 assembly language statement

The definition of a token

```
mask: .WORD 0x00FF
```

The tokens in this statement are `mask:`, `.WORD`, and `0x00FF`. Each is a set of characters from the assembly language alphabet and has meaning as a group. Their individual meanings are a symbol definition, a dot command, and a hexadecimal constant, respectively.

To a certain extent, the particular grouping of characters that you choose to form one token is arbitrary. For example, you could choose the string of characters `0x` and `00FF` to be separate tokens, `0x` for the prefix and `00FF` for the value. You would normally choose the characters of a token to be those that make the implementation of the FSM as simple as possible.

A common use of an FSM in a translator is to detect the tokens in the source string. Consider the assembler's job when confronted with this source line. Suppose the assembler has already determined that `mask:` is a symbol definition and `.WORD` is a dot command. It knows that either a decimal or hexadecimal constant can follow the dot command, so it must be programmed to accept either. It needs an FSM that recognizes both.

FIGURE 7.22(a) shows two machines for parsing a hexadecimal constant and an unsigned integer. D is the final state in the first machine, and F is the final state in the second machine for the unsigned integer. A hexadecimal constant is the digit 0, followed by lowercase x or uppercase X, followed by one or more hexdigits, which are 0..9, or a..f, or A..F. In the second machine, a digit is 0..9.

FIGURE 7.21
Removing an empty transition.

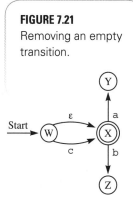

(a) The original FSM.

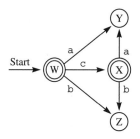

(b) The equivalent FSM without an empty transition.

FIGURE 7.22

Combining two machines to construct one FSM that recognizes both tokens.

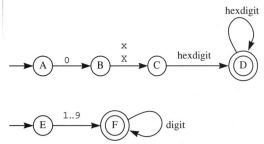

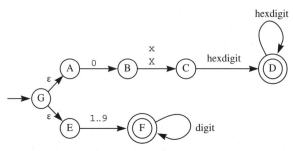

(a) Separate machines for a hexadecimal constant and an unsigned decimal integer.

(b) One nondeterministic FSM that recognizes a hexadecimal constant or an unsigned integer token.

To construct an FSM that will recognize both the hexadecimal constant and the unsigned integer, draw a new start state for the combined machine, state G in Figure 7.22(b). Then draw empty transitions from the new start state to the start state of each individual machine—in this example, from G to A and G to E. The result is one nondeterministic FSM that will recognize either token. The final state on termination tells you what token you have recognized. After the parse, if you terminate in state D, you have detected a hexadecimal constant, and if you terminate in state F, you have detected an unsigned integer.

To get the machine into a more useful form, you should eliminate the empty transitions. FIGURE 7.23(a) shows removal of the empty transitions for the FSM of Figure 7.22(b). After their removal, states A and E are

FIGURE 7.23

Transforming the FSM of Figure 7.22(b).

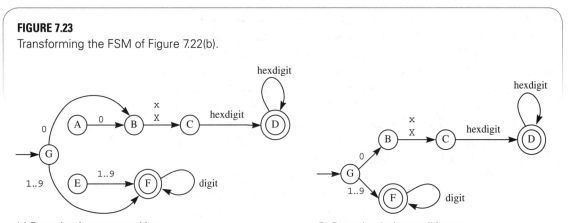

(a) Removing the empty transitions.

(b) Removing the inaccessible states.

inaccessible; that is, you can never reach them starting from the start state, regardless of the input string. Consequently, they can never affect the parse and can be eliminated from the machine, as shown in Figure 7.23(b).

As another example of when the translator needs to recognize multiple tokens, consider the assembler's job when confronted with the following two source lines:

```
NOTE: LDWA this,d ;comment 1
      NOTA           ;comment 2
```

The first token on the first line is a symbol definition. The first token on the second line is a mnemonic for a unary instruction. At the beginning of each line, the translator needs an FSM to recognize a symbol definition, which is in the form of an identifier followed immediately by a colon, or a mnemonic, which is in the form of an identifier. **FIGURE 7.24** shows the appropriate multiple-token FSM.

In the first line, this machine makes the following transitions:

A to B on N
B to B on O
B to B on T
B to B on E
B to C on :

after which the translator halts in final state C and therefore has detected a symbol definition. In the second line, it makes the transitions

A to B on N
B to B on O
B to B on T
B to B on A

Because the next input character is not a colon, the FSM does not make the transition to state C. The translator halts in final state B and therefore has detected an identifier.

Grammars Versus FSMs

Grammars and FSMs are not equivalent in power. Of the two, grammars are more powerful than FSMs. That is, there are some languages whose syntax rules are so complex that, even though they can be specified with a grammar, they cannot be specified with an FSM. On the other hand, any language whose syntax rules are simple enough to be specified by an FSM can also be specified by a grammar.

Figure 7.1 is the grammar for an identifier, and Figure 7.13 is the FSM for an identifier. The rules for forming a valid identifier are that the first

FIGURE 7.24
An FSM to parse a Pep/9 assembly language identifier or symbol definition.

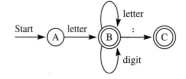

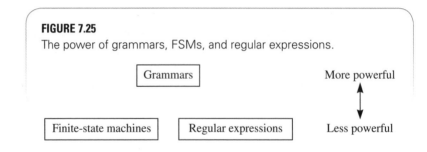

FIGURE 7.25

The power of grammars, FSMs, and regular expressions.

character must be a letter and the remaining characters must be letters or digits. These rules are so simple that an identifier can be specified by either a grammar or an FSM.

Figure 7.5 is a grammar for an expression. The language of expressions is so complex that it is mathematically impossible to specify an FSM that can parse an expression. The problem with FSMs for expressions is that you can have unlimited nested parentheses. Once the FSM scans a left parenthesis, it must transition to a state knowing that it is nested one level deep. If it scans another left parenthesis, it must transition to a state knowing that it is now nested two levels deep. If it then scans a right parenthesis, it must transition back to a state representing one level deep. It continues scanning left and right parentheses, transitioning to appropriate states for each level of nesting. To detect a valid expression, the final states must be ones with no nesting.

There is no mathematical limit in the grammar to the nesting level of an expression. Therefore, to construct an equivalent FSM, there would be no limit to the number of states. However, an FSM must have a finite number of states. Therefore, it is impossible to specify an FSM for an expression.

Although a description of regular expressions is beyond the scope of this text, how powerful are they? It turns out that for every regular expression there is an equivalent FSM, and for every FSM there is an equivalent regular expression. Consequently, FSMs and regular expressions are equal in power and are both less powerful than grammars. FIGURE 7.25 shows the power relationship between the three methods for specifying the syntax of a language.

7.3 Implementing Finite-State Machines

The remainder of this chapter shows how language translators convert a source program into an object program. It uses the Java language rather than C to illustrate the translation techniques. The syntax of the Java language is similar to that of C, and it has the advantage of being object-oriented. Java provides an extensive library of graphical user interface (GUI) elements for input and output. The programs in this chapter get their input as a string of terminal characters from a single input window and send the results of the translation to the standard output window. The GUI programming details are not shown but are available with the software for this text.

Java itself is an interpreted language based on the Java Virtual Machine (JVM). FIGURE 7.26 shows the difference between a compiled language and an interpreted language. Part (a) shows the translation process for a compiled language like C. Every run in the computation process executes a machine language program with input and output. In the first run, a C compiler converts the source code in a high-level language to the object code in machine language. In the second run, the machine language object code executes, processing the application input and producing the application output.

Part (b) shows the translation process for an interpreted language like Java and Pep/9, both of which are based on virtual machines. In the first

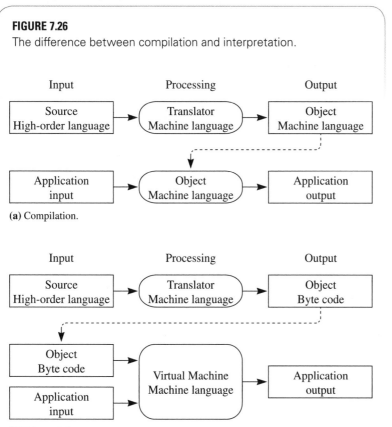

FIGURE 7.26
The difference between compilation and interpretation.

(a) Compilation.

(b) Interpretation.

run, the object code is byte code instead of machine language. In the second run, the object code does not execute directly. Instead, the virtual machine executes with two sources of input, the object byte code from the first run and the application input.

Advantage of interpretation

Advantages of interpretation include fast compilation time and ease of portability. It is faster to compile into byte code because byte code is at a higher level of abstraction than machine code and thus easier to translate. Figure 2.3 shows how a compiled language like C achieves its platform independence. The language maintainers must have a compiler for every platform. With an interpreted language like Java, the same compiler works for all platforms. The language maintainers need only to provide a virtual machine for every platform, a simpler task than providing separate compilers.

Disadvantage of interpretation

A disadvantage of interpretation is slow execution speed compared to compilation. During execution time, the application is not executing directly. Instead, the virtual machine is executing. This extra layer of abstraction provided by the virtual machine during run time makes execution of interpreted programs generally slower than execution of equivalent compiled programs.

The Compilation Process

The syntax of a programming language is usually specified by a formal grammar, which forms the basis of the parsing algorithm for the translator. Rather than specifying all the syntax, as the grammar in Figure 7.8 does, the formal grammar frequently specifies an upper level of abstraction and leaves the lower level to be specified by regular expressions or FSMs.

FIGURE 7.27 shows the steps in a typical compilation process. The low-level syntax analysis is called *lexical analysis*, and the high-level syntax analysis is called *parsing*. (This is a more specialized meaning of the word *parse*. It is sometimes used in a more general sense to include all syntax analysis.) In most translators for artificial languages, the lexical analyzer is based on a deterministic FSM whose input is a string of characters. The parser is usually based on a grammar whose input is the sequence of tokens taken from the lexical analyzer.

FIGURE 7.27

Steps in the compilation process.

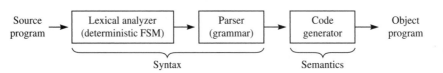

Each stage in the compilation process takes its input from the previous stage and sends its output to the following stage. The input and output of each stage are as follows:

> The input of the lexical analyzer is a string of symbols from the terminal alphabet of the source program.

> The output of the lexical analyzer and input of the parser is a stream of tokens.

> The output of the parser and input of the code generator is the syntax tree of the parse and/or the source program written in an internal low-level language.

> The output of the code generator is the object program.

A nonterminal symbol for the lexical analyzer acts like a terminal symbol for the parser. A common example of such a symbol is an identifier. The FSM has individual letters and digits as its terminal alphabet, and it inputs a string of them as it makes its state transitions. If the string abc3 is input, the FSM declares that an identifier has been detected and passes that information on to the parser. The parser uses <identifier> as a terminal symbol in its parse of the sentence from the language.

An algorithm that implements an FSM has an enumerated variable called the *state variable* whose possible values correspond to the possible states of the FSM. The algorithm initializes the state variable to the start state of the machine and gets the string of terminal characters one at a time in a loop. Each character causes a change of state. There are two common implementation techniques:

The state variable

> Table-lookup

> Direct-code

The two FSM implementation techniques

They differ in the way that the state variable gets its next value. The table-lookup technique stores the state transition table and looks up the next state based on the current state and input character. The direct-code technique tests the current state and input character in the code itself and assigns the next state to the state variable directly.

A Table-Lookup Parser

The program in **FIGURE 7.28** implements the FSM of Figure 7.11 with the table-lookup technique. Variable FSM, a two-dimensional array of integers, is the state transition table shown in Figure 7.12. The program classifies each input character as a letter or digit. Because B is the final state, it declares that the input string is a valid identifier if the state on termination of the loop is B.

FIGURE 7.28
Implementation of the FSM of Figure 7.11 with the table-lookup technique.

```java
public static boolean isAlpha(char ch) {
    return ('a' <= ch && ch <= 'z') || ('A' <= ch && ch <= 'Z');
}

// States
static final int S_A = 0;
static final int S_B = 1;
static final int S_C = 2;
// Alphabet
static final int T_LETTER = 0;
static final int T_DIGIT = 1;
// State transition table
static final int[][] FSM = {
    {S_B, S_C},
    {S_B, S_B},
    {S_C, S_C}
};

public void actionPerformed(ActionEvent event) {
    String line = textField.getText();
    char ch;
    int FSMChar;
    int state = S_A;
    for (int i = 0; i < line.length(); i++) {
        ch = line.charAt(i);
        FSMChar = isAlpha(ch) ? T_LETTER : T_DIGIT;
        state = FSM[state][FSMChar];
    }
    if (state == S_B) {
        System.out.printf("%s is a valid identifier.\n", line);
    } else {
        System.out.printf("%s is not a valid identifier.\n", line);
    }
}
```

Input/Output
```
Enter a string of letters and digits: cab3
cab3 is a valid identifier.
```

Input/Output
```
Enter a string of letters and digits: 3cab
3cab is not a valid identifier.
```

The input and output shown in the figure are a reflection of the GUI widget in the complete program, not shown here. The input comes from a dialog box with the label "Enter a string of letters and digits:" above a text input field. When the user clicks the Parse button, that event triggers execution of function `actionPerformed()`. The type `String` in the program is the Java immutable string type. Function `getText()` retrieves the user input from the text input field and gives it to variable `line`. The `for` loop processes the terminal characters one at a time with the `charAt()` function. It looks up the next state in the FSM table from the current state and the current input.

The program assumes that the user will enter only letters and digits. If the user enters some other character, it will detect the character as a digit. For example, if the user enters `cab#`, the program will detect it as a valid identifier even though it is not. A problem for the student at the end of this chapter suggests an improved FSM and corresponding implementation.

A Direct-Code Parser

The program in (FIGURE 7.29) uses the direct-code technique to parse an integer. It is an implementation of the FSM of Figure 7.20(b). Function `actionPerformed()` allows the user to enter any string of characters. If the string is not a valid integer, `parseNum` will set attribute `valid` to false and the program will issue an error message. Otherwise, `valid` will be true and `number` will be the correct integer value entered.

FIGURE 7.29

Implementation of the FSM of Figure 7.20(b) with the direct code technique.

```
public void actionPerformed(ActionEvent event) {
   String line = textField.getText();
   Parser parser = new Parser();
   parser.parseNum(line);
   if (parser.getValid()) {
      System.out.printf("Number = %d\n", parser.getNumber());
   } else {
      System.out.printf("Invalid entry.\n");
   }
}


public enum State {
   S_I, S_F, S_M, S_STOP
}
```

(continues)

FIGURE 7.29

Implementation of the FSM of Figure 7.20(b) with the direct code technique. (*continued*)

```java
public class Parser {

    private boolean valid = false;
    private int number = 0;
    public boolean getValid() {
        return valid;
    }

    public int getNumber() {
        return number;
    }

    public boolean isDigit(char ch) {
        return ('0' <= ch) && (ch <= '9');
    }

    public void parseNum(String line) {
        line = line + '\n';
        int lineIndex = 0;
        char nextChar;
        int sign = +1;
        valid = true;
        State state = State.S_I;
        do {
            nextChar = line.charAt(lineIndex++);
            switch (state) {
                case S_I:
                    if (nextChar == '+') {
                        sign = +1;
                        state = State.S_F;
                    } else if (nextChar == '-') {
                        sign = -1;
                        state = State.S_F;
                    } else if (isDigit(nextChar)) {
                        sign = +1;
                        number = nextChar - '0';
                        state = State.S_M;
```

```
            } else {
                valid = false;
            }
            break;
        case S_F:
            if (isDigit(nextChar)) {
                number = nextChar - '0';
                state = State.S_M;
            } else {
                valid = false;
            }
            break;
        case S_M:
            if (isDigit(nextChar)) {
                number = 10 * number + nextChar - '0';
            } else if (nextChar == '\n') {
                number = sign * number;
                state = State.S_STOP;
            } else {
                valid = false;
            }
            break;
        }
    } while ((state != State.S_STOP) && valid);
}
}
```

Input/Output
```
Enter a number: q
Invalid entry.
```

Input/Output
```
Enter a number: -58
Number = -58
```

Although the program is shown as one listing, it is actually fragments from three different files. The software in this chapter follows the Java coding convention of one file per class with the name of the file the same name as the class. For example, class `Parser` is in a separate file named `Parser.java`. The `State` class is also in a separate file.

Function `parseNum()` installs a newline character as a sentinel, regardless of how many or few characters the user enters. If the user enters no characters in the dialog box and simply presses the Parse button, parseNum() will install the newline character at line[0].

The procedure has a local enumerated variable called state, whose possible values are S_I, S_F, or S_M, corresponding to the states I, F, and M of the FSM in Figure 7.20(b). An additional state called S_STOP is for terminating the loop. The function initializes valid to true and state to the start state, S_I.

A do loop simulates the transitions in the FSM, which is the direct-code technique. A single switch statement determines the current state, and a single nested if statement within each case processes the next character. Assignment statements in the code change the state variable directly.

In a simplified FSM, there are two ways to stop—either you run out of input or you reach a state with no transitions from it on the next character, in which case the string is not valid. Corresponding to these termination conditions, there are two ways to quit the do loop—when the input sentinel is reached in a final state or when the string is discovered to be invalid.

The body of a do loop always executes at least once. Nevertheless, the code executes correctly even if the Parse button is pressed with an empty text input field. parseNum() installs the newline character in line[0]. It initializes state to I, enters the do loop, and immediately sets nextChar to the newline character. Then valid gets false, and the loop terminates correctly.

In addition to determining whether the string is valid, parseNum() converts the string of characters to the proper integer value. If the first character is + or a digit, it sets sign to +1. If the first character is -, it sets sign to –1. The first digit detected sets number to its proper value in state I or F. Its value is maintained correctly in state M each time a succeeding digit is detected. The magnitude is multiplied by the sign when the loop terminates with a valid number.

Integrating semantic actions with syntactic actions

The computation of the correct integer value is a semantic action, and the state assignment is a syntax action. It is easy with the direct-code technique to integrate the semantic processing with the syntactic processing because there is a distinct place in the syntax code to include the required semantic processing. For example, you know in state I that if the character is -, sign must be set to –1. It is easy to determine where to include that assignment in the syntax code.

If the user enters leading spaces before a legal string of digits, the FSM will declare the string invalid. The next program shows how to correct this deficiency.

An Input Buffer Class

The following two programs use the same technique to get characters from the input stream. Instead of duplicating the code for the input processing in each program, this section shows an implementation of an input buffer class that both programs use. It is stored in a separate file named `InBuffer.java` and is included in each program. (FIGURE 7.30) shows the implementation of the input buffer.

As shown in the following two programs, the FSM function sometimes detects a character from the input stream that terminates the current token, yet will be required from the input stream in a subsequent call to the function. Conceptually, the function must push the character back into the

FIGURE 7.30
The input buffer class included in the programs of Figures 7.32 and 7.35.

```java
public class InBuffer {

    private String inString;
    private String line;
    private int lineIndex;

    public InBuffer(String string) {
        inString = string + "\n\n";
        // To guarantee inString.length() == 0 eventually
    }

    public void getLine() {
        int i = inString.indexOf('\n');
        line = inString.substring(0, i + 1);
        inString = inString.substring(i + 1);
        lineIndex = 0;
    }

    public boolean inputRemains() {
        return inString.length() != 0;
    }

    public char advanceInput() {
        return line.charAt(lineIndex++);
    }

    public void backUpInput() {
        lineIndex--;
    }
}
```

input stream so it will be retrieved on the subsequent call. backUpInput ()
provides that operation on the buffer class. Although the FSM function needs
to access characters from the input buffer, it does not access the attributes
of the buffer directly. Only the procedures getLine (), inputRemains (),
advanceInput (), and backUpInput () access the buffer. The reason for
this design is to provide the FSM function with a more convenient abstract
structure of the input stream.

The remaining two programs in this chapter use multiline input. The
constructor for the buffer appends two newline characters to input string
and stores the result in inString. Lines are separated by the newline
character \n. Function getLine () deletes the first line from inString
using the newline character as the separater and puts it in line. Appending
two newline characters at the beginning guarantees that the last line deleted
from inString will have length 0.

A Multiple-Token Parser

If the parser of a C compiler is analyzing the string

```
total =
```

it knows that the next nonterminal could be an identifier such as amount or
an integer such as 100. Because it does not know which token to expect, it
calls an FSM that can recognize either, as in FIGURE 7.31 .

The state labeled *Ident* is a final state for detecting the identifier token.
Int is the final state for detecting an integer. The transition from Start to Start
is on the space character. It allows for leading spaces before either token. If

FIGURE 7.31
The FSM of a program that recognizes identifiers and integers.

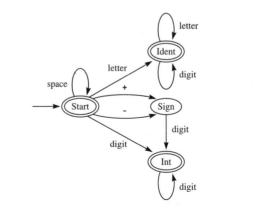

the only characters left to scan are trailing spaces at the end of a line, the FSM procedure will return the empty token. That is why the start state is also a final state.

FIGURE 7.32 shows two input/output runs from a program that implements the multiple-token recognizer of Figure 7.31. The first run has an input of two lines, the first line with five nonempty tokens and the second line with six nonempty tokens. Here is an explanation of the first run of Figure 7.32.

The machine starts in the start state and scans the first terminal, H. That takes it to the Ident state. The following terminals, e, r, and e, make transitions to the same state. The next terminal is a space. There is no transition from state Ident on the terminal space. Because the machine is in the final state for identifiers, it concludes that an identifier has been scanned. It puts the space terminal, which it could not use in this state, back into the input for use as the first terminal for the next token. It then declares that an identifier has been scanned.

The machine starts over in the start state. It uses the leftover space to make a transition to Start. A few more spaces produce a few more transitions

---

FIGURE 7.32
The input/output of a program that recognizes identifiers and integers.

Input
```
Here is A47 48B
    C-49 ALongIdentifier +50 D16-51
```
Output
```
Identifier = Here
Identifier = is
Identifier = A47
Integer   = 48
Identifier = B
Empty token
Identifier = C
Integer   = -49
Identifier = ALongIdentifier
Integer   = 50
Identifier = D16
Integer   = -51
Empty token
```

Input
```
Here is A47+ 48B
    C+49
```
```
ALongIdentifier
```
Output
```
Identifier = Here
Identifier = is
Identifier = A47
Syntax error
Identifier = C
Integer   = 49
Empty token
Empty token
Identifier = ALongIdentifier
Empty token
```

(a) First run.   (b) Second run.

to Start, after which the i and s characters produce the recognition of a second identifier, as shown in the sample output. Similarly, A47 is recognized as an identifier.

For the next token, the initial 4 sends the machine into the Integer state. The 8 makes the transition to the same state. Now the machine inputs the B. There is no transition from state Integer on the terminal B. Because the machine is in the final state for integers, it concludes that an integer has been scanned. It puts the B terminal, which it could not use in this state, back into the input for use as the first terminal for the next token. It then declares that an integer has been scanned. Notice that B is detected as an identifier the next time around.

The machine continues recognizing tokens until it gets to the end of the line, at which point it recognizes the empty token. It will recognize the empty token whether or not there are trailing spaces in the input because the buffer appends two newline characters to the input string.

The second sample input shows how the machine handles a string of characters that contains a syntax error. After recognizing Here, is, and A47, on the next call, the FSM gets the + and goes to state Sign. Because the next character is space, and there is no transition from Sign on space, the FSM returns the invalid token.

Like all multiple-token recognizers, this machine operates on the following design principle:

A design principle for multiple-token recognizers

> You can never fail once you reach a final state. Instead, if the final state does not have a transition from it on the terminal just input, you have recognized a token and should back up the input. The character will then be available as the first terminal for the next token.

The machine handles an empty line (or a line with only spaces) correctly, returning the empty token on the first call.

FIGURE 7.33 is a Unified Modeling Language (UML) diagram of the class structure of a token. AToken is an abstract token with no attributes and one public abstract operation, getDescription(). The plus sign in front of the

FIGURE 7.33
The UML diagram of the class structure of AToken.

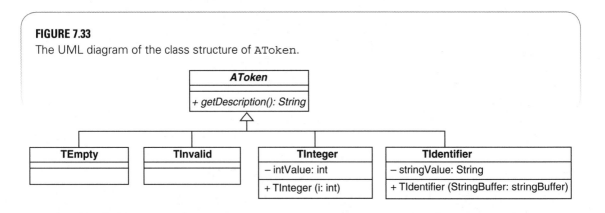

operations is the UML notation for public access. The open triangle is the UML symbol for inheritance; Figure 7.33 shows that the concrete classes TEmpty, TInvalid, TInteger, and TIdentifier inherit from AToken. The UML convention is to show abstract class names and methods in a slanted font.

Each of the concrete classes must implement the abstract methods they inherit from their superclass. Method getDescription() returns a string for the output shown in Figure 7.32. In addition to the inherited methods, class TInteger has a private attribute intValue, which stores the integer value detected by the parser, and a public constructor. The minus sign in front of the attribute is the UML symbol for private access. Class TIdentifier has a similar attribute of type String and its own constructor. Its constructor has a formal parameter of type StringBuffer, which is the Java mutable string type.

FIGURE 7.34 shows the corresponding Java implementation of the token class structure of Figure 7.33. It is a collection of code fragments from five separate files; to save space, it does not show the @Override annotation.

FIGURE 7.34
A Java implementation of class AToken in Figure 7.33.

```java
abstract public class AToken {
   public abstract String getDescription();
}

public class TEmpty extends AToken {
   public String getDescription() {
      return "Empty token";
   }
}

public class TInvalid extends AToken {
   public String getDescription() {
      return "Syntax error";
   }
}

public class TInteger extends AToken {
   private final int intValue;
   public TInteger(int i) {
      intValue = i;
   }
```

(continues)

FIGURE 7.34

A Java implementation of class `AToken` in Figure 7.33. (*continued*)

```java
    public String getDescription() {
        return String.format("Integer    = %d", intValue);
    }
}

public class TIdentifier extends AToken {
    private final String stringValue;
    public TIdentifier(StringBuffer stringBuffer) {
        stringValue = new String(stringBuffer);
    }
    public String getDescription() {
        return String.format("Identifier = %s", stringValue);
    }
}
```

FIGURE 7.35 is the direct-code implementation of the FSM of Figure 7.31. It is a collection of code fragments from three Java class files. The constructor for class `Tokenizer` sets b to the buffer that has been loaded with the input string. Method `getToken()` returns an abstract token whose dynamic type will be one of the concrete classes `TEmpty`, `TInvalid`, `TInteger`, or `TIdentifier`.

The Java `StringBuffer` class is used for efficiency. Method `getToken()` maintains a local string value, which is mutable, for processing

FIGURE 7.35

A Java implementation of the FSM of Figure 7.31.

```java
public class Util {
    public static boolean isDigit(char ch) {
        return ('0' <= ch) && (ch <= '9');
    }
    public static boolean isAlpha(char ch) {
        return (('a' <= ch) && (ch <= 'z') || ('A' <= ch) && (ch <= 'Z'));
    }
}
```

```java
public enum LexState {
   LS_START, LS_IDENT, LS_SIGN, LS_INTEGER, LS_STOP
}

public class Tokenizer {
   private final InBuffer b;
   public Tokenizer(InBuffer inBuffer) {
      b = inBuffer;
   }
   public AToken getToken() {
      char nextChar;
      StringBuffer localStringValue = new StringBuffer("");
      int localIntValue = 0;
      int sign = +1;
      AToken aToken = new TEmpty();
      LexState state = LexState.LS_START;
      do {
         nextChar = b.advanceInput();
         switch (state) {
            case LS_START:
               if (Util.isAlpha(nextChar)) {
                  localStringValue.append(nextChar);
                  state = LexState.LS_IDENT;
               } else if (nextChar == '-') {
                  sign = -1;
                  state = LexState.LS_SIGN;
               } else if (nextChar == '+') {
                  sign = +1;
                  state = LexState.LS_SIGN;
               } else if (Util.isDigit(nextChar)) {
                  localIntValue = nextChar - '0';
                  state = LexState.LS_INTEGER;
               } else if (nextChar == '\n') {
                  state = LexState.LS_STOP;
               } else if (nextChar != ' ') {
                  aToken = new TInvalid();
               }
               break;
```

(continues)

FIGURE 7.35
A Java implementation of the FSM of Figure 7.31. (*continued*)

```java
        case LS_IDENT:
            if (Util.isAlpha(nextChar) || Util.isDigit(nextChar)) {
                localStringValue.append(nextChar);
            } else {
                b.backUpInput();
                aToken = new TIdentifier(localStringValue);
                state = LexState.LS_STOP;
            }
            break;
        case LS_SIGN:
            if (Util.isDigit(nextChar)) {
                localIntValue = nextChar - '0';
                state = LexState.LS_INTEGER;
            } else {
                aToken = new TInvalid();
            }
            break;
        case LS_INTEGER:
            if (Util.isDigit(nextChar)) {
                localIntValue = 10 * localIntValue + nextChar - '0';
            } else {
                b.backUpInput();
                aToken = new TInteger(sign * localIntValue);
                state = LexState.LS_STOP;
            }
            break;
        }
    } while ((state != LexState.LS_STOP) && !(aToken instanceof TInvalid));
    return aToken;
    }
}
```

identifiers. The `append()` method mutates the string by appending `nextChar` to it. This is more efficient that appending `nextChar` to a copy of the local string value.

FIGURE 7.36 shows function `actionPerformed()`. It has a single abstract token `aToken`. The outer `while` loop executes once for each line of input, and the inner `do` loop executes once for each token in the line.

FIGURE 7.36

The `actionPerformed()` method for the tokenizer of Figure 7.35.

```
public void actionPerformed(ActionEvent event) {
   InBuffer inBuffer = new InBuffer(textArea.getText());
   Tokenizer t = new Tokenizer(inBuffer);
   AToken aToken;
   inBuffer.getLine();
   while (inBuffer.inputRemains()) {
      do {
         aToken = t.getToken();
         System.out.println(aToken.getDescription());
      } while (!(aToken instanceof TEmpty) && !(aToken instanceof TInvalid));
      inBuffer.getLine();
   }
}
```

The output relies on polymorphic dispatch to display the tokens that are detected. That is, the main program does not explicitly test the dynamic type of the token to choose how to output its value. It simply uses its abstract token to invoke the `getDescription()` method.

7.4 Code Generation

To *translate* is to transform a string of characters from some input alphabet to another string of characters from some output alphabet. The typical phases in such a translation are lexical analysis, parsing, and code generation. This section consists of a program that translates from one language to another. It illustrates all three phases of a simple automatic translator.

A Language Translator

FIGURE 7.37 shows the input/output of the translator. The input is the source and the output is the object code and a formatted program listing. The source and object languages are line oriented, as are assembly languages.

The source language has the syntax of C function calls, and the object language has the syntax of assignment statements with the assignment operator `<-`. A sample statement from the input language is

```
set (Time, 15)
```

FIGURE 7.37

The input/output of a program that translates from one language to another.

Input
```
set (Time, 15)
set (   Accel, 3)
set (TSquared   , Time)
    MUL ( TSquared, Time)
set ( Position, TSquared)
mul (Position, Accel)
dIV(Position,2)
stop
end
```

Output
```
Object code:
Time <- 15
Accel <- 3
TSquared <- Time
TSquared <- TSquared * Time
Position <- TSquared
Position <- Position * Accel
Position <- Position / 2
stop
```

```
Program listing:
set (Time, 15)
set (Accel, 3)
set (TSquared, Time)
mul (TSquared, Time)
set (Position, TSquared)
mul (Position, Accel)
div (Position, 2)
stop
end
```

(a) First run.

Input
```
set (Alpha,, 123)
set (Alpha)
sit (Alpha, 123)
set, (Alpha)
mul (Alpha, Beta
set (123, Alpha)
neg (Alpha, Beta)
set (Alpha, 123) x
```

Output
```
9 errors were detected.
```

```
Program listing:
ERROR: Second argument not an identifier or integer.
ERROR: Comma expected after first argument.
ERROR: Line must begin with function identifier.
ERROR: Left parenthesis expected after function.
ERROR: Right parenthesis expected after argument.
ERROR: First argument not an identifier.
ERROR: Right parenthesis expected after argument.
ERROR: Illegal trailing character.

ERROR: Missing "end" sentinel.
```

(b) Second run.

The corresponding object statement is

```
Time <- 15
```

The word set is reserved in the source language. The other reserved words are add, sub, mul, div, neg, abs, and end. Time is a user-defined identifier. Identifiers follow the same rules as in the C language. Integers, such as 15 in the previous example, also follow the C syntax.

The set procedure takes two arguments, separated by a comma and surrounded by parentheses. The first argument must be an identifier, but the second can be an identifier or an integer constant.

Another example of a translation is

```
mul (TSquared, Time)
```

which is written in the object language as

```
TSquared <- TSquared * Time
```

As with the set procedure, the first argument of a mul procedure call must be an identifier. To translate the mul statement, the translator must duplicate its first argument, which appears on both sides of the assignment operator.

The other procedure calls are similar, except for neg and abs, which take a single argument. For neg, the translator prefixes the argument with a dash character on the right side of the assignment operator. For abs, the translator encloses the argument in vertical bars. For example, the source statements

```
neg (Alpha)
abs (Beta)
```

are translated to

```
Alpha <- -Alpha
Beta <- |Beta|
```

The reserved word end is the sentinel for the translator. It generates no code and corresponds to .END in Pep/9 assembly language. Any number of spaces can occur anywhere in a source line, except within an identifier or integer.

The translator must not crash if syntax errors occur in the input stream. In Figure 7.37, there is also a run that shows a source file full of errors. The program generates appropriate error messages in the source listing to help the user find the bugs in the source program. If the translator detects any errors, it suppresses the object code output.

This program is based on a two-stage analysis of the syntax, as shown in Figure 7.27. Instead of using a grammar to specify the parsing problem as indicated in the figure, however, the structure of this source language is simple enough for the parser to be based on an FSM.

The complete Java project for the translator has 26 classes and 26 associated .java files. FIGURE 7.38 is the start of a listing of code fragments from the program that produces the output of Figure 7.37. The

FIGURE 7.38

The lookup maps for the translator program.

```java
public enum Mnemon {
   M_ADD, M_SUB, M_MUL, M_DIV, M_NEG, M_ABS, M_SET, M_STOP, M_END
}

public final class Maps {

   public static final Map<String, Mnemon> unaryMnemonTable;
   public static final Map<String, Mnemon> nonUnaryMnemonTable;
   public static final Map<Mnemon, String> mnemonStringTable;

   static {
      unaryMnemonTable = new HashMap<>();
      unaryMnemonTable.put("stop", Mnemon.M_STOP);
      unaryMnemonTable.put("end", Mnemon.M_END);

      nonUnaryMnemonTable = new HashMap<>();
      nonUnaryMnemonTable.put("neg", Mnemon.M_NEG);
      nonUnaryMnemonTable.put("abs", Mnemon.M_ABS);
      nonUnaryMnemonTable.put("add", Mnemon.M_ADD);
      nonUnaryMnemonTable.put("sub", Mnemon.M_SUB);
      nonUnaryMnemonTable.put("mul", Mnemon.M_MUL);
      nonUnaryMnemonTable.put("div", Mnemon.M_DIV);
      nonUnaryMnemonTable.put("set", Mnemon.M_SET);

      mnemonStringTable = new EnumMap<>(Mnemon.class);
      mnemonStringTable.put(Mnemon.M_NEG, "neg");
      mnemonStringTable.put(Mnemon.M_ABS, "abs");
      mnemonStringTable.put(Mnemon.M_ADD, "add");
      mnemonStringTable.put(Mnemon.M_SUB, "sub");
      mnemonStringTable.put(Mnemon.M_MUL, "mul");
      mnemonStringTable.put(Mnemon.M_DIV, "div");
      mnemonStringTable.put(Mnemon.M_SET, "set");
      mnemonStringTable.put(Mnemon.M_STOP, "stop");
      mnemonStringTable.put(Mnemon.M_END, "end");
   }
}
```

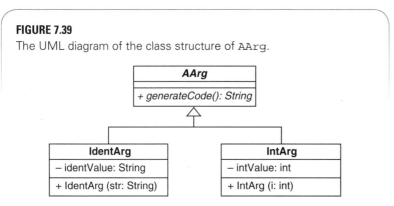

FIGURE 7.39
The UML diagram of the class structure of `AArg`.

program listing continues in the following figures. Figure 7.38 shows the setup of three Java maps used by the translator. The first two maps, one for unary instructions and one for nonunary instructions, take the string representation of a reserved word as the key and return the enumerated mnemonic representation. The third table uses enumerated mnemonic values as the key to look up the string symbol to place in the generated code. The maps use the lowercase string representation of the source code reserved word.

FIGURE 7.39 is the UML diagram of an abstract argument, and FIGURE 7.40 is its Java implementation. Because an argument in the source code can be either an identifier or an integer, the program stores a general argument as an `AArg`, which at run time is either an `IdentArg` or an `IntArg`. Class `AArg` defines the abstract method `generateCode()`, which contributes to code generation when the value of an argument must be output.

FIGURE 7.41 is the UML diagram of an abstract token, and FIGURE 7.42 is a partial listing of its Java implementation. The implementations of `TLeftParen`, `TRightParen`, `TEmpty`, and `TInvalid` are identical to the implementation of `TComma` and are not shown in the figure. This structure of a token is similar to the one in Figure 7.33 of the previous section. Classes `TIdentifier` and `TInteger` have getter methods to retrieve the values of their attributes.

The lexical analyzer returns an identifier when it encounters a reserved word and when it encounters an argument. When it encounters a reserved word, the parser needs to look up the word in the mnemonic map. It uses `getStringValue()` to get the identifier value from the token.

FIGURE 7.43 is the UML diagram of the abstract code class `ACode`, and FIGURE 7.44 is a complete listing of its Java implementation. An object of class

FIGURE 7.40

The Java implementation of class `AArg` in Figure 7.39.

```java
abstract public class AArg {
    abstract public String generateCode();
}

public class IdentArg extends AArg {
    private final String identValue;
    public IdentArg(String str) {
        identValue = str;
    }
    public String generateCode() {
        return identValue;
    }
}

public class IntArg extends AArg {
    private final int intValue;
    public IntArg(int i) {
        intValue = i;
    }
    public String generateCode() {
        return String.format("%d", intValue);
    }
}
```

FIGURE 7.41

The UML diagram of the class structure of `AToken`.

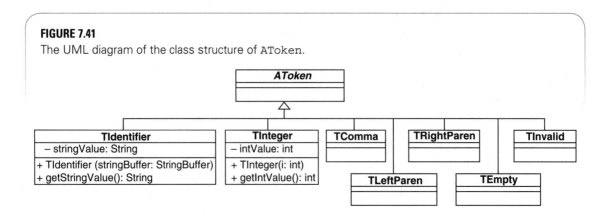

FIGURE 7.42

The Java implementation of class AToken in Figure 7.41.

```java
abstract public class AToken {
}

public class TIdentifier extends AToken {
   private final String stringValue;
   public TIdentifier(StringBuffer stringBuffer) {
      stringValue = new String(stringBuffer);
   }
   public String getStringValue() {
      return stringValue;
   }
}

public class TInteger extends AToken {
   private final int intValue;
   public TInteger(int i) {
      intValue = i;
   }
   public int getIntValue() {
      return intValue;
   }
}

public class TComma extends AToken {
}
```

ACode represents one line of source code and its corresponding object code. Execution of method generateCode() returns a string representation of the object code for that line, and execution of genereateListing() returns a string representation of the formatted source code for that line. Consequently, a code object must contain all the data it needs to output the source code and object code for that line.

For example, Figure 7.43 shows that an object of class TwoArgInstr has two attributes, firstArg, which is an abstract argument, and secondArg, also an abstract argument. In addition, it has enumerated mnemonic. Consider the last line of input from Figure 7.37(a):

```
dIV(Position,2)
```

FIGURE 7.43
The UML diagram of the class structure of ACode.

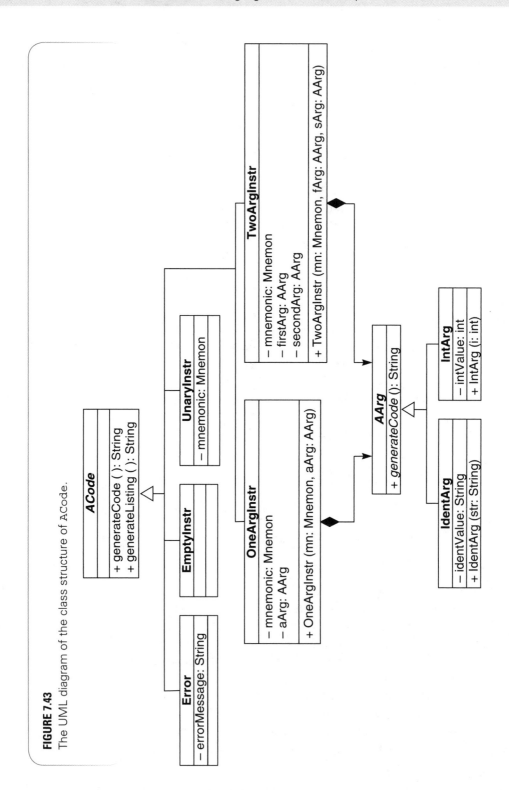

FIGURE 7.44

The Java implementation of class ACode in Figure 7.43.

```java
abstract public class ACode {
    abstract public String generateCode();
    abstract public String generateListing();
}

public class Error extends ACode {
    private final String errorMessage;
    public Error(String errMessage) {
        errorMessage = errMessage;
    }
    public String generateListing() {
        return "ERROR: " + errorMessage + "\n";
    }
    public String generateCode() {
        return "";
    }
}


public class EmptyInstr extends ACode {
    // For an empty source line.
    public String generateListing() {
        return "\n";
    }
    public String generateCode() {
        return "";
    }
}


public class UnaryInstr extends ACode {
    private final Mnemon mnemonic;
    public UnaryInstr(Mnemon mn) {
        mnemonic = mn;
    }
    public String generateListing() {
        return Maps.mnemonStringTable.get(mnemonic) + "\n";
    }
```

(continues)

FIGURE 7.44
The Java implementation of class ACode in Figure 7.43. (*continued*)

```java
    public String generateCode() {
       switch (mnemonic) {
          case M_STOP:
             return "stop\n";
          case M_END:
             return "";
          default:
             return ""; // Should not occur.
       }
    }
}

public class OneArgInstr extends ACode {
    private final Mnemon mnemonic;
    private final AArg aArg;
    public OneArgInstr(Mnemon mn, AArg aArg) {
       mnemonic = mn;
       this.aArg = aArg;
    }
    public String generateListing() {
       return String.format("%s (%s)\n",
                Maps.mnemonStringTable.get(mnemonic),
                aArg.generateCode());
    }
    public String generateCode() {
       switch (mnemonic) {
          case M_ABS:
             return String.format("%s <- |%s|\n",
                      aArg.generateCode(),
                      aArg.generateCode());
          case M_NEG:
             return String.format("%s <- -%s\n",
                      aArg.generateCode(),
                      aArg.generateCode());
          default:
             return ""; // Should not occur.
       }
    }
}
```

```java
public class TwoArgInstr extends ACode {
   private final Mnemon mnemonic;
   private final AArg firstArg;
   private final AArg secondArg;
   public TwoArgInstr(Mnemon mn, AArg fArg, AArg sArg) {
      mnemonic = mn;
      firstArg = fArg;
      secondArg = sArg;
   }
   public String generateListing() {
      return String.format("%s (%s, %s)\n",
              Maps.mnemonStringTable.get(mnemonic),
              firstArg.generateCode(),
              secondArg.generateCode());
   }
   public String generateCode() {
      switch (mnemonic) {
         case M_SET:
            return String.format("%s <- %s\n",
                    firstArg.generateCode(),
                    secondArg.generateCode());
         case M_ADD:
            return String.format("%s <- %s + %s\n",
                    firstArg.generateCode(),
                    firstArg.generateCode(),
                    secondArg.generateCode());
         case M_SUB:
            return String.format("%s <- %s - %s\n",
                    firstArg.generateCode(),
                    firstArg.generateCode(),
                    secondArg.generateCode());
         case M_MUL:
            return String.format("%s <- %s * %s\n",
                    firstArg.generateCode(),
                    firstArg.generateCode(),
                    secondArg.generateCode());
```

(continues)

FIGURE 7.44

The Java implementation of class ACode in Figure 7.43. (*continued*)

```
        case M_DIV:
            return String.format("%s <- %s / %s\n",
                    firstArg.generateCode(),
                    firstArg.generateCode(),
                    secondArg.generateCode());
        default:
            return "";  // Should not occur.
      }
    }
  }
```

The code object would have M_DIV for mnemonic, firstArg would be an IdentArg with an identValue with string value "Position," and secondArg would be an IntArg with an intValue of 2.

The concrete code classes contain the methods for generating both the object code listing and the formatted source code listing. For the preceding source line, the translator generates an object of class TwoArgInstr during the parse phase. It sets the attributes mnemonic, firstArg, and secondArg as described above. The following code in generateListing() returns the string for the formatted listing:

```
public String generateListing() {
    return String.format("%s (%s, %s)\n",
            Maps.mnemonStringTable.get(mnemonic),
            firstArg.generateCode(),
            secondArg.generateCode());
}
```

It uses mnemonic as the key to the map for looking up the string representation of the reserved word div. Then, it invokes generateCode() for the first and second arguments and formats them within parentheses. The result is the string

```
div (Position, 2)
```

formatted in the standard style.

The following code in `generateCode()` returns the string for the object code:

```
case M_MUL:
    return String.format("%s <- %s * %s\n",
            firstArg.generateCode(),
            firstArg.generateCode(),
            secondArg.generateCode());
```

The result is the string

```
Position <- Position / 2
```

The first argument occurs twice in the object code, once on the left side and once on the right side of the assignment operator.

The UML symbol for class composition is the solid diamond touching the `OneArgInstr` class box and the `TwoArgInstr` class box in Figure 7.43. The meaning of class composition is "has a" as opposed to the meaning of inheritance, which is "is a." A `OneArgInstr` object "is a" `ACode` object, and a `OneArgInstr` object "has a" `AArg` object.

FIGURE 7.45 is a partial listing of the tokenizer class. Function `getToken()` works like the `getToken()` function in Figure 7.35 except

---

FIGURE 7.45
The lexical analyzer.

```
public enum LexState {
    LS_START, LS_IDENT, LS_SIGN, LS_INTEGER, LS_STOP
}

public class Tokenizer {
    private final InBuffer b;
    public Tokenizer(InBuffer inBuffer) {
        b = inBuffer;
    }
}

public class Tokenizer {
    private final InBuffer b;
    public Tokenizer(InBuffer inBuffer) {
        b = inBuffer;
    }
}
```

(continues)

FIGURE 7.45

The lexical analyzer. (*continued*)

```
public AToken getToken() {
    char nextChar;
    StringBuffer localStringValue = new StringBuffer("");
    int localIntValue = 0;
    int sign = +1;
    AToken aToken = new TEmpty();
    LexState state = LexState.LS_START;
    do {
        nextChar = b.advanceInput();
        switch (state) {
            case LS_START:
                if (Util.isAlpha(nextChar)) {
                    localStringValue.append(nextChar);
                    state = LexState.LS_IDENT;
                } else if (nextChar == '-') {
...

            case LS_INTEGER:
                if (Util.isDigit(nextChar)) {
                    localIntValue = 10 * localIntValue + nextChar - '0';
                } else {
                    b.backUpInput();
                    aToken = new TInteger(localIntValue);
                    state = LexState.LS_STOP;
                }
                break;
        }
    } while ((state != LexState.LS_STOP) && !(aToken instanceof TInvalid));
    return aToken;
}
}
```

that it detects one of the seven tokens in Figure 7.41. As before, aToken is an abstract token returned by the function. Its dynamic type can be any of the seven concrete subclasses of aToken.

FIGURE 7.46 shows a deterministic FSM that describes the source language. The transitions of the machine are on the tokens from the lexical analyzer, indicated in the figure by the words that begin with T, as in

FIGURE 7.46

The FSM for the parser `processSourceLine` of Figure 7.47.

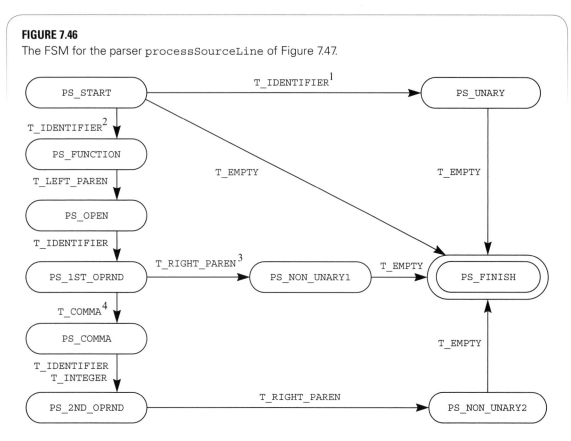

Note 1: Only the identifiers `stop` and `end`.
Note 2: Only the identifiers `set`, `add`, `sub`, `mul`, `div`, `neg`, and `abs`.
Note 3: Only for mnemonics `M_NEG` and `M_ABS`.
Note 4: Only for mnemonics `M_SET`, `M_ADD`, `M_SUB`, and `M_MUL`, `M_DIV`.

Figure 7.41. The final state `PS_FINISH` can be reached only by input of token `T_EMPTY`. The transition from `PS_START` to `PS_FINISH` will occur if there is a blank line or if there is a line that contains only spaces. The terminal strings `end` and `stop` are the only identifiers that make the transition from `PS_START` to `PS_UNARY`. The identifiers that correspond to the other reserved words—`set`, `add`, `sub`, `mul`, `div`, `neg`, and `abs`—make the transition from `PS_START` to `PS_FUNCTION`. All other identifiers are invalid when detected in the `PS_START` state.

FIGURE 7.47 is a partial listing of the translator that implements the FSM of Figure 7.46. Class `Translator` has two methods, private method `parseLine()` and public method `translate()`, which calls `parseLine()` in a loop that executes once per source line.

FIGURE 7.47
A partial listing of the translator that implements the FSM of Figure 7.46.

```
public enum ParseState {
    PS_START, PS_UNARY, PS_FUNCTION, PS_OPEN, PS_1ST_OPRND, PS_NONUNARY1,
    PS_COMMA, PS_2ND_OPRND, PS_NON_UNARY2, PS_FINISH
}

public class Translator {
    private final InBuffer b;
    private Tokenizer t;
    private ACode aCode;
    public Translator(InBuffer inBuffer) {
        b = inBuffer;
    }
    // Sets aCode and returns boolean true if end statement is processed.
    private boolean parseLine() {
        boolean terminate = false;
        AArg localFirstArg = new IntArg(0);
        AArg localSecondArg;
        Mnemon localMnemon = Mnemon.M_END; // Useless initialization
        AToken aToken;
        aCode = new EmptyInstr();
        ParseState state = ParseState.PS_START;
        do {
            aToken = t.getToken();
            switch (state) {
              case PS_START:
                if (aToken instanceof TIdentifier) {
                    TIdentifier localTIdentifier = (TIdentifier) aToken;
                    String tempStr = localTIdentifier.getStringValue();
                    if (Maps.unaryMnemonTable.containsKey(
                            tempStr.toLowerCase())) {
                        localMnemon = Maps.unaryMnemonTable.get(
                                tempStr.toLowerCase());
                        aCode = new UnaryInstr(localMnemon);
                        terminate = localMnemon == Mnemon.M_END;
                        state = ParseState.PS_UNARY;
```

```
            } else if (Maps.nonUnaryMnemonTable.containsKey(
                    tempStr.toLowerCase())) {
                localMnemon = Maps.nonUnaryMnemonTable.get(
                        tempStr.toLowerCase());
                state = ParseState.PS_FUNCTION;
            } else {
                aCode = new Error(
                        "Line must begin with function identifier.");
            }
        } else if (aToken instanceof TEmpty) {
            aCode = new EmptyInstr();
            state = ParseState.PS_FINISH;
        } else {
            aCode = new Error(
                    "Line must begin with function identifier.");
        }
        break;

...

    case PS_COMMA:
        if (aToken instanceof TIdentifier) {
            TIdentifier localTIdentifier = (TIdentifier) aToken;
            localSecondArg = new IdentArg(
                    localTIdentifier.getStringValue());
            aCode = new TwoArgInstr(
                    localMnemon, localFirstArg, localSecondArg);
            state = ParseState.PS_2ND_OPRND;
        } else if (aToken instanceof TInteger) {
            TInteger localTInteger = (TInteger) aToken;
            localSecondArg = new IntArg(
                    localTInteger.getIntValue());
            aCode = new TwoArgInstr(
                    localMnemon, localFirstArg, localSecondArg);
            state = ParseState.PS_2ND_OPRND;
        } else {
            aCode = new Error(
                    "Second argument not an identifier or integer.");
        }
        break;
```

(continues)

```
...
            case PS_NON_UNARY2:
                if (aToken instanceof TEmpty) {
                    state = ParseState.PS_FINISH;
                } else {
                    aCode = new Error("Illegal trailing character.");
                }
                break;
        }
    } while (state != ParseState.PS_FINISH && !(aCode instanceof Error));
    return terminate;
}

public void translate() {
    ArrayList<ACode> codeTable = new ArrayList<>();
    int numErrors = 0;
    t = new Tokenizer(b);
    boolean terminateWithEnd = false;
    b.getLine();
    while (b.inputRemains() && !terminateWithEnd) {
        terminateWithEnd = parseLine(); // Sets aCode and returns boolean.
        codeTable.add(aCode);
        if (aCode instanceof Error) {
            numErrors++;
        }
        b.getLine();
    }
    if (!terminateWithEnd) {
        aCode = new Error("Missing \"end\" sentinel.");
        codeTable.add(aCode);
        numErrors++;
    }
    if (numErrors == 0) {
        System.out.printf("Object code:\n");
        for (int i = 0; i < codeTable.size(); i++) {
            System.out.printf("%s", codeTable.get(i).generateCode());
        }
    }
```

```
    if (numErrors == 1) {
        System.out.printf("One error was detected.\n");
    } else if (numErrors > 1) {
        System.out.printf("%d errors were detected.\n", numErrors);
    }
    System.out.printf("\nProgram listing:\n");
    for (int i = 0; i < codeTable.size(); i++) {
        System.out.printf("%s", codeTable.get(i).generateListing());
    }
  }
}
```

The first line in `translate()` instantiates a code table as a list of abstract code objects. It maintains a count of the number of errors detected and instantiates a tokenizer, passing the input buffer for its constructor. It also maintains a Boolean flag initialized to false that is set to true when the end token is detected. It calls the `getLine()` method of the buffer to get the first line of the source. To reestablish the loop invariant, it calls `getLine()` as the last statement in the body of the loop. The loop continues executing as long as input remains in the buffer and the Boolean flag remains false.

The first statement in the `while` loop calls `parseLine()`, which returns true when it detects the end token. As a side effect, it sets the `aCode` attribute of the translator class to the concrete code object that it constructs in the parse. `translate()` stores this concrete code object in its code table. It also increments the error count if the code is an `Error` object. The remaining code in `translate()` outputs the object code and formatted source listing by looping through the code table and invoking `generateCode()` and `generateListing()` for each code object.

The structure of `parseLine()` in Figure 7.47 is identical to the structure of `getToken()` in Figure 7.45 because both functions implement an FSM. Both functions have a state variable named `state` and have a do loop that terminates when a sentinel is detected or when an error occurs. The first statement in the `getToken()` loop is

```
nextChar = b.advanceInput();
```

which gets the next terminal character from the buffer. This loop for the lexical analyzer scans enough terminal characters to comprise a single token. The first statement in the `parseLine()` loop is

```
aToken = t.getToken();
```

which gets the next token. This loop for the parser scans enough tokens to comprise a single source line. It is doing the same processing as the lexical analyzer loop but at a higer level of abstraction. A nonterminal symbol for the lexical analyzer acts like a terminal symbol for the parser.

Figure 7.47 shows code fragments of the FSM for the parser in the case of PS_START, PS_COMMA, and PS_NON_UNARY2. Code for the other cases is similar. In the case of PS_START, the parser expects either an identifier or the empty token. If it detects an identifier, it checks the maps for unary and nonunary instructions using the string it gets from the token as the key. If the map has an entry for the key, it retrieves the corresponding mnemonic from the map. It stores the retrieved mnemonic in a local variable that it uses for the rest of the parse.

If it detects a unary instruction, it has all the information necessary to instantiate a concrete code object, which it gives to aCode with the statement

```
aCode = new UnaryInstr(localMnemon);
```

This is the side effect referred to earlier. If it detects M_END, it sets the termination flag to true, which eventually terminates the loop.

If it detects a nonunary instruction, it does not have all the information necessary to instantiate a concrete code object. It simply stores the local mnemonic to be used later and sets the next state to PS_FUNCTION using the direct-code technique.

In the case of PS_COMMA, the parser has detected the comma token and expects the second argument, which can be an identifier or an integer. If it is an identifier, it instantiates a new second argument object with the statement

```
localSecondArg = new IdentArg(
    localTIdentifier.getStringValue());
```

The constructor for the argument requires a string, which the parser has gotten from the token. The parser has previously instantiated the first argument the same way. Now it can instantiate the code object using the local mnemonic and the two arguments with the statement

```
aCode = new TwoArgInstr(
    localMnemon, localFirstArg, localSecondArg);
```

The code is similar if the second argument is an integer. In both instances, the state variable is set to PS_SECOND_OPRND in accordance with the FSM of Figure 7.46.

FIGURE 7.48 is a complete listing of the actionPerformed() function that invokes the translator. It is a simple three-step process. The first statement instantiates the input buffer with the source code string that the user enters in the input dialog box. The second statement instantiates

---

FIGURE 7.48

The `actionPerformed()` function for the translator that produces the output of Figure 7.37.

```
public void actionPerformed(ActionEvent event) {
   InBuffer inBuffer = new InBuffer(textArea.getText());
   Translator tr = new Translator(inBuffer);
   tr.translate();
}
```

---

the translator, passing it the input buffer in its constructor so it will have access to the source code. The third statement invokes the void function `translate()`.

The functions that perform the three phases of the automatic translation are as follows:

> Lexical analyzer: `getToken()`

> Parser: `parseLine()`

> Code generator: `generateCode()`

The three translation phases of the program

The lexical analyzer takes as input the stream of terminal characters from the input buffer and provides as output the resulting stream of tokens for the parser. The translator calls the parser for each line of source code, and the parser calls the lexical analyzer. In general, the output of the parser and input of the code generator is the syntax tree of the parse and/or the source program written in an internal low-level language. In this translator, the output of the parser and input of the code generator is only the source program written in an internal low-level language. This low-level language is the list of code objects stored in `codeTable`. After the parse is complete, `translate()` generates the code by iterating through the code table and calling the code generation function for each code object.

Parser Characteristics

Rather than define the syntax of the source language with the FSM of Figure 7.46, you could define it with a grammar. A formal grammar for the source language would have a simple structure. For example, a production rule for a `set` statement might be

<set-statement> → set (<identifier> , <argument>)

where <argument> would be defined in another production rule as <identifier> or <integer>. Unlike in C, this grammar would contain no recursive definitions.

Parsers are usually not based on an FSM.

The simple nature of the source syntax allows the parsing of this language to be based on a deterministic FSM. Parsers for most programming languages cannot be this simple. Although it is common for lexical analyzers to be based on FSMs, it is rare that a parser can also be based on an FSM. In practice, most languages are too complex for such a technique to be possible.

Because the production rules of a real grammar invariably contain many recursive definitions, the parsing algorithm itself may contain recursive procedures that reflect the recursion of the grammar. Such an algorithm is called a *recursive descent parser*.

Regardless of the complexity of the source language or the parsing technique of the translator, the relationship of the parser to the lexical analyzer in a translation program is always the same. The parser is at a higher level of abstraction than the lexical analyzer. The lexical analyzer scans the characters and recognizes tokens, which it passes to the parser. The parser scans the tokens and produces a syntax tree and/or the source program written in an internal low-level language. The code generator uses the syntax tree and/or the low-level translation to produce the object code.

Chapter Summary

The fundamental question of computer science is: What can be automated? The automatic translation of artificial languages is at the heart of computer science. Each artificial language has an alphabet. The closure of a set, T^*, is the set of all possible strings formed by concatenating elements from T. A language is a subset of the closure of its alphabet. A grammar describes the syntax of a language and has four parts: a nonterminal alphabet, a terminal alphabet, a set of rules of production, and a start symbol. Derivation is the process by which a grammar determines a valid sentence in the language. To derive a sentence in the language, you begin with the start symbol and substitute production rules until you get a string of terminals. The parsing problem is to determine the substitution sequence to match a given string of terminals. There are hundreds of rules of production in the standard C grammar. A context-free grammar is one that restricts the left side of all the production rules to contain a single nonterminal. Although the C grammar is context-free, certain aspects of the language are context-sensitive.

A finite-state machine (FSM) also describes the syntax of a language. It consists of a set of states and transitions between the states. Each transition is marked with an input terminal symbol. One state is the start state, and at least one, possibly more, is the final state. A nondeterministic FSM may have more than one transition from a given state on one input terminal symbol. A sentence is valid if, starting at the start state, you can make a sequence of transitions dictated by the symbols in the sentence and end in a final state.

Two software implementation techniques of FSMs are the table-lookup technique and the direct-code technique. Both techniques contain loops that are controlled by a state variable, which is initialized to the start state. Each execution of the loop corresponds to a transition in the FSM. In the table-lookup technique, the transitions are assigned from a two-dimensional transition table. In the direct-code technique, the transitions are assigned with selection statements in the body of the loop.

The three translation phases of an automatic translator are the lexical analyzer, the parser, and the code generator. The input of the lexical analyzer is a stream of terminal symbols in the source program. The output of the lexical analyzer, which is the input to the parser, is a stream of tokens. The output of the parser, which is the input of the code generator, is an abstract syntax tree and/or the source program written in an internal low-level language. For most high-level languages, the lexical analyzer is based on an FSM and the parser is based on a context-free grammar. The code generator is highly dependent on the nature of the object language.

Exercises

Section 7.1

*1. What is the fundamental question of computer science?

2. What is the identity element for the addition operation on integers? What is the identity element for the OR operation on Booleans?

3. Derive the following strings with the grammar of Figure 7.1 and draw the corresponding syntax tree:

   *(a) abc123   (b) a1b2c3   (c) a321bc

4. Derive the following strings with the grammar of Figure 7.2 and draw the corresponding syntax tree:

   *(a) -d   (b) +ddd   (c) d

5. Derive the following strings with the grammar of Figure 7.3:

   *(a) abc   (b) aabbcc

6. For each of the following strings, state whether it can be derived from the rules of the grammar of Figure 7.5. If it can, draw the corresponding syntax tree:

*(a) a + (a)   (b) a * (+ a)   (c) a * (a + a)
(d) a * (a + a) * a (e) a + (- a) (f) (((a)))

7. For the grammar of Figure 7.8, draw the syntax tree for <statement> from the following strings, assuming that S1, S2, S3, S4, C1, and C2 are valid <expression>s:

*(a)
```
{ if ( C1 )
    S1 ;
  S2 ;
}
```

(b)
```
{ if ( C1 )
      if ( C2 )
        S1 ;
      else
        S2 ;
    S3 ;
}
```

(c)
```
{ if ( C1 )
      if ( C2 )
        S1 ;
      else
        S2 ;
    else
      S3 ;
  S4 ;
}
```

(d)
```
{ S1 ;
  while ( C1 )
  { if ( C2 )
      S2 ;
    S3 ;
  }
}
```

8. For the grammar of Figure 7.8, draw the syntax tree for <statement> from the following strings, assuming that alpha, beta, and gamma are valid <identifier>s and 1 and 24 are valid <constant>s:

*(a) alpha = 1 ;
(b) alpha = alpha + 1 ;
(c) alpha = (beta * 1) ;
(d) alpha = ((beta + 1) * (gamma + 24)) ;
(e) alpha (beta) ;
(f) alpha (beta, 24) ;

9. For the grammar of Figure 7.8, draw the syntax tree for \<translation-unit\> from the following string, assuming that `alpha`, `beta`, `gamma`, and `main` are valid \<identifier\>s and *C1*, *S1*, and *S2* are \<expression\>s:

```
int main()
{ int gamma;
  alpha (gamma);
  if (C1)
      S1;
  else
      S2;
}
```

10. The question this exercise poses is "Can two different grammars produce the same language?" The grammars in FIGURE 7.49 and FIGURE 7.50 are not the same because they have different nonterminal sets and different production rules. Experiment with these two grammars by deriving some terminal strings. From your experiments, describe the languages produced by these grammars. Is it possible to derive a valid string of terminals with the grammar in Figure 7.49 that is not in 7.50 or vice versa? Prove your conjecture.

Section 7.2

11. For each of the machines shown in FIGURE 7.51, (1) state whether the FSM is deterministic or nondeterministic, and (2) identify any states that are inaccessible.

12. Remove the empty transitions to produce the equivalent machine for each of the FSMs in FIGURE 7.52.

13. Draw a deterministic FSM that recognizes strings of 1's and 0's specified by each of the following criteria. Each FSM should reject any characters

FIGURE 7.49
A grammar for Exercise 10.

$N = \{A, B\}$
$T = \{0, 1\}$
$P =$ the productions
    1. $A \rightarrow 0\ B$
    2. $B \rightarrow 1\ 0\ B$
    3. $B \rightarrow \varepsilon$
$S = A$

FIGURE 7.50
Another grammar for Exercise 10.

$N = \{C\}$
$T = \{0, 1\}$
$P =$ the productions
    1. $C \rightarrow C\ 1\ 0$
    2. $C \rightarrow 0$
$S = C$

FIGURE 7.51
The FSMs for Exercise 11.

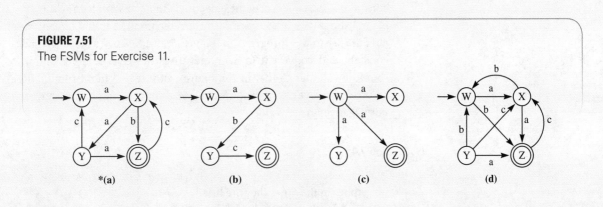

*(a)   (b)   (c)   (d)

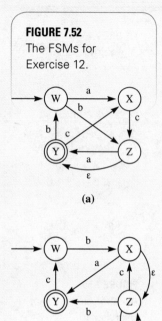

(a)

(b)

that are not 0 or 1. *(a) The string of three characters, 101. (b) All strings of arbitrary length that end in 101. For example, the FSM should accept 1101 but reject 1011. (c) All strings of arbitrary length that begin with 101. For example, the FSM should accept 1010 but reject 0101. (d) All strings of arbitrary length that contain a 101 at least once anywhere. For example, the FSM should accept all the strings mentioned in parts (a), (b), and (c), as well as strings such as 111000010111111100111.

Section 7.4

14. Design a grammar that describes the source language of the translator in Figure 7.47.

Problems

Section 7.3

15. Improve the program in Figure 7.28 as suggested in the text by defining a third enumeration in Alphabet called T_OTHER, which represents a symbol that is neither a letter nor a digit.

16. Implement each FSM in Exercise 13 using the table-lookup technique of the program in Figure 7.28. Classify a character as B_ONE, B_ZERO, or B_OTHER in the transition table.

17. Implement each FSM in Exercise 13 using the direct-code technique of the program in Figure 7.29. Write a procedure called parsePat() for a parse pattern that corresponds to parseNum(). Do not include the attribute number or method getNumber() in class Parser.

18. A hexadecimal digit is '0'..'9', or 'a'..'f', or 'A'..'F'. A hexadecimal constant is a sequence of hexadecimal digits. Examples include 3, a, 0d, and FF4e. Use the direct-code technique for implementing an FSM as in the program of Figure 7.29 to parse a hexadecimal constant and convert it to a nonnegative integer. The input/output should be similar to that in the figure, with invalid input producing an error message and a valid hexadecimal input string producing the nonnegative integer value.

Section 7.4

19. Write an assembler for Pep/9 assembly language. Complete the following milestones in the order they are listed.

(a) Write class `Tokenizer` with method `getToken()`, to implement the FSM of FIGURE 7.53 . Use class `InBuffer` from Figure 7.30. Implement method `getDescription()` for each concrete token and output the tokens with a nested do loop as in `actionPerformed()` of Figure 7.36.

Integers are stored in two bytes. When considered unsigned, the range is 0..65535. When considered signed, the range is −32768..32767. Your program must accept integers in the range −32768..65535. Each time you scan a decimal digit and update the total value, check it against this range. If inputting a decimal digit makes the total value go out of this range, return the invalid token.

FIGURE 7.53

The FSM for `getToken` in Problem 19(a).

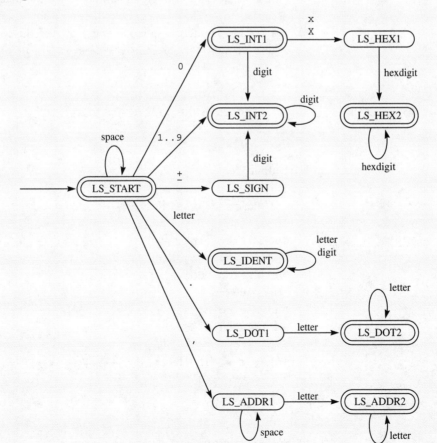

Hexadecimal constants are also stored in two bytes and are never signed. The maximum value that a hexadecimal constant can have is 65535. Each time you scan a hex digit and update the total value, check its *decimal* value against this upper limit. If inputting a hex digit makes the total greater than this upper limit, return the invalid token. You should check the limit every time you scan a hexadecimal digit. Do not test that the number of hexadecimal digits is less than five, because, for example, 0x00F4B7 is valid.

Addressing modes must be stored with a Java String attribute as with identifiers. The parser will convert the identifiers to enumerated types by table lookup.

A common mistake is to call advanceInput() within the switch statement. Make sure you do not do that .advanceInput() must be called from only one place, namely as the first statement in the body of the do loop.

Following is an example input/output. All the tokens are valid according to the FSM. For example, there is no dot command .beta, nor is there an addressing mode cat. However, the corresponding tokens are valid. The parser detects the errors later in the translation.

Input
```
alpha .beta
   b7 0x23ab ,SfX
,i , cat
-32768 65535
```

Output
```
Identifier = alpha
Dot command = beta
Empty token
Identifier = b7
Hexadecimal constant = 9131
Addressing Mode = SfX
Empty token
Addressing Mode = i
Addressing Mode = cat
Empty token
Integer = -32768
Integer = 65535
Empty token
```

(b) Design the state transition diagram for the FSM of the Pep/9 parser that corresponds to the FSM of Figure 7.46. Assume that each transition is on one of the tokens in Figure 7.53.

(c) This phase of the project is to write the parser based on your FSM of part (b). Complete the `generateListing()` methods of the code classes, and output the formatted listing of the source program but not the object code. Here is the list of instructions your program should process:

> Unary instructions—STOP, ASLA, ASRA

> Nonunary instructions—BR, BRLT, BREQ, BRLE, CPWA, DECI, DECO, ADDA, SUBA, STWA, LDWA

> Dot commands—.BLOCK, .END

> Constants—decimal, hexadecimal

Design an abstract argument `AArg` with two subclasses for a hexadecimal constant and a decimal constant, each with an integer attribute, analogous to Figure 7.40. Design your abstract code class `ACode` analogous to the code class in Figure 7.44. The class for a nonunary mnemonic must have an abstract argument for its instruction specifier and an addressing mnemonic for its addressing mode, which must be enumerated as described in part (a). Do not combine the addressing mode enumerated types with any other enumerated type. They must be separate. Set up separate Java maps for looking up unary mnemonic identifiers, nonunary mnemonic identifiers, dot commands, and addressing modes. For your code classes, do not use a Boolean attribute to distinguish unary from nonunary instructions. Instead, have separate classes for unary and nonunary instructions.

Do not use the names `OneArgInstr` or `TwoArgInstr` from the Figure 7.44 example to describe your instructions. In Pep/9 assembly language, instructions are either unary or nonunary. Do not use the names `firstArg` or `secondArg` from the figure to describe the items that follow the mnemonic. For nonunary instructions, the items following the mnemonic are the operand specifier and the addressing mode.

If you detect an illegal addressing mode or other error, you must generate an error code object to handle the error. For example, do not use the nonunary code object to generate any error messages.

The output should conform to the standard pretty-printing format of the Pep/9 assembler when you select Format From Listing in the Edit menu. For hexadecimal constants, the %X format placeholder will output an integer value in hexadecimal format. Research the Java documentation for the field width and leading zero options. For strings, the %s format placeholder has options to either left justify or right justify in a field padded with spaces.

(d) Complete the generateCode() methods of your code classes to emit the hexadecimal object code for the assembly language program in a format suitable for use by the Pep/9 loader. Following is an example input/output. Your code generator should emit one line of hex pairs for each line of source code to make it easy to visually compare the object with the source.

Input
```
BR      0x0007,  i
.BLOCK 4
deci     0x2  ,d
LDWA      +2,d
AdDa -5,   i
STWA      0x0004,d
     DECO      0x04,d
STOP
.END
```

Output
```
Object code:
12 00 07
00 00 00 00
31 00 02
C1 00 02
60 FF FB
E1 00 04
39 00 04
00
zz

Program listing:
BR        0x0007
.BLOCK    4
DECI      0x0002,d
```

```
LDWA    2,d
ADDA    -5,i
STWA    0x0004,d
DECO    0x0004,d
STOP
.END
```

To get a decimal value into hex, you can use the fact that $n/256$ is an eight-bit right shift of n. Use it to output the first byte of integer n. Also, $n\%256$ is an eight-bit remainder. Use it to output the second byte of integer n.

All hex digit pairs in the object code must be separated by exactly one space, no lines in the object code may contain a trailing space at the end of the line, and the entire sequence must terminate with lowercase zz. To test your object code, copy the hex code from the Java console, paste it into the object code pane of the Pep/9 application, and execute your program.

(e) Extend the assembler by including all 40 instructions in the Pep/9 instruction set.

(f) Extend the assembler by producing a listing that shows the object code next to the source line that produced it. Print the source line with the standard spacing conventions and uppercase and lowercase conventions of the Pep/9 assembler.

(g) Extend the assembler by permitting character constants enclosed in single quotes.

(h) Extend the assembler by permitting the dot commands .WORD and .BYTE.

(i) Extend the assembler by permitting the .ASCII dot command with strings enclosed in double quotes.

(j) Extend the assembler by permitting a source line to contain a comment prefixed by a semicolon. A line may contain only a comment, or a valid instruction followed by a comment.

(k) Extend the assembler by permitting symbols.

LEVEL 4

Operating System

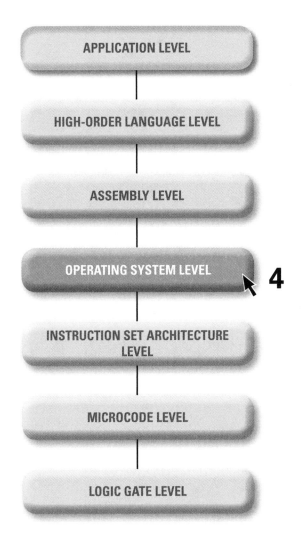

APPLICATION LEVEL

HIGH-ORDER LANGUAGE LEVEL

ASSEMBLY LEVEL

OPERATING SYSTEM LEVEL   4

INSTRUCTION SET ARCHITECTURE LEVEL

MICROCODE LEVEL

LOGIC GATE LEVEL

CHAPTER 8

Process Management

The purposes of an operating system

An operating system defines a more abstract machine that is easier to program than the machine at Level ISA3. Its purpose is to provide a convenient environment for higher-level programming and to allocate the resources of the system efficiently. The operating system level is between the assembly and machine levels. As is the case with abstraction in general, the operating system hides the details of the Level ISA3 machine from users at higher levels.

The resources of a typical computer system include CPU time, main memory, and disk memory. This chapter describes how an operating system allocates CPU time. Chapter 9 shows how it allocates main memory and disk memory.

There are three general categories of operating systems:

Three types of operating systems

> Single-user

> Multi-user

> Real-time

Mobile devices like smartphones and tablets have single-user operating systems. Such a computer is typically owned and operated by a single individual and is not shared with anyone else. Desktop and laptop computers typically have multi-user operating systems so that accounts for individual users can be set up and the computer shared. Real-time systems are used in computers that are dedicated to controlling equipment. Their inputs are from sensors and their outputs are the control signals for the equipment. For example, the computer that controls an automobile engine is a real-time system.

The Pep/9 operating system is a single-user system. It illustrates some of the techniques used to allocate CPU time. However, it does not illustrate the management of main memory or disk memory. The first two sections of this chapter include a complete listing of the Pep/9 operating system.

8.1 Loaders

An important function of an operating system is to manage the jobs that users submit to be executed. In a multi-user system, several users continually submit jobs. The operating system must decide which job to run from a list of pending jobs. After it decides which job to execute next, it must load the appropriate program into main memory and turn control of the CPU over to that program for execution.

The Pep/9 Operating System

FIGURE 8.1 shows the location of the Pep/9 operating system in main memory. The random-access memory (RAM) part of the operating system consists of the system stack, whose first byte will be allocated at FC0E, the system globals at FC0F to FC14, the input device at FC15, and the output device at FC16. The read-only memory (ROM) part of the operating system, which is shaded in the figure, consists of the loader at FC17, the trap handler at FC52, and the six machine vectors at FFF4 through FFFE. Although the Pep/9 operating system illustrates the operation of a loader, it does not illustrate the process by which the operating system must decide which job to run from a list of pending jobs.

This chapter describes the Pep/9 operating system, which is written in assembly language. Common practice is to write operating systems in a mixture of a high-order language, usually C, and the assembly language for the particular computer controlled by the operating system. Typically, more than 95% of the system is in the high-order language and less than 5% is in the assembly language. The assembly language portion is reserved for those parts of the operating system that cannot be programmed with the features available in the high-order language, or that require an extra measure of efficiency that even an optimizing compiler cannot achieve.

FIGURE 8.2 shows the global constants and variables of the Pep/9 operating system. Symbols TRUE and FALSE are declared with the .EQUATE command and thus generate no object code. They are used throughout the rest of the program.

Symbols osRAM, wordTemp, byteTemp, addrMask, opAddr, charIn, and charOut are all defined with the .BLOCK command. Normally, .BLOCK generates code, and any code generated starts at address 0000 (hex). The listing shows these .BLOCK commands generating no code and osRAM starting at FB8F instead of at 0000.

The reason for this peculiar assembler behavior is the .BURN command at FC17. When you include .BURN in a program, the assembler assumes that the program will be burned into ROM. It generates code for those instructions that follow the burn directive but not for those that precede it. The assembler also assumes that the last byte of ROM will be installed at the address given by the .BURN directive, leaving the top of memory for the application programs. It therefore calculates the addresses for the symbol table, such that the last byte generated will have the address specified by the burn directive.

In this listing, the burn directive indicates that the last byte should be at address FFFF. Figure 8.16, at the end of the operating system, shows that

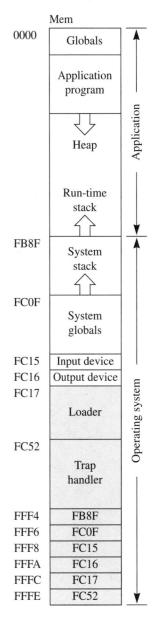

FIGURE 8.1
A memory map of the Pep/9 memory. The shaded part is read-only memory.

FIGURE 8.2

The global constants and variables of the Pep/9 operating system.

```
            ;******* Pep/9 Operating System, 2015/05/17
            ;
            TRUE:     .EQUATE 1
            FALSE:    .EQUATE 0
            ;
            ;******* Operating system RAM
FB8F        osRAM:    .BLOCK   128          ;System stack area
FC0F        wordTemp:.BLOCK    1            ;Temporary word storage
FC10        byteTemp:.BLOCK    1            ;Least significant byte of wordTemp
FC11        addrMask:.BLOCK    2            ;Addressing mode mask
FC13        opAddr:   .BLOCK   2            ;Trap instruction operand address
FC15        charIn:   .BLOCK   1            ;Memory-mapped input device
FC16        charOut: .BLOCK    1            ;Memory-mapped output device
            ;
            ;******* Operating system ROM
FC17                  .BURN    0xFFFF
```

the last byte, 52 (hex), is indeed at address FFFF. Because FFFF (hex) is 65,535 (dec), the Pep/9 computer is configured with a total of 64 KiB of main memory. You can change the value in the .BURN directive to change where the operating system is installed and the system will still work. For example, if you change the value from 0xFFFF to 0x7FFF and select the option to assemble and install the operating system, the last byte of ROM will be at address 32 Ki minus 1 instead of at 64 Ki minus 1. The symbols and machine vectors will all be recomputed and the system will still run correctly.

The Pep/9 Loader

FIGURE 8.3 shows the Pep/9 loader. To invoke the loader, you select the load option from the simulator. This triggers the following two events:

Invoking the Pep/9 loader

SP ← Mem[FFF6]
PC ← Mem[FFFC]

Because Mem[FFF6] contains FC0F, as shown in both Figure 8.1 and Figure 8.16, the stack pointer (SP) is initialized to FC0F. Similarly, the program counter (PC) is initialized to FC17, the address of the first instruction of the loader.

FIGURE 8.3

The loader of the Pep/9 operating system.

```
              ;******* System Loader
              ;Data must be in the following format:
              ;Each hex number representing a byte must contain exactly two
              ;characters. Each character must be in 0..9, A..F, or a..f and
              ;must be followed by exactly one space. There must be no
              ;leading spaces at the beginning of a line and no trailing
              ;spaces at the end of a line. The last two characters in the
              ;file must be lowercase zz, which is used as the terminating
              ;sentinel by the loader.
              ;
FC17  C80000 loader:  LDWX    0,i             ;X <- 0
              ;
FC1A  D1FC15 getChar: LDBA    charIn,d        ;Get first hex character
FC1D  B0007A          CPBA    'z',i           ;If end of file sentinel 'z'
FC20  18FC51          BREQ    stopLoad        ;  then exit loader routine
FC23  B00039          CPBA    '9',i           ;If character <= '9', assume decimal
FC26  14FC2C          BRLE    shift           ;  and right nybble is correct digit
FC29  600009          ADDA    9,i             ;else convert nybble to correct digit
FC2C  0A      shift:  ASLA                    ;Shift left by four bits to send
FC2D  0A              ASLA                    ;  the digit to the most significant
FC2E  0A              ASLA                    ;  position in the byte
FC2F  0A              ASLA
FC30  F1FC10          STBA    byteTemp,d      ;Save the most significant nybble
FC33  D1FC15          LDBA    charIn,d        ;Get second hex character
FC36  B00039          CPBA    '9',i           ;If character <= '9', assume decimal
FC39  14FC3F          BRLE    combine         ;  and right nybble is correct digit
FC3C  600009          ADDA    9,i             ;else convert nybble to correct digit
FC3F  80000F combine: ANDA    0x000F,i        ;Mask out the left nybble
FC42  91FC0F          ORA     wordTemp,d      ;Combine both hex digits in binary
FC45  F50000          STBA    0,x             ;Store in Mem[X]
FC48  680001          ADDX    1,i             ;X <- X + 1
FC4B  D1FC15          LDBA    charIn,d        ;Skip blank or <LF>
FC4E  12FC1A          BR      getChar         ;
              ;
FC51  00      stopLoad:STOP                   ;
```

The definition of a nybble

The loader begins at FC17 by clearing the index register to zero, which is the address of the first byte to load. The code from FC1A to FC42 gets the next two hex characters from the input stream into the low-order byte of the accumulator. The store byte accumulator instruction at FC45 loads the byte into memory at the address specified by the index register. The add index register instruction at FC48 increments the index register by one in preparation for loading the next byte.

The loader is in the form of a single loop that inputs a character and compares it with sentinel z. If the character is not the sentinel, the program checks whether it is in '0'..'9'. If it is not in that range, the rightmost four bits, called a *nybble* because it is half a byte, is converted to the proper value by adding 9 to it. Note that ASCII A is 0100 0001 (bin), so that when 9 is added to it the sum is 0100 1010. The rightmost nybble is the correct bit pattern for hexadecimal digit A. It will similarly be correct for hexadecimal digits B through F. If the character is in '0'..'9', the rightmost nybble is already correct.

The loader shifts the nybble four bits to the left and stores it temporarily in byteTemp. It inputs the second character of the pair, adjusts the nybble similarly, and combines both nybbles into a single byte with the ANDA at FC3F and ORA at FC42. Unfortunately, Pep/9 does not have an AND byte or an OR byte instruction. So it must use the word versions of these operations. You can see from Figure 8.2 that byteTemp is the least significant byte of wordTemp, which is why ORA can use wordTemp to access byteTemp. The loader terminates with the STOP instruction, which returns control to the simulator options.

Load modules are typically not in ASCII.

Programs to be loaded typically are not in the format of hexadecimal ASCII characters. They are already in binary, ready to be loaded. Pep/9 uses ASCII characters for the object file, so you can program directly in machine language and view the object file with a text editor.

Program Termination

The application programs presented thus far have all terminated with the STOP instruction. The STOP instruction in a real computer is rarely executed. Rather than generate a STOP instruction at the end of a program, a C compiler generates an instruction that returns control to the operating system. If your program ran on a personal computer, the operating system would set up the screen to wait for you to request another service. If your program ran on a remote timesharing system, the operating system would continue to process other users' jobs. In no case would the computer itself simply stop.

If there is only one CPU, it alternates between executing operating system jobs and application jobs. **FIGURE 8.4** shows a time line of CPU usage when

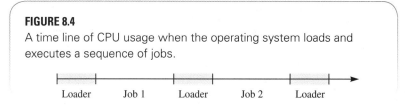

FIGURE 8.4
A time line of CPU usage when the operating system loads and
executes a sequence of jobs.

Loader　　Job 1　　Loader　　Job 2　　Loader

the operating system loads and executes a sequence of jobs. The shaded parts
represent that part of the time spent executing the operating system.

The operating system represents the overhead necessary for doing
business. When you shop at a mall, the price you pay for a widget does
not reflect just the cost of production and transportation of the widget to
the store. It also reflects the salesperson's salary, the electricity for the store
lighting, the fringe benefits for the store manager, and so on. Similarly, 100%
of a computer's resources does not go toward executing user programs. A
certain fraction of the resources, in this case CPU time, must be reserved for
the operating system.

8.2 **Traps**

When programming in assembly language at Level Asmb5, you may use
these four instructions: DECI, DECO, HEXO, and STRO. Figure 4.6 shows no
such instructions in the Level ISA3 machine. Instead, when the computer
fetches the instructions with these opcodes, the hardware executes a trap.
A trap is similar to a subroutine jump, but more elaborate. The code that
executes is called a *trap routine* or *trap handler* instead of a *subroutine*. The
operating system returns control to the application program by executing
a return from trap instruction, RETTR, instead of a return from subroutine
instruction, RET.

The trap handler implements the four instructions as if they were part of
the Level ISA3 machine. Remember that one purpose of an operating system
is to provide a convenient environment for higher-level programming.
The abstract machine provided by the Pep/9 operating system is a more
convenient machine because it contains these four additional instructions
not present at Level ISA3. In addition to DECI, DECO, HEXO, and STRO, the
operating system provides two unary trap instructions and one nonunary
trap instruction, called *no-operations*, with mnemonics NOP0, NOP1, and NOP.
These instructions do nothing when they execute and are provided so you
can reprogram them to implement new instructions of your own choosing.

The NOP *trap instructions*

The Trap Mechanism

Here is the register transfer language (RTL) specification for a trap instruction:

A Pep/9 trap

Temp	← Mem[FFF6] ;
Mem[Temp − 1]	← IR⟨0..7⟩ ;
Mem[Temp − 3]	← SP ;
Mem[Temp − 5]	← PC ;
Mem[Temp − 7]	← X ;
Mem[Temp − 9]	← A ;
Mem[Temp − 10]⟨4..7⟩	← NZVC ;
SP	← Temp − 10 ;
PC	← Mem[FFFE]

Temp represents a temporary value for notational convenience. Mem[FFF6] contains FC0F, the address of the system stack. In the first event, Temp gets FC0F. The next six events show the CPU pushing the content of all the registers onto the system stack, starting with the instruction specifier of the IR and ending with the NZVC flags. The stack pointer is then modified to point to the new top of the system stack, and the program counter gets the content of Mem[FFFE].

FIGURE 8.5 shows an example of such a trap from Figure 5.11. The program in Figure 5.11 contains the following decimal output trap:

```
003E 390003 DECO 0x0003,d ;Output the sum
```

FIGURE 8.5

A trap triggered by the execution of the DECO trap instruction 390003.

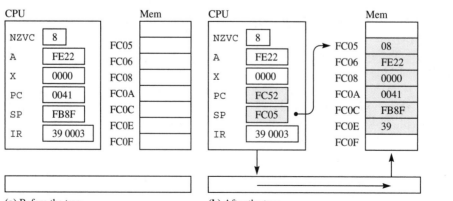

(a) Before the trap.   (b) After the trap.

where 003E is the address of the instruction and 390003 is the object code that triggered the trap during execution.

Figure 8.5(a) shows the state of the CPU before the trap executes, and Figure 8.5(b) shows the state after the trap executes. Only the instruction specifier part of the IR is pushed onto the stack. Also note that the four NZVC bits are right justified in the byte at Mem[FC05]. The leftmost nybble of the byte is zero. SP contains FC05, the new top of the system stack, and PC contains Mem[FFFE], which is FC52, the address of the first instruction of the trap handler. Figure 8.16 shows how the operating system sets up the machine vectors at FFF6 and FFFE with the .ADDRSS commands.

The RETTR Instruction

A program during execution is called a *process*. The trap mechanism temporarily suspends the process so the operating system can perform a service. The block of information in main memory that contains a copy of the trapped process's registers is called a *process control block* (PCB). The PCB for this example is stored in Mem[FC05] to Mem[FC0E], as shown in Figure 8.5(b).

The definition of a process

The process control block (PCB)

After the operating system performs its service, it must eventually return control of the CPU to the suspended process so the process can complete its execution. In this example, the service performed by the Pep/9 operating system is execution of the DECO instruction. It returns control back to the process by executing the return from trap instruction, RETTR.

Here is the RTL specification for the RETTR instruction:

$$
\begin{aligned}
\text{NZVC} &\leftarrow \text{Mem[SP]}\langle 4..7\rangle\, ; \\
\text{A} &\leftarrow \text{Mem[SP + 1]}\, ; \\
\text{X} &\leftarrow \text{Mem[SP + 3]}\, ; \\
\text{PC} &\leftarrow \text{Mem[SP + 5]}\, ; \\
\text{SP} &\leftarrow \text{Mem[SP + 7]}
\end{aligned}
$$

The RETTR instruction

RETTR pops the top nine bytes off the stack into the NZVC, A, X, PC, and SP registers. This reverses the events of the trap, except that IR is not popped. The next instruction to execute will be the one specified by the new value of PC. The last register to change is SP.

If the trap handler does not modify any of the values in the PCB, RETTR will restore the original values in the CPU registers when the process resumes. In particular, the SP will again point to the top of the application stack, as it did at the time of the trap. On the other hand, any changes that the trap handler makes to the values in the PCB will be reflected in the CPU registers when the process resumes.

The Trap Handlers

FIGURE 8.6 shows the entry and exit points of the trap handlers. `oldIR` is the stack address of the copy of the IR register stored on the system stack from the trap mechanism. FIGURE 8.7(a) shows the stack addresses of all the registers.

FIGURE 8.6
The entry and exit points of the trap handlers in the Pep/9 operating system.

```
              ;******* Trap handler
              oldIR:   .EQUATE 9              ;Stack address of IR on trap
              ;
FC52 DB0009 trap:    LDBX    oldIR,s       ;X <- trapped IR
FC55 B80028          CPBX    0x0028,i      ;If X >= first nonunary trap opcode
FC58 1CFC67          BRGE    nonUnary      ;  trap opcode is nonunary
              ;
FC5B 880001 unary:   ANDX    0x0001,i      ;Mask out all but rightmost bit
FC5E 0B              ASLX                  ;Two bytes per address
FC5F 25FC63          CALL    unaryJT,x     ;Call unary trap routine
FC62 02              RETTR                 ;Return from trap
              ;
FC63 FD6B   unaryJT: .ADDRSS opcode26      ;Address of NOP0 subroutine
FC65 FD6C            .ADDRSS opcode27      ;Address of NOP1 subroutine
              ;
FC67 0D     nonUnary:ASRX                  ;Trap opcode is nonunary
FC68 0D              ASRX                  ;Discard addressing mode bits
FC69 0D              ASRX
FC6A 780005          SUBX    5,i           ;Adjust so that NOP opcode = 0
FC6D 0B              ASLX                  ;Two bytes per address
FC6E 25FC72          CALL    nonUnJT,x     ;Call nonunary trap routine
FC71 02     return:  RETTR                 ;Return from trap
              ;
FC72 FD6D   nonUnJT: .ADDRSS opcode28      ;Address of NOP subroutine
FC74 FD77            .ADDRSS opcode30      ;Address of DECI subroutine
FC76 FEEB            .ADDRSS opcode38      ;Address of DECO subroutine
FC78 FF76            .ADDRSS opcode40      ;Address of HEXO subroutine
FC7A FFC2            .ADDRSS opcode48      ;Address of STRO subroutine
```

When a trap instruction executes, the next instruction to execute is the one at FC52, the first instruction in Figure 8.6. The trap could have been triggered by any of the following instructions:

0010 011n,	NOPn,	Unary no-operation trap
0010 1aaa,	NOP,	Nonunary no-operation trap
0011 0aaa,	DECI,	Nonunary decimal-input trap
0011 1aaa,	DECO,	Nonunary decimal-output trap
0100 0aaa,	HEXO,	Nonunary hexadecimal-output trap
0100 1aaa,	STRO,	Nonunary string-output trap

The code in Figure 8.6 determines which instruction triggered the trap and calls the specific handler that implements that instruction. There are seven trap handlers, two for the unary NOPn instructions and five for the nonunary instructions. Remember that the fetch part of the von Neumann cycle puts the instruction specifier in the instruction register (IR). After the trap occurs, the instruction specifier of the instruction that caused the trap is available on the system stack, because it was pushed there by the trap mechanism. The code in Figure 8.6 accesses the saved instruction specifier to determine which instruction triggered the trap.

The first instruction in Figure 8.6 gets the opcode from the copy of IR that was pushed onto the system stack. The NOP instruction has the first nonunary opcode, 0010 1aaa. Furthermore, 0010 1000 (bin) is 28 (hex). The CPBX instruction at FC55 compares the trap opcode with 28 (hex). If the trap opcode is less than this value, the trap instruction is unary; otherwise, it is nonunary.

If the trap instruction is unary, it must be one of the following two instructions:

| 0010 0110, | NOP0, | rightmost bit is 0 |
| 0010 0111, | NOP1, | rightmost bit is 1 |

The ANDX instruction at FC5B masks out all but the rightmost bit, which is sufficient to determine which of the two instructions caused the trap. The CALL instruction at FC5F uses the jump table technique with indexed addressing as described in the program of Figure 6.40. That figure shows how the compiler translates a C switch statement using an array of addresses with the unconditional branch instruction BR. The code in Figure 8.6 differs slightly from that in Figure 6.40 because it uses CALL instead of BR, but the principle is the same. The jump table at FC63 is an array of addresses, each element of which is the address of the first statement to execute in the trap handler for the specific instruction that triggered the trap. Because a CALL executes, it pushes a return address onto the stack. The last instruction to execute in a specific trap handler is RET, which returns control to FC62. The

FIGURE 8.7
The stack addresses of the copies of the CPU registers.

(a) Immediately after a trap.

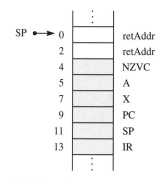

(b) With two return addresses on the run-time stack. The shaded region is the PCB.

The test for the NOPn instructions

instruction at FC62 is RETTR, which restores the registers in the CPU from the PCB and returns control to the instruction following the trap instruction.

The instructions at FC67 through FC7A do the same thing for the group of nonunary instructions. The three ASRX instructions discard the addressing mode bits, and the SUBX instruction makes an adjustment so that the content of the index register will be

The test for the nonunary trap instructions

0 if the trap IR contains 0010 1aaa, NOP
1 if the trap IR contains 0011 0aaa, DECI
2 if the trap IR contains 0011 1aaa, DECO
3 if the trap IR contains 0100 0aaa, HEXO
4 if the trap IR contains 0100 1aaa, STRO

As with the unary instructions, the CALL at FC6E branches to the trap handler for the specific instruction. After the trap handler implements the instruction, it returns control to the RETTR instruction at FC71, which in turn returns control to the statement after the one that caused the trap.

Trap Addressing Mode Assertion

Different instructions have different allowed addressing modes. For example, Figure 5.2 shows that the STWA instruction is not allowed to have immediate addressing, while the STRO instruction is only allowed to have direct, indirect, stack-relative, stack-relative deferred, and indexed addressing. Because the STWA instruction is hardwired into the CPU, the hardware detects whether an addressing error has occurred. But the trap instructions, such as STRO, are not native to the CPU. The trap handler implements them in software. The question then arises, how does a trap handler detect whether a trap instruction is attempting to use an illegal addressing mode? It does so with the addressing mode assert routine of FIGURE 8.8 .

The addressing mode assert routine must access the trap IR, which is saved on the system stack. Immediately after the trap, the IR has a stack address of 9, as Figure 8.7(a) shows. However, by the time the addressing mode assert routine is called, two additional return addresses are on top of the system stack. One comes from a CALL instruction in the trap handler code of Figure 8.6, and one comes from the CALL in the specific trap handler. Figure 8.7(b) shows the PCB on the system stack after the addressing-mode assert routine is called and the two return addresses are on the stack. The stack address of the trap IR is now 13 instead of 9 because of the four bytes occupied by the two return addresses.

The routine in Figure 8.8 has the following pre- and postconditions:

Pre- and postconditions for the addressing mode assert routine

> Precondition: addrMask is a bit mask representation of the set of allowable addressing modes, and the PCB of the trap instruction is on the system stack.

FIGURE 8.8

The trap addressing mode assertion in the Pep/9 operating system.

```
                  ;******* Assert valid trap addressing mode
                  oldIR4:   .EQUATE 13          ;oldIR + 4 with two return addresses
FC7C  D00001 assertAd:LDBA   1,i               ;A <- 1
FC7F  DB000D        LDBX    oldIR4,s           ;X <- OldIR
FC82  880007        ANDX    0x0007,i           ;Keep only the addressing mode bits
FC85  18FC8F        BREQ    testAd             ;000 = immediate addressing
FC88  0A      loop:  ASLA                       ;Shift the 1 bit left
FC89  780001        SUBX    1,i                ;Subtract from addressing mode count
FC8C  1AFC88        BRNE    loop               ;Try next addressing mode
FC8F  81FC11 testAd: ANDA   addrMask,d         ;AND the 1 bit with legal modes
FC92  18FC96        BREQ    addrErr
FC95  01            RET                        ;Legal addressing mode, return
FC96  D0000A addrErr: LDBA  '\n',i
FC99  F1FC16        STBA    charOut,d
FC9C  C0FCA9        LDWA    trapMsg,i          ;Push address of error message
FC9F  E3FFFE        STWA    -2,s
FCA2  580002        SUBSP   2,i                ;Call print subroutine
FCA5  24FFDE        CALL    prntMsg
FCA8  00            STOP                       ;Halt: Fatal runtime error
FCA9  455252 trapMsg: .ASCII "ERROR: Invalid trap addressing mode.\x00"
      . . .
```

> Postcondition: If the addressing mode of the trap instruction is in the set of allowable addressing modes, control is returned to the trap handler. Otherwise, an invalid addressing mode message is output and the program halts with a fatal run-time error.

The addressing mode assert routine is the Asmb5 version of the assert() statement found in some HOL6 languages. In C, the assert facility is in the <assert.h> library, which you can include in your programs with the #include compiler directive.

A trap handler uses the assert routine by first setting the value in global variable addrMask shown at FC11 in Figure 8.2 to indicate the allowable addressing modes for that particular instruction. Then it calls assertAd at FC7C in Figure 8.8. The routine assumes a common representation of a set known as the *bit-mapped representation*. In machine language, each bit can have a value of either 0 or 1. The bit-mapped representation of the set of allowable addressing modes associates each addressing mode with one bit in

The bit-mapped representation of a set

addrMask. If the bit has the value 0, the associated addressing mode is not in the set. If the bit has the value 1, the addressing mode is in the set.

FIGURE 8.9 shows the rightmost byte in addrMask with the precondition set by the trap handler for the STRO instruction, which can use direct, indirect, stack-relative, stack-relative deferred, or indexed addressing. The bits associated with those addressing modes have a value of 1, and the others have a value of 0. Mathematically, the mask represents the set {Direct, Indirect, Stack-relative, Stack-relative deferred, Indexed}.

To illustrate how the assert routine in Figure 8.8 tests for set membership, suppose the STRO instruction executes with stack-relative deferred addressing, so that its addressing-aaa field is 100. This is an allowable addressing mode. First, the LDBA statement at FC7C sets the rightmost byte of the accumulator to 0000 0001. The next two statements set the index register to 4 (dec) based on the addressing-aaa field of the trap instruction. A loop then counts down to zero starting from this value, shifting the 1 bit in the accumulator left each time through the loop. The accumulator ends up with 0001 0000, so that the 1 bit is at the bit position associated with stack-relative deferred addressing. The ANDA statement at FC8F takes the AND of the accumulator with the address mask in Figure 8.9. Because the 1's line up at the fifth bit from the right, the result is not zero, and control returns to the trap handler. If stack-relative deferred addressing were not allowed, the address mask would have a 0 at the fifth bit from the right, the result of the AND operation would be zero, and the assertion would fail.

FIGURE 8.9

The bits in addrMask associated with the allowable addressing modes of the STRO trap instruction.

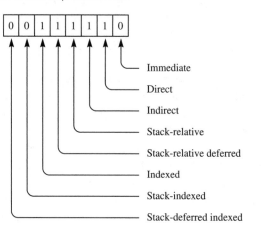

Trap Operand Address Computation

The trap operand address computation is another routine called by the nonunary trap handlers. The addressing modes for the native instructions are hardwired into the CPU. But the trap instructions are implemented in software instead of hardware. So, the eight addressing modes must be simulated in software. FIGURE 8.10 shows the routine that performs the computation.

The routine in Figure 8.10 has the following pre- and postconditions:

> › Precondition: The PCB of the stack instruction is on the system stack.

> › Postcondition: opAddr contains the address of the operand according to the addressing mode of the trap instruction.

Pre- and postconditions for the addressing mode computation routine

As with the addressing-mode assert routine in Figure 8.8, the register copies on the PCB have a stack offset four bytes greater than when the trap occurs, as Figure 8.7(b) shows. The routine uses oldIR4, defined in the addressing-mode assert routine—as well as the similarly defined oldX4, oldPC4, and oldSP4—to access the copies of the saved index register, program counter, and stack pointer.

The first four statements beginning at FCCE determine the addressing mode of the trap instruction and branch to the computation for that addressing mode. The program uses the jump table technique to switch between one of eight alternatives. The code for each of the eight alternatives computes the address of the operand by inspecting the state of the CPU at the time of the trap.

The first two instructions of each computation are

```
LDWX oldPC4,s
SUBX 2,i
```

The first two instructions of each computation

Because the trap instruction is nonunary, the program counter at the time of the trap points to the byte after the two-byte operand specifier. The first instruction loads the saved program counter into the index register, and the second instruction subtracts two from it. After these two instructions execute, the index register contains the address of the operand specifier in the instruction that caused the trap.

For immediate addressing, the operand specifier is the operand. Consequently, the statements at FCEE

```
STWX opAddr,d
RET
```

The computation for immediate addressing

simply store the address of the operand specifier in opAddr as required.

FIGURE 8.10

The trap operand address computation in the Pep/9 operating system.

```
              ;****** Set address of trap operand
              oldX4:    .EQUATE 7          ;oldX + 4 with two return addresses
              oldPC4:   .EQUATE 9          ;oldPC + 4 with two return addresses
              oldSP4:   .EQUATE 11         ;oldSP + 4 with two return addresses
FCCE DB000D setAddr: LDBX    oldIR4,s      ;X <- old instruction register
FCD1 880007          ANDX    0x0007,i      ;Keep only the addressing mode bits
FCD4 0B              ASLX                  ;Two bytes per address
FCD5 13FCD8          BR      addrJT,x
FCD8 FCE8 addrJT:  .ADDRSS addrI           ;Immediate addressing
FCDA FCF2          .ADDRSS addrD           ;Direct addressing
FCDC FCFF          .ADDRSS addrN           ;Indirect addressing
FCDE FD0F          .ADDRSS addrS           ;Stack-relative addressing
FCE0 FD1F          .ADDRSS addrSF          ;Stack-relative deferred addressing
FCE2 FD32          .ADDRSS addrX           ;Indexed addressing
FCE4 FD42          .ADDRSS addrSX          ;Stack-indexed addressing
FCE6 FD55          .ADDRSS addrSFX         ;Stack-deferred indexed addressing
              ;
FCE8 CB0009 addrI:  LDWX    oldPC4,s       ;Immediate addressing
FCEB 780002          SUBX    2,i            ;Oprnd = OprndSpec
FCEE E9FC13          STWX    opAddr,d
FCF1 01              RET
              ;
FCF2 CB0009 addrD:  LDWX    oldPC4,s       ;Direct addressing
FCF5 780002          SUBX    2,i            ;Oprnd = Mem[OprndSpec]
FCF8 CD0000          LDWX    0,x
FCFB E9FC13          STWX    opAddr,d
FCFE 01              RET
              ;
FCFF CB0009 addrN:  LDWX    oldPC4,s       ;Indirect addressing
FD02 780002          SUBX    2,i            ;Oprnd = Mem[Mem[OprndSpec]]
FD05 CD0000          LDWX    0,x
FD08 CD0000          LDWX    0,x
FD0B E9FC13          STWX    opAddr,d
FD0E 01              RET
              ;
```

```
FD0F  CB0009 addrS:   LDWX   oldPC4,s     ;Stack-relative addressing
FD12  780002          SUBX   2,i          ;Oprnd = Mem[SP + OprndSpec]
FD15  CD0000          LDWX   0,x
FD18  6B000B          ADDX   oldSP4,s
FD1B  E9FC13          STWX   opAddr,d
FD1E  01              RET
                ;
FD1F  CB0009 addrSF:  LDWX   oldPC4,s     ;Stack-relative deferred addressing
FD22  780002          SUBX   2,i          ;Oprnd = Mem[Mem[SP + OprndSpec]]
FD25  CD0000          LDWX   0,x
FD28  6B000B          ADDX   oldSP4,s
FD2B  CD0000          LDWX   0,x
FD2E  E9FC13          STWX   opAddr,d
FD31  01              RET
                ;
FD32  CB0009 addrX:   LDWX   oldPC4,s     ;Indexed addressing
FD35  780002          SUBX   2,i          ;Oprnd = Mem[OprndSpec + X]
FD38  CD0000          LDWX   0,x
FD3B  6B0007          ADDX   oldX4,s
FD3E  E9FC13          STWX   opAddr,d
FD41  01              RET
                ;
FD42  CB0009 addrSX:  LDWX   oldPC4,s     ;Stack-indexed addressing
FD45  780002          SUBX   2,i          ;Oprnd = Mem[SP + OprndSpec + X]
FD48  CD0000          LDWX   0,x
FD4B  6B0007          ADDX   oldX4,s
FD4E  6B000B          ADDX   oldSP4,s
FD51  E9FC13          STWX   opAddr,d
FD54  01              RET
                ;
FD55  CB0009 addrSFX: LDWX   oldPC4,s     ;Stack-deferred indexed addressing
FD58  780002          SUBX   2,i          ;Oprnd = Mem[Mem[SP + OprndSpec] + X]
FD5B  CD0000          LDWX   0,x
FD5E  6B000B          ADDX   oldSP4,s
FD61  CD0000          LDWX   0,x
FD64  6B0007          ADDX   oldX4,s
FD67  E9FC13          STWX   opAddr,d
FD6A  01              RET
```

For direct addressing, the operand specifier is the address of the operand. The first of the statements at FCF8

The computation for direct addressing

```
LDWX 0,x
STWX opAddr,d
RET
```

replaces the index register with the content in memory whose address is in the index register. Before the instruction executes, the index register contains the address of the operand specifier. After the instruction executes, the index register contains the operand specifier itself. Because the operand specifier is the address of the operand, that is what gets stored in opAddr.

For indirect addressing, the operand specifier is the address of the address of the operand. As with direct addressing, the first of the statements at FD05

The computation for indirect addressing

```
LDWX 0,x
LDWX 0,x
STWX opAddr,d
RET
```

replaces the index register with the operand specifier itself, which is the address of the address of the operand. The second instruction fetches the address of the operand, which gets stored in opAddr.

For stack-relative addressing, the stack pointer plus the operand specifier is the address of the operand. The first of the statements at FD15

The computation for stack-relative addressing

```
LDWX 0,x
ADDX oldSP4,s
STWX opAddr,d
RET
```

puts the operand specifier in the index register. The second instruction adds the copy of the stack pointer to it. The result is the address of the operand, which gets stored in opAddr.

The remaining four addressing modes use similar techniques to compute the address of the operand. Stack-relative deferred addressing is one extra level of indirection compared with stack-relative addressing, requiring one additional execution of LDWX 0,x. Indexed addressing is like stack-relative addressing, except the operand specifier is added to the index register instead of the stack pointer. Stack-indexed and stack-deferred indexed are variations on the same theme.

The No-Operation Trap Handlers

FIGURE 8.11 shows the code for implementation of the no-operation trap handlers. Because the no-operation instructions do not do anything, the trap handlers do no processing other than to execute RET, returning control to the exit points in Figure 8.6, and eventually to the statement following the trap.

The no-operation instructions are provided for you to write your own trap handlers. Some problems at the end of the chapter ask you to implement instructions that are not in the Pep/9 instruction set. The Pep/9 assembler lets you redefine the mnemonics for the trap instructions. To write a trap handler, you change the mnemonic of one of the no-operation instructions in Figure 8.11 to the mnemonic of your new instruction. Then, you edit the trap handler in the operating system by inserting your code at its entry point. For example, to redefine NOP0, you insert the code for your handler at FD6B. The last executable statement in your handler should be RET.

Figure 8.11 shows the implementation of nonunary NOP at FD6D. Figure 5.2 specifies that its only allowable addressing mode is immediate addressing. Therefore, the value in addrMask is set to 0000 0001, where the last 1 is at the bit position for immediate addressing, as Figure 8.9 shows.

FIGURE 8.11
The NOP trap handlers.

```
              ;******* Opcode 0x26
              ;The NOP0 instruction.
FD6B   01     opcode26:RET
              ;
              ;******* Opcode 0x27
              ;The NOP1 instruction.
FD6C   01     opcode27:RET
              ;
              ;******* Opcode 0x28
              ;The NOP instruction.
FD6D   C00001 opcode28:LDWA    0x0001,i    ;Assert i
FD70   E1FC11          STWA    addrMask,d
FD73   24FC7C          CALL    assertAd
FD76   01              RET
```

The DECI Trap Handler

This section describes the trap handler for the DECI instruction. DECI must parse the input, converting the string of ASCII characters to the proper bits in two's complement representation. It uses the finite-state machine (FSM) of (FIGURE 8.12). An outline of the logic of the FSM in the DECI trap handler appears in (FIGURE 8.13). state has enumerated type with possible values init, sign, or digit.

(FIGURE 8.14) is the listing of the DECI trap handler. The first four statements at FD77 call the addressing-mode assert routine and the routine to compute the trap operand address. At FD83, the handler allocates seven local variables on the stack—total, asciiCh, valAscii, isOvfl, isNeg, state, and temp. Each variable except asciiCh occupies two bytes, so SUBSP subtracts 13 from the stack pointer for the allocation. With application programs, SUBSP is the first executable statement in procedures with local variables. Here, SUBSP must execute after the first two routine calls, because those calls access quantities from the PCB. They assume only two return addresses on the stack, as Figure 8.7(b) shows.

The DECI trap handler must access the NZVC bits from the PCB. The handler is called by the CALL instruction at FC6E in Figure 8.6, which pushed a two-byte return address on the stack. When the handler accesses the value of NZVC stored on the stack at the trap, its stack address will be 15 greater than it is immediately after the trap because of the local variables and the return address. That is why oldNZVC equates to 15 instead of 0.

Beginning with the LDWA statement at FD86, the processing in the DECI interrupt handler follows the logic in Figure 8.13. The routine tests the input string for a value that is out of range. If so, it sets the V bit stored in the PCB during the trap. When RETTR returns control to the application, the

FIGURE 8.12

The finite-state machine in the DECI interrupt handler.

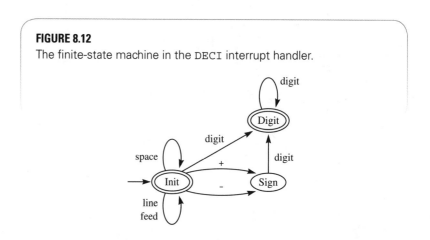

```
isOvfl ← FALSE
state ← init
do
    LDBA charIn,d
    STBA asciiCh,s
    switch state
    case init:
        if (asciiCh == '+') {
            isNeg ← FALSE
            state ← sign
        }
        else if (asciiCh == '-') {
            isNeg ← TRUE
            state ← sign
        }
        else if (asciiCh is a digit) {
            isNeg ← FALSE
            total ← value(asciiCh)
            state ← digit
        }
        else if (asciiCh is not <SPACE> or <LF>) {
            Exit with DECI error
        }
    case sign:
        if (asciiCh is a digit) {
            total ← value(asciiCh)
            state ← digit
        }
        else {
            Exit with DECI error
        }
    case digit:
        if (asciiCh is a digit) {
            total ← 10 * total + value(asciiCh)
            if (overflow) {
                isOvfl ← TRUE
            }
        }
            else {
                Exit normally
            }
        end switch
while (not exit)
```

FIGURE 8.13

The program logic of the DECI trap handler.

FIGURE 8.14

The DECI trap handler.

```
              ;****** Opcode 0x30
              ;The DECI instruction.
              ;Input format: Any number of leading spaces or line feeds are
              ;allowed, followed by '+', '-' or a digit as the first character,
              ;after which digits are input until the first nondigit is
              ;encountered. The status flags N,Z and V are set appropriately
              ;by this DECI routine. The C status flag is not affected.
              ;
              oldNZVC: .EQUATE 15             ;Stack address of NZVC on interrupt
              ;
              total:   .EQUATE 11             ;Cumulative total of DECI number
              asciiCh: .EQUATE 10             ;asciiCh, one byte
              valAscii:.EQUATE 8              ;value(asciiCh)
              isOvfl:  .EQUATE 6              ;Overflow boolean
              isNeg:   .EQUATE 4              ;Negative boolean
              state:   .EQUATE 2              ;State variable
              temp:    .EQUATE 0
              ;
              init:    .EQUATE 0             ;Enumerated values for state
              sign:    .EQUATE 1
              digit:   .EQUATE 2
              ;
FD77 C000FE opcode30:LDWA     0x00FE,i       ;Assert d, n, s, sf, x, sx, sfx
FD7A E1FC11          STWA     addrMask,d
FD7D 24FC7C          CALL     assertAd
FD80 24FCCE          CALL     setAddr        ;Set address of trap operand
FD83 58000D          SUBSP    13,i           ;Allocate storage for locals
FD86 C00000          LDWA     FALSE,i        ;isOvfl <- FALSE
FD89 E30006          STWA     isOvfl,s
FD8C C00000          LDWA     init,i         ;state <- init
FD8F E30002          STWA     state,s
              ;
FD92 D1FC15 do:      LDBA     charIn,d       ;Get asciiCh
FD95 F3000A          STBA     asciiCh,s
FD98 80000F          ANDA     0x000F,i       ;Set value(asciiCh)
FD9B E30008          STWA     valAscii,s
FD9E D3000A          LDBA     asciiCh,s      ;A<low> = asciiCh throughout the loop
FDA1 CB0002          LDWX     state,s        ;switch (state)
FDA4 0B              ASLX                    ;Two bytes per address
FDA5 13FDA8          BR       stateJT,x
              ;
```

```
FDA8   FDAE    stateJT: .ADDRSS sInit
FDAA   FE08             .ADDRSS sSign
FDAC   FE23             .ADDRSS sDigit
               ;
FDAE   B0002B  sInit:   CPBA    '+',i        ;if (asciiCh == '+')
FDB1   1AFDC3           BRNE    ifMinus
FDB4   C80000           LDWX    FALSE,i       ;isNeg <- FALSE
FDB7   EB0004           STWX    isNeg,s
FDBA   C80001           LDWX    sign,i        ;state <- sign
FDBD   EB0002           STWX    state,s
FDC0   12FD92           BR      do
               ;
FDC3   B0002D  ifMinus: CPBA    '-',i        ;else if (asciiCh == '-')
FDC6   1AFDD8           BRNE    ifDigit
FDC9   C80001           LDWX    TRUE,i        ;isNeg <- TRUE
FDCC   EB0004           STWX    isNeg,s
FDCF   C80001           LDWX    sign,i        ;state <- sign
FDD2   EB0002           STWX    state,s
FDD5   12FD92           BR      do
               ;
FDD8   B00030  ifDigit: CPBA    '0',i        ;else if (asciiCh is a digit)
FDDB   16FDF9           BRLT    ifWhite
FDDE   B00039           CPBA    '9',i
FDE1   1EFDF9           BRGT    ifWhite
FDE4   C80000           LDWX    FALSE,i       ;isNeg <- FALSE
FDE7   EB0004           STWX    isNeg,s
FDEA   CB0008           LDWX    valAscii,s   ;total <- value(asciiCh)
FDED   EB000B           STWX    total,s
FDF0   C80002           LDWX    digit,i       ;state <- digit
FDF3   EB0002           STWX    state,s
FDF6   12FD92           BR      do
               ;
FDF9   B00020  ifWhite: CPBA    ' ',i        ;else if (asciiCh is not a space
FDFC   18FD92           BREQ    do
FDFF   B0000A           CPBA    '\n',i       ;or line feed)
FE02   1AFEBE           BRNE    deciErr      ;exit with DECI error
FE05   12FD92           BR      do
               ;
```

(*continues*)

FIGURE 8.14

The DECI trap handler. (*continued*)

```
FE08  B00030 sSign:   CPBA    '0',i          ;if asciiCh (is not a digit)
FE0B  16FEBE          BRLT    deciErr
FE0E  B00039          CPBA    '9',i
FE11  1EFEBE          BRGT    deciErr         ;exit with DECI error
FE14  CB0008          LDWX    valAscii,s      ;else total <- value(asciiCh)
FE17  EB000B          STWX    total,s
FE1A  C80002          LDWX    digit,i         ;state <- digit
FE1D  EB0002          STWX    state,s
FE20  12FD92          BR      do
                  ;
FE23  B00030 sDigit:  CPBA    '0',i           ;if (asciiCh is not a digit)
FE26  16FE74          BRLT    deciNorm
FE29  B00039          CPBA    '9',i
FE2C  1EFE74          BRGT    deciNorm        ;exit normaly
FE2F  C80001          LDWX    TRUE,i          ;else X <- TRUE for later assignments
FE32  C3000B          LDWA    total,s         ;Multiply total by 10 as follows:
FE35  0A              ASLA                    ;First, times 2
FE36  20FE3C          BRV     ovfl1           ;If overflow then
FE39  12FE3F          BR      L1
FE3C  EB0006 ovfl1:   STWX    isOvfl,s        ;isOvfl <- TRUE
FE3F  E30000 L1:      STWA    temp,s          ;Save 2 * total in temp
FE42  0A              ASLA                    ;Now, 4 * total
FE43  20FE49          BRV     ovfl2           ;If overflow then
FE46  12FE4C          BR      L2
FE49  EB0006 ovfl2:   STWX    isOvfl,s        ;isOvfl <- TRUE
FE4C  0A     L2:      ASLA                    ;Now, 8 * total
FE4D  20FE53          BRV     ovfl3           ;If overflow then
FE50  12FE56          BR      L3
FE53  EB0006 ovfl3:   STWX    isOvfl,s        ;isOvfl <- TRUE
FE56  630000 L3:      ADDA    temp,s          ;Finally, 8 * total + 2 * total
FE59  20FE5F          BRV     ovfl4           ;If overflow then
FE5C  12FE62          BR      L4
FE5F  EB0006 ovfl4:   STWX    isOvfl,s        ;isOvfl <- TRUE
FE62  630008 L4:      ADDA    valAscii,s      ;A <- 10 * total + valAscii
FE65  20FE6B          BRV     ovfl5           ;If overflow then
FE68  12FE6E          BR      L5
FE6B  EB0006 ovfl5:   STWX    isOvfl,s        ;isOvfl <- TRUE
FE6E  E3000B L5:      STWA    total,s         ;Update total
FE71  12FD92          BR      do
                  ;
```

```
FE74  C30004 deciNorm:LDWA      isNeg,s      ;If isNeg then
FE77  18FE90         BREQ       setNZ
FE7A  C3000B         LDWA       total,s      ;If total != 0x8000 then
FE7D  A08000         CPWA       0x8000,i
FE80  18FE8A         BREQ       L6
FE83  08             NEGA                    ;Negate total
FE84  E3000B         STWA       total,s
FE87  12FE90         BR         setNZ
FE8A  C00000 L6:     LDWA       FALSE,i      ;else -32768 is a special case
FE8D  E30006         STWA       isOvfl,s     ;isOvfl <- FALSE
               ;
FE90  DB000F setNZ:  LDBX       oldNZVC,s    ;Set NZ according to total result:
FE93  880001         ANDX       0x0001,i     ;First initialize NZV to 000
FE96  C3000B         LDWA       total,s      ;If total is negative then
FE99  1CFE9F         BRGE       checkZ
FE9C  980008         ORX        0x0008,i     ;set N to 1
FE9F  A00000 checkZ: CPWA       0,i          ;If total is not zero then
FEA2  1AFEA8         BRNE       setV
FEA5  980004         ORX        0x0004,i     ;set Z to 1
FEA8  C30006 setV:   LDWA       isOvfl,s     ;If not isOvfl then
FEAB  18FEB1         BREQ       storeFl
FEAE  980002         ORX        0x0002,i     ;set V to 1
FEB1  FB000F storeFl: STBX      oldNZVC,s    ;Store the NZVC flags
               ;
FEB4  C3000B exitDeci:LDWA      total,s      ;Put total in memory
FEB7  E2FC13         STWA       opAddr,n
FEBA  50000D         ADDSP      13,i         ;Deallocate locals
FEBD  01             RET                     ;Return to trap handler
               ;
FEBE  D0000A deciErr: LDBA      '\n',i
FEC1  F1FC16         STBA       charOut,d
FEC4  C0FED1         LDWA       deciMsg,i    ;Push address of message onto stack
FEC7  E3FFFE         STWA       -2,s
FECA  580002         SUBSP      2,i
FECD  24FFDE         CALL       prntMsg      ;and print
FED0  00             STOP                    ;Fatal error: program terminates
               ;
FED1  455252 deciMsg: .ASCII    "ERROR: Invalid DECI input\x00"

       ...
```

programmer at Level Asmb5 will be able to test for overflow after executing DECI. isOvfl is a Boolean flag that indicates the overflow condition.

FD92 is the start of the FSM loop, identified by the do symbol. ANDA at FD98 masks out all but the rightmost four bits of the input character, which leaves the binary value that corresponds to the decimal ASCII digit. For example, ASCII 5 is represented in binary as 0011 0101. The rightmost four bits are 0101, the corresponding binary value of the decimal digit. The accumulator gets the ASCII character at FD9E and keeps it throughout the loop. stateJT at FDA8 is a jump table for the switch statement in the FSM.

The code from FDAE to FE05 is the case for state having the value sInit, the start state of the FSM. The assignments are all made via the index register instead of the accumulator, because the accumulator maintains the ASCII character for comparison throughout the loop. For example, the assignment of isNeg to FALSE at FDB4 is implemented by LDWX followed by STWX, instead of LDWA followed by STWA.

The code from FE08 to FE20 is the case for state having the value sSign, and from FE23 to FE71 is the case for state having the value sDigit. Pep/9 has no instruction to multiply a value by 10 (dec). This section of code performs the multiply with several left-shift operations. Each ASLA multiplies the value by 2. Three ASLA operations multiply the value by 8, which can be added to the value multiplied by 2 to get the value multiplied by 10. After each ASLA operation and the addition, the routine checks for overflow and sets isOvfl accordingly.

The code from FE74 to FF20 is outside the loop. The algorithm exits the loop under two conditions: normally, or when it has detected an input error. If it exits normally, it checks the isNeg flag to see if the string of digits was preceded by a negative sign. If it was, the instruction at FE83 negates the number by taking the two's complement.

The number 32768 (dec), which is 8000 (hex), must be treated as a special case. If the input is –32768, the FSM will set isOvfl to true when it adds 32760 to 8 at FE62. The problem is that 32768 is out of range, even though –32768 is in range. The routine adjusts isOvfl for this special case at FE8D.

The code from FE90 to FEB1 adjusts the copies of the N, Z, and V flags that were stored at the trap. ANDX at FE93 sets NZV to 000. Note that the mask is 01 (hex), which is 0000 0001 (bin). Because C is the rightmost bit, it remains unchanged by the AND operation. LDWA at FE96 puts the parsed value into the accumulator, setting the current N, Z, and V bits in the CPU accordingly. The code sets the copies of N and Z in the PCB equal to the current values of N and Z in the CPU. It sets the copy of V in the PCB according to the value of isOvfl computed earlier in the parse.

Now that the decimal value has been input and parsed, the trap handler must store it in memory at the location specified by the operand of the DECI that caused the trap. The instructions

```
LDWA total,s
STWA opAddr,n
```

at FEB4 perform the store. LDWA loads the computed value into the accumulator. STWA stores it to opAddr with indirect addressing, for which the operand specifier is the address of the address of the operand. Recall that the address of the operand is computed earlier at FD80 and stored in opAddr. opAddr is itself, therefore, the address of the address of the operand, as required.

The code from FEBE to FED0 executes when the input string cannot be parsed legally. It prints an error message by calling prntMsg, a procedure shown in Figure 8.16 to output a null-terminated string, and terminates the application program immediately.

The DECO Trap Handler

FIGURE 8.15 is the trap handler for the DECO instruction. This routine outputs the operand of DECO in a format that is equivalent to a C printf() function call with an integer value. Because the largest value that can be stored is 32767, the routine will output, at most, five-digit characters. It precedes the value by a negative sign, the ASCII hyphen character, if necessary.

As usual, the statements at the beginning of the trap handler at FEEB assert the legal addressing modes, call the routine to compute the address of the operand, and allocate storage for the local variables. In contrast to the DECI trap handler, the statement at FEFA

```
LDWA opAddr,n
```

accesses the operand with a load instead of a store because DECO is an output statement instead of an input statement. As with the DECI handler, the operand is accessed through opAddr with indirect addressing.

The code from FEFD to FF09 tests for a negative value. If the operand is negative, the load byte and store byte instructions at FF03 output the negative sign, and the following code negates the operand. At FF0A the accumulator contains the magnitude of the operand, which is stored in remain, which stands for *remainder*.

The code from FF0D to FF34 writes the 10,000's, 1000's, 100's, and 10's place of the magnitude of the operand. To suppress any leading zeros, it initializes outYet to false, which indicates that no digit characters have yet been output.

FIGURE 8.15
The DECO trap handler.

```
                ;******* Opcode 0x38
                ;The DECO instruction.
                ;Output format: If the operand is negative, the algorithm prints
                ;a single '-' followed by the magnitude. Otherwise it prints the
                ;magnitude without a leading '+'. It suppresses leading zeros.
                ;
                remain:   .EQUATE 0           ;Remainder of value to output
                outYet:   .EQUATE 2           ;Has a character been output yet?
                place:    .EQUATE 4           ;Place value for division
                ;
FEEB  C000FF opcode38:LDWA    0x00FF,i        ;Assert i, d, n, s, sf, x, sx, sfx
FEEE  E1FC11          STWA    addrMask,d
FEF1  24FC7C          CALL    assertAd
FEF4  24FCCE          CALL    setAddr         ;Set address of trap operand
FEF7  580006          SUBSP   6,i             ;Allocate storage for locals
FEFA  C2FC13          LDWA    opAddr,n        ;A <- oprnd
FEFD  A00000          CPWA    0,i             ;If oprnd is negative then
FF00  1CFF0A          BRGE    printMag
FF03  D8002D          LDBX    '-',i           ;Print leading '-'
FF06  F9FC16          STBX    charOut,d
FF09  08              NEGA                    ;Make magnitude positive
FF0A  E30000 printMag:STWA    remain,s        ;remain <- abs(oprnd)
FF0D  C00000          LDWA    FALSE,i         ;Initialize outYet <- FALSE
FF10  E30002          STWA    outYet,s
FF13  C02710          LDWA    10000,i         ;place <- 10,000
FF16  E30004          STWA    place,s
FF19  24FF44          CALL    divide          ;Write 10,000's place
FF1C  C003E8          LDWA    1000,i          ;place <- 1,000
FF1F  E30004          STWA    place,s
FF22  24FF44          CALL    divide          ;Write 1000's place
FF25  C00064          LDWA    100,i           ;place <- 100
FF28  E30004          STWA    place,s
FF2B  24FF44          CALL    divide          ;Write 100's place
FF2E  C0000A          LDWA    10,i            ;place <- 10
FF31  E30004          STWA    place,s
FF34  24FF44          CALL    divide          ;Write 10's place
FF37  C30000          LDWA    remain,s        ;Always write 1's place
```

```
FF3A   900030          ORA      0x0030,i      ;Convert decimal to ASCII
FF3D   F1FC16          STBA     charOut,d     ;  and output it
FF40   500006          ADDSP    6,i           ;Dallocate storage for locals
FF43   01              RET
                       ;
                       ;Subroutine to print the most significant decimal digit of the
                       ;remainder. It assumes that place (place2 here) contains the
                       ;decimal place value. It updates the remainder.
                       ;
                       remain2: .EQUATE 2              ;Stack addresses while executing a
                       outYet2: .EQUATE 4              ;  subroutine are greater by two because
                       place2:  .EQUATE 6              ;  the retAddr is on the stack
                       ;
FF44   C30002 divide:  LDWA     remain2,s     ;A <- remainder
FF47   C80000          LDWX     0,i           ;X <- 0
FF4A   730006 divLoop: SUBA     place2,s      ;Division by repeated subtraction
FF4D   16FF59          BRLT     writeNum      ;If remainder is negative then done
FF50   680001          ADDX     1,i           ;X <- X + 1
FF53   E30002          STWA     remain2,s     ;Store the new remainder
FF56   12FF4A          BR       divLoop
                       ;
FF59   A80000 writeNum:CPWX     0,i           ;If X != 0 then
FF5C   18FF68          BREQ     checkOut
FF5F   C00001          LDWA     TRUE,i        ;outYet <- TRUE
FF62   E30004          STWA     outYet2,s
FF65   12FF6F          BR       printDgt      ;and branch to print this digit
FF68   C30004 checkOut:LDWA     outYet2,s     ;else if a previous char was output
FF6B   1AFF6F          BRNE     printDgt      ;then branch to print this zero
FF6E   01              RET                    ;else return to calling routine
                       ;
FF6F   980030 printDgt:ORX      0x0030,i      ;Convert decimal to ASCII
FF72   F9FC16          STBX     charOut,d     ;  and output it
FF75   01              RET                    ;return to calling routine
```

Subroutine `divide` outputs the digit character for the place value in `place` and decreases `remain` for the next call. For example, if `remain` is 24873 before the call to `divide` at FF19, then `divide` will output 2 and leave 4873 in `remain`. It will also set `outYet` to true.

Before outputting character 0, `divide` tests `outYet` to check whether any digit characters have been output yet. If `outYet` is false, the character is a leading zero and is not output. Otherwise, it is an embedded zero and is output. For example, if remain is 761 before the call at FF22, divide prints nothing and leaves 761 in remain and false in outYet. The code beginning at FF37 writes the 1's place regardless of the value of outYet. Thus, a value of zero for the original operand gets output as 0.

The code from FF44 to FF75 is the subroutine to print the most significant digit of remain. It determines the value to output by repeatedly subtracting place from remain, counting the number of subtractions until remain is less than zero. The effect is to compute the value to output as remain / place.

The HEXO and STRO Trap Handlers and Operating System Vectors

FIGURE 8.16 is the trap handler for the HEXO and STRO instructions. They are similar in function to the DECO trap handler. Because STRO is an output instruction, the address of the operand is first fetched with

```
LDWA opAddr,d
```

at FFCE. Then it calls the prntMsg subroutine at FFD7, pushing the address of the string to print on the run-time stack. In effect, a string is an array of characters, so the processing is similar to the translations of a C program where an array is passed as a parameter. The print subroutine, therefore, uses stack-deferred indexed addressing in the statements

```
LDBA msgAddr,sfx
```

to access an element of the character array.

The machine vectors are established with the .ADDRSS assembler directive. Compare this code with the code in Figure 8.1 and Figure 8.2. The vector at FFF4 is the address of osRAM, which is the top byte of operating system RAM. The hardware initializes SP to this value when the user selects the execute option from the simulator. It is the byte at the bottom of the user stack.

The vector at FFF6 is the address of wordTemp, which is the first system global variable. Figure 8.2 shows wordTemp as the next byte below the 128-byte block of storage reserved for the system stack. The hardware initializes SP to this value when the user selects the load option from the simulator. It also pushes the PCB onto the stack starting from this point when a trap instruction executes.

The next two vectors at FFF8 and FFFA are the addresses of the input device defined by the symbol charIn and the output device defined by the symbol charOut. During translation time, the application assembler includes these symbols automatically in its symbol table. During run time,

FIGURE 8.16

The trap handlers for the HEXO and STRO instructions.

```
                ;******* Opcode 0x40
                ;The HEXO instruction.
                ;Outputs one word as four hex characters from memory.
                ;
FF76  C000FF opcode40:LDWA     0x00FF,i     ;Assert i, d, n, s, sf, x, sx, sfx
FF79  E1FC11          STWA     addrMask,d
FF7C  24FC7C          CALL     assertAd
FF7F  24FCCE          CALL     setAddr      ;Set address of trap operand
FF82  C2FC13          LDWA     opAddr,n     ;A <- oprnd
FF85  E1FC0F          STWA     wordTemp,d   ;Save oprnd in wordTemp
FF88  D1FC0F          LDBA     wordTemp,d   ;Put high-order byte in low-order A
FF8B  0C              ASRA                  ;Shift right four bits
FF8C  0C              ASRA
FF8D  0C              ASRA
FF8E  0C              ASRA
FF8F  24FFA9          CALL     hexOut       ;Output first hex character
FF92  D1FC0F          LDBA     wordTemp,d   ;Put high-order byte in low-order A
FF95  24FFA9          CALL     hexOut       ;Output second hex character
FF98  D1FC10          LDBA     byteTemp,d   ;Put low-order byte in low order A
FF9B  0C              ASRA                  ;Shift right four bits
FF9C  0C              ASRA
FF9D  0C              ASRA
FF9E  0C              ASRA
FF9F  24FFA9          CALL     hexOut       ;Output third hex character
FFA2  D1FC10          LDBA     byteTemp,d   ;Put low-order byte in low order A
FFA5  24FFA9          CALL     hexOut       ;Output fourth hex character
FFA8  01              RET
                ;
                ;Subroutine to output in hex the least significant nybble of the
                ;accumulator.
                ;
FFA9  80000F hexOut:  ANDA     0x000F,i     ;Isolate the digit value
FFAC  B00009          CPBA     9,i          ;If it is not in 0..9 then
FFAF  14FFBB          BRLE     prepNum
FFB2  700009          SUBA     9,i          ;  convert to ASCII letter
FFB5  900040          ORA      0x0040,i     ;  and prefix ASCII code for letter
FFB8  12FFBE          BR       writeHex
FFBB  900030 prepNum: ORA      0x0030,i     ;else prefix ASCII code for number
FFBE  F1FC16 writeHex:STBA     charOut,d    ;Output nybble as hex
FFC1  01              RET
                ;
```

(continues)

FIGURE 8.16
The trap handlers for the HEXO and STRO instructions. (*continued*)

```
                ;******* Opcode 0x48
                ;The STRO instruction.
                ;Outputs a null-terminated string from memory.
                ;
FFC2  C0003E  opcode48:LDWA    0x003E,i    ;Assert d, n, s, sf, x
FFC5  E1FC11          STWA    addrMask,d
FFC8  24FC7C          CALL    assertAd
FFCB  24FCCE          CALL    setAddr      ;Set address of trap operand
FFCE  C1FC13          LDWA    opAddr,d     ;Push address of string to print
FFD1  E3FFFE          STWA    -2,s
FFD4  580002          SUBSP   2,i
FFD7  24FFDE          CALL    prntMsg      ;and print
FFDA  500002          ADDSP   2,i
FFDD  01              RET
                ;
                ;******* Print subroutine
                ;Prints a string of ASCII bytes until it encounters a null
                ;byte (eight zero bits). Assumes one parameter, which
                ;contains the address of the message.
                ;
                msgAddr: .EQUATE 2           ;Address of message to print
                ;
FFDE  C80000  prntMsg: LDWX    0,i          ;X <- 0
FFE1  C00000           LDWA    0,i          ;A <- 0
FFE4  D70002  prntMore:LDBA    msgAddr,sfx  ;Test next char
FFE7  18FFF3           BREQ    exitPrnt     ;If null then exit
FFEA  F1FC16           STBA    charOut,d    ;else print
FFED  680001           ADDX    1,i          ;X <- X + 1 for next character
FFF0  12FFE4           BR      prntMore
                ;
FFF3  01      exitPrnt:RET
                ;
                ;******* Vectors for system memory map
FFF4  FB8F             .ADDRSS osRAM        ;User stack pointer
FFF6  FC0F             .ADDRSS wordTemp     ;System stack pointer
FFF8  FC15             .ADDRSS charIn       ;Memory-mapped input device
FFFA  FC16             .ADDRSS charOut      ;Memory-mapped output device
FFFC  FC17             .ADDRSS loader       ;Loader program counter
FFFE  FC52             .ADDRSS trap         ;Trap program counter
```

the hardware simulator uses these vectors to know where the I/O devices are mapped into memory.

The vector at FFFC is the address of the loader, as Figure 8.3 shows. The hardware initializes PC to this value when the user selects the load option. The vector at FFFE is the address of the interrupt handler entry point, as Figure 8.6 shows. The hardware initializes PC to this value when a trap instruction executes.

8.3 Concurrent Processes

Remember that a process is a program during execution. Section 8.2 shows how the operating system can suspend a process during its execution to provide a service. A time line of CPU activity for a process that uses DECI and DECO would look like FIGURE 8.17. The shaded regions represent those times that the CPU executes the trap service routine. The time line is similar in form to Figure 8.4 except that this figure shows the operating system suspending a process before it terminates and then restarting it when the service is complete.

The traps described in Section 8.2 are called *software interrupts* because the executing process initiates them by the unimplemented opcodes in its listing. They are also called *synchronous interrupts*, because each time the process executes, the interrupts occur at the same time. The interrupts are synchronized with the code and are predictable.

Another way to initiate a synchronous interrupt is to execute an operating system call. A common assembly-level mnemonic for an operating system call is SVC, which stands for *supervisor call*. The operand specifier normally acts as a parameter for the system call and tells the system which service the program wants to request. For example, if you want to flush the contents of a buffered stream with the equivalent of fflush(stdin) in C and the code for fflush() is 27, you might execute

Supervisor calls

```
SVC 27, i
```

FIGURE 8.17
A time line of CPU usage when the operating system executes a single program containing DECI and DECO instructions.

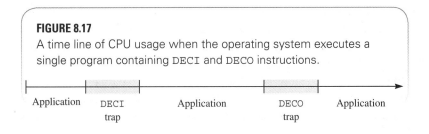

Asynchronous Interrupts

Another type of interrupt is the *asynchronous interrupt*, which does not occur at a predictable time during execution. Two common sources of asynchronous interrupts are

> Time outs

> I/O completions

To see how asynchronous interrupts can occur from time outs, consider a multi-user system, which allows several users to access the computer simultaneously. If the computer has only one CPU, the operating system must allocate the CPU to each user's job in turn with a technique known as *time sharing*. The operating system allocates a quantum of time called a *time slice*, typically about 100 ms (one-tenth of a second), to a job. If the job is not completed within that time (a condition known as *time out*), the operating system suspends the job temporarily and allocates another quantum of CPU time to the next job.

To implement time sharing, the hardware must provide an alarm clock that the operating system can set to produce an interrupt after an interval of time. The reason such an interrupt is unpredictable is that it depends on how busy the system is servicing the requests of its users. If no other job is waiting for the CPU, the system may let your job run longer than the standard time slice. Then if another user suddenly requests a service, the operating system may suspend your process immediately and allocate the CPU to the requesting job. Your process would not be interrupted at the same point as if it timed out after one time slice.

Even if the computer has more than one CPU, asynchronous interrupts occur the same way. The operating system allocates a separate time slice for each CPU in the system and manages the time outs for each CPU.

The second common source of asynchronous interrupts is I/O completions. A basic property of I/O devices is their slow speed compared to the processing speed of the CPU. If a running process requests some input from a keyboard, in the fraction of a second that it takes the user to respond, the CPU can execute hundreds of thousands of instructions for another process. Even if the process requests input from a disk file, which is much faster than keyboard input, the CPU could still execute thousands of instructions while waiting for the information to come from the disk.

To keep from wasting CPU time, the operating system can suspend the process that makes an I/O request if it appears that the process will need to wait for the I/O to complete. It can temporarily assign the CPU to a second process with the understanding that when the I/O does complete, the first process may immediately get the CPU back. Because the second process cannot predict when the I/O device will complete the I/O operation for the first process, it cannot know when the operating system might interrupt it to give the CPU back to the first process.

An operating system with one CPU that can switch back and forth between processes to keep the CPU busy is called a *multiprogramming system*. To implement multiprogramming, the hardware must provide connections for the I/O devices to send interrupt signals to the CPU when the devices complete their I/O operations.

Multiprogramming

Processes in the Operating System

One purpose of an operating system is to allocate the resources of the system efficiently. A multiprogramming time-sharing system allocates CPU time among the jobs in the system. The objective is to keep the CPU as busy as possible executing user jobs instead of being idle waiting for I/O. The operating system tries to be fair in scheduling CPU time so that all the jobs will be completed in a reasonable time.

At any given time, the operating system must maintain many suspended processes that are waiting their turn for CPU time. It maintains all these processes by allocating a separate PCB for each one, similar to the PCB the interrupt handler maintains in the Pep/9 system. A common practice is to link the PCBs together with pointers in a linked list called a *queue*. FIGURE 8.18 shows a queue of PCBs.

Each PCB includes copies of all the CPU register values at the time of the process's most recent interrupt. The register set must include a copy of the program counter so the process can continue executing from where it was when the interrupt occurred.

The PCB contains additional information to help the operating system schedule the CPU. An example is a unique process identification number

FIGURE 8.18
A queue of process control blocks.

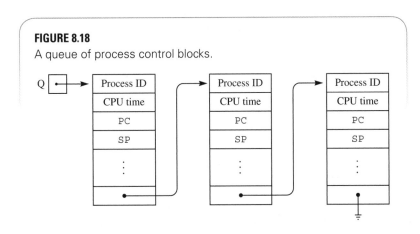

assigned by the system, labeled *Process ID* in Figure 8.18, that serves to reference the process. Suppose a user wants to terminate a process before it completes execution normally, and he knows the ID number is 782. He could issue a KILL(782) command that would cause the operating system to search through the queue of PCBs, find the PCB with ID 782, remove it from the queue, and deallocate it.

Another example of information stored in the PCB is a record of the total amount of CPU time used so far by the suspended process. If the CPU becomes available and the operating system must decide which of several suspended processes gets the CPU, it can use the recorded time to make a fair decision.

As a job progresses through the system toward completion, it passes through several states, as **FIGURE 8.19** shows. The figure is in the form of a state transition diagram and is another example of an FSM. Each transition is labeled with the event that causes the change of state.

Entering the start state

When a user submits a job for processing, the operating system creates a process for it by allocating a new PCB and attaching it to a queue of processes that are waiting for CPU time. It loads the program into main memory and sets the copy of PC in the PCB to the address of the first instruction of the process. That puts the job in the ready state.

Transition from the start state

Eventually, the operating system should select the job to receive some processing time. It sets the alarm clock to generate an interrupt after a quantum of time and puts the copies of the registers from the PCB into the CPU. That puts the job in the running state.

Transitions from the running state

While in the running state, three things can happen: (1) The running process may time out if it is still executing when the alarm clock interrupts. If so, the operating system attaches the process's PCB to the ready queue, which puts it back in the ready state. (2) The process may complete its execution normally, in which case the last instruction it executes is an SVC to request that the operating system terminate it. (3) The process may need some input, in which case it executes an SVC for the request. The operating

---

FIGURE 8.19

The state transition diagram for a job in an operating system.

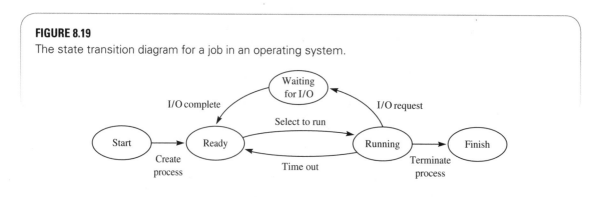

system would transfer the request to the appropriate I/O device and put the PCB in another queue of processes that are waiting for their I/O operations to complete. That puts the process in the waiting-for-I/O state.

While the process is in the waiting-for-I/O state, the I/O device should eventually interrupt the system with the requested input. When that happens, the system puts the input in a buffer in main memory, removes the process's PCB from the waiting-for-I/O queue, and puts it in the ready queue. That puts the process in the ready state, from which it will eventually receive more CPU time. Then it can access the input from the buffer.

Transition from the waiting-for-I/O state

Multiprocessing

As far as the user is concerned, a job simply executes from start to finish. The interruptions are invisible in the same way that the DECI interrupt is invisible to the assembly language programmer at Level Asmb5. The details at the operating system level are invisible to the users at a higher level of abstraction.

The only perceptible difference to the user is that it will take longer for the program to execute if many jobs are in the system. One way to speed the progress is to attach more than one CPU to the system. Each core in a multicore chip is a separate CPU. Such a configuration is called a *multiprocessing system*. FIGURE 8.20 shows a multiprocessing system with two processors.

In multiprogramming, the processes appear to be executing concurrently because the CPU switches between them so rapidly. In multiprocessing, the operating system can schedule more than one process to execute concurrently because there is more than one processor.

It would be nice if increasing the number of processors in the system increased the performance proportionally. Unfortunately, that is not usually the case. When you add more processors to the system, you place a greater demand on the communication links of the system. For example, if you attach the processors to a common bus, as in Figure 8.20, the bus may limit the performance of the system. If both CPUs request a read from the input device at the same time, one CPU will have to wait. The more processors you add, the more frequently those conflicts occur.

FIGURE 8.20
Block diagram of a multiprocessing system.

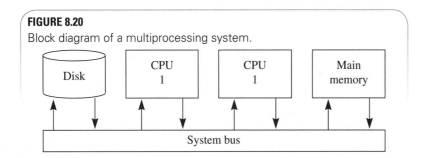

The communication overhead inherent in a multiprocessor system typically yields a performance curve as in FIGURE 8.21. The dashed line shows the theoretical maximum benefit of adding processors. On the dashed line, for example, if you double the number of processors, you double the performance. In practice, the performance does not increase that much.

A Concurrent Processing Program

The processes considered thus far have all been independent of each other. Each process belongs to a different user, and there is no interaction between the processes. Under those circumstances, the result of a computation does not depend on when an interrupt occurs. The only effect the interrupt has is to increase the amount of time it takes to execute the process.

In practice, processes managed by an operating system frequently need to cooperate with one another to perform their tasks. The program in FIGURE 8.22 describes a situation in which two processes must cooperate to avoid producing incorrect results.

Suppose the operating system must manage an airline's database, with records accessed concurrently by several users. Each flight has a record in the database that contains, among other things, the number of reservations that have been made for that flight. Travel agencies from throughout the city access the system on behalf of prospective passengers. Requests for information from the database are somewhat random because it is impossible to predict when a given agent will need to access the system.

Cooperating processes

FIGURE 8.21
The increase in performance by adding processors in a multiprocessing system.

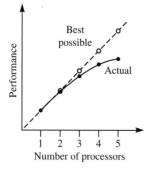

FIGURE 8.22
Concurrent processes at two levels of abstraction.

C Level

Process P1	Process P2
. . .	. . .
numRes++	numRes++
. . .	. . .

Assembly Level

Process P1	Process P2
. . .	. . .
LDWA numRes,d	LDWA numRes,d
ADDA 1,i	ADDA 1,i
STWA numRes,d	STWA numRes,d
. . .	. . .

One day, two different agents have customers who want to make reservations at exactly the same time for the same future flight. The operating system creates a process for each job called *P1* and *P2*. Figure 8.22 shows a code fragment from each process. numRes stands for *number of reservations.* It is an integer variable whose value is in main memory while P1 and P2 progress through the system.

Suppose numRes has the value 47 before either agent makes a reservation for her customer. After both transactions, numRes should have the value 49. At the C level, each process wants to increment numRes by 1 with the assignment statement numRes++. If assignment statements are *atomic*—that is, indivisible—then the code fragment at the C level will produce correct results regardless of which process executes its assignment statement first. If P1 executes first, it will make numRes 48, and P2 will make numRes 49. If P2 executes first, it will make numRes 48, and P1 will make numRes 49. In either case, numRes gets the correct value of 49.

The problem is that assignment statements at the C level are not atomic. They are compiled to LDWA, ADDA, and STWA, and are executed in a system in which an interrupt may occur between any assembly language statements. **FIGURE 8.23** is a trace of an execution sequence that shows what can go wrong. A(P1) is the content of P1's accumulator, either in the CPU when P1 is running or in the PCB when P1 is suspended. A(P2) is P2's accumulator.

In this sequence, P1 executes LDWA, which puts 47 in its accumulator, then ADDA, which increments the accumulator to 48. Then the operating system interrupts P1 and gives P2 some processor time. P2 executes all three of its statements, changing numRes in memory to 48. When P1 eventually resumes, it gives 48 to numRes as well. The net result is that numRes has the value 48 instead of 49, even though each process executed all its statements.

Nonatomic statements

Statement Executed	A(P1)	A(P2)	numRes
	?	?	47
(P1) LDWA numRes,d	47	?	47
(P1) ADDA 1,i	48	?	47
(P2) LDWA numRes,d	48	47	47
(P2) ADDA 1,i	48	48	47
(P2) STWA numRes,d	48	48	48
(P1) STWA numRes,d	48	48	48

FIGURE 8.23
A trace of one possible execution sequence of Figure 8.22.

This problem can occur whether the processes execute in a multiprocessing system with true concurrency or in a multiprogramming system where the concurrency is only apparent. In a multiprocessing system, it would be possible for P1 and P2 to execute their ADDA instructions at exactly the same time. But if they tried to execute their STWA instructions at exactly the same time, the hardware would force one process to wait while the other wrote the value to memory. From a logical point of view, the problems that can occur are the same whether the concurrency is real or not.

Critical Sections

The basic problem arises because P1 and P2 share the part of main memory that contains the value of numRes. Whenever concurrent processes share a variable, there is always the possibility that the results depend on the timing of the interrupts. To solve the problem, we need a way to ensure that when one process accesses the shared variable, the other process is prevented from accessing it until the first process has completed its access.

Sections of code in two processes that are mutually exclusive are called *critical sections*. For concurrent programs to execute correctly, the software must guarantee that if one process is executing a statement in a critical section, the other process cannot be executing a statement in its critical section. To solve the problem of Figure 8.22, we need a way of putting the assignment statements in critical sections so that the interleaved execution will not occur at the assembly level.

A critical section requires two additional pieces of code called the *entry section* and the *exit section*. The entry section for P1 is written just before its critical section. Its function is to test whether P2 is executing in its critical section and, if so, to delay somehow the execution of P1's critical section until P2 is finished with its critical section. The exit section for P1 is written just after its critical section. Its function is to alert P2 that P1 is no longer in a critical section so P2 may enter its critical section.

The code fragment at the C level for each process of Figure 8.22 must be modified as follows:

```
remainder section
entry section
numRes++ //the critical section
exit section
remainder section
```

The remainder sections are all those parts of the code that can execute concurrently with the other process with no ill effects. The critical sections are those parts of the code that must be mutually exclusive.

FIGURE 8.24
The general form of critical section programs.

Process P1	Process P2
do	do
entry section	*entry section*
critical section	*critical section*
exit section	*exit section*
remainder section	*remainder section*
while (! done1);	while (! done2);

The following programs show attempts to implement the entry and exit sections that guard the process's access to its critical section. Each program assumes that P1 and P2 have the general form of FIGURE 8.24 .

done1 and done2 are local Boolean variables (not shared) that are modified somewhere in the remainder sections.

A First Attempt at Mutual Exclusion

The program in FIGURE 8.25 , our first attempt at designing the entry and exit sections, uses turn, a shared integer variable. The entry section consists of a do loop that tests turn, and the exit section consists of an assignment statement that modifies turn. Although the listing does not show it, assume that turn is initialized either to 1 or 2 before the processes enter the do loops.

FIGURE 8.25
An attempt at programming mutual exclusion.

Process P1	Process P2
do	do
while (turn != 1)	while (turn != 2)
; //nothing	; //nothing
critical section	*critical section*
turn = 2;	turn = 1;
remainder section	*remainder section*
while (!done1);	while (!done2);

The body of the do loop in the entry section is an empty C statement that generates no code at the assembly level. The code for the entry section of P1 translates to

The nonatomic nature of the do statement

```
Loop: LDWA turn,d
      CPWA 1,i
      BRNE Loop
```

Suppose turn is initialized to 1 and both processes try to enter their critical sections at the same time. No matter how you interleave the executions of the assembly statements in the entry section, P2 will continually loop until P1 enters its critical section. When P1 finishes its critical section, its exit section will set turn to 2, after which P2 will be able to enter its critical section.

This algorithm guarantees that the critical sections are mutually exclusive. P2 can be in its critical section only if turn is 2, during which time P1 cannot be in its critical section, and vice versa. When P2 leaves its critical section, it sets turn to 1, which acts as a signal to P1 that it may enter its critical section.

Although the algorithm guarantees mutual exclusion, it has the undesirable property of requiring the processes to strictly alternate their do loops. The processes communicate through the shared variable turn, which keeps track of whose turn it is to execute a critical section. The user may want P1 to execute its do loop several times without P2 executing its loop at all. That could never happen with these entry and exit sections.

A Second Attempt at Mutual Exclusions

To allow a process to execute its do loops unrestrained by the execution of the other process (except for the mutual exclusion requirement), the program in FIGURE 8.26 uses two shared Boolean variables, enter1 and enter2. Assume that enter1 and enter2 are both initialized to false.

If P2 is in its remainder section, enter2 must be false. Then P1 can execute its do loop as often as it likes. It simply sets enter1 to true, tests enter2 once in the while loop, executes its critical section, sets enter1 to false, and executes its remainder section. It can repeat the sequence as long as it likes. Similarly, P2 can loop repeatedly if P1 is in its remainder section.

This implementation guarantees mutual exclusion. When P1 sets enter1 to true, it is signaling P2 that it is trying to enter a critical section. If P2 has just a little earlier fetched enter1 with

```
LDWA enter1,d
```

in its while test, P2 will not immediately know of P1's intentions. P2 may be executing its critical section already. However, if P2 is in its critical section, enter2 must be true, and P1's while loop will keep it from entering its

FIGURE 8.26
Another attempt at programming mutual exclusion.

Process P1	Process P2
do	do
enter1 = TRUE;	enter2 = TRUE;
while (enter2)	while (enter1)
; //nothing	; //nothing
critical section	*critical section*
enter1 = FALSE;	enter2 = FALSE;
remainder section	*remainder section*
while (!done1);	while (!done2);

critical section at the same time. When P2 finally exits, it sets enter2 to false, which allows P1 into its critical section.

The problems that confront the designer of cooperating processes can be quite subtle and unexpected. This algorithm is a case in point. Although it guarantees mutual exclusion and does not constrain the do loop execution as in the previous program, it nevertheless has a serious bug.

FIGURE 8.27 shows a trace where P1 sets enter1 to true and then experiences an interrupt. P2 sets enter2 to true and then begins executing its while loop. The while loop will continue executing until P2 times out and P1 resumes, because enter1 is true. But P1 will also loop indefinitely because enter2 is true.

P1 and P2 are in a state in which each one wants to enter a critical section. P1 cannot enter until P2 enters, executes its critical section, and sets

FIGURE 8.27
A trace of the program in Figure 8.26 that produces deadlock.

Statement Executed	enter1	enter2
	false	false
(P1) enter1 = TRUE;	true	false
(P2) enter2 = TRUE;	true	true
(P2) while (enter1);	true	true
(P1) while (enter2);	true	true

Definition of deadlock

enter2 to false. But P2 cannot enter until P1 enters, executes its critical section, and sets enter1 to false. Each process is waiting for an event that will never occur, a condition called *deadlock*. Deadlocks, like endless loops, are conditions to avoid.

Peterson's Algorithm for Mutual Exclusion

We need a solution that guarantees mutual exclusion, allows the outer do loops of each process to execute without restraint, and avoids deadlock. FIGURE 8.28 , an implementation of Peterson's algorithm, combines features from Figures 8.25 and 8.26 to achieve all these objectives. The basic idea is that enter1 and enter2 provide the mutual exclusion as in Figure 8.26, and turn allows one of the processes to enter its critical section even if both processes try to enter at the same time. enter1 and enter2 initially are false, and turn initially can be 1 or 2.

Proof that Peterson's algorithm guarantees mutual exclusion

To see that mutual exclusion is guaranteed, consider the situation if P1 and P2 were both executing their critical sections simultaneously. enter1 and enter2 would both be true. In P1, the while test would imply that turn has the value 1 because enter2 is true. But in P2, the while test would imply that turn has the value 2 because enter1 is true. This contradiction implies that P1 and P2 cannot execute their critical sections simultaneously.

But what if P1 and P2 try to enter their critical sections at about the same time? Is there some interleaving of the executions in the entry section that will permit them to both execute their critical sections simultaneously? No there is not, even though the while test with the AND operation is not atomic at the assembly level. There are two ways that P1 can get past the

---

FIGURE 8.28
Peterson's algorithm for mutual exclusion.

```
Process P1                              Process P2
do                                      do
    enter1 = TRUE;                          enter2 = TRUE;
    turn = 2;                               turn = 1;
    while (enter2 && (turn == 2))           while (enter1 && (turn == 1))
      ;  //nothing                            ;  //nothing
    critical section                        critical section
    enter1 = FALSE;                         enter2 = FALSE;
    remainder section                       remainder section
while (!done1);                         while (!done2);
```

while test into its critical section: if enter2 is false, or if turn is 1. If either of these conditions holds, P1 can enter regardless of the other condition.

Suppose that P1 gets past the while test because when it gets the value of enter2 with

```
LDWA enter2,d
```

enter2 has the value false. That can happen only when P2 is in its remainder section. Even if P1 is interrupted after it loads the value of enter2, and P2 then sets enter2 to true and turn to 1, P2 will not be able to enter its critical section because P1 has set enter1 to true and turn is now 1.

Suppose that P1 gets past the while test because when it gets the value of turn with

```
LDWA turn,d
```

turn has the value 1. Because the previous instruction in P1 set turn to 2, that can happen only if P1 was interrupted between its previous instruction and the while test, and P2 set turn to 1. But then, P2 again will be prevented from getting past its while loop into its critical section, because P1 has set enter1 to true and turn now has the value 1.

To see that deadlock cannot occur, assume that both processes are deadlocked, both executing their while loops concurrently (in a multiprocessing system) or during alternate time slices (in a multiprogramming system). The while test in P1 implies that turn must have the value 2, but the test in P2 implies that turn must have the value 1. This contradiction shows that both processes cannot be looping together.

Suppose both processes try to set turn at the same time with

Proof that Peterson's algorithm avoids deadlock

```
STWA turn,d
```

In a multiprogramming system, P1's assignment to turn will occur either before or after P2's assignment because they must execute in different time slices. In a multiprocessing system, if both processes try to store a value to turn in main memory at exactly the same time, the hardware will force one of the processes to wait while the other executes its STWA. In either system, the process that stores to turn first will enter its critical section and deadlock will not occur.

Semaphores

Although the program in Figure 8.28 solves the critical section problem while avoiding deadlock, it does have an undesirable inefficiency. The mechanism that prevents a process from entering its critical section is a while loop. The loop's only purpose is to stall the process until it is interrupted, allowing

Spin locks

time for the other process to finish executing its critical section. Such a loop is called a *spin lock* because the process is locked out of its critical section by spinning around the loop.

Spin locks are a waste of CPU time, especially if the process is executing in a multiprogramming system and has just been allocated a new time slice. It would be more efficient if the CPU were allocated to another process that could use the time to perform useful work. *Semaphores* are shared variables that most operating systems provide for concurrent programming. They enable the programmer to implement critical sections without spin locks.

A semaphore is an integer variable whose value can be modified only by an operating system call. The three operations on semaphore s are

The three operations on a semaphore

> `init(s)`

> `wait(s)`

> `signal(s)`

where `init()`, `wait()`, and `signal()` are procedures provided by the operating system. At the assembly level, the procedures would be invoked by an SVC with the appropriate operand specifier. A semaphore is another example of an abstract data type (ADT) with operations whose meanings are known to the programmer but whose implementations are hidden at a lower level of abstraction. (`wait(s)` and `signal(s)` are frequently written `p(s)` and `v(s)`, respectively.)

Each semaphore, s, has associated with it a queue of process control blocks, called `sQueue`, that represents suspended processes. The meanings of the operations are

<u>`init(s)`</u>
s = 1;
`sQueue` = *an empty list of process control blocks*

<u>`wait(s)`</u>
s--
if (s < 0)
　　　Suspend this process by adding it to `sQueue`

<u>`signal(s)`</u>
s++
if (s ≤ 0)
　　　Transfer a process from `sQueue` *to the ready queue*

An important characteristic of each operation is that the operating system guarantees them to be atomic. For example, it is impossible for two processes to execute `signal(s)` simultaneously with s incremented only by 1 as numRes is in Figure 8.22. The assembly-level statements for the assignments will never be interleaved.

FIGURE 8.29 is the state transition diagram for a job in an operating system that provides semaphores. A process in the waiting-for-s state is suspended, its PCB in sQueue, in the same way that a process in the ready state is suspended, its PCB in the ready queue. Such a process is blocked from running, because it must make a transition to the ready state before it can run.

If a running process executes `wait(s)` when s is greater than 0, then `wait(s)` simply decrements s by 1 and the process continues executing. A running process makes a transition to the waiting-for-s state by executing `wait(s)` when s is less than or equal to 0. If a running process executes `signal(s)` when s is greater than or equal to 0, it simply increments s by 1 and continues executing. A running process that executes `signal(s)` when s is less than 0 causes some other process that is waiting for s to be selected by the operating system and placed in the ready state. The process that executed `signal(s)` continues to run.

From the definitions of `wait()` and `signal()`, it follows that a negative value of s means that one or more processes are blocked in sQueue. Furthermore, the magnitude of s is the number of processes blocked. For example, if the value of s is –3, then three processes are blocked in sQueue.

The meaning of a negative semaphore value

If more than one process is blocked when `signal(s)` executes, the operating system tries to be fair in selecting the process to transfer to the ready state. A common strategy is to use *first-in, first-out* (FIFO) scheduling so the process that was blocked for the longest period of time gets sent to the ready state. FIFO is the characteristic that distinguishes a queue from a stack, which is a *last-in, first-out* (LIFO) list.

Figure 8.29 shows only one semaphore wait state. In a system that provides semaphores, the programmer can declare as many different

FIGURE 8.29

The state transition diagram for a job in an operating system that provides a semaphore.

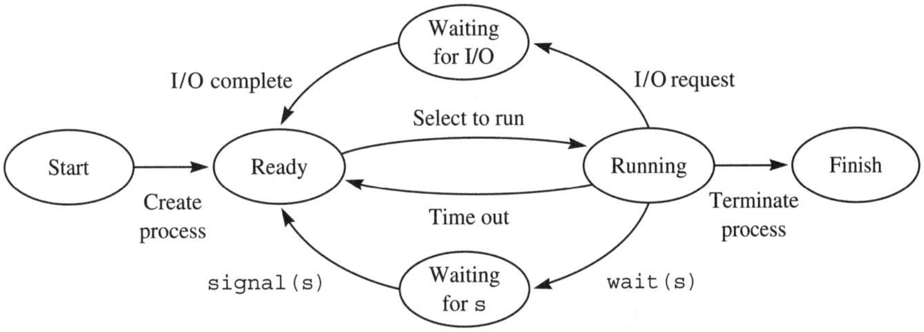

FIGURE 8.30

Critical sections with semaphore.

Process P1	Process P2
do	do
wait(mutEx);	wait(mutEx);
critical section	*critical section*
signal(mutEx);	signal(mutEx);
remainder section	*remainder section*
while (!done1);	while (!done2);

---

semaphores as she likes. The operating system will maintain a queue of blocked processes for each one.

Critical Sections with Semaphores

Critical sections are trivial to program if the operating system provides semaphores. The program in **FIGURE 8.30** assumes that mutEx is a semaphore initialized to 1 with init(mutEx).

The first process to execute wait(mutEx) will change mutEx from 1 to 0 and enter its critical section. If the other process executes wait(mutEx) in the meantime, it will change mutEx from 0 to –1, and the operating system will immediately block it. When the first process eventually leaves its critical section, it will execute signal(mutEx), which will put the other process in the ready state.

Because the operating system guarantees that wait() and signal() are atomic, the programmer need not worry about interleaving within the entry and exit sections. Also, time is not wasted on spin locks because the system immediately puts the second process on the wait queue for mutEx. Of course, hiding the details does not eliminate them. The operating system designer must use the features of the hardware, along with algorithmic reasoning such as that employed in the previous programs, to provide the semaphores. Semaphores satisfy both goals of the operating system—to provide a convenient environment for higher-level programming and to allocate the resources of the system efficiently.

8.4 Deadlocks

The program in Figure 8.26 shows how concurrent processing can produce a deadlock between two processes that share a variable in main memory. The deadlock phenomenon can occur when processes share other resources as well. Resources that an operating system must manage include printers and disk files. Sharing any of these resources among concurrent processes can lead to deadlock.

As an example of a deadlock with these resources, suppose a computer system has a hard drive with two files on it, and process P1 requests file 1 for data input. The operating system opens file 1 for P1, which holds it until it does not need the file any longer. P2 may then request input from file 2, which the operating system opens and allocates to that process.

Now suppose P1 needs to write to file 2 that P2 is accessing. It requests access, but the operating system cannot grant the request because the file is already open for P2. The operating system blocks P1 until the file becomes available. If P2 similarly requests to write to file 1, the operating system will block it as well until P1 releases the file.

In this case, the processes are in a state of deadlock. P1 cannot proceed until P2 relinquishes file 2, and P2 cannot proceed until P1 relinquishes file 1. Both are waiting for an event that will never happen, suspended by the operating system.

Resource Allocation Graphs

To manage its resources effectively, the operating system needs a way to detect possible deadlocks. It does so with a structure called a *resource allocation graph*. A resource allocation graph is a visual depiction of the processes and resources in the system that shows which resources are allocated to which processes and which processes are blocked by a request on which resources.

FIGURE 8.31 shows the resource allocation graph for the state in which P1 and P2 are deadlocked over disk file 1 and disk file 2 in the preceding scenario. Processes and resources are nodes in the graph, with processes in circles and resources as solid dots inside boxes. There are two types of edges, allocation edges and request edges.

An *allocation edge* (al) from a resource to a process means the resource is allocated to the process. In the figure, the edge labeled al from disk file 1 to P1 means the operating system has allocated file 1 to process P1. A *request edge* (req) from a process to a resource means the process is blocked, waiting for the resource. The edge labeled req from P2 to disk file 1 means P2 is blocked waiting for disk file 1 to be allocated to it.

The deadlock is evident from the fact that the edges describe a closed path from P1 to R2 to P2 to R1 and back to P1. Such a closed path in a graph is called a *cycle*. A cycle in a resource allocation graph means that a process is blocked on a resource because it is allocated to another process that is blocked on another resource, and so on, with the last resource allocated to the first process. If the cycle cannot be broken, there is a deadlock.

Sometimes the resources in a class are indistinguishable from each other. A process may request one resource from the class and not be

FIGURE 8.31
A resource allocation graph with a deadlock cycle.

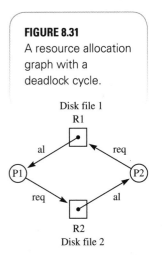

FIGURE 8.32

A resource allocation graph with a cycle but with no deadlock.

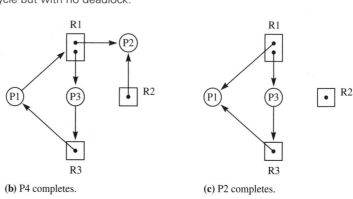

(a) Initial state.   (b) P4 completes.   (c) P2 completes.

concerned with which particular resource it gets because they are all equivalent. An example is a group of identical hard drives or identical printers. If a process needs a printer and it does not care which one, the operating system can allocate any printer that is free.

A resource allocation graph represents a class of n identical resources with n solid dots inside the rectangular box. When the operating system allocates a resource from the class, the allocation edge starts from one of the dots that represents the individual resource. A request edge, however, points to the box because the requesting process does not care which resource within the class it gets.

FIGURE 8.32(a) shows a situation in which both resources in class R1 are allocated. P1 has a request outstanding for one of those resources and does not care which resource it gets.

Even though this graph has cycle (P1, R1, P3, R3, P1), it does not represent a deadlock because the cycle can be broken. Any process in a resource allocation graph that has no request edge from it is not blocked. P4 is not blocked in this figure, and you can assume that it will eventually complete, releasing R2. The operating system will grant P2's request for resource R2. The system then changes the request edge from P2 to R2, to an allocate edge from R2 to P2, as Figure 8.32(b) shows.

Now P2 can use R2 and R1 and run to completion, eventually releasing those resources. When P2 releases an R1 resource, the operating system can allocate the resource to P1, yielding Figure 8.32(c). P1 can run to completion because it has all the resources it needs, after which P3 can complete also. All the processes can complete, so there is no deadlock.

You must consider the direction of the edges when looking for a cycle. You may be tempted to consider (R1, P1, R2, P2, R1) a cycle in FIGURE 8.33,

FIGURE 8.33

A resource allocation graph with no cycle and, therefore, no deadlock.

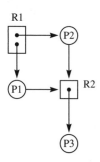

but it is not. There is no edge from R2 to P2, or from P2 to R1. A cycle is a necessary but not sufficient condition for a deadlock. In this figure, there is no cycle and, therefore, no deadlock.

Deadlock Policy

An operating system may employ one of three general policies for dealing with deadlock:

> > Prevent

> > Detect and recover

> > Ignore

Three deadlock policies

Several different policies may be found in a given operating system. The system may use one policy for one set of resources and another policy for another set.

The prevention policy employs techniques to ensure that deadlock will not occur. One technique is to require that a job request and be granted once, at the beginning of execution, all the resources it will need to run to completion. The deadlock of Figure 8.31 could not have occurred if P1 had been granted R1 and R2 simultaneously. A deadlock cycle can be set up only if a process is granted a resource and later requests another resource to complete the cycle.

The prevention policy

The detect and recover policy allows deadlocks to occur. With it, the operating system periodically executes a program to detect a deadlock cycle in the system. If the operating system discovers a deadlock, it takes away one of the resources held by a process in the cycle. Because the process has partially executed, the operating system usually must terminate the process, unless the state of the resource can be reconstructed later when it is granted to the process.

The detect and recover policy

All these policies have a cost. The prevention policy puts a constraint on the user, particularly if the resources required depend on the input and cannot be known in advance. The detect and recover policy requires CPU time for the detection and recovery algorithms—time that could be spent on user jobs.

The third policy is to ignore deadlocks. This policy is effective if the costs of the other policies are considered too great, the probability of deadlock is small, or the occurrence of deadlock is inconsequential. For example, a time-shared system may be shut down periodically for routine maintenance, at which time all jobs, including any that are deadlocked, will be removed.

The ignore policy

Chapter Summary

The goals of an operating system are to provide a convenient environment for higher-level programming and to allocate the resources of the system efficiently. One important function of an operating system is to manage the jobs that users submit to be executed. A loader is the part of the operating system that places a job into main memory for execution. After the job finishes executing, it turns control of the CPU back to the operating system, which can then load another application program.

A trap handler performs processing for a job, hiding the lower-level details from the programmer. When a trap occurs, the running job's process control block (PCB) is stored while the operating system services the interrupt. The PCB consists of the state of the process: copies of the program counter, the status bits, and the contents of all the CPU registers. To resume the job, the operating system places the PCB back into the CPU. An asynchronous interrupt functions in the same fashion as a procedure call, except that an interrupt is initiated by the operating system, not by the application programmer's code.

A process is a program during execution. In a multiprogramming system, one CPU switches between several processes. In a multiprocessing system, there is more than one CPU. Both multiprogramming and multiprocessing systems maintain concurrently executing processes. To execute cooperating processes concurrently, the operating system must be able to guarantee mutual exclusion of critical sections and avoid deadlock. Peterson's algorithm fills both these requirements. A semaphore is an integer variable provided by the operating system. Its operations include `wait()` and `signal()`, each of which is atomic, or indivisible. Semaphores can also be used to satisfy the mutual exclusion and deadlock requirements.

The deadlock phenomenon can also occur when processes share resources managed by the operating system. A resource allocation graph consists of nodes representing resources and processes, and edges between the nodes representing resource allocations and requests. If the resource allocation graph contains a cycle that cannot be broken, a deadlock has occurred.

Exercises

Section 8.1

1. What are the two purposes of an operating system?

2. The loader in Figure 8.3 executes with the following input:

```
12 00 05 00 00 31 00 03 39 00 03 D0 00 0A F1 FC
16 49 00 15 00 54 68 61 74 27 73 20 61 6C 6C 2E
0A 00 zz
```

Assume that the loop from FC1A to FC4E is executing for the 30th time. State the values in the following registers as four hexadecimal digits:

*(a) A⟨8..15⟩ after LDBA at F61A   *(b) A⟨8..15⟩before ASLA at FC2C
*(c) A⟨8..15⟩ after ASLA at FC2F   (d) A⟨8..15⟩ after LDBA at FC33
 (e) A⟨8..15⟩ after ANDA at FC3F   (f) A⟨8..15⟩ after ORA at FC42
 (g) X⟨8..15⟩ after ADDX at FC48

3. Do Exercise 2 for the 32nd execution of the loop.

Section 8.2

4. The program of (FIGURE 8.34) executes, generating an interrupt for DECI. For Figure 8.6, the entry to and exit from the trap handler, state the values in the following registers as four hexadecimal digits:

*(a) X⟨8..15⟩ after LDBX at FC52   *(b) X after ASRX at FC69
 (c) X after SUBX at FC6A   (d) PC after CALL at FC6E
 (e) PC after RETTR at FC71

*5. Do Exercise 4 for the DECO instruction.

FIGURE 8.34
The program for Exercise 4.

```
0000   120005           BR       main         ;Branch around data
0003   0000    num:     .BLOCK   2            ;Global variable
0005   310003 main:     DECI     num,d        ;Input decimal value
0008   390003           DECO     num,d        ;Output decimal value
000B   D0000A           LDBA     '\n',i
000E   F1FC16           STBA     charOut,d    ;Output message
0011   490015           STRO     msg,d
0014   00               STOP
0015   546861 msg:      .ASCII   "That's all.\x00"
       742773
       20616C
       6C2E00
0021                    .END
```

*6. Do Exercise 4 for the STRO instruction.

7. The program in Exercise 4 runs with an input of 37. For Figure 8.14, the DECI trap handler, state the values in registers a–h as four hexadecimal digits and answer the question in (i):

   *(a) A after ANDA at FD98 the first time it executes
   *(b) A after ANDA at FD98 the second time it executes
   *(c) X after LDWX at FDA1 the first time it executes
   (d) X after LDWX at FDA1 the second time it executes
   (e) PC after BR at FDA5 the first time it executes
   (f) PC after BR at FDA5 the second time it executes
   (g) A after LDWA at FE96
   (h) X before STBX at FEB1, assuming that the carry bit is zero before the trap
   (i) What statement executes just before LDWA at FE74?

*8. Do Exercise 7 with an input of -295.

9. The program in Exercise 4 runs with an input of 37. For Figure 8.15, the DECO trap handler, state the values in the following registers as four hexadecimal digits:

   *(a) A after LDWA at FEFA   *(b) A before STWA at FF0A

   In the following parts, assume that subroutine divide is called from CALL at FF2B:

   *(c) A after LDWA at FF44   (d) X before CPWX at FF59
   (e) A after LDWA at FF68

   In the following parts, assume that subroutine divide is called from CALL at FF34:

   (f) A after LDWA at FF44   (g) X before CPWX at FF59
   (h) X after ORX at FF6F

10. Do Exercise 9 with an input of -2068.

11. The program in Exercise 4 runs and executes the STRO instruction. For Figure 8.16, the STRO trap handler, state the values in the registers in hexadecimal:

   (a) A after LDWA at FFCE
   (b) A⟨8..15⟩ after LDBA at FFE4 the first time it executes
   (c) X after ADDX at FFED the first time it executes
   (d) A⟨8..15⟩ after LDBA at FFE4 the fifth time it executes
   (e) X after ADDX at FFED the fifth time it executes

12. The DECI instruction with direct addressing at 0005 in Figure 5.11 executes, generating a trap. The trap handler calls the setAddr routine in Figure 8.10. State the values in the index register as four hexadecimal digits:

(**a**) after LDWX at FCF2   (**b**) after SUBX at FCF5
(**c**) after LDWX at FCF8

13. The DECO instruction with indirect addressing at 004B in Figure 6.41 executes, generating a trap. The trap handler calls the setAddr routine in Figure 8.10. State the values in the index register as four hexadecimal digits:

(**a**) after LDWX at FCFF   (**b**) after SUBX at FD02
(**c**) after LDWX at FD05   (**d**) after LDWX at FD08

14. The DECI instruction with stack-relative addressing at 0009 in Figure 6.4 executes, generating a trap. The trap handler calls the setAddr routine in Figure 8.10. State the values in the index register as four hexadecimal digits:

(**a**) after LDWX at FD0F   (**b**) after SUBX at FD12
(**c**) after LDWX at FD15   (**d**) after ADDX at FD18

15. The DECI instruction with stack-indexed addressing at 0013 in Figure 6.36 executes for the second time, generating a trap. The trap handler calls the setAddr routine in Figure 8.10. State the values in the index register as four hexadecimal digits:

(**a**) after LDWX at FD42   (**b**) after SUBX at FD45
(**c**) after LDWX at FD48   (**d**) after ADDX at FD4B
(**e**) after ADDX at FD4E

16. The DECI instruction with stack-deferred indexed addressing at 0016 in Figure 6.38 executes for the second time, generating a trap. The trap handler calls the setAddr routine in Figure 8.10. State the values in the index register as four hexadecimal digits:

(**a**) after LDWX at FD55   (**b**) after SUBX at FD58
(**c**) after LDWX at FD5B   (**d**) after ADDX at FD5E
(**e**) after LDWX at FD61   (**f**) after ADDX at FD64

Section 8.3

17. A short notation for the interleaved execution sequence in Figure 8.23 is 112221, which represents statements executed by P1, P1, P2, P2, P2, P1 in Figure 8.22. (**a**) How many different execution sequences are possible? List each possible sequence in the short notation. For each sequence, state whether numRes has the correct value. (**b**) What percentage of the total number of possible sequences produces an incorrect value? **(c)** Would you expect that percentage to be approximately the probability of an incorrect value when the program runs? Explain.

18. The following attempt to implement critical sections is similar to the program in Figure 8.26 except for the order of the statements in the entry section:

Process P1	Process P2
do	do
while (enter2)	while (enter1)
; //nothing	; //nothing
enter1 = TRUE	enter2 = TRUE
critical section	*critical section*
enter1 = FALSE;	enter2 = FALSE;
remainder section	*remainder section*
while (!done1);	while (!done2);

***(a)** Does the algorithm guarantee mutual exclusion? If not, show an execution sequence that lets both processes run in their critical sections simultaneously. **(b)** Does the algorithm prevent deadlock? If not, show an execution sequence that deadlocks P1 and P2.

19. Show from the definitions of wait() and signal() that the magnitude of s is the number of processes blocked.

20. Let I represent an execution of init(s), W of wait(s), and S of signal(s). Then, for example, IWWS represents the sequence of calls init(s), wait(s), wait(s), and signal(s) by some processes in an operating system. For each of the following sequences of calls, state the value of s and the number of processes blocked after the last call in the sequence:

  ***(a)** IW   **(b)** IS   **(c)** ISSSW

  (d) IWWWS   **(e)** ISWWWW

21. Suppose three concurrent processes execute the following code:

Process P1	Process P2	Process P3
do	do	do
wait(mutEx);	wait(mutEx);	wait(mutEx);
critical section	*critical section*	*critical section*
signal(mutEx);	signal(mutEx);	signal(mutEx);
remainder section	*remainder section*	*remainder section*
while (!done1);	while (!done2);	while (!done3);

Explain how the code guarantees mutual exclusion of all three critical sections.

22. Suppose s and t are two semaphores initialized with init(s) and init(t). Consider the following code fragment of two concurrent processes:

Process P1	Process P2
wait(s);	wait(t);
wait(t);	wait(s);
critical section	*critical section*
signal(s);	signal(t);
signal(t);	signal(s);
remainder section	*remainder section*

*(a) Does the algorithm guarantee mutual exclusion? If not, show an execution sequence that lets both processes run in their critical sections simultaneously. (b) Does the algorithm prevent deadlock? If not, show an execution sequence that deadlocks P1 and P2.

23. Consider the code fragment of two concurrent processes:

Process P1	Process P2
Statement 1	*Statement 4*
Statement 2	*Statement 5*
Statement 3	*Statement 6*

Modify the code fragment to guarantee that Statement 5 occurs before Statement 2. Use a semaphore.

24. Each of the following code fragments contains a bug in the entry or exit section. For each fragment, state whether mutual exclusion still holds. If it doesn't, show an execution sequence that violates it. State whether deadlock can occur. If it can, show an execution sequence that produces it.

*(a)

Process P1	Process P2
do	do
wait(mutEx);	signal(mutEx);
critical section	*critical section*
signal(mutEx);	wait(mutEx);
remainder section	*remainder section*
while (!done1);	while (!done2);

(b)

Process P1	Process P2
do	do
signal(mutEx);	signal(mutEx);
critical section	*critical section*
wait(mutEx);	wait(mutEx);
remainder section	*remainder section*
while (!done1);	while (!done2);

(c)

Process P1	Process P2
do	do
wait(mutEx);	wait(mutEx);
critical section	*critical section*
signal(mutEx);	wait(mutEx);
remainder section	*remainder section*
while (!done1);	while (!done2);

(d)

Process P1	Process P2
do	do
wait(mutEx);	wait(mutEx);
critical section	*critical section*
signal(mutEx);	*remainder section*
remainder section	while (!done2);
while (!done1);	

(e)

Process P1	Process P2
do	do
wait(mutEx);	*critical section*
critical section	signal(mutEx);
signal(mutEx);	*remainder section*
remainder section	while (!done2);
while (!done1);	

Section 8.4

25. An operating system has processes P1, P2, P3, and P4 and resources R1 (one resource), R2 (one resource), R3 (two resources), and R4 (three resources). The notation (1, 1), (2, 2), (1, 2) means that P1 requests R1, then P2 requests R2, then P1 requests R2. Note that the first two requests produce allocation edges on the resource allocation graph, but the third request produces a request edge on the graph because R2 is already allocated to P2.

Draw the resource allocation graph after each sequence of requests. State whether the graph contains a cycle. If it does, state whether it is a deadlock cycle.

*(a) (1, 1), (2, 2), (1, 2), (2, 1)
*(b) (1, 4), (2, 4), (3, 4), (4, 4)
 (c) (1, 1), (2, 1), (3, 1), (4, 1)
 (d) (3, 3), (4, 3), (2, 2), (3, 2), (2, 3)
 (e) (1, 2), (1, 3), (1, 4), (2, 2), (2, 3), (2, 4)
 (f) (2, 1), (1, 2), (2, 3), (3, 3), (2, 2), (1, 3)
 (g) (2, 1), (1, 2), (2, 3), (3, 3), (2, 2), (1, 3), (3, 1)
 (h) (1, 4), (2, 3), (3, 3), (2, 1), (3, 4), (1, 3), (4, 4), (3, 1), (2, 4)
 (i) (1, 4), (2, 3), (3, 3), (2, 1), (3, 4), (1, 3), (4, 4), (3, 1), (2, 4), (4, 3)

Problems

Section 8.2

26. Implement a new unary instruction in place of NOP0 called ASL2 that does two left shifts on the accumulator. NZC should should correlate with the new value in the accumulator from the second shift. V should be set if either the first or the second shift produced an overflow. Use the test program provided in the Pep/9 app to test the features of the new instruction.

27. Implement a new nonunary instruction in place of NOP called ASLMANY whose operand is the number of times the accumulator is shifted left. Allow only direct addressing. NZC should correlate with the new value in the accumulator from the last shift. V should be set if any of the shifts produced an overflow. Use the test program provided in the Pep/9 app to test the features of the new instruction.

28. Implement a new nonunary instruction in place of NOP called MULA that multiplies the operand by the accumulator and puts the result in the accumulator. Allow only direct addressing. Use the interative shift-and-add algorithm of Problem 6.24. NZC should should correlate with the new value in the accumulator from the last addition. V should be set if any of the left shifts or additions produced an overflow. Use the test program provided in the Pep/9 app to test the features of the new instruction.

29. Direct addressing is immediate addressing deferred. Indirect addressing is direct addressing deferred. You can carry this concept one level further with double indirect addressing, which is indirect addressing deferred. Implement a new instruction in place of NOP0 with mnemonic STWADI, which stands for *store word accumulator double indirect*. It should store the accumulator using double indirect addressing. None of the status flags are affected. NOP0 is a unary instruction as far as the assembler and CPU are concerned, but your program must implement it as a nonunary instruction. You will need to increment the saved PC to skip over the operand specifier. Use the test program provided in the Pep/9 app to test the features of the new instruction.

30. Implement a new nonunary instruction in place of NOP called BOOLO, which means *Boolean output*. It should output false if the operand is zero and true otherwise. Allow immediate, direct, and stack-relative addressing. None of the status flags are affected. Use the test program provided in the Pep/9 app to test the features of the new instruction.

31. Implement a new unary instruction in place of NOP0 called STKADD. It should replace the two topmost items on the stack with their sum. Set NZVC according to the results of the addition. Use the test program provided in the Pep/9 app to test the features of the new instruction.

32. Implement a new nonunary instruction in place of NOP called XORA, which computes the bitwise exclusive OR operation with the operand and the accumulator, placing the result in the accumulator. Allow only direct addressing. Status bits NZ should be set according to the results of the operation, and VC should remain unchanged. Use the test program provided in the Pep/9 app to test the features of the new instruction.

33. This problem is to implement new nonunary instructions to process floating point numbers. Assume that floating point numbers are stored with all the special values of IEEE 754 but with a two-byte cell having one sign bit, six exponent bits, nine significand bits, and a hidden bit. The exponent uses excess 31 notation except for denormalized numbers, which use excess 30.

(a) Implement a new unary instruction in place of DECO called BINFO, which stands for binary floating point output. Permit the same addressing modes as with DECO. The value 3540 (hex), which represents the normalized number 1.101×2^{-5}, should be output as `1.101000000b011010`, where the letter b stands for two raised to a power and the bit sequence following the b is the excess 30 representation of –5. The value 0050 (hex), which represents the denormalized number 0.00101×2^{-30}, should be output as `0.001010000b-30`, where the power will always be –30 for denormalized numbers. Output a NaN value as NaN, positive infinity as inf, and negative infinity as -inf.

(b) Implement a new unary instruction in place of DECI called BINFI, which stands for *binary floating point input*. Permit the same addressing modes as with DECI. Assume that the input will be a normalized binary number. The input `1.101000000b011010`, which represents the normalized number 1.101×2^{-5}, should be stored as 3540 (hex).

(c) Implement a new unary instruction in place of NOP called ADDFA, which stands for *add floating point accumulator*. Permit the same addressing modes as with ADDA. For normalized and denormalized numbers, you may assume that the exponent fields of the two numbers to add are identical, but the exponent field of the sum may not be the same as the initial exponent fields. Your implementation will need to insert the hidden bit before performing the addition and remove it when storing the result. Take into account the possibility that one or both of the operands may be a NaN or infinity.

(d) Work part (c) assuming the exponent fields of the normalized or denormalized numbers may not be identical.

CHAPTER 9

Storage Management

The purpose of an operating system is to provide a convenient environment for higher-level programming and to allocate the resources of the system efficiently. Chapter 8 shows how the operating system allocates CPU time to the processes in the system. This chapter shows how it allocates space. The two primary classes of storage space are main memory and peripheral memory. Disk memory is the most common peripheral storage and is the type described here.

Two primary classes of storage space

9.1 Memory Allocation

Normally, programs that are not executing reside in a disk file. To execute, a program needs main memory space and CPU time. The operating system allocates space by loading the program from disk into main memory. It allocates time by setting the program counter to the address of the first instruction loaded into main memory.

The first two sections of this chapter describe five techniques for allocating main memory space:

Main memory allocation techniques

> Uniprogramming

> Fixed-partition multiprogramming

> Variable-partition multiprogramming

> Paging

> Virtual memory

The techniques are listed in order of increasing complexity. Each improves on the previous technique by solving a performance problem. A sixth technique, segmentation, is beyond the scope of this text.

Uniprogramming

The simplest memory allocation technique is *uniprogramming*, exemplified by the Pep/9 operating system. The operating system resides at one end of memory, and the application resides at the other end. The system executes only one job at a time.

Because every job will be loaded at the same place, the translators can generate object code accordingly. For example, when the Pep/9 assembler computes the symbols for the symbol table, it assumes that the first byte will be loaded at address 0000 (hex). Or, if the program contains a burn directive, it assumes that the last byte will be loaded at the address specified by the burn directive.

Advantages of uniprogramming

Uniprogramming has advantages and disadvantages. Its main advantage comes from its size. The system can be small, simple to design, and therefore relatively bug-free. It also executes with little overhead. Once an application is loaded, that application is guaranteed 100% of the processor's time, since no other process will interrupt it. Uniprocessing systems are appropriate for embedded systems like the ones that control a microwave oven.

Disadvantages of uniprogramming

The primary disadvantages are the inefficient use of CPU time and the inflexibility of job scheduling. Compared to main memory, disk memory has long access time. If the application executes a read from disk, the CPU will remain idle while waiting for the disk to deliver the input. The time could better be used executing another user's job. You can tolerate some waste of CPU time in a microcomputer, but in a computer that costs an organization hundreds of thousands of dollars you cannot, especially in a multiuser system in which other processes are executing concurrently.

Even in a single-user system, the inflexibility of job scheduling can be a nuisance. The user may want to start up two programs and switch back and forth between them without quitting either one. For example, you may want to run a word processor for a while, switch to a drawing program to create an illustration for your document, and then switch back to the word processor where you left off to continue the text.

Fixed-Partition Multiprogramming

Multiprogramming solves the problem of inefficient CPU usage by allowing more than one application to run concurrently. To switch between two processes, the operating system loads both applications into main memory. When the running process is suspended, the operating system stores its process control block (PCB) and gives the CPU to the other process.

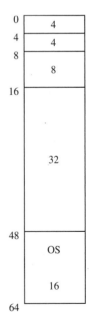

FIGURE 9.1
Fixed partitions in a 64-KiB main memory. Partition sizes and addresses are in kilobytes. The operating system occupies the bottom 16 KiB.

To implement multiprogramming, the operating system needs to partition main memory into different regions for storing the different processes while they execute. In a fixed-partition scheme, it subdivides memory into several regions whose sizes and locations do not change with time. **FIGURE 9.1** shows one possible subdivision in a fixed-partition multiprogramming system with 64 KiB of main memory. The operating system occupies 16 KiB at the bottom of memory. It assumes that the jobs will not all be the same size, so it partitions the remaining 48 KiB into two 4-KiB regions, one 8-KiB region, and one 32-KiB region.

The address problem

A problem with providing different regions of memory for different processes is that the memory references in the object code must be adjusted accordingly. Suppose an assembly language programmer writes an application that is 20 KiB long, and the operating system loads it into the 32-KiB partition. If the assembler assumes that the object code will be loaded starting at address zero, all the memory references will be wrong.

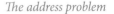

For example, suppose the first few lines of code are

```
0000 040005          BR AbsVal
0003 0000    number: .BLOCK 2
0005 310003 AbsVal: DECI number,d
```

The assembler has computed the value of symbol `AbsVal` to be 0005 because `BR` is a three-byte instruction and `number` occupies two bytes. The problem is that `BR` branches to 0005, the address of the code for the process in the first partition. Not only would this process work incorrectly, but it also may destroy some data in the other process. The operating system needs to protect processes from unauthorized tampering by other concurrent processes.

Relocatable loaders

A loader that has the capability of loading a program anywhere in memory is called a *relocatable loader*. The Pep/9 loader described in Section 8.1 is not a relocatable loader because it loads every program into memory at the same location, namely 0000 (hex).

There are several approaches to this problem. The operating system could require the assembly language programmer to decide where in memory to load the application. The assembler would need a directive that allows the programmer to specify the address of the first byte of object code. A common designation for such a directive is `.ORG`, which means *origin*. In this example, the starting address of the 32-KiB partition is 16 Ki or 8000 (hex). The first few lines of the listing would be modified as follows:

```
                 .ORG   0x8000
8000 048005      BR     AbsVal
8003 0000 number: .BLOCK 2
8005 318003 AbsVal: DECI   number,d
```

The net effect is to add 8000 to all the memory references in the application code.

If a compiler generates the object code for an application, the programmer has no concept of memory addresses. The translator would need to cooperate with the operating system to generate the correct memory references in the object code.

Logical Addresses

Requiring the programmer or the compiler to specify in advance where the object code will be loaded has several drawbacks. An applications programmer should not have to worry about partition sizes and locations. That information is not relevant to the programmer. The scheme defeats the purpose of the operating system to provide a convenient environment for higher-level programming.

It also defeats the purpose of allocating the resources of the system efficiently. Suppose the programmer specifies a 3-KiB program to be loaded in the second 4-KiB partition at address 4 Ki and sets the .ORG directive accordingly. During the course of events, the job may be waiting to be loaded while another job occupies that partition, even though the first 4-KiB partition is free. The unused memory represents an inefficient allocation of a resource.

To alleviate these problems, the operating system can let the programmer or compiler generate the object code as if it will be loaded at address zero. An address generated under this assumption is called a *logical address*. If the program is loaded into a partition whose address is not zero, the operating system must translate logical addresses to *physical addresses*.

The following equation depicts the relationship between the physical address, logical address, and address of the first byte of the partition in which the program is loaded:

Physical address = logical address + partition address

Logical address versus physical address

An example is the previous code fragment, in which the logical address of number is 0003 and the physical address is 8003.

Two address-translation techniques are possible. The operating system could provide a software utility that adds the partition address to all the memory references in the object code. The translator would need to specify those parts of the object code that need to be adjusted, because the utility cannot tell by inspection of the raw object code which parts are memory references.

Another technique depends on the availability of specialized hardware called *base* and *bound registers*. The base register solves the address-translation problem. The bound register solves the protection problem. FIGURE 9.2 shows how base and bound registers work with the previous example.

Operation of base and bound registers

The operating system loads the object program with unmodified logical addresses into the partition at 8000. It loads the base register with a value of 8000 and the bound register with a value of A000 (hex) = 48 Ki, the address of the upper bound of the partition in which the program is loaded. It turns the CPU over to the process by setting the program counter to 0000, the logical address of the first instruction.

Whenever the CPU issues a memory read request, the hardware adds the content of the base register to the address supplied by the CPU to form the physical address. It compares the physical address to the content of the bound register. If the physical address is less than the bound register, the hardware completes the memory access. Otherwise, it generates an illegal-address interrupt that the operating system must service. The bound register prevents a process from invading another process's memory partition.

FIGURE 9.2

Transformation of a logical address to a physical address with base and bound registers.

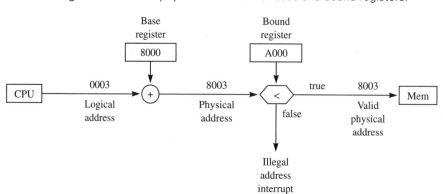

The first memory read request in this example will be from the fetch part of the von Neumann execution cycle. The CPU will request a fetch of the instruction from 0000, which the hardware will translate to a fetch from 8000. Figure 9.2 shows the translation of logical address 0003 from the DECI operand specifier. (Actually, at a lower level of abstraction, it is the operand of the STWA instruction at FEB7 in the DECI trap handler.)

To switch to another process, the operating system sets the base register to the address of the partition where the process has been loaded and the bound register to the address of the next-higher partition. When it restores the CPU registers (including the program counter) from the PCB, the process will continue executing from where it was suspended.

Scheduling problems with fixed partitions

Consider some of the problems that confront the operating system when it must schedule jobs to occupy the fixed partitions. Assume that all the partitions in Figure 9.1 are occupied except the 32-KiB partition. If a 4-KiB job requests execution, should the system put it in the 32-KiB partition or should it wait until a smaller partition becomes available? Suppose it starts the job in the 32-KiB partition, and then a 4-KiB process terminates. If a 32-KiB job now enters the system, it cannot be loaded. In retrospect, it would have been better to not schedule the small job in the large partition. Then the large job could use the large partition as soon as it requested execution, and the small job could be loaded soon anyway. Because the operating system cannot predict when a process will terminate or when a job will request execution, it cannot achieve the optimum schedule.

Another problem is how the operating system should set up the partitions in the first place. In Figure 9.1, if a 16-KiB job and a 32-KiB job request execution at the same time, only one can be loaded, even though a total of 48 KiB is available in user memory. On the other hand, if the operating system sets up user memory in two large partitions, and six or eight 4-KB jobs request execution, all but two will be delayed. Again, the optimum partition cannot be established because the operating system cannot predict the future.

Variable-Partition Multiprogramming

To alleviate the inefficiencies inherent in fixed-partition scheduling, the operating system can maintain partitions with variable boundaries. The idea is to establish a partition only when a job is loaded into memory. The size of the partition can exactly match the size of the job so more memory will be available to jobs as they enter the system.

When a job stops execution, the region of memory that it occupied becomes available for other jobs. A region of memory that is available for use by incoming jobs is called a *hole*. Holes are filled when the operating system allocates them to subsequent jobs. As in the fixed-partition scheme, the operating system attempts to schedule the jobs to maintain the largest number of processes in memory at any given point in time.

FIGURE 9.3 shows an example of a 48-KiB region of available memory before any jobs are scheduled. FIGURE 9.4 is a hypothetical sequence of job requests for the user memory in Figure 9.3. The table also indicates when a job stops executing, thereby releasing its memory for another job to use.

FIGURE 9.5 illustrates the scheduling process. The question that must be resolved is the selection criterion for determining which hole to fill when a new job requests some memory. Figure 9.5 uses what is called the *best-fit algorithm*. Of all the holes that are larger than the memory required for the job, the operating system selects the smallest. That is, the system selects the hole that the job fits best.

When J1 requests 12 KiB, there is only one hole from which to allocate memory, the initial hole in Figure 9.3. The system gives the first 12 KiB to J1, leaving a 36-KiB hole. When J2 requests 8 KiB, the system gives the first part of the smaller hole to it, and similarly for J3, J4, and J5. The result is the memory allocation in Figure 9.5(a).

Figure 9.5(b) shows the allocation when J1 stops executing, relinquishing its 12 KiB and creating a second hole at the top of main memory. When J6 requests a 4-KiB region, the operating system has the option of allocating memory for it from either hole. According to the best-fit algorithm, the system selects the 8-KiB hole rather than the 12-KiB hole, because the smaller hole is a better fit. Figure 9.5(c) shows the result.

Figure 9.5(d) shows the allocation after J5 stops, and (e) shows it after the system allocates memory from the top hole to J7. There are now three small holes scattered throughout memory. This phenomenon is called

FIGURE 9.3
The initial available user memory. Addresses are in kilobytes.

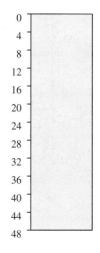

FIGURE 9.4
A job execution sequence for a variable-partition multiprogramming system. Job size is in kilobytes.

Job	Size	Action
J1	12	Start
J2	8	Start
J3	12	Start
J4	4	Start
J5	4	Start
J1	12	Stop
J6	4	Start
J5	4	Stop
J7	8	Start
J8	8	Start

FIGURE 9.5

The best-fit algorithm.

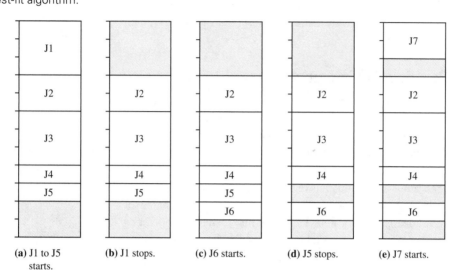

(a) J1 to J5 starts. (b) J1 stops. (c) J6 starts. (d) J5 stops. (e) J7 starts.

fragmentation. Even though J8 wants 8 KiB and available memory totals 12 KiB, J8 cannot run because the memory is not contiguous.

When confronted with a request that cannot be satisfied because of fragmented memory, the operating system could simply wait for enough processes to complete until a large enough hole becomes available. In this example, the request is so small that any job that completes will free enough memory for J8 to be loaded.

In a crowded system running many small jobs with a large request outstanding, the request may be pending for a long time before allocation. In such a case, the operating system may take time to move some processes to make a large enough hole to satisfy the request. This operation is called *compaction.*

FIGURE 9.6(a) shows the most straightforward compaction technique. The operating system shifts the processes up in memory, eliminating all the holes between them. Another possible compaction scheme is to move only enough processes to create a hole big enough to satisfy the request. In Figure 9.6(b), the system shifts only J6, leaving a large enough hole to load J8.

The idea behind the best-fit algorithm is to minimize fragmentation by using the smallest hole possible, leaving the larger holes available for future scheduling. Another scheduling technique that may not appear to be so reasonable is the *first-fit algorithm.* Rather than search for the smallest possible hole, this algorithm begins its search from the top of main memory, allocating

FIGURE 9.6

Compacting main memory.

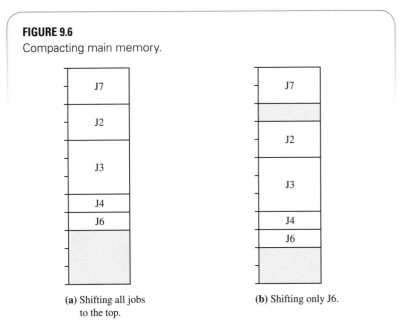

(a) Shifting all jobs
to the top.

(b) Shifting only J6.

memory from the first hole that can accommodate the request. **FIGURE 9.7** is a trace of the first-fit algorithm for the request sequence of Figure 9.4.

Figures 9.7(a) and (b) are identical to the best-fit algorithm of Figure 9.5. In Figure 9.7(c), J6 requests a 4-KB partition. Rather than allocate from the smaller hole at the bottom of memory, the first-fit algorithm finds the hole at the top of memory first, from which it allocates storage for J6.

Figure 9.7(d) shows J5 terminating. In (e), the 8-KiB request from J7 is filled by the first available hole, which is between J6 and J2. When J8 requests 8 KiB, a hole is available, and the system does not need to compact memory.

One example does not prove that first fit is better than best fit. In fact, you can devise a sequence of requests and releases that will require compaction under the first-fit algorithm before best fit. The question is "What happens on the average?" It turns out that in practice, neither algorithm is substantially superior to the other in terms of memory utilization.

First fit versus best fit

The reason first fit works so well is that storage tends to be allocated from the top of main memory. Therefore, large holes tend to form at the bottom of main memory. That is what happens in Figure 9.7.

Regardless of the allocation strategy, fragmentation is unavoidable in a variable-partition system. Noncontiguous holes represent an inefficient allocation of a resource. Even though unusable memory regions can be reclaimed with compaction, that is a time-consuming procedure.

FIGURE 9.7
The first-fit algorithm.

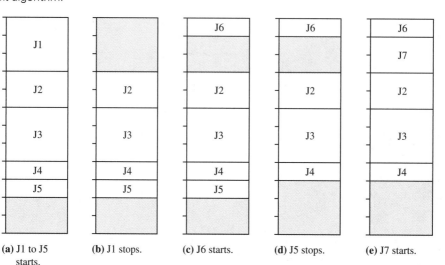

(a) J1 to J5
starts.
(b) J1 stops.
(c) J6 starts.
(d) J5 stops.
(e) J7 starts.

Paging

The idea behind paging

Paging is an ingenious idea to alleviate the fragmentation problem. Rather than coalesce several small holes to form one big hole for the program, paging fragments the program to fit the holes. Programs are no longer contiguous, but broken up and scattered throughout main memory.

FIGURE 9.8 shows three jobs executing in a paged system. Each job is subdivided into pages, and main memory is subdivided into frames that are the same size as the pages. The figure shows the first 12 KiB of a 64-KiB memory with 1-KiB frames. The page size is always a power of 2, in practice usually 4 KiB.

The code for job J3 is distributed to four noncontiguous frames in main memory. "J3, P0" in the frame at frame address 1800 represents page 0 of job J3. The second page is at 2C00, and the third and fourth pages are at 0800 and 2000, respectively. Jobs J1 and J2 are similarly scattered throughout memory. If job J4 comes along and needs 3 KB of memory, the operating system can distribute its pages to 0400, 1000, and 1400. The system does not need to compact memory to allocate it to the incoming job.

As with the previous multiprogramming memory management techniques, the application programs in paging assume logical addresses. The operating system must convert logical addresses to physical addresses during execution.

FIGURE 9.8

A paging system.

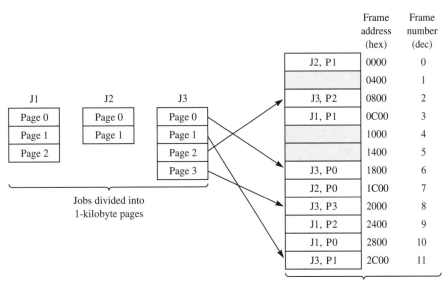

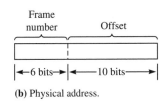

FIGURE 9.9 shows the relationship between a logical address and a physical address in the paged system of Figure 9.8. Because a page contains 1 KiB, which is 2^{10}, the rightmost 10 bits of a logical address are the offset from the top of the page. The leftmost 6 bits are the page number.

For example, consider the address 058F, which is 0000 0101 1000 1111 in binary. The leftmost six bits are 0000 01, which means that the address corresponds to a memory location in page number 1. Because 01 1000 1111 is 399 (dec), the logical address represents the 399th byte from the first byte in page number 1.

Referring to Figure 9.8, the physical address of this byte is the 399th byte from the first byte in the frame at address 2C00. To translate the logical address to the physical address, the operating system must replace the six-bit page number, 0000 01, with the six-bit frame number, 0010 11, leaving the offset unchanged.

One base register was enough to transform a logical address to a physical address in the previous memory management schemes. Paging requires a set of frame numbers, however—one for each page of the job. Such a set is called a *page table*. FIGURE 9.10 shows the page table associated with job J3 of Figure 9.8. Each entry in the page table is the frame number that must replace the page number in the logical address.

FIGURE 9.9
Logical and physical addresses in a paging system.

Page number   Offset

|←—6 bits—→|←———10 bits———→|

(a) Logical address.

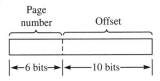

Frame number   Offset

|←—6 bits—→|←———10 bits———→|

(b) Physical address.

Page tables

FIGURE 9.10

Transformation of a logical address to a physical address with a page table.

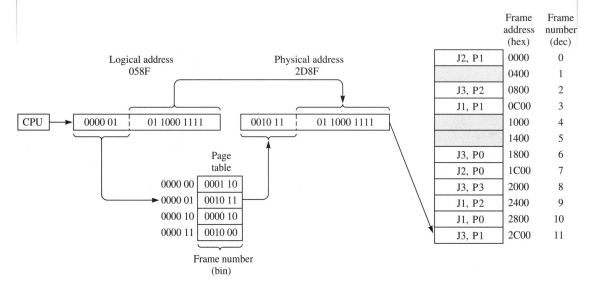

Suppose job J3 executes the statement

```
LDBA 0x058F,d
```

which causes the CPU to request a memory read from logical address 058F. The operating system extracts the first six bits, 0000 01, and uses them as an address in the page table, a special-purpose hardware memory that stores the frame numbers for the job. The frame number from the page table replaces the page number in the logical address to produce the physical address.

The byte is read from physical location 2D8F, even though the CPU issued a request for a read from location 058F. The program executes under the illusion that it has been loaded into a contiguous memory region starting at address 0000. The operating system perpetuates the illusion by maintaining a page table for each process loaded into memory. It is the ultimate scam. A process is continually interrupted in time and scattered through space without being aware of either indignity.

It is important to note that paging does not eliminate fragmentation altogether. It is rare that a job's size will be an exact multiple of the page size for the system. In that case, the last page will contain some unused memory, as FIGURE 9.11 shows for job J3. The unused memory at the end of the last page in a job is called *internal fragmentation*, in contrast to the external fragmentation that is visible to the operating system in the variable-partition scheme.

FIGURE 9.11

Internal fragmentation.

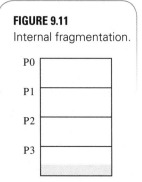

The smaller the page size, the less the internal fragmentation, on average. Unfortunately, there is a tradeoff. The smaller the page size, the greater the number of frames for a given main memory size and, therefore, the longer the page table. Because every reference to memory includes an access from a page table, the page tables usually are designed with the fastest possible circuitry. Such circuitry is expensive, so the page tables must be small to minimize the cost.

9.2 Virtual Memory

It may seem unlikely that you could improve on the memory utilization of a paged system, but the paging concept can be carried one step further. Consider the structure of a large program, say one that would fill 50 pages. To execute the program, is it really necessary for all 50 pages to be loaded into main memory at the same time?

Large Program Behavior

Most large programs consist of dozens of procedures, some of which may never execute. For example, procedures that are responsible for processing some input error condition will not execute if the input has no errors. Other procedures, such as those that initialize data, may execute only once and never be needed during the remainder of the execution.

A common control structure in any large program is the loop. As the body of a loop executes repeatedly, only that code in the loop need reside in main memory. Any code that is far from the loop (from an execution point of view) does not need to be in memory.

A program may also contain large regions of data that are never accessed. For example, if you declare an array of structures in C without knowing how many structures will be encountered when the program runs, you allocate more than you would reasonably expect to have. Pages that consist of unaccessed structures never need to be loaded.

These considerations of the typical large program show that it may be feasible to have only the active pages of the program loaded in memory. The active pages are those that contain code that is repeatedly executing and data that is repeatedly being accessed.

The set of active pages is called the *working set*. As the program progresses, new pages enter the working set and old ones leave. For example, at the beginning of execution, the pages that contain initialization procedures will be in the working set. Later, the working set will include the pages that contain the processing procedures and not the initialization procedures.

The working set

Virtual Memory

Remember that the programmer at a higher level of abstraction is under the illusion that the program executes in contiguous memory with logical addresses beginning at zero. Suppose the system can be designed to load only a few pages at a time from the executing job while still maintaining the illusion. It then becomes possible for the programmer to write a program that is too large to fit in main memory, but that will execute nonetheless. The user sees not the limited physically installed memory, but a virtual memory that is limited only by the virtual addresses and the capacity of the disk.

For example, in the older Pep/7 computer, an address contains 16 bits. It is, therefore, theoretically possible to access 2^{16} bytes (64 KiB) of memory. However, only 32 KiB of memory are installed. The application program starts at 0000 and cannot contain more than about 31,000 (dec) bytes without running into the operating system. It is common for a system to contain less memory than that permitted by the number of address bits. That situation allows the owner to upgrade the system at a later date by purchasing additional memory.

Suppose the Pep/7 computer has a virtual memory operating system. The program's physical memory is limited to 3000 bytes, but the programmer still could execute a 64-KiB program. The operating system loads the pages from disk into the memory frames as needed to execute the program. When a page needs to be loaded because it contains a statement to execute or some data to access, the operating system removes a page that is no longer active and replaces it with the one that needs to be loaded. The programmer sees the program execute in a 64-KiB virtual address space, even though the physical address space is 32 KiB.

FIGURE 9.12 shows how paging can be extended to implement a virtual memory system. It shows three jobs in the system, J1 with 10 pages, J2 with 2 pages, and J3 with 4 pages. Notice that physical memory contains only eight frames, but J1 can execute even though it is larger than physical memory. The special hardware required by the operating system includes a page table for each job and one frame table with an entry for each frame. To keep the illustration simple, frame numbers are given in decimal.

The page tables transform logical addresses to physical addresses, as in Figure 9.10. In a virtual memory system, however, some of the pages may not be loaded as the job is running. Each page table contains one extra bit per page that tells the operating system whether the page is loaded. The bit is 1 if the page is loaded and 0 if it is not. Figure 9.12 shows 1 as Y for yes, and 0 as N for no.

The frame table is needed to help the operating system allocate frames from main memory to the various jobs. The first entry is the job allocated to

FIGURE 9.12

An implementation of virtual memory.

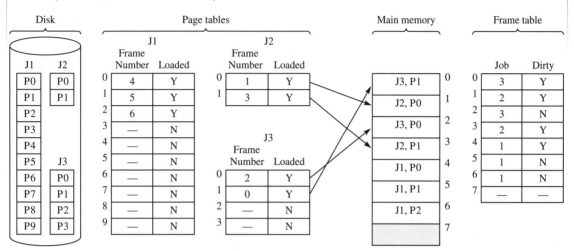

that frame. The second entry is a bit called the *dirty bit*, whose function will be explained shortly.

Demand Paging

Figure 9.12 shows that jobs J1 and J3 do not have all their pages loaded into main memory. Suppose J3 is executing some code in page P1, loaded into frame 0. It will shortly execute an LDWA instruction whose operand is in P2. How will the operating system know that J3 is going to need P2 loaded into memory? Because the system cannot predict the future, it cannot know until J3 actually executes the LDWA.

In the course of translating the logical address to a physical address, the hardware accesses the page table for J3 to determine the frame number of the physical address. Because the loaded bit says *N*, an interrupt called a *page fault* occurs. The operating system intervenes to service the interrupt.

When a page fault occurs, the operating system searches the frame table to determine whether there are any empty frames in the system. Figure 9.12 shows that frame 7 is available, so the operating system can load P2 into that frame. It updates the frame table to show that frame 7 contains a page from J3. It updates the page table for J3 to show that P2 is in frame 7, and it sets the loaded bit to Y.

When the operating system returns from the interrupt, it sets the program counter to the address of the instruction that caused the page fault. That is, it restarts the instruction. This time, when the hardware accesses the page table for J3, an interrupt will not occur, and the operand of the LDWA instruction will be brought into the accumulator.

So when does the operating system load a page into main memory? The answer is, simply, when the program demands it. In the previous example, J3 demanded that P2 be loaded via the page fault interrupt mechanism. The difference between paging and demand paging is that demand paging brings pages into main memory only on demand. If a page is never demanded, it will never be loaded.

Page Replacement

When J3 demanded that P2 be loaded, the operating system had no problem because there was an empty frame in main memory. Suppose, however, that a job demands a page when all the frames are filled. In that case, the operating system must select a page that was previously loaded and replace it, freeing its frame for the demanded page.

The replaced page may subsequently be loaded again, perhaps into a different frame. To ensure that the page is reloaded in the same state that it was in when it was replaced, the operating system may need to save its state by writing the page to disk when the page is replaced. On the other hand, it may not be necessary to write the page to the disk when it is replaced.

Deciding whether the state of the replaced page needs to be updated on disk.

In Figure 9.12, J1 has 10 pages stored on disk, 3 of which have been loaded into main memory. When J1 executes instructions such as LDWA and ASLA, the effect is to not change the state of a page in main memory. LDWA issues a memory read and places the operand in the accumulator. ASLA changes the accumulator, an action that involves neither a memory read nor a memory write. Neither instruction issues a memory write.

But when J1 executes an instruction such as STWA, the instruction changes the state of the page in main memory. STWA puts the content of the accumulator in the operand, issuing a memory write in the process. If the operand is in P0 in frame 4, P0's state will change in main memory. Page P0 on disk will no longer be an exact copy of the current P0 in main memory. If no store instruction ever executes, the image of the page on disk will be an exact replica of the page in main memory.

The dirty bit

When the operating system selects a page for replacement during a page fault, it does not need to write the page back to disk if the disk image is still a replica of the page in memory. To help the operating system decide whether the write is necessary, the hardware contains a special bit, called the *dirty bit*, in the frame table.

When a page is first loaded into an empty frame, the operating system sets the dirty bit to 0, indicated by N in Figure 9.12. If a store instruction ever issues a write to memory, the hardware sets the dirty bit for that frame to 1, indicated by Y in the figure. Such a page is said to be dirty because it has been altered from its original clean state. If a page is selected for replacement, the operating system inspects the dirty bit to check whether it must write the page back to disk before overwriting the frame with the new page.

Page-Replacement Algorithms

The operating system has two memory management tasks in a demand paged system. It must allocate frames to jobs, and it must select a page for replacement when a page fault occurs and all the frames are full.

A reasonable allocation strategy for frames is to assume that a large job will need more frames than a small job. The system can allocate frames proportionally. If J1 is twice as big as J2, it gets twice as many frames in which to execute.

Frame allocation strategy

Given that a job has a fixed number of frames in which to execute, how does the operating system decide which page to replace when a page fault occurs and all the job's frames are full? Two possible page-replacement algorithms are *first-in, first-out* (FIFO) and *least recently used* (LRU).

Page-replacement strategies

FIGURE 9.13 shows the behavior of the FIFO page-replacement algorithm in a system that has allocated three frames to a job. As a job executes, the CPU sends a continuous stream of read and write requests to main memory. The first group of bits in each address is the page number, as Figures 9.9 and 9.10 show. The page references are the sequence of page numbers that the executing job generates.

Figure 9.13 shows three empty frames available before the first request. When the job demands P6, a page fault is generated, indicated by F in the figure, and P6 is loaded into a frame.

When the job demands P8, another page fault is generated and P8 is loaded into an empty frame. The boxes do not represent particular page frames. The figure shows P6 shifting to a lower box to accommodate P8. In the computer, P6 does not shift to another frame.

The reference to P3 causes another page fault, but the following reference to P8 does not because P8 is still in the set of loaded pages. Similarly, the reference to P6 does not produce a page fault.

FIGURE 9.13
The FIFO page-replacement algorithm with three frames.

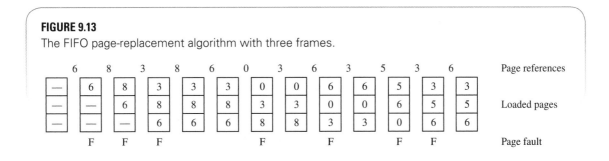

FIGURE 9.14

The FIFO page-replacement algorithm with four frames.

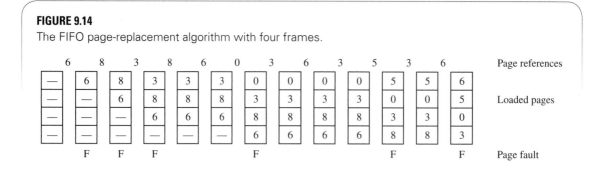

The reference to P0 triggers a page fault interrupt that must be serviced by selecting a replacement page. The FIFO algorithm replaces the page that was the first to enter the set. Because the figure shifts the pages down to accommodate a new page, the first page in is the one at the bottom, P6. The operating system replaces P6 with P0.

The given sequence of 12 page references produces 7 page faults when the job has three frames. If the job has more frames, the same sequence of page references should generate fewer page faults. **FIGURE 9.14** shows the FIFO algorithm with the same page reference sequence but with four frames. As expected, the sequence generates fewer page faults.

In general, you would expect the number of page faults to decrease with an increase in the number of frames, as **FIGURE 9.15 (a)** shows, and as the two previous examples illustrate. Early in the development of demand paging systems, however, a curious phenomenon was discovered in which a given page reference sequence with the FIFO page-replacement algorithm actually produced more page faults with a greater number of frames.

A page reference sequence with this property is

0, 1, 2, 3, 0, 1, 4, 0, 1, 2, 3, 4

Bélády's anomaly

Figure 9.15(b) is a plot of the number of page faults versus the number of frames for this sequence. It turns out that more page faults are generated with four frames than with three frames. This phenomenon is called *Bélády's anomaly* after L. A. Bélády, who discovered it.

The FIFO algorithm selects the page that has been in the set of frames the longest. That may appear to be a reasonable criterion. As the job executes, it will enter into new regions of code and data, so pages from the old region will no longer be needed. The oldest page is the one replaced.

On further reflection, however, it may be better to consider not how long a page has been in the set of frames, but how long it has been since a page was last referenced. The idea behind LRU is that a page referenced recently in the past is more likely to be referenced in the near future than a page that has not been referenced as recently.

FIGURE 9.16 illustrates the LRU page-replacement algorithm with the same sequence of page references as in Figure 9.13. The demands for P6, P8, and P3 produce a state identical to that of the FIFO algorithm. The next request for P8 brings that page to the top box to indicate that P8 is now the most-recently used. The following request for P6 brings it to the top, shifting down P8 and P3. The boxes maintain the pages in order of previous use, with the least recently used page at the bottom.

For this sequence, the LRU algorithm produced one fewer page fault than the FIFO algorithm did. One example does not prove that LRU is better than FIFO. It is possible to construct a sequence for which FIFO produces fewer faults than LRU.

In practice, operating systems have their own unique page-replacement algorithms that depend on the hardware features available on the particular computer. Most page-replacement algorithms are approximations to LRU, which generally works better than FIFO with the page request sequences from real jobs. An indication that LRU is better from a theoretical point of view is the fact that Bélády's anomaly cannot occur with LRU replacement.

The sequences of page references in the previous examples only illustrate the page-replacement algorithms and are not realistic. For a demand paging system to be effective, the page fault rate needs to be kept to less than about one fault per 100,000 memory references.

A properly designed virtual memory system based on demand paging satisfies both goals of an operating system. It offers a convenient environment for higher-level programming because the programmer can develop code without being restricted by the limits of physical memory. It also allocates the memory efficiently because a job's pages are loaded only if needed.

FIGURE 9.15
The effect of more frames on the number of page faults.

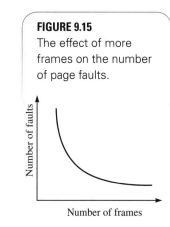

(a) Expected effect of more frames on the number of page faults.

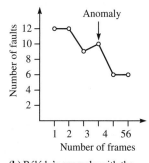

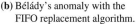

(b) Bélády's anomaly with the FIFO replacement algorithm.

9.3 **File Management**

The operating system is also responsible for maintaining the collection of files on disk. A file is an abstract data type (ADT). To the user of the system, a

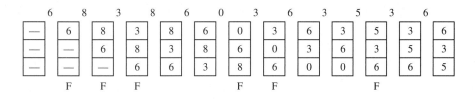

FIGURE 9.16
The LRU page-replacement algorithm with three frames.

file contains a sequence of data and can be manipulated either by a program or by operating system commands. Common operations on files include

Common operations on files

> Create a new file.
> Delete a file.
> Rename a file.
> Open a file for reading.
> Read the next data item from the file.

The operating system makes the connection between the logical organization of the file as seen by a programmer at Level HOL6 or Level Asmb5 and the physical organization on the disk itself.

Disk Drives

FIGURE 9.17 shows the physical characteristics of a disk drive. Figure 9.17(a) shows a hard disk drive that consists of several platters coated with magnetic recording material. They are attached to a central *spindle* that rotates at a typical speed of 7,200 revolutions per minute. Adjacent to each disk surface is a *read/write head* attached to an *arm*. The arm can move the heads in a radial direction across the surface of the platters.

Figure 9.17(b) shows a single disk. With the arm in a fixed position, the area under a read/write head sweeps out a ring as the disk rotates. Each

FIGURE 9.17
The physical characteristics of a disk drive.

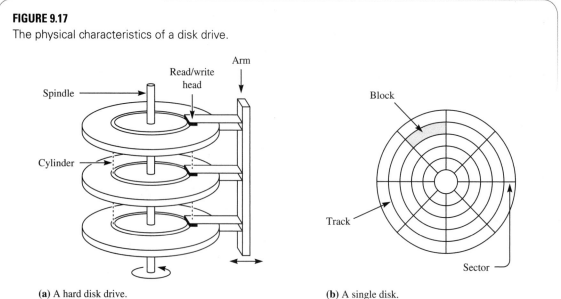

(a) A hard disk drive.   **(b)** A single disk.

ring is a *track* that stores a sequence of bits. Tracks are divided into pie-shaped *sectors*. A *block* is one sector of one track of one surface. A *cylinder* is the set of tracks on all the surfaces at a fixed arm position. A *block address* consists of three numbers—a cylinder number, a surface number, and a sector number.

In a hard disk drive, the read/write heads float just above the surface on a small cushion of air. A *head crash* in a hard disk is a mechanical failure in which the head scrapes the surface, damaging the recording material.

Reading the information from a given block is a four-step process: (1) The arm must move the heads to the designated cylinder. (2) The electronic circuitry must select the read/write head on the designated surface. (3) A period of time must elapse for the designated block to reach the read/write head. (4) The entire block must pass beneath the head to be read. Step 2 is an electronic function, which occurs in negligible time compared to the other three steps.

Reading a block from a disk

Associated with the three mechanical steps are the following times:

> Seek time

> Latency

> Transmission time

Contributions to the disk access time

Seek time is the time it takes the arm to move to the designated cylinder. *Latency* is the time it takes the block to reach the head once the head is in place. *Transmission time* is the time it takes the block to pass beneath the head. The time it takes to access a block is the sum of these three times.

File Abstraction

The user at a high level of abstraction does not want to be bothered with physical tracks and sectors. The operating system hides the details of the physical organization and presents the file with a logical organization to the user as an ADT.

For example, in C, when you execute the statement

```
fscanf(fp, "%d", &myData)
```

where fp has type FILE*, you have a logical image of fp as a linear sequence of items with a current position maintained somewhere in the sequence. The fscanf() function gets the item at the current position and advances the current position to the next item in the sequence.

Physically, the items in the file may be on different tracks and surfaces. Furthermore, there is no physical current position that is maintained by the hardware. The logical behavior of the scan statement is due to the operating system software.

Allocation Techniques

The remainder of this section describes three memory allocation techniques at the physical level—contiguous, linked, and indexed. Each technique requires the operating system to maintain a directory that records the physical location of the files. The directory is itself stored on the disk, along with the files.

If each file were small enough to fit in a single block, the file system would be simple to maintain. The directory would simply contain a list of the files on the disk. Each entry in the directory would have the name of the file and the address of the block in which the file was stored.

Contiguous allocation

If a file is too big to fit in a single block, the operating system must allocate several blocks for it. With *contiguous allocation*, the operating system matches the physical organization of the file to the logical organization by laying out the file sequentially on adjacent blocks of one track.

If the file is too big to fit on a single track, the system continues it on a second track. On a single-sided disk, the second track would be adjacent to the first track on the same surface. On a double-sided disk, the second track would be on the same cylinder as the first track. If the file is too big to fit on a single cylinder, the file would continue on an adjacent cylinder.

FIGURE 9.18 is a schematic diagram of contiguous allocation. Each row of eight blocks represents one track divided into eight sectors, as in Figure 9.17(b). The single number above each block is the block address, an

FIGURE 9.18
Contiguous allocation on a disk.

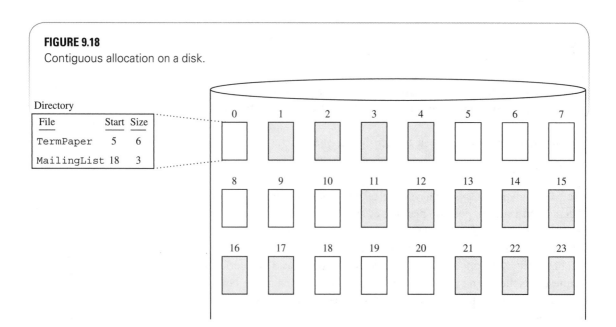

abbreviation for the three numbers required to specify the address. Block 0 contains the directory.

The directory lists the name of each file, its starting address, and its size. The file `TermPaper` starts at block 5 and contains six blocks. Its last three blocks are continued on a second track. Why wouldn't the system allocate blocks 1 through 6 for this file? The configuration in the figure could arise if another file previously occupied blocks 1 through 4, and then was deleted from the disk by the user.

The pattern of occupied and unoccupied disk memory in Figure 9.18 looks suspiciously like the pattern of occupied and unoccupied main memory in Figures 9.5 and 9.7. In fact, the memory management issues are the same. As files are created and deleted, they become fragmented. It may be impossible to create a new file because many small holes are scattered throughout the disk. To make room for the new file, the operating system supplies a disk compaction utility that shifts the files on the disk to make one large hole, as in Figure 9.6.

As with main memory, the compaction operation on disk is time-consuming. To eliminate the need for compaction, the operating system can store the file in blocks that are physically scattered throughout the disk. The linked allocation technique of **FIGURE 9.19** is one way the system can maintain the file.

Linked allocation

FIGURE 9.19

Linked allocation on a disk.

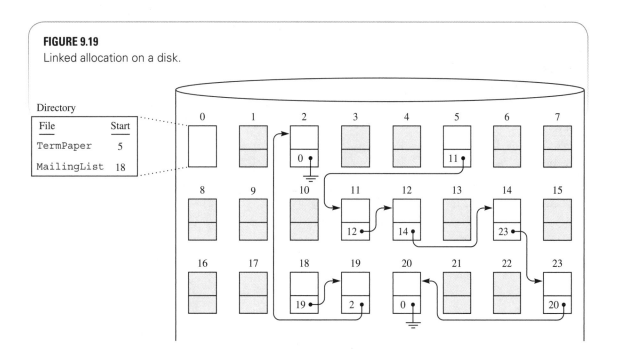

The directory contains the address of the first block of the file. The last few bytes of each block are reserved for the address of the following block. The entire sequence of blocks forms a linked list. The link field in the last block has a nil value that acts like a sentinel.

One disadvantage of the linked technique is its susceptibility to failure. In Figure 9.19, suppose that just one byte in the link field of block 12 is damaged, either by a hardware failure or by a software bug. The operating system can still access the first three blocks of the file, but it will have no way of knowing where the last three blocks are.

Indexed allocation

The indexed allocation technique in **FIGURE 9.20** collects all the addresses into a single list called an *index* in the directory. Now, if a single byte in address 12 in the index is damaged, the operating system will lose track of only one block.

Contiguous allocation does have one major advantage over noncontiguous allocation: speed. If a file is contained on one cylinder, you only need to wait for one seek and one latency period to begin the access. You can read the entire file at a speed that is limited only by the transmission time. Even if the file is not all on one cylinder, after you read the first cylinder, you only need to wait for a short seek to an adjacent cylinder.

With the blocks of one file scattered throughout the disk, you must endure a seek time and a latency time to access each block. Even with noncontiguous allocation, it is sometimes worthwhile to periodically reorganize the physical layout of the files to make their blocks contiguous. This operation is called *defragmenting* the disk.

FIGURE 9.20

Indexed allocation on a disk.

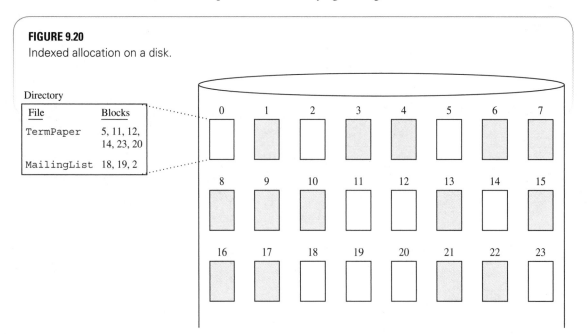

9.4 Error-Detecting and Error-Correcting Codes

To be reliable, computer systems must be able to deal with the physical errors that inevitably happen in the real world. For example, if you send an email message over the Internet, there might be some static on the transmission lines that changes one or more of your bits. The result is that the receiver does not get the same bit pattern that you sent. As another example, the system might send some data from main memory to a disk drive, which due to a transient mechanical problem, might store an altered pattern on the disk.

There are two approaches to the error problem:

> Detect the error and retransmit or discard the received message.

> Correct the error.

Both approaches use the same technique of adding redundant bits to the message to detect or correct the error.

Error-Detecting Codes

Suppose you want to send a message about weather conditions. There are four possibilities—sunny, cloudy, raining, or snowing. The sender and receiver agree on the following bit patterns to encode the information:

00, sunny
01, cloudy
10, raining
11, snowing

It is raining, so the sender sends 10. But an error occurs on the transmission line that flips the last 0 to 1. So the receiver gets 11 and concludes erroneously that it is snowing.

A simple way to detect whether an error occurs is to append a redundant bit, called the *parity bit*, to the message using some computation that the sender and receiver agree upon. A common convention is to make the parity bit 0 or 1 in such a way that the total number of 1's is even. With this scheme, the sender and receiver agree on the following bit patterns, where the parity bit is underlined:

00<u>0</u>, sunny
01<u>1</u>, cloudy
10<u>1</u>, raining
11<u>0</u>, snowing

Now the sender would send 101 for the raining message. If an error flips the 0 to 1 so that the receiver gets 111, the receiver can conclude that an error occurred, because 111 is not one of the agreed-upon bit patterns. She can then request a retransmission or discard the received message.

Note that if the error occurs in the parity bit, the received message is just as useless as if it occurs in one of the data bits. For example, if the receiver gets 111, she does not know if the error was in the first bit with 011 sent, the second bit with 101 sent, or the third bit with 110 sent. She only knows that an error occurred.

The scheme would also work if the sender and receiver agreed to use odd parity, where the parity bit is computed to make the total number of 1's odd. The only necessity is for the sender and receiver to agree on the parity computation.

What if two errors occur during transmission so that not only is the 0 flipped to 1, but the last 1 is flipped to 0? Then the receiver gets 110. But now 110 is one of the agreed-upon patterns and the receiver concludes erroneously that it is snowing.

Codes and code words

The set of bit patterns {000, 011, 101, 110} is called a *code*, and an individual pattern from the set, such as 101, is called a *code word*. The above code cannot detect two errors. It is a single-error-detecting code. Error codes operate under the realistic assumption that the probability of error on a single bit is much less than 1.0. Hence, the probability of an error in two bits is much less than the probability of error in one bit. No code can completely eliminate the possibility of an undetectable error with 100% certainty, as it is always possible for multiple errors to occur that would change one code word into another code word. Error codes are still useful because they handle such a large percentage of error events.

Code Requirements

Suppose you want to be able to detect one or two errors. You will obviously need more parity bits. The questions are "How many parity bits?" and "How do you design the code?" The answers involve the concept of distance. The

The Hamming distance

Hamming distance between two code words of the same length is defined as the number of positions in which the bits differ. It is named after Richard Hamming, who developed the theory in 1950 at Bell Labs.

Example 9.1 The Hamming distance between the code words for *cloudy*, 011, and *raining*, 101, is 2, because the code words differ in two positions— namely, the first and second positions. ∎

Inspection of the weather code {000, 011, 101, 110} should convince you that the distance between all possible pairs of code words is also 2. You can see now that a code to detect a single error cannot have any pair of code words that are separated by a distance of 1. Suppose there are two such code words, A and B. Then it would be possible for the sender to send A, have an error in transmission that flipped the single bit where A and B differ, and have the receiver conclude that B was sent. The code would fail to detect the single error.

The *code distance* is the minimum of the Hamming distance between all possible pairs of code words in the code.

The code distance

Example 9.2   The code {00110, 11100, 01010, 11101} has a code distance of 1. Although several code words, such as 00110 and 11101, are separated by a Hamming distance as great as 4, there exists a pair of words that are separated by a distance of only 1—namely, 11100 and 11101. If you used this code for sending the weather information, you could not guarantee the detection of all possible single-transmission errors.   ∎

To design a good code, you must add parity bits in such a way that you make the code distance as large as possible. To detect one error, the code distance must be 2. What must the code distance be to detect two errors? The code distance cannot be 2, as that would mean that there exists a pair of code words A and B with a Hamming distance of 2. The sender could send A, have an error in transmission that flipped both bits where it differs from B, and have the receiver conclude that B was sent.

FIGURE 9.21 is a schematic representation of this concept. A is the transmitted code word and B is the code word closest to A. The open circles in between represent words not sent but possibly received because of errors in transmission. In Figure 9.21(a), e1 comes from a single error. In Figure 9.21(b), e1 comes from a single error and e2 comes from a double error.

In general, to detect d errors, the code distance must satisfy the equation

code distance = $d + 1$

The requirement to detect d errors

For example, to be able to detect three errors, the code distance must be 4. The reason is that with a distance of at least $d + 1$ to the closest code word to A, it is impossible to transform A to any other code word by flipping d bits of A.

The concept of distance is also useful with error-correcting codes. Suppose you decide on the following code for the weather messages:

00<u>000</u>, sunny
01<u>101</u>, cloudy
10<u>110</u>, raining
11<u>011</u>, snowing

If you receive 11110, what do you conclude? You could conclude that 00000 was sent for *sunny* and that four errors occurred. But is that a reasonable

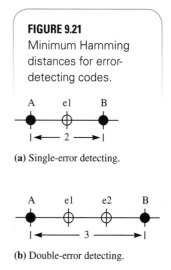

FIGURE 9.21
Minimum Hamming distances for error-detecting codes.

(a) Single-error detecting.

(b) Double-error detecting.

FIGURE 9.22

Minimum Hamming distances for error-correcting codes.

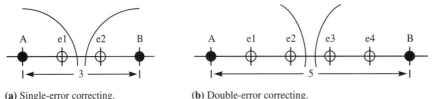

(a) Single-error correcting.   (b) Double-error correcting.

conclusion? Not really, because 11110 is closer to 10110, the code word for *raining*. With that conclusion, you assume that only one error occurred, an event of much higher probability than the event of four errors.

In general, for an error-correction code, you add enough parity bits to make the code distance large enough that the receiver can correct the errors. The receiver corrects the errors by computing the Hamming distance between the received word and every code word, and picking the code word that is closest to the received word. "Close" is defined in terms of Hamming distance.

FIGURE 9.22 is a schematic representation of the error-correction concept. As before, A is the transmitted code word, B is the code word closest to A, and the open circles are words received because of errors in transmission. Figure 9.22(a) shows the situation for a code that is capable of correcting a single error. The code distance is 3, so that even if a single error occurs, the received word e1 will be closer to A than to B, and the receiver can conclude that A was sent. If A is sent and two errors occur, so that e2 is received, then the receiver will erroneously conclude that B was sent.

Figure 9.22(b) shows a code capable of correcting two errors. If A is sent and two errors occur, so that e2 is received, e2 is still closer to A than to B. That can happen only if the distance is 5.

In general, to correct *d* errors, the code distance must satisfy the equation

The requirement to correct d errors

$$\text{code distance} = 2d + 1$$

For example, to be able to correct three errors, the code distance must be 7. The reason is based on the decision process. The receiver concludes that A was sent when it receives words close to A. But it concludes that B was sent when it receives words close to B. The line between A and B must accommodate *both* sets of received words; hence the factor of 2 in the equation. Also, the distance must be odd; hence the +1 in the equation. If the distance were even, there would be a received word equidistant between A and B, and the receiver could not conclude which code word had the higher probability of being sent.

A code that can correct single errors can alternatively be used to detect double errors, as both have a code distance of 3. It is simply a question of how the receiver wants to handle the error condition. It can correct the error assuming two errors did not occur, or it can be more conservative, assume that two errors might have occurred, and discard the message or request a retransmission.

Single-Error-Correcting Codes

The previous section describes the requirements on the code distance for error detecting and correcting codes. The question remains of how to pick the code words to achieve the required code distance. Many different schemes have been devised for codes that correct multiple errors. This section investigates the efficiency of single-error-correcting codes and describes one systematic way to construct them.

     FIGURE 9.23(a) shows the structure of a code word. There are m data bits and r parity bits, for a total of $n = m + r$ bits in the code word. Because there are n bits in a code word, there are 2^n possible received patterns. Figure 9.23(b) shows a schematic of how you can group those words that have no errors or one error. The figure shows the pattern for $n = 6$, where e1, e2, e3, e4, e5, and e6 are the six possible received words that could differ from A by one bit. If one of these is received, the receiver concludes that A was sent. Similarly, e7, e8, e9, e10, e11, and e12 are those possible words with a distance of 1 from code word B. There might be other received words

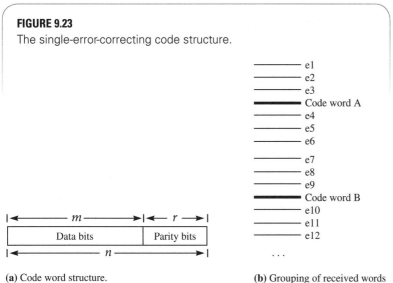

FIGURE 9.23
The single-error-correcting code structure.

(a) Code word structure.

(b) Grouping of received words with zero or one error.

that are not included in the grouping, corresponding to the event of more than one error during transmission, but resulting in a received word that is not within a distance of 1 from any code word.

In general, there are n words a distance of 1 from A. So the total number of words, including A, in the first group is $(n + 1)$. Similarly, there are $(n + 1)$ words in the B group, the C group, and so on. There is one group for each code word. So, as there are 2^m code words, there are 2^m groups. The total number of words in Figure 9.23(b) is, therefore, $(n + 1)2^m$. There could be other received words not in Figure 9.23(b), but there cannot be more than 2^n words altogether. Therefore,

$$(n + 1)2^m \le 2^n$$

Substituting $n = m + r$ and dividing both sides by 2^m gives

$$m + r + 1 \le 2^r$$

which tells how many parity bits r are necessary to correct a single error in a message with m data bits.

Perfect codes

A code for which the relationship holds with equality is called a *perfect code*. An example of a perfect code is $m = 4$, $r = 3$. Sending parity bits along with data bits increases the transmission time. For this code, for every four data bits, you must send an additional three parity bits. So, the error correction has added $3/4 = 75\%$ overhead to the transmission time. If you need to send a long stream of bits, you must subdivide the stream into chunks and apply the parity bits to each chunk. The bigger the chunk, the smaller the overhead. With computers, you usually send streams of bytes, so the chunks are usually powers of 2. **FIGURE 9.24** shows the relationship between m and r for a few values of m that are powers of 2.

FIGURE 9.24
The cost of a single-error-correcting code.

Data Bits m	Parity Bits r	Percent Overhead
4	3	75
8	4	50
16	5	31
32	6	19
64	7	11
128	8	6

FIGURE 9.25

The position of the four parity bits in a single-error-correcting code with eight data bits.

1	2	3	4	5	6	7	8	9	10	11	12
		1		0	0	1		1	1	0	0

Hamming devised an ingenious technique for determining the parity bits of a single-error-correcting code. The idea is to not append the parity bits to the end of the code word, but to distribute them throughout the code word. The advantage of this technique is that the receiver can calculate directly which bit is the erroneous one without having to compute the distance between the received word and all the code words. **FIGURE 9.25** shows the positions of the parity bits for the $m = 8$, $r = 4$ case. The bit positions are numbered consecutively from the left, and the parity bits are at locations 1, 2, 4, and 8, all powers of 2. In this example, the data to be transmitted is 1001 1100, but these bits are not stored contiguously in the code word.

The numeric position of each bit can be written as a unique sum of powers of 2 as follows:

$1 = 1$	$5 = 1 + 4$	$9 = 1 + 8$
$2 = 2$	$6 = 2 + 4$	$10 = 2 + 8$
$3 = 1 + 2$	$7 = 1 + 2 + 4$	$11 = 1 + 2 + 8$
$4 = 4$	$8 = 8$	$12 = 4 + 8$

To determine the parity bit at position 1, note that 1 occurs in the sum on the right-hand side for positions 1, 3, 5, 7, 9, and 11. Using even parity, set the parity bit so that the total number of 1's in those positions is even. There are 1's at positions 3, 7, and 9, an odd number of 1's. So, make the parity bit at position 1 a 1. The positions checked by each parity bit are:

Parity bit 1 checks 1, 3, 5, 7, 9, 11
Parity bit 2 checks 2, 3, 6, 7, 10, 11
Parity bit 4 checks 4, 5, 6, 7, 12
Parity bit 8 checks 8, 9, 10, 11, 12

You should verify that a similar computation for the other parity bits results in the code word 1 1 1 1 0 0 1 0 1 1 0 0.

Now, suppose this code word is sent, and during transmission an error occurs at position 10 so that the receiver gets 1 1 1 1 0 0 1 0 1 0 0 0. She calculates the parity bits as 1 0 1 1 0 0 1 1 1 0 0 0 and sees a discrepancy between the received parity and the calculated parity at positions 2 and 8. Because $2 + 8 = 10$, she concludes that the bit at position 10 is in error. So, she flips the bit at position 10 to correct the error. The advantage of this correction technique is that the receiver need not compare the received word with all the code words to determine which code word is closest to it.

9.5 RAID Storage Systems

In the early days of computers, disks were physically large and expensive. As technology advanced they became physically small, their data capacities increased, and they became less expensive. They finally got so cheap that it became advantageous to assemble many individual drives into an array of drives, instead of building one bigger drive when large amounts of data needed to be stored. Such a collection is called a *redundant array of inexpensive disks (RAID)* system.

Advantages of RAID systems

The idea is that an array of disks has more spindles, each with its own set of read/write heads that can operate concurrently compared to the single spindle in one big drive. The concurrency should lead to increased performance. Also, redundancy can provide error correction and detection to increase the reliability of the system. The RAID controller provides a level of abstraction to the operating system, making the array of disks appear like one big disk to the operating system. Alternatively, the abstraction can be provided in software as part of the operating system.

There are several different ways to organize an array of disks. The industry-standard terminology for the most common schemes is:

Common RAID levels

> RAID level 0: Nonredundant striped

> RAID level 1: Mirrored

> RAID levels 01 and 10: Striped and mirrored

> RAID level 2: Memory-style error-correcting code (ECC)

> RAID level 3: Bit-interleaved parity

> RAID level 4: Block-interleaved parity

> RAID level 5: Block-interleaved distributed parity

Each organization has its own set of advantages and disadvantages and is used in different situations. The remainder of this section describes the above RAID levels.

RAID Level 0: Nonredundant Striped

FIGURE 9.26 shows the organization for RAID level 0. Data that would be stored in several contiguous blocks is broken up into stripes and distributed over several disks in the array. Figure 9.18 shows blocks 0 through 7 on one

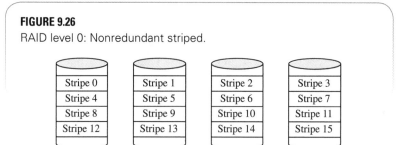

FIGURE 9.26
RAID level 0: Nonredundant striped.

track, 8 through 15 on the next track, and so on. A stripe consists of several blocks. For example, if there are two blocks per stripe, then blocks 0 and 1 in Figure 9.18 are stored in stripe 0, blocks 2 and 3 in stripe 1, and so on.

The operating system sees the logical disk as in Figure 9.18, even though the physical disks are as in Figure 9.26. If the operating system requests a disk read of blocks 0 through 7, the RAID system can read stripes 0 through 3 in parallel, decreasing the access time because of the concurrency. To service a read request of blocks 0 through 10—that is, stripes 0 through 5— the first disk would need to deliver stripes 0 and 4 sequentially, as would the second disk with stripes 1 and 5. This organization requires a minimum of two hard drives.

The advantage of level 0 is increased performance. However, it does not work well in an environment where most read/write requests are for a single block or stripe, as there is no concurrency in that case. Also, there is no redundancy as with the other levels, so reliability is not as high. The probability of a single failure with four disks running is greater than the probability of failure of a single disk running, given that all the disks have equal quality.

RAID Level 1: Mirrored

To mirror a disk is to maintain an exact mirror image of it on a separate drive, as shown in FIGURE 9.27 . There is no striping, just a strict duplication to provide redundancy in case one of the disk drives fails.

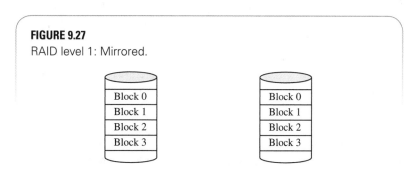

FIGURE 9.27
RAID level 1: Mirrored.

A disk write requires a write to each disk, but they can be done in parallel, so the write performance is not much worse than with a single drive. For a disk read, the controller can choose to read from the drive with the shortest seek time and latency. So a disk read is a bit better than with a single drive. If one drive fails, it can be replaced while the other continues to operate. When the replacement drive is installed, it is easily backed up by duplicating the good drive. Mirroring is usually done with only two drives. If four drives are available, it is generally better to take advantage of the increased performance with striping at level 01.

RAID Levels 01 and 10: Striped and Mirrored

There are two ways to combine RAID levels 0 and 1, and hence to obtain the advantages of both. The first is called RAID level 01, or 0+1, or 0/1, or *mirrored stripes*, as FIGURE 9.28 (a) shows. With mirrored stripes, you simply mirror the disk organization that you would have with striping at level 0. The second is RAID level 10, or 1+0, or 1/0, *striped mirrors*, as in Figure 9.28(b). Instead of using the redundant disks to duplicate the set of level 0 disks, you mirror pairs of disks, then stripe across the mirrors.

RAID level 10 is more expensive to implement than level 01. With level 01 in Figure 9.28(a), each stripe controller is a system that makes the four striped disks appear as a single disk to the mirror controller. The mirror controller is a system that makes the two mirrored disks appear as a single disk to the computer. With level 10 in Figure 9.28(b), each mirror controller is a system that makes two mirrored disks appear as a single disk to the stripe controller. The stripe controller is a system that makes the four striped disks appear as a single disk to the computer. In this example with eight physical disks, you need only three controllers for level 01 but five controllers for level 10.

The advantage of level 10 over level 01 is reliability. Suppose one physical disk goes bad, say the third one. In Figure 9.28(a), that bad disk will cause the first stripe controller to report an error to the mirror controller, which will then use its rightmost mirrored disk until the faulty drive can be replaced. In effect, during the downtime, the four physical disks of the left striped disk are out of commission. In Figure 9.28(b), the bad third disk will cause the second mirror controller to use the fourth disk (its second mirrored disk) until the faulty drive can be replaced. During the downtime, only one physical disk is out of commission.

In both cases, the computer sees uninterrupted service from its RAID disk, so it might seem that there is no difference in reliability. However, the problem comes if two disks fail. In Figure 9.28(a), if one of the physical disks fails in the left striped disk and one fails in the right striped disk, the RAID disk fails. If the two disk failures are in the same set of striped disks, the RAID disk does not fail. In Figure 9.28(b), the only way the RAID disk can

FIGURE 9.28
Combining RAID levels 0 and 1.

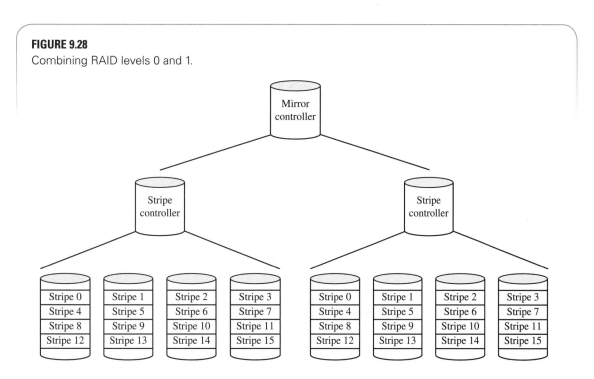

(a) RAID level 01: Mirrored stripes.

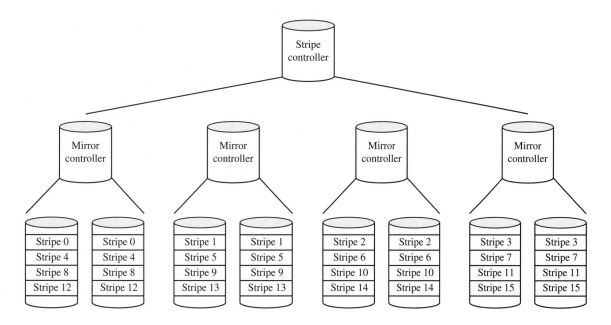

(b) RAID level 10: Striped mirrors.

fail is if both failures are in the same set of paired mirror disks, an event that is less probable than a RAID failure with level 01. See the exercises at the end of this chapter for a quantitative analysis.

Another advantage of level 10 over 01 is the time to do a mirror copy after a failed disk has been replaced. In Figure 9.28(a), the mirror controller sees each striped disk as a single entity, not as four separate disks. Once a repair has been made, the mirror controller has no choice but to copy the entire contents of the good striped disk—that is, four physical disks—to the repaired striped disk. With level 10, all mirrors are with pairs of disks, so only a single disk copy is required to restore a failed disk.

Low-end RAID systems usually support 01, with high-end systems supporting both 01 and 10. You get the performance advantage of striping and the reliability advantage of mirroring. The read performance is even better than level 0 in some cases. Consider the scenario with level 01 of a read request for stripes 0 through 5. Stripes 0 through 3 can be read concurrently on the first set of drives, with stripes 4 and 5 read concurrently on the mirrored set. Both levels 01 and 10 require an even number of hard drives, with a minimum of four.

RAID Level 2: Memory-Style ECC

The storage overhead of mirroring is tremendous—100%—because each drive is duplicated. Figure 9.24 shows that less overhead is possible with single-error-correcting codes as commonly used in high-reliability memory systems. Four data bits can be corrected with three parity bits, bringing the overhead down to 75%. With level 2, you stripe at the bit level. **FIGURE 9.29** shows each nybble (half a byte) spread out over the first four drives. The last three drives are the parity bits for the single-error-correcting code.

To maintain performance, the drives must all be rotationally synchronized. To perform a disk write, the disk controller computes the parity bits for each nybble and writes them to the parity drives along with the data. To do a read, the controller computes the parity bits from the data and compares them with the bits from the parity drives, correcting the error on the fly.

FIGURE 9.29
RAID level 2: Memory-style ECC.

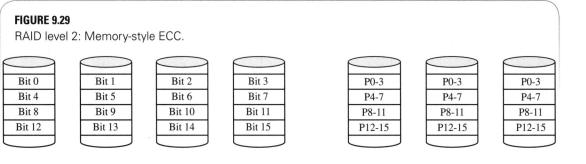

This scheme was used on some older supercomputers, usually with 32 data bits and 6 parity bits to get the overhead down. Today, inexpensive drives have their own internal error-correcting capabilities at the bit level, and so level 2 is no longer used commercially.

RAID Level 3: Bit-Interleaved Parity

By far the most common failure in a disk array is the failure of just one of the drives in the array. Furthermore, the disk controller can detect such a failure, so the system knows where the failure is. If you stripe at the bit level, and if you know which bit has failed, then you can correct the error with just one parity bit. For example, suppose you want to store the nybble 1001. With even parity, the parity bit is zero, so you store 1001 0. **FIGURE 9.30** shows 1001 stored at bit 0, bit 1, bit 2, bit 3, and parity bit 0 stored at P0-3.

Suppose the fourth drive fails, so you know that bits 3, 7, 11, 15, . . . are unavailable. You read your data as $100x\ \underline{0}$ where x is the bit you must correct. Because you are using even parity, you know that the number of 1's must be even and, therefore, that x must be 1. Your knowledge of where the error occurred allows you to decrease the overhead for single-error correcting to a single parity bit.

Although level 3 improves on the efficiency of level 2, it has several disadvantages. Recovering from a failed drive is time consuming. With mirroring, you simply clone the content of the one remaining good drive to the replacement drive. With bit-interleaved parity, the bits on the replacement drive must be computed from the bits on all the other drives, which you must, therefore, access. The rebuild is usually done automatically by the controller.

The parity drive is only used to correct errors when a drive fails and to restore the replacement drive. Consequently, it must be written on every write request to update the parity bit. Because individual disk drives have their own ECC at the bit level, you do not access the parity drive on a read request (unless a drive has failed). The access time for level 3 is not much worse than it would be for a single drive. But with levels 2 and 3, every read/

FIGURE 9.30
RAID level 3: Bit-interleaved parity.

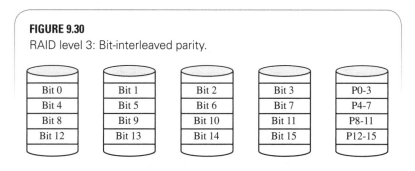

Bit 0	Bit 1	Bit 2	Bit 3	P0-3
Bit 4	Bit 5	Bit 6	Bit 7	P4-7
Bit 8	Bit 9	Bit 10	Bit 11	P8-11
Bit 12	Bit 13	Bit 14	Bit 15	P12-15

write request requires you to access every data drive, so you do not get the concurrency that you do with longer stripes.

RAID Level 4: Block-Interleaved Parity

The only difference between level 3 and level 4 is the size of the stripe. In level 3, a stripe is one bit, and in level 4, it can be one or more blocks. In Figure 9.30, P0-3 represents one bit, but in **FIGURE 9.31**, P0-3 represents an entire stripe.

For example, if each stripe is 1 KiB long, then a file is distributed over the stripes as follows:

> Stripe 0: Bits 0 through 1023
> Stripe 1: Bits 1024 through 2047
> Stripe 2: Bits 2048 through 3071
> Stripe 3: Bits 3072 through 4095

The first bit of P0-3 is the parity bit for bits 0, 1024, 2048, and 3072; the second bit of P0-3 is the parity bit for bits 1, 1025, 2049, and 3073; and so on. Because striping is not at the bit level, disks do not need to be rotationally synchronized, as they do with levels 2 and 3.

Level 4 has an advantage over level 3 with small random read requests. If each file is contained on a few stripes on different disks, the seeks, latencies, and transmissions can all happen concurrently. With level 3, to read even one small file requires all the data drives to act in concert; many small files must be read sequentially.

Although overhead with level 4 is much reduced compared to mirrored organizations, its biggest drawback is with write requests. If you are writing a file that spans stripes 0 through 3, you can compute the parity for P0-3 and write it to the parity drive at the same time. But suppose you need to write a file that is wholly contained in stripe 0. Because you are going to alter stripe 0, you also must alter P0-3. But P0-3 is the parity for stripes 1, 2, and 3 as well as 0. It would seem that you have to read stripes 1, 2, and 3 to use with your new stripe 0 to compute the new parity. There is a more efficient way,

FIGURE 9.31
RAID level 4: Block-interleaved parity.

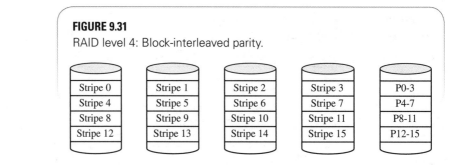

Stripe 0	Stripe 1	Stripe 2	Stripe 3	P0-3
Stripe 4	Stripe 5	Stripe 6	Stripe 7	P4-7
Stripe 8	Stripe 9	Stripe 10	Stripe 11	P8-11
Stripe 12	Stripe 13	Stripe 14	Stripe 15	P12-15

however. Instead of reading stripes 1, 2, and 3, you can read the old stripe 0 and the old P0-3. For each bit position in the new and old data stripes, if your new bit is different from your old bit, then you will be changing the number of 1's from an even number to an odd number or vice versa, and you must flip that bit in P0-3. If the new and old data bits are the same, you leave the corresponding parity bit unchanged. For four data disks, this technique reduces the number of disk reads from three to two.

Even with this shortcut, every write request requires a write to the parity disk, no matter how small the request. The parity disk becomes the performance bottleneck.

RAID Level 5: Block-Interleaved Distributed Parity

Level 5 alleviates the parity disk bottleneck. Rather than store all the parity on one disk, the parity information is scattered among all the disks, so that no one disk has the responsibility for the parity information of the whole array.

FIGURE 9.32 shows a common organization, known as *left-symmetric parity distribution*, for spreading the parity information among all the disks. It has the advantage that if you read a set of stripes sequentially, you access each disk once before accessing any disk twice. In the figure, suppose you access stripes 0, 1, 2, 3, and 4 in that order. You will access the first, second, third, fourth, and fifth disks. If you put stripe 4 where stripe 5 is in the figure and service the same request, you would access the first, second, third, fourth, and first disk; that is, you would access the first disk twice before accessing the fifth disk at all. You can see that the desirable property holds regardless of which stripe you begin with.

RAID level 5 is considered by many to be the ideal combination of good reliability, good performance, high capacity, and low storage overhead. It is one of the most popular high-end RAID systems. The most popular low-end system is probably RAID level 0, which is not really a true RAID because there is no redundancy, and hence no enhanced reliability.

FIGURE 9.32
RAID level 5: Block-interleaved distributed parity.

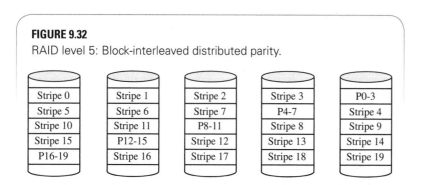

Stripe 0	Stripe 1	Stripe 2	Stripe 3	P0-3
Stripe 5	Stripe 6	Stripe 7	P4-7	Stripe 4
Stripe 10	Stripe 11	P8-11	Stripe 8	Stripe 9
Stripe 15	P12-15	Stripe 12	Stripe 13	Stripe 14
P16-19	Stripe 16	Stripe 17	Stripe 18	Stripe 19

Chapter Summary

The operating system allocates time in the form of CPU utilization and space in the form of main memory and disk allocation. Five techniques for allocation of main memory are uniprogramming, fixed-partition multiprogramming, variable-partition multiprogramming, paging, and virtual memory. With uniprogramming, only one job executes at a time from start to finish, and the job has the entire main memory to itself. Fixed-partition multiprogramming allows several jobs to execute concurrently and requires the operating system to determine the partition sizes in memory before executing any jobs. Variable-partition multiprogramming alleviates the inefficiencies inherent in fixed-partition multiprogramming by allowing the partition sizes to vary depending on the job requirements. The best-fit and first-fit algorithms are two different strategies to cope with the fragmentation problem of variable-partition multiprogramming.

Paging alleviates fragmentation by fragmenting the program to fit the memory holes. Programs are no longer contiguous but are broken up and scattered throughout main memory. Jobs are divided into equal-sized pages, and main memory is divided into frames of the same size. Logical addresses as seen by the programmer are converted to physical addresses with the help of a page table. The page table contains the frame number for each page that is stored in main memory.

Demand paging, also called *virtual memory*, postpones page loading into memory until the job demands the page. The entire program does not need to reside in main memory to execute. Instead, only its active pages, called the *working set*, are loaded. A page fault occurs when a page is referenced but has not yet been loaded into memory. First-in, first-out (FIFO) and least recently used (LRU) are two algorithms for determining which page to swap out of main memory when a frame is needed for a new page. You would normally expect the number of faults to decrease with increasing number of memory frames. But Bélády's anomaly shows that it is possible for an increase in the number of frames to produce an increase in the number of faults with the FIFO replacement algorithm.

Three contributions to disk access time are seek time, which is the time it takes for the arm to move to the designated cylinder; latency, which is the time it takes for the block to rotate to the head once the head is in place; and transmission time, which is the time it takes for the block to pass underneath the head. Three techniques of disk management are contiguous, linked, and indexed. The problem of fragmentation occurs with disk memory, as it does with main memory.

A set of redundant bits can be added to data bits in order to detect or correct errors that may occur during transmission or storage of data.

The Hamming distance between two code words is the number of bits that are different. The receiver corrects errors by choosing the code word that is closest to the received word based on the Hamming distance. With a judicious choice of the placement of the redundant bits, you can correct a single error without comparing the received word with all the code words.

A redundant array of inexpensive disks (RAID) is a grouping of disks that appears to the operating systems as a single large disk. The two benefits of a RAID system are performance, based on the concurrent access of the data with multiple spindles in the system, and reliability, based on error correction and detection with redundant drives.

Exercises

Section 9.1

1. Using the format of Figure 9.4, devise a job execution sequence for which the first-fit algorithm would require compaction before the best-fit algorithm. Sketch the fragmentation in main memory just before compaction is required for each algorithm.

2. Figure 9.10 shows how a page table in a paging system performs the same transformation of the logical address as the base register does in a multiprogramming system. The equivalent job of the bound register is not shown in the figure. *(a) To protect other processes' memory space from unauthorized access, would a paging system require a table of bound values, one for each page, or would a single bound register suffice? Explain. (b) Modify Figure 9.10 to include main memory protection from other processes.

3. Suppose the page size in a paging system is 512 bytes. (a) If most of the files are large—that is, much greater than 512 bytes—what do you suppose is the average internal fragmentation (in bytes of unused space) for each file? Explain your reasoning. (b) How would your answer to part (a) change if most of the files were much smaller than 512 bytes? (c) How would your answer to part (b) change if you expressed the fragmentation in terms of the percentage of unused space instead of the number of unused bytes?

Section 9.2

4. A computer has 12-bit addresses and a main memory that is divided into 16 frames. Memory management uses demand paging. *(a) How

many bytes is virtual memory? **(b)** How many bytes are in each page? **(c)** How many bits are in the offset of a logical and physical address? **(d)** What is the maximum number of entries in a job's page table?

5. Answer Exercise 4 for a computer with n-bit addresses and a memory divided into 2^k frames.

****6.** For which pages in Figure 9.12 is the image on disk an exact replica of the page in main memory?

7. Verify the data of Figure 9.15(b), which shows Bélády's anomaly, for the sequence of page references given in the text. Display the content of the frames in the format of Figure 9.13.

****8.** Devise a sequence of 12 page references for which the FIFO page-replacement algorithm is better than the LRU algorithm.

9. Plot the graph of Figure 9.15(b) for the page reference sequence in Figure 9.13 using the FIFO page-replacement algorithm. On the same graph, plot the data for the LRU algorithm.

****10.** If the operating system could predict the future, it could select the replacement page such that the next page fault is delayed as long as possible. Such an algorithm is called *OPT*, the *optimum page-replacement algorithm*. It is a useful theoretical algorithm because it represents the best you could possibly do. When designers measure the performance of their page-replacement algorithms, they try to get as close as possible to the performance of OPT. How many page faults does OPT produce for the sequence of Figures 9.13 and 9.16? How does that compare with FIFO and LRU?

Section 9.3

11. Suppose a disk rotates at 5,400 revolutions per minute and has each surface divided into 16 sectors. ****(a)** What is the maximum possible latency time? Under what circumstance will that occur? **(b)** What is the minimum possible latency time? Under what circumstance will that occur? **(c)** From (a) and (b), what will be the average latency time? **(d)** What is the transmission time for one block?

Section 9.4

12. ****(a)** How many data bits are required to store one of the decimal digits 0 through 9? ****(b)** How many parity bits are required to *detect* a single error? **(c)** Write a single-error detection code using even parity. Underline the parity bits. **(d)** What is the code distance of your code?

13. (a) What must the code distance be to *detect* five errors? (b) What must the code distance be to *correct* five errors?

14. (a) Which entries in Figure 9.24 represent perfect codes? (b) Augment the table in Figure 9.24 with additional entries to include all the perfect codes between $m = 4$ and $m = 128$. Be sure to include the overhead value. (c) What can you conclude about the cost of restricting the number of data bits to a power of 2?

15. (a) How many data bits are required to store one of the decimal digits 0 through 9? (b) How many parity bits are required to *correct* a single error? (c) Write a single-error correction code using even parity. Underline the parity bits. (d) What is the code distance of your code?

16. A set of eight data bits is transmitted with the single-error correction code of Figure 9.25. For each of the received bit patterns below, state whether an error occured. If it did, correct the error.

   *(a) 1 0 0 1 1 0 1 0 1 0 0 1   (b) 1 1 0 1 0 0 1 1 0 0 1 0
   (c) 0 0 0 0 1 0 1 1 0 1 0 0   (d) 1 0 1 1 0 0 1 0 0 1 0 0

Section 9.5

17. Figure 9.28 shows a RAID system with eight physical disks. (a) With six physical disks, how many mirror controllers and stripe controllers would you need for level 01 and for level 10? (b) With $2n$ disks in general (so that $n = 4$ in Figure 9.28), how many mirror controllers and stripe controllers would you need for level 01 and for level 10?

18. (a) Figure 9.28 shows the RAID level 01 and RAID level 10 systems with eight physical disks. Draw the equivalent systems for level 01 and level 10 with four physical disks. (b) Assume that two disks go bad. The sequence BBGG means that the first and second disks are bad and the third and fourth disks are good. With this scenario, the RAID level 01 disk is good because the two bad disks are in the same first striped disk, but the RAID level 10 disk is bad because the two bad disks are in the same first mirrored disk. How many permutations of four letters with two B's and two G's are there? (c) Tabulate each permutation, and for each one determine whether the RAID disk is good or bad for levels 01 and 10. (d) If two disks fail, use part (c) to determine the probability that the RAID disk fails for levels 01 and 10. Which RAID system is more reliable? (e) With $2n$ disks in general (so that $n = 4$ in Figure 9.28), how many permutations of $2n$ letters are there with 2 B's and $2n - 2$ G's? (f) How many of the permutations from part (e) cause a RAID disk failure for level 01 and for level 10? (g) If two disks fail, use part (f)

to determine the probability that the RAID disk fails for levels 01 and 10. **(h)** Use part (g) to show that the probability that the RAID disk in Figure 9.28 fails is 4/7 for level 01 and 1/7 for level 10 if two disks fail.

19. You have a RAID level 4 system with eight data disks and one parity disk. **(a)** How many disk reads and disk writes must you make to write one data stripe if you do not make use of the old data and parity values? **(b)** How many disk reads and disk writes must you make to write one data stripe if you do make use of the old data and parity values?

LEVEL
1

Logic Gate

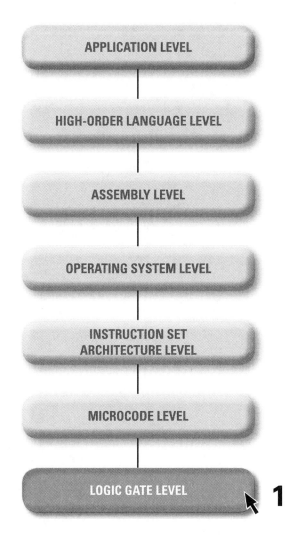

APPLICATION LEVEL

HIGH-ORDER LANGUAGE LEVEL

ASSEMBLY LEVEL

OPERATING SYSTEM LEVEL

INSTRUCTION SET
ARCHITECTURE LEVEL

MICROCODE LEVEL

LOGIC GATE LEVEL   **1**

CHAPTER
10

Combinational Circuits

Finally we come to the lowest level in our description of the typical computer system. Each level of abstraction hides the details that are unnecessary for the user at the next-higher level. The details at Level LG1 are hidden from the user at Level ISA3, the instruction set architecture level. Remember that the user at Level ISA3 sees a von Neumann machine whose language is machine language. The job of the designer at Level LG1 is to construct the Level ISA3 machine. These last three chapters describe the language and design principles at Level LG1 that are required to construct a von Neumann machine.

Omitting Level Mc2

The figures in this text consistently show the microcode level between the instruction set architecture level and the logic gate level. Some designers choose to omit the microcode level in their machines and construct the Level ISA3 machine directly from Level LG1. Others choose to design their systems with a microcode level.

What are the advantages and disadvantages of each design approach? The same as we encountered at Levels 7, 6, and 5. Suppose you need to design an application for a user at Level App7. Would you rather write it in C at Level HOL6 and compile it to a lower level or write it directly in Pep/9 assembly language at Level Asmb5? Because C is at a higher level of abstraction, one C statement can do the work of many Pep/9 statements. The C program would be much shorter than the equivalent Pep/9 program. It would, therefore, be easier to design and debug. But it would require a compiler for translation to a lower level. Furthermore, a good assembly language programmer can usually produce shorter, faster code than the object code from even an optimizing compiler. Though the program would execute faster, it would be difficult to design and debug; it would thus be more costly to develop.

The tradeoff at Levels 7, 6, and 5 is development cost versus execution speed. The same tradeoff applies at Levels 3, 2, and 1. Generally, systems that include Level Mc2 are simpler and less costly than those that omit it. But they usually execute more slowly than if they were built directly from Level LG1. A recent design trend is to build simple but fast von Neumann machines with small instruction sets, called *reduced instruction set computers* (RISCs). An important characteristic of a RISC machine is its omission of Level Mc2.

Two levels that are interesting but whose descriptions are not given in this text are the levels below the logic gate level, as FIGURE 10.1 shows. At the electronic device level (Level 0), designers connect transistors, resistors, and capacitors to make an individual logic gate at Level LG1. At the physics level (Level −1), applied physicists construct the transistors that the electrical engineer can use to construct the gates that the computer architect can use to construct the von Neumann machine. There is no level below physics, the most fundamental of all the sciences.

The languages at Levels 0 and −1 are the set of mathematical equations that model the behavior of the objects at that level. You may be familiar with some of them. At Level 0 they include Ohm's law, Kirchoff's rules, and the voltage versus current characteristics of electronic devices. At Level –1 they include Coulomb's law, Newton's laws, and some laws from quantum mechanics. At all the levels, from the calculus for relational databases at Level App7 to Newton's laws at Level –1, formal mathematics is the tool for modeling the behavior of the system.

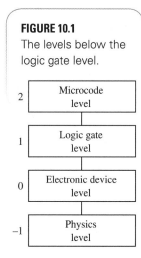

FIGURE 10.1
The levels below the logic gate level.

10.1 Boolean Algebra and Logic Gates

A *circuit* is a collection of devices that are physically connected by wires. The two basic types of circuits at Level LG1 are *combinational* and *sequential*. You can visualize either type of circuit as a rectangular block called a *black box* with a fixed number of input lines and a fixed number of output lines. FIGURE 10.2 shows a three-input, two-output circuit.

Each line can carry a signal whose value is either 1 or 0. Electrically, a 1 signal is a small voltage, usually about 3 volts, and a 0 signal is 0 volts. The circuit is designed to detect and produce only those binary values.

You should recognize Figure 10.2 as one more manifestation of the input-processing-output structure that is present at all levels of the computer system. The circuit performs the processing that transforms the input to the output.

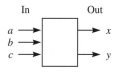

FIGURE 10.2
The black box representation of a circuit.

Combinational Circuits

With a *combinational circuit*, the input determines the output. For example, in Figure 10.2 if you put in $a = 1$, $b = 0$, $c = 1$ (abbreviated $abc = 101$) today and get out $xy = 01$, then if you put in $abc = 101$ tomorrow you will get out $xy = 01$ again. Mathematically, x and y are functions of a, b, and c. That is, $x = x(a, b, c)$ and $y = y(a, b, c)$.

This behavior is not characteristic of a sequential circuit. It may be possible for you to put $abc = 101$ into a sequential circuit and get out $xy = 01$ at one moment, but $xy = 11$ a few microseconds later. Chapter 11 shows how this seemingly useless behavior comes about and how it is, in fact, indispensable for building computers.

The three most common methods for describing the behavior of a combinational circuit are

> Truth tables

> Boolean algebraic expressions

> Logic diagrams

The remainder of this section describes those representations.

FIGURE 10.3
The truth table for
a three-input, two-
output combinational
circuit.

a	b	c	x	y
0	0	0	0	0
0	0	1	1	0
0	1	0	0	0
0	1	1	1	1
1	0	0	0	1
1	0	1	0	0
1	1	0	0	0
1	1	1	0	0

FIGURE 10.4
The truth table for a
four-input, two-output
combinational circuit.

a	b	c	d	x	y
0	0	0	0	0	0
0	0	0	1	0	0
0	0	1	0	0	0
0	0	1	1	0	0
0	1	0	0	0	1
0	1	0	1	1	1
0	1	1	0	0	0
0	1	1	1	1	0
1	0	0	0	0	0
1	0	0	1	0	0
1	0	1	0	0	0
1	0	1	1	0	0
1	1	0	0	0	1
1	1	0	1	1	1
1	1	1	0	0	0
1	1	1	1	1	0

Truth Tables

Of these three methods of representing a combinational circuit, truth tables are at a higher level of abstraction than algebraic expressions or logic diagrams. A truth table specifies what the combinational circuit does, not how it does it. A truth table simply lists the output for every possible combination of input values (hence the name *combinational circuit*).

Example 10.1 **FIGURE 10.3** is the truth table for a three-input, two-output combinational circuit. Because there are three inputs and each input can have one of two possible values, the table has $2^3 = 8$ entries. In general, the truth table for an n-input combinational circuit will have 2^n entries. ∎

Example 10.2 Another example of a combinational circuit specified by a truth table is **FIGURE 10.4**. It is a four-input circuit with 16 entries in its truth table. ∎

The black box schematic of Figure 10.2 is particularly appropriate for the truth table representation of a combinational circuit. You cannot see inside a box that is painted black. Similarly, you cannot see how a circuit produces a function that is defined by a truth table.

Boolean Algebra

An algebraic expression written according to the laws of Boolean algebra specifies not only what a combinational circuit does, but how it does it. Boolean algebra is similar in some respects to the algebra for real numbers that you are familiar with, but it is different in other respects. The four basic operations for real algebra are addition, subtraction, multiplication, and division. Boolean algebra has three basic operations: OR (denoted +), AND (denoted ·), and complement (denoted '). AND and OR are binary operations, and complement is a unary operation.

The 10 fundamental properties of Boolean algebra are

$x + y = y + x$	$x \cdot y = y \cdot x$	commutative
$(x + y) + z = x + (y + z)$	$(x \cdot y) \cdot z = x \cdot (y \cdot z)$	associative
$x + (y \cdot z) = (x + y) \cdot (x + z)$	$x \cdot (y + z) = (x \cdot y) + (x \cdot z)$	distributive
$x + 0 = x$	$x \cdot 1 = x$	identity
$x + (x') = 1$	$x \cdot (x') = 0$	complement

where x, y, and z are Boolean variables. As with real algebra, the notation is infix with parentheses to denote which of several operations to perform first. To simplify expressions with many parentheses, the Boolean operations have the precedence structure shown in (FIGURE 10.5). Using the precedence rules, the distributive properties are

$$x + y \cdot z = (x + y) \cdot (x + z) \qquad x \cdot (y + z) = x \cdot y + x \cdot z$$

and the complement properties are

$$x + x' = 1 \qquad x \cdot x' = 0$$

A striking difference between the properties of real algebra and Boolean algebra is the distributive law. With real numbers, multiplication distributes over addition. For example,

The distributive law

$$2 \cdot (3 + 4) = 2 \cdot 3 + 2 \cdot 4$$

But addition does not distribute over multiplication. It is not true that

$$2 + 3 \cdot 4 = (2 + 3) \cdot (2 + 4)$$

In Boolean algebra, however, where + represents OR and · represents AND, OR does distribute over AND.

The laws of Boolean algebra have a symmetry that the laws of real algebra do not have. Each Boolean property has a *dual* property. To obtain the dual expression,

> Exchange + and ·

> Exchange 1 and 0

Duality

The two forms of the distributive law are an example of dual expressions. In the distributive property

$$x + (y \cdot z) = (x + y) \cdot (x + z)$$

if you exchange the + and · operators, you get

$$x \cdot (y + z) = (x \cdot y) + (x \cdot z)$$

which is the other distributive property. Each fundamental property of Boolean algebra has a corresponding dual property.

The associative properties also permit simplification of expressions. Because the order in which you perform two OR operations is immaterial, you can write

The associative law

$$(x + y) + z$$

without parentheses as

$$x + y + z$$

The same is true for the AND operation.

FIGURE 10.5
Precedence of the Boolean operators.

Precedence	Operator
Highest	Complement
	AND
Lowest	OR

Boolean Algebra Theorems

Because Boolean algebra has a different mathematical structure from the real algebra with which you are familiar, the theorems of Boolean algebra may appear unusual at first. Some of the following theorems proved from the 10 basic properties of Boolean algebra are useful in the analysis and design of combinational circuits.

The *idempotent property* states that

The idempotent property

$$x + x = x$$

Proving this theorem requires a sequence of substitution steps, each of which is based on one of the 10 basic properties of Boolean algebra:

$$x + x$$
$$= \quad \langle\text{identity of AND}\rangle$$
$$(x + x) \cdot 1$$
$$= \quad \langle\text{complement of OR}\rangle$$
$$(x + x) \cdot (x + x')$$
$$= \quad \langle\text{distributive of OR over AND}\rangle$$
$$x + (x \cdot x')$$
$$= \quad \langle\text{complement of AND}\rangle$$
$$x + 0$$
$$= \quad \langle\text{identity of OR}\rangle$$
$$x$$

The dual property is

$$x \cdot x = x$$

The proof of the dual theorem requires exactly the same sequence of steps, with each substitution based on the dual of the corresponding step in the original proof:

$$x \cdot x$$
$$= \quad \langle\text{identity of OR}\rangle$$
$$(x \cdot x) + 0$$
$$= \quad \langle\text{complement of AND}\rangle$$
$$(x \cdot x) + (x \cdot x')$$
$$= \quad \langle\text{distributive of AND over OR}\rangle$$
$$x \cdot (x + x')$$
$$= \quad \langle\text{complement of OR}\rangle$$
$$x \cdot 1$$
$$= \quad \langle\text{identity of AND}\rangle$$
$$x$$

The proofs of the idempotent properties illustrate an important application of duality in Boolean algebra. Once you prove a theorem, you can assert immediately that its dual must also be true. Because each of the 10 basic properties has a dual, the corresponding proof will be identical in structure to the original proof, but with each step based on the dual of the original step.

Using duality to assert a theorem

Here are three more useful theorems with their duals. The mathematical rule for proving theorems is that you may use any axiom or previously proved theorem in your proof. So to prove the first theorem below, you may use any of the fundamental properties or the idempotent property. To prove the second theorem, you may use any of the fundamental properties, or the idempotent property, or the first theorem, and so on. The first theorem

$$x + 1 = 1 \qquad\qquad x \cdot 0 = 0$$

The zero theorem

is called the *zero theorem*. 0 is the zero for the AND operator, and 1 is the "zero" for the OR operator. The second theorem

$$x + x \cdot y = x \qquad\qquad x \cdot (x + y) = x$$

The absorption property

is called the *absorption property* because y is absorbed into x. The third theorem

$$x \cdot y + x' \cdot z + y \cdot z = x \cdot y + x' \cdot z$$
$$(x + y) \cdot (x' + z) \cdot (y + z) = (x + y) \cdot (x' + z)$$

The consensus theorem

is called the *consensus theorem*. Proofs of these theorems are exercises at the end of the chapter.

Proving Complements

The complement of x is x'. To prove that some expression, y, is the complement of some other expression, z, you must show that y and z obey the same complement properties,

$$y + z = 1 \qquad\qquad y \cdot z = 0$$

that x and x' obey.

An example of proving complements is *De Morgan's law*, which states that

$$(a \cdot b)' = a' + b'$$

De Morgan's law

To show that the complement of $a \cdot b$ is $a' + b'$, you must show that

$$(a \cdot b) + (a' + b') = 1 \qquad\qquad (a \cdot b) \cdot (a' + b') = 0$$

The first part of the proof is

$$(a \cdot b) + (a' + b')$$
$$= \quad \langle \text{commutative of OR} \rangle$$
$$(a' + b') + a \cdot b$$
$$= \quad \langle \text{distributive of OR over AND} \rangle$$
$$((a' + b') + a) \cdot ((a' + b') + b)$$
$$= \quad \langle \text{commutative and associative of OR} \rangle$$
$$(b' + (a + a')) \cdot (a' + (b + b'))$$
$$= \quad \langle \text{complement of OR} \rangle$$
$$(b' + 1) \cdot (a' + 1)$$
$$= \quad \langle \text{the zero theorem of OR, } x + 1 = 1 \rangle$$
$$1 \cdot 1$$
$$= \quad \langle \text{identity of AND, } (x \cdot 1 = 1) \ [x := 1] \rangle$$
$$1$$

and the second part of the proof is

$$(a \cdot b) \cdot (a' + b')$$
$$= \quad \langle \text{distributive of AND over OR} \rangle$$
$$(a \cdot b) \cdot a' + (a \cdot b) \cdot b'$$
$$= \quad \langle \text{commutative and associative of AND} \rangle$$
$$b \cdot (a \cdot a') + a \cdot (b \cdot b')$$
$$= \quad \langle \text{complement of AND} \rangle$$
$$b \cdot 0 + a \cdot 0$$
$$= \quad \langle \text{the zero theorem of AND, } x \cdot 0 = 0 \rangle$$
$$0 + 0$$
$$= \quad \langle \text{identity of OR, } (x + 0 = x)[x := 0] \rangle$$
$$0$$

De Morgan's second law,

$$(a + b)' = a' \cdot b'$$

follows immediately from duality.

De Morgan's laws generalize to more than one variable. For three variables, the laws are

De Morgan's law for three variables

$$(a \cdot b \cdot c)' = a' + b' + c' \qquad (a + b + c)' = a' \cdot b' \cdot c'$$

Proofs of the general theorems for more than two variables are an exercise at the end of the chapter.

Another complement theorem is $(x')' = x$. The complement of x' is x *The complement of* x′
because $x' + x = 1$ by the following proof:

$x' + x$

= ⟨commutative of OR⟩

$x + x'$

= ⟨complement of OR⟩

1

and $x' \cdot x = 0$ by the following proof:

$x' \cdot x$

= ⟨commutative of AND⟩

$x \cdot x'$

= ⟨complement of AND⟩

0

Yet another complement theorem is $1' = 0$. 1 is the complement of 0 because
$1 + 0 = 1$ by the following proof:

$1 + 0$

= ⟨identity of OR, $(x + 0 = x)$ $[x := 1]$⟩

1

and $1 \cdot 0 = 0$ by the following proof:

$1 \cdot 0$

= ⟨commutative of AND⟩

$0 \cdot 1$

= ⟨identity of AND, $(x \cdot 1 = x)$ $[x := 0]$⟩

0

The dual theorem, $0' = 1$, follows immediately.

Logic Diagrams

The third representation of a combinational circuit is an interconnection of
logic gates. This representation corresponds most closely to the hardware
because the lines that connect the gates in a logic diagram represent physical
wires that connect physical devices on a circuit board or in an integrated
circuit.

Each Boolean operation is represented by a gate symbol, shown in
FIGURE 10.6 . The AND and OR gates have two input lines, labeled a
and b. The inverter has one input line, corresponding to the fact that the
complement is a unary operation. The output is x. Also shown in the figure
are the corresponding Boolean expression and truth table for each gate.

FIGURE 10.6
The three basic logic gates.

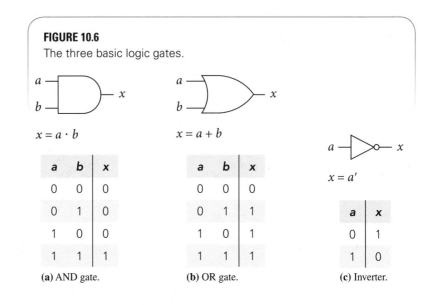

$x = a \cdot b$

a	b	x
0	0	0
0	1	0
1	0	0
1	1	1

(a) AND gate.

$x = a + b$

a	b	x
0	0	0
0	1	1
1	0	1
1	1	1

(b) OR gate.

$x = a'$

a	x
0	1
1	0

(c) Inverter.

FIGURE 10.7
Three common logic gates.

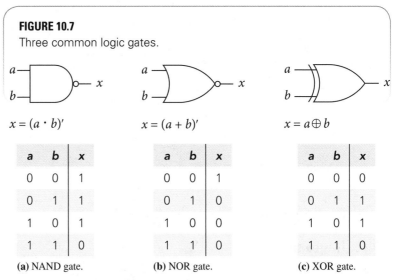

$x = (a \cdot b)'$

a	b	x
0	0	1
0	1	1
1	0	1
1	1	0

(a) NAND gate.

$x = (a + b)'$

a	b	x
0	0	1
0	1	0
1	0	0
1	1	0

(b) NOR gate.

$x = a \oplus b$

a	b	x
0	0	0
0	1	1
1	0	1
1	1	0

(c) XOR gate.

FIGURE 10.8
Two equivalent
combinational circuits.

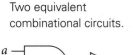

(a) AND inverter.

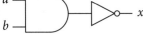

(b) NAND.

Any Boolean function can be written with only the AND, OR, and complement operations. It follows that to construct any combinational circuit, you need only the three basic gates of Figure 10.6. In practice, several other gates are common. **FIGURE 10.7** shows three of them.

The NAND gate (not AND) is equivalent to an AND gate followed by an inverter, as shown in **FIGURE 10.8**. Similarly, a NOR gate (not OR) is equivalent to an OR gate followed by an inverter. Electronically, it is frequently easier to build a NAND gate than to build an AND gate. In fact, an AND gate is often built as a NAND gate followed by an inverter. NOR gates are also more common than OR gates.

XOR stands for *exclusive* OR, in contrast to OR, which is sometimes called *inclusive* OR. The output of an OR gate is 1 if either or both of its inputs are 1. The output of an XOR gate is 1 if either of its inputs is 1 exclusive of the other input. Its output is 0 if both inputs are 1. The algebraic symbol for the XOR operation is $\oplus$. The algebraic definition of $a \oplus b$ is

$$a \oplus b = a \cdot b' + a' \cdot b$$

The precedence for the XOR operator is greater than OR but less than AND, as   FIGURE 10.9   shows.

Example 10.3   The expression

$$a + b \oplus c \cdot d$$

fully parenthesized is $a + (b \oplus (c \cdot d))$. Expanded according to the definition of XOR, the expression becomes

$$a + b \cdot (c \cdot d)' + b' \cdot (c \cdot d)$$ ∎

The AND and OR gates are also manufactured with more than two inputs.   FIGURE 10.10   shows a three-input AND gate and its truth table. The output of an AND gate is 1 only if all of its inputs are 1. The output of an OR gate is 0 only if all of its inputs are 0.

Alternate Representations

You may have recognized the similarity of the truth tables for the AND, OR, and inverter gates and the truth tables for the AND, OR, and NOT operations in C's Boolean expressions. The truth tables are identical, with NOT corresponding to the inverter and C's true and false values corresponding to Boolean algebra's 1 and 0, respectively.

The mathematical structure of Boolean algebra is important because it applies not only to combinational circuits, but also to statement logic. C uses statement logic to determine the truth of a condition contained in `if` and loop statements. A group of programming languages important in artificial intelligence makes even more extensive use of statement logic. Programs written in these languages simulate human reasoning with a technique called *logic programming*. Boolean algebra is a major component of that discipline.

Another interpretation of Boolean algebra is a description of operations on sets. If you interpret a Boolean variable as a set, the OR operation as set union, the AND operation as set intersection, the complement operation as set complement, 0 as the empty set, and 1 as the universal set, then all the properties and theorems of Boolean algebra hold for sets.

FIGURE 10.9
Precedence of the XOR operator.

Precedence	Operator
Highest	Complement
	AND
	XOR
Lowest	OR

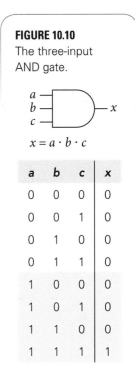

FIGURE 10.10
The three-input AND gate.

$$x = a \cdot b \cdot c$$

a	b	c	x
0	0	0	0
0	0	1	0
0	1	0	0
0	1	1	0
1	0	0	0
1	0	1	0
1	1	0	0
1	1	1	1

Statement logic interpretation

Set theory interpretation

FIGURE 10.11
The set theory
interpretation of an
absorption property.

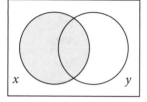

(a) x

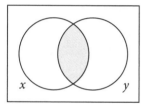

(b) $x \cdot y$

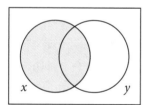

(c) $x + x \cdot y$

Example 10.4   The theorem

$$x + 1 = 1$$

states that the union of the universal set with any other set is the universal set. ∎

Example 10.5   shows the set theory interpretation of an absorption property

$$x + x \cdot y = x$$

with a Venn diagram. Figure 10.11(a) shows set x. The intersection of x and y, shown in (b), is the set of elements in both x and y. The union of that set with x is shown in (c). The fact that the region in (a) is the same as the region in (c) illustrates the absorption property. ∎

The interpretation of Boolean algebra as a description of combinational circuits and as the basis of statement logic illustrates that it is the mathematical basis of a large part of computer science. The fact that it also describes set theory shows its importance in other areas of mathematics as well.

10.2 Combinational Analysis

Every Boolean expression has a corresponding logic diagram, and every logic diagram has a corresponding Boolean expression. In mathematical terminology, there is a one-to-one correspondence between the two. A given truth table, however, can have several corresponding implementations. shows a truth table with several corresponding Boolean expressions and logic diagrams.

This section describes the correspondence among the three representations of a combinational circuit.

FIGURE 10.12
Several implementations of a given truth table.

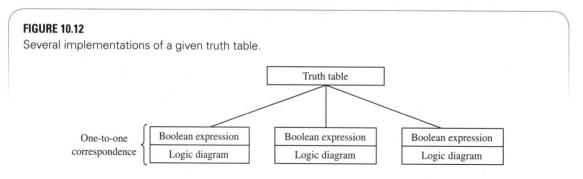

Boolean Expressions and Logic Diagrams

A Boolean expression consists of one or more variables combined with the AND, OR, and invert operations. The number of inputs to the circuit equals the number of variables. This section and the next concentrate on circuits with one output. The last section of this chapter considers circuits with more than one output.

Constructing a logic diagram from a Boolean expression

To draw the logic diagram from a given Boolean expression, draw an AND gate for each AND operation, an OR gate for each OR operation, and an inverter for each complement operation. Connect the output of one gate to the input of another according to the expression. The output of the combinational circuit is the output of the one gate that is not connected to the input of another.

Example 10.6 FIGURE 10.13 shows the logic diagram corresponding to the Boolean expression $a + b' \cdot c$.

From now on, we will omit the AND operator symbol and write the Boolean expression as

$$a + b'c$$

The output of each gate is labeled with its corresponding expression. ■

When the expression has parentheses, you must construct the subdiagram within the parentheses first.

Example 10.7 FIGURE 10.14 is the logic diagram for the three-variable expression

$$((ab + bc')a)'$$

You first form ab with one AND gate, then bc' with another AND gate. The output of those two are ORed and then ANDed with a. Because the entire expression is complemented, an inverter is the last gate. ■

FIGURE 10.13
The logic diagram for the Boolean expression $a + b' \cdot c$.

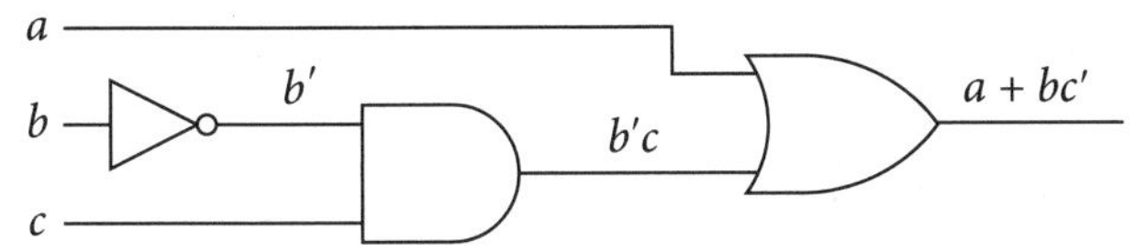

FIGURE 10.14

The logic diagram for the Boolean expression $((ab + bc')a)'$.

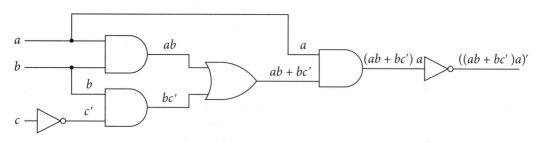

Figure 10.14 shows two junctions as small black dots where two wires are physically connected. Recall that the physical signal supplied by variable a is a voltage. When the signal from input a reaches the junction, it does not act like water in a river that encounters a fork in its path. In the river analogy, some of the water takes one path and some takes the other. In a logic diagram, it does not happen that part of the signal goes to the input of one AND gate and part goes to the other gate. The full signal from a is duplicated at the inputs at both gates.

For those who know some physics, the reason for this behavior is that voltage is a measure of electric potential. The wires have low resistance, which from Ohm's law means there is negligible potential change along a wire. So, the voltage along any wires that are physically connected is constant. The full voltage signal is, therefore, available at any point, regardless of the junction. (For those who do not know some physics, this may be an incentive to learn!)

The signal from any variable can be duplicated with a junction. The complement of any variable can be produced by an inverter, which can, in turn, also be duplicated by a junction. Rather than show variable-duplicating junctions and variable inverters, they are often omitted from the logic diagram. It is assumed that any variable or its complement is available as input to any gate.

Example 10.8 **FIGURE 10.15** shows an abbreviated version of Figure 10.14 that takes advantage of this assumption. It also recognizes that an AND gate followed by an inverter is equivalent to a NAND gate. ∎

A disadvantage of this abbreviated diagram is that the three-input nature of the network is not as evident as it is in Figure 10.14.

Example 10.9 **FIGURE 10.16** shows the logic diagram for the four-input Boolean expression

$$(a'bc \oplus c + a + d)'$$

FIGURE 10.15
An abbreviated version of Figure 10.14.

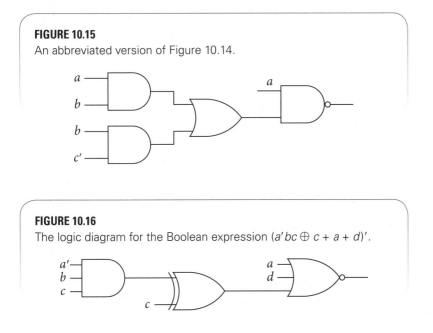

FIGURE 10.16
The logic diagram for the Boolean expression $(a'bc \oplus c + a + d)'$.

Note that the precedence of the exclusive OR operator is less than that of AND and greater than that of OR. ▮

Constructing a Boolean expression from a logic diagram

To write the Boolean expression from a given logic diagram, simply label the output of each gate with the appropriate subexpression. If you were given the logic diagram of Figure 10.16 without the Boolean expression, you would start by labeling the output of the AND gate as $a'bc$. The output of the XOR gate would be labeled $a'bc \oplus c$, which when passed through the NOR gate produces the full Boolean expression.

Truth Tables and Boolean Expressions

One method for constructing a Boolean expression from a truth table is to write the expression without parentheses as an OR of several AND terms. Each AND term corresponds to a 1 in the truth table.

Example 10.10 The truth table for $a \oplus b$ has two 1's. The corresponding Boolean expression is

$$a \oplus b = a'b + ab'$$

If a is 0 and b is 1, the first AND term will be 1. If a is 1 and b is 0, the second AND term will be 1. In either case, the OR of the two terms will be 1. Furthermore, any other combination of values for a and b will make both AND terms 0, and the Boolean expression 0. ▮

Example 10.11   Figure 10.3 shows x is 1 when $abc = 001$ and $abc = 011$; x is 0 for all other combinations of abc. A corresponding Boolean expression is

$$x = a'b'c + a'bc$$

The first AND term, $a'b'c$, is 1 if and only if $abc = 001$. The second is 1 if and only if $abc = 011$. So the OR of the two terms will be 0 except under either of those conditions, duplicating the truth table.   ∎

Example 10.12   An example with four variables is the truth table for x in Figure 10.4. A corresponding expression is

$$x = a'bc'd + a'bcd + abc'd + abcd$$

which gives 1 for the four combinations of a, b, c, and d that have 1 in the truth table.   ∎

The dual technique is to write an expression as the AND of several OR terms. Each OR term corresponds to a 0 in the truth table.

Example 10.13   The expression from FIGURE 10.17 is

$$x = (a + b' + c')(a' + b' + c)$$

If $abc = 011$, the first OR term is 0. If $abc = 110$, the second OR term is 0. Under either of these conditions, the AND of the OR terms is 0. All other combinations of abc will make both OR terms 1 and the expression 1.   ∎

Given a Boolean expression, the most straightforward way to construct the corresponding truth table is to evaluate the expression for all possible combinations of the variables.

Example 10.14   To construct the truth table for

$$x(a, b) = (a \oplus b)' + a'$$

requires the evaluation of

$$x(0, 0) = (0 \oplus 0)' + 0' = 1$$
$$x(0, 1) = (0 \oplus 1)' + 0' = 1$$
$$x(1, 0) = (1 \oplus 0)' + 1' = 0$$
$$x(1, 1) = (1 \oplus 1)' + 1' = 1$$

This example requires the evaluation of all four possible combinations of the two variables a and b.   ∎

If the expression contains more than two variables, sometimes it is easier to convert the Boolean expression into an OR of AND terms using

FIGURE 10.17

A three-variable truth table.

a	b	c	x
0	0	0	1
0	0	1	1
0	1	0	1
0	1	1	0
1	0	0	1
1	0	1	1
1	1	0	0
1	1	1	1

the properties and theorems of Boolean algebra. The truth table can then be written by inspection.

Example 10.15   The expression in Figure 10.16 reduces to

$$(a'bc \oplus c + a + d)'$$
$$= \quad \langle\text{definition of } \oplus\rangle$$
$$(a'bcc' + (a'bc)'c + a + d)'$$
$$= \quad \langle\text{complement, } cc' = 0, \text{ and zero theorem } x \cdot 0 = 0\rangle$$
$$((a'bc)'c + a + d)'$$
$$= \quad \langle\text{De Morgan}\rangle$$
$$((a + b' + c')c + a + d)'$$
$$= \quad \langle\text{distributive, complement, and identity}\rangle$$
$$(ac + b'c + a + d)'$$
$$= \quad \langle\text{absorption, } a + ac = a\rangle$$
$$(a + b'c + d)'$$
$$= \quad \langle\text{De Morgan}\rangle$$
$$a'(b'c)'d'$$
$$= \quad \langle\text{De Morgan}\rangle$$
$$a'(b + c')d'$$
$$= \quad \langle\text{distributive}\rangle$$
$$a'bd' + a'c'd'$$

The truth table has 16 entries. By inspection, insert a 1 where $abd = 010$ (two places) and $acd = 000$ (two places). All other entries are 0. The result is FIGURE 10.18 . It has three 1's instead of four because one of the places where $abd = 010$ is also one of the places where $acd = 000$.

This technique saves you from evaluating the original expression 16 times. Actually, that task may not be as difficult as it first appears. With a little thought, you can reason from the original expression that when d is 1, the expression inside the parentheses must be 1, and its inverse must be 0 regardless of the values of a, b, and c. Similarly, the expression must be 0 when a is 1. That leaves you with only the four evaluations where $ad = 00$. ∎

Two-Level Circuits

The fact that every Boolean expression can be transformed to an AND-OR expression has an important practical effect on the processing speed of the combinational circuit. When you change a signal at the input of a gate, the output does not respond instantly. Instead, there is a time delay during which the signal works its way through the internal electronic components of the gate. The time it takes for the output of a gate to respond to a change in its input is called the *gate delay*. Different manufacturing processes produce gates with different gate delays. To produce gates with short gate delays is

Gate delays

FIGURE 10.18
The truth table for the expression in Figure 10.16.

a	b	c	d	x
0	0	0	0	1
0	0	0	1	0
0	0	1	0	0
0	0	1	1	0
0	1	0	0	1
0	1	0	1	0
0	1	1	0	1
0	1	1	1	0
1	0	0	0	0
1	0	0	1	0
1	0	1	0	0
1	0	1	1	0
1	1	0	0	0
1	1	0	1	0
1	1	1	0	0
1	1	1	1	0

more expensive, and the gates require more power to operate than gates with longer delays. A typical gate delay is 2 ns (nanoseconds), although the delay varies widely depending on the device technology.

Two billionths of a second may not seem like a long time to wait for the output, but in a circuit with a long string of gates that must do its processing in a loop, the time can be significant. By way of comparison, consider the fact that the signal travels through the wires at approximately the speed of light, which is 3.0×10^8 m/s (meters per second). That is 30 cm, or about a foot, in 1 ns. In 2 ns, the time of a typical gate delay, the signal can travel through 60 cm of wire. This is such a long distance compared to the size of an integrated circuit or circuit board that the gate delay is, for all practical purposes, responsible for the limit on a network's processing speed.

Physical limits on processing speed

Example 10.16   Consider the circuit of Figure 10.16. If the gate delay is 2 ns, a change in b requires 2 ns to propagate through the AND gate, 2 ns to propagate through the XOR gate, and another 2 ns to propagate through the NOR gate. That is a total of 6 ns of propagation time. (We will ignore the propagation delay through any inverters.)

Now consider that we used Boolean algebra to write the expression for this circuit as an AND-OR expression:

$$x = (a'bc \oplus c + a + d)'$$
$$= a'bd' + a'c'd'$$

FIGURE 10.19
The two-level AND-OR circuit equivalent to the circuit of Figure 10.16.

FIGURE 10.19 shows the corresponding circuit. It is called a *two-level circuit* because a change in the input requires only two gate delays to propagate to the output. ∎

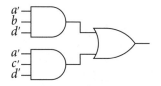

Reducing the processing time from 6 ns to 4 ns is a 33% improvement in speed, which is significant. Because any Boolean expression can be transformed to an AND-OR expression, which corresponds to a two-level AND-OR circuit, it follows that any function can be implemented with a combinational circuit with a processing time of two gate delays at most.

The same principle applies to the dual. It is always possible to transform a Boolean expression to an OR-AND expression, which corresponds to a two-level OR-AND circuit. Such a circuit has a processing time of two gate delays at most. To obtain the Boolean expression as an OR-AND expression, you can first obtain the complement as an AND-OR expression, and then use De Morgan's law.

FIGURE 10.20
The two-level OR-AND circuit of Figure 10.17.

Example 10.17   FIGURE 10.20 is the two-level OR-AND circuit of Figure 10.17 for the expression

$$x = (a + b' + c')(a' + b' + c)$$

Recall that each OR term corresponds to a 0 in the truth table. ∎

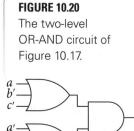

Example 10.18 The expression from Figure 10.13 is

$$x = a + b'c$$

To transform this expression into an OR-AND expression, first write its complement as

$$x' = (a + b'c)'$$
$$= a'(b'c)'$$
$$= a'(b + c')$$
$$= a'b + a'c'$$

which is an AND-OR expression. Now use De Morgan's law to write x as

$$x = (x')'$$
$$= (a'b + a'c')'$$
$$= (a'b)'(a'c')'$$
$$= (a + b')(a + c)$$

which is an OR-AND expression. ∎

It usually happens that a circuit with three or more levels requires fewer gates than the equivalent two-level circuit. Because a gate occupies physical space in an integrated circuit, the two-level circuit achieves its faster processing time at the expense of the extra space required for the additional gates.

This is yet another example of the space/time tradeoff in computer science. It is remarkable that the same space/time principle is manifest from software at the highest level of abstraction to hardware at the lowest level. It is truly a fundamental principle.

The Ubiquitous NAND

The expression $(abc)'$ represents a three-input NAND gate. De Morgan's law states that

$$(abc)' = a' + b' + c'$$

You can visualize the second expression as the output of an OR gate that inverts each input before performing the OR operation. Logic diagrams occasionally render the NAND gate as an inverted input NOR, as in `FIGURE 10.21(a)`.

The dual concept follows from the dual expression

$$(a + b + c)' = a'b'c'$$

A NOR gate is equivalent to an AND gate that inverts its inputs as in Figure 10.21(b).

FIGURE 10.21
Equivalent gates.

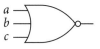

(a) A NAND gate as an inverted input OR gate.

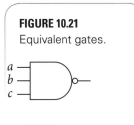

(b) A NOR gate as an inverted input AND gate.

The fundamental space/time trade-off

FIGURE 10.22

An AND-OR circuit and its equivalent NAND-NAND circuit.

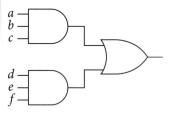

(a) An AND-OR circuit.

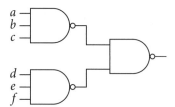

(b) The equivalent NAND-NAND circuit.

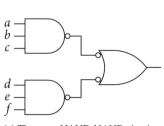

(c) The same NAND-NAND circuit as in part (b).

Carrying this idea one step further to two-level circuits, consider the equivalence of

$$abc + def = ((abc)'(def)')'$$

which again follows from De Morgan's law. The first expression represents a two-level AND-OR circuit, whereas the second represents a two-level NAND-NAND circuit. Figure 10.22 shows the equivalent circuits.

FIGURE 10.22(a) shows an AND-OR circuit with two AND gates and one OR. You can make the equivalent circuit entirely out of NAND gates, as shown in (b). Part (c) shows the same circuit as (b) but with the last NAND drawn as an inverted-input OR. This drawing style makes it apparent that the complement following the AND operation cancels the complement preceding the OR operation. The shape of the gate symbols becomes similar to those in the AND-OR circuit, which helps to convey the meaning of the circuit.

Not only can you replace an arbitrary AND-OR circuit entirely with NAND gates, you can also construct an inverter from a NAND gate by connecting the NAND inputs together, as shown in **FIGURE 10.23**. Because the NAND produces $(ab)'$ with input a and b, if you force $b = a$, the gate will produce $(a \cdot a)' = a'$, the complement of a.

Conceptually, you can construct any combinational circuit from only NAND gates. Furthermore, NAND gates are usually easier to manufacture than either AND or OR gates. Consequently, the NAND gate is by far the most common gate found in integrated circuits.

Of course, the same principle applies to the dual circuit. De Morgan's law for two-level circuits is

$$(a + b + c)(d + e + f) = ((a + b + c)' + (d + e + f)')'$$

which shows that an OR-AND circuit is equivalent to a NOR-NOR circuit. **FIGURE 10.24** is the dual circuit of Figure 10.22.

FIGURE 10.23

Three equivalent circuits.

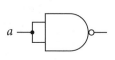

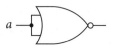

FIGURE 10.24
An OR-AND circuit and its equivalent NOR-NOR circuit.

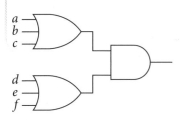 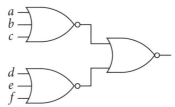 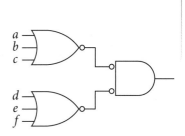

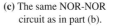

(a) An OR-AND circuit. **(b)** The equivalent NOR-NOR circuit. **(c)** The same NOR-NOR circuit as in part (b).

The same reasoning that applies to NAND circuits also applies to NOR circuits. Any combinational circuit can be written as a two-level OR-AND circuit, which can be written as NOR-NOR. Connecting the inputs of a NOR makes an inverter. You can conceptually construct any combinational circuit with only NOR gates.

10.3 **Combinational Design**

The high speed of two-level circuits gives them an advantage over circuits with more than two levels of gates. Sometimes it is possible to reduce the number of gates in a two-level circuit and retain the processing speed of two gate delays.

Example 10.19 The Boolean expression

$$x(a, b, c, d) = a'bd' + a'c'd' + a'bc'd'$$

can be simplified using the absorption property to

$$x(a, b, c, d) = a'bd' + (a'c'd') + (a'c'd')b$$
$$= a'bd' + a'c'd'$$

This expression also corresponds to a two-level circuit, but it requires only two three-input AND gates and a two-input OR gate, compared to three AND gates (one of which has four inputs) and a three-input OR gate.   ∎

Minimizing the number of gates in a two-level circuit is not always straightforward with Boolean algebra. This section presents a graphical method for designing two-level circuits with three or four variables that contain the minimum possible number of gates.

Canonical Expressions

The previous section shows that any Boolean expression can be transformed to a two-level AND-OR expression. To minimize the two-level circuit, it is desirable to first make each AND term contain all input variables exactly once. Such an AND term is called a *minterm*. It is always possible to transform an AND-OR expression into an OR of minterms.

Minterms

Example 10.20   Consider the Boolean expression

$$x(a, b, c) = abc + a'bc + ab$$

The first two AND terms are minterms because they contain all three variables, but the last is not. The transformation is

$$
\begin{aligned}
x &= abc + a'bc + ab \\
&= abc + a'bc + ab(c + c') \\
&= abc + a'bc + abc + abc' \\
&= abc + a'bc + abc'
\end{aligned}
$$

The definition of a canonical expression

The last expression is called a *canonical expression* because it is an OR of minterms in which no two identical minterms appear.   ∎

    A canonical expression is directly related to the truth table because each minterm in the expression represents a 1 in the truth table. A convenient shorthand notation for a canonical expression and its corresponding truth table is called *sigma notation*, which consists of the uppercase Greek letter sigma (Σ) followed by a list of decimal numbers that specify the rows in the truth table that contain 1's. The uppercase sigma represents the OR operation. It is understood that all the rows not listed contain 0's.

FIGURE 10.25
The truth table for a canonical expression.

Row (dec)	a	b	c	x
0	0	0	0	0
1	0	0	1	0
2	0	1	0	0
3	0	1	1	1
4	1	0	0	0
5	1	0	1	0
6	1	1	0	1
7	1	1	1	1

Example 10.21   In Example 10.20, because the canonical expression for x has three minterms, its truth table has three 1's. **FIGURE 10.25** shows the truth table for this function. It labels each row with the decimal number equivalent of the binary number abc. The corresponding sigma notation for this function is

$$x(a, b, c) = \Sigma(3, 6, 7)$$

because rows 3, 6, and 7 contain 1's.   ∎

    The dual canonical expression is an OR-AND expression, each term of which contains all variables once, with no OR terms duplicated. The corresponding notation for this canonical expression contains the list of 0's in the truth table. The uppercase Greek letter pi (Π), which represents the AND operation, is used instead of sigma.

Example 10.22 The dual canonical expression for the previous example is

$$x(a, b, c) = (a + b + c)(a + b + c')(a + b' + c)(a' + b + c)(a' + b + c')$$

which is written in pi notation as

$$x(a, b, c) = \Pi(0, 1, 2, 4, 5)$$

because these are the five rows that contain 0's in the truth table. ∎

Example 10.23 Using the sigma notation, x and y from Figure 10.3 are

$$x(a, b, c) = \Sigma(1, 3)$$
$$y(a, b, c) = \Sigma(3, 4)$$

Functions x and y from Figure 10.4 are

$$x(a, b, c, d) = \Sigma(5, 7, 13, 15)$$
$$y(a, b, c, d) = \Sigma(4, 5, 12, 13)$$
∎

Sigma and pi notation are more compact than the canonical Boolean expressions or the truth tables. The remainder of this section assumes that the function to be minimized has been transformed to its unique canonical expression, or that its truth table has been given or determined.

Three-Variable Karnaugh Maps

Minimization of two-level circuits is based on the concept of distance. The *distance* between two minterms is the number of places in which they differ.

Distance between minterms

Example 10.24 Consider the canonical expression for this function of three variables:

$$x(a, b, c) = a'bc + abc + abc'$$

The distance between minterms $a'bc$ and abc is one, because a' and a are the only variables that differ. Variables b and c are the same in both. The distance between minterms $a'bc$ and abc' is two, because a' and c in $a'bc$ differ from a and c' in abc'. ∎

Recognizing *adjacent minterms*—that is, minterms a distance of 1 from each other—is key to the minimization of an AND-OR expression. Once you identify two adjacent minterms, you can factor out the common terms with the distributive property and simplify with the complement and identity properties.

Adjacent minterms

Example 10.25 You can minimize the expression in Example 10.24 by combining the first two minterms as follows:

$$x(a, b, c) = a'bc + abc + abc'$$
$$= (a' + a)bc + abc'$$
$$= bc + abc'$$

Alternatively, you can minimize by combining the second and third minterms, as they are also adjacent.

$$x(a, b, c) = a'bc + abc + abc'$$
$$= a'bc + ab(c + c')$$
$$= a'bc + ab$$

Either way, you have improved the circuit. The original expression is for a circuit with three three-input AND gates and one three-input OR gate. Either of the simplified expressions is for a circuit with only two AND gates, one of which has only two inputs, and an OR gate with only two inputs. ∎

Recognizing adjacent minterms is the easy part. Sometimes it is helpful to make the expression temporarily more complicated to get a smaller final circuit. That happens when one minterm is adjacent to two other minterms. You can use the idempotent property to duplicate the minterm, then combine it with both of its adjacent minterms.

Example 10.26 In Example 10.25, you can duplicate abc with the idempotent property first, then combine it with both of the remaining minterms.

$$x(a, b, c) = a'bc + abc + abc'$$
$$= a'bc + abc + abc + abc'$$
$$= (a' + a)bc + ab(c + c')$$
$$= bc + ab$$

This is better than the result in Example 10.25, because both AND gates require only two inputs. ∎

Performing the minimization with Boolean algebra is tedious and error-prone. The Karnaugh map is a tool to minimize a two-level circuit that makes it easy to spot adjacent minterms and to determine which ones need to be duplicated with the idempotent property. A *Karnaugh map* is simply a truth table arranged so that adjacent entries represent minterms that differ by 1.

FIGURE 10.26(a) shows the Karnaugh map for three variables. The upper left cell is for $abc = 000$. To its right is the cell for $abc = 001$. To the right of that is the cell for $abc = 011$, and then $abc = 010$. The sequence

FIGURE 10.26
The Karnaugh map for a function of three variables.

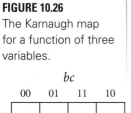

(a) The Karnaugh map.

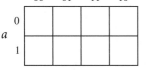

(b) The $b = 1$ region.

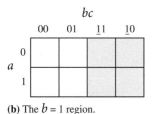

(c) The $c = 0$ region.

Karnaugh maps

000, 001, 011, 010

guarantees that adjacent cells differ by 1. That would not be the case if the cells were in numeric order

000, 001, 010, 011

because 001 is a distance 2 from 010.

The top row contains entries in the truth table where $a = 0$, and the bottom row contains entries where $a = 1$. Each column gives the values for bc. For example, the first column is for $bc = 00$ and the second for $bc = 01$. The two leftmost columns are for $b = 0$, and the two rightmost columns, Figure 10.26(b), are for $b = 1$. The two outside columns, Figure 10.26(c), are for $c = 0$, and the two middle columns are for $c = 1$.

Factoring out a common term from adjacent minterms with Boolean algebra corresponds to grouping adjacent cells on a Karnaugh map. After you group the cells, you write the simplified term by inspection of the region on the Karnaugh map.

The Karnaugh map equivalent of the distributive property

Example 10.27 (FIGURE 10.27(a)) shows the Karnaugh map for the canonical expression

$$x(a, b, c) = a'bc + a'bc'$$

The 1 in the cell for $abc = 011$ is the truth table cell for the minterm $a'bc$. The 1 in the cell for $abc = 010$ is the truth table cell for the minterm $a'bc'$. Figure 10.27(b) is the same Karnaugh map with the zeros omitted for clarity. Because the two ones are adjacent, you can group them with an oval. The cells covered by the oval are in the row for $a = 0$ and the columns for $b = 1$. Therefore, they are the regions for $ab = 01$, which corresponds to the term $a'b$. So, $x(a, b, c) = a'b$. You can write down the result by inspecting the Karnaugh map without doing the Boolean algebra. ∎

Example 10.28 (FIGURE 10.28(a)) shows the Karnaugh map for the canonical expression

$$x(a, b, c) = ab'c' + abc'$$

It may appear that the $ab'c'$ cell in the lower left and the abc' cell in the lower right are not adjacent, but in fact they are. You should think of the Karnaugh map as wrapping around so that its left and right sides are adjacent, the so-called *Pac-Man effect*. The single oval in the figure is drawn as two open-ended half ovals to convey this property of the Karnaugh map.

The group of two cells lies in the $a = 1$ row and the $c = 0$ columns, as parts (b) and (c) of the figure show. You can imagine the two cells as the

FIGURE 10.27
The Karnaugh map for the AND-OR expression of Example 10.27.

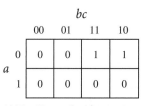

(a) The Karnaugh map.

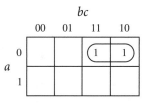

(b) The minimization.

FIGURE 10.28
The Karnaugh map for the AND-OR expression of Example 10.28.

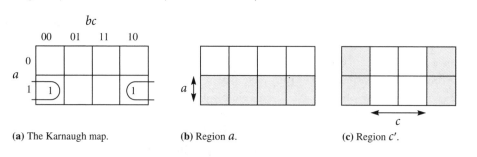

(a) The Karnaugh map.   (b) Region *a*.   (c) Region *c′*.

intersection of the shaded regions in (b) and (c). The region for the group is $ac = 10$. Therefore, the minimized function is $x(a, b, c) = ac'$. ▮

The Karnaugh map equivalent of the idempotent property

Duplicating a minterm with the idempotent property, so that it may be combined with two other minterms, corresponds to an overlap of two ovals in the Karnaugh map. If there are more than two minterms in the AND-OR expression, you are free to use a 1 in the truth table for more than one group.

Example 10.29   **FIGURE 10.29** shows the Karnaugh map for

$$x(a, b, c) = a'bc + abc + abc'$$

which is the canonical expression for Example 10.26. Part (a) shows minimization of the first and second minterms. Part (b) shows minimization of the second and third minterms. Part (c) shows that using the second term in both minimizations corresponds to an overlap of the two ovals. ▮

When the original truth table is given in sigma notation, you can use the decimal labels of **FIGURE 10.30** to insert 1's in the Karnaugh map.

The minimization procedure requires you to determine the best set of ovals that will cover all the 1's in the Karnaugh map. "Best" means the set

FIGURE 10.29
The Karnaugh map for the AND-OR expression of Example 10.26.

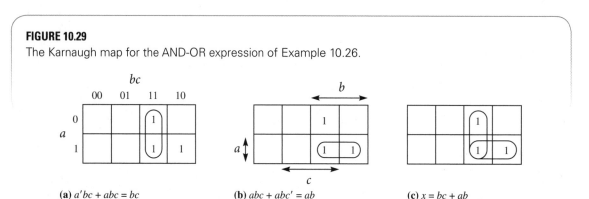

(a) $a'bc + abc = bc$ (b) $abc + abc' = ab$ (c) $x = bc + ab$

that corresponds to a two-level circuit with the least number of gates and the least number of inputs per gate. The number of ovals equals the number of AND gates. The more 1's an oval covers, the smaller the number of inputs to the corresponding AND gate. It follows that you want the smallest number of ovals, with each oval as large as possible such that the ovals cover all the 1's and no 0's. It is permissible for a 1 to be covered by several ovals. The next few examples show the general strategy.

Example 10.30 (FIGURE 10.31) shows a common minimization mistake. To minimize

$$x(a, b, c) = \Sigma(0, 1, 5, 7)$$

you may be tempted to first group minterms 1 and 5 as in Figure 10.31(a). That is a bad first choice because minterm 1 is adjacent to both 0 and 5, and minterm 5 is adjacent to both 1 and 7. On the other hand, minterm 0 is adjacent only to 1. To cover 0 with the largest possible oval, you must group it with 1. Similarly, minterm 7 is adjacent only to 5. To cover 7 with the largest possible oval, you must group it with 5.

Figure 10.31(b) shows the result of these minterm groupings. It represents the expression

$$x(a, b, c) = \Sigma(0, 1, 5, 7)$$
$$= a'b' + b'c + ac$$

which requires three two-input AND gates and a three-input OR gate. But the grouping of the first choice is not necessary. Figure 10.31(c) shows the correct minimization, which represents

$$x(a, b, c) = \Sigma(0, 1, 5, 7)$$
$$= a'b' + ac$$

This implementation requires only two two-input AND gates and a two-input OR gate. ∎

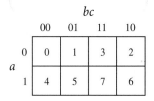

FIGURE 10.30
Decimal labels for the minterms in the Karnaugh map.

FIGURE 10.31
The result of a bad first choice.

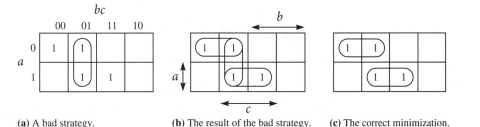

(a) A bad strategy.   (b) The result of the bad strategy.   (c) The correct minimization.

FIGURE 10.32
Failing to recognize a large grouping.

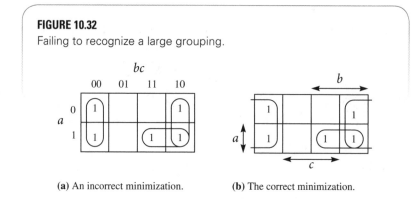

(a) An incorrect minimization.   (b) The correct minimization.

The rule of thumb that the previous example teaches us is to start a grouping with minterms that have only one nearest neighbor. Because their neighbors must be grouped with them in any event, you may be spared an unnecessary grouping of their neighbors.

Another common mistake is failing to recognize a large grouping of 1's, as Example 10.31 illustrates.

Example 10.31 (FIGURE 10.32(a)) shows the minimization of a three-variable function as

$$x(a, b, c) = \Sigma(0, 2, 4, 6, 7)$$
$$= b'c' + bc' + ab$$

which requires three two-input AND gates and one three-input OR gate. Figure 10.32(b) shows the correct minimization as

$$x(a, b, c) = c' + ab$$

which requires only one two-input AND gate and a two-input OR gate. ∎

In a three-variable problem, a grouping of four 1's corresponds to an AND term of only one variable. Because the number of 1's in a group must correspond to an intersection of regions for a, b, and c and their complements, the number of 1's in a group must be a power of 2. For example, an oval can cover one, two, or four 1's but never three or five.

Four-Variable Karnaugh Maps

Minimization of a four-variable circuit follows the same procedure as a three-variable circuit, except that the Karnaugh map has twice as many entries. (FIGURE 10.33(a)) shows the arrangement of cells. Not only is minterm 0 adjacent to 2, and 4 adjacent to 6, but minterm 12 is adjacent to 14, and 8 to

FIGURE 10.33

The Karnaugh map for a function of four variables.

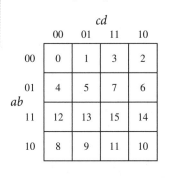

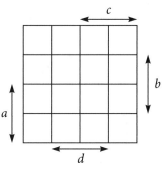

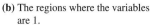

(a) Decimal labels for the minterms in the Karnaugh map.

(b) The regions where the variables are 1.

FIGURE 10.34

Minimizing a function of four variables.

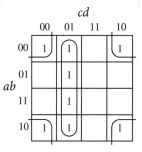

10. Also, cells on the top row are adjacent to the corresponding cells on the bottom row. Minterm 0 is adjacent to 8, 1 to 9, 3 to 11, and 2 to 10.

Each cell in a three-variable Karnaugh map has three adjacent cells. In a four-variable map, each cell has four adjacent cells. For example, the cells adjacent to minterm 10 are 2, 8, 11, and 14. Those adjacent to 4 are 0, 5, 6, and 12.

Figure 10.33(b) shows the regions of the truth table where the variables are 1. Variable a is 1 in the two bottom rows, and b is 1 in the two middle rows. Variable c is 1 in the two right columns, and d is 1 in the two middle columns.

Example 10.32 FIGURE 10.34 shows the minimization

$$x(a, b, c, d) = \Sigma(0, 1, 2, 5, 8, 9, 10, 13)$$
$$= c'd + b'd'$$

Note that the four corner cells can be grouped as $b'd'$. The second column of the Karnaugh map represents $c'd$. ∎

Example 10.33 FIGURE 10.35 shows the minimization

$$x(a, b, c, d) = \Sigma(0, 1, 2, 5, 8, 9, 10)$$
$$= a'c'd + b'c' + b'd'$$

Even though it differs from Example 10.32 by the omission of a single term, the minimization is much different.

Minterm 5 has only one adjacent 1, so it is grouped first by our rule of thumb with minterm 1. The AND term for this group is $a'c'd$, which you

FIGURE 10.35

The expression of Figure 10.34 with one minterm fewer.

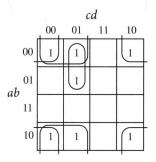

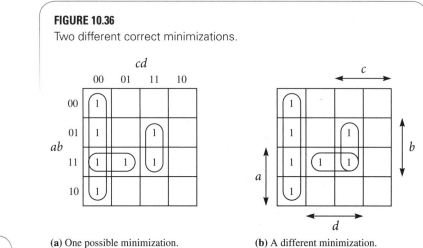

FIGURE 10.36
Two different correct minimizations.

(a) One possible minimization.　　　(b) A different minimization.

FIGURE 10.37
A complicated
minimization problem.

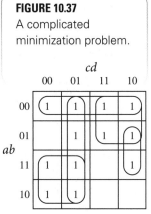

(a) A plausible but incorrect
minimization.

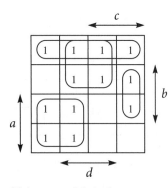

(b) A correct minimization.

can determine by visualizing the intersection of the top two rows (a'), the left two columns (c'), and the middle two columns (d).

Covering minterm 9 with the largest oval requires you to group it with minterms 0, 1, and 8, not just 8. The AND term for this group is $b'c'$, which you can determine by visualizing the intersection of the top and bottom rows (b') with the left two columns (c').

The remaining uncovered 1's are minterms 2 and 10, which are grouped with 0 and 8 as before.

Example 10.34　**FIGURE 10.36** shows that the minimization may not be unique. Two valid minimizations of this function are

$$x(a, b, c, d) = \Sigma(0, 4, 7, 8, 12, 13, 15)$$
$$= c'd' + bcd + abc'$$
$$= c'd' + bcd + abd$$

The first 1 you should group is minterm 7, because it has only one adjacent 1. Minterm 0 must be grouped with 4, 8, and 12, because there is no other possible group for it. That leaves minterm 13, which can be grouped with either 12 or 15.

Minimizing a four-variable function is not always straightforward. Sometimes you must simply experiment with several groupings in order to determine the true minimum.

Example 10.35　**FIGURE 10.37** shows such a problem. The function is

$$\Sigma(0, 1, 2, 3, 5, 6, 7, 8, 9, 12, 13, 14)$$

Figure 10.37(a) is the result of the following reasoning. Consider minterm 12. The largest group it belongs to is the group of four corresponding to ac'. Similarly, the largest group minterm 6 belongs to is the group of four, $a'c$. Given these two groupings, you can group minterm 5 in $c'd$, minterm 0 in $a'b'$, and minterm 14 in bcd'. The expression

$$ac' + a'c + c'd + a'b' + bcd'$$

is plausible because none of the groupings looks redundant. You cannot remove any oval without uncovering a 1.

Given the selection of the first two groups, the remaining three groups are the best choices possible. The problem is in the selection of the second group.

Figure 10.37(b) is the result of the following reasoning. Group minterm 12 with ac' as before. Now consider minterm 14. You must group it with either 12 or 6. Because 12 is covered, group 14 with 6. Group the remaining minterms—0, 1, 2, 3, 5, 7—most efficiently, as in Figure 10.37(b). The resulting expression,

$$ac' + a'd + a'b' + bcd'$$

requires one fewer AND gate than Figure 10.37(a).

This is a tricky problem because in general you should cover a 1 with the largest possible group. That general rule does not apply in this problem, however. Once you determine the group ac', you should not place minterm 6 in the largest possible group.

FIGURE 10.38 shows that this solution is not unique. It begins by grouping minterm 6 in $a'c$, then minterm 14 with 12. The result is

$$a'c + b'c' + c'd + abd' \qquad \blacksquare$$

How do you know which minterms and groupings to consider when confronted with a complicated Karnaugh map? It simply takes practice, reasoning, and a little experimentation.

Dual Karnaugh Maps

To minimize a function in an OR-AND expression, minimize the complement of the function in the AND-OR expression, and use De Morgan's law.

Example 10.36 FIGURE 10.39 shows the minimization of the complement of the function in Figure 10.29. The original function is

$$x(a, b, c) = \Sigma(3, 6, 7)$$
$$= \Pi(0, 1, 2, 4, 5)$$

FIGURE 10.38
Another correct minimization of the function of Figure 10.37.

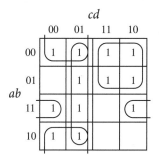

FIGURE 10.39
The complement of the function in Figure 10.29.

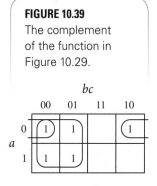

Its complement, minimized as shown in the figure, is

$$x'(a, b, c) = \Sigma(0, 1, 2, 4, 5)$$
$$= b' + a'c'$$

The original function in the minimized OR-AND expression is

$$x(a, b, c) = (x'(a, b, c))'$$
$$= (b' + a'c')'$$
$$= b(a + c)$$

which requires only two gates, compared to three with the minimized AND-OR expression,

$$x(a, b, c) = bc + ab$$

In the previous example, it pays to implement the function with a two-level NOR-NOR circuit instead of a NAND-NAND circuit. In general, you must minimize both forms to determine which requires fewer gates.

Don't-Care Conditions

Sometimes a combinational circuit is designed to process only some of the input combinations. The other combinations are not ever expected to be present in the input. These combinations are called *don't-care conditions* because you do not care what the output is if those conditions would ever appear.

Don't-care conditions give you extra flexibility in the minimization process. You can arbitrarily design the circuit to produce either 0 or 1 when a don't-care condition is present. By selectively choosing some don't-care conditions to produce 1 and others to produce 0, you can improve the minimization.

Example 10.37   **FIGURE 10.40(a)** shows minimization of

$$x(a, b, c) = \Sigma(2, 4, 6)$$
$$= bc' + ac'$$

without don't-care conditions. Now suppose that instead of requiring minterms 0 and 7 to produce 0, the problem specifies that those minterms can produce either 0 or 1. The notation for this specification is

$$x(a, b, c) = \Sigma(2, 4, 6) + d(0, 7)$$

where d preceding the minterm labels stands for a don't-care condition. Figure 10.40(b) shows × in the Karnaugh map cells for don't-care conditions.

When you minimize with don't-care conditions, you are free to cover or not cover a cell with an ×. An × acts like a wildcard in that you can treat it as

FIGURE 10.40
Don't-care conditions.

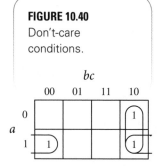

(a) Minimizing a function without don't-care conditions.

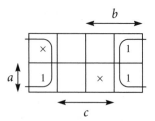

(b) Minimizing the same function with don't-care conditions.

a 0 or a 1 as you like. In this problem, if you treat minterm 0 as a 1, and 7 as a 0, the minimization is

$$x(a, b, c) = \Sigma(2, 4, 6) + d(0, 7)$$
$$= \Sigma(0, 2, 4, 6)$$
$$= c'$$

The function without don't-care conditions requires two AND gates and one OR gate, whereas this function requires no AND or OR gates. ∎

10.4 Combinational Devices

This section describes some combinational devices that are commonly used in computer design. Each device can be specified as a black box with a corresponding truth table to define how the outputs depend on the inputs. Because all devices in this section are combinational, they can be implemented with two-level AND-OR circuits. Some implementations shown here trade off processing time for less space—that is, fewer gates—and have more than two levels.

Viewpoints

Several of the following devices have an input line called *enable*. The enable line acts like the on/off switch of an appliance. If the enable line is 0, the output lines are all 0's regardless of the values of the input lines. The device is turned off, or disabled. If the enable line is 1, the output lines depend on the input lines according to the function that specifies the device. The device is turned on, or enabled.

An AND gate can implement the enable property as shown in FIGURE 10.41(a). Suppose line *a* is one of the outputs from a combinational circuit (not shown in the figure) and the circuit needs an enable line that acts like a switch to turn it on or off. You can feed line *a* into the AND gate and use the other input to the AND gate as the enable line.

When the enable line is 1,

$$x = a \cdot (\text{enable})$$
$$= a \cdot 1$$
$$= a$$

and the output equals the input, as in Figure 10.41(b). When the enable line is 0,

$$x = a \cdot (\text{enable})$$
$$= a \cdot 0$$
$$= 0$$

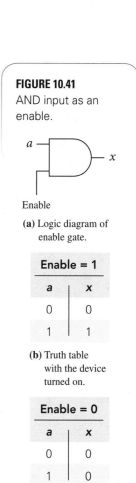

FIGURE 10.41
AND input as an enable.

(a) Logic diagram of enable gate.

Enable = 1

a	x
0	0
1	1

(b) Truth table with the device turned on.

Enable = 0

a	x
0	0
1	0

(c) Truth table with the device turned off.

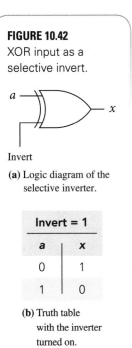

(a) Logic diagram of the
selective inverter.

Invert = 1	
a	**x**
0	1
1	0

(b) Truth table
with the inverter
turned on.

Invert = 0	
a	**x**
0	0
1	1

(c) Truth table
with the inverter
turned off.

regardless of the input as in Figure 10.41(c).

Implementing the enable property does not require a new "enable gate." It requires only that you adopt a different viewpoint of the familiar AND gate. You can think of input a as a data line and enable as a control line. The enable controls the data by either letting it pass through the gate unchanged or preventing it from passing.

Another useful gate is the *selective inverter*. For input, it has a data line and an invert line. If the invert line is 1, the output is the complement of the data line. If the invert line is 0, the data passes through to the output unchanged.

FIGURE 10.42(a) shows that the selective inverter is an XOR gate considered with a different viewpoint than it was previously. When the invert line is 1,

$$x = a \oplus (\text{invert})$$
$$= a' \cdot (\text{invert}) + a \cdot (\text{invert})'$$
$$= a' \cdot 1 + a \cdot 1'$$
$$= a'$$

and the output equals the complement of the data input, as in Figure 10.42(b). When the invert line is 0,

$$x = a \oplus (\text{invert})$$
$$= a' \cdot (\text{invert}) + a \cdot (\text{invert})'$$
$$= a' \cdot 0 + a \cdot 0'$$
$$= a$$

and the data passes through the gate unchanged.

Multiplexer

A *multiplexer* is a device that selects one of several data inputs to be routed to a single data output. Control lines determine the particular data input to be passed through.

FIGURE 10.43(a) shows the block diagram of an eight-input multiplexer. D0 to D7 are the data input lines, and S2, S1, S0 are the select control lines. F is the single data output line.

Because this device has 11 inputs, a complete truth table would require $2^{11} = 2048$ entries. Figure 10.43(b) shows an abbreviated truth table. The second entry shows that the output is D1 when the select lines are 001. That is, if D1 is 1, F is 1, and if D1 is 0, F is 0, regardless of the other values of D0 and D2 through D7.

Because n select lines can select one of 2^n data lines, the number of data inputs of a multiplexer is a power of 2. FIGURE 10.44 shows the implementation of a four-input multiplexer, which contains four data lines, D0 through D3, and two select lines, S1 and S0.

An example of where a multiplexer might be used is in the implementation of the STWr instruction in Pep/9. This instruction puts the contents of one of two registers from the CPU into memory via the bus. The CPU could do that with a two-input multiplexer that would make the selection. The select line would come from the register-r field, the inputs would come from the A and X registers, and the output would go to the bus.

Binary Decoder

A *decoder* is a device that takes a binary number as input and sets one of several data output lines to 1 and the rest to 0. The data line that is set to 1 depends on the value of the binary number that is input.

FIGURE 10.45(a) shows the block diagram of a 2 × 4 binary decoder. S1 S0 is the two-bit binary number input and D0 through D3 are the four outputs, one of which will be 1. Part (b) is the truth table.

FIGURE 10.43
The eight-input multiplexer.

D0
D1
D2
D3
D4 → F
D5
D6
D7

S2 S1 S0

(a) Block diagram.

S2	S1	S0	F
0	0	0	D0
0	0	1	D1
0	1	0	D2
0	1	1	D3
1	0	0	D4
1	0	1	D5
1	1	0	D6
1	1	1	D7

(b) Truth table.

FIGURE 10.44
Implementation of a four-input multiplexer.

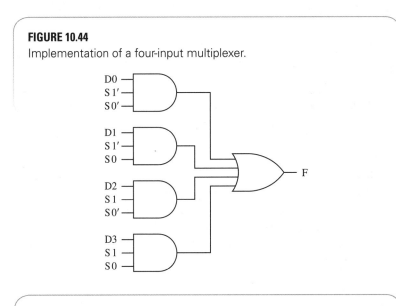

FIGURE 10.45
The 2 × 4 binary decoder.

S1	S0	D0	D1	D2	D3
0	0	1	0	0	0
0	1	0	1	0	0
1	0	0	0	1	0
1	1	0	0	0	1

S1 →   → D0
            → D1
S0 →   → D2
            → D3

(a) Block diagram.   (b) Truth table.

FIGURE 10.46
Implementation of a 2 × 4 binary decoder.

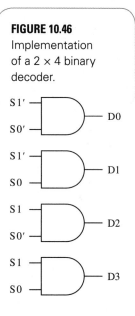

FIGURE 10.47
A 2 × 4 binary decoder with enable.

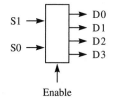

Enable

Because an *n*-bit number can have 2^n values, the number of data outputs of a decoder is a power of 2. **FIGURE 10.46** shows the implementation of a 2 × 4 decoder. Some other possible sizes are 3 × 8 and 4 × 16.

Some decoders are designed with an enable input. **FIGURE 10.47** is a block diagram of a 2 × 4 decoder with enable. When the enable line is 1, the device operates normally, as in Figure 10.45(b). When the enable line is 0, all the outputs are 0. To implement a decoder with enable requires an extra input for each AND gate. The details are an exercise at the end of the chapter.

An example of where a decoder might be used is in the CPU of Pep/9. Some instructions have a three-bit addressing-aaa field that specifies one of eight addressing modes. The hardware would have eight address computation units, one for each mode, and each unit would have an enable line. The three aaa address lines would feed into a 3 × 8 decoder. Each output line from the decoder would enable one of the address computation units.

Demultiplexer

A multiplexer routes one of several data input values to a single output line. A *demultiplexer* does just the opposite. It routes a single input value to one of several output lines.

FIGURE 10.48(a) is the block diagram of a four-output demultiplexer. Part (b) is the truth table. If S1 S0 is 01, all the output lines are 0 except D1, which has the same value as the data input line.

This truth table is similar to Figure 10.45(b), the truth table for a decoder. In fact, a demultiplexer is nothing more than a decoder with enable. The data input line, D, is connected to the enable. If D is 0, the decoder is disabled, and the data output line selected by S1 S0 is 0. If D is 1, the decoder is enabled, and the data output line selected is 1. In either case, the selected output line has the same value as the data input line. This is another example of considering a combinational device from a different viewpoint to obtain a useful operation.

FIGURE 10.48
The four-output demultiplexer.

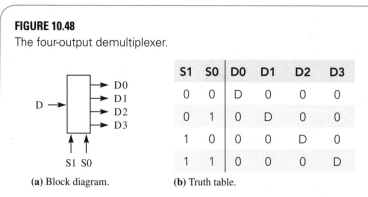

S1	S0	D0	D1	D2	D3
0	0	D	0	0	0
0	1	0	D	0	0
1	0	0	0	D	0
1	1	0	0	0	D

(a) Block diagram.   (b) Truth table.

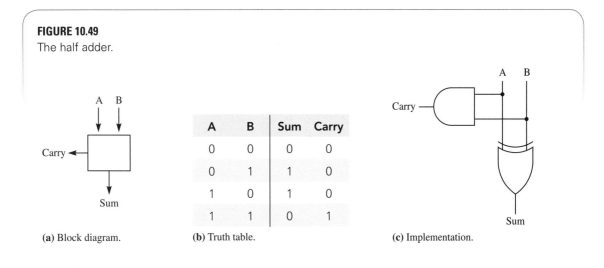

FIGURE 10.49
The half adder.

A   B

Carry

Sum

(a) Block diagram.

A	B	Sum	Carry
0	0	0	0
0	1	1	0
1	0	1	0
1	1	0	1

(b) Truth table.

A   B

Carry

Sum

(c) Implementation.

Adder

Consider the binary addition

$$
\begin{array}{ll}
 & 1011 \\
\text{ADD} & 0011 \\
\hline
C = 0 & 1110 \\
V = 0 &
\end{array}
$$

The sum of the least significant bits (LSBs) is 1 plus 1, which is 0 with a carry of 1 to the next column. To add the LSBs of two numbers requires the *half adder* of FIGURE 10.49(a). In the figure, A represents the LSB of the first number, and B the LSB of the second number. One output is Sum, 0 in this example, and the other is Carry, 1 in this example. Part (b) shows the truth table. The sum is identical to the XOR function, and the carry is identical to the AND function. Part (c) is a straightforward implementation.

To find the sum in the column next to the LSB requires a combinational circuit with three inputs: Cin, A, and B. Cin is the carry input, which comes from the carry of the LSB, and A and B are the bits from the first and second numbers. The outputs are Sum and Cout, the carry output that goes to Cin of the full adder for the next column. FIGURE 10.50(a) is the block diagram of the network, called a *full adder*. Figure 10.50(b) is the truth table. If the sum of the three inputs is odd, Sum is 1. If the sum of the three inputs is greater than 1, Cout is 1.

FIGURE 10.51 shows an implementation of the full adder that uses two half adders and an OR gate. The first half adder adds A and B. The second half adder adds the sum from the first half adder to Cin. The full adder sum

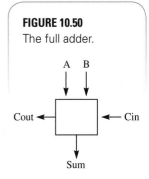

FIGURE 10.50
The full adder.

A   B

Cout   Cin

Sum

(a) Block diagram.

A	B	Cin	Sum	Cout
0	0	0	0	0
0	0	1	1	0
0	1	0	1	0
0	1	1	0	1
1	0	0	1	0
1	0	1	0	1
1	1	0	0	1
1	1	1	1	1

(b) Truth table.

FIGURE 10.51

An implementation of the full adder with two half adders.

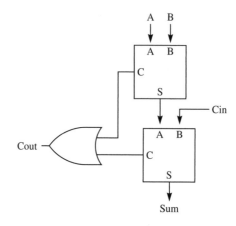

is the sum from the second half adder. If either the first or second half adder has a carry, the full adder has a carry out.

To add the two four-bit numbers requires an eight-input circuit, shown in FIGURE 10.52(a). A3 A2 A1 A0 are the four bits of the first number, with A0 the LSB. B3 through B0 are the same for the second number. S3 S2 S1 S0 is the four-bit sum, with Cout the carry bit. An implementation of the four-bit adder can use one half adder for the LSB and three full adders, one for each of the remaining columns in the addition. That implementation is called a *ripple-carry adder* because a carry that originates from the LSB must propagate, or ripple through, the columns to the left. Figure 10.52(b) shows the implementation.

The carry out of the ripple-carry adder is the Cout of its leftmost full adder. The carry bit indicates an overflow condition when you interpret the integer as unsigned. When you interpret the integer as signed using two's complement representation, the leftmost bit is the sign bit, and the bit next to it is the most significant bit of the magnitude. So with signed integers, the Cout signal of the penultimate full adder, S2 in this example, acts like the carry out.

The V bit indicates whether an overflow occurs when the numbers are interpreted as signed. You can get an overflow in only one of two cases:

The two cases for an overflow with signed integers

> A and B are both positive, and the result is negative.

> A and B are both negative, and the result is positive.

You cannot get an overflow by adding two integers with different signs. In the first case, A3 and B3 are both 0; there must be a carry from the penultimate full adder that makes S3 1, and Cout from the leftmost full adder is 0. In the second case, A3 and B3 are both 1, so there must be a

FIGURE 10.52
The four-bit ripple-carry adder.

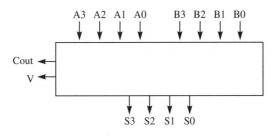

A3 A2 A1 A0   B3 B2 B1 B0

Cout

V

S3 S2 S1 S0

(a) Block diagram.

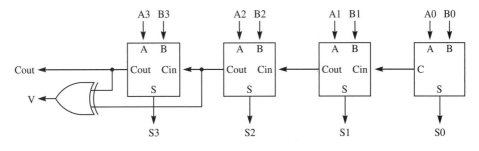

A3 B3   A2 B2   A1 B1   A0 B0

| A   B | | A   B | | A   B | | A   B |

Cout

Cout Cin   Cout Cin   Cout Cin   C

V

S   S   S   S

S3   S2   S1   S0

(b) Implementation.

carry out from the leftmost full adder, and there cannot be a carry out from the penultimate full adder, because S3 must be 0. In both of these cases, the carry out of the leftmost full adder is different from the carry out of the penultimate full adder. But that is precisely the XOR function. It is 1 if and only if its two inputs are different. So, the V bit is computed with the XOR gate taking its two inputs from the Cout signals of the leftmost and penultimate full adders.

The primary disadvantage of the ripple-carry adder is the time it takes the carry to ripple through all the full adders before a valid result is present in the output. Adder circuits have been extensively studied, because addition is such a basic mathematical operation. The carry-lookahead adder overcomes much of the speed disadvantage of the ripple-carry adder by incorporating a carry-lookahead unit in its design. More sophisticated adders are beyond the scope of this text.

Adder/Subtracter

To subtract B from A you could design a subtracter circuit along the same lines as the adder, but with a borrow mechanism that corresponds to the carry mechanism in addition. Rather than build a separate subtracter circuit, however, it is easier to simply negate B and add it to A. Recall the two's complement rule from Chapter 3:

$$\text{NEG } x = 1 + \text{NOT } x$$

To negate a number, you invert all the bits of the number and then add 1. So, to build a circuit that will function as an adder or a subtracter, we need a way to selectively invert all the bits in B and a way to selectively add 1 to it. Fortunately, the XOR gate comes to the rescue, because you can consider the XOR gate to be a selective inverter.

FIGURE 10.53 shows an adder/subtracter circuit based on this idea. Part (a) is a block diagram that differs from the block diagram of the ripple-carry

FIGURE 10.53
The four-bit ripple-carry adder/subtracter.

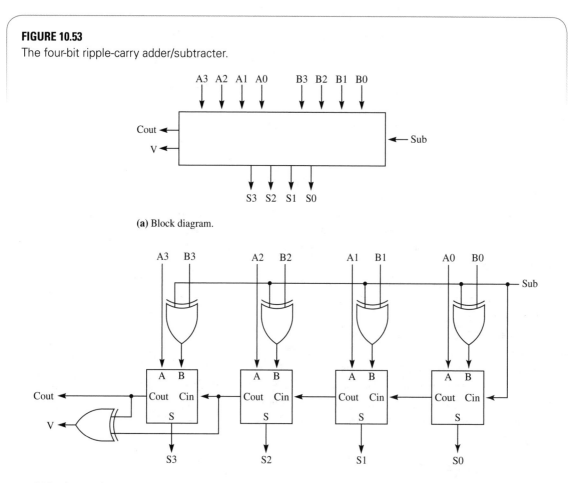

(a) Block diagram.

(b) Implementation.

adder only by the addition of a single control line labeled *Sub*. When Sub = 0, the circuit acts like an adder. When Sub = 1, the circuit acts like a subtracter.

Figure 10.53(b) is the implementation. With the adder circuit, you only need a half adder for the LSB. The adder/subtracter replaces it with a full adder. Consider the situation when Sub = 0. In that case, Cin of the least significant full adder is 0 and it acts like a half adder. Furthermore, the left input of each of the top four XOR gates is also 0, which allows the B signals to pass through them unchanged. The circuit computes the sum of A and B.

Now consider the case when Sub = 1. Because the left input of the top four XOR gates is 1, the values of all the bits in B are inverted. Furthermore, Cin of the least significant full adder is 1, adding 1 to the result. Consequently, the sum is the sum of A and the negation of B.

Arithmetic Logic Unit

The Pep/9 instructions that perform processing include ADDr, ANDr, and ORr. The addition is an arithmetic operation, whereas AND and OR are logical operations. The CPU typically contains a single combinational circuit called the *arithmetic logic unit (ALU)* that performs these computations.

FIGURE 10.54 shows the ALU for the Pep/9 CPU. A line with a slash represents more than one control line, with the number by the slash specifying the number of lines. The line labeled *ALU* represents four wires. The ALU has a total of 21 input lines—8 lines for the A input, 8 lines for the B input, 4 lines to specify the function that the ALU performs, and the Cin line. It has 12 output lines—8 lines for Result, plus the 4 NZVC values corresponding to Result. The carry output line is labeled *Cout* to distinguish

FIGURE 10.54
Block diagram of the Pep/9 ALU.

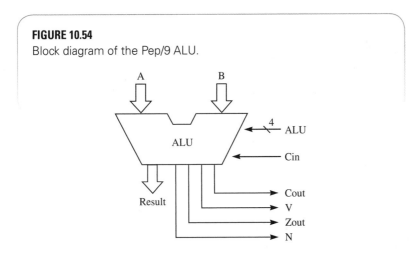

it from the carry input line Cin. The zero output line is labeled *Zout* to distinguish it from another Z line in the CPU, as described in Chapter 12.

The four ALU control lines specify which of 16 functions the ALU will perform. (FIGURE 10.55) lists the 16 functions, most of which correspond directly to the operations available in the Pep/9 instruction set. Because the + symbol is commonly used for the logical OR operation, the arithmetic addition operation is spelled out as "plus." Listed with each operation are the values of the corresponding NZVC bits. The overbar notation is another notation for negation. For example, the notation $\overline{A \cdot B}$ for the NAND function is the same as $(A \cdot B)'$.

(FIGURE 10.56) shows the implementation of the ALU. You can see the 21 input lines coming in from the top and the right, and the 12 output lines coming out from the bottom. The four ALU lines that come in from the right drive a 4 × 16 decoder. Recall that depending on the value of the ALU input, exactly one of the output lines of the decoder will be 1 and the others will all

FIGURE 10.55
The 16 functions of the Pep/9 ALU.

ALU Control			Status Bits			
(bin)	(dec)	Result	N	Zout	V	Cout
0000	0	A	N	Z	0	0
0001	1	A plus B	N	Z	V	C
0010	2	A plus B plus Cin	N	Z	V	C
0011	3	A plus $\overline{B}$ plus 1	N	Z	V	C
0100	4	A plus $\overline{B}$ plus Cin	N	Z	V	C
0101	5	$A \cdot B$	N	Z	0	0
0110	6	$\overline{A \cdot B}$	N	Z	0	0
0111	7	$A + B$	N	Z	0	0
1000	8	$\overline{A + B}$	N	Z	0	0
1001	9	$A \oplus B$	N	Z	0	0
1010	10	$\overline{A}$	N	Z	0	0
1011	11	ASL A	N	Z	V	C
1100	12	ROL A	N	Z	V	C
1101	13	ASR A	N	Z	0	C
1110	14	ROR A	N	Z	0	C
1111	15	0	A<4>	A<5>	A<6>	A<7>

FIGURE 10.56
Implementation of the ALU of Figure 10.54.

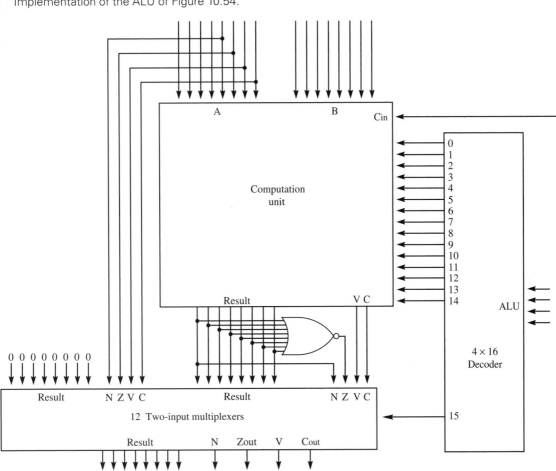

be 0. The computation unit inside the ALU performs the first 15 functions of Figure 10.55. Each of the 15 lines from the decoder into the computation unit enables a combinational circuit that performs the function.

The computation unit has 32 input lines—8 lines for the A input, 8 lines for the B input, 1 line for Cin, and 15 lines from the decoder. It has 10 output lines—8 lines for the result of the computation plus 1 line each for V and C. Computation of the N and Z bits is external to the computation unit. Figure 10.56 shows that the N bit is simply a copy of the most significant bit of Result from the computation unit. The Z bit is the NOR of all eight bits of Result. If all eight bits are 0, the output of the NOR gate is 1. If one or more inputs are 1, the output of the NOR gate is 0. These are precisely the

Computation of the N and Z bits

conditions for which the Z bit should be set, depending on the result of the computation.

The bottom box on the left is a set of 12 two-input multiplexers. The control line of each multiplexer is tied to line 15 from the decoder. The control line acts as follows:

The multiplexer of Figure 10.56

> If line 15 is 1, Result and NZVC from the left are routed to the output.

> If line 15 is 0, Result and NZVC from the right are routed to the output.

You can see how Figure 10.56 computes the last function of Figure 10.55. If the ALU input is 1111 (bin), then line 15 is 1, and Result and NZVC from the left are routed to the output of the ALU. But Figure 10.56 shows that Result from the left is tied to 0 and NZVC comes from the low nybble (half byte) of A, as required.

FIGURE 10.57 is an implementation of the computation unit of Figure 10.56. It consists of 1 A Unit, 1 arithmetic unit, and 10 logic units

FIGURE 10.57

Implementation of the computation unit of Figure 10.56.

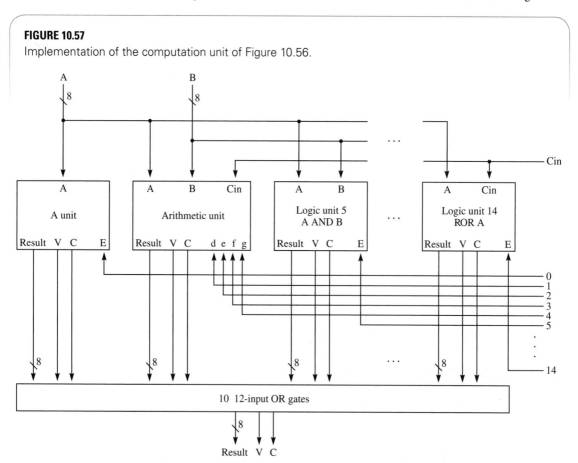

labeled *Logic unit 5* through *Logic unit 14*. The A unit and the logic units are each enabled by 1 of the 15 decoder lines. If the enable line E of any unit is 0, then all bits of Result as well as V and C are 0 regardless of any other input to the unit. The arithmetic unit is responsible for computing Result, V, and C for the arithmetic operations that correspond to functions 1, 2, 3, and 4 in Figure 10.55. The corresponding control lines for the arithmetic unit are labeled *d, e, f,* and *g,* respectively. If all four of d, e, f, and g are 0, then all bits of Result as well as V and C are 0, regardless of any other input to the arithmetic unit.

Each output line of a computation unit feeds into a 12-input OR gate. The other 11 inputs to the OR gate are the corresponding lines from the other 11 computation units. For example, the V outputs of all 12 computation units feed into one OR gate. Because 11 of the computation units are guaranteed to be disabled, exactly 11 inputs are guaranteed to be 0 for every OR gate. The one input that is not guaranteed to be 0 is the input from the unit that is enabled. Because 0 is the identity for the OR operation

$$p \text{ OR } 0 = p$$

the output from the unit that is enabled passes through the OR gate unchanged.

FIGURE 10.58 is an implementation of the A unit. It consists of eight two-input AND gates that act as enable gates for the eight bits of the A signal. Figure 10.55 specifies that V and C should be 0. Consequently, both output lines for V and C are tied to 0 in the implementation.

FIGURE 10.59 is an implementation of the arithmetic unit. It is an extension of the adder/subtracter circuit of Figure 10.53, modified to handle two additional cases for adding and subtracting 16-bit values with two 8-bit

FIGURE 10.58

Implementation of the A unit of Figure 10.57.

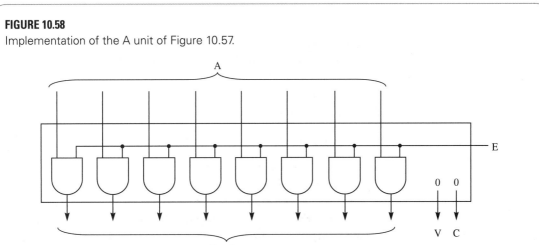

FIGURE 10.59

Implementation of the arithmetic unit of Figure 10.57.

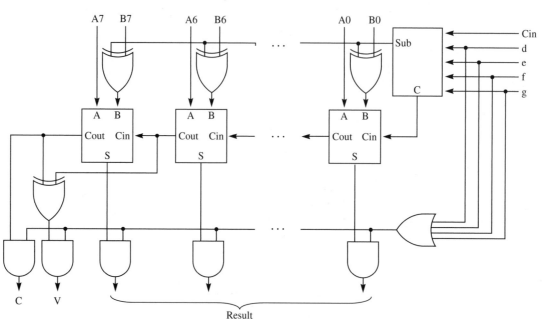

operations. FIGURE 10.60 shows how to do a 16-bit operation with two 8-bit operations. In Figure 10.60(a), you do a 16-bit add with

> A plus B

on the low-order bytes of A and B, followed by

> A plus B plus Cin

on the high-order bytes, where Cin is the Cout of the low-order operation. In Figure 10.60(b), you do a 16-bit subtraction with

> A plus $\overline{B}$ plus 1

on the low-order bytes of A and B, followed by

> A plus $\overline{B}$ plus Cin

on the high-order bytes, where Cin is again the Cout of the low-order operation. This last operation follows from the fact that subtracting B from A is performed in hardware by adding the two's complement of B to A. The carry out of the low-order operation is the carry out of an addition, not a subtraction. That is why the circuit adds Cin from the low-order operation instead of subtracting it.

FIGURE 10.60
Using two 8-bit operations to produce a 16-bit operation.

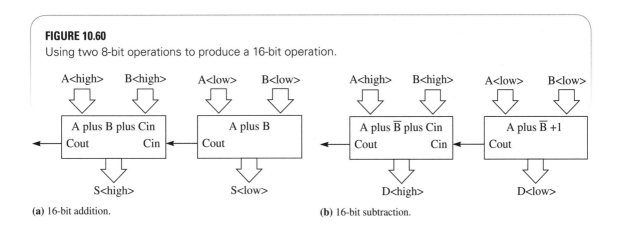

(a) 16-bit addition. (b) 16-bit subtraction.

Example 10.38 Here is how the hardware subtracts 259 from 261. As a 16-bit quantity, 259 (dec) = 0000 0001 0000 0011, so that A<high> = 0000 0001 and A<low> = 0000 0011. As a 16-bit quantity, 261 (dec) = 0000 0001 0000 0101, so that B<high> = 0000 0001 and B<low> = 0000 0101. The low-order addition is

```
              0000 0011
              1111 1010
ADD                   1
------------------------
C = 0         1111 1110
```

and the high-order addition is

```
              0000 0001
              1111 1110
ADD                   0
------------------------
C = 0         1111 1111
V = 0
```

The final difference is 1111 1111 1111 1110 (bin) = –2 (dec), as expected. The final V bit is computed from the exclusive OR of the final carry out with the penultimate carry out as follows:

$$0 \oplus 0 = 0$$ ∎

Example 10.39 Here is how the hardware subtracts 261 from 259. This time, A<high> = 0000 0001, A<low> = 0000 0101, B<high> = 0000 0001, and B<low> = 0000 0011. The low-order addition is

```
              0000 0101
              1111 1100
ADD                   1
------------------------
C = 1         0000 0010
```

and the high-order addition is

$$
\begin{array}{l}
\quad\quad 0000\ 0001 \\
\quad\quad 1111\ 1110 \\
\underline{\text{ADD}\quad\quad\quad\quad\ 1} \\
C = 1 \quad\quad 0000\ 0000 \\
V = 0
\end{array}
$$

The final difference is 0000 0000 0000 0010 (bin) = 2 (dec), as expected. The final V bit is computed from the exclusive OR of the final carry out with the penultimate carry out as follows:

$$1 \oplus 1 = 0 \quad\quad\quad\quad\quad\quad\quad\quad\quad\quad\quad\quad\quad ▮$$

The control circuit box on the top right part of Figure 10.59 controls the function of the circuit. (**FIGURE 10.61**) is its truth table. Compare the box with the Sub line that controls the adder/subtracter circuit in Figure 10.53. When Sub is 0 in the adder/subtracter, B is not inverted by the XOR gates, and the carry in of the low-order bit is 0. When Sub is 1, B is inverted, and the carry in of the low-order bit is 1. The first and third rows of Figure 10.61 duplicate these two functions. The second row of Figure 10.61 is for the high-order addition, and the last row is for the high-order subtraction.

Theoretically, the Sub and C outputs of the control box are functions of d, e, f, g, and Cin. Inspection of the truth table, however, shows that Sub can be expressed as

$$\text{Sub} = f + g$$

and C can be expressed as

$$C = (\text{Cin} + f) \cdot d'$$

with neither depending on e.

Another requirement of the arithmetic unit is that if d, e, f, and g are all 0, then all the outputs must be 0 regardless of the other inputs. The output

FIGURE 10.61
The truth table for the control circuit in Figure 10.59.

Function	d	e	f	g	Sub	C
A plus B	1	0	0	0	0	0
A plus B plus Cin	0	1	0	0	0	Cin
A plus $\overline{\text{B}}$ plus 1	0	0	1	0	1	1
A plus $\overline{\text{B}}$ plus Cin	0	0	0	1	1	Cin

of the four-input OR gate in Figure 10.59 acts as the enable signal, which allows all 10 outputs of the unit to pass through when one of d, e, f, or g is 1.

In the same way that a 16-bit addition can be composed of an 8-bit addition of the low-order bytes followed by an 8-bit addition of the high-order bytes, the shift and rotate operations can be composed of two 8-bit operations. FIGURE 10.62 shows the specification of the shift and rotate operations for the Pep/9 ALU of Figure 10.55. Although it is not shown in Figure 10.62, the V bit is set by both the ROL (rotate left) and ASL (arithmetic shift left) operations.

Figures 10.62(a) and (b) show that a 16-bit arithmetic shift right is composed first of an 8-bit arithmetic shift right of the high-order byte. That shift duplicates the sign bit and shifts its low-order bit into Cout. Following that operation, a rotate right of the low-order byte takes the Cout from the high-order shift as its Cin and rotates its low-order bit into Cout.

Figures 10.62(c) and (d) show that a 16-bit arithmetic shift left starts with an arithmetic shift left of the low-order byte in part (d). Cout gets the most significant bit, which is used as Cin for the subsequent rotate left of the high-order byte in part (c). The second step shows why the ALU sets the V bit on the ROL operation. Figure 5.2 shows that the ROLr instruction at Level Asmb5 does not affect the V bit. However, at this lower level of

FIGURE 10.62

Specification of the shift and rotate operations.

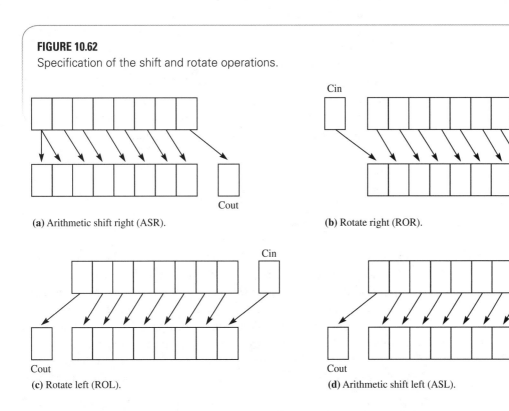

(a) Arithmetic shift right (ASR).   (b) Rotate right (ROR).

(c) Rotate left (ROL).   (d) Arithmetic shift left (ASL).

abstraction, LG1, the ALU sets the V bit because the ROL function at this level is used to implement the ASLr instruction at the higher level.

Implementation of logic units 5 through 14 is left as an exercise for the student. They are straightforward to implement, because the logic operations are available as common logic gates.

Abstraction at Level LG1

Abstract data types (ADTs) are an important design tool at Level HOL6. The idea is that you should understand the behavior of an ADT by knowing what the functions and procedures that operate on the ADT do, not necessarily how they do it. Once an operation has been implemented, you can free your mind of the implementation details and concentrate on solving the problem at a higher level of abstraction.

The same principle operates at the hardware level. Each combinational device in this section has a block diagram and a truth table that describes its function. The block diagram is to hardware what an ADT is to software. It is an abstraction that specifies the input and output while hiding the implementation details.

The block diagram as an ADT

Higher levels of abstraction in the hardware are obtained by constructing devices defined by block diagrams whose implementation is an interconnection of blocks at a lower level of abstraction. Figure 10.50 is a perfect example. This full adder block is implemented with the half adder blocks in Figure 10.51.

The highest level of abstraction for the hardware is the block diagram of the Pep/9 computer we have seen repeatedly. The three blocks—disk, CPU, and main memory with memory-mapped I/O devices—are connected by the bus. At a slightly lower level of abstraction, you see the registers in the CPU. Each register is depicted as a block. The remaining two chapters build up successively higher levels of abstraction, culminating with the Pep/9 computer at Level ISA3.

Chapter Summary

In a combinational circuit, the input determines the output. Three representations of a combinational circuit are truth tables, Boolean algebraic expressions, and logic diagrams. Of the three representations, truth tables are at the highest level of abstraction. They specify the function of a circuit without specifying its implementation. A truth table lists the output for all possible combinations of the input, hence the name *combinational circuit*.

The three basic operations of Boolean algebra are AND, OR, and NOT. The 10 fundamental properties of Boolean algebra consist of 5

laws—commutative, associative, distributive, identity, and complement—
and their duals, from which useful Boolean theorems may be proved. An
important theorem is De Morgan's law, which shows how to take the NOT
of the AND or OR of several terms.

A Boolean expression corresponds to a logic diagram, which in turn
corresponds to a connection of electronic gates. Three common gates are
NAND (AND followed by NOT), NOR (OR followed by NOT), and XOR
(exclusive OR). Two-level circuits minimize processing time, but may
require more gates than an equivalent multilevel circuit. This is another
manifestation of the fundamental space/time tradeoff. Karnaugh maps
help minimize the number of gates needed to implement a two-level
combinational circuit.

Combinational devices include the multiplexer, the decoder, the demultiplexer, the adder, and the arithmetic logic unit (ALU). A multiplexer selects
one of several data inputs to be routed to a single data output. A decoder
takes a binary number as input and sets one of several data output lines to 1
and the rest to 0. A demultiplexer routes one of several data input values to a
single output line and is logically equivalent to a decoder with an enable line.
A half adder adds two bits, and a full adder adds three bits, one of which is
the previous carry. A subtracter works by negating the second operand and
adding it to the first. An ALU performs both arithmetic and logic functions.

Exercises

Section 10.1

1. *(a) Prove the zero theorem $x + 1 = 1$ with Boolean algebra. Give a
   reason for each step in your proof. Hint: Expand the 1 on the left
   with the complement property and then use the idempotent property.
   (b) Show the dual proof of part (a).

2. (a) Prove with Boolean algebra the absorption property, $x + x \cdot y = x$.
   Give a reason for each step in your proof. (b) Show the dual proof of
   part (a).

3. (a) Prove with Boolean algebra the consensus theorem $x \cdot y + x' \cdot z +
   y \cdot z = x \cdot y + x' \cdot z$. Give a reason for each step in your proof. (b) Show
   the dual proof of part (a).

*4. Prove De Morgan's law, $(a + b)' = a' \cdot b'$, by giving the dual of the proof
   in the text. Give a reason for each step in your proof.

5. **(a)** Prove the general form of De Morgan's law,

$$(a_1 \cdot a_2 \cdot \cdots \cdot a_n)' = a_1' + a_2' + \cdots + a_n' \text{ where } n \geq 2$$

from De Morgan's law for two variables using mathematical induction. **(b)** Show the dual proof of part (a).

6. **(a)** Prove with Boolean algebra that $(x + y) \cdot (x' + y) = y$. Give a reason for each step in your proof. **(b)** Show the dual proof of part (a).

7. **(a)** Prove with Boolean algebra that $(x + y) + (y \cdot x') = x + y$. Give a reason for each step in your proof. **(b)** Show the dual proof of part (a).

8. *(a)** Draw a three-input OR gate, its Boolean expression, and its truth table, as in Figure 10.10. **(b)** Do part (a) for the three-input NAND gate. **(c)** Do part (a) for the three-input NOR gate.

9. For each of the following Boolean properties or theorems, state the set theory interpretation:

*(a)** $x + 0 = x$ **(b)** $x \cdot 1 = x$ **(c)** $x + x' = 1$ **(d)** $x \cdot x' = 0$
(e) $x \cdot x = x$ **(f)** $x + x = x$ **(g)** $x \cdot 0 = 0$

10.*(a)** Show the associative property for the OR operation using Venn diagrams with x, y, and z overlapping regions. Sketch the following regions to show that region (3) is the same as region (6):

(1) $(x + y)$ (2) z (3) $(x + y) + z$
(4) x (5) $(y + z)$ (6) $x + (y + z)$

(b) Do the dual of part (a).

11. **(a)** Show the distributive property using Venn diagrams with x, y, and z overlapping regions. Sketch the following regions to show that region (3) is the same as region (6):

(1) x (2) $y \cdot z$ (3) $x + y \cdot z$
(4) $(x + y)$ (5) $(x + z)$ (6) $(x + y) \cdot (x + z)$

(b) Do the dual of part (a).

12. **(a)** Show De Morgan's law using Venn diagrams with a and b overlapping regions. Sketch the following regions to show that region (2) is the same as region (5):

(1) $a \cdot b$ (2) $(a \cdot b)'$ (3) a' (4) b' (5) $a' + b'$

(b) Do the dual of part (a).

13. Although a Boolean variable for a combinational circuit can have only two values, 1 or 0, Boolean algebra can describe a system where a variable can have one of four possible values—0, 1, A, or B. Such a

system corresponds to the description of subsets of $\{a, b\}$ where $1 = \{a, b\}$ (the universal set), $A = \{a\}$, $B = \{b\}$, and $0 = \{\}$ (the empty set). The truth tables for two-input AND and OR operations have 16 entries instead of 4, and the truth table for the complement has 4 entries instead of 2. Construct the truth table for the following:

*(a) AND   (b) OR   (c) the complement

14. The exclusive NOR gate, written *XNOR*, is equivalent to an XOR followed by an inverter. *(a) Draw the symbol for a two-input XNOR gate. (b) Construct its truth table. (c) The XNOR is also called a *comparator*. Why?

Section 10.2

15. Draw the nonabbreviated logic diagram for the following Boolean expressions. You may use XOR gates.

*(a) $((a')')'$ (b) $(((a')')')'$
*(c) $a'b + ab'$ (d) $ab + a'b'$
(e) $ab + ab' + a'b$ (f) $((ab \oplus b')' + a'b)'$
(g) $(a'bc + a)b$ (h) $(ab'c)'(ac)'$
(i) $((ab)'(b'c)' + a'b'c')'$ (j) $(a \oplus b + b' \oplus c')'$
(k) $(abc)' + (a'b'c')'$ (l) $(a + b)(a' + c)(b' + c')$
(m) $(a \oplus b) \oplus c + ab'c$ (n) $(((a + b)' + c)' + d)'$
(o) $(ab' + b'c + cd)'$ (p) $((a + b')(b' + c)(c + d))'$
(q) $(((ab)'c)'d)'$ (r) $(((a \oplus b)' \oplus c)' \oplus d)'$

16. Draw the abbreviated logic diagram for the Boolean expressions of Exercise 15. You may use XOR gates.

17. Construct the truth tables for the Boolean expressions of Exercise 15.

18. Write the Boolean expressions for the logic diagrams of FIGURE 10.63 .

19. Write the Boolean AND-OR expression for the following:

*(a) function y in Figure 10.3
(b) function y in Figure 10.4
(c) function x in Figure 10.17
(d) the NAND gate in Figure 10.7(a)
(e) the XOR gate in Figure 10.7(c)

20. Write the Boolean OR-AND expression for the following:

*(a) function y in Figure 10.3
(b) function x in Figure 10.17
(c) the NOR gate in Figure 10.7(b)
(d) the XOR gate in Figure 10.7(c)

FIGURE 10.63

The logic diagrams for Exercise 18.

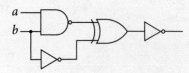

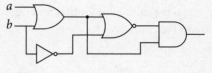

(a)   (b)

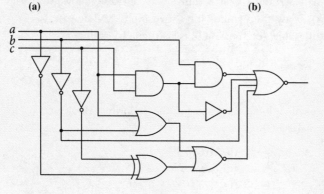

(c)

21. Use the properties and theorems of Boolean algebra to reduce the following expressions to AND-OR expressions without parentheses. The expressions may not be unique. Construct the truth table, which will be unique, by inspection of your final expression.

    *(a) $(a'b + ab')'$ (b) $(ab + a'b')'$

    (c) $(ab + ab' + a'b)'$ *(d) $(ab \oplus b')' + ab$

    (e) $(a'bc + a)b$ (f) $(ab'c)'(ac)'$

    (g) $(a \oplus b) \oplus c$ (h) $a \oplus (b \oplus c)$

    (i) $(a + b)(a' + c)(b' + c')$ (j) $((a + b)' + c)'$

*22. Construct two-level circuits for the expressions of Exercise 21 using only NAND gates.

23. Use the properties and theorems of Boolean algebra to reduce the following expressions to OR-AND expressions. The expressions may not be unique. Construct the truth table, which will be unique, by inspection of your final expression.

    (a) $a'b + ab'$ *(b) $ab + a'b$

    (c) $ab + ab' + a'b$ (d) $((ab \oplus b')' + ab)'$

    (e) $(a'bc + a)b$ (f) $(ab'c)'(ac)'$

    (g) $(a \oplus b) \oplus c$ (h) $a \oplus (b \oplus c)$

    (i) $((a + b)(a' + c)(b' + c'))'$ (j) $(a + b)' + c$

*24. Construct a two-level circuit for the expressions of Exercise 23 using only NOR gates.

25. Draw the logic diagram of a two-level circuit that produces the XOR function using the following:

    *(a) only NAND gates   **(b)** only NOR gates

26. State whether each gate in FIGURE 10.64 is the following:

    (1) an AND gate   (2) an OR gate
    (3) a NAND gate   (4) a NOR gate

Section 10.3

*27. Write each function of Exercise 21 with the sigma notation.

*28. Write each function of Exercise 23 with the pi notation.

29. In Figure 10.3, find the minimum AND-OR expression for the following:

    *(a) $x(a, b, c)$ **(b)** $y(a, b, c)$

Draw the minimized two-level circuit for each expression with only NAND gates.

30. In Figure 10.3, find the minimum OR-AND expression for the following:

    *(a) $x(a, b, c)$ **(b)** $y(a, b, c)$

Draw the minimized two-level circuit for each expression with only NOR gates.

31. Use a Karnaugh map to find the minimum AND-OR expression for $x(a, b, c)$:

    *(a) $\Sigma(0, 4, 5, 7)$ **(b)** $\Sigma(2, 3, 4, 6, 7)$ **(c)** $\Sigma(0, 3, 5, 6)$
    (d) $\Sigma(0, 1, 2, 3, 4, 6)$ **(e)** $\Sigma(1, 2, 3, 4, 5)$ **(f)** $\Sigma(1, 2, 3, 4, 5, 6, 7)$
    (g) $\Sigma(0, 1, 2, 4, 6)$ **(h)** $\Sigma(1, 4, 6, 7)$ **(i)** $\Sigma(2, 3, 4, 5, 6)$
    (j) $\Sigma(0, 2, 5)$

*32. Write each expression of Exercise 31 in pi notation. Use a Karnaugh map to find its minimum OR-AND expression.

33. Use a Karnaugh map to find the minimum AND-OR expression for $x(a, b, c, d)$:

    *(a) $\Sigma(2, 3, 4, 5, 10, 12, 13)$
    (b) $\Sigma(1, 5, 6, 7, 9, 12, 13, 15)$
    (c) $\Sigma(0, 1, 2, 4, 6, 8, 10)$
    (d) $\Sigma(7)$
    (e) $\Sigma(2, 4, 5, 11, 13, 15)$
    (f) $\Sigma(1, 2, 4, 5, 6, 7, 12, 15)$

FIGURE 10.64
The gates for Exercise 26.

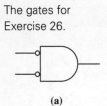

(a)

(b)

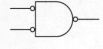

(c)

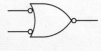

(d)

(g) $\Sigma(1, 2, 4, 5, 6, 7, 8, 11, 12, 15)$
(h) $\Sigma(1, 7, 10, 12)$
(i) $\Sigma(0, 2, 3, 4, 5, 6, 8, 10, 11, 13)$
(j) $\Sigma(0, 1, 2, 3, 4, 5, 6, 10, 11, 13, 14, 15)$
(k) $\Sigma(0, 1, 2, 3, 4, 5, 6, 7, 8, 9, 10, 11, 12, 13, 14)$

*34. Write each expression of Exercise 33 in pi notation. Use a Karnaugh map to find its minimum OR-AND expression.

35. Use a Karnaugh map to find the minimum AND-OR expression for $x(a, b, c)$ with don't-care conditions:

*(a) $\Sigma(0, 6) + d(1, 3, 7)$ **(b)** $\Sigma(5) + d(0, 2, 4, 6)$
(c) $\Sigma(1, 3) + d(0, 2, 4, 6)$ **(d)** $\Sigma(0, 5, 7) + d(3, 4)$
(e) $\Sigma(1, 7) + d(2, 4)$ **(f)** $\Sigma(4, 5, 6) + d(1, 2, 3, 7)$

36. Use a Karnaugh map to find the minimum AND-OR expression for $x(a, b, c, d)$ with don't-care conditions:

*(a) $\Sigma(5, 6) + d(2, 7, 9, 13, 14, 15)$
(b) $\Sigma(0, 3, 14) + d(2, 4, 7, 8, 10, 11, 13, 15)$
(c) $\Sigma(3, 4, 5, 10) + d(2, 11, 13, 15)$
(d) $\Sigma(5, 6, 12, 15) + d(0, 4, 10, 14)$
(e) $\Sigma(1, 6, 9, 12) + d(0, 2, 3, 4, 5, 7, 14, 15)$
(f) $\Sigma(0, 2, 3, 4) + d(8, 9, 10, 11, 13, 14, 15)$
(g) $\Sigma(2, 3, 10) + d(0, 4, 6, 7, 8, 9, 12, 14, 15)$

37. **(a)** A Karnaugh map for three variables has minterm 0 adjacent to 2, and 4 adjacent to 6. Copy Figure 10.30, cut out the Karnaugh map, and tape it in the shape of a cylinder so that adjacent minterms are physically adjacent. **(b)** For adjacent minterms to be physically adjacent in a four-variable Karnaugh map requires a three-dimensional *torus* (shaped like a doughnut). Construct a torus from clay or some other suitable material and inscribe or write on it the cells and their decimal labels of Figure 10.33(a). For example, the cell with 2 should be physically adjacent to the cells with 0, 3, 6, and 10.

Section 10.4

38. Using the viewpoint that one of the lines is a data line and the other is a control line, explain the operation of each of the following two-input gates:

*(a) OR   **(b)** NAND
(c) NOR   **(d)** XNOR

See Exercise 14 for the definition of XNOR.

39. Draw a nonabbreviated logic diagram of an eight-input multiplexer.

****40.** Construct a 16-input multiplexer from five 4-input multiplexers. Draw the 16-input multiplexer as a large block with 16 data lines labeled $D0$ through $D15$ and 4 select lines labeled $S3$ through $S0$. Inside the large block, draw each 4-input multiplexer as a small block with data lines D0 through D3 and select lines S1 and S0. Show the connections to the small blocks from the outside lines and the connections between the blocks to implement the big multiplexer. Explain the operation of your circuit.

41. Do Exercise 40 with two eight-input multiplexers without enable inputs and any other gates you need. Explain the operation of your circuit.

42. **(a)** Draw a nonabbreviated logic diagram of a 3×8 binary decoder. **(b)** Draw a nonabbreviated logic diagram of a 2×4 binary decoder with an enable input.

43. Construct a 4×16 binary decoder without an enable input from five 2×4 binary decoders with enable inputs. You may use the constant 1 as input to a device. Use the drawing guidelines of Exercise 40 to label your external and internal lines. Explain the operation of your circuit.

44. Construct a 4×16 binary decoder without an enable input from two 3×8 binary decoders with enable inputs plus any other gates you need. Use the drawing guidelines of Exercise 40 to label your external and internal lines. Explain the operation of your circuit.

45. Implement the 2×4 binary decoder with an enable input, as shown in Figure 10.47. Draw a nonabbreviated diagram of your circuit.

46. **(a)** Draw the implementation of the full adder in Figure 10.51 showing the AND and XOR gates of the half adders. **(b)** What is the maximum number of gate delays from input to output? **(c)** Design minimized two-level networks for Sum and Cout from the truth table of Figure 10.50(b). **(d)** Compute the percentage change in the number of gates and in the processing time for the design of part (c) compared to part (a). How do your results illustrate the space/time tradeoff?

47. (a) Draw the circuit of Figure 10.52 with the individual XOR, AND, and OR gates of the half adders. **(b)** What is the maximum number of gate delays from input to output? Consider an XOR gate as requiring one gate delay. This problem requires some thought. Assume that all eight inputs are presented at the same time, even though the carry will ripple through the circuit.

48. Modify Figure 10.52(b) to provide two additional outputs, one for the N bit and one for the Z bit.

49. Implement a four-bit ASL shifter with select line S. The input is A3 A2 A1 A0, which represents a four-bit number with A0 the LSB and A3 the sign bit. The output is B3 B2 B1 B0 and C, the carry bit. If S is 1, the output is the ASL of the input. If S is 0, the output is the same as the input, and C is 0.

50. Do Exercise 49 for a four-bit ASR shifter.

51. The block diagram in FIGURE 10.65 is a three-input, two-output combinational switching circuit. If s is 0, the input a is routed directly through to x, and b is routed to y. If s is 1, they are switched, with a being routed to y and b to x. Construct the circuit using only AND, OR, and inverter gates.

52. The block diagram in FIGURE 10.66 is a four-input, two-output combinational switching circuit. If $s1$ $s0$ = 00, the a input is broadcast to x and y. If $s1$ $s0$ = 01, the b input is broadcast to x and y. If $s1$ $s0$ = 10, a and b pass straight through to x and y. If $s1$ $s0$ = 11, they are switched, with a being routed to y and b to x. Construct the circuit using only AND, OR, and inverter gates. **(a)** Use Karnaugh maps to construct the minimum AND-OR circuit. **(b)** Use Karnaugh maps to construct the minimum OR-AND circuit.

53. Draw the 12 two-input multiplexers of Figure 10.56. Show all the connections to the input and output lines. You may use ellipses (. . .) for 6 of the 8 data lines.

FIGURE 10.65
The block diagram for Exercise 51.

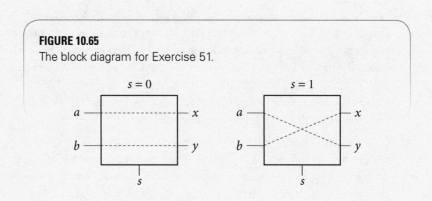

FIGURE 10.66
The block diagram for Exercise 52.

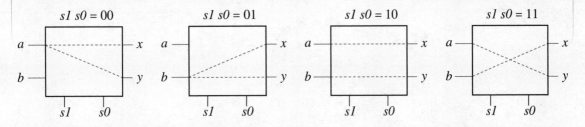

54. Implement the following logic units for the Pep/9 ALU:

    (a) logic unit 5, A · B   (b) logic unit 6, $\overline{A \cdot B}$
    (c) logic unit 7, A + B   (d) logic unit 8, $\overline{A + B}$
    (e) logic unit 9, A ⊕ B   (f) logic unit 10, $\overline{A}$
    (g) logic unit 11, ASL A   (h) logic unit 12, ROL A
    (i) logic unit 13, ASR A   (j) logic unit 14, ROR A

55. Draw the nonabbreviated implementation of the five-input, two-output
    control box of Figure 10.59.

CHAPTER 11

Sequential Circuits

Chapter 10 discusses combinational devices, which are commonly used in computer design. As useful as these devices are, however, it is impossible to build even the smallest computers as an interconnection of combinational circuits. In all the combinational devices mentioned, the output depends only on the input. When the input changes, it is only a matter of a few gate delays before that change is reflected in the output.

The distinguishing characteristic of a sequential circuit is its state.

The *state* of the circuit is the characteristic that distinguishes a sequential circuit from a combinational circuit. A sequential circuit can remember what state it is in. It has memory, in other words. The output of a sequential circuit depends not only on the input, but also on its state.

This chapter shows how to construct the basic sequential elements and how to connect them to form useful blocks at successively higher levels of abstraction. It concludes with a description of devices that are connected to build a Pep/9 computer in the following chapter.

11.1 Latches and Clocked Flip-Flops

Sequential devices are constructed from the same gates described in Chapter 10, but with a different type of connection called *feedback*. In combinational circuits and the Boolean expressions that describe them, the output of each gate goes to the input of a previously unconnected gate. A feedback connection, however, forms a loop or cycle where the output of one or more gates "feeds back" to the input of a previous gate of the circuit.

FIGURE 11.1
Simple feedback circuits.

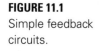

(a) An unstable circuit.

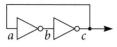

(b) A stable circuit.

Unstable states

FIGURE 11.1 shows two simple circuits with feedback connections. Part (a) is a string of three inverters with the output of the last inverter fed back to the input of the first inverter. To analyze the behavior of this circuit, suppose that point *d* has a value of 1. Because *d* is connected to *a* with the feedback loop, point *a* must also have a value of 1. One gate delay later, point *b* must have a value of 0. (Although we previously ignored the delay through an inverter for simplicity, we must take it into account with this circuit.) One more gate delay later, point *c* will have a value of 1, and after a third gate delay, *d* will have a value of 0.

The problem now is that we started our analysis assuming that point *d* has a value of 1. It will now change to 0, and three gate delays later it will become 1 again. The circuit will oscillate, with the values at each point in the circuit switching back and forth between 1 and 0 every few gate delays. A state that remains constant only for a duration of a few gate delays is called an *unstable state*.

In Figure 11.1(b), if you assume point *c* has a value of 1, then point *a* will be 1, *b* will be 0, and *c* will be 1, which is consistent with the first assumption. Such a state is stable. The points at all parts of the circuit will retain their values indefinitely.

Stable states

Another possible stable state is for points c and a to have a value of 0 and b to have a value of 1. If you construct this circuit, which state will it have? Will point c be 0 or 1? Like all electrical devices, gates require a source of electrical power and must be turned on to operate. If you construct the circuit of Figure 11.1(b) and turn it on, its state will be established at random. About half the time when you turn on the circuit, point c will be 0, and about half the time it will be 1. The circuit will remain indefinitely in the state that is established when the power is turned on.

The SR Latch

To be useful, a sequential device needs a mechanism for setting its state. Such a device is the *SR latch* of **FIGURE 11.2**. Its two inputs are S and R, and its two outputs are Q and $\overline{Q}$ (pronounced Q *bar*). The feedback connections are from Q to the input of the bottom NOR and from $\overline{Q}$ to the input of the top NOR.

To see the possibility of a stable state, suppose S and R are both 0, and Q is also 0. The two inputs to the bottom gate are both 0, which makes $\overline{Q}$ 1. The two inputs to the top NOR are 0 (from R) and 1 (from $\overline{Q}$). Thus, the output of the top NOR is 0, which is consistent with our first assumption about Q. So the stable state is $Q\overline{Q} = 01$ when SR = 00.

Starting with this stable state, consider what happens if you change input S to 1. **FIGURE 11.3** summarizes the sequence of events. T_g stands for a time interval of one gate delay, typically 2 ns.

At time 0, S changes to 1. That makes the two inputs to the bottom gate 1 (from S) and 0 (from Q). One gate delay later, the effect of that change propagates to $\overline{Q}$, which becomes 0. Now the two inputs to the top gate are 0 (from R) and 0 (from $\overline{Q}$). After another gate delay, the output of the top gate

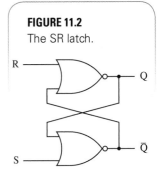

FIGURE 11.2
The SR latch.

FIGURE 11.3
Changing S to 1 in the SR latch.

Time	S	R	Q	$\overline{Q}$	Stability
Initial	0	0	0	1	Stable
0	1	0	0	1	Unstable
T_g	1	0	0	0	Unstable
$2T_g$	1	0	1	0	Stable

FIGURE 11.4

Changing S back to 0 in the SR latch.

Time	S	R	Q	Q̄	Stability
Initial	1	0	1	0	Stable
0	0	0	1	0	Stable

becomes 1. Now the input to the bottom gate is 1 (from S) and 1 (from Q). That makes the output of the bottom gate 0.

The output of the bottom gate was already 0, however, so it does not change. Because a trace through the feedback connections shows consistent values, this last state is stable. The two intermediate states in Figure 11.3 are unstable because they last for only a few gate delays.

What happens if you change S back to 0? **FIGURE 11.4** shows the sequence of events. The two inputs to the bottom gate are 0 (from S) and 1 (from Q). That makes the output of the bottom gate 0. Because it was already 0, no other changes propagate through the circuit, and the state is stable.

Figures 11.3 and 11.4 show that $\bar{Q}$ is always the complement of Q when the SR latch is in a stable state. The bar is another common notation for the complement and is equivalent to the prime notation used in Chapter 10.

Compare the first state of Figure 11.3 with the last state of Figure 11.4. In both cases the inputs are SR = 00, but in the first case the output is Q = 0 and in the second Q = 1. The output depends not only on the input, but also on the state of the latch.

Output depends on input and state.

The effect of changing S to 1 and then back to 0 was to set the state to Q = 1. If the latch begins in the state Q = 1 with SR = 00, a similar analysis shows that changing R to 1 and then back to 0 will reset the state to Q = 0. S stands for *set*, and R stands for *reset*.

An SR latch is analogous to a light switch on a wall. Changing S to 1 and back to 0 is like flipping the switch up to turn the light on. Changing R to 1 and back to 0 is like flipping the switch down. If the switch is already up and you try flipping it up, nothing changes. The switch stays up. Similarly, if Q is already 1 and you change S to 1 and back to 0, the state does not change. Q stays 1.

The normal input condition for the SR latch

The normal input condition for the SR latch is SR = 00. To set or reset the latch, you change S or R to 1 and then back to 0. Normally, S and R are not 1 simultaneously. If S and R are both 1, Q and $\bar{Q}$ will both be 0, and $\bar{Q}$ will not be the complement of Q. Furthermore, if you change SR = 11 to SR = 00 simultaneously, the state of the latch is unpredictable. About half the time it will return to Q $\bar{Q}$ = 01 and half the time to Q $\bar{Q}$ = 10. In practice, SR = 11 should not occur.

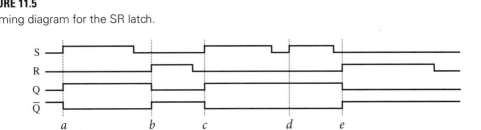

FIGURE 11.5
A timing diagram for the SR latch.

A *timing diagram* is a graphical representation of the behavior of a sequential circuit as the signals evolve in time. FIGURE 11.5 is a timing diagram that shows the change in outputs Q and $\overline{Q}$ as inputs S and R change. The horizontal axis is time, and the vertical axis is the electrical voltage that represents 1 when it is high and 0 when it is low.

The timing diagram shows the initial state as Q = 0. When S goes to 1 at time *a*, it immediately sets Q to 1 and $\overline{Q}$ to 0. The diagram shows the transitions occurring simultaneously. As shown in our previous analysis, $\overline{Q}$ will change one gate delay after S changes, and Q will change one gate delay later than that. The timing diagram assumes that the time scale is too large to show a time interval as short as a gate delay.

When S goes back to 0, the state does not change. When R goes to 1 at time *b*, it resets Q to 0. When S goes to 1 again at time *c*, it sets Q to 1. At time *d*, the 0-to-1 transition of S does not change the state of the latch because Q is already 1. At all points of the diagram, $\overline{Q}$ is the inverse of Q.

Figure 11.5 also shows the transitions as instantaneous. Nothing in nature occurs in zero time. If you magnify the time scale, the transitions will show a more gradual change with a finite slope at every point. You can think of the simultaneous and instantaneous transitions in the timing diagram as a high level of abstraction that hides the details of the gate delays and gradual slopes at a lower level of abstraction.

The Clocked SR Flip-Flop

A subsystem in a computer consists of many combinational and sequential devices. Each sequential device is like an SR latch, which is in one of two states. As the machine executes its von Neumann cycle, the states of all the sequential devices change with time. To control this large collection of devices in an orderly fashion, the machine maintains a clock and requires all the devices to change their states at the same time. The clock generates a sequence of pulses, as in FIGURE 11.6. Ck stands for *clock pulse*.

Every sequential device has a Ck input in addition to its other inputs. The device is designed to respond to its inputs only during a clock pulse. The

FIGURE 11.6
A sequence of clock pulses.

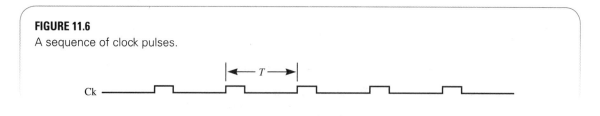

The clock period

time between pulses, indicated by T in the figure, is the *period* of the clock. The shorter the period, the more frequently the devices will change their states and the faster the circuit will compute.

FIGURE 11.7 is an SR latch with a clock input, called a *flip-flop*. It consists of the same pair of NOR gates with feedback that were shown in Figure 11.2. But instead of the SR inputs going directly into the NOR gates, they go through two AND gates that act as an enable. Figure 11.7(a) is the block diagram, and Figure 11.7(b) is an implementation. Notice that the convention for the block diagram has S opposite from Q at the top of the block, and the implementation has S opposite $\bar{Q}$.

During the time that Ck is low, the inputs to the NOR gates will be 0 regardless of the values of S and R. When there are inputs of 0 into the NOR gates, it means that the latch will not change its state. During the time that Ck is high, the values of S and R pass through the enable gates unchanged. The device behaves as the SR latch of Figure 11.2. The AND gates shield the NOR gates from the effect of S and R except during the time that Ck is high. **FIGURE 11.8** is a timing diagram that shows the behavior of the device. $\bar{Q}$ is always the complement of Q and is not shown in the figure.

When S goes to 1, that change does not affect Q because the clock is still low. At time *a* when the clock goes high, Ck allows SR = 10 to pass through the AND gates and set the latch to Q = 1. A little later when the clock goes

FIGURE 11.7AB
The clocked SR flip-flop.

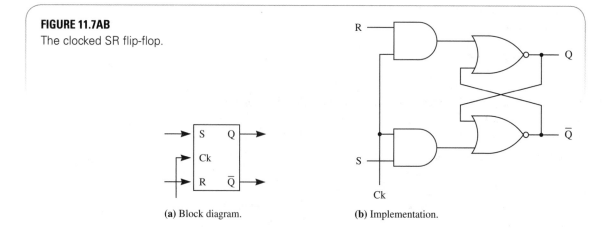

(a) Block diagram.   (b) Implementation.

FIGURE 11.8

A timing diagram of the clocked SR flip-flop.

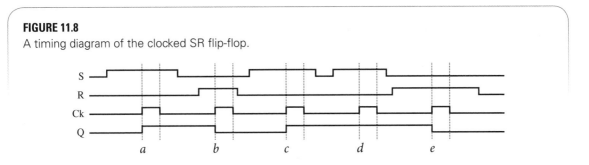

low, Ck disables the SR input from the latch. When R goes to 1 before time *b*, it cannot affect the state of the latch. Only at time *b*, when Ck goes high again, can R reset the latch.

It would be physically possible to let S and R make several transitions during a single time interval when the clock is high, but that does not happen in practice. The idea is to design the circuit to set up the SR input for the desired transition and wait for the next clock pulse. When the clock pulse arrives, the state may change according to the values of S and R. After the clock goes low, the circuit prepares the SR values for the next pulse.

The evenly spaced clock pulses force any change in state to occur only at evenly spaced time intervals. The S and R inputs of Figure 11.8 are identical to those of Figure 11.5, but the corresponding state changes in Q have been smoothed out by the clock. The effect of a clock is to make time (the horizontal axis of a timing diagram) digital in the same way that the electrical circuitry makes the voltage signal (vertical axis) digital. Just as a signal must be either high or low and never anything in between, a state change of a sequential device must occur at either one clock pulse or another—never between two pulses.

Digitizing the time axis

The Master–Slave SR Flip-Flop

The clocked flip-flop of Figure 11.7 is called *level sensitive* because the latch responds to Ck only when the clock is at a high level. Although the device is constrained to follow the clock as desired, it has a serious practical deficiency, illustrated in FIGURE 11.9 .

The figure shows a possible interconnection of an SR device. It is common for the output of a sequential device to contain a feedback loop through some combinational circuit that eventually leads to the input of the same sequential device. The figure shows a three-input, two-output combinational circuit, two of whose inputs are feedback from the output of the SR sequential device. This feedback loop is in addition to the feedback of the NOR gates not shown in the figure within the SR block.

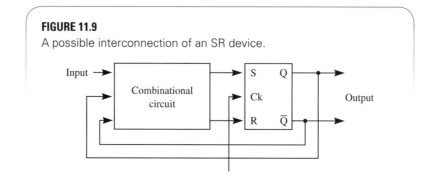

FIGURE 11.9
A possible interconnection of an SR device.

Consider what might happen if the SR flip-flop were level sensitive. Suppose SR is 10, Q $\overline{Q}$ is 01, and the clock is low. Because the clock disables SR from the NOR latch, S cannot set Q to 1. Now suppose the clock goes high, and after a few gate delays SR sets Q to 1.

Now imagine that the change in Q $\overline{Q}$, after propagating through the combinational circuit with the same external input, makes SR = 01. If Ck is still high, the clock will allow the value of SR to reset Q to 0 after a few more gate delays. Unfortunately, a value of 01 for Q $\overline{Q}$ will propagate through the combinational circuit again and change SR to 10.

You should recognize this situation as unstable. Every few gate delays, the feedback connection from the sequential device forces the SR flip-flop to change its state as long as the clock is high. The state may change hundreds of times while the clock is high. When the clock eventually goes low at the end of its pulse, it would be impossible to predict exactly what state the flip-flop would be in.

Possibility of an unstable state with feedback

Because feedback connections through combinational circuits are necessary for the construction of computer subsystems, we need a sequential device that is not only constrained to change its state during a clock pulse, but is also immune from further changes through the feedback connection. The device needs to be sensitive to its input for an extremely short period of time—so short that no matter how fast the feedback propagates through the combinational circuit and changes SR, that change cannot again affect the state of the flip-flop.

Two design solutions to the instability problem from feedback

Two techniques for designing such devices are edge-triggered and master–slave. *Edge-triggered* flip-flops are not designed to be sensitive to their inputs when the clock is at a high level, but rather when the clock is making a transition from a low level to a high level. The implementation of an edge-triggered flip-flop is more difficult to understand than the implementation of a master–slave flip-flop and will not be considered here even though it is

FIGURE 11.10

The master–slave SR flip-flop.

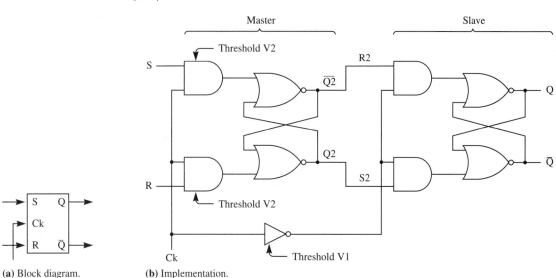

(a) Block diagram.   **(b)** Implementation.

the more common of the two. It is enough to say that both types of flip-flops solve the same problem arising from feedback connections.

 shows an implementation of the *master–slave* SR flip-flop. Both the master and the slave are level-sensitive, clocked SR flip-flops. The $\overline{Q}$ output of the master $(\overline{Q2})$ connects to the R input of the slave (R2), and the Q output of the master (Q2) connects to the S input of the slave (S2). Ck connects to the enable of the master, and the complement of Ck connects to the enable of the slave. The block diagram of a master–slave flip-flop is identical to the block diagram of the level-sensitive flip-flop.

Operation of the master–slave circuit

Because the master is an SR flip-flop, Q2 and $\overline{Q2}$ will always be the complement of each other. Because Q2 is connected to S2 of the slave and $\overline{Q2}$ is connected to R2 of the slave, when the slave is clocked, the slave will either be set or reset, depending on the state of the master. If the master is in state Q2 = 1, the master will set the slave to Q = 1 also. If the master is in state Q2 = 0, it will reset the slave to Q = 0. The reason for the master–slave terminology is that the slave obediently takes the state of the master when the slave is clocked.

The *threshold* of a gate is the value of the input signal that causes the output to change. For the master–slave circuit to function properly, the inverter and the enable gates of the master must be designed with special

The threshold of a gate

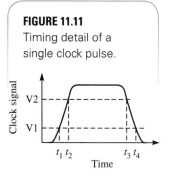

FIGURE 11.11

Timing detail of a single clock pulse.

threshold values. The threshold of the inverter, V1, must be less than the threshold of the master enable gates, V2.

FIGURE 11.11 shows V1 and V2 on a magnified timing diagram of Ck during one clock pulse. The clock does not make an instantaneous transition from a low to a high value. Instead, it gradually increases first to value V1 at time t_1, then to value V2 at time t_2 on the way to its high level. On the way down, it passes through value V2 at time t_3, and then V1 at time t_4.

Before the pulse begins its upward transition, the master is disabled from the input. Regardless of the value of SR, the master will remain in its established state. The inverter ensures that the slave input is connected to the master because the slave inputs are enabled. The slave must be in the same state as the master.

As the clock signal rises and falls, passing through times t_1, t_2, t_3, and t_4, the effect of the circuit is as follows:

> t_1: Isolate slave from master.

> t_2: Connect master to input.

> t_3: Isolate master from input.

> t_4: Connect slave to master.

At time t_1 the signal reaches the threshold of the inverter, which makes the output of the inverter change from 1 to 0. A 0 to the enable gates of the slave shields the slave from any further effects of S2 and R2. Whatever state the slave was in at time t_1, it will remain in that state as long as Ck is above the threshold value V1.

At time t_2 the signal reaches the threshold of the master enable gates, which makes the master sensitive to the SR inputs. If SR is 10, the input will set the master to Q2 = 1. If SR is 01, the input will reset the master to Q2 = 0. If SR is 00, the master will not change its state. However, if the master does change its state, its new state will not affect the slave because the slave was isolated from the master at time t_1.

Consider how this arrangement protects the flip-flop from the feedback connection of Figure 11.9. The feedback is based on the Q Q̄ output of the slave, which does not change as a result of the input to the master. The fact that V1 is less than V2 ensures that the slave will be isolated from the master before the master becomes sensitive to the input. Even if the gate delay through the combinational circuit were zero, the feedback would not affect the state of the slave.

When Ck makes its high-to-low transition, the clock reaches value V2 at time t_3. V2 is the threshold of the enable gates for the master, so now the master becomes insensitive to the input. Because V2 is greater than V1, the slave is still isolated from the effect of the master.

At time t_4 the clock signal becomes less than the threshold of the inverter. The output of the inverter changes from 0 to 1, connecting the slave to the master. Whatever state the master was in is forced on the slave. The slave may change its state. If there is feedback from the output of the slave to the input of the master, it will not affect the master because the master was isolated from the input at time t_3.

A rough analogy of the operation of a master–slave circuit is a decompression chamber in a spacecraft. Inside the craft, the astronauts do not need to wear spacesuits. To go for a space walk outside the craft, an astronaut dons a spacesuit and approaches the decompression chamber, which has two doors that are initially closed. *The decompression chamber analogy*

The astronaut opens the inner door, which connects the chamber with the craft, and steps inside the chamber. She closes the inner door, isolating the chamber from the craft, and opens the outer door, connecting the chamber with outer space. She exits the outer door, closing it behind her. At no time are both doors open at the same time. If they were, the craft would lose all its air to outer space.

Similarly, the master–slave circuit has two doors—one to isolate or connect the master to the input and one to isolate or connect the slave to the master. At no time are both doors open, with the master connected to the input and the slave connected to the master. If they were, a feedback loop might cause an unstable state in the circuit.

FIGURE 11.12 is a timing diagram of the behavior of a master–slave SR flip-flop. A change occurs in Q, the state of the slave latch, at time t_4, when the slave is connected to the master. That is during the high-to-low transition of Ck.

Because a flip-flop is not combinational, a truth table is not sufficient to characterize its behavior. Instead, flip-flops have *characteristic tables* that specify the state of the device after one clock pulse for a given input and initial state. **FIGURE 11.13** is the characteristic table for the SR flip-flop. *Characteristic tables*

$S(t)$ and $R(t)$ are the inputs at time t before a clock pulse. $Q(t)$ is the state of the flip-flop before a clock pulse, and $Q(t + 1)$ is the state after the pulse.

FIGURE 11.12

A timing diagram of the master–slave SR flip-flop.

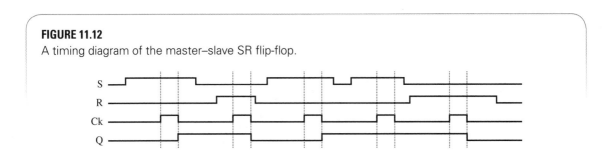

FIGURE 11.13
The characteristic table for the SR flip-flop.

S(t)	R(t)	Q(t)	Q(t + 1)	Condition
0	0	0	0	No change
0	0	1	1	
0	1	0	0	Reset
0	1	1	0	
1	0	0	1	Set
1	0	1	1	
1	1	0	–	Not defined
1	1	1	–	

The table shows that if SR is 00, the device does not change its state when clocked. If SR is 01, the device resets to Q = 0, and if it is 10, the device sets to Q = 1. It is impossible to predict what the state would be if SR = 11 when clocked.

The characteristic table is, in essence, a state transition table similar to Figure 7.11 for a finite-state machine. An SR flip-flop is a finite-state machine with two possible states, Q = 0 and Q = 1. As with any finite-state machine, its behavior can be characterized by a state transition diagram. FIGURE 11.14 is the state transition diagram for an SR flip-flop.

Circles denote the states of the machine with the value of Q inside the circle. Transitions are labeled with the values of SR that produce the given transition. For example, the transition from Q = 0 to Q = 1 is labeled with SR = 10.

FIGURE 11.14
The state transition diagram for an SR flip-flop.

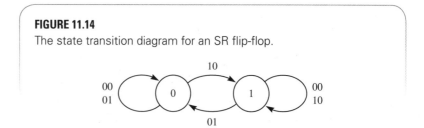

The Basic Flip-Flops

Four flip-flops are common in computer design:

> › SR   Set/reset
>
> › JK   Set/reset/toggle
>
> › D   Data or delay
>
> › T   Toggle

The previous section shows how to construct the SR flip-flop. Its characteristic table defines its behavior. The other three flip-flops have their own characteristic tables that define their behaviors. Each one can be constructed from the SR flip-flop together with a few other gates. Like the SR flip-flop, the others all have Q and $\overline{Q}$ outputs. The JK flip-flop has two inputs labeled J and K in place of S and R. The D and T flip-flops each have only one input.

There is a systematic procedure to construct the other flip-flops from the SR flip-flop. The general circuit has the structure of Figure 11.9, where the Q and $\overline{Q}$ outputs of the SR flip-flop act as the Q and $\overline{Q}$ outputs of the device under construction. For the JK flip-flop, the input line of Figure 11.9 is actually two input lines, one for J and one for K. For the D flip-flop, the one input line is labeled D, and for the T flip-flop, it is labeled T. To design each flip-flop, you must determine the logic gates and their interconnection in the box labeled *Combinational circuit*.

As with any combinational circuit design, once you determine the required input and output in the form of a truth table, you can construct the minimum AND-OR circuit with the help of a Karnaugh map. So, the first step is to write down the required input and output of the box labeled *Combinational circuit* in Figure 11.9. A useful tool to determine the specification of the circuit is the *excitation table* of the SR flip-flop in FIGURE 11.15 .

FIGURE 11.15
The excitation table for the SR flip-flop.

Q(t)	Q(t + 1)	S(t)	R(t)
0	0	0	×
0	1	1	0
1	0	0	1
1	1	×	0

Excitation tables versus characteristic tables

Contrast the excitation table with the characteristic table in Figure 11.13. The characteristic table tells you what the next state is, given the current input and the current state. But the excitation table tells you what the current input must be, given the desired transition. Here is how you build the excitation table from the characteristic table.

Constructing excitation tables

The first table entry is for the transition from Q = 0 to Q = 0. Two possible inputs permit this transition: SR = 00 and SR = 01. An SR value of 00 specifies the no-change condition. An SR value of 01 specifies the reset condition. Either of these conditions will cause the flip-flop to make the transition from Q = 0 to Q = 0. The × in the entry under R(*t*) is a don't-care value. As long as S is 0, you do not care what the value of R is. The transition will be from Q = 0 to Q = 0 regardless of the value of R.

The second entry in the table is for the transition from Q = 0 to Q = 1. The only way to force this transition is to input 10 for SR, the set condition. Similarly, the third entry is for the transition from Q = 1 to Q = 0, which can occur only with a value of 01 for SR.

The last entry is for the transition from Q = 1 to Q = 1. The two possible input conditions that permit this transition are SR = 00, the no-change condition, and SR = 10, the set condition. Regardless of the value of S, if R is 0, the transition will occur. The × under S(*t*) indicates the don't-care condition for S.

The JK Flip-Flop

The JK flip-flop resolves the undefined transition in the SR flip-flop. The J input acts like S, setting the device, and the K input acts like R, resetting the device. But when JK = 11, the condition is called the *toggle condition*. To toggle means to switch from one state to the other. In the toggle condition, if the initial state is 0, the final state will be 1, and if the initial state is 1, the final state will be 0. **FIGURE 11.16** is the block diagram and the characteristic table for the JK flip-flop.

For the JK flip-flop, the box labeled *Combinational circuit* in Figure 11.9 has three inputs and two outputs. The inputs are J, K, and Q, which comes from the feedback connection. **FIGURE 11.17** is the same figure with the J and K inputs explicit. The dashed box defines a JK flip-flop with three inputs (J, K, and Ck) and two outputs (Q and $\overline{Q}$). The Q feedback is at a lower level of abstraction and is not visible to the user of the JK flip-flop. Figure 11.17 shows only one feedback line, Q, from the output of the SR flip-flop. The $\overline{Q}$ output from the SR flip-flop is also available as a possible input to the box labeled *Combinational circuit*. However, when you design a combinational circuit, you always assume that both the input signal and its complement are available. Figure 11.17 emphasizes that the combinational

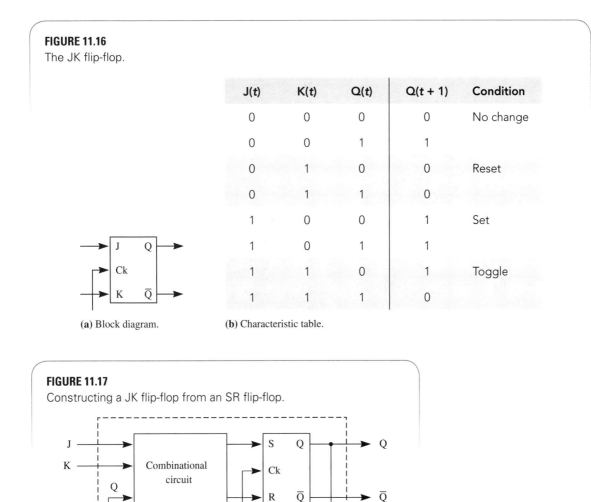

FIGURE 11.16
The JK flip-flop.

J(t)	K(t)	Q(t)	Q(t + 1)	Condition
0	0	0	0	No change
0	0	1	1	
0	1	0	0	Reset
0	1	1	0	
1	0	0	1	Set
1	0	1	1	
1	1	0	1	Toggle
1	1	1	0	

(a) Block diagram.   (b) Characteristic table.

FIGURE 11.17
Constructing a JK flip-flop from an SR flip-flop.

circuit is a three-input, two-output circuit. The outputs are S and R, and each is a function of three inputs. That is, S = S(J, K, Q) and R = R(J, K, Q). So to construct a JK flip-flop from an SR flip-flop, you need to design two three-input combinational circuits, one for S and one for R.

First, write down the design table of **FIGURE 11.18** with the help of the SR excitation table. The design table tells you the inputs that are necessary for the SR flip-flop, given the transitions that the JK flip-flop must make. The first three columns list all the possible input combinations of the

Constructing design tables

FIGURE 11.18
The design table to construct a JK flip-flop from an SR flip-flop.

Q(t)	J(t)	K(t)	Q(t + 1)	S(t)	R(t)
0	0	0	0	0	×
0	0	1	0	0	×
0	1	1	1	1	0
0	1	0	1	1	0
1	0	0	1	×	0
1	0	1	0	0	1
1	1	1	0	0	1
1	1	0	1	×	0

FIGURE 11.19
The Karnaugh maps to construct a JK flip-flop from an SR flip-flop.

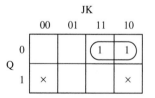

(a) Karnaugh map for S.

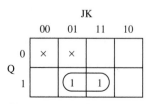

(b) Karnaugh map for R.

three inputs to the combinational circuit. It is a good idea to order the JK values as they will appear in the Karnaugh maps. The fourth column is the value of Q after the clock pulse. Each value of Q(t + 1) comes from the characteristic table of the JK flip-flop. For example, in the third row, JK = 11, which is the toggle condition. So the initial state Q(t) = 0 toggles to Q(t + 1) = 1. The last two columns come from the excitation table for the SR flip-flop, given Q(t) and Q(t + 1). For example, the third row has transition Q(t) Q(t + 1) = 01. The excitation table shows that SR must be 10 for that transition.

The next step is to write down the Karnaugh maps for the functions. The entries in FIGURE 11.19 (a) come from the column labeled S(t) in the design table, and the entries in (b) come from R(t).

By inspection of the Karnaugh maps, you can write the minimized AND-OR expression for S as $S = J\overline{Q}$, and for R as R = KQ. FIGURE 11.20 shows the complete design. You implement the JK flip-flop with an SR flip-flop and two two-input AND gates. You can see how the design works by considering all the possible values of JK. If JK = 00, then SR = 00 regardless of the state, and the state does not change. If JK = 11 and Q = 0, then SR = 10 and Q will change to 1. If Q = 1 initially, then SR = 01 and Q will change to 0. In both cases, the state toggles, as it should for JK = 11. You should convince yourself that the circuit works correctly for JK = 01 and JK = 10 as well.

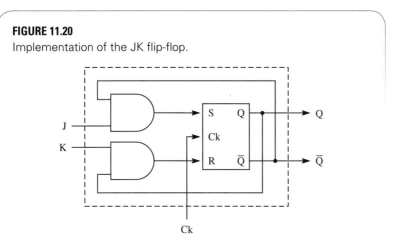

FIGURE 11.20
Implementation of the JK flip-flop.

The D Flip-Flop

The D flip-flop is a data flip-flop with only one input, D, besides the clock.
FIGURE 11.21 (a) is its block diagram and (b) is its characteristic table. The
table shows that $Q(t + 1)$ is independent of $Q(t)$. It depends only on the
value of D at time t. The D flip-flop stores the data until the next clock pulse.
Part (c) of the figure shows a timing diagram. This flip-flop is also called a

FIGURE 11.21
The D flip-flop.

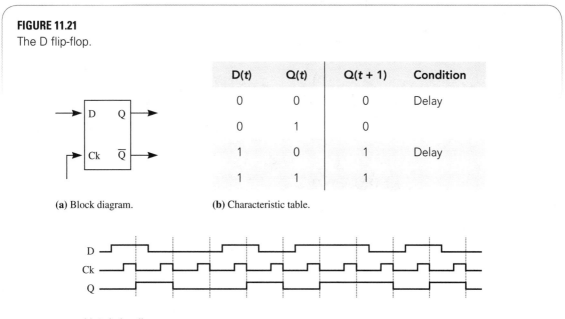

D(t)	Q(t)	Q(t + 1)	Condition
0	0	0	Delay
0	1	0	
1	0	1	Delay
1	1	1	

(a) Block diagram.   (b) Characteristic table.

(c) A timing diagram.

delay flip-flop because on the timing diagram, the shape of Q is identical to that of D except for a time delay.

To construct a D flip-flop from an SR flip-flop, first construct the design table. Because there is only one input besides Q, there are only four rows in the table, as **FIGURE 11.22** (a) shows. Parts (b) and (c) show the Karnaugh maps, which contain only four cells instead of eight. Minimization of the AND-OR circuits gives $S = D$ and $R = \bar{D}$.

FIGURE 11.23 is the implementation of the D flip-flop. It requires only a single inverter in addition to the SR flip-flop. This implementation has no feedback connections from Q or $\bar{Q}$ as the JK implementation does, because the next state does not depend on the current state.

The T Flip-Flop

The T flip-flop is a toggle flip-flop. Like the D flip-flop, it has only one input, T, besides the clock. **FIGURE 11.24** (a) is the block diagram and (b) is the characteristic table. The T input acts like a control line that specifies a

FIGURE 11.22

The design table and Karnaugh maps to construct a D flip-flop from an SR flip-flop.

Q(t)	D(t)	Q(t + 1)	S(t)	R(t)
0	0	0	0	×
0	1	1	1	0
1	1	1	×	0
1	0	0	0	1

(a) Design table.

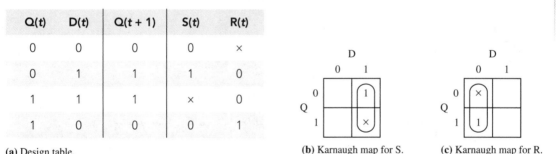

(b) Karnaugh map for S. (c) Karnaugh map for R.

FIGURE 11.23

Implementation of the D flip-flop.

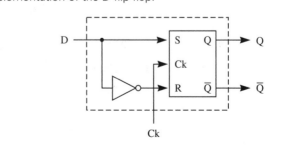

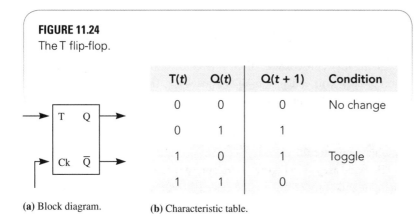

FIGURE 11.24
The T flip-flop.

T(t)	Q(t)	Q(t + 1)	Condition
0	0	0	No change
0	1	1	
1	0	1	Toggle
1	1	0	

(a) Block diagram.   (b) Characteristic table.

FIGURE 11.25
Excitation tables for the JK, D, and T flip-flops.

Q(t)	Q(t + 1)	J(t)	K(t)
0	0	0	×
0	1	1	×
1	0	×	1
1	1	×	0

(a) The JK flip-flop.

Q(t)	Q(t + 1)	D(t)
0	0	0
0	1	1
1	0	0
1	1	1

(b) The D flip-flop.

Q(t)	Q(t + 1)	T(t)
0	0	0
0	1	1
1	0	1
1	1	0

(c) The T flip-flop.

selective toggle. If T is 0, the flip-flop does not change its state, and if T is 1, the flip-flop toggles. Implementation of the T flip-flop is an exercise at the end of the chapter.

Excitation Tables

The preceding sections show how to construct the JK, D, and T flip-flops from the SR flip-flop and a few other gates. You can use the same systematic procedure to construct any flip-flop from any other flip-flop. It might seem pointless, for example, to construct a D flip-flop from a JK flip-flop, because you make a JK from an SR with two extra gates in the first place, and the D requires only an SR with an inverter. But the fact that you can construct any flip-flop from any other shows that all the flip-flops are equivalent in power. That is, any processing that you can do with any flip-flop you can do with any other with a few extra gates.

For example, assuming that you have a JK flip-flop, and you want to construct a T flip-flop, you would write the design table from the characteristic table for the T and excitation table for the JK. In general, to construct flip-flop A from flip-flop B, you need the characteristic table for A and the excitation table for B. **FIGURE 11.25** shows the excitation tables for the JK, D, and T flip-flops.

You should verify the entries of each excitation table. For example, the first entry in the JK table is for the transition from Q = 0 to Q = 0. Using the same reasoning as with the SR flip-flop, the transition will occur if JK is 00 or 01—hence, the don't-care condition under K(t). The second table entry also has a don't-care condition. The transition from Q = 0 to Q = 1 can occur under two conditions: JK can be either 10, the set condition, or 11, the toggle condition. Both allow Q to change from 0 to 1.

11.2 Sequential Analysis and Design

A sequential circuit consists of an interconnection of gates and flip-flops. Conceptually, you can group all the gates together into a combinational circuit and all the flip-flops together in a group of *state registers*, as in FIGURE 11.26. This is a generalization of Figure 11.9, which contained only one state register and whose output required no additional gates from the combinational circuit.

The solid arrows in Figure 11.26 represent one or more connecting lines. The input and output lines are the external connections to the environment of the circuit. The lines from the combinational circuit to the state registers are the input lines to SR, JK, D, or T flip-flops. The feedback lines are from the flip-flops' Q and $\overline{Q}$ outputs to the combinational circuit. The figure assumes a common clock line (not shown) to each flip-flop in the group of state registers.

Between clock pulses, the combinational part of the circuit produces its output from the external input and the state of the circuit—that is, the states of the individual flip-flops. The amount of time it takes to produce the combinational output and the state register input depends on how many gate levels are in the circuit. The Ck period is adjusted to be long enough to allow the input to propagate through the combinational circuit to the output before the next clock pulse. All the state registers are edge-triggered or master–slave to protect against multiple propagations through the feedback loop.

As in Figure 11.14, you can describe the behavior of a general sequential circuit with a state transition diagram or its corresponding state transition table. The difference is that Figure 11.14 is for a single device with two possible states, whereas Figure 11.26 is for n flip-flops. Because each flip-flop has two possible states, the sequential circuit has a total of 2^n states.

The difference between analysis and design at the hardware level is the same as the difference at the software level. FIGURE 11.27 illustrates the

FIGURE 11.26
A general sequential circuit.

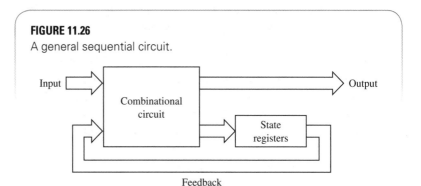

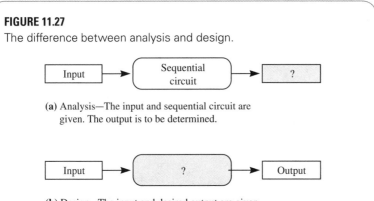

FIGURE 11.27

The difference between analysis and design.

(a) Analysis—The input and sequential circuit are given. The output is to be determined.

(b) Design—The input and desired output are given. The sequential circuit is to be determined.

difference. In analysis, the input and sequential circuit are given and the output is to be determined. In design, the input and desired output are given and the sequential circuit is to be determined.

The next section shows how to determine the output from a given sequential circuit and input stream. The general approach is to construct the analysis table from the circuit. From the analysis table, you can easily determine the state transition table, the state transition diagram, and the output stream for any given input stream.

A Sequential Analysis Problem

Suppose the circuit of **FIGURE 11.28** is given. The state registers are the two T flip-flops labeled *FFA* and *FFB*. The combinational circuit is the group of two AND gates and one OR gate. The inputs are X1 and X2, and the single output is Y. The feedback loop consists of the line from Q of FFA, labeled *A*, and the two lines from Q and $\overline{Q}$ of FFB, labeled *B* and $\overline{B}$. The input to FFA is labeled *TA*, and the input to FFB is labeled *TB*.

Because there are two flip-flops, there are four possible states,

$$AB = 00$$
$$AB = 01$$
$$AB = 10$$
$$AB = 11$$

where, for example, AB = 01 means that Q = 0 in FFA and Q = 1 in FFB. Because there are two inputs, there are four possible input combinations,

$$X1\ X2 = 00$$
$$X1\ X2 = 01$$
$$X1\ X2 = 10$$
$$X1\ X2 = 11$$

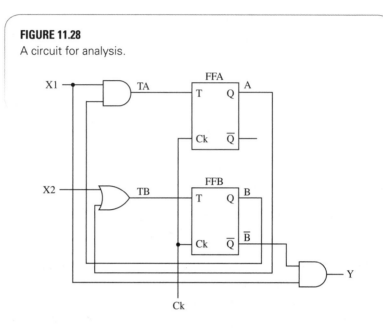

FIGURE 11.28
A circuit for analysis.

The sequential analysis
problem

Here is the problem. You are given an initial state, AB, and an initial input, X1 X2. (a) What is the initial output? (b) What will be the next state after a clock pulse occurs? Because there are four states, and with each state there are four possible input combinations, you must answer these questions 16 times. The analysis table in **FIGURE 11.29** provides a systematic tool to determine the answers.

The first four columns are a list of all possible combinations of the initial state and initial input. From Figure 11.28, the Boolean expressions for $Y(t)$, $TA(t)$, and $TB(t)$ are

$$Y(t) = X1(t) \cdot \bar{B}(t)$$
$$TA(t) = X1(t) \cdot B(t)$$
$$TB(t) = X2(t) + A(t)$$

So, you compute the column for $Y(t)$ as the AND of the column for $X1(t)$ and the complement of the column for $B(t)$. You compute the column for $TA(t)$ as the AND of the column for $X1(t)$ and the column for $B(t)$. You compute the column for $TB(t)$ as the OR of the column for $X2(t)$ and the column for $A(t)$. You compute the last two columns from the characteristic table for the T flip-flop, the initial state of a flip-flop, and its initial input.

Example 11.1 Consider the column for $B(t + 1)$. In the first row, the initial state of FFB is 0 from the column for $B(t)$. The flip-flop input is 0 from the column for $TB(t)$. From the characteristic table for the T flip-flop in

FIGURE 11.29
The analysis table for the circuit of Figure 11.28.

A(t)	B(t)	X1(t)	X2(t)	Y(t)	TA(t)	TB(t)	A(t + 1)	B(t + 1)
0	0	0	0	0	0	0	0	0
0	0	0	1	0	0	1	0	1
0	0	1	0	1	0	0	0	0
0	0	1	1	1	0	1	0	1
0	1	0	0	0	0	0	0	1
0	1	0	1	0	0	1	0	0
0	1	1	0	0	1	0	1	1
0	1	1	1	0	1	1	1	0
1	0	0	0	0	0	1	1	1
1	0	0	1	0	0	1	1	1
1	0	1	0	1	0	1	1	1
1	0	1	1	1	0	1	1	1
1	1	0	0	0	0	1	1	0
1	1	0	1	0	0	1	1	0
1	1	1	0	0	1	1	0	0
1	1	1	1	0	1	1	0	0

Figure 11.24(b), 0 is the no-change condition. So the state remains the same, and B(t + 1) is 0. ∎

Example 11.2 For the same column, consider the second row. The initial state of FFB is again 0 from the column for B(t). This time the flip-flop input is 1 from the column for TB(t). From the characteristic table for the T flip-flop, 1 is the toggle condition. So the state toggles, and B(t + 1) is 1. ∎

The state transition table in FIGURE 11.30 is a simple rearrangement of selected columns from the analysis table. For a given initial state A(t) B(t) and a given input X1(t) X2(t), it lists the next state A(t + 1) B(t + 1) and the initial

FIGURE 11.30

The state transition table for the circuit of Figure 11.28.

	X1(t) X2(t)			
A(t) B(t)	00	01	10	11
00	00, 0	01, 0	00, 1	01, 1
01	01, 0	00, 0	11, 0	10, 0
10	11, 0	11, 0	11, 1	11, 1
11	10, 0	10, 0	00, 0	00, 0
	A(t + 1) B(t + 1), Y(t)			

output Y(t). States are listed as ordered pairs. Entries in the body of the table are the next state followed by the initial output, separated by a comma.

It is usually easier to visualize the behavior of the circuit from its state transition diagram rather than its state transition table. **FIGURE 11.31** is the state transition diagram constructed from the state transition table. The standard convention is to label transitions as ordered pairs of the input followed by the initial output, separated by a slash.

Determining the output stream from the input stream

To determine the output from a given input stream, assume that you start in state AB = 11 and input the following values of X1 X2:

    11, 11, 00, 10, 01

FIGURE 11.31

The state transition diagram for the circuit of Figure 11.28. Transitions are labeled X1(t) X2(t) / Y(t).

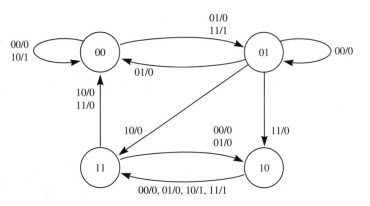

From the diagram, you will make transitions to the states

   11, 00, 01, 01, 11, 10

and generate the following output

   0, 1, 0, 0, 0

The analysis is similar for sequential circuits containing other flip-flops or even mixtures of different types of flip-flops. Using your knowledge of combinational circuits, you simply determine the input of each flip-flop for all possible combinations of inputs and states. Then, from the characteristic table of each flip-flop, you determine what the next state will be. In general, if there are m inputs and n flip-flops, you will need to analyze $2^m 2^n$ transitions.

Preset and Clear

The output sequence for the previous problem assumes that the flip-flops are both in their $Q = 1$ state. A legitimate question is: How do the flip-flops get in their start states? In practice, most flip-flops are constructed with two additional inputs, called *preset* and *clear*. These inputs are *asynchronous*; that is, they do not depend on the clock pulse to function. **FIGURE 11.32** shows the block diagram of an SR flip-flop with asynchronous preset and clear inputs.

   In normal operation, both preset and clear lines are 0. To initialize the flip-flop to $Q = 1$, send preset to 1 and back to 0. To initialize the flip-flop to $Q = 0$, send clear to 1 and back to 0. You do not need to send a clock pulse while either input is high for it to function. Implementation of the asynchronous preset and clear is an exercise at the end of the chapter.

Sequential Design

With sequential design, the behavior of the circuit is given, frequently in the form of a state transition diagram, and the implementation of the circuit with a minimum number of gates is to be determined. Also given in the problem formulation is the type of flip-flop to be used for the state registers in the sequential circuit.

   The design procedure has three steps. First, from the state transition diagram, tabulate the transitions of the circuit in a design table. For each combination of initial state and input, list the initial output and the next state. Then, from the excitation tables, list the necessary flip-flop input conditions to cause the transitions.

   Second, transfer the entries for each flip-flop input to a Karnaugh map. It helps to prevent mistakes if you look ahead in your tabulation of the design table and list the entries in the same order as a Karnaugh map. Design the

FIGURE 11.32
The block diagram of an SR flip-flop with asynchronous preset and clear.

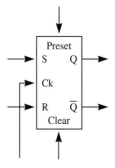

combinational part of the sequential circuit by minimizing the expressions from the Karnaugh map.

Third, draw the minimized combinational circuit. Each flip-flop input will come from a combinational circuit two gate levels deep at most. You should recognize this procedure as a generalization of the procedure to construct the JK, D, and T flip-flops from the SR flip-flop.

A Sequential Design Problem

This example illustrates the design procedure. The problem is to implement the state transition diagram of FIGURE 11.33 with SR flip-flops. As in Figure 11.31, the transitions are labeled with the input values, X1 X2, and the initial output, Y. The values in the state circles are the Q values of the first SR flip-flop, FFA, and the second SR flip-flop, FFB.

This machine has only three input combinations and four states, for a total of 12 transitions. The input combinations are 01, 11, and 10. Because the combination 00 is not expected to occur, you can treat it as a don't-care condition to help with the minimization.

To implement a finite-state machine with eight states, you need three flip-flops. To implement a machine with five to seven states also requires three flip-flops, but some of the states are not expected to occur and can be treated as don't-care states.

FIGURE 11.34 is the first step in the design process. The four columns on the left are all the possible combinations of initial state and input. The middle three columns are a simple tabulation of the initial output and next state from Figure 11.33.

FIGURE 11.33

The state transition diagram for a design problem.

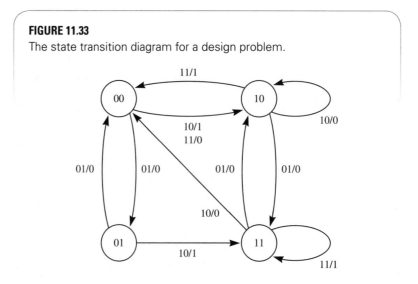

FIGURE 11.34
The design table for the state transition diagram of Figure 11.33.

Initial State		Initial Input		Initial Output	Next State		Flip-Flop Input Conditions			
							FFA		FFB	
A(t)	B(t)	X1(t)	X2(t)	Y(t)	A(t + 1)	B(t + 1)	SA(t)	RA(t)	SB(t)	RB(t)
0	0	0	1	0	0	1	0	×	1	0
0	1	0	1	0	0	0	0	×	0	1
1	1	0	1	0	1	0	×	0	0	1
1	0	0	1	0	1	1	×	0	1	0
0	0	1	1	0	1	0	1	0	0	×
0	1	1	1	0	1	1	1	0	×	0
1	1	1	1	1	1	1	×	0	×	0
1	0	1	1	1	0	0	0	1	0	×
0	0	1	0	1	1	0	1	0	0	×
0	1	1	0	1	1	1	1	0	×	0
1	1	1	0	0	0	0	0	1	0	1
1	0	1	0	0	1	0	×	0	0	×

The four columns on the right come from the fact that there are two SR flip-flops, each with two inputs. SA is the S input of FFA, RA is the R input of FFA, and so on. The flip-flop input conditions that produce the given transition come from the excitation table for the SR flip-flop, Figure 11.15.

For example, consider the first line for the transition from AB = 00 to AB = 01. The transition for FFA is from Q = 0 to Q = 0. The excitation table shows that transition is caused by a 0 for S and a don't-care condition for R. The transition for FFB is from Q = 0 to Q = 1. The excitation table shows that transition is caused by 10 for SR.

The next step is to consider that each flip-flop input is a function of four variables—the initial state, AB, and the input, X1 X2. To design the combinational circuit requires a four-variable Karnaugh map for each flip-flop input. FIGURE 11.35 shows the Karnaugh maps from Figure 11.34. The map for input SA, Figure 11.35(a), shows the row values for the state

FIGURE 11.35

The Karnaugh maps for Figure 11.34.

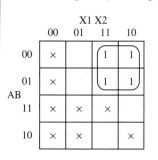

(a) SA = $\overline{A}$ X1

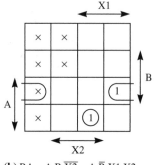

(b) RA = A B $\overline{X2}$ + A $\overline{B}$ X1 X2

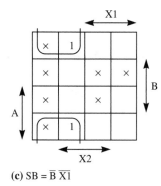

(c) SB = $\overline{B}$ $\overline{X1}$

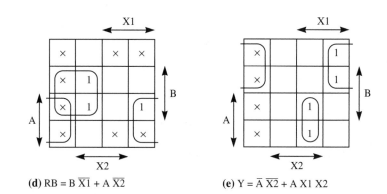

(d) RB = B $\overline{X1}$ + A $\overline{X2}$

(e) Y = $\overline{A}$ $\overline{X2}$ + A X1 X2

AB and the column values for the input X1 X2. Note that the combination X1 X2 = 00; the first column in the Karnaugh maps is a don't-care condition.

The output, Y, is also a function of the initial state and input and requires a Karnaugh map for minimization. Shown below each Karnaugh map is the corresponding minimized expression.

FIGURE 11.36 is the resulting sequential circuit. Rather than show the feedback connections explicitly, the diagram is in abbreviated form.

After completing the design, you might notice in Figure 11.35(c) and (d) that cell 8 of the Karnaugh map is covered and so appears to have the value 1. How can that be when Figure 11.35(a) and (b) do not have it covered and so it appears to have the value 0? How can it have the value 0 and 1 at the same time? Karnaugh maps do not show what happens in practice to the don't-care conditions. The specification of the circuit in Figure 11.33 assumes that the external input X1 X2 comes from some unknown source and that the combination X1 X2 = 00 will never occur in practice. Therefore, the combination represented by cell 8—namely, A B X1 X2 = 1000—will

FIGURE 11.36

The minimized sequential network for Figure 11.33.

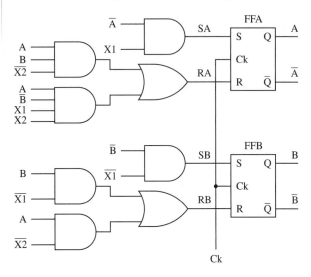

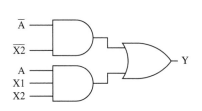

never occur. You can choose to have your circuit behave any way you want for that combination, because it will never occur.

The same consideration arises if you need to design a machine with the number of states not equal to a power of 2. Say you want to design a five-state machine. Two flip-flops are not enough, because they provide only four states. With three flip-flops, you have eight states possible, but only five will occur in practice. The other three can be don't-care conditions in the design. After you design such a circuit, the unused states will be inaccessible from the used states, but not necessarily vice versa. That is, there may be transitions from the unused to the used states, but such transitions will be irrelevant because they will never occur. They are analogous to dead code in a program.

The design procedure illustrated in this example has two flip-flops and two inputs, for a total of four variables in the Karnaugh map. Four-variable maps would also be required for a design with three flip-flops and one input, or one flip-flop and three inputs. The procedure for one flip-flop and two inputs, or two flip-flops and one input, would be identical except that three-variable Karnaugh maps would suffice for the minimization.

Some sequential circuits require minimization of a combinational circuit with more than four variables. Karnaugh maps cannot conveniently handle a problem of that size. Systematic procedures exist to deal with these larger problems, of which the most common is the Quine-McCluskey algorithm, but those are beyond the scope of this text.

11.3 Computer Subsystems

Computers are designed as a set of interconnected subsystems. Each subsystem is a black box with a well-specified interface. Sometimes the subsystem consists of an individual integrated circuit, in which case the interface is specified by the operating characteristics of the wire pins of the physical package. At a lower level of abstraction, the subsystem could be part of several subsystems within an integrated circuit. Or, at a higher level, the subsystem could be a printed circuit board made up of several integrated circuits.

However the subsystem is physically implemented, a bus connects the subsystems together. The bus could be a single wire from the output of a gate of one subsystem to the input of a gate of another subsystem. Or the bus could be a group of wires containing both data and control signals, like the bus that connects main memory to the CPU of Pep/9 shown in Figure 4.1.

Registers

A basic building block of the Level ISA3 machine is the register. You are familiar with the 16-bit registers in the Pep/9 CPU. The instruction set includes instructions to manipulate the register contents. **FIGURE 11.37** shows a block diagram and implementation of a 4-bit register.

The register has four data inputs, four data outputs, and a control input that is labeled *Load*. The block diagram shows the four data lines as a single

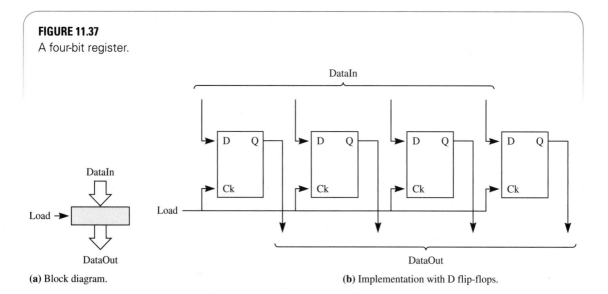

FIGURE 11.37
A four-bit register.

DataIn

Load

DataIn

DataOut

(a) Block diagram.

(b) Implementation with D flip-flops.

wide arrow. The implementation shows the data lines individually. The register is simply an array of D flip-flops. Each data input line connects to the D input of a flip-flop. Each data output line connects to the Q output of a flip-flop. The load input connects to the clock inputs of all the flip-flops. From this point on, figures that contain sequential circuits are shaded to distinguish them from combinational circuits.

The register operates by presenting the values you wish to load on the data input lines. You then clock them into the register by sending the load signal to 1 and back to 0. All four values are loaded simultaneously into the register. If each flip-flop is a master–slave device, the output appears when the slave is connected to the master at time t_4 of Figure 11.11.

Each D flip-flop is a bit in the register. An 8-bit register would have 8 flip-flops, and a 16-bit register would have 16 flip-flops. The number of flip-flops would not affect the speed of the load operation because the load into each flip-flop occurs simultaneously. The block diagram of Figure 11.37(a) is the same regardless of the number of bits in the register.

Buses

Suppose you have two subsystems, A and B, that need to send data back and forth. The simplest way to connect them is to have two unidirectional buses—one for sending data from A to B and one from B to A. The first bus would be a group of wires, each one from the output of a gate in A to the input of a gate in B. Each wire from the second would be from the output of a gate in B to the input of a gate in A.

Unidirectional buses

One problem with this arrangement is the sheer number of wires for a wide bus. If you want to send 64 bits at a time, you need two unidirectional buses, for a total of 128 wires. You can cut that number in half by using a bidirectional bus. The tradeoff is speed. With two unidirectional buses, you can send information from A to B and B to A at the same time, an impossibility with a bidirectional bus. You also must pay the price of a small setup time if you need to change the direction of the data flow on the bus before sending the data.

Bidirectional buses

FIGURE 11.38 shows the problem that must be solved to implement a bidirectional bus. An AND gate represents the master clock-enable gate of a master–slave flip-flop that is part of a register. A NOR gate represents the slave Q output gate of the flip-flop of another register. To send data from A to B, the output of gate 2 must be connected to the input of gate 3. Going from B to A, the output of gate 4 must be connected to the input of gate 1. The problem is with gates 2 and 4. You can always connect the output of one gate to the input of another, but you cannot connect the output of two gates together. Suppose gate 2 wants to send a 1 to gate 3, but the output of gate

FIGURE 11.38
The bidirectional bus problem.

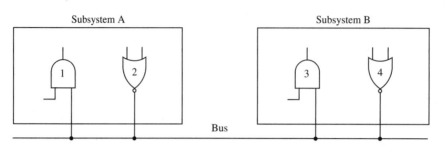

The wired-OR property

4 happens to be Ø at the time. Their outputs are in conflict, so which one predominates?

The answer depends on the technology underlying the fabrication of the gates. With some logic gate families, you can actually connect the outputs of several gates together and if one or more gates output a 1, the common bus will transfer a 1. This kind of gate is said to have the *wired-OR property* because the signal on the bus acts like the output of an OR gate. With other families, connecting the outputs of two gates together clobbers the circuit, causing unpredictable havoc. Even with wired-OR gates, the bidirectional bus problem still exists. For example, if gate 2 wants to send a Ø to gate 3, but the output of gate 4 happens to be 1 at the time, gate 3 would erroneously detect a 1.

Tri-state buffers

To make the bidirectional bus work properly, you need a way to temporarily disconnect gate 4 from the bus when gate 2 is putting data on the bus, and vice versa. A tri-state buffer can do precisely that. It has one data input, one enable control input, and one output. FIGURE 11.39 shows

FIGURE 11.39
Truth table for the tri-state buffer.

E	a	x
0	0	Disconnected
0	1	Disconnected
1	0	0
1	1	1

FIGURE 11.40
Solution to the bidirectional bus problem with the tri-state buffer.

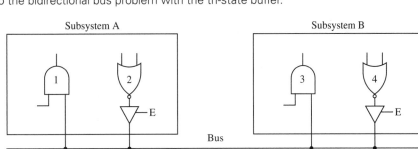

the truth table for the tri-state buffer where E is the enable control line, a is the input, and x is the output. When the device is enabled, the input passes through to the output unmodified. When it is disabled, the output is in effect disconnected from the circuit. Electrically, the output is in a high-impedance state. The device is called a *tri-state buffer* because the output can be in one of three states—0, 1, or disconnected.

FIGURE 11.40 shows how the tri-state buffer solves the bidirectional bus problem. There is a tri-state buffer between the output of every gate and the bus. To send data from A to B, you enable the tri-state buffers in A and disable the tri-state buffers in B, and vice versa. In order for this scheme to function properly, the subsystems must cooperate and never let their tri-state buffers be enabled simultaneously.

Memory Subsystems

Memory subsystems are constructed from several integrated circuit memory chips. FIGURE 11.41 shows two memory chips, each one of which stores 512 bits. Memory chips have a set of address lines labeled starting with $A0$, a set of data lines labeled starting with $D0$, and a set of control lines labeled CS, WE, and OE. The data lines have two arrowheads to indicate that they should be connected to a bidirectional bus. Part (a) shows the bits organized as a set of 64 eight-bit words. There are six address lines, because 2^6 is 64. Each possible combination of input values accesses a separate eight-bit word. Part (b) shows the same number of bits organized as a set of 512 one-bit words. There are 9 address lines because 2^9 is 512. In general, a memory chip with 2^n words has n address lines. The number of address and data lines of the chips in Figure 11.41 is unrealistically tiny to keep the examples simple. Memory chips are manufactured nowadays with billions of bits.

FIGURE 11.41

Two integrated circuit memory chips that store 512 bits.

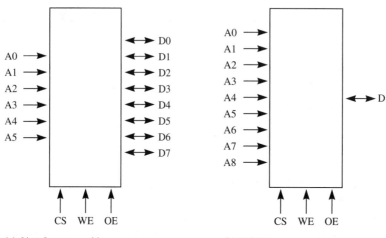

(a) 64 × 8 memory chip.   (b) 512 × 1 memory chip.

The control lines serve the following purpose:

Memory chip control lines

> CS (chip select) to enable or select the memory chip

> WE (write enable) to write or store a memory word to the chip

> OE (output enable) to enable the output buffer to read a word from the chip

Writing to a memory chip

To store a word to a chip, set the address lines to the address where the word is to be stored, set the data lines to the value that you want to store, select the chip by setting CS to 1, and execute the write by setting WE to 1.

Reading from a memory chip

To read a word from a chip, set the address lines to the address from which you want to read, select the chip by setting CS to 1, and enable the output by setting OE to 1, after which the data you want to read will appear on the

In practice, control lines are normally asserted low.

data lines. In practice, the control lines for most memory chips are asserted low. That is, they are normally maintained at a high voltage, representing 1, and are activated by setting them to a low voltage, representing 0. This text assumes that memory chip control lines are asserted high to keep the examples simple.

FIGURE 11.42 shows the implementation of a 4 × 2 memory chip with two address lines and two data lines. It stores four two-bit words. Each bit is a D flip-flop. The sequential devices are shaded to distinguish them from the combinational devices. The address lines drive a 2 × 4 decoder, one of whose

FIGURE 11.42

A 4 × 2 memory chip.

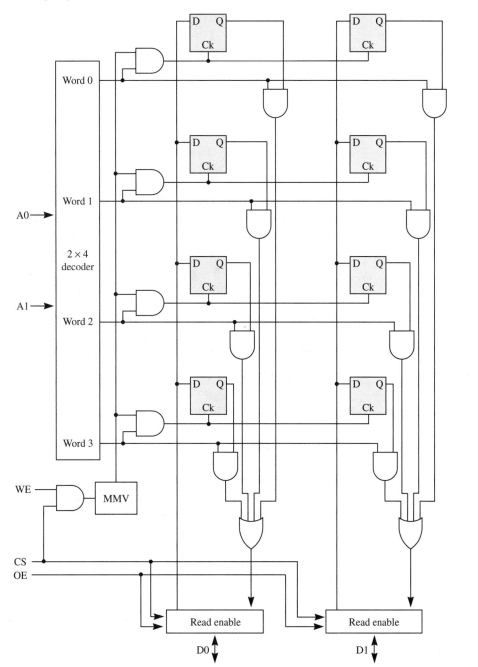

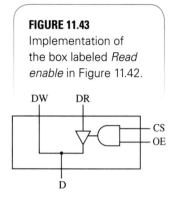

outputs is 1 and the other three 0. The decoder output line that is 1 selects the row of D flip-flops that make up the word accessed by the chip.

The box labeled *Read enable* provides the interface to a bidirectional bus. **FIGURE 11.43** shows its implementation. DR is the data read line coming from the OR gate in Figure 11.42, DW is the data write line going to the D inputs of the flip-flops, and D is the data interface to the bidirectional bus.

FIGURE 11.44 is a truth table of the circuit. The chip is normally in one of three modes.

> CS = 0: The chip is not selected.

> CS = 1, WE = 1, OE = 0: The chip is selected for write.

> CS = 1, WE = 0, OE = 1: The chip is selected for read.

It is not permitted for WE and OE to both be 1 at the same time. The truth table and its implementation show that when CS is 0, DR is disconnected from the bidirectional bus regardless of any of the other control lines. When CS is 1 and OE is 0, DR is also disconnected. This is the write mode, in which case data is being fed from the bidirectional bus to DW. When CS is 1 and OE is 1, the tri-state buffer is enabled and data is being fed from DR to the bidirectional bus.

The memory read operation
    To see how a *memory read works*, consider the following scenario, where A1 A0 = 10, CS = 1, WE = 0, and OE = 1. The values for A1 A0 make the line labeled Word 2 out of the decoder 1, and the other word lines 0. The *Word 2* line enables the AND gates connected to the Q outputs of the D flip-flops in row 2, and disables the AND gates connected to the flip-flop outputs of all the other rows. Consequently, data from the second row flows through the two OR gates into the Read enable box and onto the bidirectional bus.

*The monostable
multivibrator*
    A memory write works in conjunction with the box labeled *MMV*, which stands for *monostable multivibrator*, in Figure 11.42. Assuming that the D flip-flops are of the master–slave variety, to do a store requires a Ck pulse to go from low to high then high to low, as Figure 11.11 shows. A monostable multivibrator is a device that provides such a pulse. **FIGURE 11.45** shows the timing diagram of a monostable multivibrator with an initial delay. When the input line goes high, it triggers a delay circuit. After a predetermined time interval, the delay circuit triggers the monostable multivibrator, which emits a clock pulse with a predetermined width. Monostable multivibrators are also known as *one-shot devices* because when they are activated they emit a single "one shot" pulse.

*The memory write
operation*
    To see how a memory write works, consider the following scenario, where A1 A0 = 10, CS = 1, WE = 1, and OE = 0. Assuming that the address lines, data lines, and control lines are all set simultaneously, the

memory circuit must wait for the address signals to propagate through the decoder before clocking the data into the flip-flops. The initial delay in the monostable multivibrator is engineered to allow sufficient time for the outputs of the decoder to be set before clocking in the data. The Read enable circuit puts the data from the bidirectional bus on the input of all the flip-flops. However, when the monostable multivibrator emits the clock pulse, three of the four AND gates to which it is connected will disable the pulse from reaching their rows. It will only reach the row of Word 2, so those are the only flip-flops that will store the data.

Several types of memory chips are available on the market. The circuit model in Figure 11.42 most closely resembles what is known as *static memory*, or *SRAM*. In practice, a master–slave D flip-flop is not the basis of bit storage, as it requires more transistors than are necessary. Many static RAM devices use a circuit that is a modification of Figure 11.1(b), a stable circuit consisting of a pair of inverters with feedback. It takes only two additional transistors to implement a mechanism for setting the state. The advantage of static RAM is speed. The disadvantage is its physical size on the chip, because several transistors are required for each bit cell.

To overcome the size disadvantage of static memory, *dynamic memory*, or *DRAM*, uses only one transistor and one capacitor per bit cell. You store data by storing electrical charge on the capacitor. Because of the small size of the bit cells, DRAM chips have much higher storage capacities than SRAM chips. The problem with DRAM is that the charge slowly leaks off the capacitors within a few milliseconds of being fully charged. Before too much charge leaks off, the memory subsystem must read the data from the cell and charge the capacitor back up if necessary. As you would expect, the refresh operation takes time, and DRAM memory is slower than SRAM.

In contrast to read/write memory, *read-only memory*, or *ROM*, is designed for situations where the data to be stored never changes. The data for each bit cell can be set at the factory when the chip is manufactured, in which case the user supplies the manufacturer with the bit pattern to store. Alternatively, a *programmable ROM*, or *PROM*, chip allows the user to

FIGURE 11.44
Truth table for the Read enable box.

CS	OE	Operation
0	×	Disconnected
1	0	Disconnected
1	1	Connect DR to D

SRAM

DRAM

ROM

PROM

FIGURE 11.45
Timing diagram of a monostable multivibrator with initial delay.

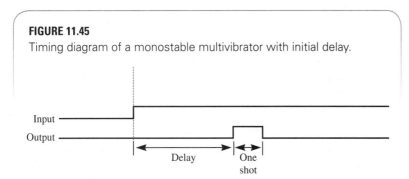

EPROM

EEPROM

Flash memory

program the bit pattern. The process is accomplished by selectively blowing out a set of fuses embedded in the chip and is irreversible. To overcome the irreversibility disadvantage, an *erasable PROM*, or *EPROM*, has the capability to erase the entire chip by exposing the circuit to ultraviolet radiation. EPROM chips, are packaged underneath a transparent window so the circuit can be exposed to the radiation. To erase an EPROM chip, you must remove it from the computer to expose it and then you must reprogram the entire chip. The *electrically erasable PROM*, or *EEPROM*, allows you to erase an individual cell with the right combination of electrical signals so that the device does not need to be removed to be reprogrammed. The circuitry to program a cell uses different voltage levels from those to read data during normal operation of the chip, and is therefore more complex to design.

SRAM and DRAM are volatile. That is, when you power off the circuit you lose the data. ROM devices are nonvolatile because they retain their data without a source of external power. *Flash memory* is popular in consumer handheld devices. It is a type of EEPROM and has the advantage of retaining its data when the device is turned off. With flash memory, you can read an individual cell, but you can only write an entire block of cells. Before writing the block, it must be completely erased. A flash card consists of an array of flash chips. A solid-state hard drive is the same thing, but with circuitry at the interface to make it appear to be a hard drive. It is not really a hard drive and has no moving parts. Compared to hard drives of the same size, flash drives are faster but hold much less data. An indication of how micro hard drive and flash memory technologies compete in the market is that manufacturers offer hard drives in a package whose interface makes them appear to be flash memory. You can plug them into your digital camera in place of the memory card. So now we have flash memory pretending to be a hard drive and a hard drive pretending to be a flash memory card, a testament to the practical power of abstraction.

Address Decoding

A single memory chip sometimes does not have the capacity to provide main memory storage for an entire computer. You must combine several chips into a memory subsystem to provide adequate capacity. Most computers are byte addressable, as is Pep/9. A chip like the one in Figure 11.41(a) would be convenient for such a machine because the word size of the chip matches the cell size that the CPU addresses.

Suppose, however, that you have a set of 4 × 2 chips like the one in Figure 11.42 and you want to use it in Pep/9. Because the word size of the chip is 2 and the size of an addressable cell for the CPU is 8, you must group four 4 × 2 chips to construct a 4 × 8 memory module. **FIGURE 11.46** shows the interconnections. You can see that the input and output lines of the

FIGURE 11.46

Constructing a 4 × 8 memory module from four 4 × 2 memory chips.

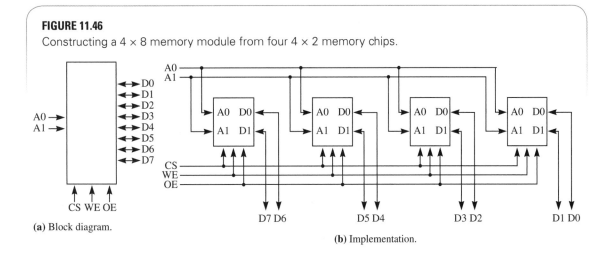

(a) Block diagram.

(b) Implementation.

module are identical to the input and output lines of what would be a 4 × 8 chip. The bits of each byte in memory are distributed over four chips. The bits of the byte at address A1 A0 = 01 are stored in the second row (Word 1) of all four chips.

Similarly, it would take eight of the chips in Figure 11.41(b) to construct a 512 × 8 memory module. For high reliability, you could use 11 of the chips for each eight-bit cell with the three extra chips used for single-error correction, as described in Section 9.4. With such an ECC system, the bits of each byte would be spread out over all 11 chips.

These examples show how to combine several $n \times m$ chips to make an $n \times k$ module where k is greater than m. In general, k must be a multiple of m. You simply hook up k/m chips, with all their address and control lines in common, and assign the data lines from each chip to the lines of the module.

A different problem in constructing memory subsystems is when you have several $n \times m$ chips, m is equal to the size of the addressable cell for the CPU, and you want an $l \times m$ module where l is greater than n. In other words, if you have a set of chips whose word size is equal to the size of the addressable cell of the CPU, how do you connect them to add memory to your computer? The key is to use the chip select line CS so that for all address requests from the CPU, no more than one chip is selected. The technique for connecting a memory chip to an address bus is called *address decoding*. There are two variations—full address decoding and partial address decoding.

Address decoding

FIGURE 11.47 shows the memory map for a CPU with eight address lines capable of storing 2^8, or 256, bytes. The scenario is unrealistically small to keep the example simple. You have four chips that you need to wire into the address space of the CPU—a 64-byte RAM to install at address 0, a

FIGURE 11.47
The memory map of a 256-byte memory with eight address lines.

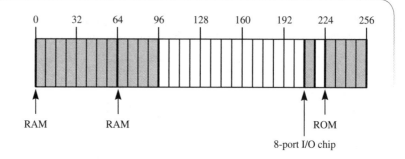

Memory-mapped input/ output

32-byte RAM to install at address 64, an eight-port memory-mapped I/O chip to install at address 208, and a 32-byte ROM to install at address 224.

The eight-port memory-mapped I/O chip corresponds to the input and output devices at charIn and charOut in Pep/9. In practice, each I/O device communicates through memory with a control register and a data register. For example, in Figure 11.47 the keyboard's control register might be at address 000 in the chip and its data register at address 001. If the chip is wired into the memory map at address 208, then the CPU will see the keyboard's control register at address 208 and its data register at address 209. It might LDBA the control register from 208 to detect that a key has been pressed, and if so, then LDBA from 209 to get the ASCII character from the keyboard buffer. For memory-mapped I/O to function, the system requires circuitry to detect when loads and stores are done to any addresses to which I/O devices are mapped. Detection of such events activates the circuitry necessary to control the I/O devices.

You determine how to connect the chips to the address bus with the help of the table in **FIGURE 11.48**. For each chip, write down in binary the minimum address (that is, the address of the starting byte of the chip) and the maximum address (that is, the address of the last byte of the chip). Comparing these two bit patterns, you determine the general form of the address range for which each chip is responsible. For example, the general address of the eight-port I/O chip is 1101 0xxx, which means that it is

FIGURE 11.48
A table for address decoding the memory map of Figure 11.47.

Device	64 × 8 RAM	32 × 8 RAM	8-port I/O	32 × 8 ROM
Minimum address	0000 0000	0100 0000	1101 0000	1110 0000
Maximum address	0011 1111	0101 1111	1101 0111	1111 1111
General address	00xx xxxx	010x xxxx	1101 0xxx	111x xxxx

responsible for the range of addresses from 1101 0000 to 1101 0111. Each letter x can be 0 or 1. Consequently, the eight-port I/O chip must be selected when, and only when, the first five digits are 11010.

FIGURE 11.49 shows the chips wired to the address bus with full address decoding. The three address lines of the eight-port I/O chip connect to the three least significant address bus lines. The most significant five address lines feed into the chip select through a pair of inverters and an AND gate. (The inverters are abbreviated in the figure and are shown as the inverted inputs to the AND gate.) You can see from the circuit that the chip select line of the eight-port I/O chip will be 1 if and only if the first five bits of the address on the bus are 11010.

To keep the figure uncluttered, it does not show the data lines of the chips. The data lines of the RAM and ROM chips all connect to an eight-bit bidirectional data bus. Also not shown are the control inputs, WE and OE, which are connected to the common WE and OE lines of the memory module.

Partial address decoding is possible if you know that your memory subsystem will never be expanded by adding more memory. A typical situation would be a small computer-controlled appliance that is not user-upgradeable. The idea is to reduce the number of gates in the decoding circuits to the bare minimum needed for the system to access the devices.

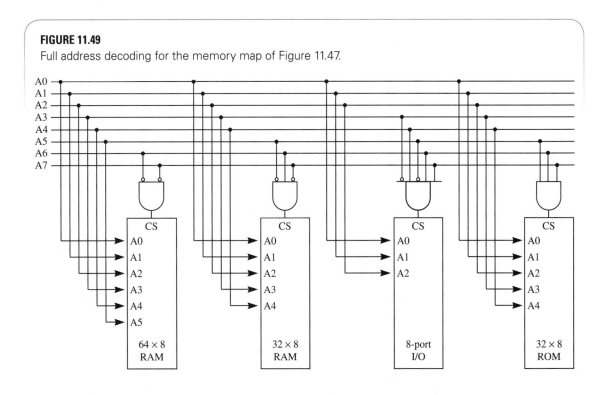

FIGURE 11.49
Full address decoding for the memory map of Figure 11.47.

The minimization technique is to write the general addresses of the chips, one per row, and inspect the columns. For the chips in Figure 11.48, the general addresses are

00xx xxxx, 64 × 8 RAM
010x xxxx, 32 × 8 RAM
1101 0xxx, 8-port I/O chip
111x xxxx, 32 × 8 ROM

Consider the first chip, and inspect the columns of the general addresses to see how you can uniquely determine the first chip with the smallest amount of information. Note that the second column, corresponding to address line A6, is 0 for the first chip and 1 for all the other chips. Therefore, you can select the first chip if A6 is 0 regardless of the value of A7.

Now consider the second chip. With full address decoding, you must test three address lines—A7, A6, and A5. Can you manage by testing only two? For example, could you test A7 A5 = 00? No, because A7 A6 A5 = 000 will select the first chip, and so both chips would be selected simultaneously. Could you test A6 A5 = 10? No, because A7 A6 A5 A4 A3 = 11010 selects the eight-port I/O chip, and again you would have a conflict. However, by inspection of the columns, none of the other chips have 01 as their first two bits. So you can test for A7 A6 = 01 to select the second chip.

Similar reasoning shows that you can select the third chip by testing A7 A6 A5 = 110 and the fourth chip by testing A7 A6 A5 = 111. **FIGURE 11.50** shows the final result of the minimization. Compared to Figure 11.49, we have eliminated one two-input AND gate and three inverters, and decreased the number of inputs of one AND gate from three to two and of another from five to three.

The question naturally arises as to the difference in behavior between the memory modules of Figures 11.49 and 11.50. There is no difference when the CPU accesses one of the shaded regions in the memory map of Figure 11.47. With full address decoding, if the CPU accesses an address outside the shaded areas, no chip will be selected and the data on the data bus is unpredictable. However, with partial address decoding, the CPU might access a chip.

Consider the 64 × 8 RAM, which has a general address of 00xx xxxx, but is selected if A6 = 0. It will be selected in two cases—with an address request of 00xx xxxx and of 10xx xxxx. The first address range is by design, but the second is a side effect of partial address decoding. In effect, you have mapped one physical device into two separate regions of the address space. The CPU sees a clone of the chip at address 0 and address 128. Similar reasoning shows that the 32 × 8 RAM is duplicated once more at address 96, and the eight-port I/O chip at three more locations. The ROM is not duplicated, as its address decode circuitry is the same for full and partial addressing. **FIGURE 11.51** shows the memory map with partial address decoding.

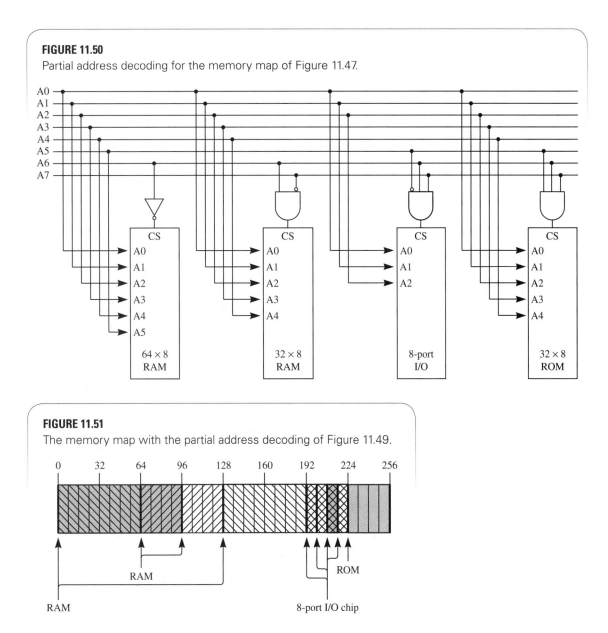

FIGURE 11.50
Partial address decoding for the memory map of Figure 11.47.

FIGURE 11.51
The memory map with the partial address decoding of Figure 11.49.

You must be careful with partial address decoding. In this example, the chips were duplicated in such a way as to completely fill the memory map with no gaps and no overlaps. If your decoding leaves gaps in the resulting map, no harm is done. If the CPU accesses a gap, then no chip is selected. If your decoding produces overlaps, however, it means that more than one chip will be selected by the CPU if it ever tries to access that region of the address space. The result could be hazardous to the system. Of course, the premise is that the CPU should never access that region, as it has no need to access a duplicated chip when it can access the original. But when is the last time you were sure there were no bugs in your program, only to discover later that there were?

A Two-Port Register Bank

The memory subsystems of the previous section all have just one set of data lines that correspond to one set of address lines. That organization is appropriate for the main memory subsystem of a computer, which normally does not reside on the same integrated circuit as the CPU. Figure 4.2 shows the registers in the Pep/9 CPU. They are organized much like a memory subsystem but are stored in a register bank in the CPU itself. The register bank in the CPU differs from the memory organization of a memory chip in two respects:

> The data buses are unidirectional instead of bidirectional.

> There are two output ports instead of one.

FIGURE 11.52 shows the 32 8-bit registers, addressed from 0 to 31. The first five registers are the ones visible to the programmer at the ISA level. Each 16-bit register is divided into two 8-bit registers. That division is invisible to the machine-level programmer.

The remaining registers, addressed from 11 to 31, are not visible to the machine-level programmer. Registers 11 to 21 comprise a group of registers for storing temporary values. Registers 22 to 31 are read-only registers that contain fixed values. They are similar to ROM in that if you try to store to them, the value in the register will not change. Their constant values are given in hexadecimal. The read-only registers are not shaded because they

FIGURE 11.52

The 32 eight-bit registers in the Pep/9 CPU.

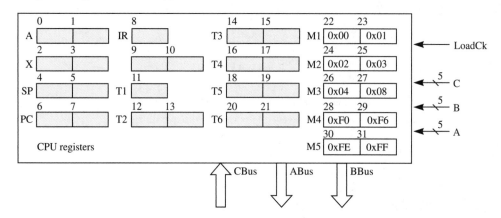

are not really sequential circuits. They act more like combinational circuits because they have no states that can change.

Where a main memory chip has one set of address lines and one set of bidirectional data lines, this register bank has three sets of addresses—A, B, and C—and three unidirectional data buses—ABus, BBus, and CBus. ABus and BBus are the two output ports, and CBus is the input port. Each data bus is eight bits wide, and each set of address lines contains five wires, capable of accessing any of the 2^5 registers. To store a value to a register, you place the address of the register on C, the data to store on the CBus, and clock the control line labeled *LoadCk*. The two output ports allow you to read two different registers simultaneously. You can put any address on A and any address on B, and the data from those two registers will appear simultaneously on ABus and BBus. You are allowed to put the same address on A and B, in which case the data from the one register will appear on both the ABus and the BBus.

FIGURE 11.53 shows the implementation of the two-port register bank. The input follows the same basic organization as a main memory chip. The

FIGURE 11.53
Implementation of the two-port register bank of Figure 11.52.

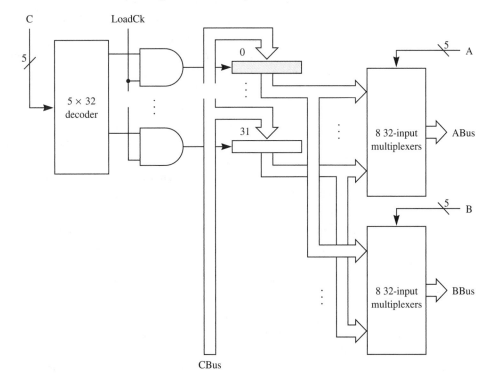

five address lines from C make one decoder output line 1 and the rest 0. CBus is connected to each of the 32 registers. When you pulse the LoadCk control line, the value on CBus is clocked into one of the registers.

The two output ports are 32-input multiplexers, each capable of routing an eight-bit quantity. Each of these multiplexers is a bank of eight individual 32-input multiplexers like the one in Figure 10.43. The five lines of A connect to the five select lines of all eight individual multiplexers in the first port. The first multiplexer routes the first bit from all 32 registers, the second multiplexer routes the second bit from all 32 registers, and so on.

Chapter Summary

A sequential circuit, constructed from logic gates with feedback loops, can remember its state. The four basic sequential devices are the SR flip-flop (set, reset), the JK flip-flop, the D flip-flop (data or delay), and the T flip-flop (toggle). The S input to the SR flip-flop sets the state to 1, and the R input resets the state to 0. The input condition SR = 11 is undefined. The JK inputs correspond to SR, except that the input condition JK = 11 is defined and toggles the state. The D input transfers directly to the state. If the T input is 1, the state toggles; otherwise, it remains unchanged. Each of these flip-flops may be constructed as master–slave devices to solve the instability problem that external feedback would produce.

A general sequential circuit consists of a combinational circuit whose output feeds into a set of state registers. The output from the state registers feeds back to the input of the combinational circuit. A sequential circuit can be characterized by a state transition diagram, which is a manifestation of a finite-state machine. When you analyze a sequential circuit, you are given the input and the sequential circuit, and you determine the output.

When you design a sequential circuit, you are given the input and the desired output, and you determine the sequential circuit. Excitation tables aid the design process. An excitation table for a flip-flop consists of the four possible state changes of the device—0 to 0, 0 to 1, 1 to 0, and 1 to 1—and the input conditions necessary to produce the change. The design process consists of tabulating the input conditions necessary to produce the given state transition diagram, and then designing the combinational circuit to produce those input conditions.

A register is a sequence of D flip-flops. The tri-state buffer makes possible the implementation of the bidirectional bus. A memory chip is (conceptually) an array of D flip-flops with a set of address lines, data lines, and control lines. The control lines usually consist of *CS* for *chip select*, *WE* for *write enable*, and *OE* for *output enable*. Address decoding is a technique for using the CS lines to construct a memory module from a set of memory chips. Partial address decoding minimizes the number of gates in the select circuitry. The two-port register bank in the Pep/9 CPU implements the registers visible to the ISA programmer, as well as the temporary registers and constant registers that are not visible.

Exercises

Section 11.1

*1. Under what circumstances will a string of an arbitrary number of inverters with a feedback loop, as in Figure 11.1, produce a stable network?

2. Construct tables analogous to Figures 11.3 and 11.4 to show that changing R to 1 and back to 0 resets the SR latch to $Q = 0$ if it starts in state $Q = 1$.

3. Define the following points in Figure 11.10: (1) A is the output of the top master AND gate. (2) B is the output of the bottom master AND gate. (3) C is the output of the inverter. (4) D is the output of the top slave AND gate. (5) E is the output of the bottom slave AND gate. Suppose $SR = 10$ and $Q = 0$ before the arrival of a clock pulse. Construct a table that shows the values of A, B, C, D, E, R2, S2, Q, and $\bar{Q}$ during each of the following intervals of Figure 11.11, assuming zero gate delay:

   *(a) before t_1 *(b) between t_1 and t_2 (c) between t_2 and t_3
   (d) between t_3 and t_4 (e) after t_4

4. Do Exercise 3 with $SR = 01$ and $Q = 1$ before the arrival of the clock pulse.

5. Draw the state transition diagram, as in Figure 11.14, for the following flip-flops:

   (a) JK   *(b) D   (c) T

6. Draw the timing diagram of Figure 11.21(c) for the toggle flip-flop with the D input replaced by T.

7. Construct the T flip-flop from an SR flip-flop.

8. This section shows how the JK and D flip-flops can be constructed from the SR flip-flop and a few gates. In fact, any flip-flop can be constructed

from any other with the help of a few gates. Construct the following flip-flops from a JK flip-flop:

*(a) D   (b) SR   (c) T

Construct the following flip-flops from a D flip-flop:

(d) SR   (e) JK   (f) T

Construct the following flip-flops from a T flip-flop:

(g) SR   (h) JK   (i) D

Section 11.2

9. Modify Figure 11.10, the implementation of the SR master–slave flip-flop, to provide asynchronous preset and clear inputs, as in Figure 11.32. When preset and clear are both 0, the device should operate normally. When preset is 1, both the master state Q2 and the slave state Q should be forced to 1 independent of the clock Ck. When clear is 1, both the master state, Q2, and the slave state, Q, should be forced to 0. You may assume that preset and clear will not both be 1 simultaneously. You can design the circuit with no extra gates if you assume that existing AND and OR gates may have three inputs instead of two.

10. Draw the logic diagram and the state transition diagram for a sequential circuit with two JK flip-flops, FFA and FFB, and two inputs, X1 and X2, with flip-flop inputs

$$JA = X1 \, B \qquad\qquad JB = X1 \, \overline{A}$$
$$KA = X2 + X1 \, A\overline{B} \qquad KB = X2 + X1 \, A$$

There is no output other than the flip-flop states.

11. Draw the logic diagram and the state transition diagram for a sequential circuit with one JK flip-flop, FFA; one T flip-flop, FFB; and one input, X, with flip-flop inputs

$$J = X \oplus B \qquad\qquad T = X \oplus A$$
$$K = \overline{X} \, B$$

and output
$$Z = A \, B$$

12. Draw the logic diagram and the state transition diagram for a sequential circuit with two SR flip-flops, FFA and FFB; two inputs, X1 and X2, with flip-flop inputs

$$SA = X1 \qquad\qquad SB = \overline{X1} \, \overline{X2} \, \overline{A}$$
$$RA = \overline{X1} \, X2 \qquad RB = X1 \, A + X2$$

and output
$$Z = X1 \, \overline{A}$$

13. Design the sequential circuit of Figure 11.33 using the following flip-flops:

*(a) D   (b) T

14. FIGURE 11.54 is a state transition diagram for a sequential circuit with three flip-flops and one input. It counts up in binary when the input is 1 and remains in the same state when the input is 0. Design the circuit and draw the logic diagram using the following flip-flops:

(a) JK   (b) SR   (c) D   (d) T

15. FIGURE 11.55 is a state transition diagram for a sequential circuit with three flip-flops and one input. It counts up in binary when the input is 1 and counts down when the input is 0. Design the circuit and draw the logic diagram using the following flip-flops:

*(a) JK   (b) SR   (c) D   (d) T

16. FIGURE 11.56 is a state transition diagram for a sequential circuit with two flip-flops and two inputs. It counts up in binary when the input is 01, counts down in binary when the input is 10, and does not change

FIGURE 11.54
The state transition diagram for Exercise 14.

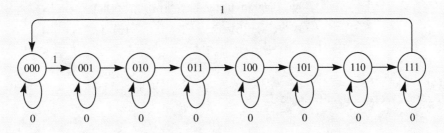

FIGURE 11.55
The state transition diagram for Exercise 15.

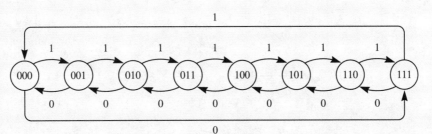

FIGURE 11.56
The state transition diagram for Exercise 16.

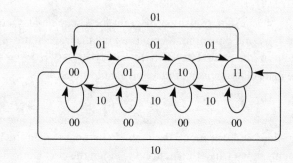

state when the input is 00. An input of 11 will never occur and can be treated as a don't-care condition. Design the circuit and draw the logic diagram using the following flip-flops:

(a) JK   **(b)** SR   **(c)** D   **(d)** T

17. FIGURE 11.57 is a state transition diagram for a sequential circuit with three flip-flops and one input. It is a three-bit shift right register. If the input is 0, a 0 is shifted into the most significant bit. If the input is 1, a 1 is shifted into the most significant bit. Design the circuit and draw the logic diagram using the following flip-flops:

(a) JK   **(b)** SR   **(c)** D   **(d)** T

FIGURE 11.57
The state transition diagram for Exercise 17.

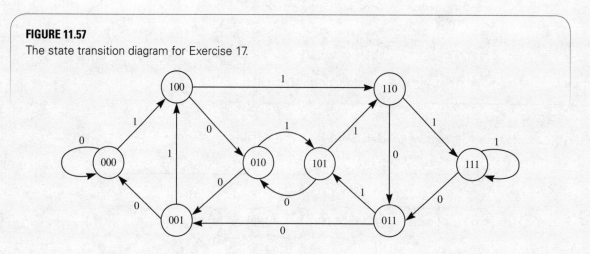

18. A sequential circuit has six state registers and three input lines. **(a)** How many states does it have? **(b)** How many transitions from each state does it have? **(c)** How many total transitions does it have?

Section 11.3

19. **(a)** How many AND gates, OR gates, and inverters are in the memory chip of Figure 11.42? Include the gates in the decoder but not in the D flip-flops. **(b)** How many of each element are in the memory chip of Figure 11.41(a)? **(c)** How many are in the memory chip of Figure 11.41(b)?

20. In practice, the chip select line of a memory chip is asserted low, and the line is labeled $\overline{CS}$ instead of CS to indicate that fact. How would Figure 11.49 change if the chip select lines on all the chips were asserted low?

21. A computer system has a 16-bit wide data bus. **(a)** If you have a box of 1 Ki × 1 dynamic RAM chips, what is the smallest number of bytes of memory this computer can have? **(b)** Answer part (a) if the 1 KiB chips you have are configured as 256 × 4 devices.

22. You have a small CPU with a 10-bit address bus. You need to connect a 64-byte PROM, a 32-byte RAM, and a 4-port I/O chip with two address lines. Chip selects on all chips are asserted high. **(a)** Show the connection for full address decoding with the PROM at address 0, the RAM at address 384, and the PIO at address 960. (These addresses are decimal.) **(b)** Show the connection for partial address decoding with the chips at the same locations. Show the memory map with partial address decoding and ensure that no duplicate regions overlap. For each chip, state (1) how many clones are produced and (2) the starting address of each clone.

23. Show how the individual multiplexers in the top port of Figure 11.53 are connected. You may use ellipses (. . .).

24. How many AND gates, OR gates, and inverters are in the two-port register bank of Figure 11.53? Include the gates necessary to construct the decoder and the multiplexers, but not the ones in the D flip-flops that make up the registers.

Microcode

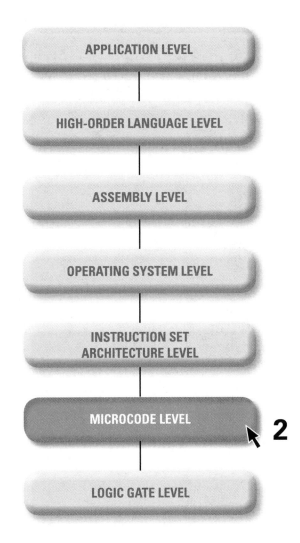

APPLICATION LEVEL

HIGH-ORDER LANGUAGE LEVEL

ASSEMBLY LEVEL

OPERATING SYSTEM LEVEL

INSTRUCTION SET
ARCHITECTURE LEVEL

MICROCODE LEVEL   **2**

LOGIC GATE LEVEL

CHAPTER 12

Computer Organization

This final chapter shows the connection between the combinational and sequential circuits at Level LG1 and the machine at Level ISA3. It describes how hardware devices can be connected at the Mc2 level of abstraction to form black boxes at successively higher levels of abstraction to eventually construct the Pep/9 computer.

12.1 Constructing a Level-ISA3 Machine

FIGURE 12.1 is a block diagram of the Pep/9 computer. It shows the CPU divided into a data section and a control section. The data section receives data from and sends data to the main memory subsystem and the disk. The control section issues the control signals to the data section and to the other components of the computer.

The CPU Data Section

FIGURE 12.2 is the data section of the Pep/9 CPU. The sequential devices in the figure are shaded to distinguish them from the combinational devices. The CPU registers at the top of the figure are identical to the two-port register bank of Figure 11.52.

The control section, not shown in the figure, is to the right of the data section. The control lines coming in from the right come from the control section. The control lines are rendered as dashed lines in Figure 12.1, but they are solid lines in Figure 12.2. There are two kinds of control signals— combinational circuit controls and clock pulses. Names of the clock pulses all end in Ck and all act to clock data into a register or flip-flop. For example,

FIGURE 12.1

Block diagram of the Pep/9 computer.

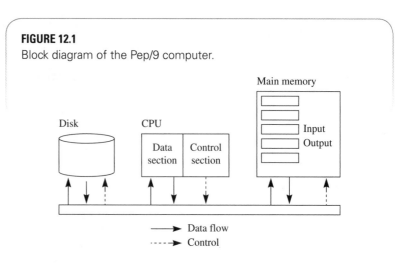

FIGURE 12.2

The data section of the Pep/9 CPU.

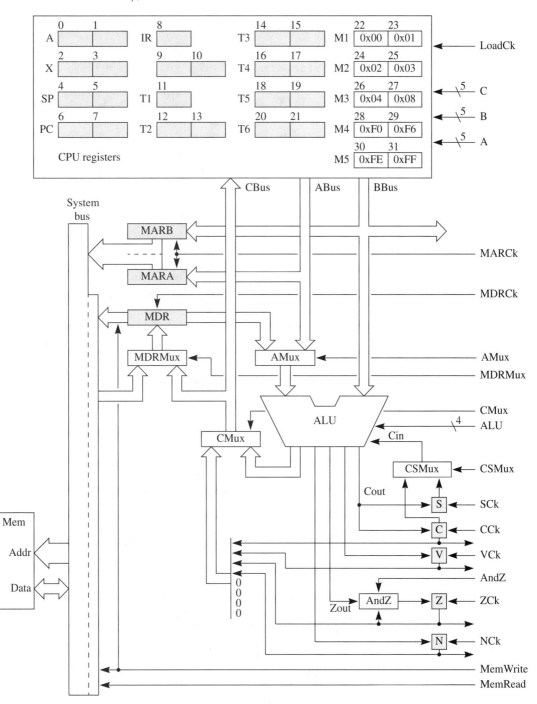

The main system bus

The memory address register, MAR

The memory data register, MDR

The multiplexers—AMux, CMux, and MDRMux

Multiplexer control signals

The status bits—N, Z, V, C, and S

MDRCk is the clock input for the MDR. When it is pulsed, the input from the MDRMux is clocked into the MDR.

The system bus on the left of the figure is the main system bus of Figure 12.1, to which main memory and the disk devices are attached. It consists of 8 bidirectional data lines, 16 address lines, and 2 control lines labeled *MemWrite* and *MemRead* at the bottom of the figure. MAR is the memory address register, divided into MARA, the high-order byte, and MARB, the low-order byte. The box labeled *Mem* is a 64-KiB memory subsystem. The 16 address lines on the bus are unidirectional, so that the output of the MAR connects to the input of the address port of the memory subsystem over the bus. MDR is the eight-bit memory data register. Because the data bus is bidirectional, there is a set of eight tri-state buffers (not shown in the figure) between MDR and the bus that are enabled by the MemWrite control line. The MemWrite line connects to the Write Enable (WE) line of the memory subsystem over the main system bus. The MemRead line connects to the Output Enable (OE) line. All the other buses in Figure 12.2 represented by the wide arrows are eight-bit unidirectional data buses, including, for example, ABus, BBus, CBus, and the bus connecting the data lines of the main system bus to the box labeled *MDRMux*.

Each multiplexer—AMux, CMux, and MDRMux—is a bank of eight two-input multiplexers with their control lines connected together to form the single control line in Figure 12.2. For example, the control line labeled *AMux* in the figure is connected to each of the eight control lines in the bank of eight multiplexers in the block labeled *AMux*. A multiplexer control line routes the signal through a multiplexer as follows:

> 0 on a multiplexer control line routes the left input to the output.

> 1 on a multiplexer control line routes the right input to the output.

For example, if the MDRMux control line is 0, MDRMux routes the content of the system bus to the MDR. If the control line is 1, it routes the data from the CBus to the MDR. Similarly, if the AMux control line is 0, AMux routes the content of MDR to the left input of the ALU. Otherwise, it routes the data from the ABus to the left input of the ALU.

The CSMux is different from the other multiplexers because it switches only one line instead of eight lines. If the CSMux control line is 0, the multiplexer sends the S bit to the Cin of the ALU. If the CSMux control line is 1, the multiplexer sends the C bit to the Cin of the ALU.

The block labeled *ALU* is the arithmetic logic unit of Figure 10.54. It provides the 16 functions listed in Figure 10.55 via the four control lines labeled ALU in Figure 12.2. The status bits—N, Z, V, C, and S—are each one D flip-flop. For example, the box labeled *C* is a D flip-flop that stores the value of the carry bit. The D input to the flip-flop is the Cout signal from the ALU. The Q output of the flip-flop is at the top, into the left input of CSMux. The Q output is also at the bottom of the box labeled C. The clock input of the flip-flop is the control signal labeled *CCk*. The outputs of each of the status bits feed into the low-order nybble of the left bus into the CMux. The high-order nybble is hardwired to four zeros. The outputs of each of the status bits are also sent to the control section.

The box labeled S is the shadow carry bit. The C bit is visible to the programmer as the carry bit at Level ISA3. The arithmetic instructions set the C bit, and the conditional branch instructions test it. The shadow carry bit S, however, is hidden from the programmer at the ISA3 abstraction level. When the ALU performs an arithmetic operation, it can take its Cin input from either the C bit or the S bit through CSMux. The system can also clock the Cout output from the ALU into either the C bit or the S bit. The question of which bit to use depends on whether the computation at Level Mc2 should alter the carry bit for the programmer at Level ISA3. If the computation is performing an arithmetic operation like ADDA for which the carry bit should be set, Cout from the ALU would be clocked into the C carry bit. If the computation is performing an internal operation like incrementing the program counter, Cout from the ALU would be clocked into the S shadow carry bit.

The shadow carry bit

At the ISA level, each register is 16 bits, but the internal data paths of the CPU are only 8 bits wide. To perform an operation on one 16-bit quantity requires two operations on 8-bit quantities at the Mc2 level. For example, the Z bit must be set to 1 if the 16 bits of the result are all zeros, which happens when the Zout signal from the ALU is 1 for both 8-bit operations. The combinational box labeled *AndZ* facilitates the computation of the Z bit. Its output is connected to the input of the D flip-flop for the Z bit. It has three inputs—the AndZ input from the control section, the Zout output from the ALU, and the Q output from the D flip-flop for the Z bit. FIGURE 12.3 shows the truth table for the box. It operates in one of the following two modes:

> If the AndZ control signal is 0, Zout passes directly through to the output.

> If the AndZ control signal is 1, Zout AND Z passes to the output.

Operation of the AndZ circuit in Figure 12.2

The Z bit is, therefore, loaded with either the Zout signal from the ALU or the Zout signal ANDed with the current value of the Z bit. Which one depends on the AndZ signal from the control section. Implementation of the AndZ circuit is an exercise at the end of the chapter.

The data flow is one big loop, starting with the 32 eight-bit registers at the top and proceeding via ABus and BBus through AMux to the ALU,

FIGURE 12.3

The truth table for the AndZ combinational circuit in Figure 12.2.

Input			Output
AndZ	Z	Zout	
0	0	0	0
0	0	1	1
0	1	0	0
0	1	1	1
1	0	0	0
1	0	1	0
1	1	0	0
1	1	1	1

through CMux, and finally back to the bank of 32 registers via CBus. Data from main memory can be injected into the loop from the system bus, through the MDRMux to the MDR. From there, it can go through the AMux, the ALU, and the CMux to any of the CPU registers. To send the content of a CPU register to memory, you can pass it through the ALU via the ABus and AMux, through the CMux and MDRMux into the MDR. From there it can go to the memory subsystem over the system bus.

The control section has 34 control output lines and 12 input lines. The 34 output lines control the flow of data around the data section loop and specify the processing that is to occur along the way. The 12 input lines come from the 8 lines of BBus plus 4 lines from the status bits, which the control section can test for certain conditions. Later in this chapter is a description of how the control section generates the proper control signals. In the following description of the data section, assume for now that you can set the control lines to any desired values for any cycle.

The von Neumann Cycle

The heart of the Pep/9 computer is the von Neumann cycle. The data section in Figure 12.2 implements the von Neumann cycle. It really is nothing more than plumbing. In the same way that water in your house runs through the pipes controlled by various faucets and valves, signals (electrons, literally) flow through the wires of the buses controlled by various multiplexers. Along the way, the signals can flow through the ALU, where they can be processed as required. This section shows the control signals necessary to implement

FIGURE 12.4
A pseudocode description at Level Mc2 of the von Neumann execution cycle.

```
do {

        Fetch the instruction specifier at address in PC
        PC ← PC + 1
        Decode the instruction specifier
        if (the instruction is not unary) {
              Fetch the high-order byte of the operand specifier as specified by PC
              PC ← PC + 1
              Fetch the low-order byte of the operand specifier as specified by PC
              PC ← PC + 1
        }
        Execute the instruction fetched
}
while ( (the stop instruction does not execute) && (the instruction is legal) )
```

the von Neumann cycle. It includes the implementation of some typical instructions in the Pep/9 instruction set and leaves the implementation of others as problems at the end of the chapter.

Figure 4.32 shows the pseudocode description of the steps necessary to execute a program at Level ISA3. The do loop is the von Neumann cycle. At Level Mc2, the data section of the CPU operates on 8-bit quantities, even though the operand specifier part of the instruction register is a 16-bit quantity. The CPU fetches the operand specifier in two steps: the high-order byte followed by the low-order byte. The control section increments PC by 1 after fetching each byte. **FIGURE 12.4** is a pseudocode description at Level Mc2 of the von Neumann execution cycle.

The control section sends control signals to the data section to implement the von Neumann cycle. **FIGURE 12.5** is the control sequence to fetch the instruction specifier and to increment PC by 1. The figure does not show the method by which the control section determines whether the instruction is unary.

Each numbered line in Figure 12.5 is a CPU clock cycle and consists of a set of control signals that are input into the combinational devices, usually followed by a clock pulse into one or more registers. The combinational signals, denoted by the equals sign, must be set up for a long enough period of time to let the data reach the register before being clocked into the register. The combinational signals are applied concurrently and are

---

FIGURE 12.5

The control signals to fetch the instruction specifier and increment PC by 1.

```
// Fetch the instruction specifier and increment PC by 1

UnitPre:  IR=0x000000, PC=0x00FF, Mem[0x00FF]=0xAB, S=0
UnitPost: IR=0xAB0000, PC=0x0100

// MAR <- PC.
1. A=6, B=7; MARCk
// Fetch instruction specifier.
2. MemRead
3. MemRead
4. MemRead, MDRMux=0; MDRCk
// IR <- instruction specifier.
5. AMux=0, ALU=0, CMux=1, C=8; LoadCk

// PC <- PC plus 1, low-order byte first.
6. A=7, B=23, AMux=1, ALU=1, CMux=1, C=7; SCk, LoadCk
7. A=6, B=22, AMux=1, CSMux=1, ALU=2, CMux=1, C=6; LoadCk
```

---

therefore separated from each other by a comma, which is the concurrent separator. The combinational signals are separated from the clock signals by a semicolon, which is the sequential separator, because the clock pulses are applied after the combinational signals have been set. Comments are denoted by double forward slashes (//).

FIGURE 12.6 shows the clock cycles corresponding to the lines numbered 1 through 5 in Figure 12.5. The period of a cycle T in seconds is specified by the frequency f of the system clock in Hz according to $T = 1/f$. The greater the frequency of your computer, as measured by its GHz rating, the shorter the period of one cycle and the faster your computer will execute, all other things being equal. So, what limits the speed of the CPU? The period must be long enough to allow the signals to flow through the combinational circuits and be presented to the inputs of the registers (which are the sequential circuits) before the next clock pulse arrives.

Transferring the PC to the MAR

For example, at the beginning of cycle 1 of Figure 12.6, A=6 sets the five A lines to 6 (dec), which is 00110 (bin), and B=7 sets the five B lines to 7 (dec), which is 00111 (bin). Figure 12.2 shows that A=6 and B=7 access the high-order byte and the low-order byte of the PC. It takes time for the A and B signals to propagate through the combinational addressing circuits in the

FIGURE 12.6

Timing diagram of the first five cycles of Figure 12.5.

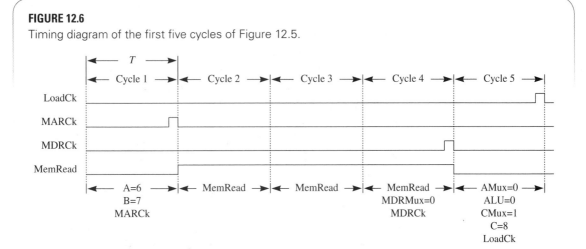

register bank and for the content of the PC to be placed on ABus and BBus. The period T is long enough to allow those signals to be set up and present at the inputs of MARA and MARB before the MARCk clock pulse occurs at the end of cycle 1 shown in Figure 12.6. After the clock pulse at the end of cycle 1, the content of PC is in MARA and MARB.

At the beginning of cycle 2, the address signals from MARA and MARB begin to propagate over the system bus to the memory subsystem. Now the MemRead signal activates the OE line on the chip in the memory subsystem that is selected by the address decoding circuitry. There are so many propagation delays in the memory subsystem that it usually takes many CPU cycles before the data is available on the main system bus. The Pep/9 computer models this fact by requiring MemRead on three consecutive cycles after the address is clocked into the MAR. So the MemRead signal is asserted high in cycles 2, 3, and 4.

At the end of cycle 4, because the same address was present in the memory address register (MAR) for three consecutive cycles and MemRead was asserted during those three cycles, the data from that address in memory is present on the system bus. In cycle 4, MDRMux=0 sets the MDR multiplexer line to 0, which routes the data from the system bus through the multiplexer to the input of the memory data register (MDR). The MDRCk pulse on cycle 4 clocks the instruction specifier into the MDR.

Cycle 5 sends the instruction specifier from the MDR into the instruction register, IR, as follows. First, AMux=0 sets the AMux control line to 0, which routes the MDR to the output of the AMux multiplexer. Next, ALU=0 sets the ALU control line to 0, which passes the data through the

Transferring a byte from memory to the MDR

Sending data from the MDR to the register bank

ALU unchanged, as specified in Figure 10.55. CMux=1 routes the data from the ALU to the CBus. Then, C=8 sets C to 8, which specifies the instruction register, as Figure 12.2 shows. Finally, LoadCk clocks the content of the MDR into the instruction register.

In cycle 5, Figure 12.6 shows the LoadCk clock pulse at the end of the cycle. The clock period T must be long enough to allow the content of the MDR to propagate through the multiplexer and the ALU before the LoadCk. The control section designer must count the number of gate delays through those combinational circuits to determine the minimum time that must elapse before the data is clocked into the instruction register. The period T is set long enough to accommodate those gate delays.

Incrementing PC by 1

Cycles 6–7 increment PC by 1. On cycle 6, A=7 puts the low-order byte of PC on ABus, and B=23 puts constant 1 on BBus. AMux=1 selects the ABus to pass through the multiplexer. ALU=1 selects the A plus B function of the arithmetic logic unit, so the ALU adds 1 to the low-order byte of PC. CMux=1 routes the sum to the CBus, and C=7 puts the sum back into the low-order byte of PC. In the same cycle, SCk saves the carry out of the addition in the shadow carry S bit. The period T is long enough for the data to flow through the combinational devices specified by the other control signals in cycle 6 before SCk stores Cout from the ALU into S and LoadCk stores the result of the ALU into the low-order byte of PC.

If the original low-order byte of PC is 1111 1111 (bin), then adding 1 will cause a carry to the high-order byte. On cycle 7, A=6 puts the high-order byte of PC onto the ABus, and B=22 puts constant 0 onto the BBus. AMux=1 routes ABus through the multiplexer to the ALU, and CSMux=1 routes the saved shadow carry S bit to Cin of the ALU. ALU=2 selects the A plus B plus Cin function for the ALU, adding the saved carry from the low-order byte to the high-order byte of PC. CMux=1 routes the result to the CBus, and C=6 directs the data on the CBus to be loaded into the high-order byte of PC, which is stored with the LoadCk pulse.

Microcode unit tests

The Pep/9 CPU software available with this text allows you to write control sequences like Figure 12.5 and simulate their execution on the Pep/9 data section. The software provides unit tests for the correctness of the sequences specified by UnitPre and UnitPost statements. A UnitPre statement can set the value of a memory location, a register bank location, or a status bit to any arbitrary value before the control sequences execute. A UnitPost statement tests the value of a memory location, a register bank location, or a status bit after the control sequences execute.

For example, in Figure 12.5 the UnitPre statement sets the IR to all zeros, the PC to 00FF (hex), Mem[00FF] to AB (hex) (the instruction specifier for CPWX this,s), and the shadow bit S to 0. With these initial conditions, fetching the instruction specifier and incrementing the program counter should put AB (hex) in the instruction register and should increment the program counter to 0100 (hex). Because the UnitPost statement specifies these values, the software automatically tests them at the conclusion of the control sequence simulation and displays a message about whether these postconditions are satisfied.

It is possible to reduce the number of cycles in Figure 12.5 by combining cycles. The control sequence in FIGURE 12.7 does the same processing as the control sequence in Figure 12.5 but with only five cycles instead of seven. Cycle 1 puts a copy of PC in the MAR, and that original copy stays in the MAR during cycles 2, 3, and 4. Consequently, the value of PC can be incremented during cycles 2 and 3 without disturbing its original value in the MAR. The control sequence in Figure 12.7 combines cycle 6 with cycle 2 from Figure 12.5. During cycle 2, the ABus, BBus, and CBus are not used in Figure 12.5. Thus, the low-order byte can be incremented by 1 in this cycle concurrently with the system waiting for the memory read. Similarly, cycle 7 is combined with cycle 3. Reducing the number of cycles from 7 to 5 is a savings in time of $2/7 = 29\%$.

Combining cycles

You cannot arbitrarily combine cycles in a control sequence. You must remember that a numbered line in a control sequence like Figure 12.5 represents one CPU cycle. Some cycles depend on the results from previous cycles. For example, you cannot combine cycles 4 and 5 in Figure 12.5, because cycle 5 depends on the results from cycle 4. Cycle 4 sets the content

FIGURE 12.7
Combining cycles of Figure 12.5.

```
// Fetch the instruction specifier and increment PC by 1

UnitPre: IR=0x000000, PC=0x00FF, Mem[0x00FF]=0xAB, S=0
UnitPost: IR=0xAB0000, PC=0x0100

// MAR <- PC.
1. A=6, B=7; MARCk
// Fetch instruction specifier, PC <- PC + 1.
2. MemRead, A=7, B=23, AMux=1, ALU=1, CMux=1, C=7; SCk, LoadCk
3. MemRead, A=6, B=22, AMux=1, CSMux=1, ALU=2, CMux=1, C=6; LoadCk
4. MemRead, MDRMux=0; MDRCk
// IR <- instruction specifier.
5. AMux=0, ALU=0, CMux=1, C=8; LoadCk
```

of the MDR, and cycle 5 uses the content of the MDR. Therefore, cycle 5 must happen after cycle 4.

Hardware concurrency is an important issue in computer organization. Designers are always on the alert to use hardware concurrency to improve performance. The seven-cycle sequence of Figure 12.5 would certainly not be used in a real machine, because combining cycles in Figure 12.7 gives a performance boost with no increase in circuitry.

Although the details of the control section are not shown, you can imagine how it would test the instruction just fetched to determine whether it is unary. The control section would set B to 8 to put the instruction specifier on BBus, which it could then test. If the fetched instruction is not unary, the control section must fetch the operand specifier, incrementing PC accordingly. The control sequence to fetch the operand specifier and increment PC is a problem at the end of this chapter.

After fetching an instruction, the control section tests the instruction specifier to determine which of the Pep/9 ISA3 instructions to execute. The control signals to execute the instruction depend not only on the opcode, but on the register-r field and the addressing-aaa field also. **FIGURE 12.8** shows the relationship between the operand and the operand specifier (OprndSpec) for each addressing mode.

A quantity in square brackets is a memory address. To execute the instruction, the control section must provide control signals to the data

FIGURE 12.8
The addressing modes for the Pep/9 computer.

Addressing mode	Operand
Immediate	OprndSpec
Direct	Mem[OprndSpec]
Indirect	Mem[Mem[OprndSpec]]
Stack-relative	Mem[SP + OprndSpec]
Stack-relative deferred	Mem[Mem[SP + OprndSpec]]
Indexed	Mem[OprndSpec + X]
Stack-indexed	Mem[SP + OprndSpec + X]
Stack-deferred indexed	Mem[Mem[SP + OprndSpec] + X]

section to compute the memory address. For example, to execute an instruction that uses the indexed addressing mode, the control section must perform a 16-bit addition of the content of the operand specifier (registers 9 and 10) and X (registers 2 and 3). The result of this addition is then loaded into MAR in preparation for a memory read in case of an LDWr instruction, or memory write in case of an STWr instruction.

The control sequence to implement the first part of the von Neumann execution cycle in Figure 12.5 looks suspiciously like a program in some low-level programming language. The sequence is the microcode language at Level Mc2. The job of control section designers is to devise circuits that, in effect, program the data section to implement the instructions at Level ISA3, the instruction set architecture level.

The next few examples show the Mc2 control sequences necessary to execute some representative ISA3 instructions. Each example assumes that the instruction has been fetched and PC incremented accordingly. Each statement in the program is written on a separate, numbered line and consists of a set of combinational signals to route data through a multiplexer or to select a function for the ALU, possibly followed by one or several clock pulses to load some registers. Keep in mind that a program at this level of abstraction (Level Mc2) consists of the control signals necessary to implement just one instruction at the higher level of abstraction (Level ISA3).

The Store Byte Direct Instruction

FIGURE 12.9 shows the control sequence to execute the instruction

    STBA there,d

where there is a symbol. The RTL specification for the STBr instruction is

byte Oprnd ← r⟨8..15⟩

Because the instruction specifies direct addressing, the operand is Mem[OprndSpec]. That is, the operand specifier is the address in memory of the operand. The instruction stores the least significant byte of the accumulator into the memory cell at that address. The status bits are not affected.

This example, as well as those that follow, assumes that the operand specifier is already in the instruction register. That is, it assumes that the fetch, decode, and increment parts of the von Neumann execution cycle have already transpired. The programs show only the execute part of the von Neumann cycle. The unit test shows that if the least significant byte of the

FIGURE 12.9

The control signals to implement the store byte instruction with direct addressing.

```
// STBA there,d
// RTL: byteOprnd <- A<8..15>
// Direct addressing: Oprnd = Mem[OprndSpec]

UnitPre: IR=0xF1000F, A=0x00AB
UnitPost: Mem[0x000F]=0xAB

// MAR <- OprndSpec.
1. A=9, B=10; MARCk
// Initiate write, MBR <- A<low>.
2. MemWrite, A=1, AMux=1, ALU=0, CMux=1, MDRMux=1; MDRCk
3. MemWrite
4. MemWrite
```

accumulator has AB (hex) and the operand specifier has 000F (hex), then after the statement executes, Mem[000F] must have AB (hex).

Transferring OprndSpec to MAR

Cycle 1 transfers the operand specifier into the memory address register. A=9 puts the high-order byte of the operand specifier on the ABus, B=10 puts the low-order byte of the operand specifier on the BBus, and MARCk clocks the ABus and BBus into the MAR registers.

Transferring A<low> to MAR

Cycle 2 transfers the low-order byte of the accumulator into the MDR. A=1 puts the low-order byte of the accumulator onto the ABus, AMux=1 routes it through the AMux into the ALU, ALU=0 passes it through the ALU unchanged, CMux=1 routes it onto the CBus, MDRMux=1 routes it through MDRMux to the MDR, and MDRCk latches the data into the MDR. This cycle also initiates the memory write.

Completing memory write

Cycles 3 and 4 complete the memory write, storing the data that is in the MDR to main memory at the address that is in the MAR. As with memory reads, memory writes require three consecutive cycles of the MemWrite line to give the memory subsystem time to get the address from the bus for routing the data. The data to be transferred needs to be in the MDR only during the last memory write cycle. The store instructions do not affect the status bits at the ISA level. Consequently, none of the cycles in the control sequence for STBA pulse NCk, ZCk, VCk, or CCk.

Bus Protocols

To fetch the instruction specifier requires a read from memory over the system bus, and to store a byte requires a write to memory over the system bus. In practice, every bus in a computer system has timing specifications that other components of the system must follow to transfer information over the bus.

The bus protocol for a memory read over the Pep/9 system bus requires three consecutive cycles, with MemRead asserted on each cycle. The read operation must adhere to the following specification:

> ❯ You must clock the address into the MAR before the first MemRead cycle.

> ❯ You must clock the data into the MDR from the system bus on or before the third MemRead cycle.

> ❯ On the third MemRead cycle, you cannot clock a new value into MAR in anticipation of a following memory operation.

The memory read bus protocol

You might be tempted to clock in a new address on the third MemRead cycle, reasoning that the address gets clocked in at the *end* of the third cycle and so would be present on the system bus during all of the first two cycles and most of the third cycle. However, the system bus protocol does not allow you to do so.

The bus protocol for a memory write requires three consecutive cycles, with MemWrite asserted on each cycle. The write operation must adhere to the following specification:

> ❯ You must clock the address into the MAR before the first MemWrite cycle.

> ❯ On the first or second MemWrite cycle, you can clock the data to be written into the MDR.

> ❯ On the third MemWrite cycle, you can clock a new data value into the MDR in anticipation of a following memory write. However, you cannot clock a new address value into the MAR in anticipation of a following memory operation.

The memory write bus protocol

Figure 12.9 shows the data value to be written to memory clocked into the MDR during cycle 2. It could just as easily be clocked into the MDR during cycle 3, which is the second MemWrite cycle. It is possible to first clock the data into the MDR, then to clock the address into the MAR, then to initiate the memory write. But that would require an extra cycle. It is more efficient to combine the clocking of the data into the MBR concurrently with one of the MemWrite cycles.

The Store Word Direct Instruction

FIGURE 12.10 shows the control sequence to execute the instruction

    STWA there,d

where there is a symbol. The RTL specification for the STWr instruction is

    Oprnd ← r

The difference between STWA and STBA is that STWA stores two bytes instead of one. Because the bytes are stored in consecutive addresses and the operand specifier is the address of where the first byte will be stored, the microcode adds 1 to that address to get the address of where to store the second byte.

FIGURE 12.10
The control signals to implement the store word instruction with direct addressing.

```
// STWA there,d
// RTL: Oprnd <- A
// Direct addressing: Oprnd = Mem[OprndSpec]

UnitPre: IR=0xE100FF, A=0xABCD, S=0
UnitPost: Mem[0x00FF]=0xABCD

// UnitPre: IR=0xE101FE, A=0xABCD, S=1
// UnitPost: Mem[0x01FE]=0xABCD

// MAR <- OprndSpec.
1. A=9, B=10; MARCk
// Initiate write, MDR <- A<high>.
2. MemWrite, A=0, AMux=1, ALU=0, CMux=1, MDRMux=1; MDRCk
// Continue write, T2 <- OprndSpec + 1.
3. MemWrite, A=10, B=23, AMux=1, ALU=1, CMux=1, C=13; SCk, LoadCk
4. MemWrite, A=9, B=22, AMux=1, CSMux=1, ALU=2, CMux=1, C=12; LoadCk

// MAR <- T2.
5. A=12, B=13; MARCk
// Initiate write, MDR <- A<low>.
6. MemWrite, A=1, AMux=1, ALU=0, CMux=1, MDRMux=1; MDRCk
7. MemWrite
8. MemWrite
```

Cycles 1 through 4 in Figure 12.10 are identical to cycles 1 through 4 in Figure 12.9, with two exceptions. First, the microcode stores the high-order (leftmost) byte of the accumulator instead of the low-order byte. Second, in parallel with the memory writes in cycles 3 and 4, it adds 1 to the operand specifier and stores it in temporary register T2.

Transferring OprndSpec to MAR and adding 1 to OprndSpec

Cycles 5 through 8 store the low-order byte of the accumulator to memory at the address computed in register T2. Cycle 5 puts the content of T2 into the MAR. Cycle 6 puts the low-order byte of the accumulator in the MDR and initiates the memory write. Cycles 7 and 8 complete the memory write. The two unit tests check for the possibility of an internal carry on the address computation. In the first test, the internal carry is 1, and in the second it is 0.

Transferring OprndSpec to MAR and writing to memory

The Add Immediate Instruction

FIGURE 12.11 shows the control sequence to implement

```
ADDA this,i
```

The RTL specification for ADDr is

$$r \leftarrow r + \text{Oprnd} ; N \leftarrow r < 0 , Z \leftarrow r = 0 , V \leftarrow \{overflow\} , C \leftarrow \{carry\}$$

The instruction adds the operand to register r and puts the sum in register r, in this case the accumulator. Because the instruction uses immediate addressing, the operand is the operand specifier. As usual, this example assumes that the instruction specifier has already been fetched and is in the instruction register.

The instruction affects all four of the status bits. However, the data section of the Pep/9 CPU can operate only on 8-bit quantities, even though the accumulator holds a 16-bit value. To do the addition, the control sequence must add the low-order bytes first and save the shadow carry from the low-order addition to compute the sum of the high-order bytes. It sets N to 1 if the two-byte quantity is negative when interpreted as a signed integer; otherwise, it clears N to 0. The sign bit of the most significant byte determines the value of N. It sets Z to 1 if the two-byte quantity is all zeros; otherwise, it clears Z to 0. So, unlike the N bit, the values of both the high-order and the low-order bytes determine the value of Z.

Cycle 1 adds the low-order byte of the accumulator to the low-order byte of the operand specifier. A=1 puts the low-order byte of the accumulator on the ABus, and B=10 puts the low-order byte of the operand specifier on the BBus. AMux=1 routes the ABus through the multiplexer, ALU=1 selects the A plus B function of the ALU, CMux=1 routes the sum to the CBus, C=1 directs the output of the ALU to be stored in the low-order byte of the accumulator,

Adding low-order byte

FIGURE 12.11

The control signals to implement the add instruction with immediate addressing.

```
// ADDA this,i
// RTL: A <- A + Oprnd; N <- A<0, Z <- A=0, V <- {overflow}, C <- {carry}
// Immediate addressing: Oprnd = OprndSpec

UnitPre:  IR=0x700FF0, A=0x0F11, N=1, Z=1, V=1, C=1, S=0
UnitPost: A=0x1F01, N=0, Z=0, V=0, C=0

// UnitPre:  IR=0x707FF0, A=0x0F11, N=0, Z=1, V=0, C=1, S=0
// UnitPost: A=0x8F01, N=1, Z=0, V=1, C=0

// UnitPre:  IR=0x70FF00, A=0xFFAB, N=0, Z=1, V=1, C=0, S=1
// UnitPost: A=0xFEAB, N=1, Z=0, V=0, C=1

// UnitPre:  IR=0x70FF00, A=0x0100, N=1, Z=0, V=1, C=0, S=1
// UnitPost: A=0x0000, N=0, Z=1, V=0, C=1

// A<low> <- A<low> + Oprnd<low>, Save shadow carry.
1. A=1, B=10, AMux=1, ALU=1, AndZ=0, CMux=1, C=1; ZCk, SCk, LoadCk
// A<high> <- A<high> plus Oprnd<high> plus saved carry.
2. A=0, B=9, AMux=1, CSMux=1, ALU=2, AndZ=1, CMux=1, C=0; NCk, ZCk, VCk, CCk, LoadCk
```

and LoadCk clocks it in. In the same cycle, AndZ=0 sends Zout through to the output of the AndZ combinational circuit, which is presented as input to the Z one-bit register (a D flip-flop). ZCk latches the bit into the Z bit, while SCk latches the carry out into the shadow carry S bit.

Adding high-order byte   Cycle 2 adds the high-order byte of the accumulator to the high-order byte of the operand specifier. A=0 puts the high-order byte of the accumulator on the ABus, and B=9 puts the high-order byte of the operand specifier on the BBus. CMux=1 routes the shadow carry bit S to Cin of the ALU, AMux=1 routes the ABus through the multiplexer, ALU=2 selects the A plus B plus Cin function of the ALU, CMux=1 routes the sum to the CBus, C=0 directs it to be stored in the high-order byte of the accumulator, and LoadCk clocks it in. AndZ=1 sends Zout AND Z through to the output of the AndZ combinational circuit, which is presented as input to the Z bit. ZCk latches the value into the status bit. A 1 will be latched into the Z bit if and only if both Zout and Z are 1. The value of Z was saved with ZCk from cycle 1, and so it contains 1 if and only if the low-order sum was all zeros. Consequently, the final value of Z is 1 if and only if all 16 bits of the sum are zeros. The other three status bits—N, V, and C—reflect the status of the high-order addition. They are saved with NCk, VCk, and CCk on cycle 2.

Figure 12.11 shows four unit tests for this ISA3 instruction implementation. Each unit test results in a different final set of values for status bits NZVC and is activated by uncommenting the test. Because the ADDA instruction affects all four status bits, their initial values are set to the opposite values they should have in the final state. For example, in the second unit test, the final values of the status bits should be NZVC = 1010. Therefore, the initial values for that unit test are NZVC = 0101.

The Load Word Indirect Instruction

FIGURE 12.12 shows the control sequence for

    LDWX this,n

The RTL specification for LDWr is

    $r \leftarrow$ Oprnd ; $N \leftarrow r < 0$, $Z \leftarrow r = 0$

This instruction loads two bytes from main memory into the index register. Because the instruction uses indirect addressing, the operand is Mem[Mem[OprndSpec]], as Figure 12.8 shows. The operand specifier is the address of the address of the operand. The control sequence must fetch a word from memory, which it uses as the address of the operand, requiring yet another fetch to get the operand.

FIGURE 12.13 shows the effect of executing the control sequence of Figure 12.12, assuming that symbol this has the value 0012 (hex) and the initial values in memory are the ones shown at addresses 0012 and 26D1. Mem[0012] contains 26D1 (hex), which is the address of the operand. Mem[26D1] contains the operand 53AC (hex), which the instruction must load into the index register. The figure shows the register addresses for each register affected by the control sequence. The first byte of the instruction register, CA, is the instruction specifier for the LDWX instruction using indirect addressing.

Cycles 1–5 transfer Mem[OprndSpec] to the high-order byte of temporary register T3. On cycle 1, A=9 and B=10 put the operand specifier on the ABus and BBus, and MARCk clocks them in to the memory address register. Cycle 2 initiates a memory read, cycle 3 continues it, and cycle 4 completes it. Cycle 5 routes the data from the MDR into the high-order byte of T3 in the usual way.

Cycles 2–3 add 1 to the operand specifier and store the result in temporary register T2 concurrently with the above operation during the memory read cycles. Cycle 2 adds 1 to the low-order byte of the operand

Transferring Mem[OprndSpec] to T3<high> and adding 1 to OprndSpec

FIGURE 12.12
The control signals to implement the load word instruction with indirect addressing.

```
// LDWX this,n
// RTL: X <- Oprnd; N <- X<0, Z <- X=0
// Indirect addressing: Oprnd = Mem[Mem[OprndSpec]]

UnitPre: IR=0xCA0012, Mem[0x0012]=0x26D1, Mem[0x26D1]=0x53AC
UnitPre: N=1, Z=1, V=0, C=1, S=1
UnitPost: X=0x53AC, N=0, ·Z=0, V=0, C=1

// UnitPre: IR=0xCA0012, X=0xEEEE, Mem[0x0012]=0x00FF, Mem[0x00FF]=0x0000
// UnitPre: N=1, Z=0, V=1, C=0, S=1
// UnitPost: X=0x0000, N=0, Z=1, V=1, C=0

// T3<high> <- Mem[OprndSpec], T2 <- OprndSpec + 1.
1. A=9, B=10; MARCk
2. MemRead, A=10, B=23, AMux=1, ALU=1, CMux=1, C=13; SCk, LoadCk
3. MemRead, A=9, B=22, AMux=1, CSMux=1, ALU=2, CMux=1, C=12; LoadCk
4. MemRead, MDRMux=0; MDRCk
5. A=12, B=13, AMux=0, ALU=0, CMux=1, C=14; MARCk, LoadCk

// T3<low> <- Mem[T2].
6. MemRead
7. MemRead
8. MemRead, MDRMux=0; MDRCk
9. AMux=0, ALU=0, CMux=1, C=15; LoadCk

// Assert: T3 contains the address of the operand.
// X<high> <- Mem[T3], T4 <- T3 + 1.
10. A=14, B=15; MARCk
11. MemRead, A=15, B=23, AMux=1, ALU=1, CMux=1, C=17; SCk, LoadCk
12. MemRead, A=14, B=22, AMux=1, CSMux=1, ALU=2, CMux=1, C=16; LoadCk
13. MemRead, MDRMux=0; MDRCk
14. A=16, B=17, AMux=0, ALU=0, AndZ=0, CMux=1, C=2; NCk, ZCk, MARCk, LoadCk

// X<low> <- Mem[T4].
15. MemRead
16. MemRead
17. MemRead, MDRMux=0; MDRCk
18. AMux=0, ALU=0, AndZ=1, CMux=1, C=3; ZCk, LoadCk
```

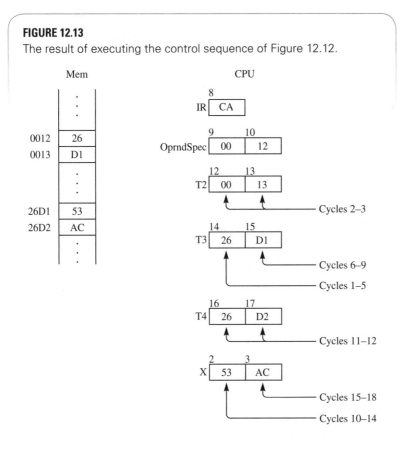

FIGURE 12.13
The result of executing the control sequence of Figure 12.12.

specifier, and cycle 3 takes care of a possible carry out from the low-order addition to the high-order addition. Cycle 5 puts the computed value of T2 into the MAR over the ABus and BBus at the same time that it puts the MDR into T3 over the CBus.

Cycles 6–9 use the address computed in T2 to fetch the low-order byte of the address of the operand. Cycle 6 initiates the memory read, cycle 7 continues the memory read, and cycle 8 completes the read and latches the byte from memory into the MDR. Cycle 9 routes the byte from the MDR through AMux and into the low-order byte of T3.

Transferring Mem[T2] to T3<low>

At this point, we can assert that temporary register T3 contains the address of the operand, 26D1 (hex) in this example. Finally, we can get the first byte of the operand and load it into the first byte of the index register. Cycles 10–14 perform that load. The RTL specification for LDWr shows that the instruction affects the N and Z bits. The N bit is determined by the sign bit of the most significant byte. Consequently, cycle 14 includes the clock

Transferring Mem[T3] to X<high> and adding 1 to T3 storing in T4

pulse NCk to save the N bit as the byte goes through the ALU. The Z bit depends on the value of both bytes, so cycle 14 also contains AndZ=0 and ZCk to save the Zout signal in the Z register. Cycles 11 and 12 increment T3, putting the result in T4 concurrently with the memory read.

Transferring Mem[T4] to X<low>

Cycles 15–18 get the second byte into the index register. Cycle 18 contains AndZ=1 so that the Z value from the low-order byte (stored in cycle 14) will be ANDed with the Zout from the high-order byte. ZCk stores the correct Z value for the 16-bit quantity that the instruction loads.

The first unit test initializes the values to correspond to the values of Figure 12.13. With these initial values, the final value of Z is 0, because the value loaded is not all zeros. The second unit test loads two bytes of all zeros into the index register, and so the final value of Z is 1. The second unit test also tests the internal carry with the shadow bit when it increments 00FF (hex).

The Arithmetic Shift Right Instruction

FIGURE 12.14 shows the control sequence to execute the unary instruction

    ASRA

The RTL specification for the ASRr instruction is

$$C \leftarrow r\langle 15 \rangle \,, r\langle 1..15 \rangle \leftarrow r\langle 0..14 \rangle \,; N \leftarrow r < 0 \,, Z \leftarrow r = 0$$

The V bit is unaffected by ASRr because it is impossible to overflow with a shift right instruction. The ASRr instruction is unary, so there are no memory accesses. That makes the control sequence nice and short.

Because the ALU computes only with 8-bit quantities, it must break the 16-bit shift into two 8-bit computations. Figure 10.62 shows the four shift and rotate computations that the ALU can perform. To do the arithmetic shift right, the control sequence does an arithmetic shift right of the high-order byte followed by a rotate right of the low-order byte.

ASR of high-order byte

In cycle 1, A=0 puts the high-order byte of the accumulator on the ABus, AMux=1 sends it to the ALU, ALU=13 selects the arithmetic shift right operation, CMux=1 and C=0 direct the result to be stored back into the accumulator, and LoadCk stores it. AndZ=0 routes the Zout from the shift operation to the Z register, and ZCk saves it. NCk saves the N bit from the high-order operation, which will be its final value. SCk saves the shadow carry S bit from the high-order operation, which will not be the final value of C.

ROR of low-order byte

In cycle 2, A=1 puts the low-order byte of the accumulator on the ABus, AMux=1 sends it to the ALU, CSMux=1 selects the shadow carry bit for Cin of the ALU, ALU=14 selects the rotate right operation, CMux=1 and C=1 direct the result to be stored back into the accumulator, and LoadCk stores it. AndZ causes the AndZ combinational circuit to perform the AND operation on

FIGURE 12.14

The control signals to implement the unary ASRA instruction.

```
// ASRA
// RTL: C <- A<15>, A<1..15> <- A<0..14>; N <- A<0, Z <- A=0

UnitPre:  IR=0x0C0000, A=0xFF01, N=1, Z=1, V=1, C=0, S=0
UnitPost: A=0xFF80, N=1, Z=0, V=1, C=1

// UnitPre:  IR=0x0C0000, A=0x7E00, N=1, Z=1, V=0, C=0, S=1
// UnitPost: A=0x3F00, N=0, Z=0, V=0, C=0

// UnitPre:  IR=0x0C0000, A=0x0001, N=1, Z=1, V=0, C=0, S=1
// UnitPost: A=0x0000, N=0, Z=1, V=0, C=1

// Arithmetic shift right of high-order byte.
1. A=0, AMux=1, ALU=13, AndZ=0, CMux=1, C=0; NCk, ZCk, SCk, LoadCk
// Rotate right of low-order byte.
2. A=1, AMux=1, CSMux=1, ALU=14, AndZ=1, CMux=1, C=1; ZCk, CCk, LoadCk
```

Zout and Z, which ZCk stores in Z as its final value. CCk stores Cout as the final value of C.

Figure 12.14 shows three unit tests for the ASRA implementation. The first tests duplication of the sign bit when it is 1 and the shadow carry bit when it is 1. The second tests duplication of the sign bit when it is 0 and the shadow carry bit when it is 0. The third tests the implementation when the final result is all zeros and the final Z bit is 1. In all three unit tests, the value of the V bit is unchanged.

The CPU Control Section

Figure 12.1 shows the CPU divided into a data section and a control section. Given a sequence of control signals necessary to implement an ISA3 instruction, such as the sequence in Figure 12.9 to implement the STBA instruction, the problem is determining how to design the control section to generate that sequence of signals.

Level Mc2

The idea behind microcode is that a sequence of control signals is, in effect, a program. Figure 12.4, which is a description of the von Neumann cycle, even looks like a C program. One way to design the control section is to create a lower-level von Neumann machine as a microcode level of abstraction that lies between ISA3 and LG1. Like all levels of abstraction, this level has its own language consisting of a set of microprogramming statements. The control section is its own micromachine with its own micromemory, uMem; its own microprogram counter, uPC; and its own microinstruction register, uIR. Unlike the machine at Level ISA3, the machine at Level Mc2 has only one program that is burned into uMem ROM. Once the chip is manufactured, the microprogram can never be changed. The program contains a single loop whose sole purpose is to implement the ISA3 von Neumann cycle.

uMem, uPC, and uIR

FIGURE 12.15 shows the control section of Pep/9 implemented in microcode at Level Mc2. The data section of Figure 12.2 has 34 control lines

FIGURE 12.15

A microcode implementation of the control section of the Pep/9 CPU.

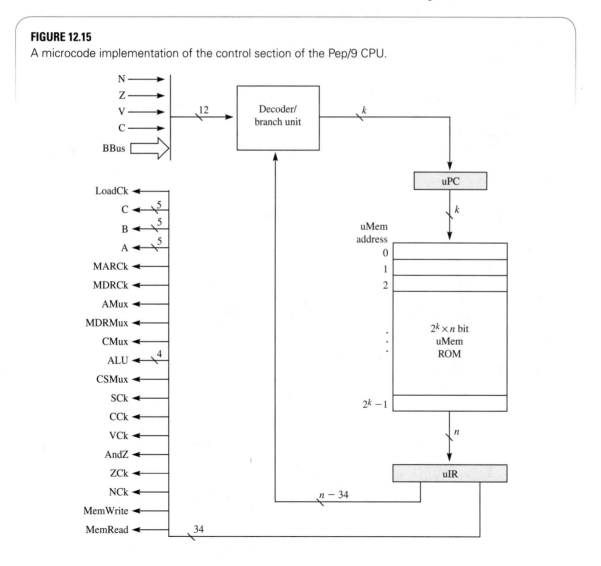

coming from the right to control the data flow. These correspond to the 34 control lines going to the left from Figure 12.15. In the data section of Figure 12.2, there are a total of 12 data lines going to the right to the control section—8 from the BBus and 4 from the status bits. These correspond to the 12 data lines coming from the right in Figure 12.15.

The microprogram counter contains the address of the next microinstruction to execute. uPC is k bits wide, so that it can point to any of the 2^k instructions in uMem. A microinstruction is n bits wide, so that is the width of each cell in uMem and also the width of uIR. At Level Mc2, there is no reason to require that the width of a microinstruction be an even power of 2. n can be any oddball value that you want to make it. This flexibility is due to the fact that uMem contains only instructions with no data. Because instructions and data are not commingled, there is no need to require the memory cell size to accommodate both.

FIGURE 12.16 shows the instruction format of a microinstruction. The rightmost 34 bits are the control signals to send to the data section. The remaining field consists of two parts—a Branch field and an Addr field. The program counter at Level ISA3 is incremented because the normal flow of control is to have the instructions stored and executed sequentially in main memory. The only deviation from this state of affairs is when PC changes due to a branch instruction. uPC at Level Mc2, however, is not incremented. Instead, every microinstruction contains within it information to compute the address of the next microinstruction. The Branch field specifies *how* to compute the address of the next microinstruction, and the Addr field contains data to be used in the computation.

For example, if the next microinstruction does not depend on any of the 12 signals from the data section, Branch will specify an unconditional branch, and Addr will be the address of the next microinstruction. In effect, every instruction is a branch instruction. To execute a set of microinstructions in sequence, you make each microinstruction an unconditional branch to the next one. The Decoder/branch unit in Figure 12.15 is designed to pass Addr straight through to uPC when the Branch field specifies an unconditional branch, regardless of the values of the 12 lines from the data section.

FIGURE 12.16

The instruction format of a microinstruction.

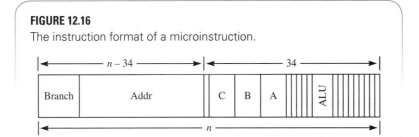

An example where a conditional microbranch is necessary is the implementation of BRLT. The RTL specification of BRLT is

$$N = 1 \Rightarrow PC \leftarrow Oprnd$$

If the N bit is 1, PC gets the operand. To implement BRLT, a microinstruction must check the value of the N bit and either do nothing or branch to a sequence of microinstructions that replaces the PC with the operand. This microinstruction would contain a Branch field that specifies that the next address is computed by combining N with Addr. If N is 0, the computation will produce one address, and if N is 1, it will produce another.

In general, conditional microbranches work by computing the address of the next microinstruction from Addr and whatever signals from the data section that the condition depends on. The biggest conditional branch of all is the branch that decides which ISA3 instruction to execute—in other words, the decode part of the von Neumann cycle. The microinstruction to decode an ISA instruction would have 8 in its B field, which would put the first byte of IR on the BBus. (See Figure 12.2 for the register address of the IR.) The Branch field would specify an instruction decode, and the Decoder/branch unit would be designed to output the address of the first microinstruction in the sequence to implement that instruction.

The details of the Branch and Addr fields in a microinstruction as well as the implementation of the Decoder/branch unit are beyond the scope of this text. Although Figures 12.15 and 12.16 ignore many practical issues in the design of a microcode level, they do illustrate the essential design elements of Level Mc2.

12.2 Performance

From a theoretical perspective, all real von Neumann computing machines are equivalent in their computation abilities. Given a mechanism to connect an infinite amount of disk memory to a machine, it is equivalent in computing power to a Turing machine. The only difference between what Pep/9 can compute and what the world's largest supercomputer can compute is the time it takes to perform the computation. Granted, it might take a million years for Pep/9 to compute the solution to a problem that a supercomputer could compute in a microsecond, but theoretically they can do the same things.

From a practical perspective, time matters. All other things being equal, faster is better. Although the data section in Figure 12.2 at Level LG1 can implement Pep/9 at Level ISA3, the question is, how fast? The fundamental source of increased performance is the space/time tradeoff. Hardware engineers can decrease the time of the computation by adding circuitry—that is, increasing the space—on the chip. There are two aspects of time in all computations—the time to perform the computation and the time to move information between components of the computer system.

Three common techniques for increasing performance in a computer system are:

> Increasing the width of the data bus

> Inserting a cache between the CPU and the memory subsystem

> Increasing hardware parallelism with pipelining

The three common techniques for increasing performance

The first two techniques decrease the time to move information between main memory and the CPU. The third technique decreases the time to perform the computation. All three techniques increase space in the system to decrease the execution time. This section describes how increasing the data bus width and using a cache improve performance. The next section describes the pipeline design of the MIPS machine.

The Data Bus Width and Memory Alignment

The most straightforward way to decrease the time to move information between main memory and the CPU is to increase the width of the data bus. If you increase the data bus width from 8 lines to 16 lines, then each memory read will get two bytes from memory instead of one. Figure 12.12 shows the implementation of a load instruction with indirect addressing. Cycles 2–4 get a low-order byte and cycles 6–8 get a high-order byte. If the data bus had 16 lines, then both bytes could be read in one memory access with only three cycles instead of six.

Figure 12.2 shows the system bus with 16 lines for addresses and 8 lines for data. To accommodate the 16-bit width of the address bus, the memory address register has two parts, MARA and MARB. If the data bus has 16 lines instead of 8, then the memory data register must have two parts as well. (FIGURE 12.17) shows the design of a Pep/9 CPU that has a data bus with 16 lines. The register bank is identical to that of Figure 12.2 and is not shown in this figure. The memory subsystem on the left is also not shown. The two parts of the memory data register are MDREven and MDROdd. The increase in space comes from the extra wires on the data bus and the circuitry for the extra memory data register. That increase in space makes possible the decrease in the computation time.

The space/time tradeoff

If the system is designed to access memory in two-byte chunks, you could design main memory to be word-addressable instead of byte-addressable. In the early days of computing, manufacturers designed memory subsystems with different cell sizes, some of which had an address

FIGURE 12.17
The data section of the Pep/9 CPU with a two-byte data bus.

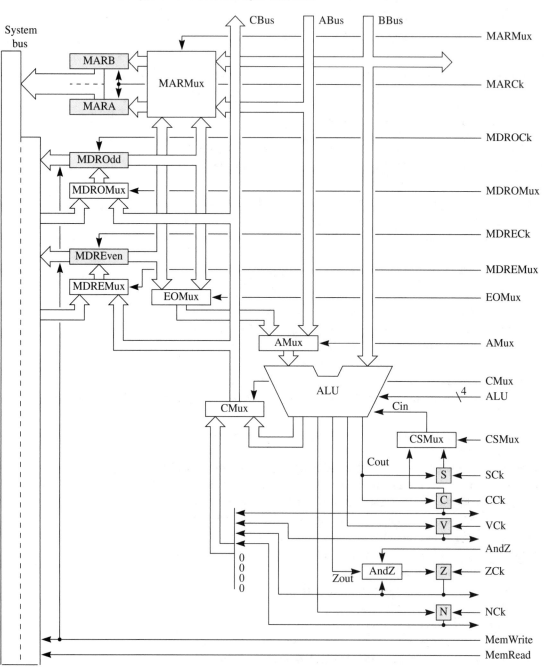

FIGURE 12.18

Addresses of data delivered by the memory subsystem to the CPU with a two-byte data bus.

CPU Address Request	Delivered	
	MDREven	MDROdd
0AB6	0AB6	0AB7
0AB7	0AB6	0AB7
0AB8	0AB8	0AB9
0AB9	0AB8	0AB9

---

for each two-byte word instead of for each byte. Today, however, virtually all computer memories are byte-addressable.

FIGURE 12.18 shows the addresses of the data delivered by the memory subsystem to the CPU in response to some example CPU requests. If the CPU puts 0AB6 in the MAR, the memory will deliver the content of Mem[0AB6] in MDREven and Mem[0AB7] in MDROdd. That is, it delivers the byte at the requested address and the byte at the *following* address. However, if the CPU puts 0AB7 in the MAR, the memory system delivers the same two bytes in the same data registers. That is, it delivers the byte at the requested address and the byte at the *preceding* address. It always delivers data from an even address to MDREven and from an odd address to MDROdd, regardless of whether the CPU memory request is even or odd.

FIGURE 12.19 shows the memory pinout of the chips for the 8-line data bus of Figure 12.2 and for the 16-line data bus of Figure 12.17. One obvious difference between the two pinouts is the set of 16 data lines for the two-byte bus as opposed to the 8 data lines for the one-byte bus. Another difference is the absence of the lowest-order address line A0 in the two-byte bus in part (b). Why is it missing? Because it is never used. Figure 12.18 shows that a memory request from 0AB6 and one from 0AB7 produce the same access—namely, Mem[0AB6] delivered to MDREven and Mem[0AB7] delivered to MDROdd. Because 0AB6 (hex) is 0000 1010 1011 0110 (bin) and 0AB7 (hex) is 0000 1010 1011 0111 (bin), the last bit A0 is irrelevant to the memory access. The address line A0 literally does not need to be on the bus, which makes it physically a 15-line address bus even though it is logically a 16-line address bus.

Figure 12.2 for the one-byte data bus shows the MDR output connected to the AMux input so you can inject it into the ABus–CBus data loop. With the two-byte data bus of Figure 12.17, however, there are two memory data registers. The EOMux, which stands for *even-odd multiplexer*, selects one of

FIGURE 12.19

The pinout diagrams for two Pep/9 main memory chips.

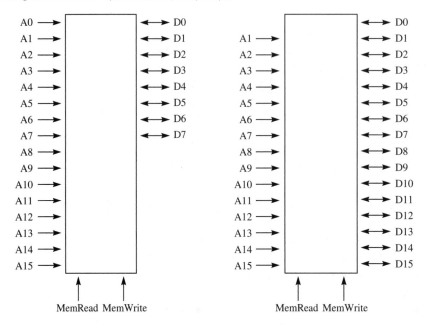

(a) The chip of Figure 12.2 with an
8-line data bus.

(b) The chip of Figure 12.17 with a
16-line data bus.

the two memory data registers to be sent to the AMux input and from there to the ABus–CBus data loop. It works like the other multiplexers, with an EOMux control value of 0 routing the MDREven output to the input of AMux and a control value of 1 routing the MDROdd output to the input of AMux.

Another performance feature of the Pep/9 CPU design of Figure 12.17 is an additional two-byte data path from the MDR registers to the MAR registers. This path alleviates a bottleneck in those cases when a memory address is read from memory and subsequently needs to be sent to the MAR. Instead of routing the address one byte at a time from the MDR registers, through the register bank, and then to the MAR, this two-byte data path allows both bytes of the MDR registers to be sent to the MAR registers in only one cycle. The box labeled *MARMux* is a 16-bit multiplexer controlled by the MARMux signal. Here is the rule for the control signal:

MARMux control signals

> 0 on the MARMux control line routes MDREven to MARA and MDROdd to MARB.

> 1 on the MARMux control line routes ABus to MARA and BBus to MARB.

Even though increasing the data bus width from one to two bytes increases the performance, it does complicate the von Neumann cycle. With the one-byte data bus, you first fetch the instruction specifier, which is one byte. If the instruction is nonunary, you then fetch the operand specifier, which is two bytes. Suppose you start the von Neumann cycle with the program loaded at address 0000. After the read from memory, you will have the instruction specifier in MDREven and the following byte in MDROdd. If the first instruction is unary, the byte in MDROdd is the instruction specifier of the following instruction. If the first instruction is nonunary, the byte in MDROdd is the first byte of the operand specifier. In either case, it is efficient to store the second byte in temporary register T1 in the register bank to be used later without having to reread it from memory.

FIGURE 12.20 shows the control sequence to fetch the instruction specifier and increment the PC. It is similar to the microcode sequence of Figure 12.5, which requires only five cycles. The extra cycle in Figure 12.20 is cycle 6, which stores the subsequent byte in register T1 in anticipation of the next fetch.

The time savings becomes apparent only when you consider the instruction specifier fetch when you know that a previous memory access has prefetched it into register T1. FIGURE 12.21 shows the control sequence

FIGURE 12.20
The fetch and increment part of the von Neumann cycle with the two-byte data bus.

```
// Fetch the instruction specifier and increment PC by 1
// Assume: PC is even and pre-fetch the next byte

UnitPre:  IR=0x000000, PC=0x00FE, Mem[0x00FE]=0xABCD, S=1
UnitPost: IR=0xAB0000, PC=0x00FF, T1=0xCD

// MAR <- PC.
1. A=6, B=7, MARMux=1; MARCk
// Initiate fetch, PC <- PC + 1.
2. MemRead, A=7, B=23, AMux=1, ALU=1, CMux=1, C=7; SCk, LoadCk
3. MemRead, A=6, B=22, AMux=1, CSMux=1, ALU=2, CMux=1, C=6; LoadCk
4. MemRead, MDREMux=0, MDROMux=0; MDRECk, MDROCk
// IR <- MDREven, T1 <- MDROdd.
5. EOMux=0, AMux=0, ALU=0, CMux=1, C=8; LoadCk
6. EOMux=1, AMux=0, ALU=0, CMux=1, C=11; LoadCk
```

FIGURE 12.21

The fetch and increment part of the von Neumann cycle with pre-fetched instruction specifier.

```
// Fetch the instruction specifier and increment PC by 1
// Assume instruction specifier has been pre-fetched

UnitPre:  IR=0x000000, PC=0x01FF, T1=0x12, S=0
UnitPost: IR=0x120000, PC=0x0200

// Fetch instruction specifier.
1. A=11, AMux=1, ALU=0, CMux=1, C=8; CCk

// PC <- PC plus 1.
2. A=7, B=23, AMux=1, ALU=1, CMux=1, C=7; SCk, LoadCk
3. A=6, B=22, AMux=1, CSMux=1, ALU=2, CMux=1, C=6; LoadCk
```

under this scenario. No memory read is required at all. The entire sequence is only three cycles. The control section can easily determine at the beginning of the cycle whether the instruction specifier was prefetched. If the program counter is even, it was not and the sequence in Figure 12.20 is necessary. If PC is odd, it uses the sequence in Figure 12.21.

A similar consideration is used for fetching the operand specifier. If the program counter is even, then no byte has been prefetched. The control section can get both bytes of the operand specifier with only one memory access. If the program counter is odd, then the first byte of the operand specifier has been prefetched. Again, only one memory access is required, which gets the second byte of the operand specifier and prefetches the subsequent instruction specifier. Another performance enhancement is the ability to increment PC by 2 only once instead of incrementing it by 1 twice, which is necessary with the one-byte data bus, as in Figure 12.4. Implementation of the control sequences to fetch the operand specifier under these scenarios is a problem for the student at the end of the chapter.

Memory Alignment

Using register T1 to store prefetched bytes increases the performance of the fetch part of the von Neumann cycle. Maximizing the performance of the execute part of the von Neumann cycle requires memory alignment of both data and program statements. For example, FIGURE 12.22(a) shows a code fragment from the program of Figure 5.27. Global variable exam1 is stored at

FIGURE 12.22

Data alignment in the program of Figure 5.26.

0000	120009		BR	main
		bonus:	.EQUATE	10
0003	0000	exam1:	.BLOCK	2
0005	0000	exam2:	.BLOCK	2
0007	0000	score:	.BLOCK	2
		;		
0009	310003	main:	DECI	exam1,d
000C	310005		DECI	exam2,d
000F	C10003		LDWA	exam1,d
0012	610005		ADDA	exam2,d

(a) Without data alignment.

0000	12000A		BR	main
		bonus:	.EQUATE	10
0003	00		.ALIGN	2
0004	0000	exam1:	.BLOCK	2
0006	0000	exam2:	.BLOCK	2
0008	0000	score:	.BLOCK	2
		;		
000A	310004	main:	DECI	exam1,d
000D	310006		DECI	exam2,d
0010	C10004		LDWA	exam1,d
0013	610006		ADDA	exam2,d

(b) With data alignment.

fixed location 0003. Consider execution of the LDWA instruction. It loads the accumulator with the value stored at 0003. Because 0003 is odd, a memory request by the CPU from this location puts Mem[0002] in MDREven and Mem[0003] in MDROdd. Even though the memory access loads two bytes from memory, it loads only the first byte of exam1 into the memory data register. The CPU can use only the value in MDROdd and needs to make a second memory access for the value from Mem[0004]. The benefit of the two-byte data bus is lost, as two memory accesses are still required.

Alignment of data

If the first byte of exam1 is stored at an even address, both bytes can be accessed with a single memory access. Figure 12.22(b) shows the same program but with an additional .ALIGN dot command inserted before the declaration of exam1. The effect of a .ALIGN command is to insert an extra zero byte if necessary so that the code generated by the following line will begin at an even address. In Figure 12.22(b), the extra byte generated by the alignment dot command forces exam1 to be stored at 0004 instead of at 0003. With this program, the LDWA instruction causes the CPU to request a memory access from 0004, which puts Mem[0004] in MDREven and Mem[0005] in MDROdd. Only one memory access is required to load the value of the integer.

The .ALIGN *assembler directive*

Alignment commands in assembly languages take an integer argument that is a power of 2. In Figure 12.22(b), the alignment command is

```
.ALIGN 2
```

The argument 2 inserts enough zero bytes in the code to force the code on the next line to be at an even address—that is, at an address divisible by 2. Suppose you increase the performace further by designing a four-byte data bus. You would then have four memory data registers—MDR0, MDR1, MDR2, and MDR3. The EOMux of Figure 12.17 would be a four-input multiplexer with two control lines instead of one. The memory chip of Figure 12.17(b) would have 32 data lines instead of 16 and would be missing address lines A0 and A1 instead of just A0. The alignment command

```
.ALIGN 4
```

would insert enough zero bytes in the code to force the code on the next line to be at the next address divisible by 4. Similarly, the alignment command

```
.ALIGN 8
```

would insert enough zero bytes in the code to force the code on the next line to be at the next address divisible by 8, appropriate for an eight-byte data bus.

Alignment on the run-time stack

Figure 12.22 shows how the alignment command maximizes performance with global variables stored at a fixed location in memory. The same optimization technique is necessary for local variables and parameters stored on the run-time stack. With a two-byte data bus, the initial value of the stack pointer is aligned to an even address. The compiler must generate assembly language code, possibly padded with zero bytes so that each variable is aligned with an even-address boundary in memory. For example, the trap mechanism described in Section 8.2 shows the process control block on the system stack. With a two-byte data bus, the instruction specifier is stored in a two-byte cell padded with a zero byte even though it is only one byte long. Each register is stored at an even address, and the NZVC bits are stored in a two-byte cell padded with a zero byte.

FIGURE 12.23 shows the implementation of the load word instruction with indirect addressing using the two-byte bus design. The unit test assumes that the operand specifier is 0012, which is even, and that Mem[0012] is 26D2, which is also even. Thus, it assumes data alignment on two-byte boundaries. Cycle 5 shows how the content of both bytes from the MDR can be sent to the MAR in one cycle. Compared to Figure 12.12, which is the implementation of the same instruction with the one-byte bus, this implementation has only two memory accesses instead of four for a total of 10 cycles instead of 18. The savings in time is thus 8 cycles out of the original 18, or 44%.

Alignment of program statements

Executing a program correctly with the two-byte data bus of Figure 12.17 requires the alignment of some program statements in memory. Branch statements cause a problem with the wide bus because they change the value of the program counter. Figure 12.21 shows the sequence for the

---

FIGURE 12.23

The two-byte bus implementation of the load word instruction with indirect addressing.

```
// LDWX this,n
// RTL: X <- Oprnd; N <- X<0, Z <- X=0
// Indirect addressing: Oprnd = Mem[Mem[OprndSpec]]

UnitPre: IR=0xCA0012, Mem[0x0012]=0x26D2, Mem[0x26D2]=0x53AC
UnitPre: N=1, Z=1, V=0, C=1
UnitPost: X=0x53AC, N=0, Z=0, V=0, C=1

// MDR <- Mem[OprndSpec].
1. A=9, B=10, MARMux=1; MARCk
2. MemRead
3. MemRead
4. MemRead, MDROMux=0, MDREMux=0; MDROCk, MDRECk

// MAR <- MDR.
5. MARMux=0; MARCk

// MDR <- two-byte operand.
6. MemRead
7. MemRead
8. MemRead, MDROMux=0, MDREMux=0; MDROCk, MDRECk

// X <- MDR, high-order first.
9. EOMux=0, AMux=0, ALU=0, AndZ=0, CMux=1, C=2; NCk, ZCk, LoadCk
10. EOMux=1, AMux=0, ALU=0, AndZ=1, CMux=1, C=3; ZCk, LoadCk
```

---

fetch part of the von Neumann cycle if PC is odd. The hardware assumes the instruction specifier is prefetched and stored in register T1. Suppose the program branches to a target statement stored at an odd location. To execute the von Neumann cycle for the target instruction, the hardware will access T1 for the instruction specifier even though it was not prefetched. For a program to work correctly with such hardware, every symbol defined on a statement that is the target of a branch instruction must be located on an even address. After the branch occurs, the program counter will be even. The fetch sequence of Figure 12.20 will execute and fetch the instruction specifier of the target instruction correctly.

FIGURE 12.24 shows the program alignment that is necessary for the program of Figure 6.8. Part (a) shows the initial branch to main as a branch

FIGURE 12.24

Program alignment in the program of Figure 6.8.

0000	120004		BR	main
		limit:	.EQUATE	100
		num:	.EQUATE	0
		;		
0003	00		.ALIGN	2
0004	580002	main:	SUBSP	2,i
0007	330000		DECI	num,s
000A	C30000	if:	LDWA	num,s
000D	A00064		CPWA	limit,i
0010	16001A		BRLT	else
0013	490022		STRO	msg1,d
0016	12001E		BR	endIf
0019	26		NOP0	
001A	490028	else:	STRO	msg2,d
001D	26		NOP0	
001E	500002	endIf:	ADDSP	2,i
0021	00		STOP	

0000	120003		BR	main
		limit:	.EQUATE	100
		num:	.EQUATE	0
		;		
0003	580002	main:	SUBSP	2,i
0006	330000		DECI	num,s
0009	C30000	if:	LDWA	num,s
000C	A00064		CPWA	limit,i
000F	160018		BRLT	else
0012	49001F		STRO	msg1,d
0015	12001B		BR	endIf
0018	490025	else:	STRO	msg2,d
001B	500002	endIf:	ADDSP	2,i
001E	00		STOP	

(a) Without program alignment.   (b) With program alignment.

to an instruction at 0003, which is odd. The .ALIGN statement in part (b) fixes that problem, forcing the main program code to begin at 0004, which is even. Inserting a .ALIGN statement at the beginning of every function, including main, is required. The program contains two other branch targets, if and endIf. To force these statements to lie on even addresses, the assembler must insert the unary no operation instruction NOP0 before each target instruction. In Pep/9, the NOP0 instruction is a trap instruction and so would cause a big performance degradation that would nullify the benefit of the wide data bus. All real processors have native no-operation instructions that execute in one cycle and are used to align program statements.

Two other statements that modify the program counter are call and ret. The call statement is a three-byte instruction that puts the incremented program counter on the run-time stack as the return address. The ret statement branches to that address. Thus, the address following the call statement must be at an even address. It follows that every call statement must be at an odd address and can therefore never be the target of a branch instruction. To fix a program that contains a branch to a call statement, you must branch instead to a no-operation instruction at an even address just before the `call`.

The Definition of an *n*-Bit Computer

The generally accepted meaning of "an *n*-bit computer" is that *n* is the number of bits in the MAR and in the CPU registers that are visible at Level ISA3. Because the registers visible at Level ISA3 can hold addresses, the registers are usually the same width as the MAR, so this definition is unambiguous. For example, Pep/9 is clearly a 16-bit computer because the registers visible at the ISA3 level that hold data, like the accumulator and the index register, are 16-bit cells. Furthermore, registers that hold addresses, like the program counter and the stack pointer, are also 16-bit cells.

There is frequently confusion about this definition, especially in marketing. An *n*-bit computer does not necessarily have *n*-bit data buses within the data section of its CPU. Nor does it necessarily have *n*-bit registers in its register bank at Level LG1. All these widths can be less than *n*. Pep/9 is an example of such a machine. Even though it is a 16-bit machine, the ABus, BBus, and CBus are only 8 bits wide. At the Mc2 level, the registers in its register bank are only 8 bits wide.

The classic example is the IBM 360 family, which was introduced in 1964. It was the first family of computers whose models all had the same ISA3 instruction sets and registers. It was a 32-bit machine, but depending on the model, the data buses in the CPU were 8-bit, 16-bit, or 32-bit. Because the LG1 details are hidden from the programmer at Level ISA3, all the software written and debugged on one model in the family ran unchanged on a different model. The only perceived difference between models was performance as measured by execution time. The concept was revolutionary at the time and promoted the design of computers based on levels of abstraction.

Nor must an *n*-bit computer have *n* address lines in the main system bus. The width of the MAR determines the maximum number of addressable bytes the system can access. An *n*-byte computer can access 2^n bytes, as FIGURE 12.25 shows. For example, Pep/9 has a 16-bit MAR and so can access a maximum of 2^{16} bytes or, equivalently, 64 KiB.

Many laptop computers today have 64-bit processors with a theoretical maximum main memory size of 2^{64} bytes, or 17,179,869,184 GiB. Because it will never be physically possible to have that much main memory installed, such systems simply advertise a maximum main memory size and design the system with the corresponding number of lines in the address bus. For example, suppose a computer manufacturer advertises a 64-bit computer for which you can install a maximum of 32 GiB of memory. Because the CPU is a 64-bit processor, its internal MAR is 64 bits wide. To save space on

FIGURE 12.25

Maximum memory limits as a function of the MAR width.

MAR Width	Number of Addressable Bytes
8	256
16	64 Ki
32	4 Gi
64	17,179,869,184 Gi

the circuit board, however, the manufacturer designs the system bus with only 35 address lines connected to MAR lines A0 through A34. Lines A35 through A63 of the MAR remain unconnected. Because 2^{35} bytes is 32 GiB, the product will allow the user to install up to 32 GiB of memory.

It is even possible for the number of data lines in the main system bus to be greater than n. For example, Pep/9, which is a 16-bit computer, could have a 32-bit wide data bus that would fetch 8 bytes with each memory read. In the same way that the microcode sequence in Figure 12.20 prefetches an additional byte that eliminates the need for a later memory access, all the unused bytes from the 8-byte memory access can be saved in the CPU, possibly eliminating many future memory accesses. The idea of prefetching more data than necessary to eliminate future memory accesses is the basis of cache memories described in the next section.

Assuming that the internal registers, the internal buses, and the data/address buses on the system bus all have the same width, increasing that common width will increase the performance. Increasing the common width of these components has a large impact on the size of the chip. All the circuits, including the ALU, the multiplexers, and the registers, must be increased to accommodate the larger width. The history of computers shows a progression toward ever-wider buses and registers. FIGURE 12.26 shows how the Intel CPUs increased in bus width from 4 bits to 64 bits. The 4004 was the first microprocessor on a chip. The first 64-bit processor from Intel was a version of the Pentium 4 chip. The market is in the process of completing the transition from 32-bit machines to 64-bit machines. Most desktop and laptop machines today have 64-bit processors, while most mobile devices have 32-bit processors.

The progression is possible only because technology advances at such a regular pace. Gordon Moore, the founder of Intel, observed in 1965 that the density of transistors in an integrated circuit had doubled every year and would continue to do so for the foreseeable future. The rate has slowed

FIGURE 12.26

Historic register/bus widths.

Chip	Date	Register Width
4004	1971	4-bit
8008	1972	8-bit
8086	1978	16-bit
80386	1985	32-bit
x86–64	2004	64-bit

somewhat, so that today the so-called *Moore's law* now states that the density of transistors in an integrated circuit doubles every 18 months. This pace cannot be maintained forever, because the miniaturization will eventually reach the dimensions of an atom, which cannot be subdivided. Exactly when Moore's law will cease has been hotly debated in the past, with many people predicting its demise, only to see it continue on.

Moore's law

The big push for 64-bit computers was because multimedia applications and large databases needed an address space greater than 4 GiB. The transition to 64-bit computers will probably be the last of its kind, however, because 64 address lines can access 16 billion GiB. The increase from one generation to the next is not polynomial, but exponential. For many years, 32-bit computers had 32-bit MARs but only 24 address lines on the main memory bus. The 8 high-order address bits were ignored. Users could install up to 16 MiB (2^{24}) on such machines, which was plenty of memory at the time. It will be the same with 64-bit computers long into the future, where the number of external address lines will be less than the internal width of the MAR, depending on the needs of the market.

Cache Memories

The Pep/9 control sequence has a requirement that memory reads and writes require three cycles because of the excessive time it takes to access the memory subsystem over the main system bus. Although this requirement puts some realism into the model, in practice the speed mismatch between main memory access time and the CPU cycle time is more severe. Suppose it took 10 cycles instead of just 3 for a main memory access. You can imagine what the control sequences would look like—many cycles of MemReads. Most of the time the CPU would be waiting for memory reads, wasting cycles that could be used for making progress on the job.

But what if you could predict the future? If you knew which words from memory would be required by the program ahead of time, you could set up a small amount of expensive, high-speed memory right next to the CPU, called a *cache*, and fetch the instructions and data from main memory ahead of time. The information would then be available for the data section immediately. Of course, no one can predict the future, so this scheme is impossible. Still, even if you could not predict the future with 100% accuracy, what if you could predict it with 95% accuracy? Those times your prediction was correct, the memory access time from the cache would be nearly instantaneous. If the percentage of time you were correct was high enough, the time savings would be substantial.

Cache memory

The problem is determining how to make the prediction. Suppose you could tap the address lines and monitor all the memory requests that a CPU makes when it executes a typical job. Would you expect to see the sequence of addresses come out at random? That is, given one address request, would you expect to see the next one close to it, or would you expect the next one to be at some random location far away?

There are two reasons you should expect to see successive memory requests close together, based on the two things stored in memory. First, the CPU must access instructions during the fetch part of the von Neumann cycle. As long as no branches execute to faraway instructions, it will be requesting from addresses that are all clumped together. Second, the CPU must access data from memory. Recall that the assembly language programs in Chapter 6 all have their data clumped together in memory. It is true that applications and the heap are stored in low memory, and the operating system and the run-time stack are stored in high memory, but you should be able to visualize that for periods of time, the accesses will all be of bytes from the same neighborhood.

The phenomenon that memory accesses are not random is called *locality of reference*. If memory accesses were totally random, then a cache would be totally useless because it would be impossible to predict which bytes from memory to preload. Fortunately, typical access requests exhibit two kinds of locality:

The two types of locality of reference

> *Spatial locality*—An address close to the previously requested address is likely to be requested in the near future.

> *Temporal locality*—The previously requested address *itself* is likely to be requested in the near future.

Temporal locality comes from the common use of loops in programs.

Cache hits and misses

When the CPU requests a load from memory, the cache subsystem first checks to see if the data requested has already been loaded into the cache, an event called a *cache hit*. If so, it delivers the data straightaway. If not, an event called a *cache miss* occurs. The data is fetched from main memory, and the CPU must wait substantially longer for it. When the data finally arrives, it is loaded into the cache and given to the CPU. Because the data was just requested, there is a high probability that it will be requested again in the near future. Keeping it in the cache takes advantage of temporal locality. You can take advantage of spatial locality by bringing into the cache not only the data that is requested, but also a clump of data in the neighborhood of the requested byte. Even though you have brought in some bytes that have not been requested yet, you are preloading them based on a prediction of the future. The probability that they will be accessed in the near future is high because their addresses are close to the address of the previously accessed byte.

Why not build main memory with high-speed circuits like the cache, put it where the cache is, and dispense with the cache altogether? Because high-speed memory circuits require so much more area on a chip. There is a huge size and speed difference between the fastest memory technology and the slowest. It is the classic space/time tradeoff. The more space you are willing to devote per memory cell, the faster you can make the memory operate.

Memory technology provides a range of designs between these two extremes. Corresponding to this range, three levels of cache are typical between the CPU and the main memory subsystem:

> Split L1 instruction and data cache—smallest, fastest, closest to the CPU

> Unified L2 cache—between the L1 and L3 caches

> Unified L3 cache—largest, slowest, farthest from the CPU

Three levels of cache in a computer system

FIGURE 12.27 shows the three levels for a quad-core CPU. In the figure, the dashed line marks the boundary of a single package—that is, a single part

FIGURE 12.27
Three levels of cache in a typical computer system.

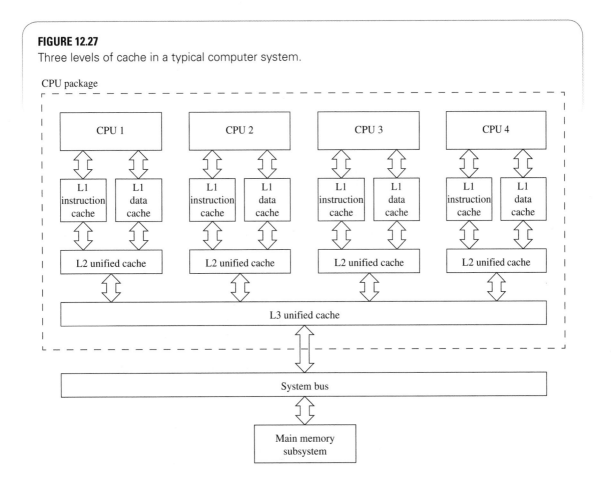

that is mounted on the circuit board of the computer system. The L1 cache is smaller and faster than the L2 cache, which is smaller and faster than the L3 cache, which is smaller and faster than the main memory subsystem. Typical sizes are 32 to 64 KiB per core for the L1 cache. (To show how tiny Pep/9 is, its entire main memory would fit inside a typical L1 cache.) The L1 cache runs at CPU speeds. The L2 cache usually runs at one-half or one-quarter the speed of the L1 cache and is four to eight times larger. The L3 cache is usually another factor of four to eight times slower and larger than the L2 cache. The cache next to main memory is also called *last-level cache*. Some designs omit the L3 cache altogether, and others have more than three levels.

The CPU makes a distinction between an instruction fetch as part of the von Neumann cycle and a data fetch of an operand. Accordingly, the L1 cache is split between an instruction cache and a data cache. The L1 cache receives memory requests from the CPU and passes the requests on to the L2 cache in case of a cache miss. The L2 cache is known as a *unified cache* because it stores instructions and data intermixed with no distinction between them. Each core also has its own L2 cache. In the event of a cache miss in the L2 cache, the L2 cache passes the requests on to the L3 cache, a unified cache that is shared between all the cores. In the event of a cache miss in the L3 cache, the L3 cache passes the requests on to the main memory subsystem.

There are two kinds of cache design:

Two types of cache design

> Direct-mapped cache

> Set-associative cache

The simpler of the two is direct-mapped cache, an example of which is shown in (FIGURE 12.28). As usual, the example is unrealistically small to help facilitate the description.

The example is for a system with 16 address lines and $2^{16} = 64$ KiB main memory. Memory is divided into 16-byte chunks called *cache lines*. On a cache miss, the system loads not only the requested byte, but also all 16 bytes of the cache line that contains the requested byte. The cache itself is a miniature memory with eight cells addressed from 0 to 7. Each cell is divided into three fields—Valid, Tag, and Data. The Data field is that part of the cache cell that holds a copy of the cache line from memory. The Valid field is a single bit that is 1 if the cache cell contains valid data from memory and 0 if it does not.

The address field is divided into three parts—Tag, Line, and Byte. The Byte field is 4 bits, corresponding to the fact that $2^4 = 16$, and there are 16 bytes per cache line. The Line field is 3 bits, corresponding to the fact that $2^3 = 8$, and there are eight cells in the cache. The Tag field holds the remainder of the bits in the 16-bit address, so it has $16 - 3 - 4 = 9$ bits. A cache cell holds a copy of the Tag field from the address along with the data

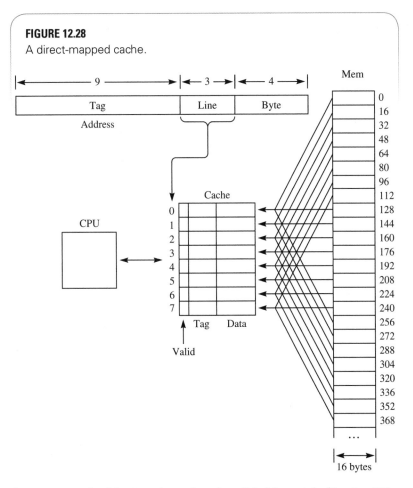

FIGURE 12.28

A direct-mapped cache.

from memory. In this example, each cache cell holds a total of $1 + 9 + 128 =$ 138 bits. As there are eight cells in the cache, the entire cache holds a total of $138 \times 8 = 1104$ bits.

FIGURE 12.29 is a pseudocode descritption of the operation of a direct-mapped cache. When the system starts up, it sets all the Valid bits in the cache to 0. The very first memory request will be a miss. The address of the cache line from memory to be loaded is simply the Tag field of the address, with the last four bits set to 0. That line is fetched from memory and stored in the cache cell with the Valid bit set to 1 and the Tag field extracted from the address and stored as well.

If another request asks for a byte in the same line, it will be a hit. The system extracts the Line field from the address, goes to that line in the cache, and determines that the Valid bit is 1 and that the Tag field of the request matches the Tag field stored in the cache cell. It extracts the byte or word from the Data part of the cache cell and gives it to the CPU without a memory read. If the Valid bit

FIGURE 12.29

A pseudocode description of the operation of a direct-mapped cache.

> *Extract the Line field from the CPU memory address request*
> *Retrieve the Valid/Tag/Data cache entry from the Line row*
> `if (Valid == 0) {`
>   *Cache miss, memory fetch*
> `} else if (Tag` *from cache* `!=` *Tag* `from memory request) {`
>   *Cache miss, memory fetch*
> `} else {`
>   *Cache hit, use Data field from cache*
>
> `}`

is 1 but the Tag fields do not match, it is a miss. A memory request is necessary, and the Tag and Data fields replace the old ones in the same cache cell.

Example 12.1   The CPU requests the byte at address 3519 (dec). What are the nine bits of the Tag field, what are the four bits of the Byte field, and which cell of the cache stores the data? Converting to binary and extracting the fields gives

3519 (dec) = 000011011 011 1111 (bin)

The nine bits in the Tag field are 000011011, the four bits in the Byte field are 1111, and the data is stored at address 011 (bin) = 3 (dec) in the cache. ∎

A deficiency of direct-mapped caches

Figure 12.28 shows that the blocks of memory at addresses 16, 144, 272, . . . , all contend for the same cache entry at address 1. Because there are nine bits in the Tag field, there are $2^9 = 512$ blocks in memory that contend for each cache cell, which can hold only one at a time. There is a pattern of requests resulting in a high cache miss rate that arises from switching back and forth between two fixed areas of memory. An example is a program with pointers on the run-time stack at high memory in Pep/9 and the heap at low memory. A program that accesses pointers and the cells to which they point will have such an access pattern. If it happens that the pointer and the cell to which it points have the same Line field in their addresses, the miss rate will increase substantially.

Set-associative caches

Set-associative caches are designed to alleviate this problem. Instead of having each cache entry hold just one cache line from memory, it can hold several. **FIGURE 12.30(a)** shows a four-way set-associative cache. It duplicates the cache of Figure 12.29 four times and allows a set of up to four blocks of memory with the same Line fields to be in the cache at any

FIGURE 12.30

A four-way set-associative cache.

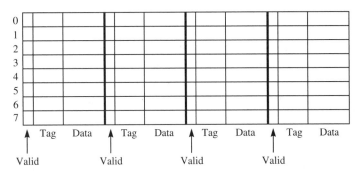

(a) Block diagram of cache storage.

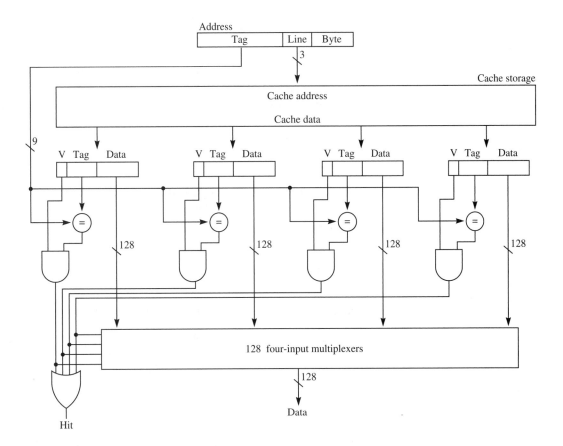

(b) Implementation of read circuit.

time. The access circuitry is more complex than the circuitry for a direct-mapped cache. For each read request, the hardware must check all four parts of the cache cell in parallel and route the one with the matching Line field if there is one.

Figure 12.30(b) shows the details of the read circuit. The circle with the equals sign is a comparator that outputs 1 if the inputs are equal and 0 otherwise. The bank of 128 multiplexers is simpler than usual. Four-input multiplexers usually have two select lines that must be decoded, but the four select lines of this multiplexer are already decoded. The output labeled *Hit* is 1 on a cache hit, in which case the output labeled *Data* is the data from the cache line with the same Tag field as the one in the requested address. Otherwise Hit is 0.

Set-associative cache line replacement

Another complication with set-associative caches is the decision that must be made when a cache miss occurs and all four parts of the cache cell are occupied. The question is, which of the four parts should be overwritten by the new data from memory? One technique is to use the least recently used (LRU) algorithm. In a two-way, set-associative cache, only one extra bit is required per cache cell to keep track of which cell was least recently used. But in a four-way set-associative cache, it is considerably more complicated to keep track of the least recently used. You must maintain a list of four items in order of use and update the list on every cache request. One approximation to LRU for a four-way cache uses three bits. One bit specifies which group was least recently used, and the bits within each group specify which item in that group was least recently used.

Regardless of whether the cache is direct-mapped or set-associative, system designers must decide how to handle memory writes with caches. There are two possibilities with cache hits:

Two cache write policies with cache hits

> *Write through*—Every write request updates the cache and the corresponding block in memory.

> *Write back*—A write request updates only the cache copy. A write to memory happens only when the cache line is replaced.

FIGURE 12.31 shows the two possibilities. Write through is the simpler design. While the system is writing to memory, the CPU can continue processing. When the cache line needs to be replaced, the value in memory is guaranteed to already have the latest update. The problem is an excessive amount of bus traffic when you get a burst of write requests. Write back minimizes the bus traffic, which could otherwise affect performance of other components wanting to use the main system bus. At any given time, however, memory does not have the most recent copy of the current value of the variable. Also, there is a delay when the cache line must be replaced,

FIGURE 12.31
Cache write policies with cache hits.

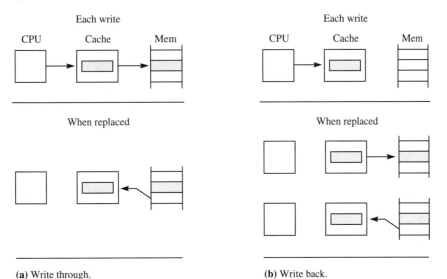

(a) Write through.   (b) Write back.

because memory must be updated before the new data can be loaded into the cache. By design, this event should happen rarely with a high percentage of cache hits.

Another issue to resolve with caches is what to do with a write request in conjunction with a cache miss. The policy known as *write allocation* brings the block from memory into the cache, possibly replacing another cache line, and then updates the cache line according to its normal cache write strategy. Without write allocation, a memory write is initiated, bypassing the cache altogether. The idea here is that the CPU can continue its processing concurrently with the completion of the memory write.

Cache write policies with cache misses

FIGURE 12.32 shows the cache write policies without and with write allocation. Although either cache write policy with cache misses can be combined with either cache write policy with cache hits, write allocation is normally used in caches with write back for cache hits. Write-through caches also tend to not use write allocation in order to keep the design simple. The design choice of most caches is either parts (a) of Figures 12.31 and 12.32 on the one hand or parts (b) of Figures 12.31 and 12.32 on the other.

The discussion of cache memories should sound familiar if you have read the discussion of virtual memory in Section 9.2. In the same way that the motivation behind virtual memory is the mismatch between the small size of main memory and the size of an executable program stored on a hard drive, the motivation behind caches is the mismatch between the small size

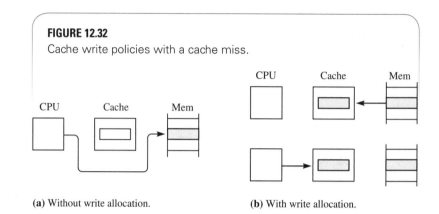

FIGURE 12.32

Cache write policies with a cache miss.

(a) Without write allocation.   **(b)** With write allocation.

of the cache and the size of main memory. The LRU page replacement policy in a virtual memory system corresponds to the LRU replacement policy of a cache line. Cache is to main memory as main memory is to disk. In both cases, there is a *memory hierarchy* that spans two extremes of a small high-speed memory subsystem that must interface with a large low-speed memory subsystem. Design solutions in both hierarchies rely on locality of reference. It is no accident that designs in both fields have common issues and solutions. Another indication of the universality of these principles is the hash table data structure in software. In Figure 12.28, you should have recognized the mapping from main memory to cache as essentially a hash function. Set-associative caches even look like hash tables where you resolve collisions by chaining, albeit with an upper limit on the length of the chain.

Memory hierarchies

The System Performance Equation

The ultimate performance metric of a machine is how fast it executes. FIGURE 12.33 , the system performance equation, shows that the time it takes to execute a program is the product of three factors. The word *instruction* in

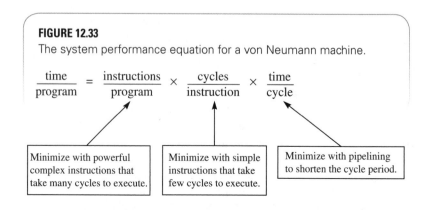

FIGURE 12.33

The system performance equation for a von Neumann machine.

$$\frac{time}{program} = \frac{instructions}{program} \times \frac{cycles}{instruction} \times \frac{time}{cycle}$$

| Minimize with powerful complex instructions that take many cycles to execute. | Minimize with simple instructions that take few cycles to execute. | Minimize with pipelining to shorten the cycle period. |

the equation means Level-ISA3 instruction, and the word *cycle* means the von Neumann cycle.

There is a relationship between the first two factors that is not shared by the third. A decrease in the first factor usually leads to an increase in the second factor, and vice versa. That is, if you design your ISA3 machine in such a way that you decrease the number of instructions it takes to execute a given program, you usually must pay the price of increasing the number of cycles it takes to execute each instruction. Conversely, if you design your ISA3 machine so that each instruction takes as few cycles as possible, you usually must make the instructions so simple that it takes more of them to execute a given program.

The third factor in the equation is based on parallelism and comes into play by reorganizing the control section so that more subsystems on the integrated circuit can operate concurrently. There is no tradeoff between it and either of the first two factors. You can introduce pipelining in the design to decrease the time per cycle, and the time per program will decrease, whether you have chosen to minimize the first factor at the expense of the second, or the second at the expense of the first.

RISC Versus CISC

Early in the history of computing, designers concentrated on the first factor. That approach was motivated in part by the high cost of main memory. Programs needed to be as small as possible just so they could fit in the available memory. Instruction sets and addressing modes were designed to make it easy for compilers to translate from HOL6 to Asmb5. Pep/9 is an example of such a design. In this case, the motivation is for pedagogical reasons and not for reasons of limited main memory. The assembly language is designed to teach the principles of translation between levels of abstraction typical in computer systems. Those principles are easiest to learn when the translation process is straightforward.

By the early 1980s, the computing landscape had changed. Hardware was getting cheaper, and memory subsystems were getting bigger. Some designers, notably John Cocke at IBM, David Patterson at UC Berkeley, and John Hennessy at Stanford, began to promote designs based on decreasing the second factor at the expense of increasing the first. Their designs were characterized by a much smaller number of ISA3 instructions and fewer addressing modes. The moniker for their designs was *reduced instruction set computer* (RISC, pronounced *risk*). In contrast, the older designs began to be called *complex instruction set computers* (CISCs, pronounced *sisks*).

RISC and CISC

The following is a list of RISC design principles. The first principle is the primary one from which the others necessarily follow.

1. Each ISA3 instruction except for load and store executes in one cycle.

2. The control section has no microcode.

3. Every ISA3 instruction is the same length.

4. There are only a few simple addressing modes.

5. All arithmetic and logic operations take place entirely in the CPU.

6. Data sections are designed for deep pipelining.

Pep/9, although it is a tiny processor, is a complex instruction set computer.

The first RISC design principle

The first RISC design principle is that each ISA3 instruction except for load and store executes in one cycle. The second factor in the system performance equations shows that you can minimize the execution time of a program by minimizing the number of cycles per instruction. The RISC design principle takes this optimization technique to the extreme by making the second factor exactly one. RISC machines execute with one cycle per ISA3 instruction, even including the fetch part and the increment part of the von Neumann cycle.

The second RISC design principle

The second RISC design principle is that the control section has no microcode. Figure 12.15 shows the control section of Pep/9, a CISC machine. Because a Pep/9 ISA3 instruction takes many cycles to execute, its control section must deliver a sequence of control signals to the data section. In a RISC machine, the Mc2 level is missing altogether because a sequence of control signals is no longer necessary to drive the data section.

The third RISC design principle

The third RISC design principle is that every ISA3 instruction is the same length. The fetch part of the Pep/9 von Neumann cycle fetches the instruction specifier, determines if the instruction is unary, and if not, fetches the operand specifier. The fetch process must, therefore, take more than one cycle. If each instruction must execute in one cycle, then every instruction must be the same length.

The fourth RISC design principle

The fourth RISC design principle is that there are only a few simple addressing modes. Pep/9 has the eight addressing modes of Figure 12.8. Of these eight modes, a RISC machine could not have the complex modes indirect, stack-relative deferred, or stack-deferred indexed because each one would take multiple memory fetches. Operand address computations that would be provided at the Mc2 level in hardware must be provided by the compiler in software. For example, if an HOL6 program has a data structure that needs stack-deferred indexed addressing, the compiler must generate the code to compute Mem[SP + OprndSped] + X] at the ISA3 level because it is not provided by the hardware at the Mc2 level. Consequently, the application code for a RISC machine is larger than the equivalent application code for a CISC machine.

The fifth RISC design principle

The fifth RISC design principle is that all arithmetic and logic operations take place entirely in the CPU. Consider the Pep/9 ADDA instruction with direct addressing. It adds Mem[OprndSpec] to the accumulator and puts the result in the accumulator. The addition operation requires a memory access, which consumes many memory access cycles. To minimize memory accesses, RISC machines have a large bank of general-purpose registers instead of a small bank of special-purpose registers. The processor performs arithmetic and logic operations with a register addressing mode.

For example, the Pep/9 translation of

```
x = y + z;
```

into assembly language is

```
LDWA y,d
ADDA z,d
STWA x,d
```

Code for an accumulator machine

where x, y, and z are global variables stored in a fixed location of memory. All three assembly language statements require a memory access. The preceding translation pattern makes Pep/9 a so-called *accumulator machine*. In a RISC machine, the equivalent code would be

```
LDW r1,y,d   ;Load y into register r1
LDW r2,z,d   ;Load z into register r2
ADD r3,r1,r2 ;Add r1 + r2 and put the sum in r3
STW r3,x,d   ;Store register r3 into x
```

Code for a load/store machine

Registers r1, r2, and r3 are three registers from a large set of general-purpose registers. The ADD instruction uses the register addressing mode and does not access memory. The preceding translation pattern makes RISC processors so-called *load/store machines*.

It may seem like the execution time would increase on the RISC machine with the above example because there are still three memory accesses plus the addition. In the long run, memory accesses are minimized over the CISC machine because the large register bank acts like a cache for recently used variables. The compiler maintains an internal symbol table for the set of recently used variables. The first time a variable is accessed, the compiler assigns it to one of the registers. When arithmetic and logic operations are performed in a function with the variables, only the register copies are used, with no memory accesses. The generated code stores variable values to memory only when necessary—for example, when a return statement executes.

The sixth RISC design principle is that data sections are designed for deep pipelining. This principle is not unique to RISC processors, as CISC processors also use pipelining to decrease the cycle period. However, the simplicity of the instruction set and the small number of simple addressing modes allow RISC processors to more efficiently implement deep pipelining.

The sixth RISC design principle

Microcode in x86 Systems

The x86 processors built by Intel and AMD are the most widely used CISC processors on the market. The details of their internal designs, including the design of their Mc2 level microcode control units, are proprietary and considered to be company secrets. The companies even encrypt the microcode on the chip in an effort to keep it hidden. Through limited publications and reverse engineering, however, we do have a partial picture of the designs.

Modern x86 chips use microcode only for those instructions in their ISA3 instruction set that are complex. Simple instructions that require just a few cycles are implemented with finite-state machines directly in the hardware that output RISC-like operations (ROPs) of a fixed length. More complex instructions use a full Mc2 layer of abstraction.

FIGURE 12.34 shows the microcode sequence for an AMD chip that implements the complex movsb instruction, whose mnemonic stands for *move string byte*. This one ISA3 instruction copies a string of ASCII bytes from one memory location to another. It uses two index registers in the x86 register bank—ESI, the index register for the source, and EDI, the index register for the destination—and one register ECX for the byte count. The CPU also has a direction flag that the assembly language programmer can set and clear. To use the movsb instruction, the programmer first puts the address of the source string in ESI, puts the address of the destination in EDI, puts the byte count in ECX, and sets or clears the direction flag, depending on whether the copy should be left to right or right to left. Then, the single execution of movsb at the ISA3 level performs the entire copy using a loop at the Mc2 microcode level.

The microcode in Figure 12.34 is more symbolic than Pep/9 microcode. For example, the microcode instruction at cycle 2 sets the Z bit if the content of the ECX register is all zeros. It takes the OR operation of the ECX register with itself and sets the Z bit accordingly. The equivalent Pep/9 microcode sequence for testing the high-order byte of the index register and setting the Z bit accordingly is

```
2. A=2, B=2, AMux=1, ALU=7, AndZ=0; ZCk
```

In the Pep/9 version, the numeric address of the register 2 is required, while the AMD microcode version uses the symbolic name ecx. Pep/9 microcode requires the numeric value 7 on the ALU control line to select the OR operation, while the AMD microcode version uses the symbolic name OR. The Pep/9 version requires explicit control values for the multiplexer and clock pulse, while these signals are implicit in the AMD microcode. The AMD microassembler must generate these control signals and values when it translates the microcode.

FIGURE 12.34
AMD microcode for the movsb instruction.

```
1. LDDF             ;load direction flag to latch in functional unit
2. OR ecx, ecx      ;test if ECX is zero
3. JZ end           ;terminate string move if ECX is zero
loop:
4. MOVFM+ tmp0, [esi] ;move to tmp data from source and inc/dec ESI
5. MOVTM+ [edi], tmp0 ;move the data to destination and inc/dec EDI
6. DECXJNZ loop       ;dec ECX and repeat until zero
end:
7. EXIT
```

12.3 The MIPS Machine

Since the 1980s, almost all newly designed CPUs have been RISC machines. Two prominent RISC machines are the ARM chip, which dominates the mobile phone and tablet markets, and the MIPS chip, which is based on the Stanford design and is used in servers and Nintendo game consoles. *MIPS* is an acronym for *microprocessor without interlocked pipeline stages*. There is one CISC design that continues to dominate the desktop and laptop market—namely, Intel's x86-64 family of processors, the latest chip family listed in Figure 12.26. Its continued dominance is due in large part to the compatibility that each family has maintained with its predecessor. It is expensive to migrate applications and operating systems to chips with different ISA3 instructions and addressing modes. Furthermore, CISC designers were able to adopt the RISC philosophy by creating a level of abstraction with a RISC core, the details of which are hidden at a low level, that implemented the CISC machine at Level ISA3.

The Register Set

The MIPS machine is a classic example of a commercially produced load/store machine. The 32-bit version has 32 32-bit registers in its CPU. The 64-bit version of MIPS also has 32 registers, but each register is 64 bits wide. FIGURE 12.35 is a drawing to scale of the registers in the 32-bit MIPS CPU compared to those in Pep/9.

Each register has a special assembler designation that begins with a dollar sign. $zero is a constant zero register similar to register 22 in Figure 12.2 but visible at Level ISA3. $v0 and $v1 are for values returned by a subroutine, and $a0 through $a3 are for arguments to a subroutine, similar to the calling protocol for operator `malloc` in Section 6.5. Registers that begin with $t are temporary, not preserved across a function call; and those that begin with $s are saved registers, preserved across a function call. The $k registers are reserved for the operating system kernel. $gp is the global pointer, $sp is the stack pointer, $fp is the frame pointer, and $ra is the return address.

Pep/9 is a tiny machine compared to most microprocessors. Figure 12.25 shows that there are 16 times more bits in the MIPS CPU registers than the Pep/9 CPU registers. And that does not count another set of floating-point registers that MIPS has and Pep/9 does not. Even with this big mismatch in size, in two respects MIPS is simpler than Pep/9—it has fewer addressing modes, and its instructions are all the same length, namely, four bytes. For enhanced performance, the memory alignment issue forces

FIGURE 12.35
Comparison of the 32-bit MIPS and Pep/9 CPU registers.

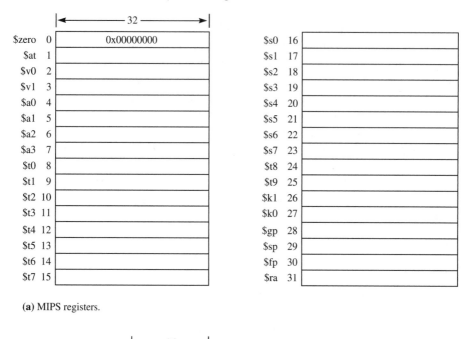

(a) MIPS registers.

(b) Pep/9 registers.

the first byte of each instruction to be stored at an address evenly divisible by four. (FIGURE 12.36) shows the von Neumann cycle for the MIPS machine. There is no if statement to determine the size of the instruction.

Figure 12.36 shows the von Neumann cycle for MIPS as an endless loop, which is more realistic than the cycle for Pep/9. Real machines have no STOP instruction because the operating system continues to execute when an application terminates.

The Addressing Modes

In contrast to Pep/9, which has eight addressing modes, MIPS has the five addressing modes of (FIGURE 12.37). Each of the five addressing modes uses one of the three instruction types—either I-type, R-type, or J-type.

FIGURE 12.36
A pseudocode description of the MIPS von Neumann execution cycle.

```
do {
      Fetch the instruction at the address in PC
      PC ← PC + 4
      Decode the instruction specifier
      Execute the instruction fetched
}
while (true)
```

FIGURE 12.37
The MIPS addressing modes.

Addressing Mode	Instruction Type	Operands		
		Destination	Source	Source
Immediate	I-type	Reg[rt]	Reg[rs]	SE(im)
Register	R-type	Reg[rd]	Reg[rs]	Reg[rt]
Base with load	I-type	Reg[rt]	Mem[Reg[rb] + SE(im)]	
Base with store	I-type	Mem[Reg[rb] + SE(im)]	Reg[rt]	
PC-relative	I-type	PC	PC + 4	SE(im × 4)
Pseudodirect	J-type	PC	(PC + 4)⟨0..3⟩ : (ta × 4)	

FIGURE 12.38 shows the instruction format for each addressing mode. Instructions with the addressing modes immediate, base, and PC-relative are I-type instructions. Instructions with register addressing are R-type, and instructions with pseudodirect addressing are J-type instructions. A MIPS instruction always consists of a six-bit opcode to specify the instruction and one or more operand specifiers. The rs field, when present, is always at bit location 6..10, the rt field is always at 11..15, and rd is always at 16..20. This chapter specifies bit locations starting with the leftmost bit as 0 and numbering from left to right to be consistent with Pep/9 notation. Standard MIPS notation is to start with the rightmost bit as 0 and to number from right to left.

MIPS bit numbering notation

FIGURE 12.38

The MIPS instruction formats corresponding to the addressing modes.

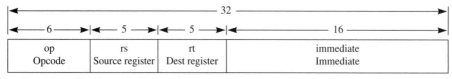

op	rs	rt	immediate
Opcode	Source register	Dest register	Immediate

(a) Immediate addressing with the I-type instruction.

op	rs	rt	rd	shamt	funct
Opcode	Source register	Source register	Dest register	Shift amount	Function field

(b) Register addressing with the R-type instruction.

op	rs	rt	immediate
Opcode	Base register	Target register	Address displacement

(c) Base addressing with the I-type instruction.

op	rs	rt	immediate
Opcode	Source register	Branch cond	Branch displacement

(d) PC-relative addressing with the I-type instruction.

op	target
Opcode	Target address

(e) Pseudodirect addressing with the J-type instruction.

Because there are 32 registers in the register bank in Figure 12.35(a), and 2^5 is 32, it takes five bits to access one of them. The designations rs, rt, and rd are standard MIPS notations for five-bit register fields in an instruction. Figure 12.37 shows that rs is always a source register, and rd is always a destination register; but rt, which stands for *target register*, can be either a source or a destination register. The notation *Reg* in Figure 12.37 stands for *register* and is analogous to *Mem*, which stands for *memory*. Reg[r] indicates the content of the register r. For example, if an instruction with immediate addressing executes, Figure 12.37 shows Reg[rt] as the destination operand. If the five-bit rt field in Figure 12.38(a) has the value 10011 (bin), which is 19 (dec), then the destination register $s3 will contain the result of the operation because $s3 is register 19 in Figure 12.35.

The function SE(im) is sign extension of the immediate operand. If the sign bit of the 16-bit operand is 0, indicating a positive quantity, the 16-bit operand is expanded to 32 bits by prepending 16 additional zeros. If the sign bit of the 16-bit quantity is 1, the operand is expanded by prepending 16 additional ones. For example, the 16-bit quantity 7C9B (hex) expands to the 32-bit quantity 00007C9B, and 8C9B expands to FFFF8C9B. Sign extension does not change the decimal value of the operand. *Sign extension*

Figure 12.38(a) shows the instruction format for immediate addressing. The immediate operand cannot contain 32 bits because it must be part of a 32-bit instruction. It is sign extended to 32 bits and combined with the other source operand Reg[rs], and the result is put in Reg[rt]. With immediate addressing, rt is a destination register. *Immediate addressing*

Figure 12.38(b) shows the instruction format for register addressing. All the arithmetic and logic operations use register addressing with two source registers and one destination register. For example, one instruction can add the values of two different variables and give their sum to a third. The function field is, in effect, an expanded opcode. If the opcode field is 000000 (bin), the instruction uses register addressing and the function field determines the operation. For example, if the function field is 100000, the operation is addition, and if it is 100010, the operation is subtraction. The Pep/9 shift instructions shift only one bit location either to the left or to the right. The MIPS processor can shift a register multiple times in one cycle. The shift amount field specifies how many bits to shift. With register addressing, rt is a source register. *Register addressing*

Figure 12.38(c) shows the instruction format for base addressing. Of all the addressing modes, this is the only one that accesses main memory. The rs field designates the base register field and is written as *rb* in Figure 12.37. The instruction computes the memory address by adding the sign-extended immediate field to the content of the base register. For load instructions, memory is the source and register rt is the destination. For store instructions, register rt is the source and memory is the destination. *Base addressing*

Figure 12.38(d) shows the instruction format for PC-relative addressing. The conditional branch instructions use this addressing mode to change the program counter. If the condition of the branch is satisfied, the program counter is changed with the following specification: *PC-relative addressing*

$$PC \leftarrow (PC + 4) + SE(im \times 4)$$

MIPS instructions are 32 bits in length, so they are aligned on 4-byte boundaries when stored in main memory. Because you would never access an instruction that is not aligned, the immediate operand is multiplied by 4, which is equivalent to a left shift by 2. The shifted operand is sign extended and added to the incremented value of the program counter. The quantity added to the PC is a signed 18-bit quantity—16 bits from the immediate operand, then shifted left 2 more bits. The range of values for an 18-bit signed integer is -2^{17} to $2^{17} - 1$. Therefore, with PC-relative addressing, you can branch backward and forward from the current PC by 128 KiB. To branch beyond this limit requires the use of another addressing mode. Most conditional branches are within this limit. For example, an endFor symbol is not far from its corresponding for symbol because the body of the loop is usually smaller than 128 KiB.

Figure 12.38(d) shows that the rt field specifies the branch condition. The rt field with PC-relative addressing is another instance of an expanded opcode. If the six-bit opcode field is 000001, then the instruction is a conditional branch, and the rt field specifies the condition. For example, if the rt field is 00000, the branch is on rs less than zero, but if the rt field is 00001, the branch is on rs greater than or equal to zero. Some conditional branch instructions have a six-bit opcode field different from 000001.

All processors have some form of PC-relative addressing that is used by branch instructions. Chapter 6 gives examples of PC-relative addressing in the x86 architecture. Pep/9 does not need PC-relative addressing because every application program is loaded into memory starting at address 0000. The assembler can know the absolute memory address of every global variable and instruction of the program and calculate the value of each symbol accordingly. With Pep/9, a branch to endFor uses the symbol as the absolute address of the instruction.

In practice, operating systems manage multiple processes simultaneously, with the code for the processes scattered at various locations throughout the memory map. It is impossible for the assembler to know at translation time where in memory the program will be loaded and executed, so direct addressing is rarely useful. When a MIPS assembler encounters a branch to endFor, it counts the number of bytes between the use of the symbol and the definition of the symbol, which it generates as the immediate value in the PC-relative branch. Regardless of where the program is loaded in memory, the number of bytes between the use of the symbol and its definition is unchanged, and the code will execute correctly. The same concept is used in Pep/9 stack-relative addressing, where the memory location of a local variable is specified by its offset from the stack pointer. With PC-relative addressing, the offset is from the program counter instead of the stack pointer.

Pseudodirect addressing

Figure 12.38(e) shows the instruction format for pseudodirect addressing used with the unconditional branch instruction j, which stands for *jump*. The program counter is changed with the following specification.

$$PC \leftarrow (PC + 4) \langle 0 .. 3 \rangle : (ta \times 4)$$

Quantity ta is the 26-bit target address, which is shifted left 2 bits, increasing its length to 28 bits. The colon in the specification is the concatenation operator. The first 4 significant bits of the incremented program counter are concatenated with the 28 bits of the shifted target address to produce a 32-bit address for the PC.

With pseudodirect addressing, you are still limited to one-sixteenth of the memory map specified by the first four bits of the program counter. Neither PC-relative nor pseudodirect addressing modes allow unrestricted access to the entire 4 GiB address space. MIPS provides the jump register instruction jr with base addressing to access any address in the entire address space. The program counter is changed with the following specification:

$$PC \leftarrow Reg[rb]$$

The jump register instruction

where rb is the base register in the rs field of Figure 12.38(c). It requires the programmer to compute the address and put it in the base register before executing the unconditional branch.

The Instruction Set

FIGURE 12.39 is a summary of some MIPS instructions. The first column is the mnemonic of the instruction for MIPS assembly language. Operand specifiers labeled sssss and ttttt are five-bit source register fields, those labeled ddddd are five-bit destination register fields, and those labeled bbbbb are five-bit base register fields. A field of i characters is an immediate operand specifier, which is sign-extended for addition and zero-extended for AND and OR. A field of a characters is an address operand specifier, which is a sign-extended offset in an address calculation. Operand specifiers labeled hhhhh are five-bit shift amounts for the shift instructions.

Following are some examples of C code fragments with their translation into MIPS assembly language. The MIPS processor uses its bank of 32 registers as a cache for variables. The first time a variable is accessed, the compiler associates a register with that value. Later accesses use the variable copy in the register instead of accessing memory again. With Pep/9, global variables are stored at a fixed absolute address in memory. With MIPS, global variables are accessed relative to $gp, the global pointer.

Example 12.2 Figure 5.27 declares three global variables, exam1, exam2 and score, as well as a constant bonus, which equates to 10. The C compiler might install the three globals with offsets 0, 4, and 8 from $gp and associate them with registers $s1, $s2, and $s3 in the register bank. It translates the Cstatement

```
score = (exam1 + exam2) / 2 + bonus;
```

FIGURE 12.39

A few instructions from the MIPS instruction set.

Mnemonic	Meaning	Binary Instruction Encoding							
add	Add	0000	00ss	ssst	tttt	dddd	d000	0010	0000
addi	Add immediate	0010	00ss	sssd	dddd	iiii	iiii	iiii	iiii
sub	Subtract	0000	00ss	ssst	tttt	dddd	d000	0010	0010
and	Bitwise AND	0000	00ss	ssst	tttt	dddd	d000	0010	0100
andi	Bitwise AND immediate	0011	00ss	sssd	dddd	iiii	iiii	iiii	iiii
or	Bitwise OR	0000	00ss	ssst	tttt	dddd	d000	0010	0101
ori	Bitwise OR immediate	0011	01ss	sssd	dddd	iiii	iiii	iiii	iiii
sll	Shift left logical	0000	0000	000t	tttt	dddd	dhhh	hh00	0000
sra	Shift right arithmetic	0000	0000	000t	tttt	dddd	dhhh	hh00	0011
srl	Shift right logical	0000	0000	000t	tttt	dddd	dhhh	hh00	0010
lb	Load byte	1000	00bb	bbbd	dddd	aaaa	aaaa	aaaa	aaaa
lw	Load word	1000	11bb	bbbd	dddd	aaaa	aaaa	aaaa	aaaa
lui	Load upper immediate	0011	1100	000d	dddd	iiii	iiii	iiii	iiii
sb	Store byte	1010	00bb	bbbt	tttt	aaaa	aaaa	aaaa	aaaa
sw	Store word	1010	11bb	bbbt	tttt	aaaa	aaaa	aaaa	aaaa
beq	Branch if equal to	0001	00ss	ssst	tttt	aaaa	aaaa	aaaa	aaaa
bgez	Branch if greater than or equal to zero	0000	01ss	sss0	0001	aaaa	aaaa	aaaa	aaaa
bgtz	Branch if greater than zero	0001	11ss	sss0	0000	aaaa	aaaa	aaaa	aaaa
blez	Branch if less than or equal to zero	0001	10ss	sss0	0000	aaaa	aaaa	aaaa	aaaa
bltz	Branch if less than zero	0000	01ss	sss0	0000	aaaa	aaaa	aaaa	aaaa
bne	Branch if not equal to	0001	01ss	ssst	tttt	aaaa	aaaa	aaaa	aaaa
j	Jump	0000	10aa	aaaa	aaaa	aaaa	aaaa	aaaa	aaaa
jr	Jump register	0000	00bb	bbb0	0000	0000	0000	0000	1000

to MIPS assembly language as

```
lw $s1,0($gp)    # Load exam1 into register $s1
lw $s2,4($gp)    # Load exam2 into register $s2
add $s3,$s1,$s2  # Register $s3 gets exam1 + exam2
sra $s3,$s3,1    # Shift right register $s3 one bit
addi $s3,$s3,10  # Register $s3 gets $s3 + 10
sw $s3,8($gp)    # score gets $s3
```

Comments begin with the # character. In MIPS assembly language, the first argument after the mnemonic is usually the destination. For example, in the first lw instruction, $s1 is the destination register, and in the add instruction, $s3 is the destination register. The sw instruction is an exception to this general rule. The RTL specification of the lw instruction is

Reg[rt] ← Mem[Reg[rb] + SE(im)]   *The* lw *instruction*

and the specification of the sw instruction is

Mem[Reg[rb] + SE(im)] ← Reg[rt]   *The* sw *instruction*

In both of these instructions, the base register $gp is in parentheses preceded by the immediate operand in decimal notation. The RTL specification of the add instruction is

Reg[rd] ← Reg[rs] + Reg[rt]   *The* add *instruction*

The destination register rd is $s3, the source register rs is $s1, and the target register rt is $s2. The mnemonic addi stands for *add immediate* and obviously uses immediate addressing. The machine language translation of these instructions is

```
100011 11100 10001 0000000000000000
100011 11100 10010 0000000000000100
000000 10001 10010 10011 00000100000
000000 00000 10011 10011 00001 000011
001000 10011 10011 0000000000001010
101011 11100 10011 0000000000001000
```

For base addressing, Figure 12.38(c) shows the base register field next to the opcode field. The above lw and sw instructions have $gp as the base register. Figure 12.35 shows $gp as register 28 (dec) = 11100 (bin), which is the register field next to the opcode field in the preceding machine code. For the add instruction with register addressing, the fields in the machine code are in the order rs, rt, rd, consistent with Figure 12.38(b), while the fields in the assembly code are in the order rd, rs, rt, with the destination field first. In Figure 12.35, you can identify the binary fields in the preceding machine code for the global variables as follows:

> > $s1 is register 17 (dec) = 10001 (bin).
> > $s2 is register 18 (dec) = 10010 (bin).
> > $s3 is register 19 (dec) = 10011 (bin).   ∎

It is not feasible to store an entire array in the register bank because most arrays have too many elements to fit the available registers. To process arrays, the C compiler associates a register with the address of the first element of the array and uses base addressing to access an element of the array. Pep/9 accesses the element of an array with indexed addressing, for which the operand is specified as

Oprnd = Mem[OprndSpec + X]

A significant difference between Pep/9 and MIPS is the use of the register to access an array element. In Pep/9, the register X contains the value of the index. In the MIPS machine, the register rb contains the address of the first element of the array—in other words, the base of the array. That is why register rb is called the *base register* and this addressing mode is called *base addressing*.

Example 12.3   Suppose the C compiler associates $s1 with array a, $s2 with variable g, and $s3 with array b. It translates the statement

```
a[2] = g + b[3];
```

to MIPS assembly language as

```
lw $t0,12($s3)  # Register $t0 gets b[3]
add $t0,$s2,$t0 # Register $t0 gets g + b[3]
sw $t0,8($s1)   # a[2] gets g + b[3]
```

The load instruction has 12 for the address field, because it is accessing b[3], each word is four bytes, and $3 \times 4 = 12$. Similarly, the store instruction has 8 in the address field because of the index value in a[2]. The machine language translation of these instructions is

```
100011 10011 01000 0000000000001100
000000 10010 01000 01000 00000 100000
101011 10001 01000 0000000000001000
```

Figure 12.35 shows that $t0 is register 8 (dec) = 01000 (bin), $s3 is register 19 (dec) = 10011 (bin), $s2 is register 18 (dec) = 10010 (bin), and $s1 is register 17 (dec) = 10001 (bin).   ∎

The situation is a bit more complicated if you want to access the element of an array whose index is a variable. MIPS has no index register that does what the index register in Pep/9 does. Consequently, the compiler must generate code to add the index value to the address of the first element of the array to get the address of the element referenced. In Pep/9, this addition is done automatically at Level Mc2 with indexed addressing. But, the design philosophy of load/store machines is to have few addressing modes even at the expense of needing more statements in the program.

In Pep/9, words are two bytes, and so the index must be shifted left once to multiply it by 2. In MIPS, words are four bytes, and so the index must be shifted left twice to multiply it by 4. The MIPS instruction sll, for *shift left logical*, uses the shamt field in Figure 12.38(b) to specify the amount of the shift.

A word is four bytes in MIPS.

Example 12.4 The MIPS assembly language statement to shift the content of $s0 seven bits to the left and put the result in $t2 is

```
sll $t2,$s0,7
```

The machine language translation is

```
000000 00000 10000 01010 00111 000000
```

The first field is the opcode. The second field is not used by this instruction and is set to all zeros. The third is the rt field, which indicates $s0, register 16 (dec) = 10000. The fourth is the rd field, which indicates $t2, register 10 (dec) = 01010 (bin). The fifth is the shamt field, which indicates the shift amount. The last is the funct field used with the opcode to indicate the sll instruction. ∎

Example 12.5 Assuming that the C compiler associates $s0 with variable i, $s1 with array a, and $s2 with variable g, it translates the statement

```
g = a[i];
```

into MIPS assembly language as follows.

```
sll $t0,$s0,2    # $t0 gets $s0 times 4
add $t0,$s1,$t0  # $t0 gets the address of a[i]
lw $s2,0($t0)    # $s2 gets a[i]
```

Note the 0 in the address field of the load instruction. ∎

Like Pep/9, the MIPS machine has a stack register $sp in its register bank. Unlike Pep/9, there is no special ADDSP instruction because the addi instruction can access any of the 32 registers in the register bank, including $sp. To allocate storage on the run-time stack, execute addi with a negative immediate value and with $sp as both the source and destination register.

Example 12.6   To allocate four bytes of storage on the run-time stack, you would execute

```
addi $sp,$sp,-4 # $sp <- $sp - 4
```

where −4 is not an address but the immediate operand. The machine language translation is

```
001000 11101 11101 1111111111111100
```

where $sp is register 29.   ∎

You may have noticed a limitation with the addi instruction. The constant field is only 16 bits wide, but MIPS is a 32-bit machine. You should be able to add constants with 32-bit precision using immediate addressing. Here is another example of the RISC architecture philosophy. The goal is simple instructions with few addressing modes. The Pep/9 design permits instructions with different widths—that is, both unary and nonunary instructions. Figure 12.4 shows how this decision complicates the fetch part of the von Neumann cycle. The hardware must fetch the instruction specifier, then decode it to determine whether to fetch an operand specifier. This complexity is completely counter to the load/store philosophy, which demands simple instructions that can be decoded quickly. The simplicity goal demands that all instructions be the same length.

But if all instructions are 32 bits wide, how could one instruction possibly contain a 32-bit immediate constant? There would be no room in the instruction format for the opcode. Here is where decreasing the second factor in Figure 12.33 at the expense of the first factor comes into play. The solution to the problem of a 32-bit immediate constant is to require the execution of two instructions. For this job, MIPS provides lui, which stands for *load upper immediate*. It sets the high-order 16 bits of a register to the immediate operand and the low-order bits to all zeros. A second instruction is required to set the low-order 16 bits, usually the OR immediate instruction ori.

Example 12.7   Assuming that the compiler associates register $s2 with variable g, it translates the C statement

```
g = 491521;
```

to MIPS assembly language as

```
lui $s2,0x0007
ori $s2,$s2,0x8001
```

The decimal number 491521 requires more than 16 bits in binary, and 491521 (dec) = 0007 8001 (hex). ▮

MIPS Computer Organization

FIGURE 12.40 shows the data section of the MIPS CPU. The box labeled *Register bank* is a two-port bank of the 32-bit registers in Figure 12.35(a). The data section has the same basic organization as the data section of Pep/9 in Figure 12.2 with an ABus and BBus that feed through the primary ALU, whose output eventually goes over the CBus to the bank of CPU registers. A significant difference in the organization is the L1 instruction and data caches in the path. As most cache memories exhibit a hit rate above 90%, we can assume that memory reads and writes operate at full CPU speed. There are no MemRead or MemWrite delays, except on those rare occasions when you get a cache miss. The ABus, BBus, and CBus and the buses into and out of the ALU; the L1 data cache; and the JMux, PCMux, and CMux multiplexers are all 32 bits.

Unlike Pep/9, the program counter is not one of the general registers in the register bank. Instead, it is in effect the memory address register to the L1 instruction cache. There is no separate MAR other than the program counter itself. Similarly, the output of the ALU is, in effect, the memory address register to the L1 data cache. Likewise, there is no separate MDR. Instead, the ABus is, in effect, the memory data register to the L1 data cache.

The CPU does not write to the instruction cache. It simply requests a read from the address specified by PC. The cache subsystem delivers the instruction from the cache immediately on a hit. On a miss, it delays the CPU and eventually reads the instruction from the L2 cache, writes it to the L1 cache, and notifies the CPU that it can continue. Because the CPU never writes to the instruction cache, it treats the cache as if it were a combinational circuit. That is why the instruction cache is not shaded in Figure 12.40.

The primary design goal of a RISC machine is for every ISA3 instruction to execute in one von Neumann cycle, including the fetch and increment part of the cycle. The next value of the program counter must be computed concurrently with the computation of the execute part of the cycle. The data section contains a set of specialized combinational circuits for the program counter that operate concurrently with the ALU. The ASL2 units output an arithmetic shift left by 2 bits. The Sign extend unit outputs a 32-bit sign extension from a 16-bit input. The Plus4 unit is hardwired to add 4 to a 32-bit quantity. Its bottom and right outputs are the 32-bit sum, but its left output is the 4 most significant bits of the sum. Because all instructions are exactly four bytes long, the increment part of the von Neumann cycle is simpler than that of Pep/9 and can be implemented with these specialized hardware units without tying up the main ALU or consuming cycles.

FIGURE 12.40
The MIPS data section. Sequential circuits are shaded.

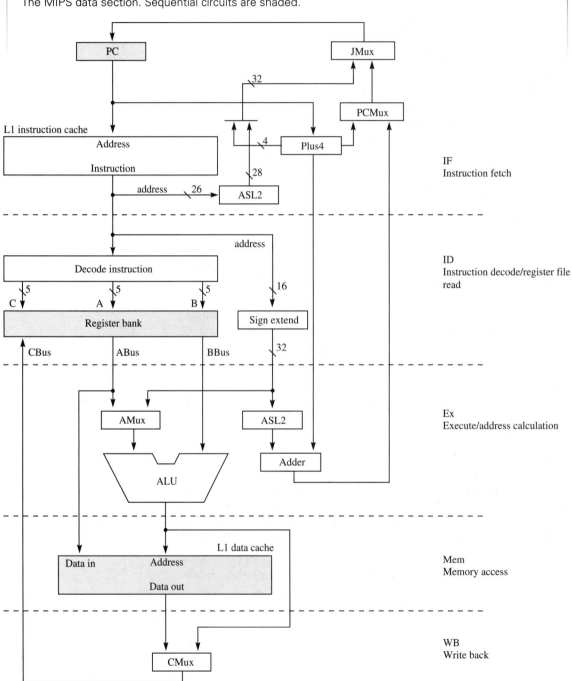

The box labeled *Decode instruction* in Figure 12.40 is a circuit whose 32 inputs are all the bits of the instruction that is executing. MIPS has no Mc2 level that emits a sequence of control signals. The Decode unit corresponds to the control section of a CISC machine and outputs the control signals for the single cycle to implement the instruction. Its bottom outputs are the three five-bit fields A, B, and C, which feed into the register bank and correspond to the A, B, and C control signals into the Pep/9 register bank of Figure 12.2. FIGURE 12.41 hides the specialized hardware units of the previous figure and shows the other control outputs of the Decode unit. Besides the A, B, and C outputs, there are eight other control signals, as follows:

> *JMux control*—If 0, select left input. If 1, select PCMux.

> *PCMux control*—If 0, select Plus4. If 1, select Adder.

> *AMux control*—If 0, select ABus. If 1, select Sign extend.

> *CMux control*—If 0, select Data out. If 1, select ALU.

> *ALU control*—Multi-line function select.

> *PCCk*—Clock pulse for program counter.

> *LoadCk*—Clock pulse for write to Register bank.

> *DCCk*—Clock pulse for write to L1 data cache.

The MIPS control signals

The multiplexer control signals follow the Pep/9 convention for consistency. Specifically, a zero-control signal selects the left input, and a one-control signal selects the right input. Actual MIPS hardware differs from this convention. MIPS hardware documentation also differs from the naming convention for the hardware units, which is used in this text for consistency with the Pep/9 system.

PC is clocked on every cycle and drives the primary loop. The register bank and the data cache are not always clocked, depending on the instruction executed. The following examples show the control signals from the Decode unit to implement some ISA3 MIPS instructions.

Example 12.8 The jump instruction uses pseudodirect addressing. The ASL2 box in the IF section of Figure 12.40 shifts the address two places to the left with the result concatenated with the first four (high-order) bits of the incremented PC. This is the hardware implementation with specialized hardware units of the pseudodirect addressing mode of Figure 12.37. The jump instruction requires the following control signals:

```
1. JMux=0; PCCk
```

Jump instruction

Before the cycle executes, PC has the address of the jump instruction, the 26-bit address field is presented to the ASL2 input, the first 4 bits of

FIGURE 12.41
The control signals from the Decode unit in the MIPS data section.

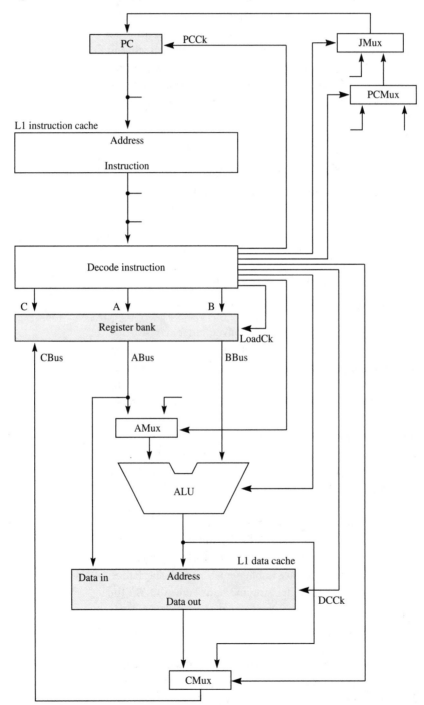

the incremented PC concatenated with the ASL2 output are presented to JMux, and the output of JMux is presented to PC. The clock pulse updates PC. ∎

Unlike Pep/9, the MIPS processor has no NZVC status bits for its conditional branch instructions. Instead, the comparison is always between two registers in the register bank, one of which might be the $zero register. To test for overflow with an arithmetic instruction, programs use a version of the instruction that generates a trap on overflow. Otherwise, they use an unsigned version, which does not trap on overflow. For example, the add instruction triggers a system trap on overflow. The addu instruction, which stands for *add unsigned*, does the same operation but does not trap on overflow.

MIPS has no status bits.

Example 12.9 The conditional branch instructions alter the program counter in one of two ways, depending on the condition. The Decode unit compares two registers and outputs different control signals, depending on the outcome of the test. If the branch is not taken, it outputs

```
1. PCMux=0, JMux=1; PCCk
```

Branch instructions

Before the cycle executes, PC has the address of the conditional branch instruction, and the incremented value from Plus4 is presented to PCMux, passed through JMux, and clocked into PC. If the branch is taken, it outputs

```
1. PCMux=1, JMux=1; PCCk
```

Before the cycle executes, PC has the address of the conditional branch instruction *and* the 16-bit address field is presented to the ASL2 input in the Ex section, the ASL2 output and incremented PC are presented to the adder in the Ex section, the adder output is presented to PCMux, the PCMux output is presented to JMux, and the output of JMux is presented to PC. The clock pulse updates PC. ∎

The store instructions are facilitated by a clever arrangement of components in the data section. ABus provides a path from the register bank directly to the data input of the L1 data cache. Furthermore, the output of the primary ALU output goes to the address lines of the data cache. Hence, the addition for the address computation of a store instruction is done by the primary ALU and not a special-purpose hardware unit. PC is updated and the data is written to the data cache simultaneously.

Example 12.10 The store word instruction sw has RTL specification

$$Mem[Reg[rb] + SE(im)] \leftarrow Reg[rt]$$

Because it updates PC and writes to memory, the cycle requires simultaneous clock pulses PCCk and DCCk. The control signals are

Store instruction

```
1. PCMux=0, JMux=1, A=rt, AMux=1, B=rb, ALU=A plus B;
   PCCk, DCCk
```

The PCMux=0 and JMux=1 signals simply present the incremented PC to PC. The A=rt signal puts the content of the rt source register on ABus, which is presented as data to the cache. The AMux=1 signal selects the address field of the instruction as the left input to the ALU, and the B=rb signal puts the base register on BBus as the right input to the ALU. Selecting the addition function presents the address computation on the address lines of the data cache. ∎

The register instructions use the primary ALU for their processing but do not write to memory. Therefore, the output of the ALU has a path through CMux to the register bank. As with store instructions, PC and the register bank are updated simultaneously.

Example 12.11   The add instruction add has RTL specification

Reg[rd] ← Reg[rs] + Reg[rt]

Because it updates PC and writes to the register bank, the cycle requires simultaneous clock pulses PCCk and LoadCk. The control signals are

Add instruction

```
1. PCMux=0, JMux=1, A=rs, AMux=0, B=rt, ALU=A plus B,
   CMux=1, C=rd; PCCk, LoadCk
```

The PCMux=0 and JMux=1 signals present the incremented PC to PC. The A=rs signal puts the content of the rs source register on ABus, which is presented as data to the cache through AMux with the AMux=0 signal. The B=rt signal puts the base register on BBus as the right input to the ALU. Selecting the addition function presents the result on CBus through CMux with the CMux=1 signal. Signal C=rd addresses the register bank for the destination register rd. ∎

The control signals for the load instructions are left as an exercise at the end of the chapter.

Pipelining

The instant PC changes at the beginning of a cycle, the data must propagate from it through the combinational circuits in the following order:

Stages in the MIPS data section

    1. IF: The instruction cache, the Plus4 adder, the shifter and multiplexers

2. ID: The Decode instruction box, the Register bank, the sign extend box

3. Ex: The AMux, the ASL2 shifter, the ALU, the adder

4. Mem: The data cache

5. WB: The CMux, the address decoder of the Register bank

The CPU designers must set the period of the clock long enough to allow for the data to be presented to the sequential circuits—PC, Register bank, and data cache—before clocking the data into them. FIGURE 12.42 shows a time line of several instructions executing, one after the other. The boxes represent the propagation time of each stage.

The situation in Figure 12.42 is analogous to a single craftsman who must build a piece of furniture. He has a shop with all the tools to do three things—cut the wood, assemble with clamps and glue, and paint. As there is only one craftsman, he builds his furniture in the same sequence, one piece of furniture after the other. With two other craftsmen, there are several ways to increase the number of pieces produced per day. The other craftsmen could acquire their own tools, and all three could work concurrently, cutting the wood for three pieces at the same time, assembling the three pieces at the same time, and painting them at the same time. It is true that output per time is tripled, but at the cost of all those extra tools.

A more economical alternative is to recognize that when one person is using the clamps and glue, the tools for cutting the wood could be used for starting the next piece of furniture. Similarly, when the first piece is being painted, the second can be assembled and the wood for the third can be cut. You should recognize this organization as the basis of the factory assembly line.

The assembly line analogy

The resources corresponding to the tools are the combinational circuits in the five areas listed above—instruction fetch, instruction decode/register

FIGURE 12.42

Instruction execution without pipelining.

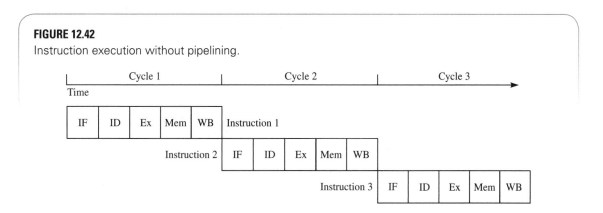

file read, execute/address calculation, memory access, and write back. The idea of our CPU pipeline is to increase the number of cycles it takes to execute an instruction by a factor of five, but to decrease the period of each cycle by a factor of five. It might seem at first glance that there would be no net benefit. But by overlapping the execution of one instruction with the next, you get parallelism that increases the number of instructions executed per second.

To implement this idea requires a modification to the data path of Figure 12.40. The results of each stage must be saved to be used as input for the next stage. At the boundary of each of the five stages, you must put a set of registers, as **FIGURE 12.43** shows. At the end of each new shortened cycle, the data from every data path that crosses to the next stage below it gets stored in a boundary register.

Boundary registers

You can get a perfect five-times decrease in the cycle time only if the propagation delays at each stage are exactly equal. In fact, they are only approximately equal. So the new cycle time must be the propagation time of the lengthiest delay of all the shortened stages. When choosing where to put the boundary registers to implement a pipeline, a designer must strive to evenly divide the stages.

FIGURE 12.44 shows how pipelining works. At startup the pipeline is empty. In cycle 1, the first instruction is fetched. In cycle 2, the second instruction is fetched concurrently with the first instruction being decoded and the register bank being read. In cycle 3, the third instruction is fetched concurrently with the second instruction being decoded and the register bank being read and the first instruction executing, and so on. The speedup comes from putting more parts of the circuit to use at the same time. Pipelining is a form of parallelism. In theory, a perfect pipeline with five stages increases by five times the number of instructions executing per second, once the pipeline is filled.

That's the good news. The bad news is that a whole host of problems can throw a monkey wrench into this rosy scenario. There are two kinds of problems, called *hazards*:

Piplining hazards

> Control hazards from unconditional and conditional branches

> Data hazards from data dependencies between instructions

Each of these hazards is due to an instruction that cannot complete the task at one stage in the pipeline because it needs the result of a previous instruction that has not finished executing. A hazard causes the instruction that cannot continue to stall, which creates a bubble in the pipeline that must be flushed out before peak performance is restored.

FIGURE 12.45(a) shows the execution of a pipeline from startup with no hazards. The second group of five boxes on the first line represents the

FIGURE 12.43
The MIPS data section with pipelining.

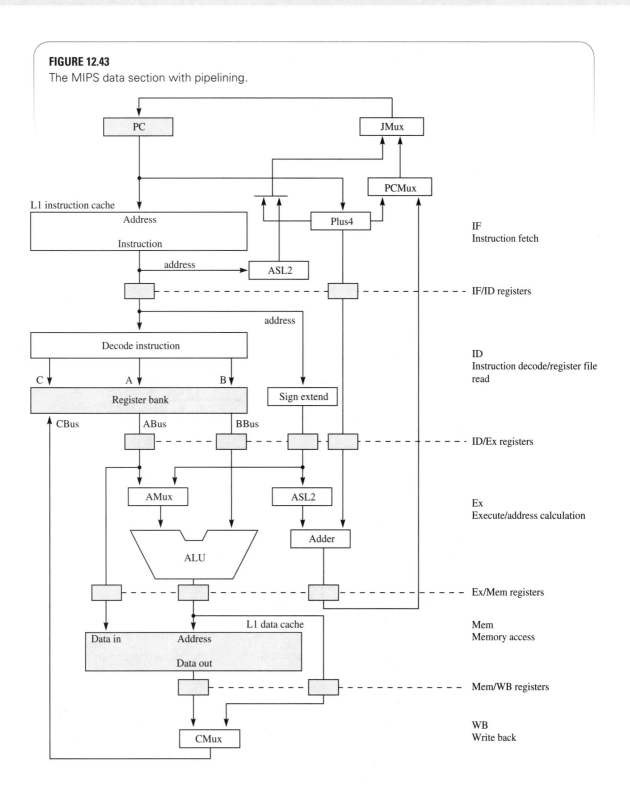

FIGURE 12.44

Instruction execution with pipelining.

Cycle | 1 | 2 | 3 | 4 | 5 | 6 | 7 | 8 |
Time

Instruction 1 | IF | ID | Ex | Mem | WB

Instruction 2 | IF | ID | Ex | Mem | WB

Instruction 3 | IF | ID | Ex | Mem | WB

Instruction 4 | IF | ID | Ex | Mem | WB

FIGURE 12.45

The effect of a hazard on a pipeline.

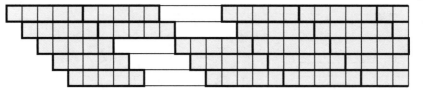

(a) No hazards.

(b) A branch hazard.

sixth instruction to execute, the second on the second line represents the seventh, and so on. Starting with cycle 5, the pipeline operates at peak efficiency.

Consider what happens when a branch instruction executes. Suppose instruction 7, which starts at cycle 7 on the second line, is a branch instruction. Assuming that the updated program counter is not available for the next instruction until the completion of this instruction, instruction

8 and every instruction after it must stall. Figure 12.45(b) shows the bubble as not shaded. The effect is as if the pipeline must start over at cycle 12. FIGURE 12.46 shows that branch instructions account for 15% of executing statements in a typical program on a MIPS machine. So roughly every seventh instruction must delay four cycles.

There are several ways to reduce the penalty of a control hazard. Figure 12.45(b) assumes that the result of the branch instruction is not available until after the write-back stage. But branch instructions do not modify the register bank. So, to decrease the length of the bubble the system could eliminate the write-back stage of branch instructions under the assumption that the next instruction has been delayed. The extra control hardware to do that would decrease the length of the bubble from four cycles to three.

Eliminate the write-back stage of the branch instructions.

Conditional branches present another opportunity to minimize the effects of the hazard. Suppose the branch penalty is three cycles with the addition of the extra control hardware, and the computer is executing the following MIPS program:

```
beq $s1,$s2,4
add $s3,$s3,$s4
sub $s5,$s5,$s6
andi $s7,$s7,15
sll $s0,$s0,2
ori $s3,$s3,1
```

The first instruction is a branch if equal. The address field is 4, which means a branch to the fourth instruction after the next one. Consequently, if the branch is taken, it will be to the `ori` instruction. If the branch is not taken, `add` will execute next.

Figure 12.45(b) shows a lot of wasted parallelism. While the bubble is being flushed out of the pipeline, many stages are idle. You do not know whether you should be executing `add`, `sub`, and `andi` while waiting for the results of `beq`. But you can execute them anyway assuming that the branch is not taken. If the branch is in fact not taken, you have eliminated the bubble altogether. If it is taken, you are no worse off in terms of bubble delay than you would have been if you had not started the instruction after `beq`. In that case, flush the bubble from the pipeline.

Assume that conditional branches are not taken.

The problem is the circuitry required to clean up your mess if your assumption is wrong and the branch is taken. You must keep track of any instructions in the interim, before you discover whether the branch is taken, and not allow them to irreversibly modify the data cache or register bank. When you discover that the branch is not taken, you can commit to those changes.

FIGURE 12.46
Frequency of execution of MIPS instructions.

Instruction	Frequency
Arithmetic	50%
Load/Store	35%
Branch	15%

Dynamic branch prediction

Assuming the branch is not taken is really a crude form of predicting the future. It is like going to the racetrack and betting on the same horse regardless of previous outcomes. You can let history be your guide with a technique known as *dynamic branch prediction*. When a branch statement executes, keep track of whether the branch is taken or not. If it is taken, store its destination address. The next time the instruction executes, predict the same outcome. If it was taken the previous time, continue filling the pipeline with the instructions at the branch destination. If it was not, fill the pipeline with the instructions following the branch instruction.

The scheme described above is called *one-bit branch prediction* because one bit is necessary to keep track of whether the branch was taken or not. A one-bit storage cell defines a finite-state machine with two states, corresponding to whether you predict the branch will be taken or not. **FIGURE 12.47** shows the finite-state machine.

Using the racetrack analogy, perhaps you should not be so quick to change the horse to bet on. Suppose the same horse you have been betting on has won three times in a row. The next time out, another horse wins. Would you really want to change your bet to the other horse based on only one result, discounting the history of previous wins? It is similar to what happens when you have a program with nested loops. Suppose the inner loop executes four times each time the outer loop executes once. The compiler translates the code for the inner loop with a conditional branch that is taken four times in a row, followed by one branch not taken to terminate the loop. Here is the sequence of branches taken and the one-bit dynamic prediction based on Figure 12.47:

```
Taken:       Y Y Y Y N Y Y Y Y N Y Y Y Y N Y Y Y Y N
Prediction: N Y Y Y Y N Y Y Y Y N Y Y Y Y N Y Y Y Y
Incorrect:  x         x x         x x         x x         x
```

With one-bit dynamic branch prediction, the branch of every inner loop will always be mispredicted twice for each execution of the outer loop.

To overcome this deficiency, it is common to use two bits to predict the next branch. The idea is that if you have a run of branches taken and you

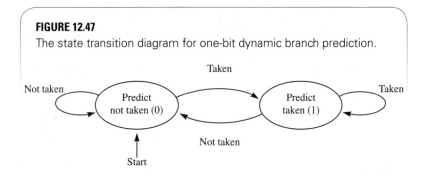

FIGURE 12.47

The state transition diagram for one-bit dynamic branch prediction.

encounter one branch not taken, you do not change your prediction right away. The criterion to change is to get two consecutive branches not taken. FIGURE 12.48 shows that you can be in one of four states. The two shaded states are the ones where you have a run of two consecutive identical branch types—the two previous branches either both taken or both not taken. The states not shaded are for the situation where the two previous branches were different. If you have a run of branches taken, you are in state 00. If the next branch is not taken, you go to state 01, but still predict the branch after that will be taken. A trace of the finite-state machine of Figure 12.48 with the branch sequence above shows that the prediction is correct every time after the outer loop gets started.

Another technique used on deep pipelines, where the penalty would be more severe if your branch assumption is not correct, is to have duplicate pipelines with duplicate program counters, fetch circuitry, and all the rest. When you decode a branch instruction, you initiate both pipelines, filling one with instructions assuming the branch is not taken and the other assuming it is. When you find out which pipeline is valid, you discard the other and continue on. This solution is quite expensive, but you have no bubbles regardless of whether the branch is taken or not.

Build two pipelines.

A data hazard happens when one instruction needs the result of a previous instruction and must stall until it gets it. It is called a read-after-write (RAW) hazard. An example is the code sequence

```
add $s2,$s2,$s3 # write $s2
sub $s4,$s4,$s2 # read $s2
```

A RAW data hazard

FIGURE 12.48

The state transition diagram for two-bit dynamic branch prediction.

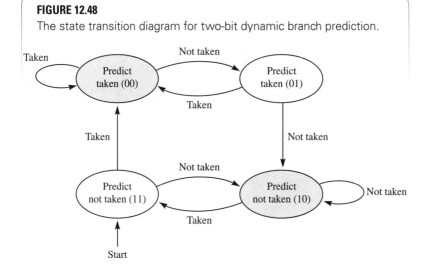

The add instruction changes the value of $s2, which is used in the sub instruction. Figure 12.43 shows that the add instruction will update the value of $s2 at the end of the write-back stage, WB. Also, the sub instruction reads from the register bank at the end of the instruction decode/register file read stage, ID. **FIGURE 12.49(a)** shows two instructions without a RAW hazard, and 12.49(b) shows how the two instructions must overlap with the data hazard. The sub instruction's ID stage must come after the add instruction's WB stage. The result is that the sub instruction must stall, creating a three-cycle bubble.

If there were another instruction with no hazard between add and sub, the bubble would be only two cycles long. With two hazardless instructions between them, the bubble gets reduced to one cycle in length, and with three, it disappears altogether. This observation brings up a possibility: If you could find some hazardless instructions nearby that needed to be executed sometime anyway, why not just execute them out of order, sticking them in between the add and sub instructions to fill up the bubble? You might object that mixing up the order in which instructions are executed will change the results of the algorithm. That is true in some cases, but not in

Instruction reordering

all. If there are many arithmetic operations in a block of code, an optimizing compiler can analyze the data dependencies and rearrange the statements to reduce the bubbles in the pipeline without changing the result of the algorithm. Alternatively, a human assembly language programmer can do the same thing.

This is an example of the price to be paid for abstraction. A level of abstraction is supposed to simplify computation at one level by hiding the details at a lower level. It would certainly be simpler if the assembly language

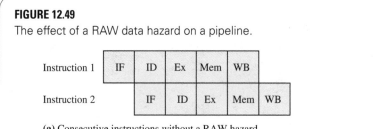

FIGURE 12.49
The effect of a RAW data hazard on a pipeline.

(a) Consecutive instructions without a RAW hazard.

(b) Consecutive instructions with a RAW hazard.

programmer or the compiler designer could generate assembly language statements in the most convenient order at Level ISA3, without knowing the details of the pipeline at Level LG1. Adding a level of abstraction always comes with a performance penalty. The question is whether the performance penalty is worth the benefits that come with the simplicity. Using the details of Level LG1 is a tradeoff of the simplicity of abstraction for performance. Another example of the same tradeoff is to design ISA3 programs while taking into account the properties of the cache subsystem.

Trading off abstraction for performance

Another technique called *data forwarding* can alleviate data hazards. Figure 12.43 shows that the results of the add instruction from the ALU are clocked into an Ex/Mem boundary register at the conclusion of the Ex stage. For the add instruction, it is simply clocked into a Mem/WB boundary register at the end of the Mem stage and finally into the register bank at the end of the WB stage. If you set up a data path between the Ex/Mem register containing the result of the add and one of the ID/Ex registers from which sub would normally get the result from the register bank, then the only alignment requirement in Figure 12.49(b) is that the ID stage of sub follows the Ex stage of add. Doing so still leaves a bubble, but it is only one cycle long.

Data forwarding

A *superscalar* design exploits the idea that two instructions with no data dependencies can execute in parallel. **FIGURE 12.50** shows two approaches. In part (a), you simply build two separate pipelines. There is one fetch unit that is fast enough to fetch more than one instruction in one cycle. It can

Superscalar machines

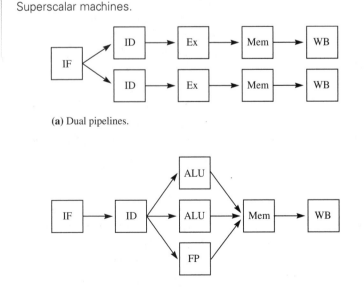

FIGURE 12.50
Superscalar machines.

(a) Dual pipelines.

(b) Multiple execution units.

issue up to two instructions per cycle concurrently. Scheduling is complex, because data dependencies across the two pipelines must be managed.

Figure 12.50(b) is based on the fact that the execution unit Ex is usually the weakest link in the chain, because its propagation delays are longer than those in the other stages in the pipeline. Floating point units are particularly time consuming compared to integer-processing circuits. The box labeled *FP* in the figure is a floating point unit that implements IEEE 754. Each one of the execution units can be three times slower than the other stages in the pipeline. However, if their inputs and outputs are staggered in time and they work in parallel, the execution stage will not slow down the pipeline.

With superscalar machines, the instruction scheduler must consider other types of data hazards. A write-after-read (WAR) hazard occurs when one instruction writes to a register after the previous one reads it. An example is the following MIPS code:

A WAR data hazard

```
add $s3,$s3,$s2 # read $s2
sub $s2,$s4,$s5 # write $s2
```

In the pipelined machine of Figure 12.43, this sequence is not a hazard, because add clocks $s2 into the ID/Ex register at the end of its ID stage, and sub writes it at the end of its WB stage. A superscalar machine reorders instructions to minimize bubbles, so it might start the execution of sub before it starts add. If it does so, it must ensure that the WB stage of sub comes after the ID stage of add.

In a perfect pipeline, increasing the clock frequency by a factor of k using a pipeline with k stages increases the performance by a factor of k. What is to prevent you from carrying this design to its logical conclusion with a cycle time equal to one gate delay? What prevents you are all the complexities from control hazards and data hazards that reduce the performance from the ideal. There comes a point at which increasing the length of the pipeline and increasing the frequency decrease performance.

But there is one more benefit to increasing the clock frequency—advertising. The megahertz rating on personal computers can be a factor in a consumer's mind when making a decision of which computer to purchase.

The megahertz myth

The *megahertz myth* says that of two machines with two different megahertz ratings, the one with more megahertz has higher performance. You can now understand why the myth is not true. Increasing the frequency by increasing the number of stages in the pipeline increases the hazard performance penalties. The question is how effective the design is in combating those penalties. Using only megahertz as a measure of performance also neglects the interplay between the factors of the performance equation in Figure 12.33. The ultimate question is not just how many cycles per second your CPU can crank out; it is also how much useful work is done per cycle to get the program executed.

At this time in computing history, pipelining technology has hit a plateau. Although advances in clock speed still occur in commercial CPU chips, they do not do so at the same pace as before. Moore's law continues to hold, with digital circuit engineers providing more total gates per square millimeter on the chips. But the current trend in CPU design is to use the extra circuitry to simply duplicate the entire CPU, fitting multiple CPU cores into a single package. This trend is expected to accelerate in the future. The big challenge will be for software designers to use parallel programming techniques, like those introduced in Section 8.3, to harness the power provided by these multicore CPU chips.

Future trends

12.4 Conclusion

Pep/9 illustrates the fundamental nature of a von Neumann computer. The data section consists of combinational and sequential circuits. It is one big finite-state machine. Input to the data section consists of data from main memory and control signals from the control section. Output from the data section is also sent to main memory and the control section. Each time the control section sends a clock pulse to a state register, the machine makes a transition to a different state.

In a real computer, the number of states is huge but finite. The Pep/9 data section of Figure 12.2 has 25 writable 8-bit registers and 5 status bits, for a total of 205 bits of storage, or 2^{205} states. With 8 inputs from the data lines on the main system bus and 34 control inputs from the control section, the number of transitions from each state is 2^{42}. Considered as a finite-state machine, the machine has a total number of transitions of 2^{205} times 2^{42}, or $2^{247} = 10^{74}$. The number of atoms in the earth is estimated to be only about 10^{50}. And Pep/9 is a tiny computer! At the most fundamental level, no matter how complex the system, computing is nothing more than executing a finite-state machine with peripheral storage.

Finite-state machines are the basis of all computing.

Simplifications in the Model

The Pep/9 computer illustrates the basic organizational idea behind all real von Neumann machines. Of course, many simplifications are made to keep the machine easy to understand.

One low-level detail that is different in real hardware implementations is the use of edge-triggered flip-flops throughout the integrated circuit instead of master–slave. Both kinds of flip-flop solve the feedback problem. Because the master–slave principle is easier to understand than the edge-triggered principle, that is the one that is carried throughout the presentation.

Another simplification is the interface of the CPU and main memory with the main system bus. With real computers, the timing constraints are more complex than simply putting the addresses on the bus, waiting for three cycles with MemRead asserted, and assuming that data can be clocked into MDR. A single memory access requires more than just two cycles, and there is a protocol that specifies in more detail how long the address lines must be asserted and precisely when the data must be clocked into a register on the CPU side.

Direct memory access

Another issue with the main system bus is how it is shared among the CPU, main memory, and the peripheral devices. In practice, the CPU is not always in control of the bus. Instead, the bus has its own processor that arbitrates between competing devices when too many of them want to use the bus at the same time. An example is with *direct memory access* (DMA), in which data flows directly from a disk over the bus to main memory not under control of the CPU. The advantage of DMA is that the CPU can spend its cycles doing useful work executing programs without diverting them to control the peripherals.

Other topics beyond the scope of this text include assembler macros, linkers, popular peripheral buses like USB and Thunderbolt, supercomputers, and the whole field of computer networks. When you study computer networks, you will find that abstraction is central. Computer systems are designed as layers of abstraction with the details of each level hidden from the level above, and Internet communication protocols are designed the same way. Each level of abstraction exists to do one thing and provides a service to the next higher level, hiding the details of how the service is provided.

The Big Picture

Now consider the big picture from Level App7 all the way down to Level LG1. Suppose a user is entering data in a database system with an application at Level App7. She wants to enter a numerical value, so she types it and executes an Enter command. What lies behind such a seemingly innocuous action?

A C programmer wrote the database system, including the procedure to input the numeric value. The C program was compiled to assembly language, which in turn was assembled into machine language. A compiler designer wrote the compiler, and an assembler designer wrote the assembler. The compiler and assembler, being automatic translators, both contain a lexical analysis phase, a parsing phase, and a code-generating phase. The lexical analysis phase is based on finite-state machines.

The C programmer also used a finite-state machine in the numeric input procedure. The compiler translated each C statement in that procedure to many assembly language statements. The assembler, however, translated each assembly language statement into one machine language statement. So the code to process the user's Enter command was expanded into many C commands, each of which was expanded into many ISA3-level commands.

Each ISA3-level command in turn was translated into the control section signals to fetch the instruction and to execute it. Each control signal is input to a multiplexer or some other combinational device, or it is a pulse to clock a value into a state register. The sequential circuits are governed by the laws of finite-state machines.

Each register is an array of flip-flops, and each flip-flop is a pair of latches designed with the master–slave principle. Each latch is a pair of NOR gates with simple cross-coupled feedback connections. Each combinational part of the data section is an interconnection of only a few different types of gates. The behavior of each gate is governed by the laws of Boolean algebra. Ultimately, the user's Enter command translates into electrical signals that flow through the individual gates.

The user's Enter command may be interrupted by the operating system if it is executing in a multiprogramming system. The Enter command may generate a page fault, in which case the operating system may need to execute a page replacement algorithm to determine the page to copy back to disk.

Of course, all these events happen without the user getting any hint of what is going on at the lower levels of the system. Design inefficiencies at any level can tangibly slow the processing to the extent that the user may curse the computer. Remember that the design of the entire system from Level App7 to Level LG1 is constrained by the fundamental space/time tradeoff.

The connection between one signal flowing through a single gate in some multiplexer at Level LG1 and the user executing an Enter command at Level App7 may seem remote, but it does exist. Literally millions of gates must cooperate to perform a task for the user. So many devices can be organized into a useful machine only by structuring the system into successive levels of abstraction.

It is remarkable that each level of abstraction consists of a few simple concepts. At Level LG1, either the NAND or NOR gate is sufficient to construct any combinational circuit. There are only four basic types of flip-flops, all of which can be produced from the SR flip-flop. The simple von Neumann cycle is the controlling force at Level ISA3 behind the operation of the machine. At Level OS4, a process is a running program that can be interrupted by storing its process control block. Assembly language at Level Asmb5 is a simple one-to-one translation to machine language. A high-order language at Level HOL6 is a one-to-many translation to a lower-level language.

Levels of abstraction

The concept of a finite-state machine permeates the entire level structure. Finite-state machines are the basis of lexical analysis for automatic

Finite-state machines

translators, and they also describe sequential circuits. The process control block stores the state of a process.

Simplicity is the key to harnessing complexity.

All sciences have simplicity and structure as their goals. In the natural sciences, the endeavor is to discover the laws of nature that explain the most phenomena with the fewest number of mathematical laws or concepts. Computer scientists have also discovered that simplicity is the key to harnessing complexity. It is possible to construct a machine as complicated as a computer only because of the simple concepts that govern its behavior at every level of abstraction.

Chapter Summary

The central processing unit (CPU) is divided into a data section and a control section. The data section has a bank of registers, some or all of which are visible to the Level-ISA3 programmer. Processing occurs in a loop, with data coming from the register bank on the ABus and BBus, through the ALU, then back to the register bank on the CBus. Data is injected into the loop from main memory via the main system bus and the memory data register at the address specified by the memory address register.

The function of the control section is to send a sequence of control signals to the data section to implement the ISA3 instruction set. The machine is controlled by the von Neumann cycle—fetch, decode, increment, execute, repeat. In a CISC machine like Pep/9, the control signals must direct the data section to fetch the operand, which may take many cycles because of complex addressing modes. A RISC machine like MIPS has few addressing modes and simple instructions so that each instruction executes with only one cycle.

Three common sources of increased performance are increasing the data bus width, inserting cache memory between the CPU and main memory, and pipelining. All three are based on the fundamental space/time tradeoff.

Increasing the data bus width requires more space for the wires on the bus and additional data registers and buses in the data section of the CPU. This increase in space makes possible a decrease in the time to move information between main memory and the CPU. All computer memories are byte-addressable. Exploiting the increased parallelism with a bus that is wider than one byte requires memory alignment of data and programs in assembly language.

Cache memory solves the problem of the extreme mismatch between the fast speed of the CPU and the slow speed of main memory. A cache is a small high-speed memory unit that contains a copy of data from main memory likely to be accessed by the CPU. It relies on the spatial and temporal locality of reference present in all real programs.

Performance enhancements are based on three components of execution time specified by the performance equation

$$\frac{\text{time}}{\text{program}} = \frac{\text{instructions}}{\text{program}} \times \frac{\text{cycles}}{\text{instruction}} \times \frac{\text{time}}{\text{cycle}}$$

CISC machines minimize the first factor at the expense of the second. RISC machines, also called *load/store machines*, minimize the second factor at the expense of the first. Both organizations can use the third factor to increase performance, primarily through pipelining.

Computers with complex instructions and many addressing modes were popular early in the history of computing. They are characterized by the Mc2 level of abstraction, in which the control section has its own micromemory, microprogram counter, and microinstruction register. The microprogram of the control section produces the control sequences to implement the ISA3 instruction set. A characteristic of load/store computers is the absence of Level Mc2 because each of its simple instructions can be implemented in one cycle.

Pipelining is analogous to an assembly line in a factory. To implement a pipeline, you subdivide the cycle by putting boundary registers in the data path of the data section. The effect is to increase the number of cycles per instruction but decrease the cycle time proportionally. When the pipeline is full, you execute one instruction per cycle through the parallelism inherent in the pipeline. However, control hazards and data hazards decrease the performance from the theoretical ideal. Techniques to deal with hazards include branch prediction, instruction reordering, and data forwarding. Superscalar machines duplicate pipelines or execution units for greater parallelism.

Exercises

Section 12.1

1. Draw the individual lines of the eight-bit bus between MDR and the main memory bus. Show the tri-state buffers and the connection to the MemWrite line.

2. Design the three-input, one-output combinational circuit AndZ of Figure 12.2. **(a)** Minimize the AND-OR circuit with a Karnaugh map.

(b) Minimize the OR-AND circuit with a Karnaugh map. (c) Which one is better?

3. Figure 12.7 combines cycle 6 with cycle 2 and cycle 7 with cycle 3 in Figure 12.5 to speed up the von Neumann cycle. Can you combine cycle 6 with cycle 3 and cycle 7 with cycle 4 instead? Explain.

4. Figure 12.7 combines cycle 6 with cycle 2 and cycle 7 with cycle 3 in Figure 12.5 to speed up the von Neumann cycle. Can you combine cycle 6 with cycle 4 and cycle 7 with cycle 5 instead? Explain.

Section 12.2

*5. The text predicts that we will never need to transition from 64-bit computers to 128-bit computers because we will never need main memories bigger than 16 billion GiB. Silicon crystals have a plane consisting of 0.5-nm square tiles, each tile containing two atoms. (a) Assuming that you could manufacture a memory so dense as to store one bit per atom on one plane of silicon atoms (and neglecting the interconnection issues with the wires), what would be the length of the side of a square chip necessary to store the maximum number of bytes addressable by a 64-bit computer? Show your calculation. (b) Does this calculation support the prediction? Explain.

6. The CPU requests the byte at address 4675 (dec) with the cache of Figure 12.28. (a) What are the nine bits of the Tag field? (b) What are the four bits of the Byte field? (c) Which cell of the cache stored the data?

7. A CPU can address 16 MiB of main memory. It has a direct-mapped cache in which it stores 256 eight-byte cache lines. (a) How many bits are required for a memory address? (b) How many bits are required for the Byte field of the address? (c) How many bits are required for the Line field of the address? (d) How many bits are required for the Tag field of the address? (e) How many bits are required for the Data field of each cache entry? (f) How many bits total are required for all the fields of one cache entry? (g) How many bits total are required for the entire cache?

8. If the CPU of Exercise 7 had a two-way set-associative cache, again with 256 eight-byte cache lines, how many bits would be required for each cache entry?

9. For Figure 12.30, (a) draw the implementation of a comparator, the circle with the equals sign. (*Hint:* Consider the truth table of an XOR followed

by an inverter, sometimes called an *XNOR gate*.) **(b)** Draw the input and output connections to and from the 128 four-input multiplexers. **(c)** Draw the implementation of one of the 128 four-input multiplexers. You may use ellipses (. . .) in parts (a) and (b) of the exercise.

10. A direct-mapped cache is at one extreme of cache designs, with set-associative caches in the middle. At the opposite extreme is the *fully associative cache,* where there is in essence only one entry in the cache of Figure 12.29(a), and the Line field of the address has zero bits—that is, it is missing altogether. An address consists of only the Tag field and the Byte field. **(a)** In Figure 12.29, instead of having 8 cache cells, each with 4 lines, you could use the same number of bits with 1 cache cell having 32 lines. Would this design increase the cache hit percentage over that in Figure 12.29? Explain. **(b)** How many comparators in the read circuit would be required for the cache of part (a)?

Fully associative caches

11. Suppose a CPU can address 1 MByte of main memory. It has a fully associative cache (see Exercise 10) with 16 32-byte cache lines. **(a)** How many bits are required for a memory address? **(b)** How many bits are required for the Byte field of the address? **(c)** How many bits are required for the Tag field of the address? **(d)** How many bits are required for the Data field of each cache entry? **(e)** How many bits total are required for the entire cache?

Section 12.3

*12. **(a)** Suppose a C compiler for the MIPS machine associates $s4 with array a, $s5 with variable g, and $s6 with array b. How does it translate

```
a[4] = g + b[5];
```

into MIPS assembly language? **(b)** Write the machine language translation of the instructions in part (a).

13. **(a)** Write the MIPS assembly language statement to shift the content of register $s2 nine bits to the left and put the result in $t5. **(b)** Write the machine language translation of the instruction in (a).

14. **(a)** Suppose a C compiler for the MIPS machine associates $s4 with variable g, $s5 with array a, and $s6 with variable i. How does it translate

```
g = a[i];
```

into MIPS assembly language? **(b)** Write the machine language translation of the instructions in part (a).

15. **(a)** Suppose a C compiler for the MIPS machine associates $s4 with variable g, $s5 with array a, and $s6 with variable i. How does it translate

    ```
    a[i] = g;
    ```

    into MIPS assembly language? **(b)** Write the machine language translation of the instructions in part (a).

16. **(a)** Suppose a C compiler for the MIPS machine associates $s4 with variable g, $s5 with array a, and $s6 with variable i. How does it translate

    ```
    g = a[i+3];
    ```

    into MIPS assembly language? **(b)** Write the machine language translation of the instructions in part (a).

17. **(a)** Suppose a C compiler for the MIPS machine associates $s5 with array a and $s6 with variable i. How does it translate

    ```
    a[i] = a[i+1];
    ```

    into MIPS assembly language? **(b)** Write the machine language translation of the instructions in part (a).

18. **(a)** Write the MIPS assembly language statement to allocate 12 bytes of storage on the run-time stack. **(b)** Write the machine language translation of the instruction in part (a).

19. **(a)** Suppose a C compiler for the MIPS machine associates $s5 with variable g. How does it translate

    ```
    g = 529371;
    ```

    into MIPS assembly language? **(b)** Write the machine language translation of the instructions in part (a).

20. **(a)** What is the RTL specification for the lw instruction? **(b)** For Figure 12.40, write the control signals to execute the lw instruction.

21. In Figure 12.43, **(a)** how many bits are in each of the two IF/ID boundary registers? **(b)** How many bits are in each of the four ID/Ex boundary registers? **(c)** How many bits are in each of the three Ex/Mem boundary registers? **(d)** How many bits are in each of the two Mem/WB boundary registers?

22. For Figure 12.45(b), place a checkmark for each circuit that is idle in each of the cycles in the table below, and list the total number of circuits that are idle for each cycle.

Cycle	7	8	9	10	11	12	13	14	15	16
IF										
ID										
Ex										
Mem										
WB										
Number idle										

23. Suppose the five-stage pipeline of Figure 12.45(a) executes a branch 15% of the time, each branch causing the next instruction that executes to stall until the completion of the branch, as in Figure 12.45(b). **(a)** What is the percentage increase in the number of cycles over the ideal pipeline with no bubbles? **(b)** Suppose an n-stage pipeline executes a branch x% of the time, each branch causing the next instruction that executes to stall until the completion of the branch. What is the percentage increase in the number of cycles over the ideal pipeline with no bubbles?

24. The text states that you can eliminate the write-back stage of an unconditional branch under the assumption that the next instruction has been delayed. **(a)** Draw cycles 7 through 16 of Figure 12.45(b) with that design. **(b)** Complete the table of Exercise 22 with that design.

25. **(a)** In Figure 12.47 for one-bit dynamic branch prediction, what pattern of Taken outcomes will produce the maximum percentage of incorrect predictions? What is the maximum percentage? **(b)** In Figure 12.48 for two-bit dynamic branch prediction, what pattern of Taken outcomes will produce the maximum percentage of incorrect predictions? What is the maximum percentage?

26. Construct the one-input finite-state machine of Figure 12.48 to implement two-bit dynamic branch prediction. Minimize your circuit with a Karnaugh map. **(a)** Use two SR flip-flops. **(b)** Use two JK flip-flops. **(c)** Use two D flip-flops. **(d)** Use two T flip-flops.

27. The finite-state machine of Figure 12.48 for branch prediction moves from predicting no branch to predicting branch only if two consecutive branches were made (and similarly for moving from predicting branch

to predicting no branch). **(a)** Draw a finite-state machine that moves from predicting no branch to predicting branch only if *three* consecutive branches were made (and similarly for moving from predicting branch to predicting no branch). **(b)** How many prediction bits would be necessary for the implementation of the machine?

Problems

The problems in this chapter are to write the control sequences to implement ISA3 instructions at Level Mc2. For each problem, write your implementation in the Pep/9 CPU simulator. The Help feature of the application has unit tests for each problem, which you must use to test your implementation. For all problems, use the fewest cycles possible.

Section 12.1

28. Write the control sequence with the one-byte data bus for the von Neumann cycle to fetch the operand specifier and increment PC accordingly. Assume the instruction specifier has been fetched and the control section has determined that the instruction is nonunary.

29. Write the control sequence with the one-byte data bus to implement the following unary ISA3 instructions. Assume the instruction has been fetched and the program counter has been incremented.

*(a) MOVSPA   (b) MOVFLGA
(c) MOVAFLG   (d) NOTA
(e) NEGA   (f) ROLA
(g) RORA

30. Write the control sequence with the one-byte data bus to implement the ASLA instruction, which does an arithmetic shift left of the accumulator and puts the result back in the accumulator. The RTL specification of ASLA at the ISA3 level shows that, unlike ASRA, the V bit is set to indicate an overflow when the quantity is interpreted as a signed integer. At the Mc2 level, an ASLA instruction is implemented as an ASL on the low-order byte followed by an ROL on the high-order byte. Even though the ROL operation does not set the V bit at the ISA3 level, Figure 10.55 shows that the ALU function for ROL does compute the V bit at the Mc2 level. So, you can access the V output from the ALU on the ROL operation. Assume the instruction has been fetched and the program counter has been incremented.

31. Write the control sequence with the one-byte data bus to implement the following nonunary ISA3 instructions. Assume that the instruction has been fetched and the program counter has been incremented. Note that the operand is already in the instruction register (IR).

    *(a) SUBA this,i   (b) ANDA this,i
    (c) ORA this,i   (d) CPWA this,i
    (e) CPBA this,i   (f) LDWA this,i
    (g) LDBA this,i

32. Write the control sequence with the one-byte data bus to implement the following nonunary ISA3 instructions. Assume that the instruction has been fetched and the program counter has been incremented.

    *(a) LDWA here,d   (b) LDWA here,s
    (c) LDWA here,sf   (d) LDWA here,x
    (e) LDWA here,sx   (f) LDWA here,sfx
    (g) STWA there,n   (h) STWA there,s
    (i) STWA there,sf   (j) STWA there,x
    (k) STWA there,sx   (l) STWA there,sfx

33. Write the control sequence with the one-byte data bus to implement the following flow of control ISA3 instructions. Assume that the instruction has been fetched and the program counter has been incremented. Because DECO is a trap instruction, its addressing mode is irrelevant to its implementation. All trap instructions have the same implementation at the ISA3 level.

    (a) BR main   (b) BR guessJT,x
    (c) CALL alpha   (d) RET
    (e) DECO 0x0003,d   (f) RETTR

Section 12.2

34. Write the control sequence with the two-byte data bus for the von Neumann cycle to fetch the operand specifier and increment PC accordingly. (a) Assume the program counter is even so that the first byte of the operand specifier has not been prefetched. (b) Assume the program counter is odd so that the first byte of the operand specifier has been prefetched. Prefetch the following instruction specifier.

35. Write the control sequence with the two-byte data bus to implement the ISA3 instructions of Problem 32. Assume that all addresses and word operands are aligned at even addresses. Compare the number of cycles with the corresponding number of cycles for the one-byte data bus and

compute the percentage savings in the number of cycles for the two-byte bus design.

36. Write the control sequence with the two-byte data bus to implement the ISA3 instructions of Problem 33. Assume that all addresses and word operands are aligned at even addresses. Compare the number of cycles with the corresponding number of cycles for the one-byte data bus and compute the percentage savings in the number of cycles for the two-byte bus design. Part (e) is a trap instruction, and part (f) is the return from trap instruction. Both parts assume an aligned system stack. The modified RTL specification for the aligned system stack is provided in the Pep/9 CPU simulator along with the usual unit tests.

37. Insert the .ALIGN dot command and the NOP0 instruction to align the following Pep/9 assembly language programs for the Pep/9 processor with the two-byte data bus. Remember that all CALL statements must be at odd addresses so the return address will be at an even address. The source code for the original nonaligned program is available in the Help facility of the Pep/9 application. Test your aligned programs.

(a) Figure 5.22   *(b) Figure 6.10
(c) Figure 6.12   (d) Figure 6.18
(e) Figure 6.21

APPENDIX

Pep/9 Architecture

This appendix summarizes the architecture of the Pep/9 computer.

FIGURE A.1
The hexadecimal conversion chart.

	0	1	2	3	4	5	6	7	8	9	A	B	C	D	E	F
0_	0	1	2	3	4	5	6	7	8	9	10	11	12	13	14	15
1_	16	17	18	19	20	21	22	23	24	25	26	27	28	29	30	31
2_	32	33	34	35	36	37	38	39	40	41	42	43	44	45	46	47
3_	48	49	50	51	52	53	54	55	56	57	58	59	60	61	62	63
4_	64	65	66	67	68	69	70	71	72	73	74	75	76	77	78	79
5_	80	81	82	83	84	85	86	87	88	89	90	91	92	93	94	95
6_	96	97	98	99	100	101	102	103	104	105	106	107	108	109	110	111
7_	112	113	114	115	116	117	118	119	120	121	122	123	124	125	126	127
8_	128	129	130	131	132	133	134	135	136	137	138	139	140	141	142	143
9_	144	145	146	147	148	149	150	151	152	153	154	155	156	157	158	159
A_	160	161	162	163	164	165	166	167	168	169	170	171	172	173	174	175
B_	176	177	178	179	180	181	182	183	184	185	186	187	188	189	190	191
C_	192	193	194	195	196	197	198	199	200	201	202	203	204	205	206	207
D_	208	209	210	211	212	213	214	215	216	217	218	219	220	221	222	223
E_	224	225	226	227	228	229	230	231	232	233	234	235	236	237	238	239
F_	240	241	242	243	244	245	246	247	248	249	250	251	252	253	254	255

FIGURE A.2

The relationship between hexadecimal and binary.

Hexadecimal	Binary	Hexadecimal	Binary	Hexadecimal	Binary	Hexadecimal	Binary
0	0000	4	0100	8	1000	C	1100
1	0001	5	0101	9	1001	D	1101
2	0010	6	0110	A	1010	E	1110
3	0011	7	0111	B	1011	F	1111

FIGURE A.3

The American Standard Code for Information Interchange (ASCII).

Char	Bin	Hex	Char	Bin	Hex	Char	Bin	Hex	Char	Bin	Hex
NUL	000 0000	00	SP	010 0000	20	@	100 0000	40	`	110 0000	60
SOH	000 0001	01	!	010 0001	21	A	100 0001	41	a	110 0001	61
STX	000 0010	02	"	010 0010	22	B	100 0010	42	b	110 0010	62
ETX	000 0011	03	#	010 0011	23	C	100 0011	43	c	110 0011	63
EOT	000 0100	04	$	010 0100	24	D	100 0100	44	d	110 0100	64
ENQ	000 0101	05	%	010 0101	25	E	100 0101	45	e	110 0101	65
ACK	000 0110	06	&	010 0110	26	F	100 0110	46	f	110 0110	66
BEL	000 0111	07	'	010 0111	27	G	100 0111	47	g	110 0111	67
BS	000 1000	08	(	010 1000	28	H	100 1000	48	h	110 1000	68
HT	000 1001	09	)	010 1001	29	I	100 1001	49	i	110 1001	69
LF	000 1010	0A	*	010 1010	2A	J	100 1010	4A	j	110 1010	6A
VT	000 1011	0B	+	010 1011	2B	K	100 1011	4B	k	110 1011	6B
FF	000 1100	0C	,	010 1100	2C	L	100 1100	4C	l	110 1100	6C
CR	000 1101	0D	–	010 1101	2D	M	100 1101	4D	m	110 1101	6D
SO	000 1110	0E	.	010 1110	2E	N	100 1110	4E	n	110 1110	6E
SI	000 1111	0F	/	010 1111	2F	O	100 1111	4F	o	110 1111	6F
DLE	001 0000	10	0	011 0000	30	P	101 0000	50	p	111 0000	70
DC1	001 0001	11	1	011 0001	31	Q	101 0001	51	q	111 0001	71
DC2	001 0010	12	2	011 0010	32	R	101 0010	52	r	111 0010	72
DC3	001 0011	13	3	011 0011	33	S	101 0011	53	s	111 0011	73
DC4	001 0100	14	4	011 0100	34	T	101 0100	54	t	111 0100	74
NAK	001 0101	15	5	011 0101	35	U	101 0101	55	u	111 0101	75
SYN	001 0110	16	6	011 0110	36	V	101 0110	56	v	111 0110	76
ETB	001 0111	17	7	011 0111	37	W	101 0111	57	w	111 0111	77
CAN	001 1000	18	8	011 1000	38	X	101 1000	58	x	111 1000	78
EM	001 1001	19	9	011 1001	39	Y	101 1001	59	y	111 1001	79
SUB	001 1010	1A	:	011 1010	3A	Z	101 1010	5A	z	111 1010	7A
ESC	001 1011	1B	;	011 1011	3B	[	101 1011	5B	{	111 1011	7B
FS	001 1100	1C	<	011 1100	3C	\	101 1100	5C			111 1100	7C
GS	001 1101	1D	=	011 1101	3D	]	101 1101	5D	}	111 1101	7D
RS	001 1110	1E	>	011 1110	3E	^	101 1110	5E	~	111 1110	7E
US	001 1111	1F	?	011 1111	3F	_	101 1111	5F	DEL	111 1111	7F

Abbreviations for Control Characters

NUL	null, or all zeros	**FF**	form feed	**CAN**	cancel
SOH	start of heading	**CR**	carriage return	**EM**	end of medium
STX	start of text	**SO**	shift out	**SUB**	substitute
ETX	end of text	**SI**	shift in	**ESC**	escape
EOT	end of transmission	**DLE**	data link escape	**FS**	file separator
ENQ	enquiry	**DC1**	device control 1	**GS**	group separator
ACK	acknowledge	**DC2**	device control 2	**RS**	record separator
BEL	bell	**DC3**	device control 3	**US**	unit separator
BS	backspace	**DC4**	device control 4	**SP**	space
HT	horizontal tabulation	**NAK**	negative acknowledge	**DEL**	delete
LF	line feed	**SYN**	synchronous idle		
VT	vertical tabulation	**ETB**	end of transmission block		

FIGURE A.4

The central processing unit of the Pep/9 computer.

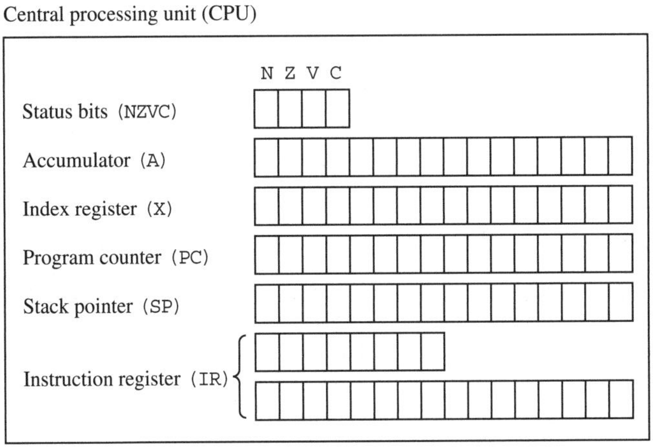

FIGURE A.5

The Pep/9 instruction format.

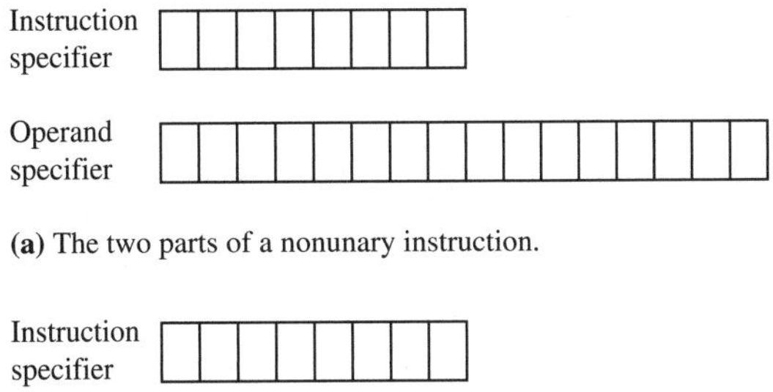

(a) The two parts of a nonunary instruction.

(b) A unary instruction.

FIGURE A.6

The Pep/9 instruction specifier fields.

aaa	Addressing Mode
000	Immediate
001	Direct
010	Indirect
011	Stack-relative
100	Stack-relative deferred
101	Indexed
110	Stack-indexed
111	Stack-deferred indexed

(a) The addressing-aaa field.

a	Addressing Mode
0	Immediate
1	Indexed

(b) The addressing-a field.

r	Register
0	Accumulator, A
1	Index register, X

(c) The register-r field.

FIGURE A.7

The Pep/9 addressing modes.

Addressing Mode	aaa	Letters	Operand
Immediate	000	i	OprndSpec
Direct	001	d	Mem[OprndSpec]
Indirect	010	n	Mem[Mem[OprndSpec]]
Stack-relative	011	s	Mem[SP + OprndSpec]
Stack-relative deferred	100	sf	Mem[Mem[SP + OprndSpec]]
Indexed	101	x	Mem[OprndSpec + X]
Stack-indexed	110	sx	Mem[SP + OprndSpec + X]
Stack-deferred indexed	111	sfx	Mem[Mem[SP + OprndSpec] + X]

FIGURE A.8

The Pep/9 instruction set at Level Asmb5.

Instruction Specifier	Mnemonic	Instruction	Addressing Mode	Status Bits
0000 0000	STOP	Stop execution	U	
0000 0001	RET	Return from CALL	U	
0000 0010	RETTR	Return from trap	U	
0000 0011	MOVSPA	Move SP to A	U	
0000 0100	MOVFLGA	Move NZVC flags to A⟨12..15⟩	U	
0000 0101	MOVAFLG	Move A⟨12..15⟩ to NZVC flags	U	
0000 011r	NOTr	Bitwise invert r	U	NZ
0000 100r	NEGr	Negate r	U	NZV
0000 101r	ASLr	Arithmetic shift left r	U	NZVC
0000 110r	ASRr	Arithmetic shift right r	U	NZC
0000 111r	ROLr	Rotate left r	U	C
0001 000r	RORr	Rotate right r	U	C
0001 001a	BR	Branch unconditional	i, x	
0001 010a	BRLE	Branch if less than or equal to	i, x	
0001 011a	BRLT	Branch if less than	i, x	
0001 100a	BREQ	Branch if equal to	i, x	
0001 101a	BRNE	Branch if not equal to	i, x	
0001 110a	BRGE	Branch if greater than or equal to	i, x	
0001 111a	BRGT	Branch if greater than	i, x	
0010 000a	BRV	Branch if V	i, x	
0010 001a	BRC	Branch if C	i, x	
0010 010a	CALL	Call subroutine	i, x	
0010 011n	NOPn	Unary no operation trap	U	
0010 1aaa	NOP	Nonunary no operation trap	i	

(continued)

FIGURE A.8

The Pep/9 instruction set at Level Asmb5. (*continued*)

0011 0aaa	DECI	Decimal input trap	d, n, s, sf, x, sx, sfx	NZV
0011 1aaa	DECO	Decimal output trap	i, d, n, s, sf, x, sx, sfx	
0100 0aaa	HEXO	Hexadecimal output trap	i, d, n, s, sf, x, sx, sfx	
0100 1aaa	STRO	String output trap	d, n, s, sf, x	
0101 0aaa	ADDSP	Add to stack pointer (SP)	i, d, n, s, sf, x, sx, sfx	NZVC
0101 1aaa	SUBSP	Subtract from stack pointer (SP)	i, d, n, s, sf, x, sx, sfx	NZVC
0110 raaa	ADDr	Add to r	i, d, n, s, sf, x, sx, sfx	NZVC
0111 raaa	SUBr	Subtract from r	i, d, n, s, sf, x, sx, sfx	NZVC
1000 raaa	ANDr	Bitwise AND to r	i, d, n, s, sf, x, sx, sfx	NZ
1001 raaa	ORr	Bitwise OR to r	i, d, n, s, sf, x, sx, sfx	NZ
1010 raaa	CPWr	Compare word to r	i, d, n, s, sf, x, sx, sfx	NZVC
1011 raaa	CPBr	Compare byte to r⟨8..15⟩	i, d, n, s, sf, x, sx, sfx	NZVC
1100 raaa	LDWr	Load word r from memory	i, d, n, s, sf, x, sx, sfx	NZ
1101 raaa	LDBr	Load byte r⟨8..15⟩ from memory	i, d, n, s, sf, x, sx, sfx	NZ
1110 raaa	STWr	Store word r to memory	d, n, s, sf, x, sx, sfx	
1111 raaa	STBr	Store byte r⟨8..15⟩ to memory	d, n, s, sf, x, sx, sfx	

FIGURE A.9

The pseudo-ops of Pep/9 assembly language.

Pseudo-op	Assembler Directive
.ADDRSS	The address of a symbol
.ALIGN	Padding to align at a memory boundary
.ASCII	A string of ASCII bytes
.BLOCK	A block of zero bytes
.BURN	Initiate ROM burn
.BYTE	A byte value
.END	The sentinel for the assembler
.EQUATE	Equate a symbol to a constant value
.WORD	A word value

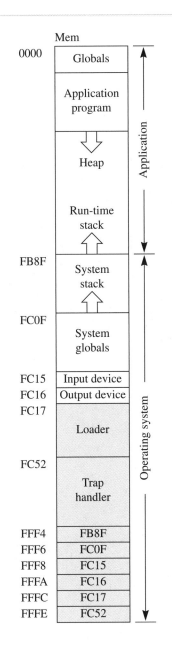

Mem

0000	Globals
	Application program
	Heap
	Run-time stack
FB8F	System stack
FC0F	System globals
FC15	Input device
FC16	Output device
FC17	Loader
FC52	Trap handler
FFF4	FB8F
FFF6	FC0F
FFF8	FC15
FFFA	FC16
FFFC	FC17
FFFE	FC52

Application

Operating system

FIGURE A.10
A memory map of the Pep/9 memory. The shaded part is read-only memory.

FIGURE A.11
The RTL specification of Pep/9 instructions.

Instruction	Register Transfer Language Specification
STOP	Stop execution
RET	PC ← Mem[SP] ; SP ← SP + 2
RETTR	NZVC ← Mem[SP]⟨4..7⟩ ; A ← Mem[SP + 1] ; X ← Mem[SP + 3] ; PC ← Mem[SP + 5] ; SP ← Mem[SP + 7]
MOVSPA	A ← SP
MOVFLGA	A⟨8..11⟩ ← 0 , A⟨12..15⟩ ← NZVC
MOVAFLG	NZVC ← A⟨12..15⟩
NOTr	r ← ¬ r ; N ← r < 0 , Z ← r = 0
NEGr	r ← −r ; N ← r < 0 , Z ← r = 0 , V ← {overflow}
ASLr	C ← r⟨0⟩ , r⟨0..14⟩ ← r⟨1..15⟩ , r⟨15⟩ ← 0 ; N ← r < 0 , Z ← r = 0 , V ← {overflow}
ASRr	C ← r⟨15⟩ , r⟨1..15⟩ ← r⟨0..14⟩ ; N ← r < 0 , Z ← r = 0
ROLr	C ← r⟨0⟩ , r⟨0..14⟩ ← r⟨1..15⟩ , r⟨15⟩ ← C
RORr	C ← r⟨15⟩ , r⟨1..15⟩ ← r⟨0..14⟩ , r⟨0⟩ ← C
BR	PC ← Oprnd
BRLE	N = 1 ∨ Z = 1 ⇒ PC ← Oprnd
BRLT	N = 1 ⇒ PC ← Oprnd
BREQ	Z = 1 ⇒ PC ← Oprnd
BRNE	Z = 0 ⇒ PC ← Oprnd
BRGE	N = 0 ⇒ PC ← Oprnd
BRGT	N = 0 ∧ Z = 0 ⇒ PC ← Oprnd
BRV	V = 1 ⇒ PC ← Oprnd
BRC	C = 1 ⇒ PC ← Oprnd
CALL	SP ← SP − 2 ; Mem[SP] ← PC ; PC ← Oprnd
NOPn	Trap: Unary no operation
NOP	Trap: Nonunary no operation
DECI	Trap: Oprnd ← {decimal input}
DECO	Trap: {decimal output} ← Oprnd
HEXO	Trap: {hexadecimal output} ← Oprnd
STRO	Trap: {string output} ← Oprnd
ADDSP	SP ← SP + Oprnd
SUBSP	SP ← SP − Oprnd
ADDr	r ← r + Oprnd ; N ← r < 0 , Z ← r = 0 , V ← {overflow} , C ← {carry}
SUBr	r ← r − Oprnd ; N ← r < 0 , Z ← r = 0 , V ← {overflow} , C ← {carry}

ANDr	$r \leftarrow r \wedge \text{Oprnd}$; $N \leftarrow r < 0$, $Z \leftarrow r = 0$
ORr	$r \leftarrow r \vee \text{Oprnd}$; $N \leftarrow r < 0$, $Z \leftarrow r = 0$
CPWr	$T \leftarrow r - \text{Oprnd}$; $N \leftarrow T < 0$, $Z \leftarrow T = 0$, $V \leftarrow \{overflow\}$, $C \leftarrow \{carry\}$; $N \leftarrow N \oplus V$
CPBr	$T \leftarrow r\langle 8..15 \rangle - \text{byte Oprnd}$; $N \leftarrow T < 0$, $Z \leftarrow T = 0$, $V \leftarrow 0$, $C \leftarrow 0$
LDWr	$r \leftarrow \text{Oprnd}$; $N \leftarrow r < 0$, $Z \leftarrow r = 0$
LDBr	$r\langle 8..15 \rangle \leftarrow \text{byte Oprnd}$; $N \leftarrow 0$, $Z \leftarrow r\langle 8..15 \rangle = 0$
STWr	$\text{Oprnd} \leftarrow r$
STBr	$\text{byte Oprnd} \leftarrow r\langle 8..15 \rangle$
Trap	$T \leftarrow \text{Mem[FFF6]}$; $\text{Mem[T − 1]} \leftarrow \text{IR}\langle 0..7 \rangle$; $\text{Mem[T − 3]} \leftarrow \text{SP}$; $\text{Mem[T − 5]} \leftarrow \text{PC}$; $\text{Mem[T − 7]} \leftarrow X$; $\text{Mem[T − 9]} \leftarrow A$; $\text{Mem[T − 10]}\langle 4..7 \rangle \leftarrow \text{NZVC}$; $\text{SP} \leftarrow T − 10$; $\text{PC} \leftarrow \text{Mem[FFFE]}$

FIGURE A.12
The 16 functions of the Pep/9 ALU.

ALU Control			Status Bits			
(bin)	(dec)	Result	N	Zout	V	Cout
0000	0	A	N	Z	0	0
0001	1	A plus B	N	Z	V	C
0010	2	A plus B plus Cin	N	Z	V	C
0011	3	A plus $\overline{B}$ plus 1	N	Z	V	C
0100	4	A plus $\overline{B}$ plus Cin	N	Z	V	C
0101	5	A · B	N	Z	0	0
0110	6	$\overline{A \cdot B}$	N	Z	0	0
0111	7	A + B	N	Z	0	0
1000	8	$\overline{A + B}$	N	Z	0	0
1001	9	A $\oplus$ B	N	Z	0	0
1010	10	$\overline{A}$	N	Z	0	0
1011	11	ASL A	N	Z	V	C
1100	12	ROL A	N	Z	V	C
1101	13	ASR A	N	Z	0	C
1110	14	ROR A	N	Z	0	C
1111	15	0	A<4>	A<5>	A<6>	A<7>

FIGURE A.13

The data section of the Pep/9 CPU.

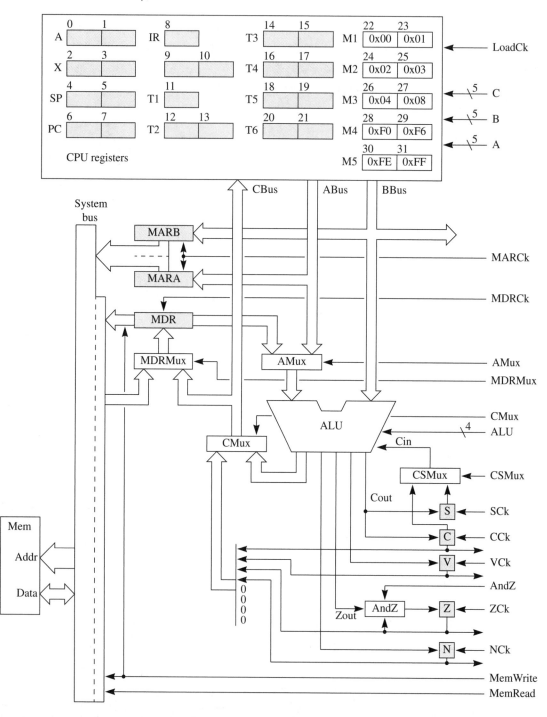

FIGURE A.14

The Pep/9 CPU with a two-byte data bus.

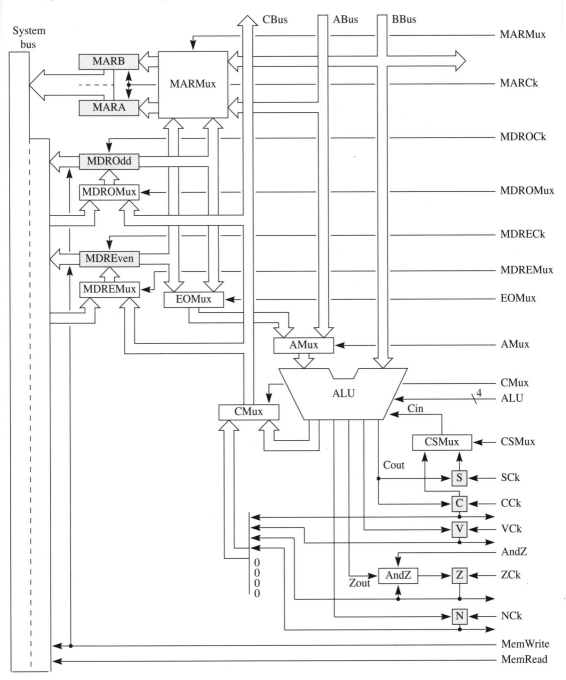

Solutions to Selected Exercises

Chapter 1

2. (a) 11,110 not counting Khan

3. (a)

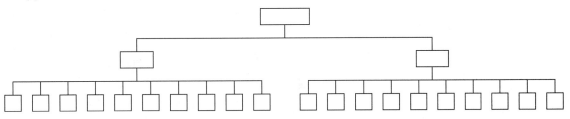

4. (a)

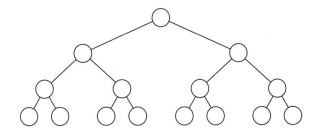

   (b) 31

9. 43 ms

12. 32 b/s

15. (a) 1936 b   (b) 152 characters

21. `Temp5`

`F.Name`	`F.Major`	`F.State`
Ron	Math	OR

`Temp6`

`S.Name`	`S.Class`	`S.Major`	`S.State`
Beth	Soph	Hist	TX
Allison	Soph	Math	AZ

22. (a) `select Sor where S.Name = Beth giving Temp`
       `project Temp over S.State giving Result`

Chapter 2

1. (a) Called four times.

2.

(a, part 1)   (a, part 2)

```
Main program
   Call BC(4, 1)
       Call BC(3, 1)
              Call BC(2, 1)
                  Call BC(1, 1)
              Return to BC(2, 1)
                  Call BC(1, 0)
              Return to BC(2, 1)
          Return to BC(3, 1)
              Call BC(2, 0)
          Return to BC(3, 1)
      Return to BC(4, 1)
          Call BC(3, 0)
      Return to BC(4, 1)
Return to main program
```

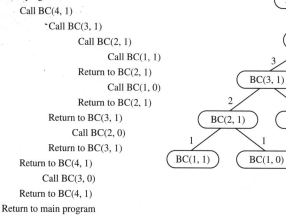

(a, part 3)   Called seven times.

(a, part 4)   Maximum of five stack frames.

(a, part 5)

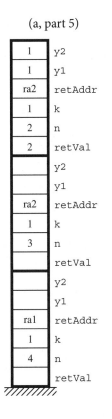

Chapter 3

1. (a) Octal: 267, 270, 271, 272, 273, 274, 275, 276, 277, 300, 301

   (b) Base 3: 2102, 2110, 2111, 2112, 2120, 2121, 2122, 2200, 2201, 2202, 2210

   (c) Binary: 10101, 10110, 10111, 11000, 11001, 11010, 11011, 11100, 11101, 11110, 11111

   (d) Base 5: 2433, 2434, 2440, 2441, 2442, 2443, 2444, 3000, 3001, 3002

3. (a) 18   (b) 6   (c) 11   (d) 8   (e) 31   (f) 85

5. (a) 11001   (b) 10000   (c) 1   (d) 1110   (e) 101   (f) 101001

7. (a) 00 to 11 (bin) and 0 to 3 (dec)   (b) 000 to 111 (bin) and 0 to 7 (dec)

8. (a) 111 0100, C = 0   (b) 001 0000, C = 1

   (c) 111 1110, C = 1   (d) 000 0000, C = 0

11. (a) $7 \times 8^4 + 0 \times 8^3 + 1 \times 8^2 + 4 \times 8^1 + 6 \times 8^0$

13. (a) 0110001   (b) 1100101   (c) 0000000   (d) 1000000   (e) 1111111

   (f) 111 1110   (g) 100 0000 to 011 1111 (bin) and −64 to 63 (dec)

15. (a) 29   (b) −43   (c) −4   (d) 1   (e) −64   (f) −63

17. (a) 011 1001, NZVC = 0000   (b) 000 0110, NZVC = 0001
    (c) 001 1011, NZVC = 0011   (d) 101 0110, NZVC = 1001
    (e) 100 0001, NZVC = 1011   (f) 111 0100, NZVC = 1000

19. (a) 10 to 01 (bin) and −2 to 1 (dec)
    (b) 100 to 011 (bin) and −4 to 3 (dec)

20. (a) 010 1000, NZ = 00   (b) 000 0101, NZ = 00   (c) 110 1110, NZ = 10
    (d) 101 1111, NZ = 10   (e) 100 0110, NZ = 10   (f) 101 1010, NZ = 10
    (g) 101 0100   (h) 001 0101

22. (a) 24 (dec) = 001 1000 (bin)
        ASL 001 1000 = 011 0000 (bin) = 48 (dec), NZVC = 0000
        ASR 001 1000 = 000 1100 (bin) = 12 (dec), NZC = 000
    (b) 37 (dec) = 010 0101 (bin)
        ASL 010 0101 = 100 1010 (bin) = −54 (dec), NZVC = 1010
        ASR 010 0101 = 001 0010 (bin) = 18 (dec), NZC = 001
    (c) −26 (dec) = 110 0110 (bin)
        ASL 110 0110 = 100 1100 (bin) = −52 (dec), NZVC = 1001
        ASR 110 0110 = 111 0011 (bin) = −13 (dec), NZC = 100
    (d) 1 (dec) = 000 0001 (bin)
        ASL 000 0001 = 000 0010 (bin) = 2 (dec), NZVC = 0000
        ASR 000 0001 = 000 0000 (bin) = 0 (dec), NZC = 011
    (e) 0 (dec) = 000 0000 (bin)
        ASL 000 0000 = 000 0000 (bin) = 0 (dec), NZVC = 0100
        ASR 000 0000 = 000 0000 (bin) = 0 (dec), NZC = 010
    (f) −1 (dec) = 111 1111 (bin)
        ASL 111 1111 = 111 1110 (bin) = −2 (dec), NZVC = 1001
        ASR 111 1111 = 111 1111 (bin) = −1 (dec), NZC = 101

25. (a) C = 1, ROL 010 1101 = 101 1011, C = 0
    (b) C = 0, ROL 010 1101 = 101 1010, C = 0
    (c) C = 1, ROR 010 1101 = 101 0110, C = 1
    (d) C = 0, ROR 010 1101 = 001 0110, C = 1

28. (a) 3AB7, 3AB8, 3AB9, 3ABA, 3ABB, 3ABC

29. (a) 11,614

30. (a) 68CF

32. (a) 5D (hex) = 101 1101 (bin) = −35 (dec)
    (b) 2F (hex) = 010 1111 (bin) = 47 (dec)
    (c) 40 (hex) = 100 0000 (bin) = −256 (dec)

34. (a) −27 (dec) = 110 0101 (bin) = 65 (hex)
    (b) 63 (dec) = 011 1111 (bin) = 3F (hex)
    (c) −1 (dec) = 111 1111 (bin) = 7F (hex)

36. Have a nice day!

38. 101 0000   110 0001   111 1001   010 0000   010 0100
    011 0000   010 1110   011 1001   011 0010

40. (a) D5 82

43. (a) An octal digit represents three bits.

44. (a) 6.640625   (b) 0.046875   (c) 1.0

46. (a) 1101.00101   (b) 0.000101   (c) 0.1001100110011 . . .

50. (a) −12.5 (dec) = −1100.1 (bin), which is stored as 1 110 1001

51. (a) 0.90625

53. (a) 1.0×2^6

Chapter 4

1. (a) 65,536 bytes   (b) 32,768 words   (c) 524,288 bits
    (d) 92 bits   (e) 5699 times bigger

3. For instruction 6AF82C   For instruction D623D0
    (a) opcode = 0110   (a) opcode = 1101
    (b) It adds to register r   (b) It loads a byte from memory to register r
    (c) r = 1   (c) r = 0
    (d) The index register, X   (d) The accumulator, A
    (e) aaa = 010   (e) aaa = 110
    (f) Indirect   (f) Stack-indexed
    (g) OprndSpec = F82C   (g) OprndSpec = 23D0

5.

	A	X	Mem[0A3F]	Mem[0A41]
Original content	19AC	FE20	FF00	103D
(a) C1 = Load word accumulator	FF00	FE20	FF00	103D
(b) D1 = Load byte accumulator	19FF	FE20	FF00	103D
(c) D9 = Load byte index register	19AC	FE10	FF00	103D
(d) F1 = Store byte accumulator	19AC	FE20	FF00	AC3D
(e) E9 = Store word index register	19AC	FE20	FE20	103D
(f) 79 = Subtract index register	19AC	EDE3	FF00	103D
(g) 71 = Subtract accumulator	1AAC	FE20	FF00	103D
(h) 91 = OR accumulator	FFAC	FE20	FF00	103D
(i) 07 = Invert index register	19AC	01DF	FF00	103D

9. (a) M

Chapter 5

1. (a) ORX 0xEF2A,n   (b) MOVSPA   (c) LDBA 0x003D,sfx

3. (a) 0A   (b) 33 00 0F   (c) 1A 01 E6

5. (a) 42 65 61 72 00   (b) F8   (c) 03 16

7. mug

10. -57

72

0048

Hi

12. (a) Object code is:

38 00 6D D0 00 0A F1 FC 16 38 6D 6D D0 00 0A F1
FC 16 D0 00 26 F1 FC 16 00 zz

Output is:

109

28013

&

13. Object code is:

12 00 05 00 09 39 00 03 00 zz

Symbol here has value 0003 (hex). Symbol there has value 0005 (hex).

15. Symbol this has value 0000 (hex). The output is 4100. The output comes from the hexadecimal output instruction, which outputs its own instruction specifier followed by the first byte of its operand specifier.

18. The compiler uses its symbol table to store the type of each variable. It consults the symbol table whenever it encounters an expression or assignment statement to verify that the types are compatible.

Chapter 6

3. Because the current value of j will be in the accumulator regardless of whether control comes from the STWA at 0009 or from the BR at the bottom of the loop. Before the BR at the bottom of the loop, the accumulator was used to increment j; hence, its current value will still be in the accumulator when CPWA executes.

6.

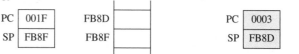

PC	001F	FB8D	
SP	FB8F	FB8F	

PC	0003	FB8D	001F
SP	FB8D	FB8F	

(a) Before execution of the second CALL.   (b) After execution of the second CALL.

8. The branch address is calculated as

Oprnd = Mem[OprndSpec + X]

= Mem[0013 + 8]

= Mem[001B]

= 4900

You cannot tell from the program listing what bits are at 4900, but as-suming that they are all 0's, the von Neumann cycle blindly interprets the 00 at address 4900 as the STOP instruction.

Chapter 7

1. The fundamental question of computer science is: What can be automated?

3. (a)

<identifier>

⇒ <identifier> <digit>	Rule 3
⇒ <identifier> 3	Rule 9
⇒ <identifier> <digit> 3	Rule 3
⇒ <identifier> 23	Rule 8
⇒ <identifier> <digit> 23	Rule 3
⇒ <identifier> 123	Rule 7
⇒ <identifier> <letter> 123	Rule 2
⇒ <identifier> c123	Rule 6
⇒ <identifier> <letter> c123	Rule 2
⇒ <identifier> bc123	Rule 5
⇒ <letter> bc123	Rule 1
⇒ abc123	Rule 4

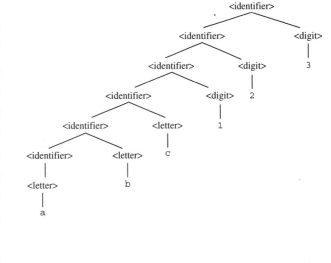

4. (a)

I ⇒ FM	Rule 1
⇒ −M	Rule 3
⇒ −d	Rule 6

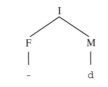

5. (a)

A ⇒ abC	Rule 2
⇒ abc	Rule 5

6. (a)

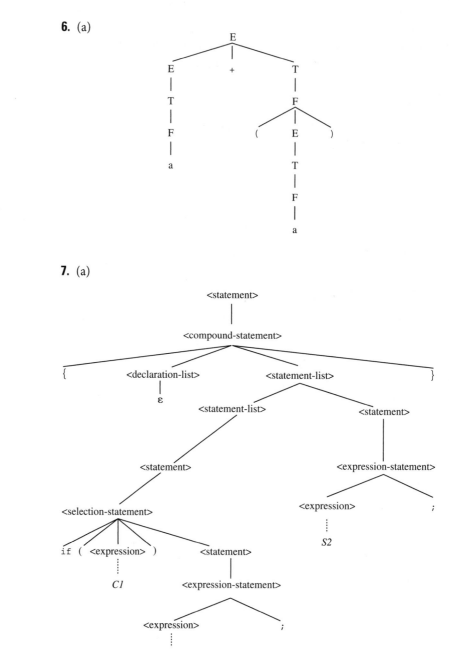

7. (a)

8. (a)

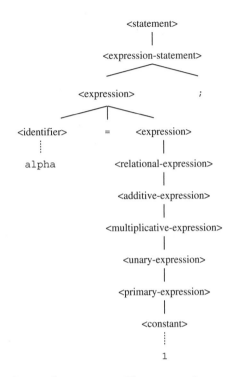

11. (a) The machine is deterministic. There are no inaccessible states.

13. (a)

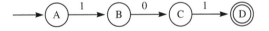

Chapter 8

2. (a) 36 (hex), the ASCII code for 6 in the 30th byte, 6C

(b) 36 (hex)

(c) 60 (hex)

4. (a) 31 (hex), the instruction specifier of the interrupted instruction

(b) 0006 (hex)

5. (a) 39 (hex) the instruction specifier of the interrupted instruction

(b) 0007

6. (a) 49 (hex) the instruction specifier of the interrupted instruction

(b) 0009

7. (a) 0003 (hex), the numeric value of the ASCII character 3

(b) 0007 (hex), the numeric value of the ASCII character 7

(c) 0000 (hex), the value of the `init` state

8. Hint: The first character input is the ASCII hyphen character

9. (a) 0025 (hex), which is 37 (dec) (b) 0025 (hex), not negated because it was already nonnegative (c) The CALL from FF78 is for writing the 100's place. The accumulator still contains 0025 (hex), which is 37 (dec), because 37 mod 100 is 37.

18. (a) The algorithm no longer guarantees mutual exclusion. Suppose P1 and P2 are both in their remainder sections with enter1 and enter2 both false. P1 could execute its while loop test and be interrupted, after which P2 could execute its while loop test. They could then assign their respective enter variables to true and enter their critical sections simultaneously.

20. (a) s = 0 and there are no blocked processes.

22. (a) The algorithm does guarantee mutual exclusion. If you remove the t semaphore altogether, you get the algorithm of Figure 8.20, which guarantees mutual exclusion regardless of any other code present in the algorithm.

24. (a) Mutual exclusion is no longer guaranteed. Can you find a trace that allows P1 and P2 to enter their critical sections simultaneously? Deadlock, however, cannot occur.

25.

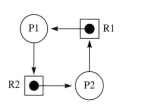

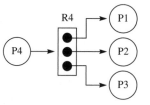

(a) Contains a deadlock cycle.   (b) Does not contain a cycle and therefore does not have a deadlock.

Chapter 9

2. (a) A single bound register would suffice because only one process at a time can execute. If a user process tries to access a memory location outside its logical address space, the hardware must interrupt the access before the page table because there is no such page in main memory. The operating system must keep track of one bound value for each process.

4. (a) 2^{12} or 4096 bytes

6. Those that have a dirty bit value of N—namely, the ones in frames 2, 5, and 6.

8. The start of one page reference sequence for a job that has three frames allocated is 1, 2, 3, 1, 4, 2, . . . , which has four faults for FIFO and five for LRU. Can you complete the sequence in such a way that FIFO is better in this special case?

10. It produces five faults compared to seven for FIFO and six for LRU. You should trace the algorithm to verify this figure.

11. (a) Hint: The worst case occurs when the start of the block has just rotated past the read/write head when the head has reached the track. Hence, it is time for the disk to make one complete revolution. You can calculate it from the RPM number.

12. (a) Four data bits.   (b) One parity bit.

16. (a) An error did occur in position 2. The corrected code word is 1101 1010 1001.

Chapter 10

1. (a)

$x + 1$

= $\langle$complement of OR$\rangle$

$x + (x + x')$

= $\langle$associative of OR$\rangle$

$(x + x) + x'$

= $\langle$idempotent of OR$\rangle$

$x + x'$

= $\langle$complement of OR$\rangle$

1

4. To show that the complement of $a + b$ is $a' \cdot b'$, you must show that

$(a + b) \cdot (a' \cdot b') = 0$ and $(a + b) + (a' \cdot b') = 1$

First part:

$(a + b) \cdot (a' \cdot b')$

= $\langle$commutative of AND$\rangle$

$(a' \cdot b') \cdot (a + b)$

= $\langle$distributive of AND over OR$\rangle$

$(a' \cdot b') \cdot a + (a' + b') \cdot b$

= $\langle$commutative and associative of AND$\rangle$

$b' \cdot (a \cdot a') + a' \cdot (b \cdot b')$

= $\langle$complement of AND$\rangle$

$b' \cdot 0 + a' \cdot 0$

$=$ $\langle$the zero theorem of AND, $x \cdot 0 = 0\rangle$

$0 + 0$

$=$ $\langle$idempotent of OR$\rangle$

0

8. (a)

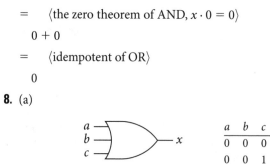

$x = a + b + c$

a	b	c	x
0	0	0	0
0	0	1	1
0	1	0	1
0	1	1	1
1	0	0	1
1	0	1	1
1	1	0	1
1	1	1	1

9. (a) The union of any set with the empty set is the set itself.

10. (a)

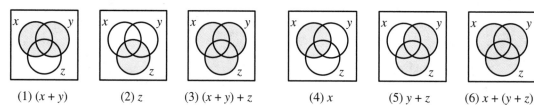

(1) $(x + y)$ (2) z (3) $(x + y) + z$ (4) x (5) $y + z$ (6) $x + (y + z)$

13. (a)

x	y	x AND y
0	0	0
0	A	0
0	B	0
0	0	0
A	1	0
A	0	A
A	A	0
A	B	A
B	1	0
B	0	0
B	A	B
B	B	B
1	1	0
1	A	A
1	B	B
1	1	1

14. (a)

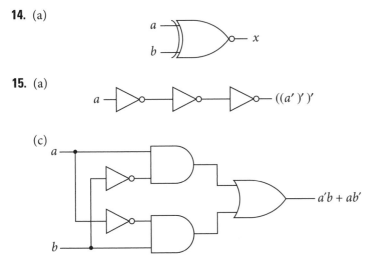

15. (a) a —▷o—▷o—▷o— $((a')')'$

(c)

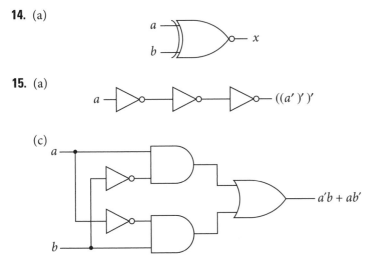

$a'b + ab'$

19. (a) $y(a, b, c) = a'bc + ab'c'$

20. (a) $y(a, b, c) = (a+b+c)(a+b+c')(a+b'+c)(a'+b+c')(a'+b'+c)$
$\qquad\qquad (a' + b' + c')$

21. (a) $ab + a'b$ \qquad (d) $a'b + ab$

a	b	21(a)	21(d)
0	0	1	0
0	1	0	1
1	0	0	0
1	1	1	1

22.

(a)

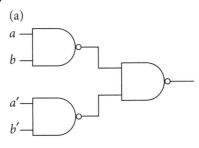

(b)

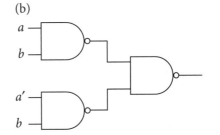

23. (b) $(a' + b)(a + b')$

a	b	
0	0	1
0	1	0
1	0	0
1	1	1

24. (b)

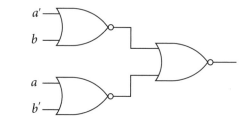

25. (a)

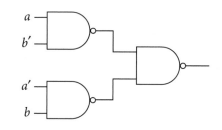

27. (a) $\Sigma(0,3)$ (d) $\Sigma(1,3)$
28. (b) $\Pi(1,2)$
29. (a) $x = a'c$

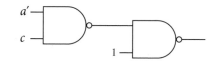

30. (a) $x = (a')(c)$

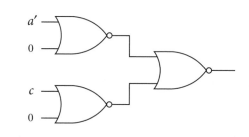

31. (a) $x(a, b, c) = ac + b'c'$
32. (a) $x(a, b, c) = \Pi(1, 2, 3, 6) = (a + c')(b' + c)$
33. (a) $x(a, b, c, d) = bc' + a'b'c + b'cd'$
34. (a) $\Pi(0, 1, 6, 7, 8, 9, 11, 14, 15)$, $x(a, b, c, d) = (b + c)(b' + c')$
$(a' + c' + d')$ or $x(a, b, c, d) = (b + c)(b' + c')(a' + b + d')$
35. (a) $x(a, b, c) = a'b' + ab$

36. (a) $x(a, b, c, d) = bc + bd$

38. (a) The control line acts as an enable that passes the data through unchanged when it is 0. When the control line is 1, it disables the output, which is set to 1, regardless of the data input.

40.

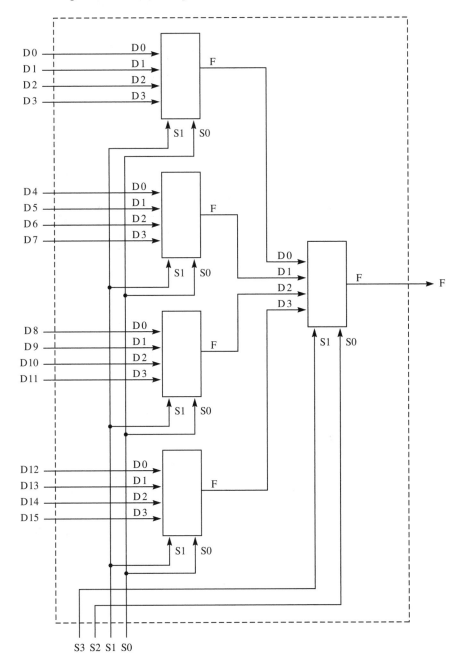

42. (a)

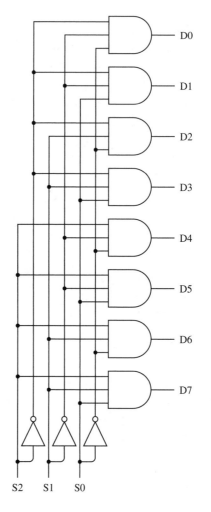

46. (a)

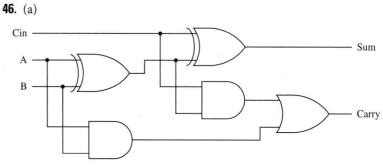

(b) Maximum of three gate delays.

47. (b) Hint: If you look at Figure 10.52 and use the fact that a full adder has three gate delays and a half adder has one gate delay, you might conclude that the total gate delay is 10. However, it is less than that.

Chapter 11

1. The network will be stable if there is an even number of inverters.

3.

	A	B	C	D	E	R2	S2	Q	$\bar{Q}$
(a)	0	0	1	1	0	1	0	0	1
(b)	0	0	0	0	0	1	0	0	1

5. (b)

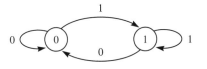

8. (a)

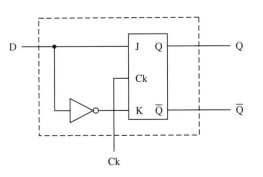

13 (a)

$$DA = A\,\overline{X1} + \overline{A}\,X1 + A\,B\,\overline{X2} + B\,X1\,X2$$
$$DB = \overline{B}\,\overline{X1} + B\,X1\,X2 + \overline{A}\,B\,X1$$
$$Y = \overline{A}\,X2 + A\,X1\,X2$$

15 (a)

$$JA = \overline{B}\,\overline{C}\,\overline{X} + B\,C\,X \qquad KA = \overline{B}\,\overline{C}\,\overline{X} + B\,C\,X$$
$$JB = \overline{C}\,\overline{X} + C\,X \qquad KB = \overline{C}\,\overline{X} + C\,X$$
$$JC = 1 \qquad KC = 1$$

Chapter 12

5. Hint: (a) Using 16 billion GiB equal to 16×1024^6 bytes, the chip would be 4.3×4.3 meters square, but you must show your calculation. (b) Yes, but you must explain.

12. (a)

```
lw $t0,20($s6)   # Register $t0 gets b[5]

add $t0,$s5,$t0  # Register $t0 gets g + b[5]

sw $t0,16($s4)   # a[2] gets g + b[5]
```

(b)

```
100011 10110 01000 0000000000010100

000000 10101 01000 01000 00000 100000

101011 10100 01000 0000000000010000
```

Index